*THIRD
EDITION*

# Issues and Ethics
# in the Helping Professions

*THIRD*
*EDITION*

# Issues and Ethics
# in the Helping Professions

■ **Gerald Corey**

*California State University, Fullerton*
*Diplomate in Counseling Psychology,*
*American Board of Professional Psychology*

■ **Marianne Schneider Corey**

*Private Practice*

■ **Patrick Callanan**

*Private Practice*

*Brooks/Cole Publishing Company*
*Pacific Grove, California*

Brooks/Cole Publishing Company
A Division of Wadsworth, Inc.

Printed in the United States of America

10  9  8  7  6  5  4

**Library of Congress Cataloging-in-Publication Data**

Corey, Gerald.
    Issues and ethics in the helping professions.

    Rev. ed. of: Issues & ethics in the helping
professions.  2nd ed.  c1984.
    Bibliography: p.
    Includes indexes.
      1. Psychotherapists—Professional ethics.
2. Counselors—Professional ethics.    I. Corey,
Marianne Schneider [date]    II. Callanan, Patrick.
III. Corey, Gerald.    Issues & ethics in the helping
professions.    IV. Title.    [DNLM: 1. Counseling.
2. Ethics, Professional.  3. Professional-Patient
Relations.  4. Psychotherapy.  WM 62 C797i]
RC455.2.E8C66    1987      174′.2      87–13194
ISBN 0–534–08082–0 (pbk.)

Sponsoring Editor:  *Claire Verduin*
Editorial Assistant:  *Linda Ruth Wright*
Production Editor:  *Fiorella Ljunggren*
Production Assistant:  *Dorothy Bell*
Manuscript Editor:  *William Waller*
Permissions Editor:  *Carline Haga*
Interior and Cover Design:  *Sharon L. Kinghan*
Typesetting:  *Bi-Comp, Inc., York, Pennsylvania*
Printing and Binding:  *R. R. Donnelley & Sons Company, Crawfordsville, Indiana*

*Dedicated to
the significant people in our lives;
to our friends and colleagues*

**GERALD COREY,** Professor and Coordinator of the Human Services Program at California State University at Fullerton and a licensed psychologist, received his doctorate in counseling from the University of Southern California. He is a Diplomate in Counseling Psychology, American Board of Professional Psychology; is registered as a National Health Service Provider in Psychology; is a National Certified Counselor; is a licensed marriage, family, and child counselor; and is a Fellow of the American Psychological Association (Counseling Psychology). He teaches courses in professional ethics, counseling theory and practice, and group counseling. With his colleagues he has conducted workshops in the United States, Mexico, China, and Europe, with a special focus on training in group counseling. He was the recipient of the 1986 Award in the Field of Professional Ethics of the Association for Religious and Value Issues in Counseling; the 1984 Distinguished Service Award in the Field of Group Work of the Association for Specialists in Group Work; and the Distinguished Faculty Member Award in 1984 from the School of Human Development and Community Service of California State University at Fullerton.

The recent books he has authored or co-authored (all published by Brooks/Cole Publishing Company) include:

- *Group Techniques*, Revised Edition (1988)
- *Groups: Process and Practice*, 3rd Edition (1987)
- *Theory and Practice of Counseling and Psychotherapy*, 3rd Edition (and *Manual*) (1986)
- *Case Approach to Counseling and Psychotherapy*, 2nd Edition (1986)
- *I Never Knew I Had a Choice*, 3rd Edition (1986)
- *Theory and Practice of Group Counseling*, 2nd Edition (and *Manual*) (1985)
- *Casebook of Ethical Guidelines for Group Leaders* (1982)

**MARIANNE SCHNEIDER COREY** is a licensed marriage and family therapist in Idyllwild, California, and is a National Certified Counselor. She received her master's degree in marriage, family, and child counseling from Chapman College. She is a Clinical Member of the American Association for Marriage and Family Therapy and holds memberships in the California Association of Marriage and Family Therapists, the American Association for Counseling and Development, the Association for Specialists in Group Work, and the Western Psychological Association. Marianne and Jerry Corey were the co-chairpersons of the Professional Standards and Ethics Committee of the Association for Specialists in Group Work in 1981–1982. Marianne Corey's professional interests are in counseling individuals and couples, as well as leading therapeutic groups and training groups. With her colleagues she has conducted professional workshops in the United States, Mexico, China, and Europe. She donates her time each year to California State University at Fullerton for training and supervising student leaders in a group counseling class and for co-leading week-long residential growth groups. She received an Award for Contributions to the Field of Professional Ethics from the Association for Religious and Value Issues in Counseling in 1986.

She has co-authored several journal articles as well as the following books (published by Brooks/Cole Publishing Company):

- *Group Techniques*, Revised Edition (1988)
- *Groups: Process and Practice*, 3rd Edition (1987)
- *I Never Knew I Had a Choice*, 3rd Edition (1986)
- *Casebook of Ethical Guidelines for Group Leaders* (1982)

**PATRICK CALLANAN** is a licensed marriage and family therapist in private practice in Santa Ana, California, and is a National Certified Counselor. He graduated with a bachelor's degree in Human Services from California State University at Fullerton and then received his master's degree in clinical psychology from United States International University. In his private practice he works with individuals, couples, and families and regularly leads several therapy groups. He is also a consultant for mental-health practitioners, and he presents workshops and training groups at conventions and for professional organizations. He donates his time each year to California State University at Fullerton to assist in training and supervising group leaders, to co-lead week-long residential growth groups, and to teach field-work and internship seminars. He is a member of the California Association of Marriage and Family Therapists, the Association for Specialists in Group Work, the American Association for Counseling and Development, and the Western Psychological Association. He received an Award for Contributions to the Field of Professional Ethics from the Association for Religious and Value Issues in Counseling in 1986.

He has co-authored several articles published in the *Journal for Specialists in Group Work*, as well as the following books (published by Brooks/Cole Publishing Company):

- *Group Techniques*, Revised Edition (1988)
- *Casebook of Ethical Guidelines for Group Leaders* (1982)

# Preface

*Issues and Ethics in the Helping Professions* is written for both graduate and undergraduate students in the helping professions. It is suitable for courses involving human-services delivery, from counseling psychology to social work. It can be used as a core textbook in courses such as practicum, fieldwork, internship, and ethical and professional issues or as a supplementary text in courses dealing with skills or theory. Because the issues we discuss are likely to be encountered throughout one's professional career, we have tried to use language and concepts that will be meaningful both to students doing their fieldwork and to professionals interested in improving their skills through continuing-education seminars or independent reading.

This book is meant to help the reader learn to deal with the professional and ethical issues that most affect the actual practice of counseling and related helping professions throughout the practitioner's career. To this end we raise the following questions: How do the therapist's values and life experiences affect the therapeutic process? What are the rights and responsibilities of both the client and the helper? As professionals, how can we determine our level of competence? How can we provide quality services for culturally diverse populations? What are some major ethical issues facing practitioners in community agencies and in private practice? in marital and family therapy? in group work?

Our goal is both to provide a body of information and to teach readers a process of focusing on and dealing with the basic issues they will face as practitioners. For most of the issues we raise, we present a number of viewpoints to stimulate discussion and reflection. We also present our views, when appropriate, to help readers formulate their own positions.

To assist in this process, we cite the ethical codes of various professional organizations, which offer some guidance for practice. These guidelines, however, leave many questions unanswered. We believe that students and professionals alike must ultimately struggle with the issues of responsible practice, deciding how accepted ethical standards apply in the specific cases they encounter.

We have tried to make this book a personal one that will involve our readers in an active and meaningful way. To this end we have provided many opportunities to respond to our discussions and to draw on personal experiences. Each chapter begins with a self-inventory designed to help readers focus on the key topics to be discussed in the chapter. Within the chapters we frequently ask readers to think about how the issues apply to them. Open-ended cases and situations are presented to stimulate thought and assist readers in formulating their own positions. Related literature is cited when we are exploring ethical and professional issues. Suggestions for further reading are provided throughout the text.

This book combines the advantages of a textbook, student manual, and instructor's resource manual. Instructors will find an abundance of material and suggested activities, surely more than can be covered in a single course. Ethical decision making is an ongoing process, and in this sense the book is designed to raise many more questions than it will neatly answer.

It is good to see the increase in journal articles and books dealing with ethical and professional issues in the helping professions. The reception and response from users of the previous editions of this book also please us, because these people continue to say that studying ethics can be an exciting adventure that provokes lively classroom discussion.

This third edition of *Issues and Ethics in the Helping Professions* has been extensively revised, with at least 50% new material. It provides new topics and more comprehensive coverage than the previous editions. Some of the additions and expanded areas are:

- a new introductory chapter on ethical decision making
- a new chapter on issues in multicultural counseling
- a new chapter on ethical issues specific to marriage and family therapy
- inclusion in the Appendix of revised codes of ethics of many of the major mental-health professional organizations
- expansion of trends in the teaching of ethics
- new material on stress in the helping professions
- an increased focus on informed consent and the rights of clients
- updated coverage of guidelines for working with special populations, such as women, gays and lesbians, and ethnic minorities
- discussions of landmark court cases, with implications for professional practice
- updated coverage of confidentiality and privileged communication
- new material on the duty to warn and protect
- guidelines for assessment of and intervention with suicidal clients
- methods of preventing malpractice suits
- increased coverage of counseling supervision
- updated coverage of the client/counselor relationship
- expanded discussion of dual relationships in therapy and in supervision
- new material on trends and practices in the field of counselor education
- an updated and expanded discussion of sexual attractions and intimacies in the client/therapist relationship
- expanded coverage of the training of paraprofessionals
- inclusion of material on ethics in consultation

- increased attention to legal issues
- expanded coverage of transference and countertransference issues
- inclusion of many new case illustrations and examples
- new material on the ethical issues involved in using certain therapeutic techniques, such as paradoxical interventions
- new material on the role of peer review as an approach to ensuring professional competency
- an updated discussion of ethical issues in group work
- sources of information about certificates, licenses, and professional organizations
- an updated survey of the literature dealing with ethical and professional issues, with emphasis on recent journal articles

We have also prepared an objective final examination based on this book. Instructors can obtain a copy by writing to the publisher.

A note on terminology: We frequently use the terms *mental-health professional, practitioner, counselor, therapist,* and *helper.* Generally, we use these as interchangeable terms, but we have also tried to reflect the differing nomenclature of the various professions we cover.

## Acknowledgments

We thank the following people, who reviewed the manuscript and offered valuable suggestions for improvement: Virginia Allen of Idaho State University; Patricia Arredondo, Director of Empowerment Workshops in Maine; James H. Bray of Texas Women's University; John R. Cochran of the University of Akron; A. Michael Dougherty of Western Carolina University; Richard Ellis of New York University; Harold Engen of the University of Iowa; William K. Gabrenya of the Florida Institute of Technology; Wayne Huey of Gordon High School; Wallace Kahn of West Chester University; Marva J. Larrabee of the University of South Carolina; Arlene Lewis of Western Washington University; Donald MacDonald of Seattle Pacific University; Edward Neukrug of Notre Dame College; Paul Pedersen of Syracuse University; Anthony Preus of the State University of New York at Binghamton; Theodore Remley of George Mason University; Holly Stadler of the University of Missouri at Kansas City; and Bea Wehrly of Western Illinois University.

We thank our student reviewers, who included Andrea Mark, Mitch Simon, Jane Sipe, Deborah Soucy, and Veronika Tracy. Recognition and appreciation go to Joanna Quintrell, who did her usual fine job of preparing the index.

We received extra help on the new chapter on multicultural counseling from a number of reviewers. The following people provided many useful suggestions and helped us focus on the most salient issues in multicultural counseling: Patricia Arredondo of Empowerment Workshops in Maine; A. Michael Dougherty of Western Carolina University; William K. Gabrenya of the Florida Institute of Technology; Mikel Garcia of California State

University at Fullerton; Beverly Palmer of California State University at Dominguez Hills; Paul Pedersen of Syracuse University; Bea Wehrly of Western Illinois University; George Williams of the University of New Orleans; and Jerome Wright of California State University at Fullerton.

Soraya Colely of California State University at Fullerton reviewed Chapter 9, "The Counselor in the Community and in a System."

Finally, we want to express our appreciation to those people in the Brooks/Cole family who have contributed their talents to making this a better book. Claire Verduin, managing editor and psychology editor, and Fiorella Ljunggren, senior production coordinator, continue to demonstrate their special interest in all of our books. Special recognition also goes to William Waller, manuscript editor, who meticulously labored on these pages and who provided many helpful suggestions that resulted in greater clarity and better flow of exposition.

*Gerald Corey*
*Marianne Schneider Corey*
*Patrick Callanan*

# Contents

# Introduction to Professional Ethics

- How This Book Came into Being
- Ethical Decision Making
- Some Suggestions for Using This Book
- Self-Assessment: An Inventory of Your Attitudes and Beliefs about Professional and Ethical Issues in the Helping Professions
- Chapter Summary
- Suggested Activities
- Suggested Readings

# How This Book Came into Being

For a number of years the three of us have worked as a team co-leading therapy and personal-growth groups. During this time we have watched one another grow and change personally and professionally. Although we have developed our own therapeutic styles and sometimes challenge one another's ideas, we do share a common view of people and of helping relationships.

Over the years we have worked independently in our own counseling practices as well as with one another. All three of us have had to confront many professional and ethical issues that do not have clear-cut solutions. Exchanging our ideas has helped each of us formulate, revise, and clarify our positions on these issues. Our interactions with students and fellow professionals have shown us that others wrestle with similar questions. It has become clear to us that students in the counseling field should confront the issues that will be a large part of their professional experience and would benefit by giving serious thought to their positions on these issues before they begin practicing.

Some of the issues we are referring to arise out of the fact that counselors, no less than clients, are *people*; they have their own personalities, private lives, strengths, and personal struggles. In Chapter 2, for instance, we point out that it's impossible to separate the kind of person a counselor is from the kind of help the counselor will be able to provide. Whether a counselor is willing and able to form honest and caring relationships with his or her clients is one particularly significant issue. To take another example, in Chapter 2 we talk about the problem of counselor "burn-out." How can we, as people who have our own limits of energy and emotional resources and who have our own lives to think of, stay alive as therapists, both to our own feelings and to those of our clients?

Other issues involve the nature of the therapeutic process and the helping relationship. What theoretical stance should we choose, and how important is it to have a clear theoretical approach to counseling? What role do our personal values play in the counseling relationship? What ethical responsibilities and privileges do clients and counselors have? What considerations are involved in counseling culturally different clients? What special ethical issues are raised by marital and family therapy? What ethical and professional problems are involved in group counseling? What is the counselor's role in the community and in the institutional structure within which he or she must work?

In considering these questions, we decided to write a book that would be meaningful to experienced practitioners as well as to students about to embark on their professional careers. Many of the issues that are relevant to beginning professionals surface again and again and take on different meanings at the various stages of one's professional development.

Just as we have found no easy answers to most of the issues that have confronted us in our professional practice, we have attempted to write a book that does not fall into the trap of dispensing prescriptions or providing simple solutions to complex problems. Our main purpose is to provide you with the basis for discovering your own guidelines within the broad limits of professional codes of ethics and divergent theoretical positions. We raise what we consider to be central issues, present a range of diverse views on these issues, discuss our position, and provide you with many opportunities to refine your own thinking and to actively develop your position.

In making the statement that you are the one who will ultimately discover your own guidelines for responsible practice, we are not endorsing a position of absolute freedom. We're not implying that students are free to choose any set of ethics merely on the basis that it "feels right." The various human-services professions have developed codes of ethics that are binding on the members of professional organizations. Any professional should, of course, know the ethical code of his or her specialty and should be aware of the consequences of practicing in ways that are not sanctioned by the appropriate professional organization. Even within the broad guidelines of ethical codes, responsible practice implies that professionals base their practice on informed, sound, and responsible judgment. To us, this implies that professionals should consult with colleagues, keep themselves current in their specialties through reading and periodic continuing-education activities, and be willing to engage in an honest and ongoing process of self-examination. Codes of ethics provide general standards, but these guidelines are not sufficiently explicit to deal with every situation. Often it is difficult to interpret them in practice, and there are differences of opinion concerning their application in specific cases. Consequently, counselors retain a significant degree of freedom and will meet many situations that demand the exercise of sound judgment. They will face issues in which there are no obvious answers, and they will have to struggle with themselves in an honest way to decide how they should act in order to further the best interests of their clients.

It is worth emphasizing that the issues dealt with in the text need to be periodically reexamined throughout your professional life. Even if you thoughtfully resolve some of these issues at the initial stage of your professional development, there is no guarantee that everything will be worked out once and for all. They may take on new dimensions as you gain more experience, and questions that are of relatively minor importance at one time may become major concerns at another time as you progress in your profession. In addition, it may not be possible or even desirable to have solutions for all the professional concerns you will encounter. Many students burden themselves with the expectation that they should resolve all possible issues before they are ready to begin practicing, but we see the definition and refinement of the issues we raise as being an evolutionary process that requires a continually open and self-critical attitude.

# Ethical Decision Making

## Foundations of an Ethical Perspective

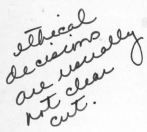

Ethical decisions in counseling are usually not clear-cut. The issues involved are often complex and multifaceted, and they defy simplistic solutions. There are many "gray areas" that demand both reflection and the use of decision-making skills. This process requires more than learning information about ethical standards; it entails learning how to define and work with a variety of problem situations.

**Law and Ethics.**    Ethical issues in the mental-health professions are regulated both by legislation and by professional codes. Laws and codes, by their very nature, tend to be reactive, emerging from what has occurred rather than anticipating what may occur. We hope that practitioners will not limit their behavior simply to following established statutes and ethical standards but will develop a sensitivity to doing what is best for their clients. It is very important that mental-health practitioners develop this ethical sense at the beginning of their professional program. Otherwise, they are likely to get the impression that ethics are unimportant, making it more difficult for them to develop an ethical sense later. Professionals may take a very narrow stance of merely staying within the boundaries of the law and concluding that being ethical means doing just what is legal. Although the law and ethics share common elements, they are not synonymous. At times there may be conflicts between the two, and in these cases the values of the counselor come into the picture. Mappes, Robb, and Engels (1985) note that codes of ethics are designed to guide practitioners, protect clients, safeguard the autonomy of professional workers, and enhance the status of the profession. Conflicts between these codes and the law may arise in areas such as advertising, confidentiality, and clients' rights of access to their own files.

In making ethical decisions we must ask questions such as "Which values should I rely upon? What values do I hold? How do my values affect my work with clients? Why do I hold certain values?" Our ethical perspective is bound up with the way we treat others. In the helping professions we are not merely sensitive to the welfare of others but are committed to the welfare of clients above all else.

We agree with Tennyson and Strom (1986) that acting responsibly is an inner quality, not something merely imposed by authority. One way of conceptualizing professional ethics is by contrasting lower-level ethical functioning with higher-level ethical functioning. The first level of ethical functioning is characterized by compliance with the law and by following the ethical codes of one's profession. This is called "mandatory ethics." Practitioners who comply at this level are generally safe from legal action or professional censure. At the higher level of ethical functioning, called "aspirational ethics," practitioners do more than comply with the law and the

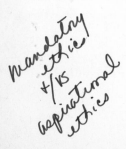

codes. They are continuously open to the effects of their interventions on the welfare of their clients.

**The Role of Professional Codes.**    Various professional organizations have established codes of ethics that provide broad guidelines for mental-health practitioners. Examples of such ethical standards are presented in the Appendix. At this time we encourage you to review these standards so that you can apply them to the issues we raise in the remaining chapters of this book. Some of the organizations that have formulated codes of ethics are the National Association of Social Workers (NASW), the American Psychological Association (APA), the American Association for Counseling and Development (AACD), and the American Association for Marriage and Family Therapy (AAMFT).

Although you have or will become familiar with the ethical standards of your specialization, you will be challenged to develop your own personal code of ethics to govern your practice. The ethical guidelines offered by most professional organizations are general and usually represent minimal standards of conduct. Your own ethical awareness and problem-solving skills will determine how you interpret and translate general guidelines into your professional day-to-day behavior.

From what we have said, it is clear that ethical codes are necessary but not sufficient for the exercise of professional responsibility. Thus, it is essential that you be aware of the limitations of professional codes. The following limitations are noted by Mabe and Rollin (1986):

- Some issues cannot be handled by ethical codes alone.
- There are problems with enforcing codes; courts may decide that the codes are not applicable.
- There are conflicts within codes and between them.
- The values of a practitioner may conflict with a code.
- Codes may conflict with institutional policies and practices.
- Codes tend to spring from past events.

Codes are not intended as a blueprint that would remove all need for the use of judgment and ethical reasoning (Welfel & Lipsitz, 1984). Ethical codes tend to be conservative by nature. They were developed to protect the profession from outside regulation, and thus they reflect what most professionals can agree on, as opposed to reflecting ideal practice (Kitchener, 1984b). Thus, as Tennyson and Strom (1986) note, ethical standards cannot tell helpers what to do or why they should behave in a certain way. Final authority must rest with the helper in determining what is right in a particular situation.

To illustrate the complexity of making ethical decisions, we present the following case, involving child abuse. Put yourself in the place of a counselor who works with the family described in the case. Consider this case as an example of how laws and ethical codes do not relieve the practitioner of resolving difficult ethical dilemmas.

## A Case of Child Abuse

**The Situation.**    This case involves a mother, father, and their daughter. One night, in a rare moment of intoxication, the father stumbles into his 12-year-old daughter's bedroom, and he initiates some sexual contact. The daughter's cries bring the mother into the room, and the incident does not go further. Later, the father does not recall the incident. There has been no previous history of molestation. During therapy the family is able to talk openly about the incident and is working through the pain that resulted. The family is adamant that this situation should not be reported to social services. The therapist is aware that the law clearly specifies that she is required to report this incident, even if it happened in the past and was not repeated. What follows are a few glimpses of the inner dialogue of the therapist as she attempts to deal with the issue of whether to report the incident. Think about your reactions to each course of action that occurs to the helper.

• "There are many hazards involved if I do not report this incident. If this family ever broke up, the mother or daughter could sue me for having failed to report what happened. I would be obeying the law and protecting myself totally by reporting it, and I could justify my actions by citing the requirement of the law."

• "But this is a one-time incident. The father was intoxicated, and the situation did not progress beyond the fondling stage. The daughter was traumatized by the incident, but she seems to be able to talk about it in the family now. If I just obey the law, my actions may be more detrimental to the family at this time than beneficial."

• "But the law is there for a reason. A child has been abused—that is no minor incident—and there was trauma for some time afterward."

• "What is the most ethical thing to do? I may be following the law by reporting it, but is this the most ethical course in this case? Is this in the best interest of this family now, especially since none of the members wants it reported? My ethical sense tells me that my interventions should always be in the best interests of all three members of this family."

• "Before I act, perhaps I should consult an attorney for advice on how to proceed."

• "I need to call the Child Protective Services to find out what I must do."

• "I could call the Board of Ethics of my professional organization and get some advice on how to proceed."

• "I don't know what action to take. Maybe I should consult with a colleague."

**Discussion.**   This case illustrates some of the difficulties a counselor can find herself in when her inner ethical sense conflicts with the law or an ethical code. This counselor must struggle with herself to determine whether she will follow her clinical intuitions by doing what she thinks is in the best interests of this family or whether she will do what is required by the law. If she simply reported this case, she would be acting on the lower level of ethical functioning. Her action would be characterized by compliance with the law and by following the ethical code of her profession. If the therapist called the ethics committee of her professional organization or a colleague, she would be acting on a slightly higher level of ethical functioning because of her willingness to consult. Consulting colleagues is always recommended in cases such as the one described. The consultation process would help from a legal perspective, because if other professionals agreed with her course of action, she would have a good chance of demonstrating that she had acted in good faith. In addition, consulting colleagues would provide her with one or more different perspectives on a difficult case. Perhaps the therapist is acting on the highest level of ethical functioning in examining all the factors and special circumstances of this family before acting. She is struggling to act appropriately, not just to protect herself, and is truly concerned with the best interests of everyone in the family. The welfare of the family members does not require her to violate the law, but it does require her to think beyond merely coping with the law.

## Perspectives on the Teaching of Ethics

**The Formation of an Ethical Sense.**   Developing an ethical sense includes committing yourself to your education, being an active learner, learning from role models such as your professors, and immersing yourself in related course work. From our perspective the cultivation of an ethical sense begins with your commitment to your education in the helping professions. The way you approach your education has a bearing on the way you will approach your professional career. If you are the kind of person who is motivated to fully commit yourself to your studies on both an intellectual and emotional level, you will probably bring this enthusiasm and dedication to your professional practice. We all know students who are committed to manipulating the system so that they can merely get by with minimal effort. Some take the shortest route to earning a degree and getting a license, and once they attain these goals, they stop learning. We are convinced that these people are limited in their capacity to help others. Their limitations may not be apparent to the consumer, however.

   In addition to being an active learner, we think, it is essential that you be aware of your own motivations for choosing the helping professions as a career. Your motivations for being a helper are related to the development of your ethical sense. Although many personal needs can be met through helping others, it is crucial that these needs not be met at the expense of the client. Those who make a lifetime commitment to helping others have a responsibility to be clear about what they are getting from their work and how their personal characteristics play a vital role in their ability to make appropriate ethical decisions. To this end, the next chapter focuses on the counselor as both person and professional and asks you to examine your needs and motivations.

We contend that the faculty of any program in the helping professions plays a major role in modeling an ethical sense. The ways in which the faculty members teach their courses and relate to and supervise students have a significant impact. For example, supervisors may model confidentiality or the lack of it by how they talk about their own clients. As Kitchener (1984b) has pointed out, one way of teaching students what it means to be an ethical professional is by being truthful, honest, and direct with them. The faculty members must be open to honest self-exploration of the ethical issues they face if they hope to have an impact on their students' ability to think from an ethical perspective. Kitchener puts this matter well:

> By modeling, through discussions, and by valuing ethical behavior, counselor educators can encourage young professionals to develop a sense of responsibility to act in an ethically responsible manner. Also, they can help them learn to tolerate the ambiguity involved in ethical decision making; first, however, counselor educators must learn to tolerate it themselves [1986, p. 310].

**The Goals of Ethics Education and Training.**    Kitchener (1986) has suggested that ethics training should create sensitivity to the ethical issues in the profession and to the implications of professional actions; should improve the ability to reason about ethical issues; should develop moral responsibility and the determination to act in ethical ways; and should teach tolerance of ambiguity in ethical decision making.

**Ways of Teaching Ethical Decision Making.**    We endorse the practice of teaching students the process of making ethical decisions from the very beginning of their training program. The teaching of ethics can be conceptualized as progressing from a focus on theoretical issues to a stress on practical issues. When you are introduced to ethics education, it is likely that the emphasis will be on teaching general and fundamental principles of ethical reasoning. Specific application can involve creating situations in the classroom in which students are challenged to apply ethical principles to specific cases. Through feedback from our students, we have found that discussing case vignettes is an effective way to develop decision-making attitudes and skills. We encourage you, as you read and think about the cases we present in this book, to formulate your personal ethical perspective on the issues raised by the cases.

**Teaching Ethics at the Graduate Level.**    Graduate courses in ethics at both the beginning and the end of the program are an ideal way to provide students with opportunities to grapple with ethical principles by applying them to practice. What are the current practices in teaching ethics? A national survey of 289 terminal master's programs in psychology assessed the type of ethics training that was available (Handelsman, 1986a). The results of this survey indicated that 87% of these programs had some format for teaching ethics; 29% had a formal and separate course in ethics; 47% taught ethics as a part of a formal course; and 11% dealt with ethical issues in informal ways through discussion during practicum and internship supervision sessions. Although 98.5% of the respondents believed that ethics could be taught adequately at the master's level, only 57% of them would recommend a formal course devoted entirely to ethics. Handelsman concluded that ethical thinking should be regarded as a skill, which can and should be taught in formal courses.

As Welfel and Lipsitz (1984) point out, however, more research is needed to determine the impact of formal course work in ethics. These authors contend that the literature only very weakly supports the interpretation that ethics courses have a positive impact on students. There is no study dealing with the influence of ethics training on actual behavior with clients. There are also no data to determine whether ethics is better taught in a separate course or integrated into existing courses in the curriculum. Welfel and Lipsitz raise the question of whether knowing ethical codes and learning a way of thinking and dealing with ethical dilemmas will actually be translated into actual practice. They acknowledge that progress has been made over the last 30 years in ethics education, but they ask if this increased attention to ethics training says much about the quality of this training. They assert that ethics courses are likely to fall short of their ultimate goals despite the best intentions of those who teach them.

**Trends in the Teaching of Ethics.**    The recent focus on ethics education is related to an increase in malpractice litigation. The greater consciousness in the human-services professions about ethical and legal responsibilities parallels a concurrent rise in public consciousness about legal rights. There is a great deal of professional concern over identifying appropriate actions in the face of conflicting ethical, legal, and professional demands (Haas, Malouf, & Mayerson, 1986).

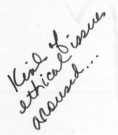

Most of the attention has been given to violations of confidentiality and to sexual intimacies with clients. Other types of unethical behaviors have been documented, however, such as misrepresentation of skills, problems in the methods of collecting fees, improper use of assessment techniques, failure to respect client integrity, inappropriate public statements, and unethical research practices (Lipsitz, 1985).

Lipsitz (1985) reports that the literature reveals a sevenfold increase in the availability of training experiences over the last 30 years. It appears that both formal and integrated ethics training are well respected by students who have been exposed to them. Ninety-two percent of the participants in the Lipsitz study were exposed to some systematic attempt to incorporate the topic of professional ethics into their curriculum. Of this group, 51%

had a formal course in ethics, and 41% received ethics training that was integrated throughout their program.

Handelsman (1986b) presents a persuasive case for reconceptualizing ethics education. Contending that there are problems with ethics training by "osmosis," he maintains that ethical thinking is a skill that must be developed through formal courses devoted primarily to ethics. For him, relying exclusively on informal methods alone, such as teaching ethics in the context of supervision, is a dangerous practice.

We do not assume that course work in ethics is sufficient to bring about ethical practice on your part. We do think that formal course work in ethics, both in separate courses and through an integrated approach with the rest of the curriculum, will significantly help you benefit from supervised field-work. The course work can alert you to ethical, legal, and professional issues that you might not have looked for, and you will be able to bring to your fieldwork questions about the ethical dimensions of your dealings with clients.

## Some Suggestions for Using This Book

If you're like many students, you've probably found some textbooks difficult to relate to in a personally meaningful way, because they seemed dry and abstract. Perhaps you found yourself reading passively just to acquire information, without being challenged to make a real synthesis of the ideas in the text with your own ideas and experiences or to formulate your own positions. Because we believe that this passive relationship of reader to material is unfortunate, we've tried to write a book that will involve you in an active way. This book deals with the central professional and ethical issues that you are likely to encounter in your work with clients, and we have made every effort to make it a practical book without making it a source of ready-made answers. Our aim has been to provide a context within which you can actively formulate your own positions.

In writing this book we frequently imagined ourselves in conversations with our students, and we hope you will find it informal and personal. Whenever it seems appropriate, we state our own thinking and discuss how we came to the positions we hold. We think it's important to openly state our biases, views, convictions, and attitudes, so that you can critically evaluate our stance. On many issues we present a range of viewpoints so that you'll have material to use in formulating your own thoughts. Our hope is that you will give constant attention to ways of integrating your own thoughts and experiences with the issues we explore, so that you will not only absorb information but also deepen your understanding.

The format of this book is therefore different from that of most traditional textbooks. This is a personal manual that can be useful to you at various stages in your professional development. The many questions and exercises interspersed in the text are intended to stimulate you to become an active reader and learner. If you take the time to do these exercises and complete the surveys and inventories, the book will become both a challenge to reflect personally on the issues and a record of your reactions to them.

You should know that we have intentionally provided an abundance of exercises in each chapter, more than can be integrated in one semester or in one course. We invite you to look over the questions and other exercises to decide which of them have the most meaning for you. At a later reading of the book you may want to consider questions or activities that you omitted on your initial reading.

We'd like to make several other specific suggestions for getting the most from this book and your course. Many of these ideas come from students who have been in our classes. In general, you'll get from this book and course whatever you're willing to invest of yourself, so it's important to clarify your goals and to think about ways of becoming actively involved. The following suggestions may help you become more active as a learner.

1. *Preparation.* You can best prepare yourself to become active in your class by spending time outside of class reading and thinking about the questions we pose. Completing the exercises and responding to the questions and open-ended cases will help you focus on where you stand on some controversial issues.

2. *Dealing with your expectations.* Often students have unrealistic expectations of themselves. Even though they have had very little counseling experience, they may think that they should have all the right answers worked out once and for all before they begin to work with people, or they may feel that they lack appropriate experiences. If you haven't had much experience in counseling clients, you can begin to become involved in the issues we discuss by thinking about situations in which friends have sought you out when they were in need of help. You can also reflect on the times when you were experiencing conflicts and needed someone to help you gain clarity. In this way you may be able to relate the material to events in your own life even if your counseling experience is limited.

3. *Self-assessment.* At the end of this chapter there is a multiple-choice survey designed to help you discover your attitudes concerning most of the issues we deal with in this book. We encourage you to take this inventory before you read the book to see where you stand on these issues at this time. You may want to take the inventory in more than one sitting, so that you can give careful thought to each question. We also encourage you to take the inventory again after you complete the book. You can then compare your responses to see what changes have occurred in your attitudes as a result of the course and your reading of the book.

4. *Pre-chapter self-inventories.* Each chapter begins with a self-inventory designed to stimulate your thinking about the issues that will be explored in the chapter. You may want to bring your responses to class and compare your views with those of fellow students. You may also find it

useful to retake the inventory after you finish reading the chapter to see whether your views have changed.

5. *Examples, cases, and questions.*   Many examples in this book are drawn from actual counseling practice in various settings with different types of clients. We frequently ask you to consider how you might have worked with a given client or what you might have done in a particular counseling situation. We hope you'll take the time to think about these questions and briefly respond to them in the spaces provided.

6. *End-of-chapter exercises and activities.*   Each chapter ends with exercises and activities intended to help you integrate and apply what you've learned in the chapter. They include suggestions for things to do both in class and on your own, as well as ideas for thought and discussion that you can consider alone or use for small-group discussions in class. The purpose of these aids is to make the issues come alive and to help you apply your ideas to practical situations. We think the time you devote to these end-of-the-chapter activities can be most useful in helping you achieve a practical grasp of the material treated in the text.

7. *Selected outside reading.*   Near the end of the book you'll find a reading list of additional sources you might want to consult. By developing the habit of doing some reading on issues that have meaning to you, you can gain insights that can be integrated into your own frame of reference.

Most of all, we encourage you to use this book in any way that assists you to become involved in the issues. We hope that you'll feel free to focus selectively on the questions and activities that have the most meaning for you at this time and that you'll remain open to new issues as they assume importance for you.

## Self-Assessment: An Inventory of Your Attitudes and Beliefs about Professional and Ethical Issues in the Helping Professions

The purpose of this inventory is to survey your thoughts on various professional and ethical issues in the field of counseling and psychotherapy. Most of the items relate directly to topics that are explored in detail later in the book. The inventory is designed to introduce you to these issues and to stimulate your thought and interest. You may want to complete the inventory in more than one sitting, so that you can give each question your full concentration.

This is *not* a traditional multiple-choice test in which you must select the "one right answer." Rather, it is a survey of your basic beliefs, attitudes, and values on specific topics related to the practice of therapy. For each question, write in the letter of the response that most clearly reflects your viewpoint at this time. In many cases the answers are not mutually exclusive, and you may choose more than one response if you wish. In addition, a blank line is included for each item. You may want to use this line to provide another response more suited to your thinking or to qualify a chosen response.

Notice that there are two spaces before each item. Use the spaces on the left for your answers at the beginning of the course. At the end of the course you can retake this inventory using the spaces on the right and covering your initial answers so that you won't be influenced by how you originally responded. Then you can see how your attitudes have changed as a result of your experience in this course.

You may want to bring the completed inventory to your beginning class session so that you can compare your views with those of others in the class. Such a comparison might stimulate some debate and help get the class involved in the topics to be discussed. In choosing the issues you want to discuss in class, you might go back over the inventory and circle the numbers of those items that you felt most strongly about as you were responding. You may find it instructive to ask others how they responded to these items in particular.

 1. The personal characteristics of counselors are
    a. not really that relevant to the counseling process.
    b. the most important variable in determining the quality of the counseling process.
    c. shaped and molded by those who teach counselors.
    d. not as important as the skills and knowledge the counselors possess.
    e. _____

 2. Which of the following do you consider to be the most important personal characteristic of a good counselor?
    a. willingness to serve as a model for clients
    b. courage
    c. openness and honesty
    d. a sense of being "centered" as a person
    e. _____

 3. Concerning self-disclosure on the part of counselors to their clients, I believe that
    a. it is essential if a relationship is to be established.
    b. it is inappropriate and merely burdens the client.
    c. it should rarely be done and only when the therapist feels like sharing.
    d. it is useful for counselors to reveal how they feel toward their clients in the context of the therapy sessions.
    e. _____

 4. A client/therapist relationship characterized by warmth, acceptance, caring, nonjudgmentalness, empathy, and respect is

a. a necessary and sufficient condition of positive change in clients.

b. a necessary but not sufficient condition of positive change in clients.

c. neither a necessary nor a sufficient condition of positive change in clients.

d. _____

_c_ __ 5. Of the following factors, which is the most important in determining whether counseling will result in change?

a. the kind of person the counselor is

b. the skills and techniques the counselor uses

c. the motivation of the client to change

d. the theoretical orientation of the therapist

e. _____

__ __ 6. Of the following, which do you consider to be the most important attribute of an effective therapist?

a. knowledge of the theory of counseling and behavior

b. skill in using techniques appropriately

c. genuineness and openness

d. ability to specify a treatment plan and evaluate the results

e. _____

__ __ 7. I believe that, for those who wish to become therapists, personal psychotherapy

a. should be required for licensure.

b. is not an important factor in developing the capacity to work with others.

c. should be encouraged but not required.

d. is needed only when the therapist has *real* problems.

e. _____

__ __ 8. I believe that, in order to help a client, a therapist

a. must like the client personally.

b. must be free of any personal conflicts in the area in which the client is working.

c. needs to have experienced the very same problem as the client.

d. needs to have experienced feelings similar to those being experienced by the client.

e. _____

__ __ 9. In regard to the client/therapist relationship, I think that

a. the therapist should remain objective and anonymous.

b. the therapist should be a friend to the client.

c. a personal relationship, but not friendship, is essential.

d. a personal and warm relationship is not essential.

e. _____

\_\_ \_\_ 10. I should be open, honest, and transparent with my clients
   a. when I like and value them.
   b. when I have negative feelings toward them.
   c. rarely, if ever, so that I will avoid negatively influencing the client/therapist relationship.
   d. only when it intuitively feels like the right thing to do.

   e. _____

\_\_ \_\_ 11. I expect that I will experience professional burn-out if
   a. I get involved in too many demanding projects.
   b. I must do things in my work that aren't personally meaningful.
   c. my personal life is characterized by conflict and struggle.
   d. my clients complain a lot and fail to change for the better.

   e. _____

_C_ \_\_ 12. I think that professional burn-out
   a. can be avoided if I'm involved in personal therapy while working as a professional.
   b. is inevitable and that I must learn to live with it.
   c. can be lessened if I find ways to replenish and nourish myself.
   d. may or may not occur, depending on the type of client I work with.

   e. _____

\_\_ \_\_ 13. If I were an intern and were convinced that my supervisor was encouraging trainees to participate in unethical behavior in an agency setting, I would
   a. first discuss the matter with the supervisor.
   b. report the supervisor to the director of the agency.
   c. ignore the situation for fear of negative consequences.
   d. report the situation to the ethics committee of the state professional association.

   e. _____

_B_ \_\_ 14. Practitioners who work with culturally diverse groups without having cross-cultural knowledge and skills
   a. are violating the civil rights of their clients.
   b. are probably guilty of unethical behavior.
   c. should realize the need for specialized training.
   d. can be said to be practicing ethically.

   e. _____

\_\_ \_\_ 15. If I had strong feelings, positive or negative, toward a client, I think that I would most likely
   a. discuss my feelings with my client.
   b. keep them to myself and hope they would eventually disappear.

    c. discuss them with a supervisor or colleague.

    d. accept them as natural unless they began to interfere with the counseling relationship.

    e. _____

\_\_ \_\_ 16. I won't feel ready to counsel others until

    a. my own life is free of problems.

    b. I've experienced counseling as a client.

    c. I feel very confident and know that I'll be effective.

    d. I've become a self-aware person and developed the ability to continually reexamine my own life and relationships.

    e. _____

\_\_ \_\_ 17. If a client evidenced strong feelings of attraction or dislike for me, I think that I would

    a. help the client work through these feelings and understand them.

    b. enjoy these feelings if they were positive.

    c. refer my client to another counselor.

    d. direct the sessions into less emotional areas.

    e. _____

\_\_ \_\_ 18. Practitioners who counsel clients whose sex, race, age, social class, or sexual orientation is different from their own

    a. will most likely not understand these clients fully.

    b. need to understand the differences between their clients and themselves.

    c. can practice unethically if they do not consider cross-cultural factors.

    d. are probably not going to be effective with such clients because of these differences.

    e. _____

\_\_ \_\_ 19. When I consider being involved in the helping professions, I value most

    a. the money I expect to earn.

    b. the security I imagine I will have in the job.

    c. the knowledge that I will be intimately involved with people who are searching for a better life.

    d. the personal growth I expect to experience through my work.

    e. _____

\_\_ \_\_ 20. I see counseling as

    a. a process of reeducation for the client.

    b. a process whereby clients are taught new and more appropriate values to live by.

    c. a process that enables clients to make decisions regarding their own lives.

d. a process of giving advice and setting goals for clients.

e. _____

___ ___ 21. With respect to value judgments in counseling, therapists should
    a. feel free to make value judgments about their clients' behavior.
    b. actively teach their own values when they think that clients need a different set of values.
    c. remain neutral and keep their values out of the therapeutic process.
    d. encourage clients to question their own values and decide upon the quality of their own behavior.

    e. _____

___ ___ 22. Counselors should
    a. teach desirable behavior and values by modeling them for clients.
    b. encourage clients to look within themselves to discover values that are meaningful to them.
    c. reinforce the dominant values of society.
    d. very delicately, if at all, challenge clients' value systems.

    e. _____

___ ___ 23. In terms of appreciating and understanding the value systems of clients who are culturally different from me,
    a. I see it as my responsibility to learn about their values and not impose mine on them.
    b. I would encourage them to accept the values of the dominant culture for survival purposes.
    c. I would attempt to modify my counseling procedures to fit their cultural values.
    d. I think it is imperative that I learn about the specific cultural values my clients hold.

    e. _____

___ ___ 24. If a client came to me with a problem and I could see that I would not be objective because of my values, I would
    a. accept the client because of the challenge to become more tolerant of diversity.
    b. tell the client at the outset about my fears concerning our conflicting values.
    c. refer the client to someone else.
    d. attempt to influence the client to adopt my way of thinking.

    e. _____

___ ___ 25. I believe that the real reason for professional licensing and certification is

a. to provide information to the public about mental-health services.
b. to protect the public by setting minimum levels of competence for psychological services.
c. to upgrade the helping professions by assuring that the highest standards of excellence are promoted.
d. to protect the self-serving interests of various helping professions and to reduce competition.

e. _____

___ ___ 26. I would tend to refer a client to another therapist
a. if I had a strong dislike for the client.
b. if I didn't have much experience working with the kind of problem the client presented.
c. if I saw my own needs and problems getting in the way of helping the client.
d. if the client seemed to distrust me.

e. _____

___ ___ 27. My ethical position regarding the role of values in therapy is that, as a therapist, I should
a. never impose my values on a client.
b. expose my values, without imposing them on the client.
c. teach my clients what I consider to be proper values.
d. keep my values out of the counseling relationship.

e. _____

___ ___ 28. If I were to counsel lesbian and gay clients, a major concern of mine would be
a. maintaining objectivity.
b. not knowing and understanding enough about this type of life-style.
c. establishing a positive therapeutic relationship.
d. pushing my own values.

e. _____

___ ___ 29. Of the following, I consider the most unethical form of therapist behavior to be
a. promoting dependence in the client.
b. becoming sexually involved with clients.
c. breaking confidentiality without a good reason to do so.
d. accepting a client who has a problem that goes beyond the therapist's competence.

e. _____

___ ___ 30. Regarding the issue of counseling friends, I think that
a. it is seldom wise to accept a friend as a client.
b. it should be done rarely, and only if it is clear that the

friendship will not interfere with the therapeutic relationship.

c. friendship and therapy should not be mixed.

d. it should be done only if it seems appropriate to both the client and the counselor.

e. _____

___ ___ 31. Regarding confidentiality, I believe that

a. it is ethical to break confidence when there is reason to believe that the client may do serious harm to himself or herself.

b. it is ethical to break confidence when there is reason to believe that the client will do harm to someone else.

c. it is ethical to break confidence when the parents of a client ask for certain information.

d. it is ethical to inform the authorities when a client is breaking the law.

e. _____

___ ___ 32. Therapists should terminate therapy with a client when

a. the client decides to do so and not before.

b. they judge that it is time to terminate.

c. it is clear that the client is not benefiting from the therapy.

d. the client reaches an impasse.

e. _____

___ ___ 33. A sexual relationship between a client and therapist is

a. ethical if the client initiates it.

b. ethical if the therapist decides it is in the best interests of the client.

c. ethical only when client and therapist discuss the issue and agree to the relationship.

d. never ethical.

e. _____

___ ___ 34. Concerning the issue of physically touching a client, I think that touching

a. is unwise, because it could be misinterpreted by the client.

b. should be done only when the therapist genuinely feels like doing it.

c. is an important part of the therapeutic process.

d. is ethical when the client requests it.

e. _____

___ ___ 35. A clinical supervisor has initiated sexual relationships with former trainees (students). He maintains that, because he no longer has any professional responsibility to them, this practice is acceptable. In my view, this behavior is

a. clearly unethical, because he is using his position to initiate contacts with former students.

b. not unethical, because the professional relationship has ended.

c. not unethical but is unwise and inappropriate.

d. somewhat unethical, because the supervisory relationship is similar to the therapeutic relationship.

e. _____

____ ____ 36. Regarding the place of theory in counseling, I think that therapists should

a. ignore it, since it has no practical application.

b. select *one* theory and work within its framework.

c. select something from most of the theories of therapy.

d. select a theory on the basis of the client's personality and presenting problem.

e. _____

____ ____ 37. In the practice of marital and family therapy, I think that

a. the therapist's primary responsibility is to the welfare of the family as a unit.

b. the therapist should focus primarily on the needs of individual members of the family.

c. the therapist should attend to the family's needs and try to hold the amount of sacrifice by any one member to a minimum.

d. the therapist has an ethical obligation to state his or her bias and approach at the outset.

e. _____

____ ____ 38. On the matter of developing sexual relationships with *former* clients, my position is that

a. it is strictly up to the people involved to make that decision.

b. it is always unethical.

c. it is an example of taking advantage of a client.

d. it can be either ethical or unethical, depending on the case.

e. _____

____ ____ 39. Regarding the issue of who should select the goals of counseling, I believe that

a. it is primarily the therapist's responsibility to select goals.

b. it is primarily the client's responsibility to select goals.

c. the responsibility for selecting goals should be shared equally by the client and therapist.

d. the question of who selects the goals depends on what kind of client is being seen.

e. _____

___ ___ 40. Concerning the role of diagnosis in counseling, I believe that
        a. diagnosis is essential for the planning of a treatment program.
        b. diagnosis is counterproductive for therapy, since it is based on an external view of the client.
        c. diagnosis is dangerous in that it tends to label people, who then are limited by the label.
        d. whether to use diagnosis depends on one's theoretical orientation and the kind of counseling one does.

        e. _____

___ ___ 41. Concerning the place of testing in counseling, I think that
        a. tests generally interfere with the counseling process.
        b. tests can be valuable tools if they are used as adjuncts to counseling.
        c. tests are essential for people who are seriously disturbed.
        d. tests can be either used or abused in counseling.

        e. _____

___ ___ 42. Regarding the issue of psychological risks associated with participation in group therapy, my position is that
        a. clients should be informed at the outset of possible risks.
        b. these risks should be minimized by careful screening.
        c. this issue is exaggerated, since there are no real risks.
        d. careful supervision will offset some of these risks.

        e. _____

___ ___ 43. Concerning the counselor's responsibility to the community, I believe that
        a. the counselor should educate the community concerning the nature of psychological services.
        b. the counselor should attempt to change patterns that need changing.
        c. community involvement falls outside the proper scope of counseling.
        d. counselors should become involved in helping clients use the resources available in the community.

        e. _____

___ ___ 44. My view of personal counseling or psychotherapy for practitioners is that
        a. it is most desirable for beginning counselors.
        b. it is of great value for experienced counselors as well as beginning practitioners.
        c. it should be a strongly recommended component of any counselor-preparation program.

       d. it should not be necessary for most practitioners, unless they are faced with a personal crisis.

       e. _____

\_\_ \_\_ 45. As an intern, if I thought my supervision was inadequate, I would

       a. talk to my supervisor about it.

       b. continue to work without complaining.

       c. seek supervision elsewhere.

       d. feel let down by the agency I worked for.

       e. _____

\_\_ \_\_ 46. My view of supervision is that it is

       a. something that I could use on a permanent basis.

       b. a threat to my status as a professional.

       c. valuable to have when I reach an impasse with a client.

       d. a way for me to learn about myself and to get insights into how I work with clients.

       e. _____

\_\_ \_\_ 47. When it comes to working within institutions, I believe that

       a. I must learn how to survive with dignity within a system.

       b. I must learn how to subvert the system so that I can do what I deeply believe in.

       c. the institution will stifle most of my enthusiasm and block any real change.

       d. I can't blame the institution if I'm unable to succeed in my programs.

       e. _____

\_\_ \_\_ 48. If my philosophy were in conflict with that of the institution I worked for, I would

       a. seriously consider whether I could ethically remain in that position.

       b. attempt to change the policies of the institution.

       c. agree to whatever was expected of me in that system.

       d. quietly do what I wanted to do, even if I had to be devious about it.

       e. _____

\_\_ \_\_ 49. In working with clients from different ethnic groups, I think it is most important to

       a. be aware of the sociopolitical forces that have affected these clients.

       b. understand how language can act as a barrier to effective cross-cultural counseling.

       c. refer these clients to some professional who shares their ethnic and cultural background.

    d. help these clients modify their views so that they will be accepted and not have to suffer rejection.

    e. _____

___ ___ 50. To be effective in counseling clients from a different culture, I think that a counselor must

    a. possess specific knowledge about the particular group he or she is counseling.

    b. be able to accurately "read" nonverbal messages.

    c. have had direct contact with this group.

    d. treat these clients no differently from clients from his or her own cultural background.

    e. _____

# Chapter Summary

This introductory chapter has focused on the foundations of creating an ethical sense and has explored various perspectives on teaching the process of making ethical decisions. The central point has been that professional codes of ethics are indeed essential for ethical practice but that merely knowing these codes is not enough. The challenge comes with learning how to think critically and knowing ways to apply general ethical principles to particular situations.

We have encouraged you to become active in your education and training. We also suggest that you try to keep an open mind about the issues you encounter during this time and throughout your professional career. An important part of this openness is a willingness to focus on yourself as a person and as a professional, as well as on the questions that are more obviously related to your clients.

# Suggested Activities

1. As a practitioner, how will you determine what is ethical and what is unethical? Think about how you will go about developing your guidelines for ethical practice, and make up a list of behaviors that you judge to be unethical. After you've thought through this issue by yourself, you may want to explore your approach with fellow students.

2. Look over all of the professional codes of ethics in the Appendix. What are your impressions of each of these codes? To what degree are they complete? To what degree do they provide you with the needed guidelines for ethical practice? What are the values of such codes? What limitations do you see in them? What do the various codes of ethics have in common?

3. Assume that you were a member of a committee that was making recommendations for the professional training program in which you are now involved. What changes would you most want to make in your training program? As you see it, what are the strengths and the weaknesses of your program? After you have done this exercise, bring some of your ideas to your professors.

   *Note to the student:* We want to remind you that we do not expect you to systematically think about and work on *every* suggested activity that we have at the end of each chapter. Our purpose is to invite you to personalize the material and develop your own positions on the issues we raise. Use your judgment in selecting those activities that you find the most challenging and meaningful.

■
## Suggested Readings

At the end of each chapter we provide some suggestions for further reading on many of the topics we have explored. Because the cutting edge in the development of professional ethics is found in the journals, we emphasize the more recent journal articles. Here we provide only the author and the date, along with brief annotations. For the full bibliographic entry, consult the References and Reading List at the back of the book.

On the role of ethical codes see Mabe and Rollin (1986), Tennyson and Strom (1986) and Van Hoose (1986). On conflicts between ethics and the law see Mappes, Robb, and Engels (1985). On the teaching of ethics see Tymchuk (1981), Tymchuk and Associates (1979, 1982), Welfel and Lipsitz (1984), Lipsitz (1985), Baldick (1980), and Handelsman (1986a, 1986b). For models of ethical decision making see Pelsma and Borgers (1986), Hillerbrand and Stone (1986), and Kitchener (1984a, 1984b, 1986). On ethics education and adjudication within psychology see Mills (1984). For an interesting discussion of the failure of graduate students in clinical psychology to apply to practice what they know about ethical principles, see Bernard and Jara (1986). For the results of a national survey of ethical dilemmas in psychological practice, see Haas, Malouf, and Mayerson (1986). For a casebook see Callis, Pope, and DePauw (1982). For a few textbooks in professional ethics see Van Hoose and Kottler (1985), Loewenberg and Dolgoff (1985), Keith-Spiegel and Koocher (1985), and Carroll, Schneider, and Wesley (1985).

# TWO

# The Counselor as a Person and as a Professional

■

# Pre-Chapter Self-Inventory

The pre-chapter self-inventories can help you identify and clarify your attitudes and beliefs about the issues to be explored in the chapter. Keep in mind that the "right" answer is the one that best expresses your thoughts at the time. We suggest that you complete the inventory before reading the chapter; then, after reading the chapter and discussing the material in class, you can retake the inventory to see whether your positions have changed in any way.

*Directions:*    For each statement, indicate the response that most closely identifies your beliefs and attitudes. Use the following code:

3 = I *agree*, in most respects, with this statement.
2 = I am *undecided* in my opinion about this statement.
1 = I *disagree*, in most respects, with this statement.

\_\_\_\_    1. Therapists' attitudes are more important than their theoretical orientations in initiating positive personality changes in clients.

\_\_\_\_    2. The personal qualities of therapists are at least as important as their knowledge and skills in effecting client change.

\_\_\_\_    3. Therapists should remain relatively anonymous and avoid disclosing much of themselves, so that they don't unduly influence their clients.

\_\_\_\_    4. For therapy to be successful, the relationship between client and therapist must be characterized by acceptance, trust, and personal warmth.

\_\_\_\_    5. Part of the counselor's task is to serve as a model for clients, because clients learn a great deal by imitating the behavior of the therapist.

\_\_\_\_    6. The ability of a therapist to establish a good personal relationship with a client is essential, but it is not sufficient by itself to bring about behavioral change.

\_\_\_\_    7. Unless therapists have a high degree of self-awareness, there is a real danger that they will use their clients to satisfy their own needs.

\_\_\_\_    8. Before therapists begin to practice, they should be free of personal problems and conflicts.

\_\_\_\_    9. Counselors or therapists should be required to undergo their own therapy before they are licensed to practice.

\_\_\_\_    10. Counselors who satisfy personal needs through their work are behaving unethically.

\_\_\_\_    11. Most professionals in the counseling field face a high risk of burnout because of the demands of their jobs.

\_\_\_\_    12. Counselors who know themselves can avoid experiencing overidentification with their clients.

\_\_\_\_    13. Strong feelings about a client are a sign that the counselor needs further therapy for himself or herself.

___ 14. Feelings of anxiety in a beginning counselor indicate unsuitability for the counseling profession.

___ 15. A competent counselor can work with any client.

___ 16. I fear that I'll have difficulty challenging my clients.

___ 17. A professional counselor will avoid both getting involved socially with clients and counseling friends.

___ 18. A major fear I have is that I'll make mistakes and seriously hurt a client.

___ 19. Real therapy does not occur unless a transference relationship is developed.

___ 20. A professional counselor will not withhold anything personal about himself or herself from a client.

___ 21. The most important personal quality of a therapist is empathy, for this is the basis for forming relationships.

___ 22. For a counselor to be effective with a client, he or she must have experienced the same type of problems as the client.

___ 23. For a counselor to be effective with a client, the two must have a similar "world view"; that is, they must share a common set of values, beliefs, cultural mores, and experiences in life.

___ 24. As a counselor, I think it is important that I be willing to adapt my therapeutic style (techniques and approaches) to the cultural backgrounds of my clients.

___ 25. An experienced and competent counselor should not need either periodic or ongoing personal psychotherapy.

# Introduction

One of the most basic issues in the helping professions concerns the role of the counselor *as a person* in the therapeutic relationship. Since counselors are asking people to take an honest look at themselves and to make choices concerning how they want to change, it seems critical to us that counselors themselves be searchers who hold their own lives open to the same kind of scrutiny. Counselors should repeatedly ask themselves such questions as the following: "What makes me think I have a right to counsel anyone else? What do I personally have to offer others who are struggling to find their way? Am I doing in my own life what I urge others to do?"

Counselors and psychotherapists usually acquire an extensive theoretical and practical knowledge and make that knowledge available to their clients. But to every therapeutic session they also bring themselves as persons. They bring their human qualities and the life experiences that have molded them. It is our belief that professionals can be well-versed in psychological theory and can learn diagnostic and interviewing skills and still be ineffective as helpers. It seems obvious to us that, if counselors are to promote growth and change in their clients, they must be willing to promote growth in their own lives by exploring their own choices and decisions and by striving to become aware of the ways in which they sometimes ignore their own potential for growth. This willingness to attempt to live in accordance with what they teach and thus to be positive models for their clients is what makes counselors "therapeutic persons."

It is difficult to talk about the counselor *as a professional* without considering the personal qualities that influence the kind of professional he or she becomes. A counselor's values, beliefs, personal attributes, life experiences, and way of living are intrinsically related to the way he or she functions as a professional. Counselors do have a professional identity, however, and some issues are specifically related to their professionalism as counselors. Although some of the questions we discuss are of special concern to the beginning counselor, you'll probably find yourself struggling with most of these issues again and again throughout your professional career.

## Personal Characteristics of Effective Counselors

*✻ Key ✻* <

We see the personal attributes of the therapist as the single most important determinant of successful therapy. In this section we examine some of the characteristics that we think are important for effective counselors to have, and we ask you to think of the personal attributes *you* deem to be vital. Of course, no counselor is likely to possess all the attributes we mention; we're not contending that being a successful counselor is synonymous with being a model of perfection! But those counselors who are willing to look within themselves and struggle toward becoming more effective human beings are the ones most likely to make a positive difference in the lives of their clients.

The following is a list of personal traits and characteristics that we believe counselors might aim for. As you read over our list, ask yourself whether you agree with each item and whether there are other traits that you think are important. Then you can use your list of significant personal characteristics as a starting point for reflection on your own struggle to become a more effective person.

1. *Good will.*   Effective counselors must have a sincere interest in the welfare of others. The way they relate to others shows that they respect, trust, and value other people. Caring about others doesn't necessarily imply merely showing warmth and giving support. It may involve challenging others to look at aspects of their lives they would prefer to ignore. It may involve a refusal to tolerate dishonest behavior and a corresponding willingness to encourage others to live without their masks and shields. Caring is perhaps best shown when counselors avoid using clients to meet their own needs.

2. *The ability to be present for others.*   By being emotionally present for clients, we mean being with them in their experience of pain or joy. This ability stems from the counselor's openness to his or her own struggles and feelings. This is not to say that counselors must talk with their clients about

their own experiences but, rather, that being in contact with their own emotions enables them to be compassionate and empathic with their clients.

3. *A recognition and acceptance of one's personal power.*    Effective counselors recognize their personal power, not in the sense that they dominate or exploit their clients but that they are in contact with their own strength and vitality. They feel confident and alive and have no need to diminish others or feel superior to them. They recognize that two persons in a relationship can both be powerful, and they don't have to assume a superior role to feel competent. Indeed, one of their aims is to help clients discover their own autonomy and competence.

4. *A personal counseling style.*    Effective practitioners strive to develop counseling styles that are expressions of their own personalities. They are open to learning from others and may borrow concepts and techniques from different schools of therapy, but their styles are ultimately their own.

5. *A willingness to be vulnerable and open.*    Ideally, counselors exemplify in their own lives the courage and openness they hope to promote in their clients. Thus, they are willing to take risks, to be vulnerable at times, to trust their intuitions even when they're unsure of the outcome, to be emotionally touched by others, to draw on their own experiences in order to identify with the feelings and struggles of other people, and to disclose what they think and feel about their clients when it is appropriate to do so.

6. *Self-respect and self-appreciation.*    Counselors will be most effective if they feel like "winners." In other words, they should have a strong sense of self-worth that enables them to relate to others out of their strengths rather than out of their weaknesses.

7. *A willingness to serve as models for clients.*    One of the best ways to teach others is by example. Accordingly, effective counselors don't ask their clients to do things they aren't willing to do themselves. If they genuinely value risk taking, openness, honesty, self-examination, and so on, then they will exhibit some degree of these qualities in their own lives.

8. *A willingness to risk making mistakes and to admit having made them.*    Effective counselors realize that they will accomplish little if they rarely take the chance of failing. They know they will make mistakes, and they try to learn from them without burdening themselves excessively with self-recrimination.

9. *A growth orientation.*    The most effective counselors remain open to the possibility of broadening their horizons instead of telling themselves they have "arrived." They question the quality of their existence, their values, and their motivations. Just as they encourage their clients to become more autonomous, they attempt to live by their own values and standards rather than by the expectations of others. They are committed to a continual search for self-awareness, and they know that an appreciation of their own limitations, strengths, fears, and vulnerabilities is essential if they are to foster this kind of self-understanding in their clients.

10. *A sense of humor.*   Effective practitioners take counseling seriously, but they are also able to laugh *at themselves* and *with clients*. This humor does not mock the client; rather, it is a function of the strength of the relationship with the client. Humor is one way for counselors to maintain a sense of perspective in their work.

Now that we've listed some traits that we think are important for effective counselors to have, we'd like to give you the chance to reflect a moment on your reactions.

- From our list, select one or two traits that you think are most important, and state why. Also, think of people who were helpful to you. What were their characteristics?
- At this point in your evolution as a helping person, what major *personal strengths* do you consider will be assets to you in your profession?
- What personal areas do you see as being potential liabilities for you as a counselor?

# Self-Awareness and the Influence of the Therapist's Personality and Needs

Since counselors ask clients to examine their behavior and lives in order to understand themselves more fully, it is incumbent on them to be equally committed to awareness of their own lives. Moreover, without a high level of self-awareness, counselors will obstruct the progress of their clients. The focus of the therapy will shift from meeting the client's needs to meeting the needs of the therapist. Consequently, counselors and therapists should be aware of their own needs, areas of "unfinished business," personal conflicts, defenses, and vulnerabilities—*and* how these may intrude on their work with their clients. In this section we consider some specific areas that we think counselors need to examine.

## Personal Benefits

One critical question that counselors can ask themselves is "What do I personally get from doing counseling?" There are many answers to this question. Many therapists experience excitement and a deep sense of satisfaction from being with people who are struggling to achieve self-understanding, who recognize that their lives aren't the way they want them to be, and who are willing to experience pain as they seek a better life for themselves. Some counselors enjoy the feeling of being instrumental in others' changes; others appreciate the depth and honesty of the therapeutic relationship. Still other therapists value the opportunity to question their own lives as they work with their clients. Therapeutic encounters can in many ways serve as mirrors in which therapists can see their own lives reflected. As a

a catalyst for therapist change

result, therapy can become a catalyst for change in the therapist as much as in the client.

Therapeutic progress can be blocked, however, when therapists use their clients, perhaps unconsciously, to fulfill their own needs. Out of a need to nurture others or to feel powerful, for example, people sometimes feel that they have the answers concerning how others should live. The tendency to give advice and try to direct another's life can be especially harmful in a therapist, because it leads to excessive dependence on the part of clients and only perpetuates their tendency to look outside themselves for answers. Therapists who need to feel powerful or important may begin to think that they are indispensable to their clients or, worse still, make themselves so.

The goals of therapy can also suffer when therapists who have a strong need for approval focus on trying to win the acceptance, admiration, respect, and even awe of their clients. Some therapists may be primarily motivated by a need to receive confirmation of their value as persons and as professionals from their clients. It is within their power as therapists to control the sessions in such a way that these needs are continually reinforced. Because clients often feel a need to please their therapists, they can easily encourage therapists who crave continuous reinforcement of their sense of worth.

teach problem solving

One of the goals of therapy, as we see it, is to teach the *process* of problem solving, not just to solve problems. When clients have learned the process, they have less and less need of their therapists. Therapists who tell clients what to do or use the sessions to buttress their own sense of self-worth diminish the autonomy of their clients and invite increased dependence in the future.

When therapists are not sufficiently aware of their own needs, they may abuse the power they have in the therapeutic situation. Some therapists and counselors gain a sense of power by assuming the role of directing others toward solutions instead of encouraging them to seek alternatives for themselves. A solution-oriented approach to counseling may also spring from the therapist's need to feel a sense of achievement and accomplishment. Some therapists feel very ill at ease if their clients fail to make instant progress; consequently, they may either push their clients to make decisions prematurely or even make decisions for them. This tendency can be encouraged even more by clients who express gratitude for this kind of "help."

Of course, therapists *do* have their own personal needs, but these needs don't have to assume priority or get in the way of clients' growth. Most people who enter the helping professions do want to nurture others, and they do need to know that they are being instrumental in helping others to change. In this sense, they need to hear from clients that they are a significant force in their lives. In order to keep these needs from interfering with the progress of their clients, therapists should be clearly aware of the danger of working primarily to be appreciated by others instead of working toward the best interests of their clients. If they are open enough to recognize this potential danger, the chances are that they will not fall into using their clients to meet their own needs.

As Kottler (1986) has written, in the practice of psychotherapy our personal and professional roles can complement each other. Our knowledge and skills are equally useful with clients, friends, or family. Also, our life experiences, both joys and sorrows, provide the background for what we do in our therapeutic sessions with clients.

It's hard to find fault with therapists who find excitement in their work. The rewards of practicing psychotherapy are many, but one of the most significant rewards is the joy of seeing clients move from being victims to assuming control over their lives. Therapists can achieve this reward only if they avoid abusing their influence and maintain a keen awareness of their role as facilitators of others' growth. As you consider your own needs and their influence on your work as a therapist, you might ask yourself the following questions:

- How can I know when I'm working for the client's benefit and when I'm working for my own benefit?
- How much might I depend on clients to tell me how good I am as a person or as a therapist? Am I able to appreciate myself, or do I depend primarily on others to validate my worth and the value of my work?
- How can I deal with feelings of inadequacy, particularly if I seem to be getting nowhere with a client?

## Unresolved Personal Conflicts

We have suggested that the personal needs of a therapist can interfere with the therapeutic process, to the detriment of the client, if the therapist is unaware of their impact on his or her work. The same is true for personal problems and unresolved conflicts. This is not to say that therapists must resolve all their personal difficulties before they begin to counsel others; such a requirement would eliminate almost everybody from the field. In fact, it's possible that a counselor who rarely struggles or experiences anxiety may have real difficulty in relating to a client who feels desperate or caught in a hopeless conflict. Moreover, if therapists flee from anxiety-provoking questions in their own lives, they probably won't be able to effectively encourage clients to face such questions. The important point is that counselors can and should be *aware* of their biases, their areas of denial, and the issues they find particularly hard to deal with in their own lives.

To illustrate, suppose that you're experiencing a rough time in your life. You feel stuck with unresolved anger and frustration. Your home life is tense, and you're wrestling with some pivotal decisions about how you want to spend the rest of your life. Perhaps you're having problems with your clients or your spouse. You might be caught between fears of loneliness and a desire to be on your own, or between your fear of and need for close relationships. Can you counsel others effectively while you're struggling with your own uncertainty?

To us, the critical point isn't *whether* you happen to be struggling with personal questions but *how* you're struggling with them. Do you see your part in creating your own problems? Are you aware of your alternatives for action? Do you recognize and try to deal with your problems, or do you invest a lot of energy in denying their existence? Do you find yourself generally blaming others for your problems? Are you willing to consult with a therapist, or do you tell yourself that you can handle it, even when it becomes obvious that you're not doing so? In short, are you willing to do in your own life what you encourage your clients to do?

If you're not working on being aware of your own conflicts, then you'll be in a poor position to pay attention to the ways in which your personal life influences your work with clients, especially if some of their problem areas are also problem areas for you. For example, suppose a client is trying to deal with feelings of hopelessness and despair. How can you intensively explore these feelings if, in your own life, you're busily engaged in cheering everybody up? If hopelessness is an issue you don't want to face personally, you'll probably steer the client away from exploring it. As another example, consider a client who wants to explore her feelings about homosexuality. Can you facilitate this exploration if you are homophobic? If you feel discomfort in talking about homosexual feelings and experiences and don't want to have to deal with your discomfort, can you stay with your client emotionally when she brings up this topic?

Since you'll have difficulty staying with a client in an area that you're reluctant or fearful to deal with, consider what present unfinished business in your own life might affect you as a counselor. What unresolved conflicts are you aware of, and how might these conflicts influence the way you counsel others?

# Common Concerns of Beginning Counselors

Students in counselor-training programs tend to bring up the same fears, resistances, self-doubts, concerns, and questions. They may wonder whether they have what it takes to be ethically sensitive professional counselors, or they may seriously question the nature of their impact on the people they counsel. Moreover, students inevitably discover that there is a gap between their formal, academic learning and the actual work they do when they come face to face with clients. The discovery that they have mainly themselves to work with—that, although techniques can be helpful, they must ultimately draw on themselves as persons—can be a frightening one. You should keep in mind, however, that these concerns are rarely resolved once and for all; even as an experienced counselor, you'll probably find yourself struggling from time to time with doubts and anxieties about your adequacy or the value of your work.

The following questionnaire is drawn from statements we frequently hear in practicum and internship courses; they represent a sampling of the issues faced by those who begin to counsel others. Apply these statements to yourself, and decide to what degree you see them as your concerns. If a statement is more true than false for you, place a "T" in front of it; if it is more false than true for you, place an "F" in front of it.

\_\_\_\_ I'm afraid that I'll make mistakes.

\_\_\_\_ My clients will really suffer because of my blunders and my failure to know what to do.

\_\_\_\_ I have real doubts concerning my ability to help people in a crisis situation.

\_\_\_\_ I demand perfection of myself, and I constantly feel I should know more than I do.

\_\_\_\_ I would feel threatened by silences in counseling situations.

\_\_\_\_ It's important to me to know that my clients are making steady improvement.

\_\_\_\_ It would be difficult for me to deal with demanding clients.

\_\_\_\_ I expect to have trouble working with clients who are not motivated to change or who are required to come to me for counseling.

\_\_\_\_ I have trouble deciding how much of the responsibility for the direction of a counseling session is mine and how much is my client's.

\_\_\_\_ I think that I should be successful with all my clients.

\_\_\_\_ I expect to have trouble in being myself and trusting my intuition when I'm counseling.

\_\_\_\_ I am afraid to express feelings of anger to a client.

\_\_\_\_ I worry that my clients will see that I am a beginner and wonder if I am competent.

\_\_\_\_ I am concerned about looking and acting like an ethical professional.

\_\_\_\_ Sometimes I'm concerned about how honest I should be with clients.

\_\_\_\_ I'm concerned about how much of my personal reactions and my private life I should reveal in counseling sessions.

\_\_\_\_ I tend to worry about whether I'm making the proper intervention.

\_\_\_\_ I sometimes worry that I may overidentify with my client's problems to the extent that they become *my* problems.

\_\_\_\_ During a counseling session I would frequently find myself wanting to give advice.

\_\_\_\_ I'm afraid that I may say or do something that might greatly disturb a client.

\_\_\_\_ I'm concerned about counseling clients whose values are very different from my own.

\_\_\_\_ I would be concerned about whether my clients liked and approved of me and whether they would want to come back.

\_\_\_\_ I'm concerned about being mechanical in any counseling, as though I were following a book.

Now go back and select the issues that represent your greatest concerns. You can then begin to challenge some of the assumptions behind these concerns. Suppose, for example, that you feel greatly afraid of making mistakes. You may be saying to yourself: "I should know more than I do, and I should have answers for my clients. If I were to get stuck and not know what to do with a given client, that would be terrible; it would completely erode my self-confidence. If I made mistakes, I might drive my clients away, and they would be far worse off than when they began counseling with me." If you are burdening yourself with these or similar expectations, you can begin to challenge your basic assumptions by asking yourself such questions as these:

- Why should I be all-knowing?
- Who told me that making mistakes would be fatal?
- Am I really expected to provide solutions for clients?
- Are my clients so fragile that they won't be able to survive my mistakes?

As we discuss some of the issues encountered by practicing counselors, ask yourself how you relate to these issues and whether you should begin to question some of your assumptions. You might also find it useful to write about other concerns you now have as you think about becoming a professional counselor. What issues are most pressing for you? What assumptions underlie your concerns? How valid are these assumptions?

## Anxiety

Many counselors experience some anxiety over their work, particularly if they have had little or no experience. As you think of facing your first clients, you may ask yourself: "What will my clients want? Will I be able to give them what they want? What will I say, and how will I say it? Will they want to come back? If they do, what will I do then?"

Although raising such questions can be part of a process of self-inquiry and growth for even an experienced counselor, it's possible to become so anxiety-ridden that you cannot deal with the questions effectively. Your anxiety may feed on itself, especially if you think that it's abnormal or tell yourself that you wouldn't be experiencing so much anxiety if you were really suited for the counseling profession. It may help to realize that a certain amount of anxiety indicates an awareness of the uncertainty that surrounds your work with clients. Although anxiety can get out of hand and freeze a counselor into inactivity, some anxiety is certainly to be expected. In fact, we become concerned when we encounter student counselors who never exhibit any kind of self-doubt or self-questioning, which we believe to be part of the evolutionary process of becoming a counselor. The experience of anxiety can lead to honest self-appraisal. We often hear students say that their peers seem so much more knowledgeable, skilled, and confident than they themselves feel. When such students have the courage to bring their feelings of inadequacy into the open, they frequently discover that they aren't alone and that those who appear the most self-confident also have doubts about their capabilities as counselors.

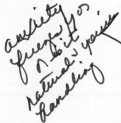

*regular meetings w/ peers helpful*

This is where regular meetings with your fellow students and your instructor are vitally important. There are no easy solutions to the kind of anxiety you are likely to experience; in any event, we think it's counterproductive to try to remove all anxiety. With your peers you can discuss your fears, worries, and questions, and you can gain a sense of how they deal with such feelings. You can also explore with them how much of your anxiety reflects a genuine appreciation of the uncertainties inherent in your chosen profession. This kind of exchange offers invaluable opportunities for personal and professional growth. And, since it takes courage to share your feelings, doing so may defuse some of the anxiety that is unrealistic.

Before you continue reading, take a few moments to reflect on some areas of your professional work that might cause you anxiety.

## Expecting Instant Results

Many beginning counselors become discouraged when they don't see immediate, positive results in their clients. These counselors may be assuming that their role is to solve any and all problems their clients bring to the sessions. Accordingly, they ask: "Is my client getting better or worse? How do I know if what I'm doing during our sessions is really worth anything?"

The fact is that clients generally don't make immediate gains. Indeed, it's far more common for them to report an increase in anxiety in the early stages of counseling and at various points later on. In trying to be honest with their counselors and with themselves, they are giving up many of their defenses and are likely to experience an acute sense of vulnerability. Counselors therefore need to be able to continue working without knowing the full extent to which they're having positive effects on a client. They may not know the nature of their impact until months after the conclusion of a therapeutic relationship, if then.

## Dealing with 'Difficult' Clients

To a beginning counselor almost every client seems difficult, in part because any counselor wants to succeed and needs to see signs of progress in the client. Even for experienced counselors, however, there are genuinely difficult clients. Some of these clients pose particular problems that tend to come up fairly often in a counseling practice. As we describe each of these clients, allow yourself to imagine that you are their counselor. What kinds of feelings and thoughts do they evoke in you? How do you imagine you would deal with each one? And how would you deal with the impact that "difficult" clients might have on you?

**Silent Clients.** The silent client is particularly troublesome for beginning counselors, who may interpret a client's silence as evidence that they aren't using the "right technique." For some counselors a silent moment in a therapeutic session may seem to last an hour. Out of their anxiety they may employ a barrage of questions in an attempt to get the client to open up. Or they may break silences with noisy chatter because of their own discomfort and fail to pursue what the silence means.

Although silence *may* be an indication that the sessions are not very fruitful, there are some distinct values to silence, and counselors need to learn that silence can have many meanings. The client may be waiting for the therapist to initiate a direction, particularly if the therapist has developed a style of asking many questions, making suggestions, or otherwise taking major responsibility for the sessions. The client may be quietly thinking or simply allowing himself or herself to experience some feelings aroused by the session. The client may feel stuck and not know what to say next or feel bored and anxious for the session to end. Both client and therapist may be resisting moving to a deeper level of interaction. Thus, silence may or may not be counterproductive, and it's important to explore the particular meaning of silence in each instance. You might ask yourself: "How do I generally respond to long silences? Am I able to communicate with another person through silence as well as through words? What would I be likely to do if a client habitually said very little?"

**Overly Demanding Clients.**    Overly demanding clients are especially troublesome for counselors who feel that their function is to meet all the demands of their clients. Because they perceive themselves as helpers, they may convince themselves that they should give unselfishly, regardless of the nature of the demands made on them. They may, therefore, have difficulty dealing with clients who call them at home to talk at length about ever-present crises, who want to be seen more frequently, or who become so dependent that they need to be told what to do at every turn. Such clients may insist that, if their counselors really cared for them, they would be more "giving." Counselors can easily become entangled with such clients and not know how to extricate themselves. Out of a sense of guilt or out of a failure to be assertive in setting realistic limits, they may allow themselves to be controlled by excessive demands.

If you've had some counseling experience, review any encounters you've had with overly demanding clients. What were some of the demands placed on you? In what ways were these demands unrealistic or unreasonable? Do you find that you're able to set reasonable limits? Are you able to make demands for yourself?

In dealing with overly demanding clients you may have to work through your own need to be needed. An extremely dependent client who continually tells you that you're indispensable is relating to you as a child to a parent. It's easy to keep this kind of client dependent on you, so that you can continue to feel needed. You might convince yourself that you're expected to be available to your clients at all times, while ignoring the benefit you obtain from being needed.

**Unmotivated Clients.**    Some clients have little investment in their counseling or little motivation to change in any significant way. Perhaps their main motivation for being in counseling is that someone else thought it would be

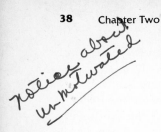

*notice about un-motivated*

a good idea. Again, counselors need to be alert to the dangers of allowing themselves to be perpetually drawn into games with their clients. If you find that you're doing most of the work and that you seem to care more about some clients than they care about themselves, you have good reason to believe that your own needs, not those of your clients, are being served.

We have discussed only a few examples of clients who may pose special problems for you. What other kinds of clients might be "difficult" for you? How do you see yourself reacting to them? Since we can only briefly describe the topic of dealing with difficult clients, we refer you to our book *Groups: Process and Practice* (Corey & Corey, 1987) for a more detailed discussion of the issues involved.

## Learning Your Limits

All counselors are faced with the task of learning their limits and learning to operate ethically within them. This includes recognizing that they aren't going to succeed with every client. Even experienced therapists sometimes doubt their effectiveness with clients they just can't seem to reach. For new counselors the inability to reach a client can be even more threatening, particularly since it's easy to believe at first that they should be able to work effectively with any client. Many beginning counselors tell themselves that they should like all the people who come to them for help or that they should be willing to work with anyone.

*takes wisdom & courage to admit you can't work w/ everybody*

It takes courage as well as wisdom to admit that you can't work effectively with everyone. You might work well with children but have real problems in trying to understand adolescents. Or you might be very close to certain children but feel removed and distant from others. Some counselors find meaning in working with the elderly, whereas others become depressed and discouraged. At some point you may need to consider whether it's better to accept a client you feel you cannot relate to or to admit to the client that another counselor would be more suitable.

*· ask what's your most liked kind of client.*

Ask yourself what kinds of clients you would most like to work with and what clients you would least like to work with. Then it might be useful to look honestly at some of your motivations for preferring certain clients over others. What clients would most challenge your personal or professional values? Do you want only those clients with whom you feel comfortable or who promise the greatest hope of success, or are you willing to endure some level of discomfort as you learn to work with a greater range of people? Are you able to admit to yourself and to your prospective clients that you don't *have* to succeed with everyone?

## On Demanding Perfection

Many counselors burden themselves with the belief that they must be perfect—that they must always know the appropriate thing to say or do, must never make mistakes, and must always have the skill needed to deal with any kind of counseling situation. Yet the fact is that all of us, new or experienced, are going to make mistakes. We fail to do our clients justice when we think of them as being so fragile that they will fall apart if we make mistakes. By overemphasizing the importance of avoiding mistakes, we diminish our clients' role in working toward their own decisions. Furthermore, if most of our energies go into presenting the image of the polished professional, we have little energy left for actually working with the client. Perhaps this is where the client is really cheated. It's hard to conceive of a genuine therapeutic relationship growing from such a situation.

*practicum*

A practicum in which you're getting supervision and have an opportunity to discuss your work might be a good place to bring up the issue of perfection. Sometimes students involved in group supervision are reluctant to talk about their inadequacies for fear of what their peers or instructors will think. It can take a good deal of ego strength to be willing to share your mistakes and apprehensions. It isn't easy to say: "I'd like some time to talk about the difficulties I'm having with one of my clients. Our relationship is stirring up a lot of feelings in me at this point, and I'm not sure how to proceed." Although it does take courage to ask for others' perceptions and feedback, this is an excellent way to learn not only about how to proceed with the client but also about your own dynamics. In this connection you might ask yourself the following questions:

- Am I reluctant to use my practicum (group supervision) sessions to talk freely about what I'm experiencing as I work with certain clients? If so, what is holding me back?
- If I feel insecure about making mistakes and about how I'll be perceived by my instructor and my peers, am I willing to share my insecurities with them? If not, what is holding me back?
- What specific insecurities would I be willing to explore with fellow students and an instructor or supervisor?

## Self-Disclosure and Being Yourself

Many counselors, regardless of their years of experience, struggle with the issue of how much self-disclosure to clients is appropriate. It is not uncommon to be guilty of either extreme—disclosing too little or disclosing too much.

*extremes*
*too little*
*too much*

**Excessive Self-Disclosure: Denying Your Professional Role.**    Most beginning counselors (and many experienced ones) have a need to be approved of by their clients. It's easy for these counselors to share intimate details so that their clients will perceive them as being human. They may talk about themselves a great deal, regardless of how appropriate their self-disclosure is for a given client, in the hope that their openness will encourage their clients to trust them and share more of themselves.

*aloof role*

Counselors who engage in excessive self-disclosure are often trying to avoid getting lost in a professionally aloof role. Some of these counselors would rather be seen as a friend than as a professional with specialized helping skills, and some use the client/counselor relationship to explore their own needs. The danger of this approach is that an artificiality can develop out of their need to be seen as human. Trying too hard to prove their humanness, they may not only fail to be authentic but also limit their potential effectiveness. When therapists disclose detailed stories about themselves, they take the focus away from the client. Although they are supposedly sharing their problems and experiences for the benefit of their clients, more often than not such sharing serves their own needs.

Van Hoose and Kottler (1985) admit that self-disclosure by the therapist has many values, but they caution that there is a fine distinction between appropriate, timely self-disclosure and self-disclosure that serves the therapist's own needs. They contend that, whenever therapists take the focus off their clients and put it on themselves, they are in danger of abusing their clients. They put the issue bluntly:

> Whenever the therapist engages in long-winded stories or anecdotes irrelevant to the client's pressing concern, he is keeping the focus on himself and acting unethically. Each and every time that the therapist takes the focus off the client and puts in on himself he is wasting valuable time in the interview and negating the client's importance [p. 123].

Self-disclosure on the part of the counselor need not be excessive, however. Facilitative disclosure, which is hard for many of us to learn, enhances the therapeutic process. It admits the client into the therapist's private world when to do so is relevant and timely within the context of the therapeutic relationship. Appropriate disclosure can focus on the reactions of the therapist to the client in the here-and-now encounter between them. With a few words, and sometimes even nonverbally, the therapist can express feelings of identification and understanding. The focus thus remains on the client, and the self-disclosure is not a contrived technique to get the client to open up. Appropriate self-disclosure is one way of being yourself without trying to prove your humanity to the point of being inauthentic or serving your own needs at the expense of the client. At this point, take some time to reflect on the following questions and on your own criteria for determining whether your self-disclosure is facilitative. You might bring these questions up for class discussion:

- How important is it to you that your clients like you?
- How much of your outside life are you willing to make known to your clients? For what reasons would you reveal your personal life?
- How might your clients be helped or hindered when you talk about yourself?
- How do you decide whether to share your personal reactions and feelings, positive and negative, concerning the client and your relationship?
- Would you tell a client that you were finding it difficult to concentrate on him or her during a particular session if you were in turmoil over some personal matter of your own? Why or why not?

**Too Little Self-Disclosure: Hiding behind Your Professional Role.** If some counselors go to the extreme of denying their professional role in order to be seen as friendly and human, some go to the opposite extreme. They hide behind a professional facade, becoming so caught up in maintaining stereotyped role expectations that they let little of themselves show in their interactions. Perhaps out of a fear of appearing unprofessional or otherwise losing the respect of their clients, they tend to keep their personal reactions out of the counseling session. Consider for a moment whether it's possible to perform your functions as a professional without being aloof and impersonal. Is it possible that the more insecure, frightened, and uncertain you are in your professional work, the more you will tend to cling to the defense afforded by a professional image?

We believe that "professional" aloofness may stem from unrealistic expectations that some counselors have concerning their role in therapy. Trying to live up to these expectations neither helps clients nor fosters your own growth. Consider the following statements, and check the ones that describe your expectations of yourself:

_____ I should always know what to say and do in a counseling session, for I need to appear competent if I am to earn the trust of my clients.

_____ I should always care for my clients, and I should care for all of them equally.

_____ I should like and enjoy my clients; I must be all-accepting, all-understanding, and fully empathic.

_____ To be an effective counselor I must have everything "together" in my own life; any indication that I have personal problems diminishes my effectiveness.

_____ I should be able to figure out what my clients want and need, even if they don't know themselves or don't reveal their wants and needs to me. Further, I should be able to provide them with solutions to their problems.

_____ I must remain neutral and objective at all times and avoid having personal feelings and reactions toward my clients.

We believe that such notions of what it means to be a professional lead counselors to hide behind a facade instead of being themselves in a nonmechanical and real way. By accepting these and other lofty standards, counselors end up playing roles that aren't always congruent with the way they feel. In moments of uncertainty with clients they may act all-knowing; if they find it difficult to care about or like certain clients, they may deny their negative feelings by focusing on positive ones; if they feel uninterested or bored, they may try to force themselves to pay attention. If you find that you tend to adopt an inauthentic professional role, you might ask yourself whether you can realistically expect your clients to shed inauthentic behavior and become increasingly genuine with themselves and with you. After all, what kind of behavior are you modeling for your clients if you fail to be authentic with them?

*transparent*

Sidney Jourard (1971) makes a helpful distinction between hiding be-hind professional roles (which is undesirable) and being a person who plays many roles (which is inevitable). He points to the fact that, when we get lost in our roles, we become alienated from ourselves. For Jourard, one of the major goals of therapists is to be transparent with their clients, at least with respect to their experiences in the counseling relationship. This kind of authenticity is basic to effective psychotherapy, he argues, because it offers the possibility of a genuine encounter between therapist and client. Clients will not be fooled if therapists attempt to hide their basic feelings by resort-ing to expert techniques: "Patients are seldom that insensitive. Moreover, if a therapist thus hides his being, he is engaging in the same inauthentic behavior that generated symptoms in the patient, and supposedly, he is trying to undo this self-alienating process" (p. 148).

Pause a moment now to consider specific kinds of feelings that you would *not* be willing to disclose to your clients. Why would you be unwilling to make these disclosures? Think also about the kinds of feelings and experi-ences you can see yourself sharing with your clients.

## Self-Deception

Even with the best of intentions and motives, both counselors and clients can fall prey to the phenomenon of self-deception. Self-deception occurs in subtle ways and is not to be confused with conscious lying. The client and the therapist both want to see productive results come out of the therapeutic relationship, and both may convince themselves that what they are doing is worthwhile, regardless of the reality. Let's consider client self-deception first.

It's safe to assume that people who are clients by choice have an invest-ment in experiencing positive changes. They are committing themselves financially and emotionally to a relationship in the hopes that they will experience less conflict, feel better about themselves, get along with others better, and feel more in charge of their own lives. Given these expectations and the personal investment involved, there is always the possibility that clients will overestimate what they are really getting from counseling. Some may have to feel they are benefiting in order to justify the personal sacrifices they are making to obtain counseling. In failing to be open to the reality of the situation, however, they render the counseling experience less effective.

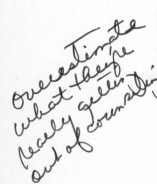

*Overestimate what they're really getting out of counseling*

Counselor self-deception sometimes operates in subtle ways to reinforce the self-deception of clients. Counselors, too, have an investment in seeing clients make progress. Less experienced counselors, in particular, may find it very hard to tolerate periods in which their clients seem to make little progress or actually seem to regress. Counselors whose egos are heavily invested in a successful outcome may not want their clients to talk about their ambivalent feelings concerning the value of their counseling. Simi-larly, if counselors need to feel that they are solving problems and "straightening out" their clients, they are likely to be less skeptical than they should be in evaluating therapeutic outcomes. Although there is no sure-fire method of avoiding self-deception, being aware of the hazard may lessen the chance that you'll "see" nonexistent results in order to satisfy your expectations and those of your clients. As a way of exploring how self-deception can arise in counseling, consider the following questions:

- How would you feel if several of your clients complained that they weren't really getting anywhere? How would you respond?
- How would you be affected if you couldn't detect any signs of progress with a client?

# The Issue of Personal Therapy for Counselors

Throughout this chapter we have stressed the importance of counselors' self-awareness. A closely related issue is whether those who wish to become counselors should themselves undergo therapy and whether continuing personal therapy is valuable for practicing therapists.

## Therapy during Training

There are several reasons, we think, why potential counselors should be encouraged to experience their own therapy. First of all, those who expect to counsel others should know what the experience of being a client is really like. We don't assume that most potential therapists are "sick" and in need of being "cured," but then we don't make that assumption about most clients, either. Many clients are attracted to counseling because they want to explore the quality of their lives and the alternatives they have for a richer existence. Potential counselors can approach therapy in much the same way. Therapy can help us take an honest look at our motivations in becoming helpers. It can help us explore how our needs influence our actions, how we use power in our lives, what our values are, and whether we have a need to persuade others to live by them. We can look at our need to be recognized and appreciated, at painful memories and past experiences that have shaped our ways of living, and at the sources of meaning in our lives. In the process, we can experience firsthand what our clients experience in therapy.

Another reason for undergoing therapy is that all of us have blind spots and unfinished business that may interfere with our effectiveness as therapists. All of us have areas in our lives that aren't fully developed and that keep us from being as effective as we can be, both as persons and as counselors. Personal therapy is one way of coming to grips with these and other issues.

Ideally, we'd like to see potential counselors undergo a combination of individual and group therapy, because the two types supplement each other. Individual therapy provides the opportunity to look at ourselves in some depth. Many counselors will experience a reopening of old psychic wounds as they engage in intensive work with their clients. For example, their therapeutic work may bring to the surface guilt feelings that need to be resolved. If they are in private therapy at the same time as they are doing their internship, they can productively bring such problems to their sessions.

Group therapy, on the other hand, can provide the opportunity to get feedback from others on how they experience us. It allows us to become increasingly aware of our personal styles and gives us a chance to experiment with new behavior in the group setting. The reactions we receive from others can help us learn about personal attributes that could be either strengths or limitations in our work as counselors.

Many training programs in counselor education recognize the value of having students involved in personal-awareness groups with their peers. A group can be set up specifically for the exploration of personal concerns, or such exploration can be made an integral part of training and supervision groups. Whatever the format, students will benefit most if they are willing to focus on themselves personally and not merely on their "cases." Unfortunately, many beginning counselors would rather focus exclusively on client dynamics. Their group learning would be more meaningful if they were open to exploring such questions as "How am I feeling about my own value as a counselor? Do I like my relationship with my client? What kinds of reactions are being evoked in me as I work with this client?" In short, if counselors in training are willing to become personally invested in the therapy process, they can use their training program as a real opportunity for expanding their own awareness.

Concerning either requiring or strongly recommending personal therapy as a part of a graduate program, one ethical issue needs to be considered. Faculty members in some programs do offer individual and group counseling for students. In one study 72% of the faculty reported having seen students for short-term personal counseling, and 56% of the educators reported that counseling students would be ethical if the students were not currently in their classes (Roberts, Murrell, Thomas, & Claxton, 1982). The ethical codes of both the American Association for Counseling and Development and the American Psychological Association imply that mixing personal therapy with education constitutes a dual relationship and is therefore unethical. The argument is that the student is at a disadvantage if he or she receives personal therapy from supervisors or faculty members, since they exert power over the student in the form of grading and evaluation. In Chapter 7 we will address the ethics of this type of dual relationship in more detail.

## Therapy for Practitioners

We do not want to convey the idea that practicing professionals are exempt from periodic and ongoing introspection. At times, experienced practitioners can profit from a program that will challenge them to reexamine some of their beliefs and behaviors, especially as these pertain to their effectiveness in working with clients. We hope that honest practitioners will see the value of making it a lifelong practice to engage in a variety of ways of self-examination as a means of keeping honest with themselves and others.

To what extent do practicing professionals make use of therapeutic resources? Deutsch (1985) found that 47% of practicing therapists had entered therapy for relationship problems, and 27% had entered for depression.

In their article "Personal Therapy for the Experienced Psychotherapist: A Discussion of Its Usefulness and Utilization," Guy and Liaboe (undated-a) comment that there is a puzzling silence among mental-health professionals concerning the need for periodic or ongoing therapy for experienced professionals. They concluded from their study that the majority of psychotherapists appear to resist entering personal therapy, even during times of distress when it may be both useful and appropriate. They contend that personal therapy is largely underutilized by the very providers of this service. It seems ironic that so little attention is given to promoting the psychological health of therapists, who have made a professional commitment to promoting the emotional well-being of others.

Guy and Liaboe suggest that a periodic course of psychotherapy seems justified solely because it may improve the quality and character of the personal relationships and general well-being of therapists. Among their list of recommendations for ways to promote personal therapy among practicing therapists are the following:

- Students in graduate training programs can be encouraged to remain open to the benefits of personal therapy, not merely as a way of sharpening their skills but as a way to minimize the potential negative consequences of later therapeutic practice.
- Professional organizations and licensing boards can consider a policy requiring periodic return to personal therapy.
- A referral network can be provided for experienced therapists seeking their own therapy.
- Research can be conducted to determine whether therapy is actually helpful in reducing negative consequences of therapeutic practice and improving the overall emotional well-being of the therapist.
- Increased therapist awareness and acceptance of the need for therapy can be accomplished through professional workshops, seminars, and symposia.

Clark (1986) reviewed empirical studies that explored the question "Can therapists who have undergone psychotherapy be shown to be more effective with clients than colleagues who have not received such treatment?" A review of seven empirical studies that dealt with this question revealed:

- Only one of the studies showed a slight and insignificant trend supporting the assumption that personal therapy would improve the therapist's performance.

- Five studies found no relationship between client outcome and whether the therapist had experienced therapy.
- One study of student therapists found that therapy could be detrimental to client outcome.

Clark concluded that further research is needed in order to clarify this important training issue. Apparently, this question has generated considerably more discussion than it has research. Clark suggests that future research should control for the level of experience of the therapist, the motivation of the therapist for entering therapy, and the point in the practitioner's career that personal therapy occurs.

If it is assumed that therapists themselves are their most important therapeutic instruments, then their own vitality as persons and as professionals is crucial to their work. We would encourage practitioners, both those who are beginning and those with many years of experience, to pay attention to what they are giving to and getting from their work. If they are not committed to doing for themselves what they are teaching their clients, one wonders about their chances of successfully inspiring clients to act in self-directed and responsible ways. An ethical guideline is for counselors to take care of themselves and to heal themselves. In addition to the formal therapeutic relationship, there are many creative avenues that lead to nurturing for the helper.

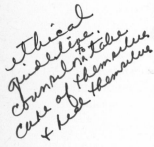

Therapists must also be prepared to recognize and deal with their unresolved personal issues and their reactions to their clients. A high degree of self-awareness on the therapist's part and a deep respect and concern for clients are safeguards. In the next section we explore ways that transference and countertransference can either facilitate or interfere with therapy. The following discussion provides a rationale for the importance of therapists' being willing to experience their own therapy. In addition to personal therapy, practitioners need training to deal with their own and their clients' feelings, which is often best received through the process of supervision and consultation.

# Dealing with Transference and Countertransference

You will inevitably have to come to grips with issues relating to transference and countertransference, regardless of your therapeutic orientation or whether you practice short-term or long-term therapy. We agree with Gelso and Carter (1985), who assume that transference and countertransference are universal and that they occur to varying degrees in most relationships. With its emphasis on a special kind of controlled helping, the therapeutic relationship intensifies this natural reaction. We believe that the ways in which you deal with both your own feelings and your clients' feelings will have a direct bearing on therapeutic outcomes. Since dealing with such feelings in ineffective ways is likely to block successful therapy, this matter has implications from ethical, legal, and clinical perspectives.

*the feelings of client toward the therapist*

# Transference: The 'Unreal' Relationship in Therapy

*Transference* refers to the unconscious process whereby clients project onto their therapist past feelings or attitudes they had toward significant people in their lives. Transference typically has its origin in one's early childhood, and it constitutes a repetition of past conflicts. Through this process a client's unfinished business produces a distortion in the way he or she perceives and reacts to the therapist. The feelings that are experienced in transference may be positive or negative; they may include love, hate, anger, ambivalence, and dependency. The essential point is that these feelings are rooted in past experiences but are now directed toward the therapist. Gelso and Carter (1985) refer to transference as the "unreal" relationship, because such projections are an error, even though the therapist's actions may serve to trigger them. Transference entails a misperception or a misinterpretation of the therapist, either positive or negative.

Watkins (1983) identifies the following five transference patterns in counseling and psychotherapy:

1. *Counselor as ideal.* The client sees the counselor as the ideal person. This perfect person does everything right, without flaws. Psychoanalytically, the counselor is given an idealized image, which may be the way the client's parents were viewed at one time. Transference is conceptualized as a carryover of interpersonal relationships from childhood into current relationships. Clients behave toward others in ways that are dynamically much like their behavior in their early years. The danger here is that counselors, their egos fed, can come to believe these projections! Yet not challenging clients to work through these feelings results in infantilizing them. When clients elevate the therapist, they put themselves down. They lose themselves by trying to be just like their ideal. Clients may attempt to identify with the counselor in many respects, and in doing so they become carbon copies and lose themselves in the process.

2. *Counselor as seer.* Clients view the counselor as expert, all-knowing, and all-powerful. Clients look to the counselor for direction, based on the conviction that the counselor has all the right answers and that they themselves cannot find their own answers. Again, a danger is that the counselor may feed on this projection and give clients advice based on his or her own need to be treated as an expert. The ethical issue here is that clients are encouraged to remain dependent.

3. *Counselor as nurturer.* Some clients look to the counselor for nurturing and feeding, as a small child would. They play the helpless role, and they feel that they cannot act for themselves. They may seek touching and hugs from the therapist. A danger here is that the counselor may get lost in giving sympathy and feeling sorry for the client. The counselor may become a nurturing parent and take care of the client. In the process, the client never learns the meaning of personal responsibility.

4. *Counselor as frustrator.* The client is defensive, cautious, and guarded and is constantly testing the counselor. Such clients may want

advice or simple solutions and may expect the counselor to deliver according to their desires. They may be frustrated if they don't receive such prescriptions. Counselors need to be aware that merely giving easy solutions will not help the client in the long run, and they should be careful not to get caught in the trap of perceiving this client as fragile. Also, it is essential that counselors avoid reacting defensively to this client, a response that would further entrench the client's resistance.

5. *Counselor as nonentity.*   In this form of transference the client regards the counselor as an inanimate figure without needs, desires, wishes, or problems. Often clients use a barrage of words and keep their distance with these outbursts. The counselor is likely to feel overwhelmed and discounted. If counselors depend on feedback from their clients as the sole means of validation of their worth as counselors, they may have difficulty in managing cases in which this phenomenon exists.

The potential effect of transference in these examples shows how essential it is for counselors to be clearly aware of their own needs, motivations, and personal reactions. If they are unaware of their own dynamics, they will be less effective with their clients. They will avoid important therapeutic issues instead of focusing on challenging their clients to understand and resolve the feelings they are bringing into the present from their past.

It should be recognized that transference is not a catch-all intended to explain every feeling that clients express toward their therapists. For example, if a client expresses anger toward you, it may be justified. If you haven't been truly present for the client, instead responding in a mechanical fashion, your client may be expressing legitimate anger and disappointment. Similarly, if a client expresses affection toward you, these feelings may be genuine; simply dismissing them as infantile fantasies can be a way of putting distance between yourself and your client. Of course, most of us would probably be less likely to interpret positive feelings as distortions aimed at us in a symbolic fashion than we would negative feelings. It is possible, then, for therapists to err in either direction—to be too quick to explain away negative feelings or too willing to accept whatever clients tell them, particularly when they are hearing how loving, wise, perceptive, or attractive they are. In order to understand the real import of clients' expressions of feelings, therapists must actively work at being open, vulnerable, and honest with themselves. Although they should be aware of the possibility of transference, they should also be aware of the danger of discounting the genuine reactions their clients have toward them.

We will now present a series of brief, open-ended cases in which we ask you to imagine yourself as the therapist. How do you think you would respond to each client? What are your own reactions?

*Your client, Shirley, seems extremely dependent on you for advice in making even minor decisions. It is clear that she does not trust herself and that she often tries to figure out what you might do in her place. She asks you personal questions about your marriage and your family life. Evidently, she has elevated you to the position of one who always makes wise choices, and she is trying to emulate you in every way. At other times she tells you that her decisions typically turn out to be poor ones. Consequently, when faced with a decision she vacillates and becomes filled with self-doubt. Although she says she realizes that you cannot give her "the" answers, she keeps asking you what you think about her decisions.*

- How would you deal with Shirley? What would you say to her?
- What direction would you take in trying to understand her dependence and lack of self-trust?
- How would you respond to her questions about your private life?
- If many of your clients expressed the same thoughts as Shirley, what elements in your counseling style might you need to examine?

*Marisa says she feels very let down by you. She complains that you are not very available and asks if you really care about her. She also says she feels that she is "just one of your caseload." She tells you that she would like to be more special to you.*

- How would you deal with Marisa's expectations?
- How would you explain your position?
- How would you explore whatever might be behind her stated feelings instead of defending your position?
- Would you be inclined to tell her how she affected you?

*Carl seems to treat you as an authority figure. He once said that you were always judging him and that he was reluctant to say very much because you would consider everything he said to be foolish. Although he has not confronted you directly since then, you sense many digs and other signs of hostility. On the surface, however, Carl seems to be trying very hard to please you by telling you what he thinks you want to hear. He seems convinced that you will react negatively and aggressively if he tells you what he really thinks.*

- How would you respond to Carl?
- How might you deal with his indirect expression of hostility?
- How might you encourage him to express his feelings and work through them?

## Countertransference: Ethical and Clinical Implications

So far we have focused on transference and the feelings of clients toward their counselors, but counselors also have emotional reactions to their clients, some of which may involve their own projections. We agree with Watkins's (1985) contention that such *countertransference* has both positive and negative elements. It can be for better or worse in counseling. It can prove constructive, but it can also be a destructive element in the therapy

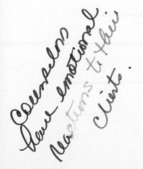
Counselors have emotional reactions to their clients.

*becomes ethical issue when* [handwritten margin note]

relationship. Destructive countertransference occurs when a counselor's own needs or unresolved personal conflicts become entangled in the therapeutic relationship, obstructing or destroying a sense of objectivity. In this way, countertransference becomes an ethical issue.

Regardless of how self-aware and insightful counselors are, the demands of practicing counseling or therapy are great. The emotionally intense relationships they develop with their clients can be expected to tap into their own unresolved conflicts. Because countertransference may be a form of identification with the client, the counselor can easily get lost in the client's world and thus be of little therapeutic value. When counselors become so concerned with meeting their own needs that they even use the client for this purpose, their behavior is unethical.

Thus, ethical practice requires that counselors remain alert to their emotional reactions to their clients, that they attempt to understand such reactions, and that they do not meet their own needs at the expense of their clients' needs. Questions counselors might ask of themselves are "What am I feeling as I am with this person? What am I experiencing? What do I want to say and do? What am I aware of *not* saying to the client? Do I find myself hoping the client will fail to show up? Do I find myself wanting the client to stay longer?" If countertransference is recognized by counselors, they can seek supervision as one way of sorting out their feelings. Watkins (1985) mentions five methods that counselors can use to combat acting out in counseling situations: self-analysis, genuineness and self-disclosure, undergoing personal counseling, supervision, and referral of the client.

Countertransference can show itself in many ways, some of which we will now discuss:

1. *Being overprotective with clients manifests itself in an oversolicitous attitude.* Counselors may see clients as fragile and infantile and thus soften their remarks. They protect clients from experiencing pain and anxiety and may thwart them in their struggle. Clients are not challenged to grapple with personal conflicts, and thus they do not learn how to face and cope with their issues (Watkins, 1985).

- Are you aware of reacting to certain types of people in overprotective ways? If so, what might this reveal about you?
- Do you find that you are able to allow others to experience their pain, or do you have a tendency to want to take their pain away quickly?

2. *Treating clients in benign ways may stem from the counselor's fears of the clients' anger.* To guard against this anger, the counselor creates a bland, benign counseling atmosphere. This tactic results in exchanges that are superficial. Watkins mentions the danger of losing therapeutic distance, with the result that the client/counselor interchange degenerates into either a friendly conversation or a general "rap session."

- Do you ever find yourself saying things to guard against another's anger?
- What might you say or do if you became aware that your exchanges with a client were primarily superficial?

fear anger
or disapproval
of client —

3. *Rejection of clients may be based on perceiving them as needy and dependent.*    Yet instead of moving toward them to protect them, the counselor moves away from such clients. The counselor remains cool and aloof, keeps distant and unknown, and does not let clients get too close (Watkins, 1985).

- Are there certain types of people that you find yourself wanting to move away from?
- What can you learn about yourself by looking at those people that you are likely to reject?

4. *The need for constant reinforcement and approval* can be a source of countertransference. Just as clients may develop an excessive need to please their therapists in order to feel liked and valued, therapists may have an inordinate need of reassurance concerning their effectiveness. Ellis (1973) contends that therapists must be willing to let go of the irrational idea that their clients must think well of them. They need to challenge and confront their clients' irrational and self-defeating thinking, and they can do so only if they are willing to risk their clients' disapproval.

- Do you feel you need to have the approval of your clients? How willing are you to confront them even at the risk of being disliked?
- If you have some counseling experience, what is your style of confronting a client? Do you tend to confront certain kinds of clients more than others? What does this tell you about yourself as a therapist?

5. *Seeing yourself in your clients* is another form of countertransference. This is not to say that feeling close to a client and identifying with that person's struggle is necessarily an instance of countertransference. However, one of the problems many beginning therapists have is that they identify with clients' problems to the point that they lose their objectivity. They become so lost in their clients' worlds that they are unable to separate their feelings from those of their clients. Or they may tend to see in their clients traits that they dislike in themselves.

- Have you ever found yourself so much in sympathy with others that you could no longer be of help to them? What would you do if this were to happen with a client?
- From an awareness of your own dynamics, list some personal traits of clients that would be most likely to elicit overidentification on your part.

6. One of the common manifestations of transference or countertransference is the development of *sexual or romantic feelings* between clients and therapists. Therapists can exploit the vulnerable position of their clients, whether consciously or unconsciously. Seductive behavior on the part of a client can easily lead to the adoption of a seductive style by the therapist, particularly if the therapist is unaware of his or her own dynamics and motivations. On the other hand, it's natural for therapists to be attracted to some clients more than to others, and the fact that they have sexual feelings toward some clients does not have to mean that they cannot counsel these

sexual and/or
romantic

clients effectively. More important than the mere existence of such feelings is the manner in which therapists deal with them. Feelings of attraction can be recognized and even acknowledged frankly without becoming the focus of the therapeutic relationship. The possibility that therapists' sexual feelings and needs might interfere with their work is one important reason why therapists should experience their own therapy when starting to practice and should continue to be willing to consult another professional when they encounter difficulty because of their feelings toward certain clients.

- What do you think you would do if you experienced intense sexual feelings toward a client?
- How would you know if your sexual attraction to a client was countertransference or not?

7. Countertransference can also take the form of *compulsive advice giving*. Many nonprofessionals and even some professionals equate counseling with giving advice. A tendency to advise can easily be encouraged by clients who are prone to seek immediate answers to ease their suffering. The opportunity to give advice places therapists in a superior, all-knowing position—one that some of them can easily come to enjoy—and it isn't difficult for them to delude themselves into thinking that they do have answers for their clients. They may also feel uncomfortable if they're unable to be prescriptive or may find it difficult to be patient with their clients' struggles toward autonomous decision making.

In all these cases the needs of the therapist are taking priority over those of the client. Even if a client has asked for advice, there is every reason to question whose needs are being served when therapists fall into advice giving.

- Do you ever find yourself giving advice? What do you think giving advice does for you?
- Are there any times when advice is warranted? If so, when?

8. A *desire to develop social relationships with clients* may stem from countertransference, especially if it is acted on while therapy is taking place. Occasionally clients let their therapist know that they would like to develop more of a relationship than is possible in the limiting environment of the office. They may, for instance, express a desire to get to know their therapist as "a regular person." Even experienced therapists sometimes must struggle with the question of whether to blend a social relationship with a therapeutic one. When this question arises, therapists should assess whose needs would be met through such a friendship and decide whether effective therapy can coexist with a social relationship. Some questions you might ask yourself in this context are:

- If I establish social relationships with certain clients, will I be as inclined to confront them in therapy as I would be otherwise?
- Will my own needs for preserving these friendships interfere with my therapeutic activities and defeat the purpose of therapy?

- Am I sensitive to being called a "cold professional," even though I may strive to be real and straightforward in the therapeutic situation?

In writing about the dynamics of countertransference, Gelso and Carter (1985) point out the differences between the counselor's inner experience and the counselor's actions toward clients. They comment that the early literature on countertransference focused on the therapist's behavior toward clients. In this context there was the implication that countertransference was "evil" and something to be avoided. More recent literature, however, addresses the inner experience of therapists and the potential benefits to both them and to clients if they pay attention to the subtle ways in which clients' behavior stimulates this internal experience.

> In fact, we think that facing, and indeed inspecting, countertransference-based feelings is one of the most difficult tasks of the therapist. It requires considerable courage and a willingness to deal with one's own painful feelings for the sake of the therapeutic work. There are no easy answers to the question of how to accomplish this, but at the same time doing so is a crucial aspect of effective therapy [Gelso & Carter, 1985, pp. 182–183].

*very difficult task*

It is not possible to deal fully here with all the possible nuances of transference and countertransference. If you are interested in a more in-depth treatment of this subject, we highly recommend the excellent article by Gelso and Carter.

# Stress in the Counseling Profession

## Warning: Bumpy Road ✓

There is agreement in the literature that counseling is a hazardous profession and that its stresses stem both from the nature of the work and from the professional role expectations of counselors. (For an excellent discussion of the inner strains of healing work, see Jaffe, 1986.) Counselors are typically not given enough warning about the hazards of the profession they are about to enter. Many counselors-in-training look forward to a profession in which they can help others and, in return, feel a deep sense of self-satisfaction. Yet they are not told that the commitment to self-exploration and to inspiring this search in clients is fraught with difficulties. Effective practitioners use their own life experiences and personal reactions as a way to understand their clients and as a method of working with them. The process of working therapeutically with people opens up the therapist's own deepest issues. As a partner in the therapeutic journey, the therapist is deeply affected by seeing the client's pain. There is a resonance within the therapist's own life experiences that comes about through the activation of painful memories. Unfinished business is stirred up, and old wounds are opened. Conflicts that were repressed tend to surface. In short, working with clients who are in pain often opens up therapists to their own pain.

## Sources of Stress

Deutsch (1984) and Farber (1983a) found surprisingly similar results in their surveys of therapists' perceptions of stressful client behavior. In both studies therapists reported that suicidal statements were the most stressful source of client behavior. In the accompanying box are comparisons between these two studies with respect to which behaviors of clients are perceived by counselors as stressful.

### Most-Stressful Client Behaviors for Therapists

**Deutsch's Findings**

1. suicidal statements
2. anger toward the therapist
3. severely depressed clients
4. apathy or lack of motivation
5. client's premature termination

**Farber's Findings**

1. suicidal statements
2. aggression and hostility
3. premature termination of therapy
4. agitated anxiety
5. apathy and depression

Other sources of stress that therapists reported in the Deutsch (1984) study included:

- inability to help distressed clients to feel better
- seeing more than the usual number of clients
- not liking clients
- self-doubts on the therapist's part about the value of therapy
- professional conflicts with colleagues
- feeling isolated from other professionals
- overidentification with clients and failure to balance empathy with appropriate professional distance
- inability to leave client concerns behind when leaving work
- sexual attraction to a client
- absence of expression of gratitude from clients

A growing body of research suggests that many therapists experience negative effects with respect to their ability to relate meaningfully with family and friends (Guy & Liaboe, 1986). More than half of the therapists in Farber's study (1983a, 1983b) reported that conducting therapy had decreased their emotional investment in their own family. In the area of friendships, some therapists reported that their work had hindered their ability to be genuine, spontaneous, and comfortable with friends (Farber, 1983a). Farber notes a trend for therapists to reduce their circle of friends and to socialize less during their career. One interpretation of these findings is that many therapists experience stress and negative consequences from their work.

Stress is related to irrational beliefs that many therapists hold. Practitioners with exceptionally high goals or perfectionistic strivings related to helping others often report a high level of stress. Deutsch (1984) gives the following examples of the three most stressful beliefs that produce stress, all of which pertain to doing perfect work with clients:

1. I should always work at my peak level of enthusiasm and competence.
2. I should be able to cope with any client emergency that arises.
3. I should be able to help every client.

The other irrational beliefs that lead to stress are (1) When a client does not make progress, it is my fault. (2) I should not take off time from work when I know that a particular client needs me. (3) My job is my life. (4) I should be able to work with every client. (5) I should be a model of mental health. (6) I should be "on call" at all times. (7) A client's needs always come before my own. (8) I am the most important person in my client's life. (9) I am responsible for my client's behavior. (10) I have the power to control my client's life.

It is interesting to note that these beliefs are related to the basic reasons why many people choose the helping professions. The needs of helpers are to be needed by others, to feel important, to have an impact on the lives of others, to have power to control others, and to be significant. When helpers are able to successfully do these things, they are likely to feel that they are making a significant difference in the lives of their clients. When they feel that they are not making a difference and are not reaching clients, stress affects them more dramatically.

Deutsch makes the point that therapists' cognitions provide clues to the experience of stress. Beliefs that create stress are those that goad the counselor to constantly produce at maximum levels, a pace that eventually leads to burn-out. When therapists do not live up to unrealistically high levels of performance, they often experience frustration. When they fall short of their own idealized expectations, they view the slow progress in their clients as evidence of their failure and lack of competence. The underlying assumption that creates stress is "If I do not live up to my high expectations, I am personally incompetent and inadequate." From this vantage point the crucial factor in therapists' experience of stress is not merely difficult client behaviors; rather, it is the beliefs therapists hold about their role in helping others. If we assume that we are completely responsible for the success or failure of therapy, we are burdening ourselves needlessly and creating our own stress. We are also depriving our clients of assuming their rightful share of responsibility for what they choose to do with their life. Kottler counsels that "it is necessary for us to accept our own limits and share with the client the responsibility for success of treatment" (1986, p. 82).

The ethical and professional question is to what degree a therapist's behavior resulting from stress has negative implications for the client's progress.

### The Myth of the Wounded Healer

Jaffe (1986) presents arguments for a change in the way most professional helpers perceive their role. He argues that health professionals must see that they cannot simply give and remain detached from their feelings; rather, they must look inward at their personal needs and roles. He describes the professional myths that healers are not supposed to have needs, that personal feelings are not relevant, and that helpers should detach themselves from their own responses of pain. He also describes the wounded-healer myth. Greek mythology attributed healing powers to the wounded healer. Although such healers possess the wisdom of life and death, they are not able to heal their own incurable wound. According to Jaffe, those in the healing professions must recognize the impact on their own life of working with suffering people. Not only must they become aware of their inner responses, but they must do something about them if they are to avoid burn-out and impairment in their personal and professional life. If they pay attention to their inner experience, major personal changes tend to occur as well as changes in their way of approaching their work.

# Professional Burn-Out

The phenomenon of professional burn-out has been the topic of numerous publications and is receiving increasing attention at professional conferences and conventions. What is professional burn-out? What are its causes? How are professionals who work in institutions particularly susceptible to losing their vitality? What can be done to prevent burn-out? How can counselors stay alive personally and professionally?

### Nature and Scope of the Problem

Burn-out is a state of physical, emotional, and mental exhaustion. It is the result of repeated emotional pressures, often associated with intense involvement with people over long periods of time. Professionals who are burned out are characterized by physical depletion and by feelings of hopelessness and helplessness. They tend to develop negative attitudes toward themselves, others, work, and life (Pines & Aronson, with Kafry, 1981). Many people in the helping professions find that they grow tired and lose the energy and enthusiasm they once experienced in their work. They talk of feeling drained, empty, and fragmented by the pull of many different projects. Since burn-out is an occupational hazard that most professional helpers face at one time or another, it is important to be prepared for it. Burn-out can rob you of the vitality you need if you are to communicate hope and provide healthy modeling for your clients.

*isolation*

*mechanical*

Professional helpers need to see that what they do is worthwhile; yet the nature of their profession is such that they often don't see immediate or concrete results. This lack of reinforcement can have a debilitating effect as counselors begin to wonder whether anything they do makes a difference to anyone. The danger of burn-out is all the greater if they practice in isolation, have little interchange with fellow professionals, have demanding or disturbed clients, or fail to seek an explanation of their feelings of deadness.

Professionals who limit their work to one type of activity are particularly susceptible to burn-out. Many therapists who work alone in their own practice report that they often get caught in the routine of seeing client after client. They find it increasingly difficult to be fully present for their clients, especially when it seems that they are dealing with the same kind of problem over and over again. After a while they may well find themselves responding almost mechanically. It may be very difficult to deal with this kind of situation if one's livelihood seems to depend on maintaining one's own private practice. Nevertheless, therapists can question whether sticking to one kind of practice is worth the price they're paying in deadness and lack of excitement.

The problem of burn-out is particularly critical for people working in systems in the human-services field. With the emphasis in this kind of work on giving to others, there is often not enough focus on giving to oneself. According to Pines and her associates (1981), people who perform human services share three basic characteristics: (1) they are involved in emotionally taxing work; (2) they tend to be sensitive to others' problems and have a desire to relieve suffering; and (3) they often see their work as a calling to be givers to those who feel powerless and helpless. Unfortunately, some who enter the helping professions have high hopes that are never realized. If they meet with constant frustration, see almost no positive change in their clients, and encounter obstacles to meeting their goals of helping others, their hopes may eventually be replaced by the hopelessness and powerlessness that are prime characteristics of many of the clients they see. Farber and Heifetz (1982) note the following basic characteristics associated with burned-out professionals: they lose concern for clients; they come to treat the people they work with in ways that are detached and even dehumanizing; they become cynical toward their clients and often blame them for creating their own problems; and they experience a wide range of symptoms, such as emotional frustration and psychosomatic ailments.

*ignore signs for years*

Kottler (1986) observes that therapists who are psychologically impaired have probably ignored the signs of their condition for months and even years. Unfortunately, their sense of cynical hopelessness affects many other colleagues and clients. Kottler lists a number of these symptoms of burn-out: (1) when clients call to cancel, the therapist celebrates with a bit too much enthusiasm; (2) daydreaming and escapist fantasies are common; (3) there is a tendency to cope with prolonged stress by abusing drugs; (4) therapy sessions lose their excitement and spontaneity; (5) the therapist gets

*yes!*

behind in paperwork and billings; (6) the therapist's social life suffers; and (7) therapists are reluctant to explore the causes and cures of their burned-out condition.

## Causes of Burn-Out

Farber and Heifetz (1982) found that therapists had the following perceptions of the causes of burn-out:

- The majority of the therapists interviewed (54.7%) felt that burn-out resulted from the nonreciprocated attentiveness, giving, and responsibility demanded by the therapeutic relationship.
- Other causes of burn-out included overwork (22.2%), the general difficulty in dealing with the patient problems (20.4%), discouragement as a function of tedious work tasks (18.5%), the tendency of therapeutic work to bring out their own personal conflicts (13%), the general passivity of counseling work (13%), and the isolation involved in therapy (11.1%).
- If they experienced stresses at home, therapists felt that they were particularly prone to transient feelings of burn-out. Their own family problems lowered their threshold for the demanding work of therapy and impaired their ability to attend effectively to the needs of their clients.
- Most practitioners (73.7%) cited "lack of therapeutic success" as the single most stressful aspect of their work.

The Farber and Heifetz study suggests that therapists expect their work to be difficult and even stressful but that they also expect that their efforts will be appreciated and that they will see positive results. Constant giving without the reinforcement of some measure of success apparently produces burn-out. Although working conditions, such as excessive work load and organizational politics, can create an added burden of stress for therapists who work in institutions, many therapists can accept these realities of working in the system. When therapeutic work is only minimally successful and often frustrating, however, the chances of experiencing disillusionment are particularly high. For example, therapists who work primarily with suicidal, homicidal, depressed, severely regressed, and chronically resistant clients are likely to experience signs of burn-out.

We encourage you now to look at the factors that are most likely to cause burn-out in you. A common denominator in many cases of burn-out is the question of _responsibility_. Counselors may feel responsible for what their clients do or don't do; they may assume total responsibility for the direction of therapy; or they may have extremely high expectations of themselves. How does this apply to you? In what ways could your assumption of an inordinate degree of responsibility contribute to your burn-out?

There are other causes of burn-out besides an excessive sense of responsibility. Consistently working with clients whom you don't like, who are unmotivated and yet demanding, or who don't appreciate or value you can cause burn-out. How would working with such clients affect you? What other factors can you think of that would lead to your burn-out?

## Fragmentation

✓ Fragmentation is a <u>problem that is closely related to burn-out</u>. People may feel that they're doing too much in too little time and not doing justice to any of their activities. Or they may feel as if they're here, there, and everywhere but at the same time nowhere. Some of the factors that can lead to a sense of fragmentation are driving great distances to and from work or from one appointment to another; never taking a break between involvements in different activities; taking on diverse and sometimes conflicting commitments; being swamped with paper work; and attending innumerable meetings. Although we suggested earlier that a way to prevent burn-out is to introduce some diversity into your work, there is also the danger of becoming overextended—pulled in so many different directions that you lose all sense of yourself. At such times you may feel that there is little time between activities and that one experience seems to blur into the next.

Counselors who begin to feel fragmented should stop to ask themselves such questions as these: What effect is my work having on my clients and me? Am I merely doing chores that have been assigned to me and that give me little sense of accomplishment? If I'm in an administrative position, how willing am I to delegate responsibility to others? Do I need to have a finger in every pie?

*Green House* Fragmentation is especially likely to be a problem in institutional settings, where many demands are made on professionals that have little to do with counseling expertise. Counselors in such settings who begin to feel fragmented might need to ask questions like the following:

- Am I so conscious of my security in the system that I never make any waves?
- Am I so convinced that I'm the only one capable of doing the work that I never delegate any of it?
- Do I take on work that is beyond my ability to do?
- Do I ever ask myself whether I'm doing what I really want to do?
- Do I ever say no?

Fragmentation is often a problem for beginning counselors, who may spread themselves thinner than they might wish in order to make a living. Like burn-out, however, fragmentation is an issue that can be handled only by counselors themselves. They are their own monitors; they need to pay attention to their internal workings and decide on their own limits.

## Staying Alive Personally and Professionally

B-O obvious to others only in late stages — Since professional burn-out is an internal phenomenon that becomes obvious to others only in its advanced stages, you should take special care to recognize your own limits. How you approach your tasks and what you get from doing them are more important than how much you're doing. Some people are able to put much more of themselves into a project than others without feeling drained. One person, for example, may feel exhausted after conducting a group-therapy session, whereas another may come out of it energized and excited. One helpful suggestion is to find what Jourard (1971) calls a "check-out" place where you can briefly meditate and experiment with different ways of living without pressure from others. Ultimately, whether you experience burn-out depends on how well you monitor your own responses to the stresses of your work and the effects these stresses have on you and on the quality of your counseling.

**Ways of Preventing Burn-Out.**   Perhaps the most basic way to retain your vitality as a person and as a professional is to realize that you are not a bottomless pit and cannot give and give without replenishing yourself. Counselors often ignore signs that they are becoming depleted. They may view themselves as having unlimited capacities to give, and at the same time they may not pay attention to taking care of their own needs for nurturing, recognition, and support. However, simply recognizing that they cannot be universal givers without getting something in return is not enough to keep them alive as people and professionals. What follows are some specific suggestions for preventing burn-out. As you read them, apply them to yourself to see how they might fit for you. Although there are no sure ways to avoid feelings of disillusionment and fatigue at times, you can learn practices and attitudes to reduce the risk of being chronically burned out:

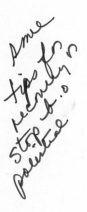

• Learn to set limits with demanding clients; take care to avoid overextending yourself in a system.
• Learn the value of a sense of humor. Some therapists adopt a "heavy" attitude toward life and forget how to laugh. Humor may be one of the best ways to keep matters in perspective.
• Develop a circle of associates and colleagues whom you can trust. Meetings can be used to discuss difficult cases, personal concerns, and ways of surviving with dignity in a system.
• It is a good idea to have activities and interests besides therapy as a way of renewing yourself. These diversions can serve as a temporary escape from the stresses of therapeutic work and can prevent the therapeutic mode from totally dominating your perspective. Also, related activities (such as consulting, teaching, supervising, or working with colleagues) can give you a new perspective on therapeutic work. Of course, hobbies and recreational activities apart from work can be valuable sources of replenishing you personally.
• Keeping in mind your most important professional objectives is helpful. We often get involved in unrewarding tasks and forget to pay attention to our priorities. We can at least learn to ask ourselves: "Is what I am doing now really important? Are there ways I can learn to delegate certain tasks? Do I need to learn to say no more often?"
• Learn the value of expressing negative feelings about your work, rather than keeping all your reactions to yourself. Unfortunately, we may not often hear or read about the fears, failures, and doubts experienced by colleagues.

• Attending some exciting seminars, conferences, and conventions (especially workshops on ways to stay alive as a person and as a professional) can keep you vital.

• Professionals in public agencies and institutions have adopted various ways of lessening the pressures inherent in their environments. Some vary their activities by teaching, supervising and training interns, doing public-relations work in the community, consulting with other colleagues or agencies, or working on their own special projects. Exchanging positions with someone from a different agency is another way of generating new vitality. Counselors from different agencies can trade places with one another for periods varying from a week to several months. This procedure allows counselors to share their special talents with another staff and to work with new people for a time. It can thus benefit both the counselors who make the exchange and the staffs that play host to the visiting counselors.

As a further strategy to prevent burn-out, graduate training programs in therapy should prepare students for the disappointments they will encounter in the course of their training, as well as in the jobs they eventually secure. If students are not given adequate preparation, they may be especially vulnerable to early disenchantment and high rates of burn-out, for they are saddled with unrealistic expectations.

**Your Personal Strategy.**    Now think of some ways of preventing burn-out or regaining your vitality. The following is a list of suggestions for dealing with burn-out. Of course, counselors need to find their own way of remaining vital as professionals; our purpose in presenting this list is simply to stimulate you to think of your own ways of preventing or treating burn-out. After you think about each suggestion, rate each one by using the following code: A = this approach would be very meaningful to me; B = this approach would have some value for me; C = this approach would have little value for me.

____ Think of ways to bring variety into my work.

____ Become involved in peer-group meetings where a support system is available.

____ Find other interests besides my work.

____ Attend to my health and take care of my body by exercising and eating well.

____ Take stock of what I'm doing to determine whether it is meaningful or draining.

____ Do some of the things now that I plan to do when I retire.

____ Take time for myself to do some of the things that I enjoy doing.

____ Refuse to get caught in the trap of assuming an inordinate amount of responsibility.

____ Attend a personal-growth group or some type of personal-therapy experience to work on my level of vitality.

____ Travel or seek new experiences.

___ Read stimulating books and do some personal writing.

___ Exchange jobs for a time with a colleague.

___ Find nourishment with family and friends.

___ Find a person who will confront and challenge me and who will encourage me to look at what I'm doing.

## Chapter Summary

In this chapter we've discussed one of the most basic issues in the practice of therapy and counseling—the counselor's own personality as an instrument in therapeutic practice. We have stressed the idea that counselors might possess knowledge and technical skills and still be ineffective in significantly reaching clients. Our belief is that the life experiences, values, attitudes, and caring that counselors bring to their therapy sessions are crucial factors in the establishment of effective therapeutic relationships.

We have also discussed a broad range of issues related to the professional identity of counselors. They do not by any means represent an exhaustive list. By reflecting on these issues now, however, you may be better able to recognize and struggle with these and related questions as you grow in your chosen profession. We have tried to emphasize that you may need to review your resolutions of these issues periodically throughout your career. This kind of openness and honest self-appraisal is an essential quality of those who wish to be effective helpers.

## Suggested Activities

These activities and questions are designed to help you apply your learning. Many of them can profitably be done alone in a personal way or with another person; others can be done in the classroom as discussion activities, either with the whole class or in small groups. We suggest that you select those that seem most significant to you and do some writing on these issues in your journal. Many of these questions are ones that prospective employers ask during job interviews. Practicing answering these questions can help you clarify your thinking and your positions, which in the long run could help you land a job.

1. In small groups in your class explore the issue of why you're going into a helping profession. This is a basic issue, and one that many students have trouble putting into concrete words. What motivated you to seek this type of work? What do you think you can get for yourself? What do you see yourself as being able to do for others?

2. What personal needs do you have that may be met by counseling others? To what degree do you think that they might get in the way of your work with clients? How can you recognize and meet your needs—

which are a real part of you—without having them interfere with your work with others?

3. What are some of the major problems you expect to be faced with as a beginning counselor? What are some of your most pressing concerns?

4. In small groups share your own anxieties over becoming a counselor. What can you learn about yourself from a discussion of these anxieties?

5. This exercise deals with the fundamental question "Who has a right to counsel anybody?" Form small groups of perhaps three persons. Take turns briefly stating the personal and professional qualities that you can offer people. The others give feedback. Afterwards, explore any self-doubts you have concerning your ethical right to counsel others.

6. What kind of results would you look for in working with clients? How would you determine the answers to such questions as "Is the counseling doing any good? Is my intervention helping my client make the changes he or she wants to make? How effective are my techniques?"

7. Think of the type of client you might have the most difficulty working with. Then become this client in a role-playing fantasy with one other student. Your partner attempts to counsel you. After you've had a chance to be the client, change roles and become the counselor. Your partner then becomes the type of client you just role-played.

8. In subgroups explore the issue of how willing you are to disclose yourself to your clients. Discuss the guidelines you would use to determine the appropriateness of self-disclosure. What are some areas you would feel hesitant about sharing? How valuable do you think it is to share yourself in a personal way with your clients? What are some of your fears or resistances about making yourself known to your clients?

9. In subgroups discuss some possible causes of professional burn-out. Then examine specific ways that you could deal with this problem. After you've explored this issue in small groups, reconvene as a class and make a list of the causes and solutions that your groups have come up with.

10. In dyads, one person assumes the role of the therapist, the other of a client whom the therapist is having difficulty with. Role-play a session in which the therapist informs the client of his or her feelings. Afterwards, discuss how each of you experienced the interaction.

# Suggested Readings

On transference see Gelso and Carter (1985), Kottler (1986), and Watkins (1983); on countertransference see the first two sources above plus Watkins (1985), Cerney (1985), and Lorion and Parron (1985). On the hardships of therapeutic practice see Kottler (1986). On stress in the helping professions and therapists' personal problems see Deutsch (1984, 1985), Farber (1983a, 1983b), Guy and Liaboe (1986), Laliotis and Grayson (1985), Jaffe (1986), Kilburg, Nathan, and Thoreson (1986), and Freudenberger (1986). For a discussion of alcoholism among psychologists see Thoreson, Budd, and Krauskopf (1986). For a review and discussion of the impact of the therapist's illness or accident on psychotherapeutic practice, see Guy and Souder (1986). For a review of seven empirical studies on the value of personal therapy for therapists see Clark (1986). On professional burn-out see Farber and Heifetz (1982), Maslach (1982), Pines and Aronson with Kafry (1981), Edelwich with Brodsky (1980), Kottler (1986), and Pines (1986). For a book that deals with the risks, challenges, and satisfactions of being a psychotherapist see Kottler (1986). For a textbook on the topic of personal themes of choice that apply to the counselor as a person see Corey with Corey (1986). For a treatment of the client/therapist relationship from the perspective of a foundation for eclectic psychotherapy see Patterson (1985b).

# THREE

# Values and the Helping Relationship

- Pre-Chapter Self-Inventory
- Introduction: Clarifying Your Values and Their Role in Your Work
- Value Conflicts with Clients
- Differences in Life Experiences and Philosophies
- Controversial Issues: Implications for Counseling
- Ethical Issues in Counseling Gay and Lesbian Clients
- Chapter Summary
- Suggested Activities
- Suggested Readings

# Pre-Chapter Self-Inventory

*Directions:* For each statement, indicate the response that most closely identifies your beliefs and attitudes. Use the following code:

3 = I *agree*, in most respects, with this statement.
2 = I am *undecided* in my opinion about this statement.
1 = I *disagree*, in most respects, with this statement.

___ 1. It is both possible and desirable for counselors to remain neutral and keep their values from influencing clients.

___ 2. Counselors should influence clients to adopt values that seem in their opinion to be in the clients' best interests.

___ 3. It is appropriate for counselors to express their values, as long as they don't try to impose them on clients.

___ 4. The search for meaningful values is a central part of psychotherapy.

___ 5. Counselors should challenge clients to make value judgments regarding their own behavior.

___ 6. I can work only with clients whose value systems are similar to my own.

___ 7. Before I can effectively counsel a person, I have to decide whether our life experiences are similar enough that I'll be able to understand that person.

___ 8. The clarification of values is a major part of the counseling process.

___ 9. I could work effectively with people who had certain values that I did not respect.

___ 10. I might be inclined to subtly influence my clients to consider my values.

___ 11. I consider it my job to challenge my clients' philosophies of life.

___ 12. I have a clear idea of what I value and where I acquired my values.

___ 13. I see the clarification of my own values as an ongoing process.

___ 14. Gay and lesbian clients are best served by gay and lesbian counselors.

___ 15. I tend to have difficulty with people who think differently from the way I do.

___ 16. I see part of the counseling task as teaching clients a more effective way of living.

___ 17. I see my values as the lenses through which I view the world.

___ 18. Ultimately, I think, the choice of living or dying rests with my clients, and therefore I do not have the right to persuade them to make a different choice.

___ 19. I have an ethical obligation to ask myself what types of clients I am unable to effectively work with and to seek referral in such cases.

___ 20. As a condition for licensure, counselors should have some specialized training for counseling gay and lesbian clients.

— 21. A counselor who is lesbian is unlikely to be effective in dealing with heterosexual female clients.

— 22. Sometimes I think that it is ethical to impose my values on my clients, especially if I have their best interests at heart.

# Introduction: Clarifying Your Values and Their Role in Your Work

The question of values permeates the therapeutic process. This chapter is intended to stimulate your thinking about your values and life experiences and the influence they will have on your counseling. We ask you to consider the possible impact of your values on your clients, the effect your clients' values will have on you, and the conflicts that may arise when you and your client have different values.

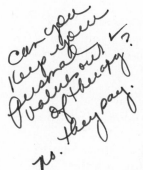

Perhaps the most fundamental question we can raise about values in the therapeutic process is whether it is possible for counselors to keep their values out of their counseling sessions. In our view it is neither possible nor desirable for counselors to be scrupulously neutral with respect to values in the counseling relationship. Although we don't see the counselor's function as persuading clients to accept a certain value system, we do think it's crucial for counselors to be clear about their own values and how they influence their work and the directions taken by their clients. Since we believe that counselors' values do inevitably affect the therapeutic process, we also think it's important for counselors to be willing to express their values openly when they are relevant to the questions that come up in their sessions with clients.

Not everyone who practices counseling or psychotherapy would agree with this position. At one extreme, some counselors who have definite, absolute value systems believe that their job is to exert influence on clients to adopt proper values. These counselors tend to direct their clients toward the attitudes and behaviors that *they* judge to be in their clients' best interests. At the other extreme are the counselors who are so anxious to avoid influencing their clients that they immobilize themselves. They keep themselves and their values hidden so that they won't contaminate their clients' choices. We'd like to comment briefly on each of these extremes.

First, we don't view counseling as a form of indoctrination; nor do we believe that the therapist's function is to teach clients the right way to live. We think it's unfortunate that some well-intentioned counselors believe that their job is to help people conform to socially acceptable standards or to straighten out their clients. It seems arrogant to suppose that counselors know what's best for others. We question the implication that counselors have greater wisdom than their clients and can prescribe ways of being happier. No doubt, teaching is a part of counseling, and clients do learn in both direct and indirect ways from the input and example of their counselors; but this is not to say that counseling is synonymous with preaching or instruction.

*I like this!*

On the other hand, we don't favor the opposite extreme of trying so hard to be "objective" that we keep our personal reactions and values hidden from our clients. Counselors who adopt this style are unlikely to do more than mechanical, routine counseling. Clients demand a lot more involvement from their therapists than mere reflection and clarification. They often want and need to know where their therapists stand in order to test their own thinking. We think that clients deserve this kind of honest involvement on the part of their therapists.

The following questions may help you to begin thinking about the role of your values in your work with clients:

- Is it possible for therapists to interact honestly with their clients without making value judgments? Is it desirable for therapists to avoid making such judgments?
- Do you have a need to see your clients adopt your beliefs and values?
- Can you remain true to yourself and at the same time allow your clients the freedom to select their own values, even if they differ sharply from yours?
- How do you determine whether a conflict between your values and those of your client necessitates a referral to another professional?
- How does honestly exposing your clients to your viewpoint differ from subtly "guiding" them to accept your values?
- To what degree do you need to have life experiences that are similar to those of your clients? Is it possible that too much similarity in values and life experiences might result in therapy that is not challenging for the client?

If, as we have maintained, your values will significantly affect your work with clients, it is incumbent on you to clarify your values and the ways they enter the therapeutic process. For example, counselors who have "liberal" values may find themselves working with clients who have more traditional values. If these counselors privately scoff at conventional values, can they truly respect clients who don't think as they do? Or if counselors have a strong commitment to values that they rarely question, whether these values are conventional or radical, will they be inclined to promote these values at the expense of hindering their clients' free exploration of their own attitudes and beliefs? If counselors never reexamine their own values, can they expect to provide a climate in which clients can reexamine theirs?

Whatever your own values are, there may be many instances in which they present some difficulty for you in your work with clients. In the following sections we examine some sample cases and issues that may help you clarify what you value and how your values might influence your counseling. As you read through those examples, you might keep the following questions in mind:

- What is my position on this particular issue?
- Where did I develop my views?
- Are my values open to modification?
- Have I challenged my views, and am I open to being challenged by others?
- Do I insist that the world remain the same now as it was earlier in my life?
- Do I feel so deeply committed to any of my values that I'm likely to push my clients to accept them?
- How would I communicate my values to my clients without imposing those values?
- How do my own values and beliefs affect my eclectic and personalized approach to working with clients?

As you work through the rest of this chapter, we suggest that you look for areas where you'd be inclined to "push" your values instead of challenging your clients to discover and clarify their own values.

# Value Conflicts with Clients

Even if you think it's inappropriate or unethical to impose your values on clients, you may unintentionally influence them in subtle ways to embrace your values. What you pay attention to during counseling sessions will reinforce what your clients choose to talk about. Even your nonverbal clues and body messages give them indications of when you like or dislike what they do. Since your clients may feel a need to have your approval, they may respond to these clues by acting in ways that they imagine will meet with your favor instead of developing their own inner direction. Suppose, for example, that an unhappily married man knew or surmised that you really thought he was wasting good years of his life in the marriage. This client might be influenced to obtain a divorce simply because he thought you would approve. So, even though you've made a clear decision not to push clients to believe and act in ways that agree with your own values, you still need to be sensitive to the subtle messages that can be powerful influences on their behavior.

## To Refer or Not to Refer

Being clear about your own values doesn't eliminate the possibility that a conflict of values between you and your client may interfere with effective therapy. Do you see yourself as being able to work effectively with anyone who seeks counseling from you? Some counselors believe that they can work with any kind of client or with any type of problem. They may be convinced that being professional means being able to assist anyone. On the other hand, some counselors are so unsure of their abilities that they are quick to refer anyone they feel uncomfortable with to another counselor.

Somewhere between these extremes are the cases in which your values and those of your client clash to such an extent that you question your ability to function in a helping way. Obviously there are no easy ways to determine what to do when this happens. The burden must be on counselors to honestly assess whether their values are likely to interfere with the objectivity they need to be useful to their clients. To make such an assessment, counselors must be clear about their feelings concerning value-laden issues, they must be honest about their own limitations, and they must be honest with potential clients when they think value conflicts will interfere with the therapeutic relationship. At times counselors may need to tell clients that, because of their own views, they cannot work effectively with them and that a referral to another professional would be in their best interests.

Consider the circumstances in which you would be inclined to refer a client to someone else because of a conflict of value systems. For each of the following, indicate the response that best fits you. Use the following code: A = I could work with this type of person; B = I would have difficulty working with this type of person; C = I could not work with this type of person.

___  1.  a man with fundamentalist religious beliefs
___  2.  a woman who claims that she is seeking a way to put Christ in the center of her life and that, if she only could turn her life to Christ, she would find peace
___  3.  a person who shows little development of a conscience, who is strictly interested in his or her own advancement, and who uses others to achieve personal aims
___  4.  a homosexual couple hoping to work on conflicts in the relationship
___  5.  a man who wants to leave his wife and children for the sake of sexual adventures with other women that might bring zest to his life
___  6.  a woman who has decided to leave her husband and children in order to gain her independence, but who wants to explore her fears of doing so
___  7.  a woman who wants an abortion but wants help in making her decision
___  8.  a man who is disturbed because he periodically becomes violent with his wife and has beaten her severely a number of times
___  9.  a man who lives by extremely rigid "macho" expectations of what a man should be
___ 10.  a person who lives by logic and is convinced that feelings are confusing and should be avoided
___ 11.  a man who believes that the only way to discipline his children is through the use of corporal punishment
___ 12.  an interracial couple coming for premarital counseling

___ 13. a husband and wife who seek counseling to discuss conflicts they are having with their adopted son, who is from a different culture
___ 14. a lesbian couple wanting to adopt a child
___ 15. a person whose way of life includes a consistent reliance on marijuana as a means of coping with stress
___ 16. a man who has found a way of beating the system and getting more than his legal share of public assistance
___ 17. a man and his wife, who is unwilling to give up her affair
___ 18. an interracial couple wanting to adopt a child and being faced with their respective parents' opposition to the adoption
___ 19. a client from another culture who has values very different from your own
___ 20. clients who have values that you strongly disapprove of or goals that you do not respect

Now go back over the list, and pay particular attention to the items you marked "C." Why do you think you'd have particular difficulty in working with these types of people? What other kinds of people do you envision you'd have trouble working with because of a clash of values?

## Case Studies of Possible Value Conflicts

In this section we present some case studies of possible value conflicts. Try to imagine yourself working with each of these clients. How do you think your values would affect your work with each one?

■ *The case of Candy.*    Candy is a 14-year-old client whom you are seeing because of family conflicts. Her parents have recently divorced, and Candy is having problems coping with the breakup. Eventually, she tells you that she is having sexual relations with her boyfriend. Moreover, she tells you that she's opposed to any birth-control devices because they seem so contrived. She assures you that she won't be one to get pregnant.

What are your feelings about Candy's having sex? If you sense that her behavior is an attempt to overcome her feelings of isolation, how might you deal with it? How would you respond to her decision not to use birth-control measures? Is she a danger to herself or others?

After you've been working with Candy for a few months, she discovers that she is pregnant. Her boyfriend is also 14 and is obviously in no position to support her and a baby. Candy tells you that she has decided to have an abortion but feels anxious about following through on her decision. How would you respond? In the blanks put an "A" if you agree more than disagree with the statement, and put a "D" if you mainly disagree.

___ I'd encourage Candy to do whatever she wants to do.
___ I'd encourage her to consider other options besides abortion, such as adoption, keeping the child as a single parent, marrying, and so on.

___ I'd reassure her about having an abortion, telling her that thousands of women make this choice.

___ I'd consult with a supervisor or a colleague about possible legal implications in this case.

___ I'd attempt to arrange for a family session, or at least a session with Candy and her parents, as a way to open up communication on this issue.

___ I'd encourage her to explore all the options and consequences of each of her choices.

___ I'd inform her parents, because I believe they have a right to be a part of this decision-making process.

___ I'd refer Candy to a family-planning center and encourage her to at least seek abortion counseling so that she could deal with her fears, guilt, and ambivalence pertaining to abortion as one option.

___ I'd pay particular attention to helping Candy clarify her value system; I'd be sensitive to her religious and moral values and the possible implications of specific choices she might make.

___ I'd refer Candy to another professional because of my opposition to abortion.

___ I'd tell Candy that I am personally opposed to (or in favor of) abortion but that I want to remain her counselor during this difficult time and will support whatever decision she makes for herself.

___ I would reprimand Candy and tell her that I knew this was going to happen.

___ I would check out the legal issues concerning a 14-year-old having sex.

Candy's case illustrates several thorny problems. What do you do if you feel that you cannot be objective because of your views on abortion? Do you refer Candy to someone else? If you do, might she feel that you are rejecting her because she has committed some horrible offense? If you're firmly opposed to abortion, could you support Candy in her decision to go ahead with it? Would you try to persuade her to have the baby because of your views on abortion?

A possible course of action would be to tell Candy about your values and how you felt they would influence your work with her. If you felt that you couldn't work effectively with her, perhaps you should ask yourself why. Why is it crucial that her decision be compatible with your values? Do you necessarily have to approve of the decisions your clients make?

Consider the possible decisions Candy might make, and ask yourself what your goals in working with her would be. What are *your* values in a case such as Candy's?

**Value issues.**   As can be seen in Candy's case, women are often unprepared or unwilling to include a child in their lives. When it comes to the subject of abortion, many women are reluctant to consider this as an option, either because of their value systems or because of their feelings of guilt, shame, and fear. Thus, an unwanted pregnancy and its termination constitute a crisis for most women. In writing about counseling women who find themselves unexpectedly pregnant, Kahn-Edrington (1979) states that the counselor's goal is to mobilize each woman's coping skills, deal with the many complex aspects of each client's situation, and provide support and information during the time of crisis. She suggests that counseling should deal with areas such as the following: the woman's total life perspective (including her life plans, her economic and social situation, and her role expectations for her age and background); her attitudes toward the pregnancy (including her values pertaining to abortion, the fetus, and contraception); her relationship with the man, other children, and family members; the reactions of others to her being pregnant and to having a child; alternatives and possible consequences; her motivation for having the child or for having an abortion; and her fears or misconceptions regarding abortion. Kahn-Edrington also presents her views on the knowledge, skills, and attitudes needed by those who counsel pregnant women. (See the accompanying box.)

## Principles for Effective Abortion Counseling

1. *Knowledge*: Counselors involved in abortion counseling:
   * are aware of the definition, prevalence, myths, procedures, risks, and sequels of abortion
   * are aware of alternatives to problem pregnancy: abortion, adoption, marriage
   * have information about sexuality, contraception, and community resources
   * have knowledge of value systems of other cultures and religions
2. *Skills*: Counselors have crisis-intervention and problem-solving skills.
3. *Attitudes*: In dealing with women with problem pregnancies, counselors:
   * evaluate personal attitudes toward birth and adoption
   * believe that the client has the right and responsibility to make her own decisions regarding abortion

Adapted from "Abortion Counseling" by M. Kahn-Edrington, 1979, *The Counseling Psychologist*, 8(1), pp. 37–38. Reprinted by permission.

■ *The case of Paul.* Paul comes to a counselor with many difficulties and anxieties, one of which is his antipathy toward interracial marriage. He expresses disappointment in his daughter and in himself as a father because of her engagement to a man of another race. Paul has gone as far as threatening to write her out of his will if she marries this man. What this client does not know is that the therapist herself is a partner in an interracial marriage. The therapist discloses this fact and lets him know of her difficulties with what she perceives as his prejudices.

* How do you react to her self-disclosure? (Was it ethical for her to do so? Would it have been ethical not to do so? Explain.)
* Would a referral be in order? Why or why not?

• What are your values in this situation, and what might you do or say if you were the counselor?

*Value issues.*   Your views on racial issues can have an impact on your manner of counseling in certain situations. As we encouraged you to clarify your values in other areas, we suggest that you take the following inventory and then think about what your responses tell you about how your values might operate in cases pertaining to racial concerns. In the space, write an "A" if you agree more than you disagree with the statement, and put a "D" if you disagree more than you agree.

___ 1. I could effectively counsel a person of a different race.

___ 2. I'd be inclined to refer a person of a different race to a counselor of that race, since the client is bound to have more trust in a therapist of the same race.

___ 3. My approach to counseling would entail modifying my practices and techniques in working with clients who are racially and culturally different.

___ 4. Interracial marriages in this society are almost doomed to failure because of the extra pressures on them.

___ 5. Interracial marriages pose no greater strain on a relationship than do interfaith marriages.

___ 6. I have certain racial (cultural) prejudices that would affect my objectivity in working with clients of a different race (culture) from mine.

Reflect on values you hold that would influence your way of working with clients such as Paul who present interracial issues.

■ *The case of Lupe.*   Lupe is a social worker in a community mental-health agency. Her agency is sponsoring workshops aimed at prevention of the spread of acquired immune deficiency syndrome (AIDS). Lupe's agency has attempted to involve the local churches in these workshops. One church withdrew its support because the workshops encouraged "safe" sexual practices, including the use of condoms, as a way of preventing AIDS. A church official contended that the use of condoms implies either homosexual behavior or promiscuous heterosexual activities, both of which are contrary to church teachings. Being a member of this church, Lupe finds herself struggling with value conflicts. She is in basic agreement with the teachings of the church, and she thinks that the official had a right to withdraw his support of these workshops, based on his beliefs and the church's position. But she is also aware that many people in the community she serves are at high risk for contracting AIDS, because of both drug usage and sexual practices. In her attempt to resolve her value conflicts she seeks out several of her colleagues, each of whom responds differently:

Colleague A says: "I would encourage you to tell your clients and others in the community that you agree with the position of the church. Then actively attempt in your workshops to change people's risky behavior. You could try to get them to give up their drug use, and you could steer them in the direction of monogamous sex practices."

Colleague B says: "I hope you will be up front with the people you come in contact with by telling them of your values and then providing them with adequate referrals where they can get information about prevention of this disease. But you do owe it to them not to steer them in the direction you think they should move."

Colleague C says: "I think it is best that you not disclose your values or let them know that you agree with the church's views. Instead, work toward changing their behavior and modifying their values indirectly. After all, in this case the end justifies the means."

Colleague D says: "More harm can come by your failure to provide necessary information. Even though your values are in sympathy with the church's position, I think that ethically you owe it to the community to teach them methods of safe sex."

**Value issues.**    If Lupe were to seek you out and ask for your advice, consider what you might say to her. In formulating your position, consider these questions:

- Which of her colleagues comes closest to your thinking, and why?
- With which colleague do you find yourself disagreeing the most, and why?
- Do you think that Lupe would be ethical if she did not disclose her values to her clients? Why or why not?
- Given the gravity of this situation and considering the possibility of the spread of disease, do you think that Lupe is ethically bound to provide community people who are at high risk with facts and information about prevention?
- What kind of advice would you be inclined to give Lupe, and what does this tell you about your values in this situation?

## Differences in Life Experiences and Philosophies

Many people would contend that the life experiences and value systems of counselors must be similar to those of their clients. The idea is that counselors can understand and empathize with their clients' conflicts only if they have had the same kinds of subjective experiences. Thus, an elderly person may feel that a counselor who hasn't reached this stage of life cannot hope to understand what it means to cope with loss, physical decline, loneliness, and anxiety about the future. Many people who belong to racial or ethnic minorities think it is extremely important to seek counselors of their own ethnic group, in the belief that counselors who haven't had to contend with discrimination and prejudice cannot really understand how they see the world. Similarly, many women are convinced that men cannot effectively counsel women, because their life experiences and biases prevent them from being able to understand women's needs. People who are committed to a homosexual life-style may seek gay therapists because they are convinced that heterosexual counselors lack the experience and understanding to work with them on their conflicts. Many drug addicts and alcoholics reveal failure after failure in their psychotherapy experiences with professionals who haven't experienced drug and alcohol problems.

The growth of self-help groups reflects the idea that people who have encountered and resolved certain difficulties possess unique resources for helping others like themselves. Thus, overweight people share their problems in Overeaters Anonymous. Alcoholics who have chosen to live one day at a time without alcohol provide support for fellow alcoholics who are trying to quit drinking. Many drug addicts who have entered Synanon have found that they cannot deceive former addicts with their games and that being confronted by people who once played the same games forces them to look at how they are living. Members of Recovery Incorporated find support in facing the world once they have left state mental hospitals.

To what degree do you share the view that you must have had life experiences similar to those of your clients? Do you think you need to have the same philosophy of life that your clients have in order to work effectively with them? Do you think that you can be helpful to people whose experiences, values, and problems are different from yours by tuning in to their feelings and relating them to your own? Consider for a moment whether you could communicate effectively with:

- an elderly person
- a person with a strict religious background
- a person of a different race or ethnic group
- a physically handicapped person
- a delinquent or a criminal
- an alcoholic
- a person with a different sexual orientation
- an obese person

Our position is that counselors need not have experienced each of the struggles of their clients to be effective in working with them. When the counselor and the client are relating on a *feeling* level, cultural and age differences are transcended. It is possible for a relatively young counselor to work effectively with an elderly client in spite of the fact that the counselor has not yet experienced some of the problems of the older client. For example, the client may be experiencing feelings of loss, guilt, sadness, and hopelessness over a number of situations in life. The counselor still has the capacity to empathize with these feelings, for he or she can tie into different experiences that resulted in some of the same feelings. Our point is that there can be a connection between the client and the counselor even though they have had different life experiences. What is essential is that the counselor must be sensitive to the differences in their backgrounds.

Sue. Counseling the
Culturally Different
Values and the Helping Relationship  **77**

In his excellent book *Counseling the Culturally Different: Theory and Practice*, D. W. Sue (1981a) points out that many counselors are "culturally blind" in the sense that they perceive reality exclusively through the filters of their own life experiences. He thinks that what is important is for counselors to become "culturally aware"—to be able to critically evaluate their conditioned values and assumptions and the conditioning of their clients. Sue sees it as imperative that counselors have a broad perspective of diverse cultural value systems. Those counselors who remain victims of their own cultural conditioning risk further oppressing minority clients.

To facilitate your reflection on the issue of whether you need to have life experiences or value systems that are similar to those of your clients, we'll present a number of situations that you might be faced with as a counselor. In each case, assess what factors in your life would either help or hinder you in establishing a good working relationship with the client we describe.

*Frances is a 60-year-old teacher who is thinking about going to law school because it's something she has wanted to do for a long time. For 30 years she has taught government and history in community colleges, and now she wants to retire early in order to take up a new profession. Frances wonders whether she has the stamina to endure long hours of study, and she is asking herself whether leaving teaching at this stage in life would be a wise move.*

- What experiences have you had that could help you understand Frances's desires and conflict?
- How do you respond to a person's beginning law school at the age of 60?
- Would you be inclined to encourage Frances to take a risk, or would you favor her staying with a secure job in her situation?
- How might your answers to the preceding questions affect the way you would counsel Frances?

*Alberto, a minority-group client, comes to a community mental-health clinic on the recommendation of one of his friends. His presenting problem is depression, chronic sleep disturbance, and the imminent threat of losing his job. During the initial session you are aware that he is extremely guarded. He discloses little about himself or how he is feeling in this situation with you. Although he will answer your questions briefly, you sense that he is withholding much information from you, and you meet with a variety of stubborn resistances during the session. As a counselor, you may assume that self-disclosure and openness to feeling enhance one's life. In working with Alberto, consider these questions:*

- How sensitive are you to the client's sense of privacy? Have you considered that keeping one's thoughts and feelings to oneself might be a value in certain cultures? How might this be a survival mechanism in some cultures?

- Assume that you succeed in getting Alberto to be more self-disclosing and expressive, not only with you but also within his environment. What potential hazards can you see in terms of his reentry into his environment?
- Is it ethical to convert him to your point of view without first understanding the cultural context? Explain.
- One of your aims might be to teach Alberto to be more autonomous (to become less dependent on his parents and his extended family). How might this be an expression of your value system, and how might that affect your client as he attempts to deal with his family?
- How might your intervention reflect your lack of understanding of the importance of the extended family in certain cultures?
- Some might label Alberto's behavior as bordering on paranoia. How might his cautiousness be more adaptive than maladaptive?

*At a community clinic Sylvia, who is 38, tells you that she is an alcoholic. During the intake interview she says: "I feel so much remorse, because I've tried to stop my drinking and haven't succeeded. I'm fine for a while, and then I begin to think that I have to be a 'perfect' wife and mother. I see all the ways in which I don't measure up, how I let my kids down, the many mistakes I've made with them, the embarrassment I've caused my husband, and then I get so down I feel compelled to take that next drink to stop my shaking and to blur my depression. I see that what I'm doing is self-destructive, but I haven't been able to stop, in spite of going to A.A."*

- What experiences have you had that would help you understand what it's like for Sylvia to feel compelled to drink?
- How do you see Sylvia? As having a disease? As suffering from a lack of willpower? As an irresponsible, indulgent person?
- How does the fact that Sylvia is a woman affect your view of her problem?
- What is your reaction to Sylvia's being in Alcoholics Anonymous? Do you see it as a desirable adjunct to therapy? Or do you see it as potentially working at cross purposes with your therapy? Explain.

■ *The case of Jan, a man who lives mainly by reason.*    Jan is a physicist, born and educated in northern Europe. He has several degrees from prestigious universities. Jan's life-style and interests center on intellectual pursuits, and he tends to show very little affect in most situations. His wife is having an affair, and he seeks your counsel, not so much on his own initiative but because of the encouragement of colleagues who think he can use some guidance. Jan talks calmly about the potential breakup of his family and indicates that he has discussed the matter with his wife. In essence, he has asked her to decide on the outcome. Jan is in your office to find a logical explanation for why the affair occurred, yet he does not display any strong emotional reactions to the situation. He gives no clues to how he is feeling about it.

- Would you consider Jan's cultural and educational background in dealing with his reaction to his situation?

- Would you immediately pursue the expression of feeling? Can you see yourself saying: "Cut out the intellectualizing and tell me how you feel?" Why or why not?

   ***Commentary.***     This example is used to illustrate another type of cultural difference. Although we do not deny the value of expressing one's emotional reactions to a situation such as Jan's, we would be especially sensitive to his cultural background and his conditioning. In certain cultures openly admitting having been affected by a situation such as this is equivalent to a loss of face or pride. Jan might never show the degree of emotionality that we deem appropriate, but that does not mean that he cannot express an emotional reaction. Our main point is that to push for the "norm" of "getting at feelings" could be counterproductive and potentially unethical. Although this example could apply to many American males as well, it is even more representative of Jan's cultural conditioning not to share his feelings.

   *You are the probation counselor for Mike, who has a history of being expelled from school. He has spent much of his life in and out of juvenile court. The customs of the gang he belongs to dictate how he lives. He's silent during most of your first session, but he does let you know that he doesn't really trust you, that he's only there because the court sent him, and that you can't possibly understand what his life is about.*

- Have you had any life experiences that would qualify you to counsel Mike?
- What are your immediate reactions to Mike?
- Would you want to convert him to any of your values? For example, would you want to see him finish school? stop being involved in gang fights? take counseling seriously?
- If you haven't had the kinds of experiences growing up that he has had, could you still communicate effectively with him and understand his view of the world?

   *Luigi is a middle-aged businessman who says that he's not seeking personal counseling but rather wants advice on how to manage his teenage daughter. According to Luigi, his daughter is immature and unruly. She isn't learning self-discipline, she socializes too much and works too little, she doesn't respect her parents, and in other ways she is a disappointment and a worry to him. Luigi seems to be oppressive rather than loving, and to him the full responsibility for the conflict in his family rests with his daughter. You surmise that he doesn't see any need to examine his own behavior or his role in contributing to the family's difficulties.*

- How do you imagine you might relate to Luigi?
- Would your own values get in the way of understanding his values?
- Do you think you might want to get him to look at his own part in the family disturbances? Would you want to challenge his values as they pertain to his daughter's behavior?

- Would you accept him as a client, even if he wanted to focus on how he could change his daughter?
- Would family therapy be indicated?

You can add your own examples of clients whom you might have difficulty in counseling because of a divergence in values or life experiences. How would you deal with such clients? You could decide to refer most of them to other counselors, but you might also look at how to broaden yourself so that you could work with a wider range of personalities. If you have difficulty relating to people who think differently from the way you do, you can work on being more open to diverse viewpoints. This openness doesn't entail accepting other people's values as your own. Instead, it implies being secure enough in your own values that you aren't threatened by really listening to, and deeply understanding, people who think about life differently. It implies listening to your clients with the intent of understanding what their values are, how they arrived at them, and the meaning these values have for them and then communicating this acceptance. This kind of accepting attitude requires a willingness to let your clients be who they are without trying to convince them that they should see life the way you do. Achieving this acceptance of your clients can significantly broaden you as a person and as a professional.

# Controversial Issues: Implications for Counseling

In the two previous sections you have seen that differences in life experiences and values are bound to influence the interventions you make. As you counsel a variety of clients, you may find yourself struggling with how your beliefs affect the way you work with them. This is especially true in controversial cases pertaining to the right to die, religion, and sexuality. As you read this section, attempt to clarify your values in these areas and think about how your views might either enhance or interfere with your ability to establish contact with certain clients.

## The Right to Die and the Issue of Suicide

How do you react to the following statement?

> The choice of suicide is ours to make. It is our life we are giving up, and our death we are arranging. The choice does not infringe on the rights of others. We do not need to explain and excuse.[1]

In the article from which this quotation is taken, Doris Portwood (1978) makes a case for the right of elderly people to choose to end their own lives if they decide that each day there is less to live for or if they are in a state of

---

[1] From "A Right to Die?" by D. Portwood, January 1978, *Psychology Today*, p. 68.

physical and psychological deterioration. Pointing out that many old people are subjected to an undignified ending to life, particularly if they have certain terminal illnesses, she argues persuasively that they have the right to end their lives before they become utterly miserable and a drain on their families.

Apply this argument to yourself. Might there come a time in your life when there is nothing for you to live for? Imagine yourself in a rest home, growing more and more senile. You are unable to read, to carry on meaningful conversation, or to go places, and you are partially paralyzed by a series of strokes. Would you want to be kept alive at all costs, or might you want to end your life? Would you feel justified in doing so? What might stop you?

Now apply this line of thought to other situations in life. If you accept the premise that your life is yours to do with as you choose, do you believe it is permissible to commit suicide at *any* period in your life? In many ways, people who choose suicide are really saying that they want to put an end to the way they are living *now*. Suppose you felt this way even after trying various ways of making your life meaningful, including getting intensive psychotherapy. Imagine that you felt as if nothing worked, as if you always wound up in a dead-end street. Would you continue to live until natural causes took you? Would you feel justified in ending your own life if your active search had failed to bring you peace?

Perhaps thinking about conditions that might lead you to consider suicide is so unpleasant that you have never really allowed yourself to imagine such situations. If you give some thought to how this issue applies to you, however, you may feel less threatened in entering into real dialogues with individuals who are contemplating the balance sheet of their lives. If you are closed to any personal consideration of this issue, you may tend to interrupt these dialogues or cut off your clients' exploration of their feelings.

The ethical questions associated with suicide can come up in other ways as well. Consider the following example.

■ *The case of Emily.*   Emily, who is in her early 20s, is dying painfully of cancer. She expresses her wish to forgo any further treatment and to take an overdose of pills to end her suffering. Her parents cling to hope, however, and in any event they deeply believe that it is always wrong to take one's own life. If her parents were coming to you for counseling, what might you say to them? Do you feel that Emily has the right to end her life? What role should your opinion play in your counseling? How might your values affect the things you say to the family?

Now assume that Emily herself comes to you, her therapist of long standing, and says: "I am dying and I have no desire to suffer. I don't want to involve you in it, but as my therapist, I would like you to know my last wishes." She tells you of her plan to take an overdose of pills, an action she sees as more humane than continuing to endure her suffering. Consider the following questions:

- What are the legal implications involved here?
- Do you think you have the ethical and legal responsibility to prevent Emily from carrying out her intended course of action?
- If you were in full agreement with her wishes, how might this influence your intervention?
- What do you consider to be the ethical course of action?

■ *The case of Betina.*   Let's consider a different case involving the termination of one's life. An adolescent girl named Betina, who is living at a boarding school, has made light suicidal overtures. Although these attempts seem to be primarily attention-getting gestures, there have been several of them. Betina's counselor feels manipulated and has not reported these episodes to the girl's parents. During one of these attempts, however, Betina seriously hurts herself and ends up in the hospital.

- Did the counselor take the "cry for help" too lightly?
- What are the ethical and legal implications of the counselor's deciding that the client's attempts were more manipulative than serious and therefore should be ignored?
- What can a counselor do in a situation in which he or she determines that the attempts are manipulative rather than serious?
- Assume that the counselor had told Betina that she was going to inform Betina's parents about these suicidal attempts. Betina had responded by saying that she would quit counseling if the counselor did so. What do you think the counselor should have done?

**Issues Involved in Right-to-Die Cases.**   Although the cases of Emily and Betina are different, they do raise similar issues that are worth considering. What is your position on these issues pertaining to the right to die?

- Do counselors have the responsibility and the right to forcefully protect people from the potential harm that their own decisions may bring?
- Do helpers have an ethical right to block clients who have clearly chosen death over life?
- What are the ethical and legal considerations of right-to-die decisions?
- Once a therapist determines that a significant risk exists, must some course of action be taken? What are the consequences of failing to take steps to prevent clients from ending their lives? Do factors such as the age of the client, the client's level of competence, and the special circumstances of each case make a difference?

In his paper *Adolescence and the Right to Die,* Powell (1982) discusses the issues of autonomy, competence, and paternalism as directly related to the right to die. Although Powell's article focuses on adolescents, his paper has broader implications, since the three concepts he discusses can be applied to all age levels. *Autonomy* refers to a person's independence, self-reliance, and ability to make decisions that affect his or her life. Autonomy, in turn, is based on a presumption of the person's *competence*. Competence is determined in part by the person's degree of ability to understand the potential consequences of his or her decisions. Thus, people experiencing trauma and extreme crisis and those who are actively hallucinating and clinging to false beliefs (or displaying other psychotic behaviors) are not viewed as competent to make certain critical decisions. In cases in which clients are found to be unable to direct their own lives or incompetent to make decisions of life and death, *paternalism* comes into the picture. This concept implies that the therapist (or some agent of the client) makes decisions and acts in the "best interests" of the client. In his discussion Powell states that he has been unable to find a clear constitutional or legal statement of a person's right to choose death. What does appear to have a constitutional basis, however, is the right to refuse treatment, even life-saving treatment. Powell cites an adolescent girl, dying from bone cancer, whose refusal of a leg operation was supported by the courts. In this case, her own wishes were considered to be crucial.

## Religion

What role does religion play in your life? Does it provide you with a source of meaning? What are your views concerning established and organized religion? Has religion been a positive, negative, or neutral force in your life? Even if religious issues are not the focus of a client's concern, religious values may enter into the sessions indirectly as the client explores moral conflicts or grapples with questions of meaning in life. Do you see yourself as being able to keep your religious values out of these sessions? How do you think they will influence the way you counsel? If you're hostile to organized religions, can you empathize with clients who feel committed to the teachings of a particular church?

Some take the position that psychotherapy and religion can and should work together. Quackenbos, Privette, and Klentz (1986) argue that religion is a pervasive force in our society and yet is excluded from most psychotherapy. They see a clear need to integrate religious values with psychotherapy for many people. These authors assert that the clergy need rigorous preparation in counseling and that secular counselors also need special preparation for dealing with religious issues:

> The time is ripe for seriously considering specialized education or certification in religious counseling for secular psychotherapists. Secular psychotherapists then could function not as ministers or religious teachers, but as facilitators for clients with religious questions as well as concerns in the secular realm [p. 85].

As you formulate your own position on the place of religious values in the practice of counseling, we suggest that you reflect on these questions: Is it appropriate to deal with religious issues in an open and forthright manner as a client's needs arise in the counseling process? Do clients have the right to explore their religious concerns in their therapy? Are therapists forcing their values on their clients when they decide what topics can and cannot be discussed during therapy?

Religious beliefs and practices affect many dimensions of human experience that are brought into counseling situations. How people handle guilt feelings, authority, and moral questions are just a few of these areas. The key issue here is whether you can understand your clients' religious beliefs and their meaning for your clients, even if these views differ from your own. For example, you may think that a client has accepted an unnecessarily strict and authoritarian moral code. Yet you need to be able to understand what these beliefs mean to your client, whatever your own evaluation of them for yourself might be.

Suppose you have a client, Janet, who seems to be suffering from a major conflict because her church would disapprove of the way she is living. Janet experiences a great deal of guilt over what she sees as her transgressions. If you sharply disagreed with the values she accepted from her church or thought they were unrealistic, how might your views affect your counseling? Do you think you might try to persuade Janet that her guilt is controlling her and that she would be better off freeing herself from her religious beliefs? Why or why not?

*Consider the case of Susan, who is a devout Catholic. She was married for 25 years, until her husband left her. Later, she fell in love with another man and very much wanted a relationship with him. But her moral upbringing resulted in her having guilt feelings about her involvement with another man. She sees her situation as hopeless, for there is no way in her mind to resolve an impossible situation. She might live alone for the rest of her life, and that scares her. She might marry the man, but she fears that her guilt feelings would eventually ruin the relationship.*

- What are your values that pertain to this case, and how do you think they would influence your interventions?
- Would you recommend that she see a priest to help her resolve her guilt feelings? Explain.
- Assume that Susan asks you what she should do, or at least what you think about her dilemma. What do you think you'd say to her?

*In this final case, assume that Jeremiah is in a group that you are leading. He calls himself a "born-again Christian" and feels that he has found peace and strength in his own life. In a sincere and caring way, Jeremiah wants to pass on to other members in the group what has become very meaningful to him. Several members respond negatively, asserting that he is pushing his values on them and that he comes across in a superior way.*

- As a group leader, how would you intervene?
- What reactions do you think you'd have toward a person who holds very strong religious values, and how might your reactions either inhibit or enhance your ability to work with such a person?

- If your views were very similar to this person's, what interventions might you make, and how might you react?

## Sexuality

What are your values with respect to sexual behavior? Do they tend to be liberal or conservative? What are your attitudes toward:

- the belief that sex should be reserved for marriage only
- sex as an expression of love and commitment
- casual sex
- group sex
- extramarital sex
- premarital sex
- homosexuality
- teenage sex

An important issue is whether you can counsel people who are experiencing conflict over their sexual choices if their values differ dramatically from your own. For example, if you have very liberal views about sexual behavior, will you be able to respect the conservative views of some of your clients? If you think their moral views are giving them difficulty, will you try to persuade them to become more liberal and adopt your views? How will you view the guilt they may experience? Will you treat it as an undesirable emotion that they need to free themselves of? Or, if you have fairly strict sexual standards that you use as guidelines for your own life, will you tend to see the more permissive attitudes of some of your clients as a problem? Can you be supportive of choices that conflict with your own values?

■ *The case of an extramarital affair.*   Virginia and Tom find themselves in a marital crisis when she discovers that he has been having sexual affairs with several women. These affairs have been going on for several years. Tom agrees to see a marriage counselor, and the couple comes for a counseling session. Tom says that he has no intention of giving up his life-style, because he doesn't think the affairs are interfering in his relationship with his wife. He says that he loves his wife and that he does not want to end the marriage. His involvements with the other women are sexual in nature rather than committed love relationships. Virginia says that she would like to accept her husband's affairs but that she finds it too painful to continue living with him while knowing of his activities.

*Counselor A.*   This counselor has a definite bias in favor of Tom. She points out that the two seem to have a basically sound marriage, and she suggests that with some individual counseling Virginia can learn to accept and live with her husband's affairs.

- With her bias, is it ethical for this counselor to accept this couple for counseling? Should she suggest a referral to another professional?
- Is the counselor ignoring the wife's needs and values?
- Is there an ethical issue in siding with the husband?
- Would it be a better course of action for the counselor to keep her values and attitudes to herself so that she would be less likely to influence the couple's decisions?

**Counselor B.**    From the outset, this counselor makes it clear that she sees affairs as disruptive in any marriage. She maintains that they are typically started because of a deep dissatisfaction within the marriage. In her view affairs are symptomatic of other real conflicts. The counselor suggests that, with couples therapy, Tom and Virginia can get to the basis of their problem. She further says that she will not work with them unless Tom is willing to give up his affairs, since she is convinced that counseling will not work unless he is fully committed to doing what is needed to work on his relationship with Virginia.

- Do you see this counselor as imposing her values?
- Is this approach appropriate, since the counselor is openly stating her conditions and values from the outset?
- To what degree do you agree or disagree with this counselor's thinking and approach?

**Counselor C.**    This counselor tells the couple at the initial session that from her experience extramarital affairs add many strains to a marriage, that many people tend to get hurt in such situations, and that affairs do pose some problems for couples seeking counseling. However, she adds that affairs sometimes actually have positive benefits for both the wife and the husband. She says that her policy is to let the husband and wife find out for themselves what is acceptable to them. She accepts Virginia and Tom as clients and asks them to consider as many options as they can to resolve their difficulties. Counselor C asks Virginia to consider the possibility of getting involved with other men.

- Do you see this counselor as neutral or biased? Explain.
- Does it seem practical and realistic to expect the couple to make the decision by coming up with some alternatives?
- Is it ethical for the counselor to suggest that Virginia consider becoming sexually involved with other men?

# Ethical Issues in Counseling Gay and Lesbian Clients

Gay and lesbian life-styles evoke much negative reaction. This issue often presents a challenge to those who hold traditional value systems. Even counselors who are intellectually accepting may be emotionally rejecting of this life-style. Counselors who have negative emotional or intellectual reac-

tion, become this client and bring her problem to another student, who plays the part of a counselor.

6. For this exercise, work in small groups. Discuss the kinds of life experiences you've had that you think will enable you to effectively counsel others. You might also talk about the *limitations* of your life experiences so far as they might hinder your understanding of certain clients.

7. Interview some practicing counselors about their experiences with values in the counseling process. You could ask such questions as "What are some kinds of clients that you've had difficulty working with because of your value system? How do you think your values influence the way you counsel? How are your clients affected by your values? What are some of the main value issues that clients bring into the counseling process?"

8. Do this exercise in pairs. One student plays a counselor; the other plays a client. The counselor actively tries to convert the client to some value or point of view that the counselor holds. The job of the counselor is to try to persuade the client to do what the counselor thinks would be best for the client. This exercise can give you a feel for what it's like to persuade a person to adopt your point of view and what it's like to be subjected to persuasion. Then, the two students can switch roles.

9. This exercise can also be done in pairs. Each person interviews the other on the following issue: What are some of your central values and beliefs, and how do you think they will inhibit or facilitate the work you will do as a counselor?

## Suggested Readings

For a discussion of goals and values in psychotherapy see Patterson (1985b). For a personal exploration of values pertaining to topics such as marriage and the family, sex-role identity, work, meaning in life, death and loss, love and intimate relationships, and sexuality see Corey with Corey (1986). For a book that deals with value issues and both sides of the ethical controversies on topics such as the right to die, suicide, withholding the truth from dying patients, abortion, and screening for antibodies to the AIDS virus see Levine (1987). For a persuasive case against suicide prevention see Szasz (1986). For an article that discusses the thesis that religion and psychotherapy should be integrated, see Quackenbos, Privette, and Klentz (1986). On ethical issues in counseling gay and lesbian clients see Graham, Rawlings, Halpern, and Hermes (1984). For a description and evaluation of a workshop designed to train mental-health providers to work with gay and lesbian adolescents see Schneider and Tremble (1986). On issues pertaining to counseling clients with AIDS see Price, Omizo, and Hammett (1986). On counseling gay parents and their children see Cramer (1986). For textbooks pertaining to counseling gay clients see Moses and Hawkins (1982) and Woodman and Lenna (1980).

# FOUR

# Theory and Practice in Counseling and Psychotherapy

- Pre-Chapter Self-Inventory
- Introduction
- Developing a Counseling Stance
- The Trend toward Eclectic Counseling
- Four Basic Models of Helping
- The Use of Techniques in Counseling and Therapy
- The Division of Responsibility in Therapy
- Roles and Functions of Counselors
- Deciding on the Goals of Counseling
- Diagnosis as a Professional Issue
- The Issue of Using Tests in Counseling
- Ethical Issues in Psychotherapeutic Research
- Chapter Summary
- Suggested Activities
- Suggested Readings

# Pre-Chapter Self-Inventory

*Directions:*   For each statement, indicate the response that most closely identifies your beliefs and attitudes. Use the following code:

3 = I *agree*, in most respects, with this statement.
2 = I am *undecided* in my opinion about this statement.
1 = I *disagree*, in most respects, with this statement.

_____   1. I have settled on a definite theory of counseling.
_____   2. I would rather combine insights and techniques derived from various theoretical approaches to counseling than base my practice on a single model.
_____   3. My view of people is that they are basically capable of and responsible for changing their behaviors.
_____   4. What happens in counseling sessions is more my responsibility than it is my client's.
_____   5. I would find it difficult to work for an agency if I was expected to perform functions that I didn't see as appropriate counseling functions.
_____   6. I have the power to define my own role and professional identity as a counselor.
_____   7. Clients should always select the goals of counseling.
_____   8. I'd be willing to work with clients who didn't seem to have any clear goals or reasons for seeking counseling.
_____   9. Giving advice is a legitimate part of counseling.
_____  10. Enhancing a client's social adjustment is a legitimate goal of counseling.
_____  11. A diagnosis is helpful, if not essential, when a client begins counseling.
_____  12. There are more dangers than values associated with diagnosis in counseling.
_____  13. Testing can be a very useful adjunct to counseling.
_____  14. I think the medical model of mental health can be fruitfully applied in counseling and psychotherapy.
_____  15. There is a real danger that counseling techniques can be used to keep the therapist hidden as a person.
_____  16. Skill in using a variety of techniques is one of the most important qualities of a therapist.
_____  17. Theories of counseling can limit counselors by encouraging them to pay attention only to behavior that fits their particular theory.
_____  18. Counselors should develop and modify their own theories of counseling as they practice.
_____  19. A theory should be more than an explanation of disturbed behavior; it should challenge my philosophy of human nature.

___ 20. Counselors can identify their theoretical preferences by paying attention to the way they actually practice.

___ 21. In my view of human nature, people are responsible both for creating and for solving their problems.

___ 22. Although I do not see people as responsible for creating their problems, I do see them as responsible for finding ways to deal effectively with these problems.

___ 23. It can be unethical for practitioners to fail to do some type of assessment and diagnosis, especially with "high-risk" (suicidal and dangerous) patients.

___ 24. It is questionable for therapists to help minority clients assimilate into the majority culture.

___ 25. In assessment and diagnosis it is critical to take cultural factors into consideration if the therapist hopes to gather accurate data and come up with a valid perspective on a client.

# Introduction

*Important*
*to understand*
*theoretical bias*

Professional counselors should be able to conceptualize *what* they are doing in their counseling sessions and *why* they're doing it. Too often practitioners are unable to explain why they use certain counseling procedures. For example, when you meet a new client, what guidelines should you use in structuring your first interview? What do you want to accomplish at this initial session? Rank in order of importance the following factors that you would be interested in knowing about your client:

- the presenting problem (the reason the client is seeking counseling)
- the client's present style of coping with demands, stresses, and conflicts
- the client's early experiences as a child, particularly in relationship to parents and siblings
- the client's ego strength
- the client's history of successes and failures
- the client's developmental history
- the client's struggle with current choices
- the client's goals and agenda for counseling
- the client's current support system
- the client's motivation to change
- the client's level of reality testing

What are some of the interventions you might make during your initial session in getting to know your client? How would you want to structure your future sessions? Consider the following questions, and briefly write your responses.

- Would you begin with a detailed case history? Why or why not?
- Do you consider diagnosis a necessary prerequisite to counseling? Why or why not?

- Are tests important as a prerequisite to counseling? Would you decide whether to test, or would you allow your client to make this decision?
- How much would you structure the session to obtain *current* information about your client's life? How much would you want to know about the client's past?
- Would you do most of the talking? Why or why not?
- Who would set the goals of therapy? Who would be primarily responsible for what was discussed? Why?
- Who would take the greater responsibility for *directing* the initial session? Would you ask many questions? Would you encourage your client to structure the session?
- Would you develop contracts with your clients specifying what they can expect from you, what they want from counseling, and what they are willing to do to meet their goals? Why or why not?
- Would you be inclined to use directive, action-oriented techniques, such as homework assignments? Why or why not?
- What aspects of the client's life would you stress?

In this chapter we focus on how your theoretical positions and biases influence your actual practice. Ideally, theory should help you make sense of what you do in your counseling sessions. Since your answers to the preceding questions depend on your view of personality and of counseling, looking at how you responded to these questions is one way to begin clarifying your theoretical approach. Another way of thinking about this issue is to imagine a client asking you to explain your view of counseling in clear and simple terms. Would you be able to tell your client *what* you most hoped to accomplish and *how* you would go about it?

You might consider how open you are to challenging your theoretical stance and how this openness or lack of it might influence the therapeutic outcome for your clients. Think about how your theoretical viewpoint influences your stand on questions such as these: What is the role and function of the counselor? What are some goals for counseling? What is the proper place of diagnosis and testing in the counseling process? What techniques are most appropriate in reaching certain goals of counseling?

# Developing a Counseling Stance

Developing a counseling stance is more complicated than merely accepting the tenets of a given theory. We believe that the theoretical approach you use to guide you in your practice is an expression of your uniqueness as a person and an outgrowth of your life experience. Further, your counseling stance must be appropriate for the type of counseling you do and the unique needs of your clients.

We believe that a theoretical approach becomes more useful and meaningful after you've taken a critical look at the *theorist* who developed the theory, as well as its key concepts, since a theory of counseling is often an expression of the personality of the theorist. Blindly following any single theory, however, can lead you to ignore some of the insights that your life opens up to you. This is our bias, of course, and many would contend that providing effective therapy depends on following a given theory.

A major consideration in developing or evaluating a theory is the degree to which that perspective helps you understand what you're doing. Does your framework provide a broad base for working with diverse clients in different ways, or does it restrict your vision and cause you to ignore variables that don't fit the theory? If you are a "true believer" of one theory, there's a danger of forcing your clients to conform to your expectations. It's important, therefore, to evaluate what you are emphasizing in your counseling work. The following questions may help you make this evaluation:

- Where did you acquire your theory? Did you incorporate many of the views of your instructors or training supervisors? Has one theory intrigued you to the point that it is the sole basis for your orientation?
- Do you embrace a particular theory because it is a justification of your own life-style, experiences, and values? For instance, do you adopt a theory that stresses an active, didactic role for the therapist because you see yourself as "straightening out" your clients? What does your approach stress, and why does it appeal to you?
- To what degree does your theory challenge your own previous frame of reference? Does your theory cause you to test your hypotheses, beliefs, and assumptions? Does it encourage you to think of alternatives? To what degree does your theory reinforce your present world view? Does your theory force you to extend your thinking, or does it merely support your biases?
- How do you see your own life experiences as an influence in your counseling style? In what ways have your life experiences caused you to modify your theoretical viewpoint?
- What are the ethical implications of a counselor's practicing without a theoretical orientation? Does ethical practice demand having a rationale for the interventions you make?

Your assumptions about the nature of counseling and the nature of people have a direct impact on your manner of practice. The goals that you think are important in therapy, the techniques and methods you employ to reach these goals, the way in which you see the division of responsibility in the client/therapist relationship, your view of your role and functions as a counselor, and your view of the place of diagnosis and testing in the therapeutic process—these are largely determined by your theoretical orientation.

Practicing counseling without an explicit theoretical rationale is somewhat like flying a plane without a map and without instruments. We do not see a theoretical orientation (or a counseling stance) as a rigid structure that prescribes the specific steps of what to do in a counseling situation. Rather, we see theory as a set of general guidelines that counselors can use to make sense of what they are doing.

In the following sections we look at some current theoretical trends in counseling and psychotherapy; we examine the assumptions underlying the basic models of helping; and we focus on theoretical differences over the issue of how responsible clients are for creating their own problems and for solving them.

## The Trend toward Eclectic Counseling

Smith (1982) asked clinical and counseling psychologists what theoretical orientations they adhered to. He received 422 usable questionnaires, yielding the following results:

| | |
|---|---|
| Transactional analysis | 0.96% |
| Reality | .96% |
| Rational-emotive | 1.69% |
| Gestalt | 1.69% |
| Existential | 2.17% |
| Family | 2.65% |
| Adlerian | 2.89% |
| Behavioral | 6.75% |
| Person-centered | 8.67% |
| Other | 9.16% |
| Cognitive behavioral | 10.36% |
| Psychoanalytic | 10.84% |
| Eclectic | 41.20% |

*...developmental, social learning career theory, personal-effectiveness training...*

The "other" category included developmental orientation, social-learning theory, career theory, and personal-effectiveness training. The findings indicated a continued decline in the popularity of psychoanalytic therapy and a trend toward the cognitive behavioral therapies.

Smith cites literature indicating a trend in the direction of "creative synthesis, masterful integration, and systematic eclecticism." Clearly, with 41% of the respondents indicating "eclectic" as their primary theoretical orientation, this sample preferred drawing concepts and techniques from various approaches rather than being restricted by a single theory. "These findings strongly suggest that the trend in psychotherapy is away from the exclusiveness of schools and toward some kind of eclectic system that transcends both the narrowness in schools and the mediocrity of traditional eclecticism" (p. 807).

*eclectic n rise*

## Theoretical Orientations of Faculty Members in Counselor-Education Programs

In a survey of faculties of counselor-preparation programs, Hollis and Wantz (1983) found that the vast majority of members identified themselves by an eclectic orientation. Below are the rankings:

1. Eclectic
2. Person-centered
3. Existential/humanistic
4. Behavioral
5. Cognitive
6. Systems approach
7. Interpersonal relationship
8. Rational-emotive
9. Gestalt
10. Psychoanalytic
11. Social-learning
12. Adlerian
13. Transactional analysis
14. Transpersonal
15. Art therapy

An increasing number of writers point to the advantages of developing an eclectic approach. One of the reasons for this trend is the recognition that no single theory is comprehensive enough to account for the complexities of human behavior, especially when the range of client types and their specific problems are taken into consideration. It is important to stress that genuine eclecticism is not a haphazard borrowing of techniques from several theories. Rather, it is a thoughtful integrating of concepts and procedures from various approaches. Thus, eclecticism should not be an excuse for sloppy practice or a failure to think about the implications of theory for practice. Unfortunately, some practitioners who call themselves "eclectic" really have no theoretical stance at all but have simply collected a "bag of techniques" that they use in shotgun fashion in the hope that some will work if others won't.

One advantage of an eclectic orientation is that theory can become a growing, open-ended framework. We agree with Ivey, Ivey, and Simek-Downing (1987) that theory need not be fixed but is best seen as an opening to new and greater possibilities in the future. Palmer (1980) proposes an eclectic approach that includes both the psychodynamic and the behavioral trends in psychotherapy. According to Palmer, since the client is a unity—an individual with internal and external experiences that interact—the task of the eclectic psychotherapist is to bring together the *psychodynamic* theory (which focuses on internal events such as ideas, dreams, projections, fears, and attitudes) and the *behavioral* theory (which stresses responses and coping behavior of the individual to the external environment).

Messer (1986) indicates that recent trends in behavior therapy and psychoanalytic therapy suggest some confluence of these perspectives. Messer notes that there are changing visions of both branches of therapy and that many therapists of both schools welcome integration. "For them, the mutual influence of one therapy on the other, the convergence of certain perspectives, and the particular shift of visions and values that this entails constitute a creative challenge both to the theory of each therapy and to its practice" (p. 1270).

Garfield (1980) summarizes the challenges of the(eclectic perspective.

> Although the eclectic therapist would appear to have the advantage of having a broader orientation to psychotherapy and potential access to a wider variety of therapeutic techniques and procedures than his school-oriented colleagues, it must also be acknowledged that his path is less clearly illuminated. There is some personal comfort for the therapist in believing in and adhering to a given theoretical system. He can follow certain stated procedures and explain certain phenomena in terms of his theoretical system [p. 234].

The eclectic therapist does not have the specific structure and kind of support that many practitioners have who follow a particular theory. This can be a disadvantage. It can also be a challenge to the therapist to develop a creative integration that is an expression of his or her own unique personality and therapeutic style. According to Garfield, given the theoretical development in the field of psychotherapy and the current state of knowledge, it seems to be defensible and justifiable for the eclectic therapist to place confidence in empirical results and tenable hypotheses instead of adhering to a single theory. In the absence of research data, Garfield contends, therapists must rely on their clinical experiences and evaluations and evaluate their interventions as therapy proceeds. His view of the eclectic approach places responsibility on the therapist to make an adequate appraisal of the client and then to work out a plan of therapy that seems appropriate. Such a plan includes selecting procedures from a variety of approaches that are relevant to the specific problems presented by particular clients.

Although we encourage the development of an eclectic perspective in counselor-education programs, C. H. Patterson (1985a) would take strong exception to our position. He writes: "Telling students to make their own choices is admitting that we have no basis for teaching, that counseling is not a profession" (p. 349). In a critique of recent textbooks that present an eclectic perspective, Patterson asserts: "They are lacking in an adequate systematic theoretical integration. Moreover, they have little in common. Attempts to develop an eclectic approach are essentially uncritical compendia of the many and varied methods and techniques, with a minimal ordering or organization or theoretical basis" (p. 350).

## Four Basic Models of Helping

As a way of conceptualizing the variety of theoretical orientations to therapeutic practice, we rely on the analysis of Brickman, Rabinowitz, Karuza, Coates, Cohn, and Kidder (1982). In our opinion their four models of helping provide a framework for analyzing some basic assumptions of the contemporary psychotherapies mentioned earlier. Their analysis is based on a distinction between attribution of responsibility (who is to be held accountable for a present or past event) and attribution of responsibility for a solution (who is to control future events). They describe four general models: In the *moral model* people are held responsible for both the problems in their

lives and the solutions to them and are believed to need only proper motivation. In the *compensatory model* people are seen as not responsible for their problems but as responsible for solutions, and they are believed to need power. In the *medical model* people are seen as responsible for neither their problems nor the solutions and are believed to need treatment. In the *enlightenment model* people are seen as responsible for their problems but as unable or unwilling to provide the solutions, and they are believed to need discipline.

Practitioners are not always aware of the assumptions they make about human behavior and how these assumptions affect their interventions. Therapists can function with more direction when they become aware of their assumptions about responsibility for problems and for solutions. Each of these four sets of assumptions is internally consistent, and to some degree each is incompatible with the other three.

## The Moral Model

The moral model is based on the assumption that people are responsible both for creating and for solving their problems. Under this model people see themselves and are seen by others as unmotivated and as not making the effort needed for changing. If they hope to change, they must develop the motivation to do what is necessary to bring about change, for nobody but they can act in ways that will result in change. Practitioners with this orientation remind clients how they are responsible for creating their life situations and how only they can utilize their resources to control their future. Several current theories of therapy are grounded on this model of human behavior—reality therapy, rational-emotive therapy, existential therapy, person-centered therapy, and Gestalt therapy.

## The Compensatory Model

The model in which people are not held responsible for their problems but are still held responsible for solving these problems is the compensatory model. This model holds that people have to compensate for obstacles placed before them by their situation with a special kind of effort and collaboration with others. Brickman and his associates (1982) write that the strength of this model is that it allows people to direct their efforts toward the future by trying to transform their environment without blaming themselves for creating their problems. Although clients are not blamed for their problems that originated in the past, they are given credit for coming up with solutions. Under this model we classify these approaches: Adlerian, behavioral, and transactional analysis.

## The Medical Model

The basic premise of the medical model is that people are not held responsible for either the origin of their problems or the solution to their problems. People are seen as victims of a disease and are considered to be subject to forces beyond their control. This model views people as incapacitated, and they are expected to accept that condition, which involves exempting them from responsibility. They must seek expert help in coping with their problems. The advantage of the medical model for coping is that it allows people to accept help without being blamed for their weakness (Brickman et al., 1982). The drawback of the model is that it fosters dependency and a sense of powerlessness.

## The Enlightenment Model

Under the enlightenment model, people are held accountable for contributing to or causing their problems, but they are not believed to be responsible for solving them. People with addictive personalities, for example, often blame themselves for their drinking problems, for the fact that they cannot live without drugs, or for their obsession with eating. Because their impulses are out of control, they believe, they need the discipline provided from some external authority or some type of therapeutic community.

Therapeutic communities such as Alcoholics Anonymous, Daytop Village, Overeaters Anonymous, Weight Watchers, and other peer self-help groups are based on the assumption that some form of structured therapeutic community is necessary to help addictive personalities control their impulses. Some drug and alcohol rehabilitation programs, for example, use recovered alcoholics and drug addicts, who have the goal of rehabilitating fellow substance abusers. Many of these organizations provide a highly structured environment that directs its members in the specifics of everyday living. An example of an organization based on the enlightenment model is Alcoholics Anonymous. Members must take responsibility for their past drinking problems and the consequences of their life-style rather than continuing to blame others for their drinking patterns. They admit that they are alcoholics, that they have a disease, and that they are powerless to control their drinking. Thus, they turn their lives over to a higher power and to the community of fellow alcoholics who have been successful in giving up drinking.

## Mixing Your Models: A Case Study

The point we want to make at this juncture is that, even though these four models help us understand the views of human nature held by the different theories of counseling, they are not to be viewed in a rigid fashion. Let us add a note of confusion to the picture by way of a case study.

*A Southeast Asian refugee adolescent has seen little except war, hunger, destruction, and chaos. He is a patient in a mental institution, for in a delusional moment he killed his adoptive parents. He is diagnosed as a paranoid schizophrenic and is still actively delusional.*

How can this person be treated in light of the four contrasting models just described?

- He may need medication for his delusional state to calm him down (medical model). In your opinion, would it be ethical to deny him medication because of your view that he is responsible for his past and his actions (moral model)?
- The medication sedates him to the point at which you can converse with him. At this point, which models can you draw from, and which can you not draw from?
- To what degree do you hold him responsible for his past? Given his unusual life experiences, do you see him as a victim of these circumstances? Why or why not? Is he responsible for changing his behavior, or does he need help? How would your answer affect your approach and your interventions in working with him? What would your approach tell you about rigid delineations of various models?

*your approach to a client is ultimately influenced by client circumstances*

   ***Commentary.***   It is our point of view that your approach to a client is ultimately influenced by the client's circumstances and welfare, not by your loyalty to a particular view of human nature. There may be a time when the therapist needs to draw from several theoretical approaches. In the above-cited case, the therapist from the moral school may need help from the doctor (medical model) before any understanding or changing of behavior can begin.

## Your Views on the Models of Helping

Now that you have been briefly introduced to four models of helping, we hope that you will clarify your own position on people's responsibility for creating their problems and for finding solutions to these problems. Examine the following questions on your own, and bring your positions to class for a general discussion.

- What are the advantages and strengths of each of these four models? What are the disadvantages and weaknesses?
- Which model comes closest to your thinking? Why? What are the implications of embracing this model with respect to your counseling practice?
- Do you think it is important that you convey to your clients your basic assumptions and the model from which you function? Should clients know your views on the degree to which they are responsible for their problems and solutions? Explain your stand.

# The Use of Techniques in Counseling and Therapy

Your view of the use of techniques in counseling and therapy is closely related to your theoretical model. The issue of techniques includes such questions as *what* techniques, procedures, or intervention methods you would use and *when* and *why* you would use them. Some counselors are very eager to learn new techniques, treating them almost as if they were a bag of tricks. Others, out of anxiety over not knowing what to do in a given counseling situation, may try technique after technique in helter-skelter fashion. However, counselors should have a rationale for using particular methods of intervention, and we question the benefit to the client of an overreliance on technique.

## Learning and Evaluating Techniques

It can be very illuminating to see yourself working with a client on videotape or to listen to a session you've tape-recorded. Instead of focusing your attention on what your client said or did, you can monitor your own responses and get some general sense of how you related to your client. We suggest that you review your sessions with several clients in this way, paying attention to questions such as the following:

- Do you ask many questions? If so, are the questions mainly to get information, or are they open-ended ones designed to challenge your client? Do you raise questions merely because you don't know what else to do and hope that your questions will keep things moving?
- Do you tend to give advice and work quickly toward solutions? Or do you allow your client to explore feelings in depth instead of focusing on solutions to problems?
- How much direction do you give to the sessions? Who typically structures the sessions?
- How much support and reassurance do you give? Do you allow your clients to fully express what they're feeling before you offer support? Do your attempts to give support tend to cut them off from what they're feeling?
- Do you challenge your clients when you think they need it? Do your interventions get them to think about what they're saying on a deeper level?
- Who does most of the talking? Do you hear yourself as preaching or persuading? Are you responsive to what your client is saying?
- How often do you clarify what you hear? Do you check whether you're hearing what your client means to express?
- Do you reflect back to your clients what you hear them saying? If so, is your reflection done mechanically, or does it encourage a deeper self-exploration?
- Do you interpret much, telling your clients what you think certain behaviors mean? Or do you leave it to them to discover what their behavior means from their own perspectives?
- Do you use techniques primarily to get clients moving, or do you wait until they express some feelings and then use a technique geared to helping them experience their feelings on a more intense level?
- Do you use techniques that "feel right" for you and that you're comfortable using? Have you experienced these techniques yourself as a client?
- Are the procedures you use drawn from one counseling approach? Or do

you borrow techniques from various approaches and use them when they seem appropriate?
- When you use a particular technique, does it seem mechanical to you? Or do you feel that your techniques are appropriate and unforced?
- How do your clients generally respond to the techniques you use? Do they react negatively to any of your counseling methods?

Monitoring your own work in light of these questions can help you discover your counseling style, ask yourself why you're making the interventions you make, and evaluate the impact these counseling procedures have on your clients. This willingness to reflect on the effects your interventions have on clients is of the utmost importance.

We believe that the purpose of techniques is to facilitate movement in a counseling session and that your counseling techniques really cannot be separated from your personality and your relationship with your client. When counselors fall into a pattern of mechanically employing techniques, they become technicians and are not responding to the particular individuals they're counseling. You can lessen the chances of falling into a mechanical style by deliberately paying attention to the ways you tend to use techniques. Particular techniques may be better suited to some therapists' personalities and styles of counseling than to others'. At times you may try a technique that you've observed someone else using very skillfully, only to find that it fails for you. In essence, your techniques should fit your counseling style, and you should feel comfortable and real in using them.

## Issues regarding Paradoxical Interventions

One technique that has received much recent attention in the professional literature is the so-called paradoxical intervention. Although there are many types of paradoxical interventions, and thus a variety of definitions, all of these techniques attempt to place clients in a double bind, so that therapeutic change occurs regardless of their responses to paradoxical directives. Thus, clients are often asked to exaggerate and even perfect a problematic style of behavior. For instance, clients who suffer from insomnia may be directed to attempt to stay awake, or clients who are anxious may be instructed to continue to perform problem behaviors in an exaggerated fashion so as to heighten their anxiety. By accepting the therapist's directives and thus maintaining the symptom, clients demonstrate control of a problem behavior and are no longer helpless. On the other hand, if clients resist the therapist's directives and discontinue a particular symptom, the behavior is not only controlled but eliminated. For a more detailed review of current schools of paradoxical interventions and a compilation of paradoxical techniques, see Weeks and L'Abate (1982) and Dowd and Milne (1986).

Paradoxical interventions are gaining popularity among mental-health professionals of nearly all theoretical orientations, but particularly practitioners who adhere to systems approach and strategic therapists. Weeks and L'Abate (1982) observe that since the mid-1970s paradoxical therapy has mushroomed, as evidenced by conferences, seminars, journal articles, and books dealing with this approach. They contend that there are still many problems in learning how and when to work paradoxically; they add that paradoxical therapy has no underlying theory to guide its development and practice.

We give special coverage of the use of paradoxical techniques because of their ethical implications. Since this approach is powerful and risky, certain factors need to be carefully considered in employing it.

**Applications of Paradoxical Techniques.**    Huddleston and Engels (1986) summarize the research findings on the use of paradoxical techniques. Successful applications of paradox have been reported in areas such as behavior therapy, couples therapy, family therapy, behavioral medicine, anxiety disorders, agoraphobia, depression, the inpatient treatment of children, and insomnia, among others. Paradox appears to be especially well suited for resistant clients with specific behaviorally defined problems.

Dowd and Milne (1986) charge that paradoxical interventions have been applied indiscriminately and inappropriately, almost as though they were equally useful for all individuals in all situations with all problems. Cautioning practitioners to be sensitive to client cues that paradox is being overused, they suggest that these interventions should be interspersed with other techniques. In agreement with this position are Weeks and L'Abate (1982), who contend that practitioners who overuse paradoxical methods with every client are intervening irrelevantly. They further suggest that paradox is best applied in selected cases and usually in combination with a variety of other techniques. Dowd and Milne call for more controlled research to determine if clinical lore is correct that paradoxical strategies are particularly useful for behavioral disorders such as insomnia, enuresis, and child management. It appears that there is much to learn about how paradox works, when and where to use these methods, whether therapeutic gains carry over into a client's "real world," and how effective treatment is in the long term. There is agreement in the literature that much more research is necessary in order to understand and evaluate paradoxical strategies (Huddleston & Engels, 1986).

Ethical practice dictates that it is essential to know when paradoxical interventions should be avoided. The use of these techniques is obviously neither wise nor ethical in those situations where harmful consequences to the client are likely. Paradoxical intervention is inadvisable in crisis situations, suicide, homicide, violence, abuse, or excessive drinking. Paradox in these situations is most likely to be unhelpful and irresponsible (Weeks & L'Abate, 1982). Encouraging a suicidal client to carry out impulses into action, for example, could lead to highly negative outcomes for both the client and the therapist.

**Ethical and Clinical Considerations.**    Some key questions raised in this approach are "Who is competent to use these interventions? How and when should paradox be used? What are the potential benefits and risks involved?

*paradox is not a gimmick!*

*carefully formulated & Timed*

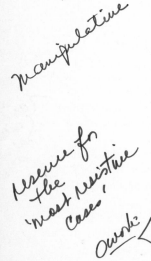

*malpractice suit.*

*manipulative*

*Reserve for the most resistive cases!*

*Overt?*

Are paradoxical strategies by their very nature manipulative and tricky? Is deceiving a client ever ethically justifiable, even if it happens to produce desired results?"

It is essential that paradox not be used as a gimmick. Practitioners must possess the necessary training and supervision before using these strategies. Also, therapists have an ethical obligation to inform clients concerning experimental techniques. Practitioners who plan to use paradoxical methods must carefully consider their own training, experience, and preparedness to implement such methods (Huddleston & Engels, 1986). Another guideline is that "Paradoxical interventions must be carefully formulated, appropriately timed, convincingly delivered, and followed up. In order to make paradoxical interventions, the therapist must first have skills necessary to make active and directive interventions" (Weeks & L'Abate, 1982, p. 249).

Does this approach necessarily involve manipulation and deception of the client? Mahoney (1986) implies that paradoxical interventions too often reflect a detached, gurulike stance on the therapist's part, which results in disempowering the client. "I fear, however, that popularized versions of 'strategic psychotherapy' may be playing—sometimes recklessly—with the power inherent in all helping relationships" (Mahoney, 1986, p. 289). Johnson (1986) is also concerned about the denial of client freedom. Her objection to paradoxical techniques is their deceptiveness, and she asks: Are the ends worth the means? Are the ends as effective as other ends? Schmidt (1986) also raises ethical and legal considerations in using these interventions. If practitioners are manipulative in their conduct, are their methods in compliance with ethical codes? If clients either do not improve or worsen, he asks, might they conclude that the therapist's directive was responsible? In light of the illogical nature of the technique, might the therapist be vulnerable to a malpractice suit?

On the issue of whether paradoxical interventions are unnecessarily manipulative, Weeks and L'Abate (1982) cite three specific areas of ethical concern: (1) definition of the problem and goals, (2) selection of a method that is not controlling in the client's view, and (3) informed consent. They shed a different light on the issue of these "manipulative interventions." First, the client and therapist should make a careful analysis of the problem and agree on what is to be changed. Furthermore, clinicians should not impose their own definition of the problem; rather, specific behavioral goals are established whenever possible. The second issue is that of selecting a technique that is not restrictive, controlling, or intrusive. Paradoxical interventions should be reserved for the more resistive cases. Only when some of the more straightforward therapeutic interventions fail is the use of paradox indicated. The treatment with the lowest risk is tried first. The third issue pertains to informed consent. As applied to paradoxical therapy, the question is whether clients understand and agree to the methods used to change their behavior. Weeks and L'Abate have found that paradoxical methods work even when they are explained to clients, if the task is acted on. They see the real issue as the client's being changed without insight or conscious recognition. Paradoxical therapy conflicts with the traditional assumption that insight is necessary for lasting change to occur.

**Evaluation.**    The value of paradoxical interventions may well depend on the training and experience of those who employ them. Certainly there is a danger of misusing these techniques if counselors seek quick and easy solutions (Mahoney, 1986) or use these interventions for their shock value or as a gimmick because they have failed at everything else (Weeks & L'Abate, 1982). Both the therapist and the client need to be aware that using paradoxical techniques involves considerable risk.

When paradoxical interventions are used by practitioners who are trained and experienced in these techniques, they can be powerful therapeutic tools that can lead to positive change in clients. When they are inappropriately used as a gimmick to effect a "quick cure" or to enhance the therapist's power, however, they have a potential for serious consequences for both the client and the therapist. Dowd and Milne (1986, p. 278) suggest that the appropriate use of paradoxical interventions requires that the standard counseling psychology question be asked: "What technique used by what counselor causes what change with what type of client in what situation?"

**What Is Your Stand?**    Consider these questions as a way of clarifying your own position on the ethical implications of using paradoxical procedures.

- Would you be inclined to use paradoxical interventions? Why or why not? If so, with what type of clients and in what settings?
- Many therapists believe that clients have a right to be informed of the rationale for the procedures that will be used as a part of their therapy. On the other hand, providing too detailed a rationale by explaining the paradoxical intervention may interfere with therapeutic effectiveness. How might you provide informed consent without ruining the impact of the technique?
- Think of a problematic behavior that you would like to change. How do you imagine that you would respond to a paradoxical technique?
- To what degree do you believe that paradoxical interventions involve manipulation and deception of the client? Do you think that this behavior by a therapist is ever justified, even if it produces positive change in a client?
- What guidelines can you think of for the ethical use of paradoxical techniques?

# The Division of Responsibility in Therapy

Earlier in this chapter we briefly discussed four models of human nature and the responsibility for change these models do or do not place on the client. As you consider the range of viewpoints on the division of responsibility in therapy, think about your own position on this issue. What do you see as your responsibility, both to your client and to yourself? What do you expect from your client? Do you burden yourself with the total responsibility for what happens in therapy?

We've observed that many beginning counselors tend to deprive their clients of their rightful responsibility for their experience in therapy, because they anxiously take so much of this responsibility on themselves. If clients don't progress fast enough, these counselors may blame themselves for not knowing enough, not having the necessary skill and experience, or not being sensitive or caring enough. They may worry constantly about their adequacy as counselors and transmit their anxiety to their clients. *If only* they were better therapists, their clients would be changing in more positive directions. This may be true, of course, but overly anxious counselors frequently fail to see the role their clients play in the outcomes of their own therapy, whether for better or for worse.

We believe that counselors do well to bring up the question of responsibility during the initial sessions, so that clients can begin to think about their part in their own therapy. One way of clarifying the sharing of responsibility in a therapeutic relationship is a contract. A contract is based on a negotiation between the client and the therapist to define the therapeutic relationship. It encourages the client and the therapist to specify the goals of the therapy and the methods likely to be employed in obtaining these goals. Other aspects of a contract include the length and frequency of sessions, the duration of therapy, the cost and method of payment, provisions for the renegotiation of the contract, any factors limiting confidentiality, the extent of responsibility for each partner, and ways of determining the effectiveness of the therapeutic relationship.

We see therapy as a joint venture of the client and the therapist. Both have serious responsibilities for the direction of therapy, and this issue needs to be clarified during the initial stages of counseling. In our view counselors who typically decide what to discuss and are overdirective run the risk of perpetuating their clients' dependence. We'd like to see clients encouraged from the start to assume as much responsibility as they can. Even directive therapies such as transactional analysis, behavior therapy, rational-emotive therapy, and reality therapy stress client-initiated contracts and homework assignments as ways clients can fulfill their commitment to change. These devices help to keep the focus of responsibility on the clients by challenging them to decide what *they* want from therapy and what *they* are willing to do to get what they want.

Although we have stressed the tendency of some therapists to take on too much responsibility, we do believe that therapists have responsibilities to their clients, including:

- being emotionally present for their clients
- keeping themselves enthused and energetic
- taking on only as many clients as they can handle effectively
- being willing to live up to their contracts with their clients
- being honest with clients

- refusing to accept clients whom they are not personally or professionally competent to counsel
- discussing any factors that may influence a client's decision to enter the therapeutic relationship
- discussing and structuring the various dimensions of the relationship

■ ***The case of Ivan.***   Ivan is a member of an ongoing weekly group. At the 16th meeting he unexpectedly tells the group that he has often thought of suicide. He has never developed a detailed plan, but suicide is weighing heavily on his mind, and it frightens him.

*Counselor A.*   "Ivan, this is news to me! I'm very willing to work with you on your suicidal ideation, but I hold you responsible for your life. If you choose to kill yourself, that is your responsibility. If you choose to challenge yourself and live, that, too, is your responsibility. I refuse to burden myself with the responsibility of your life."

*Counselor B.*   "Ivan, this really surprises me! If I'd known this, I wouldn't have put you in the group. I'd like to switch you from group treatment to individual treatment twice a week. Furthermore, I'll check in with you by telephone every day, and I'd like you to call me at any time if you become frightened by your impulses. Perhaps later on, when you have worked through this problem, you may be able to be in a group again."

*Counselor C.*   "This is a surprise. I'd like you to tell me more about what's going on in your life now. Perhaps you can address the members in the group and give each person a reason why life isn't worth living. This will give you an opportunity to explore at a deeper level the meaning of your suicidal thinking."

At the end of the session, the therapist adds: "Ivan, you are ultimately responsible for your life, but I'd like to make myself available to you to explore and understand what you are experiencing. I think you could also use this group as a tool to help you in this struggle."

In reviewing these three approaches, consider your own stand.

- Which approach are you most likely to take and why?
- Imagine yourself as Ivan. Which of these approaches would you find most helpful and why? Least helpful?
- How can this case help you formulate your own ideas about the division of responsibility in counseling?

# Roles and Functions of Counselors

The roles and functions of counselors depend on their theoretical perspectives, the type of counseling they do, where they work, and the kinds of people they counsel. We think that counselors are responsible, to a large

degree, for defining their own roles and choosing their own functions as part of creating their professional identities. Too often counselors passively allow others to define their roles for them. Even if their positions involve job descriptions that limit their options, often they fail to exercise the freedom they *do* have in deciding on their job priorities.

Of course, the type of counseling you do will determine some specific functions. The functions performed by career counselors are different from those performed by crisis-intervention counselors. The roles of counselors who work primarily with severely disturbed people in institutional settings will differ from those of counselors who specialize in personal-growth approaches for people without major dysfunctional behavior. Functions that are appropriate in some counseling situations, then, may be inappropriate in others.

You can begin to consider now what functions would be appropriate for you to perform in the kind of position you hope to obtain. How would you deal with being required to perform functions that you thought were inappropriate or interfered with your effectiveness as a counselor? Could you work in an agency that expected you to perform such functions? If you accepted such a job, would it be worth the price you would have to pay?

Counselors may need to provide auxiliary helping services, such as teaching grooming, before they can do more direct counseling. Because basic physical and security needs must be met before attention can be devoted to a higher-order needs (such as self-actualization), some counselors consider assisting clients to meet basic needs to be part of their work.

## Deciding on the Goals of Counseling

Aimless therapy is unlikely to be effective, yet too often practitioners fail to devote enough time to thinking about the goals they have for their clients and the goals clients have for themselves. In this section we discuss possible goals of therapy, how they are determined, and who should determine them. Counselors' answers to these questions are directly related to their theoretical orientations.

In considering therapeutic goals it is important to keep in mind the cultural determinants of therapy. The goals of therapy are specific to a particular culture's definition of psychological health. Levine and Padilla (1980) note that the goals for therapy in any culture can range from removal of symptoms to attitude change, behavior change, insight, improved relations with others, social effectiveness, personal adjustment, and preventive health. They give an example of Morita therapy, a popular treatment in Japan that involves discussion of the concepts of Zen Buddhism. This therapy directs the person toward an Eastern conception of mental health based on an inner-directed life acquired through peace and meditation.

As you read about therapeutic goals, think of how certain theoretical approaches represent a cultural bias. The experiential therapies, for example, have the goal of helping people move in the direction of becoming self-actualizing and autonomous, which is typically a goal of Western cultures. It should be noted, however, that this is not the goal valued in all cultures, especially Eastern ones.

*Cultural goals.*

## Your Goals as a Counselor

What are some of the basic goals that you would use to guide your work with clients? The following list presents 20 therapeutic goals. Indicate how much you would emphasize each by using the following code: A = an extremely important goal; B = a somewhat important goal; C = a relatively unimportant goal. A goal of therapy is that clients will:

\_\_\_\_ 1. take risks that may result in increased awareness of themselves and others

\_\_\_\_ 2. critically examine their cultural conditioning and determine whether they want to embrace the values of their particular culture

\_\_\_\_ 3. develop increased pride and respect for the unique values that are a part of their culture

\_\_\_\_ 4. strive for and be able to form a personal as well as cultural identity

\_\_\_\_ 5. learn how to question a given society's definition of mental and psychological health to determine whether they want to strive toward an "ideal level of functioning" as set by the society

\_\_\_\_ 6. learn both the advantages and the disadvantages of living by the norms of the dominant culture in which they live

\_\_\_\_ 7. accept responsibility for internal support, as opposed to depending on external support

\_\_\_\_ 8. acquire inner peace and tranquility

\_\_\_\_ 9. learn ways to reach out to social networks for support, especially with their families

\_\_\_\_ 10. make value judgments about their own behavior and then decide on a plan of action for change should they determine that their behavior is not working effectively for them

\_\_\_\_ 11. learn certain coping skills that will help them deal effectively with present and future problems so that they will ultimately rely on themselves to solve problems rather than on the therapist

\_\_\_\_ 12. recall past events and work through emotions that are blocking their enjoyment of the here and now

\_\_\_\_ 13. come to recognize that they have the capacities within themselves to make new choices

\_\_\_\_ 14. begin to question their values and assumptions about life and determine the degree to which these beliefs are valid for them now

\_\_\_\_ 15. reduce or eliminate specific behavioral problems and replace their faulty learning with more effective behavior

\_\_\_\_ 16. learn the process of using their resources for solving their own problems

_____ 17. become more conscious of their options and more willing to make choices for themselves and accept the consequences

_____ 18. experience the range of their own personal power so that they can give up feeling and behaving like victims

_____ 19. uncover the influence of the past on their present behavior

_____ 20. learn to translate their insights into action

## Who Determines Therapeutic Goals?

Most counseling approaches agree that effective counseling does not result when the therapist imposes goals; rather, goals should be set by the client and the therapist working together. However, some therapists believe that they know what is best for their clients and try to persuade their clients to accept certain goals. Others are convinced that the specific goals of counseling ought to be determined entirely by their clients and try to keep their own views out of their counseling.

Of course, the issue of who sets the goals of counseling must be seen in the light of the theory you operate from, the type of counseling you offer, the setting in which you work, and the nature of your clientele. If you work in crisis intervention, your goals are likely to be short-term and practical, and you may be very directive. If you're working with children in a school setting, you may aim at combining educational and therapeutic goals. As a counselor with institutionalized elderly people, you may stress teaching survival skills and ways of relating to others on their ward. What your goals are and how actively involved your client will be in determining them depend to a great extent on the type of counseling you provide and the type of client you see.

*[handwritten margin note: Goals that are set together while client are not therapist imposed. But...]*

*[handwritten margin note: example]*

# Diagnosis as a Professional Issue

The main purpose of the diagnostic approach is to allow the therapist to plan treatments tailored to the special needs of the client. There are different kinds of diagnosis. *Medical diagnosis* is the process of examining physical symptoms, inferring causes of physical disorders or diseases, providing some kind of category that fits the pattern of a disease, and prescribing an appropriate treatment. *Psychodiagnosis* (or *psychological diagnosis*) is a general term covering the process of identifying an emotional or behavioral problem and making a statement about the current status of a client. This process also includes the identification of the possible causes of the person's emotional, psychological, and behavioral difficulties, and it entails suggesting the appropriate therapy techniques to deal effectively with the identified problem and estimating the chances for a successful resolution. *Differential diagnosis* is the process of distinguishing one form of disease or psychological disorder from another by determining which of two (or more) diseases or disorders with similar symptoms the person is suffering from. The third

*[handwritten margin note: · Medical · Psychodiagnosis · Differential diagnosis]*

edition of the American Psychiatric Association's (1980) *Diagnostic and Statistical Manual of Mental Disorders* (DSM III) is the standard reference for pathology.

Whether diagnosis should be part of psychotherapy is a controversial issue. Some mental-health professionals see diagnosis as an essential step in any treatment plan, but others view it as an inappropriate application of the medical model of mental health to counseling and therapy. Even though you may not yet have had to face the practical question of whether to diagnose a client, you will probably need to come to terms with this issue at some point in your work. In this section we briefly review some of the arguments for and against the use of diagnosis in therapy and ask you to consider how valuable diagnosis is from your viewpoint.

## Arguments for Psychodiagnosis

Practitioners who favor the use of diagnostic procedures in therapy generally argue that such procedures enable the therapist to acquire sufficient knowledge about the client's past and present behavior to develop an appropriate plan of treatment. This approach stems from the medical model of mental health, according to which different underlying causal factors produce different types of disorders. Goldenberg (1977) cites six purposes of psychodiagnosis that are generally mentioned by those who support its use in therapy:

1. Each diagnostic label encompasses a wide range of behavioral characteristics, and this allows professionals to communicate common meanings effectively.
2. Diagnosis facilitates the selection of the most suitable form of therapy.
3. A diagnostic explanation of the causal factors involved in a client's problems can suggest measures that will alleviate the client's symptoms.
4. Diagnosis is useful in predicting the course and outcome of a person's disorder.
5. Diagnosis provides a framework for research into the effectiveness of various treatment approaches.
6. Diagnostic classifications facilitate such administrative tasks as the collection of statistical data regarding the incidence of particular disorders and the type of psychological services provided in the community.

Psychoanalytically oriented therapists favor psychodiagnosis, since this form of therapy was patterned after the medical model of mental health and stresses the understanding of past situations that have contributed to a dysfunction. Some psychological-assessment devices used in psychodiagnosis involve projective techniques that rest on psychoanalytic concepts.

For different reasons, practitioners with a behavioristic orientation also favor a diagnostic stance, inasmuch as they emphasize specific treatment programs. Although they may not follow the medical model, these practitioners value observation and other objective means of appraising both a client's specific symptoms and the factors that have led up to the client's malfunctioning. Such an appraisal, they would argue, enables them to use the techniques that are appropriate for a particular disorder and to evaluate the effectiveness of the treatment program.

Brammer and Shostrom (1982) see diagnosis as being broader than simply labeling clients with some category from DSM III. They argue in favor of diagnosis as a general descriptive statement identifying a client's style of functioning. Such information can motivate clients to change their behavior. They contend that practitioners must make some decisions, do some therapeutic planning, and be alert for signs of pathology in order to avoid serious mistakes in therapy. They propose that a therapist "simultaneously understand diagnostically and understand therapeutically" (p. 136). In favoring this broad type of diagnostic process, which involves developing hunches, Brammer and Shostrom caution against accepting a narrow and rigid diagnostic approach.

## Arguments against Psychodiagnosis

Although many professionals see diagnosis as an essential component of psychotherapy, there are as many critics who view it as unnecessary or harmful. Generally, "existential or relationship-oriented therapists" fall into this group. Their arguments against diagnosis include the following:

1. Diagnosis is typically done by an expert observing a person's behavior and experience from an external viewpoint, without reference to what they mean to the client.
2. Diagnostic categories can rob people of their uniqueness.
3. Diagnosis can lead people to accept self-fulfilling prophecies or to despair over their condition.
4. Diagnosis can narrow the therapist's vision by encouraging the therapist to look for behavior that fits a certain disease category.
5. The best vantage point for understanding another person is through his or her subjective world, not through a general system of classification.
6. There are many potential dangers implicit in the process of reducing human beings to diagnostic categories.

Many psychologists and some psychiatrists have objected to the use of diagnosis in therapy. Rogers (1942, 1951, 1961) has consistently maintained that diagnosis is detrimental to counseling because it tends to pull clients away from an internal and subjective way of experiencing themselves and to foster an objective and external conception *about* them. The result may be to increase tendencies toward dependence and cause clients to act as if the responsibility for changing their behavior rested with the expert and not with themselves. Of course, client-centered therapy is grounded on the belief that clients are in the best position to understand and resolve their personal difficulties. Rogers (1951) states: "When the client perceives the locus of judgment and responsibility as clearly resting in the hands of the clinician, he is, in our judgment, further from therapeutic progress than when he came in" (p. 223).

Rogers (1951) is also concerned about psychological diagnosis because of the long-range implications of the "social control of the many by the few" (p. 224). A similar concern is expressed by Szasz (1974), who has labeled the whole concept of nonorganic mental illness a "myth." According to Szasz's theory of human behavior, people are always responsible for their actions. What we call mental "diseases" aren't diseases at all, in the medical sense, but social-psychological phenomena. Szasz sees the classification of behavior as a control strategy. Like Rogers, he emphasizes the dangers of demeaning human beings by giving them psychiatric labels that miss the essence of the person.

R. D. Laing (1967), a psychiatrist who has criticized traditional types of diagnosis, expresses concern about the effects of diagnosis on those who are being classified *and* on those who are doing the categorizing. For the person being classified, diagnosis can result in a self-fulfilling prophecy whereby the person acts as he or she is expected to act. Thus, a person who knows he or she has been diagnosed as a schizophrenic may take great delight in telling ward attendants "After all, I'm crazy! What can you expect from me?" In turn, hospital or ward personnel may see people only through the stereotypes associated with various diagnoses. If they expect certain behaviors from the patients, there is a good chance that the patients will adopt these behaviors and live up to the staff's expectations.

## Our Position on Psychodiagnosis

We believe that diagnosis, broadly construed, is a legitimate part of the therapeutic process. The kind of diagnosis we have in mind is the result of a joint effort by the client and the therapist. Both should be involved in discovering the nature of the client's difficulty, a process that commences with the initial sessions and continues until therapy is terminated. Even practitioners who oppose conventional diagnostic procedures and terminology need to raise such questions as:

- What is going on in this client's life at this time?
- What are the client's resources for change?
- What does the client want from therapy, and how can it best be achieved?
- What should be the focus of the sessions?
- What factors are contributing to the client's problems, and what can be done to alleviate them?
- What are the prospects for meaningful change?

The counselor and the client can discuss each of these questions as a part of the therapeutic process. Counselors will develop hypotheses about their clients, and they can talk about their conjectures with their clients in an ongoing way. The diagnosis performed by counselors does not have to be a matter of categorizing their clients; rather, counselors can describe behavior and think about its meaning. In this way, instead of being done mechanically and technically by an expert, diagnosis becomes a process of thinking *about* the client *with* the client.

From our perspective, diagnosis should be associated with treatment, and it should help the practitioner conceptualize a case. Ethical dilemmas are often created when diagnosis is done strictly for insurance purposes, which often entails arbitrarily assigning a client a diagnostic classification. As we have seen earlier, many practitioners use diagnosis for a variety of reasons other than thinking about the dynamics of a client and an appropriate treatment plan.

We also think that it is an ethical (and sometimes legal) obligation of therapists to screen clients for life-threatening problems such as organic disorders, schizophrenia, manic-depression, and suicidal types of depression. Students need to learn the clinical skills necessary to do this type of screening, which is a form of diagnostic thinking.

## Current Issues in Diagnosis

Those who support the traditional forms of diagnosis agree that there are limitations to present classification systems and that some of the problems mentioned by the critics of diagnosis do exist. Rather than abandoning diagnostic classifications altogether, however, they favor updating diagnostic manuals to reflect improvements in diagnosis and treatment procedures.

Another important issue is whether clients should know their diagnosis and have access to all the information concerning themselves that their therapists have. Some practitioners contend that they should decide how much information to reveal to their clients. Others believe that it is unethical to keep pertinent information from their clients. Can you think of situations in which you would not be willing to share your hunches or information about a client with that client?

There is also a practical matter pertaining to diagnosis—the fact that many insurance companies who pay for psychological services require a diagnosis on the insurance form. Presumably, clients who consult a therapist regarding problems that don't fit a standard category are not to be reimbursed for their psychotherapy. These insurance carriers take the position that psychotherapy is for treatment of specific mental or emotional disorders; consequently, if a therapist doesn't write down a specific diagnosis, the client's insurance may not cover his or her expenses.

We think that Smith (1981) hits the heart of the current controversy over the traditional diagnostic system when he addresses informed-consent procedures. He points out that, while unprecedented attention is being given to informed decisions by clients regarding treatment plans and expectations, most practitioners remain virtually silent on clients' rights to be informed regarding diagnostic classifications for the purpose of securing third-party payments. Smith contends that psychologists are compromising their integrity and sacrificing the dignity of their clients for economic gain

by using the DSM system <u>without the informed consent</u> of the client. He makes a case for amending the APA's (1981a) *Ethical Principles of Psychologists* to spell out clearly that the use of categorizing and coding for insurance purposes must include informed-consent procedures. He argues for psychologists to make a bold gesture to declare to their clients whether they are advocates or opponents of the mental-illness model. They will have taken another commendable step when they begin to lobby with other mental-health professionals to persuade legislative bodies to enact laws to protect consumers from the wholesale abuse of diagnostic codes and classifications.

### Questions on Diagnosis

What is your position on diagnosis? The following questions may help you formulate such a position.

- After reviewing the arguments for and against psychodiagnosis, which position do you tend to support? Why?
- Some contend that clients have a right to know their diagnoses on the ground of informed consent, whereas others maintain that clients should not be told their diagnoses because of the dangers of their living up to a self-fulfilling prophecy. What is your thinking on this matter?
- Smith (1981) asserts that practitioners should take a stand against classification and coding for the purpose of third-party payments unless clients know of their diagnoses and agree to provide this information to insurance companies. Do you see an ethical issue in this practice? Do you agree or disagree that therapists who do not accept the medical model, yet who provide diagnoses for reasons of third-party payments, are compromising their integrity? What options are open to them?
- What ethical and professional issues can you raise pertaining to diagnosis? In your view what is the most critical issue?

## The Issue of Using Tests in Counseling

At some point in your career you may need to decide on the place that testing will occupy in your counseling. This section focuses on when and how you would use tests in your work with clients.

As is true of diagnosis, the proper use of testing in counseling and therapy is the subject of some debate. Generally, those therapeutic approaches that emphasize an objective view of counseling are inclined to use testing procedures as <u>tools to acquire information</u> about clients or as resources that <u>clients themselves</u> can use to help them in their decision making. The <u>client-centered</u> and <u>existential approaches</u> tend to view testing in much the same way that they view diagnosis—as an <u>external</u> frame of reference that is of <u>little use</u> in counseling situations.

*the ? —*
*— what circumstances*
*& for what purposes —*

## When to Use Tests

We think that the core of the issue is not whether you will use tests as an adjunct to counseling but rather under what circumstances, and for what purposes, you may want to use tests. Many types of tests can be used for counseling purposes, including measures of aptitude, ability, achievement, intelligence, values and attitudes, vocational interests, and personality characteristics. The following questions may help you think about the circumstances in which you might want to use tests for counseling purposes.

1. What do you know about the tests you may use? It's important for counselors to be familiar with any tests they use and to have taken them themselves. They should know the purpose of each test and how well it measures what it purports to measure. You'll need to decide whether you're willing to invest the time necessary to become acquainted with the tests you might want to use. In many counseling centers, one person assumes the responsibility for administering and interpreting tests. If you or your clients want to use a test, you may want to refer them to a person who specializes in testing.

2. How much say do you think clients should have in the selection of tests? Some counselors assume the responsibility for deciding whether and when to use tests and prescribe specific tests for clients. Other counselors believe that clients should decide whether they want testing and, if so, what general type of testing they want (aptitude, interest, achievement, personality). These counselors claim that clients who are not actively involved in decisions about tests may become passive, relying too heavily on test results to determine what they should do instead of using the results to make informed decisions of their own.

3. Do you know *why* you want to use a particular test? Is it merely because a client asks for it? Is it because you don't know what to do next and hope that a test will point to a direction? Does your agency require that you administer certain tests? Your reasons for using tests will depend on the particular circumstances. If you're doing vocational counseling, your client may want to take a vocational-interest inventory, and you may agree that such a test could be useful in helping the client to pinpoint some areas of interest. In another case a client's behavior may concern you, and you may want to administer some projective tests or other personality-assessment devices to help you determine the severity of his or her difficulty. Whatever your reasons for testing are, you should be able to state a clear rationale for any test you use.

4. If a client requests testing, do you explore the reasons for the request with the client? Some clients may think that a test will give them answers and, in effect, make decisions *for* them. Clients need to be aware that tests are only tools that can provide useful information about themselves, which they can proceed to explore in their counseling sessions. They also need to know what the tests are designed for and what they expect from the testing. Are you willing to explore the values and limitations of tests with your clients, as well as their reasons for wanting to take them?

5. How do you integrate the test results into the counseling sessions? How might you use them for counseling purposes? In general, it's best to give test *results*, not simply test *scores*. In other words, you should explore with your client the *meaning* the results have for him or her. However, just as clients need to be involved in the selection of tests, they also should be involved in the interpretation of the results. In this connection you'll need to evaluate your clients' readiness to receive and accept certain information, and you'll need to be sensitive to the ways in which they respond to the test results. Your clients may need an opportunity to express and explore discrepancies between what they think their abilities and interests are and what the test results indicate. Are you willing to allow your clients to talk about any possible disappointments? Do you use this opportunity to encourage them to ask whether some of their prior decisions were realistic?

6. Are you concerned about maintaining the confidentiality of test results? Test results may be handled in different ways, depending on the purpose and type of each test. Nevertheless, your clients need to feel that they can trust you and that test results will neither be used against them nor revealed to people who have no right to this information. The uses and confidentiality of test results are matters that you may want to discuss with your clients.

7. Are you critical in evaluating tests? Too often mistakes have been made because counselors have had blind faith in tests. If personality assessments have low reliability and validity, will giving a battery of these tests result in more accurate information? You should know the limitations of the tests you use, and you should keep in mind that a test can be useful and valid in one situation, yet inappropriate in another. Are you willing to acquire the knowledge you need to properly evaluate the tests you use?

## Ethical Considerations in Using Tests

One of the key principles in using tests and other psychological-assessment techniques is that the counselor should make every effort to protect and promote the welfare of the client. Unfortunately, tests have been misused in many ways. They can be misused when they are given routinely to unwilling clients, when the clients receive no feedback, when tests are used for the wrong purposes, or when they are given by people who are not qualified. According to one set of ethical guidelines, psychologists

> guard against the misuse of assessment results. They respect the client's right to know the results, the interpretations made, and the bases for their conclusions and recommendations. Psychologists make every effort to maintain the security of tests and other assessment techniques within limits of legal mandates. They strive to ensure the appropriate use of assessment techniques by others [APA, 1981a].[1]

[1] The codes of ethics of the major mental-health organizations can be found in the Appendix.

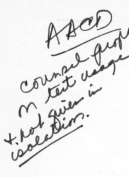

The American Association for Counseling and Development (1981) has developed a number of specific standards that provide guidance for the ethical use of tests in counseling. First of all, people taking a test should know what it is for, how it relates to their situation, and how the results will be used. Further, tests should not be used in isolation, without other relevant data. Each test should be presented in such a way that it can be placed in proper perspective with other relevant factors.

**Cross-Cultural Considerations in Using Tests.** When it comes to interpreting the test scores of minority-group members, it is especially important that all the factors that influence test results be given consideration. In its *Ethical Standards* the AACD (1981) warns counselors to proceed with caution in testing minorities if the norm group on which the instrument was standardized did not include the minority population. It is also important to be aware that minority clients might react to testing with suspicion, since tests have been used to discriminate against them in schools and employment. To minimize such negative reactions it is a good practice to explore a minority-group member's views and feelings about testing and to work with the client in resolving attitudes that are likely to affect the outcome of a test. Ibrahim and Arredondo (1986) have recommended that the *Ethical Standards* of the AACD be extended to address cross-cultural factors in assessment. They propose the addition of the following two standards:

> *Standard 1.* Counselors need to appraise the client as a cultural entity before any other assessment strategy is undertaken. Understanding the client as a cultural entity implies an understanding of the client's philosophy of life, beliefs, values, and assumptions in the context of his or her primary and secondary cultures and in the context of the larger societal system.
> *Standard 2.* Counselors need to use multisource, multilevel, and multimethod approaches to assess the capabilities, potentials, and limitations of the client [p. 350].

Ibrahim and Arredondo (1986) indicate that multimethod assessment protects the interests of cross-cultural clients by increasing the probability that language or reading barriers do not result in underestimates of their capabilities.

Ibrahim (1986) has proposed specific revisions of the APA ethical principles (1981a). Principle 8, Assessment Techniques, needs to be expanded to include the recognition that, since there are very few cross-cultural instruments, clients must first be assessed in a cross-cultural context, according to Ibrahim. Conducting psychological assessments without clarifying the world view of clients and the primary group they identify with should be codified as unethical, he contends.

**Other Ethical Considerations.** Lonner and Sundberg (1985) make a series of recommendations concerning ethical responsibilities associated with cross-cultural assessment. Their guidelines are as follows:

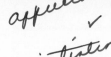

- Understand and appreciate the culture of the person being assessed.
- Be aware of ethnocentric tendencies in yourself, and be aware of how even unintentional bias can prevent objective assessment.
- Avoid the dangers of "overculturalizing." Look for universal human themes (such as uncertainties about the future, loss, loneliness) that provide a basis for rapport.
- Avoid the dangers of "overassessing." Realize that all assessment devices have limitations. If time is limited, it might be better to interview the client rather than to use some assessment instrument.

Another ethical issue pertaining to testing is competence. Sometimes mental-health workers find themselves expected to give and interpret tests as a basic function of their job. If they have not had adequate training in this area, they are in an ethical bind. In-service training and continuing-education programs are ways of gaining competence in using psychological-assessment devices. The AACD (1981) offers this guideline on the matter: "Different tests demand different levels of competence for administration, scoring, and interpretation. Members must recognize the limits of their competence and perform only those functions for which they are prepared."

Perhaps the most basic ethical guideline for using tests is to keep in mind the primary purpose for which they were designed: to provide objective and descriptive measures that can be used by clients in making better decisions. Further, a wide range of appraisal techniques, including both test and nontest data, should be used in providing clients with useful information. And it is wise to remember that tests are tools that should be used in the service of clients, not against clients.

## Ethical Issues in Psychotherapeutic Research

As can be seen, most of the questions that we have raised in this chapter have a direct relationship to one's therapeutic theory. Matters such as the use of specialized techniques, the balance of responsibility in the client/therapist relationship, the functions of the therapist, and the goals of treatment are tied to one's theory. Surely one critical ethical question is "Does a given psychotherapeutic approach or technique work?" Failing to at least attempt to base one's practice on the findings of research is tantamount to asking consumers to simply trust that practitioners know what they are doing.

Although the topic of ethical implications of conducting research in counseling and psychotherapy is vast, we do want to address a few selected ethical issues and encourage you to think about your responsibilities in this area. Some of the questions that we encourage you to keep open are as follows:

- In conducting research in a counseling setting, must the informed consent of participants always be given? Can you think of situations in which it might be justified *not* to obtain informed consent for the sake of a better research design?

- Is it ever ethical to use deception in psychological research? Is deception justified if the subjects are given the accurate details *after* the research study is completed?
- Can practitioners be considered ethical if they practice without conducting any research on the techniques employed or without having them empirically validated?

## Ethics and Research: Some Situations

Considering the vast number of studies on psychotherapeutic research, there is little discussion in the literature regarding ethical problems in designing and conducting studies. Yet there are critical ethical issues in this field that deserve the careful attention of investigators (Imber, Glanz, Elkin, Sotsky, Boyer, & Leber, 1986). In this section we consider some of these issues, including informed consent, using deception in psychological research, withholding of treatment, the use of placebos, research with training and personal-growth groups, and cross-cultural considerations in research.

**Situations Involving Informed Consent.**   Informed consent is defined as the participant's assent to being involved in a research study after having received full information about the procedures and their associated risks and benefits. The basic elements of informed consent include competence, voluntarism, full information, and comprehension, which are summarized below (Imber et al., 1986).

*Competence* refers to the legal capacity of the subject to give consent. Ethical issues here pertain to subjects who are not able to make decisions. *Voluntarism* implies that subjects be allowed to make their decision about whether to participate in a study without being pressured. It is essential that clients understand that they may refuse to participate in a study and that they will still be eligible for alternative services. They should also know that, even if they do consent to participate, they are still free to withdraw or drop out without penalty and with the provision of appropriate referrals. *Full information* implies that potential subjects be fully advised of the potential risks and benefits involved in participation. Full information about research is somewhat a contradiction in terms, however, because research designs require a withholding of certain information. In general, potential research subjects have a right to know what is going to happen to them in the study, what risks they are facing and whether their personal rights are jeopardized, and what safeguards will be taken. *Comprehension* implies that consent forms be written in language that can be understood by most people.

Informed consent is important for a variety of reasons (Lindsey, 1984): it protects people's autonomy, because it allows them to make decisions about matters that directly concern them; it guarantees that the participants will be exposed to certain risks only if they agree to them; it decreases the possibility of an adverse public reaction to experimenting with human subjects; and it helps researchers scrutinize their designs for inherent risks. The researcher might be guided by the question "What would the person who is interested in his or her own welfare need to know before making a decision?" With these points in mind consider the following situation to determine the ethics of the researcher's behavior.

■ *A case of informed consent.*    Dr. Hamner is committed to designing research procedures to evaluate the process and outcome of her treatment programs. She is convinced that in order to obtain valid data she must keep the research participants ignorant in many respects. Thus, she thinks that it is important that the clients she sees be unaware that they are being studied and be unaware of the hypotheses under investigation. Although Dr. Hamner agrees that some ethical issues may be raised by her failing to inform her clients, she thinks that good research designs call for such procedures. She does not want to influence her clients and thus bias the results of her study, so she chooses to keep information from them. She contends that her practices are justified because there are no negative consequences or risks involved with her research. She further contends that, if she is able to refine her therapeutic techniques through her research efforts with her clients, both they and future clients will be the beneficiaries.

*Commentary.*    Although some of Dr. Hamner's contentions have some merit, we think that the ends are not justified by the means she employs in this case. Further, although she might be justified in withholding some of the details of her research studies (or the hypotheses under investigation), it seems unethical for her to fail even to mention to her clients that she is actually doing research with them as a part of her therapeutic approach. Since her clients are investing themselves both emotionally and financially in their therapy, it seems to us that they have the right to be informed about procedures that are likely to affect them. They <u>further have the right to agree or refuse</u> to be a part of her study. Her approach does not give them that right.

### Some questions on informed consent

- What are your thoughts about Dr. Hamner's ethics and the rationale she gives for not obtaining informed consent?
- Assume that Dr. Hamner was interested in studying the effects of therapist reinforcement of certain client statements during sessions. Do you think that, if the clients knew she was using certain procedures and studying certain behaviors, this would bias the results?
- If the values of the research seem to be greater than the risks involved to participants, do you think that the researcher is justified in not obtaining the informed consent of the subjects?

**Situations Involving Deception.**   Baumrind (1985) defines intentional deception as "withholding information in order to obtain participation that the participant might otherwise decline, using deceptive instructions and confederate manipulations in laboratory research, and employing concealment and staged manipulations in field settings" (p. 165). The case against deception in psychological research has been strongly made. The arguments against deception are that it violates the individual's right to voluntarily choose to participate, abuses the trusting relationship between experimenter and subject, contributes to deception as a societal value, is contrary to the professional roles of educator or scientist, and will eventually erode the trust in the profession of psychology (Adair, Dushenko, & Lindsay, 1985). Baumrind (1985) has argued that the use of intentional deception in the research setting is unethical, imprudent, and unwarranted scientifically. With these points in mind, consider the following situation and determine whether deception is justified.

■   *A case of deception.*   In this case a family therapist routinely videotapes his initial session with families without their knowledge. He does so on the ground that he wants to have a basis for comparing the family's behavior at the outset with their behavior at the final session. He assumes that, if the family members knew they were being videotaped at the initial session, they would behave in self-conscious and fearful ways. At this stage in the therapy he does not think that they could handle the fact of being taped. Yet he likes to have *them* be able to look at themselves on videotape at their final session, at which time he tells them that he taped their initial session. He also explains to them his reasons for not having informed them.

### Some questions on deception

- Since the therapist eventually does tell this family that it was taped at the initial session, do you think that he is guilty of deception? Explain.
- An APA research guideline reads: "Openness and honesty are essential characteristics of the relationship between investigator and research participant" (1973a, p. 1). Do you think that this therapist's motivations for this practice justify his lack of openness and honesty?
- To what degree do you think that the practice of taping clients without their knowledge affects the trust level in the therapeutic relationship? Are the possible benefits of this practice worth the potential risks to the practitioner's reputation?

**Commentary.**   We think that the therapist's policy of videotaping clients without their knowledge and consent is unethical. Most of the professional codes of the national organizations explicitly state that such a practice is to be avoided. Since we contend that the therapeutic relationship is built on good will and trust, we oppose any practices that are likely to jeopardize the trust that clients have toward the helping professionals. Deception cuts to the core of the helping professions, and it fosters distrust among the public toward the profession.

**Situations Involving Withholding of Treatment.**    Is it ethical to withhold treatment from a particular group so that it can be used as a control group? Consider this situation as you explore the question:

■    *A case of withholding treatment.*    Dr. Hope works with depressive psychotics in a state mental hospital. In the interest of refining therapeutic interventions that will help depressed clients, she combines therapy and research procedures. Specifically, she employs cognitive behavioral approaches in a given ward. Her research design specifies treatment techniques for a particular group of patients, and she carefully monitors their rate of improvement as a part of the treatment program. Dr. Hope says that she believes in the value of cognitive behavioral approaches for depressive patients, yet she feels a professional and ethical obligation to empirically validate her treatment strategies. For her to know whether the treatment procedures alone are responsible for changes in the patients' behaviors, she deems it essential to have a comparable group of patients that does not receive the treatment. When Dr. Hope is challenged on the ethics of withholding treatment that she believes to be potent from a particular group of patients on the ward, she justifies her practice on the ground that she is working within the dictates of sound research procedures.

*Some questions on withholding treatment*

• Some researchers contend that they are necessarily caught in ethical dilemmas if they want to use a control group. Do you see an apparent contradiction between the demands of sound research methodology and sound ethical practice?
• Do you think Dr. Hope is ethical in withholding treatment so that she can test her therapeutic procedures? Would it be better for her to simply forget any attempts at empirical validation of her procedures and devote her efforts to treating as many patients as she can? Is it ethical for her to use procedures that are untested?

■    *A modification of the case.*    In a second case Dr. Hope uses *placebo controls*. That is, rather than merely denying treatment to a group or keeping members on a waiting list, she meets with a control group whose members think they are receiving therapy but actually are not receiving standard treatment. In short, the group is led to believe that it is benefiting from therapy.

• What are the ethics of using placebos in counseling and clinical research?
• Does the placebo approach by its very nature constitute deception of patients? Can you think of any situations that justify the use of this approach?

*unethical if treat available*

*suicide risks?*

✓

``

"*might be given*"

***Commentary.*** Parloff (1979) writes that the definitive answer to the question of the role of the placebo in various forms of therapy has yet to be found. On this ground we assert that using placebos borders on unethical practice. Stricker (1982) comments that it is possible in institutional settings either to withhold treatment for a control group or to employ placebos. He argues, however, that to do so is grossly unethical if treatment is available.

The inclusion of placebos places a good deal of responsibility on the investigators to protect subjects. Safeguards that might be built into the research design include screening out individuals judged to be imminent suicide risks, provision of regular contact with a pharmacotherapist, periodic independent evaluations, and the specification of clear procedures for clients who drop out and referral to appropriate treatment resources (Imber et al., 1986).

In a discussion of the ethical dilemma posed by the use of placebos Lindsey (1984) makes the point that, when people enter treatment and develop a contract with an agency, they do so with the understanding that they will receive active treatment aimed to help them. If they receive placebos in place of this active treatment, he asserts, then this contract is violated. He adds that, if and when clients discover that they have received placebo treatment in place of the treatment they thought they were getting, they might well feel betrayed by the profession. He concludes that their autonomous choice is violated by using inaccurate and insufficient information, unless they willingly assent to be in a research study knowing that placebo treatments might be given.

**Situations Involving Research with Training and Personal-Growth Groups.**    In many graduate programs it is common for trainees in counseling internships to participate in personal-growth groups. Sometimes these groups are integrated with training or supervision groups in which the interns are encouraged to explore their own personal issues that arise in conjunction with their placements in the field.

■ *A case of research with trainees.*    A professor, Dr. White, makes it a practice to conduct research on the process and outcomes of the personal-growth groups he leads for these counselor trainees. To begin with, all the students in Dr. White's graduate counseling program are required to attend the sessions of a personal-growth group for a full academic year. In addition to leading these growth groups for trainees, Dr. White also teaches theory courses and supervises students in writing master's theses and doctoral dissertations. His primary theoretical orientation is Gestalt therapy, with emphasis on other experiential and role-playing techniques. He expects the students to come to the sessions and be willing to work on personal concerns. These personal concerns often pertain to issues that arise as a result of problems they encounter with difficult client situations in their internship. At the beginning of the group he asks students to take psychological tests that assess traits such as openness, dogmatism, degree of self-acceptance, level of self-esteem, and other dimensions of personality that he deems to be related to one's ability to counsel others. He again administers these same devices at the end of the year so that he has a comparison of specific dimensions. During the year he asks a group of experts to observe his trainees in the group sessions at various points. This is done so that outsiders can assess the level of growth of individuals at different points as well as get a sense of the progress of the group as a whole.

As a part of informed consent Dr. White tells the trainees what he is attempting to evaluate during the year, and he discusses fully with them the rationale for using outsiders to observe the group. He also promises the students that he will meet with them individually at any time during the semester if they want to discuss any personal issues. He also meets with them individually at the end of the group to discuss changes in scores on the psychological tests. As a way to correct for his bias in the investigation Dr. White submits his research design to a university committee. The function of this committee is to review his design for any ethical considerations and to give him suggestions for improving his study.

### Some questions on research with training groups

- Do you think it is ethical for a program to require student attendance at personal-growth groups? And is it ethical for the leader of such a group to also have these same students in academic classes and to evaluate and supervise them?
- What ethical steps, if any, do you commend Dr. White for?
- What research practices, if any, would you say are ethically questionable?
- Do you think that it is ethically sound to have observers as a part of the design? The students know about these outsiders, but the observers will be a part of the process even if some students do not like the idea. Do you see pressure being exerted? If so, is it justified in this case?
- What recommendations can you make for improving Dr. White's research design as well as improving the quality of the learning experience for the students?

**Situations Involving Research in a Cross-Cultural Context.**    Although research is considered basic to the development of theory, cultural factors are often neglected in both research and theory. This neglect of cultural factors leads Triandis and Brislin (1984) to question the universality of psychological theories and to argue instead for the cultural relativity of these theories. In psychotherapeutic research with minority groups, the assumptions of the study must include the minority culture's view of mental health, the value of self-disclosure, privacy, language, sociocultural experiences, and social interactions. Ibrahim and Arredondo (1986) emphasize that attending to cultural issues in research is not only ethical behavior but also good scientific practice. They propose the following two standards for addition to the AACD (1981) *Ethical Standards*:

> *Standard 1.* Research studies recognize and address such cultural factors as ethnicity, race, gender, life-style, and social class.
> *Standard 2.* Research methodology is culturally appropriate to the group and topic under study [p. 350].

## A Commentary on Ethical Dilemmas in Therapy Research

We hope that you will see that ethical problems in research cannot be solved by enunciating simple principles that are based on absolutes of what is "right" and "wrong." As noted in the APA's (1973a) *Ethical Principles in the Conduct of Research with Human Participants*, ethical questions typically involve balancing the advantages and disadvantages of a particular research design. In considering benefits and costs, the APA writes, the contribution that research might make to human welfare must be weighed against the cost to individual research participants. "The general ethical question always is whether there is a negative effect upon the dignity and welfare of the participants that the importance of the research does not warrant" (p. 11).

According to the APA, the clearest guiding principles are that the participants must emerge from their research experience unharmed, that the risks must be minimized, and that participants must understand and consent to these risks as reasonable side effects of the research.

Adair, Dushenko, and Lindsay (1985) have concluded that research ethics and research methods are closely intertwined, for one cannot be addressed without the other, and that there needs to be a concern for balancing them. Lindsey (1984) has emphasized that ethical rigor must be given a central place in psychotherapeutic research alongside methodological rigor. Stricker (1982) asserts that the way out of the dilemma between violating a person's rights and doing research poorly or not at all is to make ethics and methodology consistent. This can be done by seeking alternatives for research procedures that violate a code of ethics. Stricker agrees with the research principle of the APA that the central issue may not be ethics (standards of rightness and wrongness of actions) but values (what a person holds to be significant). He contends that what is ethical, rather than being absolute, usually varies as a function of values.

Stricker makes a case for designing psychotherapeutic research on a model based on collegiality and informed consent—that is, a model in which research subjects are treated like colleagues rather than objects of study, are given the information they need to be aware of all the variables, and are asked to give their consent to certain research procedures.

In writing about general considerations pertaining to research with human beings, the APA (1973a) acknowledges that, given the ethical obligation of therapists to conduct the best research possible, ethical conflicts are at times unavoidable. It is not a matter of advocating ethical absolutes but of learning ways of resolving conflict.

### Inventory of Your Position on Research

As a way of concluding this discussion, we suggest that you clarify your own thinking on the matter of balancing scientific rigor with ethical rigor. If you agree more than you disagree with the following statements, place an "A" in the space; if you disagree more than you agree, place a "D" in the space. After you've finished the inventory, we suggest that you discuss some of your answers with fellow students.

_____ 1. To use therapy techniques or interventions that lack a sufficient research base is irresponsible and unethical.

_____ 2. Deception is sometimes a necessary evil in psychological research.

_____ 3. The failure to obtain the informed consent of participants in research is always unethical.

_____ 4. If a research study contains any risks to the participants, its design should be changed, for by its very nature it is unethical.

_____ 5. The use of placebo groups can be justified, for if these controls are not used, practitioners will have difficulty in evaluating the efficacy of the interventions they use.

_____ 6. I think that researchers will ultimately get the best results if they are open and honest about the research design with the participants in the study.

_____ 7. In cases where "debriefing" of the subjects is used after deception has been a part of the study, the practice can be justified.

_____ 8. Practitioners should use no techniques that have not been empirically shown to be of value.

_____ 9. If we are concerned about producing sound research studies of therapy, we must be willing to tolerate some ethical violations.

# Chapter Summary

To a large degree your therapeutic techniques and procedures flow from your theoretical assumptions; in this sense counseling theory and practice are closely related. Whether or not you have a clearly articulated theory, you tend to operate on the basis of fundamental views of people and of the therapeutic process. Consequently, in this chapter we've asked you to consider your basic assumptions, some aspects of various theories that most appeal to you, the role of techniques in counseling, the issue of responsibility, your role as a counselor, therapeutic goals, and practical issues related to the use of diagnosis and testing.

Although it's unrealistic to expect that you'll operate from a clearly defined and unified theory at the outset of your practice, we do think that you can at least raise the issues that we've focused on in this chapter. We believe that counselors who give little thought to the theoretical issues that affect their professional practice will spend a lot of time floundering. Reflecting on why you make the interventions you do will enable you to have a more meaningful impact on your clients and to develop a framework for assessing the effects of your therapeutic work.

## Suggested Activities

1. Do this exercise in dyads. Describe your theoretical stance, and tell your partner how you view human nature. How will this view determine the way you counsel?

2. How do you determine for yourself the proper division of responsibility in counseling? How might you avoid assuming responsibility that you think belongs to your client? How might you ensure that you will accept your own share of responsibility?

3. Suppose you were applying for a job as a counselor, and the following question appeared on the application form: "Describe in not more than three lines how you see your role as a counselor." How would you respond to this question? In class, form small groups and discuss your responses.

4. Suppose the same application form asked, "What are the *most important* goals you have for your clients?" How would you respond?

5. In class, debate the role of diagnosis in therapy. One person makes a case *for* diagnosis as a valuable part of the therapeutic process, and the other person argues *against* the use of diagnosis. Or have a class discussion on trends in diagnosis, its uses and abuses, and its purpose and value.

6. Suppose that a client came to you and asked you to administer a battery of interest, ability, and vocational tests. How would you respond? What kinds of questions would you ask the client before agreeing to arrange for the testing?

7. What is your position on the use of techniques in counseling? When do you think they are appropriate? How can you determine for yourself whether you're using techniques as gimmicks to allay your anxiety or as extensions of your personal style as a counselor?

8. Interview at least one practicing therapist in order to discuss how theoretical orientation affects his or her practice. Ask the practitioner the kinds of questions that were raised in this chapter. Bring the results of your interview to class.

9. Suppose that you were applying for a job in a community mental-health center and that the following question was asked of you during the interview: "Many of our clients represent a range of diverse cultural and ethnic backgrounds. To what degree do you think that you will be able to form positive therapeutic relationships with clients who are culturally different from you? How do you think that your own acculturation will influence the way you counsel ethnically and culturally diverse clients? Can you think of any factors that might get in the way of forming trusting relationships with these clients?"

# Suggested Readings

For readings about theoretical perspectives on counseling and therapy see Corey (1986b) and Tremblay, Herron, and Schultz (1986). On trends in eclecticism in counseling practice see Ward (1983), Beutler (1983), Brabeck and Wolfel (1985a, 1985b), Patterson (1985a, 1985b, 1986), Rychlak (1985), Smith (1982), Garfield (1980), Palmer (1980), and Ivey, Ivey, and Simek-Downing (1987). On the question "Are all psychotherapies equivalent?" see Stiles, Shapiro, and Elliott (1986). For the models of helping see Brickman and his associates (1982). A useful book on the subject of paradoxical psychotherapy is Weeks and L'Abate (1982). Huddleston and Engels (1986) discuss the ethical and practical issues related to the use of paradoxical techniques. Dowd and Milne (1986) also discuss such interventions and survey the research literature on the subject. For other useful and interesting articles on the technique of paradoxical interventions see Mahoney (1986), Ascher (1986), Johnson (1986), Ridley and Tan (1986), and Schmidt (1986). For a discussion of the ethics and acceptability of paradoxical interventions, see Brown and Slee (1986), Cavell, Frentz, and Kelley (1986), and Kolko and Milan (1986). On broadening the ethical standards pertaining to assessment and testing in multicultural situations see Ibrahim and Arredondo (1986), Ibrahim (1986), and Lonner and Sundberg (1985). On ethical issues in psychotherapeutic research see Imber and his associates (1986), Baumrind (1985), Ibrahim and Arredondo (1986), Strupp (1986), Lindsey (1984), Adair, Dushenko, and Lindsay (1985), Garfield (1987), and Gendlin (1986). For both sides of the question "Can deception in research be justified?" see Levine (1987).

# FIVE

# Professional Competence, Training, and Supervision

# Pre-Chapter Self-Inventory

*Directions:* For each statement, indicate the response that most closely identifies your beliefs and attitudes. Use the following code:

3 = I *agree*, in most respects, with this statement.
2 = I am *undecided* in my opinion about this statement.
1 = I *disagree*, in most respects, with this statement.

____ 1. Counselors are ethically bound to refer clients to other therapists when working with them is beyond their professional training.

____ 2. Ultimately, practitioners must create their own ethical standards.

____ 3. Possession of a license or certificate from a state board of examiners shows that a person has therapeutic skills and is competent to practice psychotherapy.

____ 4. Professional licensing protects the public by setting minimum standards of preparation for those who are licensed.

____ 5. The present processes of licensing and certification encourage the self-serving interests of the groups in control instead of protecting the public from incompetent practice.

____ 6. Continuing education should be a requirement for renewal of a license to practice psychotherapy.

____ 7. Health-care professionals should be required to demonstrate continuing competency in their field as a prerequisite for renewal of their licenses.

____ 8. Institutions that train counselors should select trainees on the basis of *both* their academic records and the degree to which they possess the personal characteristics of effective therapists (as determined by current research findings).

____ 9. I think that the arguments for licensing counselors and therapists outweigh the arguments against licensing.

____ 10. Peer review, or the analysis and judging of a professional's practice by other practitioners, provides a high degree of assurance to consumers that they will receive competent services.

____ 11. A major problem of the peer-review process involves the difficulty in determining the qualifications of the reviewer.

____ 12. Ethical guidelines are needed for the supervisors of counselors in order to protect the client, the supervisor, and the supervisee.

____ 13. Supervisors should be held legally accountable for the actions of the trainees they supervise.

____ 14. Supervisors have the responsibility to monitor and assess the trainee's performance in a consistent and careful manner.

____ 15. I think that supervision is the most important component in my development as a competent practitioner.

____ 16. Supervisors must be sure that the trainee's clients are fully informed about the limits of confidentiality.

___ 17. I think that the focus of supervision should be on myself as a person, rather than on the client's problem.

___ 18. Ideally, supervision sessions should not be aimed at providing therapy for the trainee.

___ 19. I see nothing wrong in counselor educators' counseling their students, provided the students request it.

___ 20. It is clearly unethical for counselor educators to date their students.

# Introduction

In this chapter and the next two we provide you with an opportunity to reflect on the personal ethical system you will draw on in making sound therapeutic judgments. We present general ethical principles from the various professional organizations, as well as open-ended cases and examples that explore the therapist's responsibilities with regard to client welfare.

We suggest that you devote some time to reviewing the basic similarities and differences among the various professional organizations with respect to their ethical standards and guidelines. By knowing the general content of the codes of ethics (given in the Appendix) you will be in a better position to apply established ethical guidelines to the practical problems that we will pose in this and later chapters. In reading the professional codes you should examine the assets and limitations of these codes. In a discussion of the reasons why professional codes exist Van Hoose and Kottler (1985) pay particular attention to the following:

- Ethical standards are designed to protect the profession from governmental interference. Professional codes are self-imposed as an alternative to having regulations imposed by legislative bodies.
- Ethical standards are designed to prevent internal disagreement and bickering within the profession.
- Ethical codes are designed to protect the practitioner in cases of malpractice, for therapists who conscientiously practice in accordance with accepted professional codes do have some measure of protection in case of litigation. In a lawsuit a counselor's conduct would probably be judged in comparison with that of other professionals with similar qualifications and duties. Actually, the legal standard—what professionals *actually* do—is less rigorous than ethical standards—what professionals *should* do.

Our thoughts on ethical consciousness can be partially summed up with Patrick Callanan's statement that "ethics should be taken out of governing bodies and put into human bodies." As you read this and the remaining chapters, we hope you will apply the principles and issues that we explore to your own behavior. Rather than pointing your finger in shame at others and proclaiming, "That's unethical!" we encourage you to challenge your own thinking and apply professional standards to your behavior. The key question, "Is it in the best interests of the client?" always needs to be in the background of any of these discussions. In Chapter 1 we established that ethical practices typically involve complex factors and thus defy simple solutions. As you read and think about the professional codes of ethics, identify any areas of possible disagreement that you might have with a particular standard. If your practice goes against a standard, you surely need a rationale for your course of action. Realize also that there are consequences for going against the codes of your profession. Must you follow *all* the ethical codes of your profession to be considered an ethical practitioner? If you agree with and follow all the ethical codes of your profession, does this necessarily mean that you are an ethical professional?

In this chapter we discuss the ethical and legal aspects of professional competence, with special attention given to professional licensing and certification. The role of peer review is examined as one way of ensuring professional competency. Because clinical supervision is so vitally related to producing competent practitioners, we consider both the ethical and legal issues central to the supervisory process.

# Therapist Competence: Ethical and Legal Aspects

This section examines what therapist competence is, how we can assess it, and what some of its ethical and legal dimensions are. The topic of competence is developed by giving attention to such questions as "What ethical standards do various mental-health professions have regarding competence? What are some ethical issues in the training of therapists? To what degree is professional licensing an accurate and valid measure of competence? What are some alternatives to professional licensing and certification? What are the ethical responsibilities of therapists to continue to upgrade their knowledge and skills?"

## Various Perspectives on Competence

We begin this discussion of competence with an overview of specific guidelines from various professional organizations. They are summarized in the accompanying box.

A reading of the guidelines shows that several questions are left unanswered. What are the boundaries of one's competence, and how do professionals know when they have exceeded them? How can they determine whether they should accept a client when they lack the experience or training they would like to have?

These questions become more complex when we consider the issue of what criteria to use in evaluating competence. Is completing a professional degree a necessary or sufficient condition of competence? There are many people who complete doctoral programs and yet lack the skills or knowledge

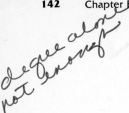

needed to carry out certain therapeutic tasks. Obviously, degrees alone don't confer competence to perform any and all psychological services.

You also need to assess how far you can safely go with clients and when you should refer them to other specialists. Similarly, it's important to learn when to consult another professional if you haven't had extensive experience in working with a certain problem. If you were to refer all the clients you encountered difficulties with, you'd probably have few clients. Keep in mind that many beginning counselors experience a great deal of self-doubt about their general level of competence; in fact, it's not at all unusual for even experienced therapists to wonder seriously at times whether they have the personal and professional abilities needed to work with some of their clients. Thus, difficulty in working with some clients doesn't by itself imply incompetence.

One way to develop or upgrade your skills is to work with colleagues or professionals who have more experience in certain areas than you do. You can also learn new skills by going to conferences and conventions, by taking additional courses in areas you don't know well, and by participating in workshops that combine didactic work with supervised practice. The feedback you receive can give you an additional resource for evaluating your readiness to undertake certain therapeutic tasks.

## Professional Codes of Ethics and Competence

*American Association for Marriage and Family Therapy (1985):*

- "A therapist will not attempt to diagnose, treat, or advise on problems outside the recognized boundaries of their competence."

*American Psychological Association (1981a):*

- "Psychologists recognize the boundaries of their competence and the limitations of their techniques. They only provide services and only use techniques for which they are qualified by training and experience."

*American Psychiatric Association (1986):*

- "A psychiatrist who regularly practices outside his/her area of professional competence should be considered unethical. Determination of professional competence should be made by peer review boards or other appropriate bodies."

*National Association of Social Workers (1979):*

- "The social worker should accept responsibility or employment only on the basis of existing competence or the intention to acquire the necessary competence."
- "The social worker should not misrepresent professional qualifications, education, experience, or affiliations."

*American Association for Counseling and Development (1981):*

- "With regard to the delivery of professional services, members should accept only those positions for which they are professionally qualified."

## Making Referrals

Therapists have a responsibility to know *when* and *how* to refer clients to appropriate resources. It is crucial for professionals to know the boundaries of their own competence and to refer clients to other professionals when working with them is beyond their professional training or when personal factors would interfere with a fruitful working relationship. After counseling with a client for a few sessions, for example, you might determine that he or she needs more intensive therapy than you're qualified to offer. Even if you have the skills to undertake long-term psychotherapy, the agency you work for may, as a matter of policy, permit only short-term counseling. Or you and a client may decide that, for whatever reason, your relationship isn't productive. The client may want to continue working with another person rather than discontinue counseling. As we discussed in Chapter 3, there may be times when the discrepancy or conflict between your values and those of a client necessitates a referral. For these and other reasons you will need to develop a framework for evaluating *when* to refer a client, and you'll need to learn *how* to make this referral in such a manner that your client will be open to accepting your suggestion.

To make the art of referral more concrete, consider the following exchange between a client and her counselor. Helen is 45 years old and has seen a counselor at a community mental-health center for six sessions. Helen suffers from periods of deep depression and frequently talks about how hard it is to wake up to a new day. In other respects it is very difficult for her to express what she feels. Most of the time she sits silently during the session.

The counselor decides that Helen's problems warrant long-term therapy that he doesn't feel competent to provide. In addition, the center has a policy of referring clients who need long-term treatment to therapists in private practice. The counselor therefore approaches Helen with the suggestion of a referral:

*Counselor:* Helen, during your intake session I let you know that we're generally expected to limit the number of our sessions to six visits. Since today is our sixth session, I'd like to discuss the matter of referring you to another therapist.

*Helen:* Well, you said the agency *generally* limits the number of visits to six, but what about exceptions? I mean, after all, I feel like I've just started with you, and I really don't want to begin all over again with someone I don't know or trust.

*Counselor:* I can understand that, but you may not have to begin all over again. I could meet with the therapist you'd be continuing with to talk about what we've done these past weeks.

*Helen:* I still don't like the idea at all. I don't know whether I'll see another person if you won't continue with me. Why won't you let me stay with you?

*Counselor:*  Well, there are a couple of reasons. I really think you need more intensive therapy than I feel I'm trained to offer you, and, as I've explained, I'm expected to do only short-term counseling.

*Helen:*  Intensive therapy! Do you think I'm *that* sick?

*Counselor:*  It's not a question of being sick, but I *am* concerned about your prolonged depressions, and we've talked about my concerns over your suicidal fantasies. I'd just feel much better if you were to see someone who's trained to work with depression.

*Helen:*  *You'd* feel better, but *I* sure wouldn't! The more you talk, the more I feel crazy—like you don't want to touch me with a ten-foot pole. You make me feel like I'm ready for a mental hospital.

*Counselor:*  I wish I could make you understand that it isn't a matter of thinking you're crazy; it's a matter of being concerned about many of the things you've talked about with me. I want you to be able to work with someone who has more training and experience than I do, so that you can get the help you need.

*Helen:*  I think you've worked with me just fine, and I don't want to be shoved around from shrink to shrink! If you won't let me come back, then I'll just forget counseling.

This exchange reflects a common problem. Even though the counselor explains why he wants to refer Helen to another therapist, she seems determined to reject the idea. She doesn't want to open herself up to anyone else right now. She clings to her feeling that she is being helped by her counselor, and she interprets the suggestion to see someone else as a sign that her counselor won't work with her because she's too sick.

What do you think of the way Helen's counselor approached his client? Can you see anything you would have done differently? If you were Helen's counselor, would you agree to continue seeing her if she refused to be referred to someone else?

If you didn't want Helen to discontinue counseling, a number of alternatives would be open to you. You could agree to see her for another six sessions, provided that your director or supervisor approved. You could let her know that you would feel a need for consultation and close supervision if you were to continue seeing her. Also, you could say that, although this might not be the appropriate time for a referral, you would want to work toward a referral eventually. Perhaps you could obtain Helen's consent to have another therapist sit in on one of your sessions so that you could consult with him or her. There may be a chance that Helen would eventually agree to begin therapy with this person. What other possibilities can you envision? What would be the consequences if you refused to see Helen or could not obtain approval to see her?

The National Association of Social Workers' code of ethics (1979) contains some principles that can help the practitioner clarify some of the issues involved:

- "The social worker should terminate service to clients, and professional relationships with them, when such service and relationships are no longer required or no longer serve the clients' needs or interests."
- "The social worker should withdraw services precipitously only under unusual circumstances, giving careful consideration to all factors in the situation and taking care to minimize possible adverse effects."
- "The social worker who anticipates the termination or interruption of service to clients should notify clients promptly and seek the transfer, referral, or continuation of services in relation to the clients' needs and preferences."

## Ethical Issues in the Training of Therapists

Training is obviously a basic aspect of therapist competence. In our opinion Grayson (1982) has pinpointed the most salient issues of training in his excellent article "Ethical Issues in the Training of Psychotherapists." His discussion is concerned with four key questions: (1) How do we select whom to train? (2) What should we teach? (3) What are the best ways of training? (4) What should be the criteria for certification? The following discussion is primarily a summary of the points with which we are most in agreement with Grayson.

**How Do We Select Whom to Train?**    Some questions that can be raised here are:

- Should the selection of trainees be based solely on traditional academic standards, or should it take into account the latest findings on the personal characteristics of effective therapists?
- To what degree is the candidate for training open to learning and to considering new perspectives?
- Does the candidate have problems that are likely to interfere with training and with the practice of psychotherapy?
- Whom do we select to work with which populations?

On the matter of selecting minority-group members Grayson writes:

> Do we select minority group members to work with their own minority groups, or do we select only those minority group members who are culturally similar enough to the young, white, successful middle-class group that when they graduate, they will simply join the abundant ranks of therapists serving this group? Do our training programs even attract minority group members who are enough a part of their own groups to be able to understand and to work effectively with them? And if this selection barrier is surmounted, would the training program itself prepare the minority therapist to work effectively with a variety of minority populations [p. 52]?

**What Should Be Taught?**    Although Grayson does not think that all specialty training should be abolished, he does take the position that it is unethical to train practitioners in only one therapeutic orientation (without also providing unbiased introductions to other systems). Thus, there is merit in an analytically trained therapist's learning about alternative therapy systems such as behavior therapy. By the same token, a behavior therapist should be able to recognize the role of transference and countertransference in the therapeutic process. Therapists should learn when a particular approach is contraindicated, especially if it is their own specialty.

We are in complete agreement with Grayson's view that therapists should be objectively introduced to all of the major systems of therapy so that they can be in a position to decide which aspects of the available current therapies they will include in their own personal style. He writes: "I do not intend to present a case against specialization because I believe that it increases another kind of competence, but only if it does not produce tunnel vision as a side effect" (p. 55).

Grayson also notes that there is an ethical issue involved in presenting therapeutic approaches that have very limited applicability to working with certain ethnic or cultural populations. "Students of all ethnic and social backgrounds learn primarily white, middle-class theories and techniques of psychotherapy, many of which are not directly applicable to the minority populations, and may be particularly irrelevant for minority students who intend to work with these populations" (p. 55). Among his suggestions is that trainees find ways of broadening their life experiences and opening themselves to diverse cultural and social backgrounds.

Questions that Grayson raises on the issue of what to teach include:

- Is there a universal definition of mental health, or is mental health culturally defined?
- What are the implications of training therapists who will work with clients whose culture drives people to a variety of stress-related diseases? Should therapy help clients adjust to their culture? Or should therapy encourage clients to find ways of constructively changing their culture?
- Does the curriculum give central attention to the ethics of professional practice? Is it ethical to leave out training in ethics? Is it enough to hope that ethical issues will be addressed through the supervision process alone?

**How Can We Best Train?** Grayson stresses that trainees learn largely through the modeling of their professors and supervisors. There are clear implications here concerning the type of modeling that is provided to the trainees. Another ethical issue involves the requirement that trainees experience their own personal psychotherapy (or some other type of personal-growth experience). We fully agree with his assertion that training programs have an obligation to address the issue of what personality factors are likely to interfere with trainees' work with clients, as well as what traits are assets in developing effective therapeutic alliances.

**What Should the Criteria Be for Certification or Graduation?**    A key question here is whether personality factors are part of the criteria for certification or whether meeting academic requirements is the sole criterion. According to Grayson, the training institution has an ethical responsibility to screen candidates so that the public will be protected from incompetent practitioners.

Regardless of the type of professional program one completes, it is rarely the end of the road to becoming a competent professional who is able to practice independently. For licenses in areas such as clinical social work, clinical or counseling psychology, and marriage and family therapy, most states have established specific requirements of supervised practice beyond the receipt of a master's or doctor's degree. We now turn our attention to the issues involved in the debate over whether licensing procedures actually assess competence.

## Professional Licensing and Certification as a Sign of Competence

Licenses assure the public that the licensees have completed *minimum* educational programs, have had a certain number of hours of supervised training, and have gone through some type of evaluation and screening. Licenses do not ensure that practitioners can effectively and competently *do* what their licenses permit them to do. The main advantage of licensure is the protection of the public from grossly unqualified and untrained practitioners.

Most licenses are generic in nature; that is, they usually don't specify the types of clients or problems the licensee is competent to work with, nor do they specify the techniques that a practitioner is competent to use. A licensed psychologist may possess the expertise needed to work with adults yet lack the competencies for working with children. The same person might be qualified to do individual psychotherapy yet have neither the experience nor the skills required for family counseling or group therapy. Most licensing regulations do specify that licensees are to engage only in those therapeutic tasks for which they have adequate training, but it is up to the licensee to put this rule into practice. A license permits the professional to provide a wide range of services, and it is the professional's responsibility to determine which services he or she is actually competent to provide.

This section focuses on some of the basic assumptions of the practice of licensing, the relationship of licensing to competency, some arguments for and against licensing and certification for mental-health professionals, and alternatives to current licensing practices. Although licensing and certification differ in their purposes, they have some features in common. Both require applicants to meet specific requirements in terms of education and training; both generally rely on tests of competence to determine those applicants who have met the standards and who deserve to be granted a credential (Shimberg, 1981). Fretz and Mills (1980) define licensure as "the statutory process by which an agency of government, usually a state, grants permission to a person meeting predetermined qualifications to engage in a given occupation and/or use a particular title and to perform specified functions" (p. 7).

**The Pros and Cons of Professional Licensing.** According to Fretz and Mills (1980), more has been written in the psychological literature in opposition to licensing than in favor of it, yet licensing legislation has accelerated during the 1970s and 1980s. Following are some of the central arguments over the values of licensing, along with some criticisms of the licensing process for health-care providers.

In their discussion of the pros and cons of licensure Fretz and Mills write that most of the arguments in support fall under one of five major premises.

The first premise is that licensure is designed to protect the public by setting minimum standards of service and to hold professionals accountable if they do not provide these minimum standards. This argument contends that the consumer would be harmed by the absence of such standards, because incompetent practitioners can cause long-term negative consequences.

Other writers, however, challenge the assumption that licensing does indeed protect consumer interests. According to Gross (1978), substantial evidence suggests that existing licensing practices are a rather confused array of policies that promise public protection but may actually serve to institutionalize a lack of public accountability. He argues that licensing of a profession does not guarantee quality or responsible behavior, and he cites medicine and law to support his argument. He asserts, in fact, that "research refutes the claim that licensing protects the public" (p. 1009). In a review of the status of licensing processes in the United States, Cottingham (1980) concludes that there is no clear evidence that a lack of regulation would result in any danger to the public's welfare. Furthermore, he finds no evidence that licensure protects the quality of service or directly affects the competencies of health-care providers. He also maintains that, while failing to produce a valid system of assessing competence, the licensing process at the same time excludes many competent health professionals.

The second major argument listed by Fretz and Mills is that licensing is designed to protect the public from ignorance about mental-health services. This argument rests on the assumption that the consumer who needs psychological services typically does not know how to choose an appropriate practitioner or how to judge the quality of services received. According to Gill (1982), it is not clear that credentialing by itself provides the necessary information. Further, he asserts that certification and licensing tend to be more confusing than helpful for consumers. Most people do not know the basic differences between a licensed psychologist, a licensed social worker, a certified mental-health counselor, or a person who simply uses the general title of "counselor." Gross (1978) contends that licensing tends to mystify the therapeutic process by reducing the amount of information that is actually provided to the consumer. Fretz and Mills write that no controlled studies have compared unlicensed practitioners and licensed practitioners in their effects on consumers.

Fretz and Mills give three other reasons for licensure. One is the assumption that licensing increases the chances that practitioners will be more competent and that their services will be better distributed. Hogan (1979) writes that, when a group becomes licensed, it gains increased status, privileges, and income. As a result, the group's services usually cost more after licensure, which means that the profession tends to be less willing to provide service to the poor and to minority groups. According to Cottingham (1980), there is no research evidence that licensure protects the quality of service or directly affects the specific competencies of providers.

Another reason offered by Fretz and Mills is the view that licensing upgrades the profession. This argument holds that a licensed profession will have more practitioners committed to improving the profession and maintaining the highest standards of excellence. By way of criticism of this position, Rogers (1980) contends that, as soon as criteria are set up for certification, the profession is inevitably frozen in a past image. He adds that there are as many *certified* charlatans as there are uncertified practitioners. Another drawback to licensing, from his viewpoint, is that professionalism builds up a rigid bureaucracy (pp. 243–248).

Finally, Fretz and Mills hold the view that licensing allows the profession to define for itself what it will and will not do. Accordingly, the profession is assumed to be more independent, since other professions or the courts cannot specify its functions. On the other hand, licensing has a tendency to incite challenges to a profession that makes definite claims, particularly in cases involving the right to offer certain services or to obtain payments from insurance companies. Thus, licensing both protects a profession's domain and also invites attack on it (Fretz & Mills, 1980).

In summary, the essence of the argument for licensure revolves around the contention that the welfare of the consumer is better safeguarded with legal regulation than without it. Challengers to this assumption often maintain that licensing is designed to create and preserve a "union shop." Cottingham (1980) writes that licensure may serve to strengthen the self-protection of practitioners and create monopolistic helping professions rather than protecting the public from misrepresentation and poor services. He adds that the licensing process appears to be more a political issue than an objective and professional assessment of specific skills necessary for effective professional practice. In agreement with this point of view is Davis (1981), who cautions the profession to be aware of practices that encourage the self-serving interests of the groups in control of licensure, instead of protecting the public from incompetent practice.

**Alternatives to Licensing and Certification.**   The diversity of licensing procedures from state to state gives the public little confidence in the license as a sign of minimal competence in health-care practice. Although the ineffectiveness of professional licensing laws has led some (Gross, 1977, 1978; Hogan, 1979) to encourage deregulation, others who have written on this issue see that action as too extreme. One option to current licensing practices is a model based on competence, as proposed by Bernstein and

*"union" shop "political" than profession?*

Lecomte (1981). They contend that the nature of the regulatory process (rather than regulation itself) is what should be challenged. Their proposal includes a number of specific ways to assess competency. One is to review candidates who apply for entry-level licenses on a range of factors that have a demonstrable relationship to positive client outcomes. Further, those who earned a license would be required to continue to demonstrate competent performance at regular intervals as a condition for renewal.

As another alternative, Hogan (1979) proposes that the present licensing practices be replaced by full disclosure of background information about a practitioner. Gross (1977) also recommends that professionals inform clients about themselves and about the therapeutic process through the use of a professional-disclosure statement. As a result of the consumer movement the practice of disclosure appears to be gaining in popularity. In addition to giving potential clients information they need to make informed choices, disclosure also has several benefits for the professional (Gill, 1982). Writing a statement that clarifies one's professional identity is of value as a self-assessment experience. This process entails an honest examination of personal beliefs, values, strengths and weaknesses, and goals regarding the therapeutic relationship. In addition, through concisely stating who they are and what they do, counselors can begin to define for themselves the competencies that are integral to the profession.

Bernstein and Lecomte (1981), as a part of their competency-based alternative to current practices, call for licensed practitioners to participate in professional disclosure. They recommend that a disclosure statement be updated annually and filed with the licensing board. It would include information for clients about the psychologist's academic and professional background. Information would also be provided individually to clients about the proposed length of treatment and anticipated outcomes.

Gross (1977) provides a rather complete description of how professional disclosure can provide regulation that protects the consumer better than current licensing and certification laws. In addition to providing basic information, each practitioner would include a philosophy of counseling, information about his or her education and professional experiences, and a fee schedule.

Although disclosure can take many forms, it is essentially a process of informing prospective clients about the qualifications of a practitioner, the nature of the psychotherapeutic process, and the details of the services provided. This is done to provide clients with the data necessary for making intelligent decisions regarding the use of a particular practitioner's services.

Our position is that professional disclosure is an excellent practice, for both the consumer and the practitioner. Although it may be one alternative to current licensing practices, it can also be used by practitioners who have licenses. Disclosure provides some basis for an assessment of how well services are being provided. We support the view that it can no longer be taken for granted that, simply because professionals are licensed, they are making a significant difference in their clients' lives. Even if practitioners can legally practice by automatically renewing their licenses, ethical practice demands an approach that will keep them abreast of needed knowledge and skills. Further, we applaud the trend toward expecting professionals to demonstrate that they are indeed accomplishing what they say they are doing. Accountability procedures are part of the current debate over licensure and continued competency demonstration. A few examples of the trend toward accountability in practice are the attention given to consumer rights, attempts to provide for informed consent, efforts to demystify the therapy process, descriptions of the nature of the client/therapist relationship through contracts that guide the process, and efforts to educate the public about psychotherapy and related services. Before proceeding to the next section, consider these questions:

• What are your views on alternatives to licensing? What do you think of the suggestions presented? Can you come up with some other ideas?

• Some states have proposed "sunset legislation," which requires professionals to reconvince the legislature periodically that their profession needs to be regulated to protect the public. The assumption is that licensing procedures have become too rigid and restrictive and that bureaucratic factors have contributed to excluding many competent practitioners from legally practicing (while creating a restricted guild based on survival of those with licenses). Do you think that sunset legislation is a workable solution to the problems associated with licensure and certification? What might you want to say if you were on a committee that had the task of evaluating and modifying existing licensing regulations?

• What do you think the likely consequences would be if all professional licensing laws were eliminated? What would the results be for the various mental-health professions? What might the consequences be for the public?

We have presented this overview merely as an illustration of some of the requirements for license in one field of counseling. We encourage you to write to the appropriate agency in your state to find out the specific requirements for licensing or certification of social workers, counselors, psychologists, marriage and family counselors, and other types of mental-health professionals. The specific requirements for even the same category of licensure vary considerably from state to state. If you are seeking a professional license, it behooves you to keep informed of the changing requirements for the type of license you hope to obtain.

The Appendix lists general information about counselor certification. You can ask the appropriate organizations about specific requirements for certification.

## Continuing Education and Demonstration of Competence

Most professional organizations support efforts to make continuing education a mandatory condition of relicensure. In the past, people could obtain licenses to practice professionally and then act as though there were no need to obtain any further education. We question how ethical it is to neglect taking substantive steps to keep current with new developments. In any event, the trend now is to encourage professionals to engage in ongoing education and training in areas related to their specializations.

It should be noted that one of the weak points of mandatory continuing education is that professional organizations can require practitioners to accumulate the necessary hours, but they cannot require intellectual and emotional involvement. A practitioner's résumé can look very impressive in terms of knowledge acquired; the reality might be much less than the paper indicates.

If a state does not mandate continuing education as a condition for relicensure, many professional organizations have a voluntary program. For example, all clinical members of the American Association for Marriage and Family Therapy are encouraged to complete 150 hours every three years. The AAMFT regards the program, known as Continuing Education in Family Therapy, as a part of an ongoing process of professional development, which has as its goal the maintenance of high-quality services to consumers.

In terms of models of assuring competence, Vitulano and Copeland (1980) describe three options. One is the continuing-education model, in which credits are given for participation in approved workshops, courses, seminars, and other avenues of ongoing professional training. Under this model the psychologist must accumulate a given number of credits over a period of time as a prerequisite for relicensure. A second option is the examination model, which would entail psychologists' taking periodic examinations to demonstrate expertise as a prerequisite for relicensure or recertification. A third model is the peer-review system. This approach would involve an elaborate system of comparing the practitioner's record of clinical practice with an established set of standards of care for the profession as a whole.

## The Role of Peer Review

Peer review refers to an organized system by which practitioners within a profession assess other practitioners' services. This approach is gaining in popularity. It provides some assurance to consumers that they will receive competent services.

**Peer Review as a Way to Ensure Quality.**　Regarded as a means rather than an end in itself, peer review has as its ultimate goals not only determining whether a practitioner's present professional activity is adequate but also ensuring that future services will be acceptable. In a discussion of the philosophical underpinnings of peer review, Secrest and Hoffman (1982) make a case for such a system as the heart of a mature profession. They assert that the peer-review model can unite professionals by promoting the highest level of responsible practice. Like earlier means to ensure quality, peer review continues the tradition of self-regulation. It makes collegial account-ability a continuing presence in professional practice. If the approach works well, it will promote self-discipline within the profession (Theaman, 1984). A possible drawback of the peer-review model is implied in these questions we raise: Who determines the qualifications of the peer reviewer? What criteria should be used to determine the effectiveness of counseling practice?

**Peer-Consultation Groups.**   Greenburg, Lewis, and Johnson (1985) de-scribe peer-consultation groups as an important means for helping private practitioners improve their therapeutic effectiveness and counter the loneli-ness that is associated with this profession. Following is a summary of the key points of their article.

The goals of peer-consultation groups are to provide mutual support and help in dealing with problematic cases and various sources of stress in private practice; to provide a source of objectivity in dealing with counter-transference issues; and to share information about referral resources, ther-apeutic procedures, research, and professional meetings. The content of peer-consultation group sessions also includes topics such as ethical issues; professional issues, such as third-party payments; legal decisions that affect the professional; fees; political issues; problems pertaining to private prac-tice; and burn-out. At these group meetings, which in one case were four hours in duration once a month, leadership is a shared function, and the agenda is flexible and determined by the needs of the members.

Peer groups can provide a consistent means of identifying and address-ing sources of negative feelings and loss of objectivity. Without relationships with colleagues, private practitioners are cut off from vital sources of sup-port. In private practice there is no built-in provision for sharing problems, and peer-consultation groups can provide that setting.

The type of group just described is primarily designed not for review and evaluation but for further learning by association with colleagues with simi-lar interests and struggles. Peer consultation, especially in a group setting, is an excellent source of continuing professional development.

## Clarifying Your Views on Maintaining Competence

Having finished this summary of continuing-education practices and the discussion of peer review and peer consultation, think about your position on the following questions:

- What effects on individual practitioners do you think the trend toward increased accountability is likely to have?
- Do you think it is ethical to continue practicing if one does not engage in any type of continuing education? Why or why not?
- What are some advantages and disadvantages to using continuing-educa-tion programs solely as the basis for renewing a license? Is continuing education enough? Explain.

- What are your reactions to competency examinations (oral and written) as a basis for entry-level applicants and as a basis for renewal of licenses? What kinds of exams might be useful?
- Should evidence of continuing education be required (or simply strongly recommended) as a basis for recertification or relicensure? If you support mandatory continuing education, who do you think should determine the nature of this education? What standards should be used in making this judgment?
- Can you think of both advantages and disadvantages to basing license renewal strictly on peer-review procedures?
- What are some potential difficulties with the peer-review model? For instance, who would decide on the criteria for assessment?
- Assume that the peers who reviewed you had been chosen because they had a similar orientation to counseling (behavioral). Would they be assessing your competency or your fidelity to the tenets of the particular school? If the peers who reviewed your work had a different theoretical orientation from yours (psychoanalytic), how competent would they be to assess you within the framework of your practice?
- What are some kinds of continuing education you want for yourself? Through what means do you think you can best acquire new skills and keep current with advances in your field?

Before concluding this discussion of competence, we want to mention the danger of rarely allowing yourself to experience any self-doubt and being convinced that you can handle any therapeutic situation. There are therapists who feel this way; they tell themselves they have it made and attend conventions to show off how much they know and impress their colleagues with their competence. Sidney Jourard (1968) has warned about this delusion that one has nothing new to learn. He maintains that contact at exciting workshops or with challenging colleagues can keep therapists growing. He urges professionals to find colleagues they can trust, so that they can avoid becoming "smug, pompous, fat-bottomed and convinced that they have *the word*." Such colleagues can "prod one out of such smug pomposity, and invite one back to the task" (p. 69).

With Jourard, we see the development of competence as an *ongoing process, not* a goal that counselors ever attain once and for all. This process involves a willingness to continually question whether you're doing your work as well as you might and to search for ways of becoming a more effective person and therapist.

# Ethical and Legal Issues in Clinical Supervision

The relationship between the clinical supervisor and the trainee (or student of psychotherapy) is of critical importance in the development of competent and responsible therapists. Specific guidelines for ethical behavior between a supervisor and trainee have not been delineated in all of the professional codes. If we take into consideration the dependent position of the trainee and the similarities between the supervisory relationship and the therapy relationship, the establishing of further guidelines outlining the rights of trainees and the responsibilities of supervisors is very much needed (Newman, 1981).

## The Supervisor's Responsibilities

Supervisors are responsible for the actions of their trainees. They must check on the trainees' progress and be familiar with their case loads. The trainee has the right to know about training objectives, assessment procedures, and evaluation criteria. It is the responsibility of supervisors to inform trainees about these matters at the beginning of supervision (Cormier & Bernard, 1982).

Supervisors also have the responsibility to monitor and assess the trainee's performance in a consistent and careful manner. Trainees have a legal right to periodic feedback and evaluation so that they have a basis for improving their clinical skills (Cormier & Bernard, 1982). Supervision is perhaps the most important component in the development of a competent practitioner. It is within the context of supervision that trainees begin to develop a sense of professional identity and to examine their own beliefs and attitudes regarding clients and therapy. Thus, the supervisor fosters the trainees' professional development by serving as teacher, role model, and evaluator (Newman, 1981).

**Training Competent Supervisors.**    One basic issue is the preparation of the supervisor for supervision. The profession needs to set down some guidelines for appropriate supervision. On this issue Hess and Hess (1983) found that the supervisors in their study had an average of 9.3 years of clinical experience and 7.6 years of supervisory experience. They apparently lacked adequate preparation in psychotherapy supervision, however, since only one-third of the facilities where they were working reported having training supervisors.

The Hess and Hess study suggests that many supervisors are functioning without the benefit of adequate and current training. The authors assert that a more focused and central role for supervision is necessary. Supervisors need to become familiar with more supervisory methods, and supervisees must receive effective training.

**The Focus of the Supervision Process.**    We think there is a good rationale for supervision that includes attention to the trainee as a person. Thus, when we supervise, we focus on the dynamics between supervisees and their clients. Our style of supervision can be grasped by the kinds of questions we explore: "What is going on with you? How are you reacting to your clients? How is your behavior affecting them? Which clients bring out your own

resistances? How are your values manifested by the way you interact with your clients?"

We do not focus merely on the cases that trainees bring to the supervision sessions; rather, we focus on the interpersonal and intrapersonal variables. Although we see supervision as a separate process from psychotherapy and do not attempt to make supervisory sessions into therapy sessions, we think that the supervision process can be therapeutic and growth-producing.

## Legal Aspects of Supervision

The legal considerations pertaining to the supervisory relationship involve informed consent, confidentiality and its limits, and the concept of liability. First, supervisors must see that trainees provide the information to clients that they need to make informed choices. This requirement implies that clients be made fully aware that the counselor they are seeing is a trainee; that he or she is meeting on a regular basis for supervision sessions; that the client's case may be discussed in group supervision meetings with other trainees; and that sessions may be taped or observed.

Second, supervisors have an ethical obligation to respect the confidentiality of client communications. There may be certain exceptions, however, such as cases when the supervisor determines that the client is potentially dangerous to himself or herself or to others. Supervisors must make sure that clients are fully informed about the limits of confidentiality.

Third, supervisors ultimately bear the legal responsibility for the welfare of those clients who are counseled by their trainees. Cormier and Bernard (1982) point out that supervisors must be familiar with each case of every supervisee, in order to prevent negligent supervision. This may not be practical in the sense that supervisors cannot be cognizant of all details of every case. But they should at least know the direction in which the cases are being taken. Cormier and Bernard add that the supervisor is legally responsible for knowing when counselors are involved in a case beyond their level of competence. Also, university training programs have a responsibility to clients to make some kind of formal assessment of each trainee before allowing the person to counsel clients.

## Ethical Standards and the Supervisory Process

Upchurch (1985) discusses the need for establishing further ethical guidelines for counseling supervision. Some of her major points are summarized below:

• Guidelines can make clear the details of the beginning supervisory relationship, including appropriate fees for supervision, behavioral objectives for the supervisee, and information about grievance procedures to deal with the failure to meet training objectives.

- Guidelines can encourage the appropriate use of consultation and can help in prescribing a course of action if there are problems in the supervisory relationship.
- Guidelines can encourage the supervisor and supervisee to discuss the purpose, goals, techniques, uses, and limitations of counseling supervision. Attention should be given to each supervisee's unique interests.
- Guidelines are useful for clarifying the nature of the supervisor/supervisee relationship. This is especially true when the relationship extends beyond supervision to include therapy, social relationships, sexual intimacies, services other than supervision, and administrative supervision of the supervisee.
- Guidelines are needed to avoid sex-role stereotyping in supervision.
- Guidelines are needed for the protection of the client, the supervisor, and the supervisee, all of whom are vulnerable in different ways.

The current trend toward accountability in the counseling process itself also has implications for the process of supervising counselors. Engaging in the supervision of counseling without specific ethical guidelines seems to be equivalent to practicing counseling without an adequate set of ethical standards.

## Dual Relationships and the Supervision Process

As in the case of sexual contact between therapists and clients, sex in the supervisory relationship can result in an abuse of power because of the difference in status between supervisees and supervisors. Further, there is the matter of poor modeling for trainees for their future relationships with clients.

**Sexual Intimacies during Professional Training.**    It can be argued that trainees are in a position of diminished consent. Thus, they are in a poor position to give voluntary consent to participate in any type of dual relationship with a supervisor. Other problems with dual relationships are pointed out by Cormier and Bernard (1982): there is the possibility of exploitation of trainees; there could be a reduction in the supervisor's power in some aspects of supervision; and the supervisor's objectivity can be impaired, thus clouding his or her ability to supervise effectively. (Such a situation might entail legal liability for failure to provide adequate supervision.)

Pope, Schover, and Levenson (1980) have discussed the multiple roles of clinical supervisors, including those of teacher, evaluator, and therapist. Considering the effects of each of these roles we can see that ethical issues are raised when sexual intimacies become mixed up with the supervisory relationship.

- *Supervisors function as teachers.* It can easily be seen that teachers who gain sexual satisfaction through students are likely to have considerable difficulty in keeping their students' interests and welfare as primary concerns.

• *Supervisors function as evaluators*. Sexual intimacy can obstruct the supervisor's ability to provide careful, objective, and valid evaluations.

• *Supervisors function as therapists*. Most training programs involve some type of experiential learning as part of the supervision process and as a part of the trainee's personal-growth sessions. Thus, there are similarities between the supervisory relationship and the therapy relationship, in that both clients and trainees are likely to develop transference relationships. It is obvious that sexual relationships will increase feelings of transference and countertransference and will thus get in the way of effective personal learning.

The question of what constitutes appropriate relationships between faculty members and students was explored by Roberts, Murrell, Thomas, and Claxton (1982). In their study of the attitudes and practices of counselor educators pertaining to dual relationships, they found the following:

• Seventy-two percent of the faculty members believed it was ethical to have nonsexual relationships with students but that sexual relationships were unethical.

• Twenty-one percent thought that close relationships with students in their classes, even of a nonsexual nature, were unethical under any circumstances.

• Seven percent viewed it as ethical to have noncoerced sexual relationships with students.

Glaser and Thorpe (1986) conducted an anonymous survey of 464 female members of APA's Division 12 (Clinical Psychology) that examined (1) their experiences during graduate training of sexual intimacy with and sexual advances from psychology educators and (2) their past and current perceptions and evaluations of these experiences in terms of coercion, ethicality, and impact on the professional working relationship. Glaser and Thorpe found that sexual contact was quite prevalent between graduate students and supervisors or educators. The overall rate was 17%; among recent doctoral graduates it was 22%; and among students divorcing or separating during graduate training the rate was 34%.

An earlier survey (Pope, Levenson, & Schover, 1979) had similar results: 16.5% of female respondents reported such sexual contact. Also, of the respondents who had received their degrees within the previous six years, 25% had experienced sexual contact with their psychology educators.

The 1979 survey (Pope et al.) reported that 77% of respondents did not believe that sexual relationships between students and their educators could be beneficial. To the statement "I believe that sexual relationships between students and their psychology teachers, administrators, or clinical supervisors can be beneficial to both parties" 2% said yes, 77% said no, and the remaining 21% said "perhaps." The survey revealed a predominant pattern:

An older, higher-status man becomes sexually active with a younger, subordinate woman. In each of these higher-status roles, a much higher percentage of men than women engage in sex with those students or clients for whom they have assumed professional responsibility. These findings support the contention that sexual contact with students or clients represents the unethical behavior of a therapist acting out of his own needs for power, esteem, acceptance, and sexual fulfillment.

In the study of Glaser and Thorpe (1986) the judgments of the majority of the respondents were very negative: over 95% of them evaluated such contact as unethical, coercive, and harmful to the working relationship to a considerable degree. Sexual advances were reported by 31% and were judged by most to be overwhelmingly negative. Almost all judged sexual contact between an educator and a student during a working relationship to be highly unethical.

The core ethical implication pertains to the difference in power or status between teacher and the student. The student is in an extremely vulnerable position. Faced with a faculty member who makes a sexual proposition, the student may be intimidated and thus accept the offer (Pope, Schover, & Levenson, 1980).

In summary, the Glaser and Thorpe survey indicates that 20% to 25% of female psychology graduate students over the past decade have had sexual relationships with psychology educators, most often during a working relationship. Although these intimate relationships were evaluated by many respondents as coercive and exploitive, one-half of the respondents who had experienced sexual contact during a working relationship perceived no professional ethical problem at the time of the relationship. Several studies indicate that the preponderance of sexual relationships involve men in the more powerful social role and women in the less powerful role.

Consider the following assumptions: sexual relationships between graduate students and their professors or supervisors cannot be equated with relationships between a client and a therapist because:

• Students are not emotionally unstable and are not seeking therapy.
• Students in the counseling field who purport to teach responsibility to clients later in their profession must themselves be responsible for what they do and cannot blame others for "what was done to them."

What is your evaluation of these assumptions? What are your views on the ethical and professional implications of sexual intimacies between students and faculty members?

Assume that you are a trainee, and your clinical supervisor consistently harasses you sexually, along with touching you in questionable ways. During your individual supervision sessions the supervisor makes many comments with double meanings. The supervisor frequently looks at you in flirtatious ways. From what your supervisor says and does, you get the distinct impression that your evaluations will be more favorable if you engage in "playing the game." What course of action might you take in such a situation?

**Educators Who Counsel Students.**    Besides inappropriate sexual contact between faculty members or supervisors and students, there are other dual relationships related to one's professional training. We now consider the issue of counselor educators or supervisors who also provide counseling for their students or supervisees. When researchers raised the question "What is the appropriateness of faculty members' serving as counselors for their students?" their survey (Roberts et al., 1982) revealed that:

*Supervisor & therapist at same time*

- Fifty-six percent of the counselor educators responding to the survey thought that such relationships would be ethical if the students were not in their classes at the time.
- Thirty-four percent saw no ethical conflict even if these students were still in their classes.
- Seventy-two percent reported that they had seen their students for short-term personal counseling, and nineteen percent had done so on a long-term basis.

Counselor educators must struggle with the issue of how far to extend the boundaries of educational relationships to include the affective and personal dimensions along with the cognitive components of counseling. Supervisors must also give serious consideration to how they can help students understand their own dynamics but avoid converting supervision sessions into therapy sessions. Stadler (1986) holds the opinion that the dual-relationship standard of ethical conduct can and should be used to establish limits on the methods used to train counselors. On the issue of educators serving as counselors for their students, Stadler concluded that there were many negative repercussions of the practice that could sour student/faculty relationships. These consequences are summarized in the box on p. 161.

There is no clear answer to the ethical question raised by counselor educators who provide some form of counseling for their students. As we mentioned in Chapter 2, many professional programs strongly recommend, if not require, some type of personal therapeutic experience. Some programs expect students to undergo individual therapy for a time, and other programs provide a growth-group experience. At the very least, students have a right to know of these requirements before they make a commitment to begin a program. Further, we think that students should generally be allowed to decide what type of therapeutic experience is most appropriate for them. The practice of faculty members' providing counseling for students in a program for a fee is highly questionable.

Some situations are not so clear-cut, however. Once students complete a program, for example, what are the ethics of a psychology professor's taking them on as clients? Can it still be argued that the prior role as educator might negatively affect the current role as therapist? If this matter is fully

## Negative Effects of Dual Relationships

• *Effects on the student*. Students' autonomy may be compromised if they fear that an academic evaluation will be influenced by information divulged during counseling. Further, students who seek counseling from a faculty member are likely to assume that dual relationships are ethical and may go on to engage in those types of relationships as a professional.

• *Effects on other students*. Assuming that students are aware that dual relationships in most cases violate ethical standards, they may lose respect for the counselor educator involved as well as the graduate program and a profession that appears to support unethical behavior. Further, resentment may build up with those who have not been singled out for what may appear to be a privileged relationship with a faculty person.

• *Effects on other faculty members*. Fellow counselor educators can be placed in the difficult position of having to either confront their colleague or condone this behavior.

• *Effects on the counseling profession*. Ethical violations are especially detrimental when violators are those responsible for the education of beginning professionals.

• *Effects on the counselor educator*. The faculty person who violates an ethical standard by engaging in dual relationships is also adversely affected. Dual relationships may lead to conflicts of interest that would otherwise not occur.

discussed by the former student and the professor/therapist and both agree that there are no problems in entering into a therapeutic relationship, is doing so ethically justified? To clarify your position on this issue, you might reflect upon this case that follows.

■ *A case of counseling students.*    The situation involves a psychology professor, Dr. Hilda Uppertown, who teaches counseling classes, supervises interns, and also provides individual counseling at the university counseling center. One of her current graduate students, Kent, approaches her with a request for personal counseling. Even though Dr. Uppertown tells him of her concern over combining roles, Kent is persuasive and adds that he trusts her and sees no problem in being both her student and her counselee. He also informs her that he will be in her internship class next semester.

• Would Dr. Uppertown be unethical if she accepted Kent as a client, given his feelings about the matter?
• Would you see any difference if he approached her for counseling after he had completed the course with her?
• Would the situation take on a different ethical dimension if the professor had a private practice? Is the matter partly one of the professor's charging a fee for her service?
• Assume that Dr. Uppertown was leading a therapy group during the semester and that Kent wanted to join the group. Do you think that being a client in a group is different from being an individual client? Would it be unethical for her to accept Kent into the group? Would it be unethical for

her to reject him from the group on the ground that he was a student, especially if she believed that the group would benefit him?

• Do you think that the lack of availability of other resources in the area should make a difference in whether to accept Kent as a client?

## Some Questions to Consider

What is your position on some of the ethical and legal issues raised in this section? Specifically, take a stand on the following situations:

• Your supervisor does not provide what you consider to be adequate supervision. You are left mainly on your own with a difficult case load. The staff members where you work all are overloaded, and when you do get time with a supervisor, the person feels burdened with many responsibilities. Thus, you do not get quality time for supervision or for discussion of cases. What would you be inclined to do?

• You have a conflict with your supervisor over the ethical way to deal with a client. What would you do?

• You are aware that a clinical supervisor that you are scheduled to work with has a reputation of being sexually involved with supervisees. What course of action, if any, would you take?

• You do not get ongoing feedback on your performance as a trainee. At the end of the semester your supervisor gives you a negative evaluation. What are the ethical and legal issues involved? What might you do or say?

• Do you think it is unethical for a supervisor to initiate social or sexual relationships with trainees after they have graduated (and when the supervisor has no professional obligations to the trainee)? Explain your position.

# Chapter Summary

This chapter has focused on the therapist's ethical and legal responsibilities, particularly with respect to client welfare, referrals, and competence. We have looked at ethical issues in the training of therapists, the debate over whether professional licensure is a sign of competence, the role of peer review and continuing education in ensuring professional competence, and some ethical and legal issues in clinical supervision.

Another focus of this chapter has been the scope of professionals' responsibilities. Besides their duties to the client, therapists also have responsibilities to their agencies, to the profession, to the community, to the members of their clients' families, and to themselves. Ethical dilemmas arise when there are conflicts of responsibilities—for instance, when the agency's expectations conflict with the concerns or wishes of clients. Members of the helping professions need to know and observe the ethical code of their professional organization and the standards of ethics that have been generally agreed on by members of the profession. Furthermore, many times they are called on to exercise judgment by applying and interpreting these guidelines to specific instances. In this chapter we've encouraged you to think about specific ethical issues and to develop a sense of professional ethics and knowledge of state laws so that your judgment will be based on more than what "feels right."

■_____

# Suggested Activities

1. Invite several practicing counselors to talk to your class about the ethical and legal issues they encounter in their work. You might have a panel of practitioners who work in several different settings and with different kinds of clients.

2. In small groups explore the topic of when and how you might make a referral. Role-play a referral, with one student playing the client and another the counselor. After a few minutes the "client" and the other students can give the "counselor" feedback on how he or she handled the situation.

3. In small groups explore what you think the criteria should be for determining whether a therapist is competent. Let a student role-play an "incompetent" therapist and defend himself or herself. Make up a list of specific criteria, and share it with the rest of the class. Are you able as a class to come up with some common criteria?

4. Several students can look up the requirements for licensure or certification of the major mental-health specializations in your state. What are some of the common elements? Present your findings to the class.

5. Work out a proposal for a continuing-education program. In small groups the class can develop a realistic model of ensuring competency for professionals once they have been granted a license. What kind of design most appeals to you? A peer-review model? Competency examinations? Taking courses? Other ideas?

6. Assume that you are applying for a job or writing a résumé to be used by you in private practice. Write up your own professional disclosure statement in a page or two. Another suggestion is to bring your disclosure statements to class and have fellow students review what you've written. They can then interview you, and you can get some practice in talking with "prospective clients." This exercise can help you clarify your own positions and give you valuable practice for job interviews.

7. As a class project several students can form a committee to investigate some of the major local and state laws that apply to the practice of psychotherapy. You might want to ask mental-health professionals what major conflicts they have experienced between the law and their professional practice.

8. Interview several clinical supervisors to determine what they consider to be some of the most pressing ethical and legal issues in the supervisory relationship. Some questions you might ask supervisors are: What are the rights of trainees? What are the main responsibilities of supervisors? To

what degree should supervisors be held accountable for the welfare of the clients who are counseled by their trainees? What kind of specialized training have they had in supervision? Who is the proper focus of supervision—the client? the trainee? What are some common problems faced by supervisors in effectively carrying out their duties?

9. Assume that you are in a field placement as a counselor in a community agency. The administrators tell you that they do not want you to inform your clients that you are a student intern. They explain that your clients might feel that they were getting second-class service if they found out that you were in training. The administrators contend that your clients are paying for the services they receive (on a sliding scale, or ability-to-pay basis) and that it is not psychologically good to give them any information that might cause them to conclude that they are not getting the best help available. What would you say and do if you found yourself as an intern in this situation? Would it be ethical to follow this directive and not inform your clients that you were a trainee and that you were receiving supervision? Do you agree or disagree with the rationale of the administrators? Might you accept the internship assignment under the terms outlined if you could find any other field placements?

# Suggested Readings

This would be a good time to review the ethical codes of the various professions, which are found in the Appendix. Look for commonalities as they pertain to the topics explored in this chapter.

On ethical issues in the training of therapists see Grayson (1982). For a discussion of training graduate students in methods of short-term psychotherapy see Schneider and Pinkerton (1986). On professional regulation (licensure and certification) of mental-health services see Cottone (1985), Shimberg (1981), Fretz and Mills (1980), Gross (1977, 1978), Cottingham (1980), Hogan (1979), Gill (1982), Rogers (1980), Davis (1981), Bernstein and Lecomte (1981), Hedgeman (1985), Messina (1985), Stone (1985), and Smith and Karpati (1985). On issues pertaining to peer review as a way to ensure competence see Theaman (1984), Biskin (1985), Claiborn, Stricker, and Bent (1982), and Secrest and Hoffman (1982). On peer consultation groups see Greenburg, Lewis, and Johnson (1985). On the need for establishing ethical guidelines for counseling supervision see Upchurch (1985). On ethical issues in counseling supervision see Cormier and Bernard (1982) and Newman (1981). On effective supervision in groups see Savickas, Marquart, and Supinski (1986). On training of clinical supervisors see Hess and Hess (1983) and Grater (1985). On ethical concerns of counselor educators see Roberts, Murrell, Thomas, and Claxton (1982), Glaser and Thorpe (1986), Pope, Levenson, and Schover (1979), and Pope, Schover, and Levenson (1980). On dual relationships in counselor education see Stadler (1986).

# SIX

# Client Rights, Confidentiality, and Duty to Warn and Protect

■ Pre-Chapter Self-Inventory
■ Introduction
■ The Rights of Clients
■ Confidentiality, Privileged Communication, and Privacy
■ Duty to Warn and Protect
■ Chapter Summary
■ Suggested Activities
■ Suggested Readings

# Pre-Chapter Self-Inventory

*Directions:* For each statement, indicate the response that most closely identifies your beliefs and attitudes. Use the following code:

3 = I *agree*, in most respects, with this statement.
2 = I am *undecided* in my opinion about this statement.
1 = I *disagree*, in most respects, with this statement.

\_\_\_\_ 1. If there is a conflict between a legal and an ethical standard, a therapist must follow the law.

\_\_\_\_ 2. Practitioners who do not use written consent forms are derelict in their duty.

\_\_\_\_ 3. In order to practice ethically therapists must become familiar with the laws related to their profession.

\_\_\_\_ 4. Clients in therapy should have the right of access to their files.

\_\_\_\_ 5. Clients should be made aware of their rights at the outset of a diagnostic or therapeutic relationship.

\_\_\_\_ 6. It is unethical for a counselor to alter the fee structure once it has been established.

\_\_\_\_ 7. Ethical practice demands that therapists develop procedures to ensure that clients are in a position to make informed choices.

\_\_\_\_ 8. Therapists have the responsibility to become knowledgeable about community resources and alternatives to therapy and to present these alternatives to their clients.

\_\_\_\_ 9. Before entering therapy clients should be made aware of the purposes, goals, techniques, policies, and procedures involved.

\_\_\_\_ 10. Therapists have an ethical responsibility to discuss a termination date with clients during the initial session(s) and then to review this matter with them periodically.

\_\_\_\_ 11. Involuntary commitment is *not* a violation of the human rights of people who are unable to be responsible for themselves or their actions.

\_\_\_\_ 12. Mental patients in institutions should be consulted about the treatment they might receive.

\_\_\_\_ 13. Clients should be informed at the initial counseling session of the limits of confidentiality.

\_\_\_\_ 14. There are no situations in which I would disclose what a client had told me without the client's permission.

\_\_\_\_ 15. Absolute confidentiality is necessary if effective psychotherapy is to occur.

\_\_\_\_ 16. If I were working with a client whom I had assessed as potentially dangerous to another person, I would see it as my duty to warn the possible victim.

\_\_\_\_ 17. As a therapist who might work with potentially dangerous clients, I see it as my responsibility to both warn and protect any intended victims.

___ 18. Once I make an assessment that one of my clients is suicidal or at a high risk of self-destructive acts, it is my ethical obligation to take action.

___ 19. We should make it more difficult for suicidal persons to reject responsibility for deliberately taking their own life.

___ 20. If a suicidal client does not want my help or actively rejects it, I would be inclined to leave the person alone.

# Introduction

If we hope to practice in an ethical and legal manner, the rights of clients cannot be taken for granted. In this chapter we deal with ways of educating clients about their rights and responsibilities as partners in the therapeutic process. Special attention is given to the role of informed consent as well as ethical and legal issues that arise when therapists fail to provide for consent.

Perhaps the central right of a client is the guarantee that disclosures in therapy sessions will be respected. As you will see, however, you cannot legally make a blanket promise to your clients that *everything* that they talk about will *always* remain confidential. It becomes critical that you become aware of the ethical and legal ramifications of confidentiality. You need to inform your clients from the outset of therapy of those circumstances that limit confidentiality. Because issues pertaining to confidentiality are rarely clear-cut, we present a number of cases to help you develop ethical decision-making skills in problematic situations.

Landmark court cases have shed new light on the therapist's duty to warn and to protect both clients and others who may be directly affected by a client's behavior. As a professional, for example, you have both ethical and legal responsibilities to protect innocent people who might be injured by a dangerous client. You also have responsibilities to assess and intervene effectively with clients who are likely to try to take their own life. To the end of helping you think about your position in dealing with potentially dangerous clients or suicidal clients we offer guidelines and case illustrations.

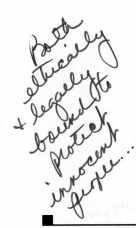

Both ethically + legally bound to protect "innocent people..."

# The Rights of Clients

Part of ethical practice is talking with clients about their rights. Depending on the setting and the situation, this discussion can involve such questions as the circumstances that may affect the client's decision to enter the therapeutic relationship, the responsibilities of the therapist toward the client, the possibility of involuntary hospitalization, the possibility of being forced to submit to certain types of medical and psychological treatment, matters of privacy and confidentiality, and the possible outcomes and limitations of therapy.

Frequently, clients don't realize that they have rights. Because they are vulnerable and sometimes desperate for help, they may unquestioningly accept whatever their therapist says or does. There may be an aura about the therapeutic process, and clients may have an exaggerated confidence in the therapist. It is much like the trust that many patients have in their physician. For most clients the therapeutic situation is a new one, so they are unclear about what is expected of them and what they should expect from the therapist. For these reasons we think that it is the responsibility of the therapist to protect clients' rights and teach them about these rights. The ethical codes of most professional organizations require that clients be given adequate information to make informed choices about entering and continuing the client/therapist relationship. (See the accompanying box.) By helping clients accept their rights and responsibilities, the practitioner is encouraging them to develop a healthy sense of autonomy and personal power.

### The Rights of Clients and Informed Consent: Some Ethical Codes

*American Psychological Association (1981a):*

- "Psychologists fully inform consumers as to the purpose and nature of an evaluative, treatment, educational or training procedure, and they freely acknowledge that clients, students, or participants in research have freedom of choice with regard to participation."

*National Association of Social Workers (1979):*

- "The social worker should provide clients with accurate information regarding the extent and nature of the services available to them."
- "The social worker should apprise clients of their risks, rights, opportunities, and obligations associated with social service to them."

*American Association for Counseling and Development (1981):*

- "The member must inform the client of the purposes, goals, techniques, rules of procedure, and limitations that may affect the relationship at or before the time that the counseling relationship is entered."

## The Right to Informed Consent

One of the best ways of protecting the rights of clients is to develop procedures to help them make informed choices. This process of providing clients with information they need to become active participants in the therapeutic relationship begins with the intake interview and continues throughout counseling. Informed consent entails a balance between telling clients too much and telling them too little. Although most professionals agree on the ethical principle that it is crucial to provide clients with information about

*[handwritten margin note: don't overwhelm client]*

the client/counselor relationship, in practice there is little consensus about how much or what should be revealed (Goodyear & Sinnett, 1984). On the one hand, it is a mistake to overwhelm clients with too much detailed information at once. On the other hand, it is a mistake to withhold important information that clients need if they are to make wise choices about their therapy program. What and how much is told to clients is determined in part by the clientele. Surely, any unusual practices should be clarified and discussed. It helps to consider informed consent as an ongoing process, especially during the initial stages of counseling, and not something that must be completed at the intake session.

*[handwritten margin note: a Responsibility Ethically &]*

Professionals have a responsibility to their clients to make reasonable disclosure of all significant facts, the nature of the procedure, and some of the more probable consequences and difficulties inherent in the procedure. To the extent that counselors do not provide information about the counseling process, they promote paternalism. In addition, issues of violating the rights of clients are raised when practitioners fail to provide clients with adequate information that may affect their welfare. Bray, Shepherd, and Hays (1985) specify two types of liability that face practitioners who fail to obtain informed consent. One is that of negligence or malpractice. The failure to make a complete disclosure of possible risks or deviations from standard professional practice may result in a judgment of negligent practice. The second liability is breach of contract. If therapists guarantee that a certain treatment will "cure" a person and it does not, they are liable to be sued.

*[handwritten margin note: Legally]*

Legally, there are three elements to adequate informed consent: capacity, comprehension of information, and voluntariness (Bray et al., 1985). *Capacity* means that the client has the ability to make rational decisions. When this capacity is lacking, a parent or guardian is typically responsible for giving consent. *Comprehension of information* means that therapists must give clients information in a clear way and check to see that they understand it. The information must include the benefits and risks of procedures, the risk of forgoing treatment, and alternate procedures that are available. *Voluntariness* means that the person giving consent is acting freely in the decision-making process; the person is legally and psychologically able (competent) to give consent. Informed consent implies that the professional and the client discuss the nature of the problem and possible treatments for it. Before treatment begins, the client must consent to it and, thus, give the therapist the power to act.

Some questions that clients would do well to have the answers to at the outset of the counseling relationship are:

- What are the goals of the therapeutic program?
- What services will the counselor provide?
- What behavior is expected of the client?
- What are the risks and benefits of therapeutic procedures?
- What are the risks and benefits of alternatives to psychotherapy?

- What are the qualifications of the provider of the services?
- What are the financial considerations?
- What is the estimated duration of the therapy?
- Is counseling a voluntary arrangement?
- What are the limitations of confidentiality?
- In what cases does the counselor have mandatory reporting requirements?

A number of writers on this subject suggest using written informed-consent procedures. It is important to note that either the client or the therapist has the option to revise the therapeutic contract.

In a study on the use, content, and readability of informed-consent forms for treatment, Handelsman, Kemper, Kesson-Craig, McLain, and Johnsrud (1986) found that only 29% of psychologists in private practice reported using such forms. The major reason given for not using them was a preference for oral agreements. The content of the forms dealt mainly with the financial arrangements of therapy. The authors write that practitioners seem to be attempting to avoid malpractice suits with the forms but are not meeting the ethical requirements of informed consent. Some of the conclusions of Handelsman and his colleagues are as follows:

- Practitioners who do not use consent forms are not necessarily derelict in their duty.
- Clinicians who do use consent forms are not doing all that they need to do.
- Therapists need to evaluate their practices regarding informed consent in relationship to ethical guidelines such as autonomy, the ability of their clients to understand the forms used, and the kind of information that clients should have in order to make informed choices about their therapy.

There is a danger of becoming overly legalistic with clients, and there is no assurance that practitioners won't be involved in a suit even if they do obtain written informed consent. Rather than focusing on legalistic documents, it is a good idea to develop informed-consent procedures that will increase client understanding about the counseling process and will be likely to forestall dissatisfaction and, therefore, legal action (Deardorff, Cross, & Hupprich, 1984). We now look in more detail at some of the topics about which clients should be informed.

**The Therapeutic Process.**   Although it may be difficult to give clients a detailed description of what occurs in therapy, some general ideas can be explored. We support the practice of letting clients know that counseling might open up levels of awareness that could cause pain and anxiety. Clients who want ongoing counseling need to know that they may experience changes that could produce disruptions and turmoil in their lives. Some clients may choose to settle for a limited knowledge of themselves rather than risking this kind of disruption. We believe that a frank discussion of the chances for change and its personal and financial costs is an appropriate way to spend some of the initial sessions. Clients should have a knowledge of the procedures and goals of therapy. This is especially true if any unusual or experimental approaches or techniques are to be employed.

*esp. true when...*

**Background of the Therapist.**  The matter of therapists' developing professional disclosure statements was covered in the previous chapter. Such a statement is an excellent way to help clients decide whether they will make use of the practitioner's services. Therapists should provide clients with a description of their training and education, any specialized skills, and the types of clients and types of problems that they are best trained to deal with. If the counseling will be done by an intern or a paraprofessional, the clients should know this. This clear description of the practitioner's qualifications, coupled with a willingness to answer any questions clients have about the process, reduces the unrealistic expectations of clients about therapy.

*Ethics: Intern paraprofessional*

**Costs Involved in Therapy.**  Morton Berger (1982) lists as part of the "patient's bill of rights" the right to a reasonable financial arrangement. According to Berger, this right entails several therapist responsibilities, some of which are:

- providing information regarding all fees by the end of the initial session, including the arrangement for a payment schedule
- avoiding exploitation of clients by prolonging therapy needlessly or convincing them to undergo unnecessary diagnostic or treatment procedures
- making clients aware of insurance reimbursement, and taking whatever steps are necessary to help them collect payments from a third party
- not springing unexpected costs upon the client

*costs are a delicate issue*

Matters of finance are delicate, and if they are handled poorly, they can easily result in a strained relationship between the client and therapist. Thus, the manner in which fees are handled has much to do with the tone of the therapeutic partnership.

**The Length of Therapy.**  Some therapists make it a practice to discuss with their clients an approximate length for the therapeutic process. They may make this matter a part of the written or verbal contract during the initial session(s). Other therapists maintain on theoretical grounds that, since the problems that brought the client into therapy are typically complex and long-standing, therapy will necessarily be long-term. These therapists may be unwilling to talk during the initial phase about the length of treatment, simply because of their conviction that individual differences among clients make such a prediction impossible.

Regardless of the therapist's theoretical orientation, we think, clients do have a right to expect that their therapy will end when they have realized the maximum benefits from it or have obtained what they were seeking when they entered it. We think that the issue of termination needs to be openly

*clients have right to expect to effect their therapy end...*

explored by the therapist and client and that the decision to terminate ultimately rests with the client. Berger (1982) maintains that therapists have the responsibility to set a tentative termination date with clients and then review this date and revise it when appropriate.

As we saw in the last chapter, many agencies have a policy of *limiting* the number of sessions that a client can have. In this case, clients need to be informed at the outset that they cannot receive long-term therapy. They should not be informed at the next-to-last session that they will not be allowed to return. Also, clients have the right to expect a referral so that they can continue exploring whatever concerns initially brought them to therapy.

*agencies have policy of 'limiting number of sessions'*

**Consultation with Colleagues.**  Student counselors generally meet regularly with their supervisors and fellow students to discuss their progress and any problems they encounter in their work. It is good policy for counselors to inform their clients that they are meeting with others and may be talking with them about some of the sessions. Clients can be assured that their identities will not necessarily be disclosed, and they can be informed of the reasons for these meetings with supervisors and others. Even though it is ethical for counselors to discuss their cases with other counselors, it's wise to routinely let clients know about this possibility. Clients will then have less reason to feel that the trust they are putting in their counselors is being violated. Counselors can explain that these discussions may well focus on what *they* are doing and feeling as counselors, rather than on their clients as "cases."

✓ **Clients' Right of Access to Their Files.**  An area of potential conflict between ethics and the law pertains to the right of clients to have access to their files and records. This matter is not directly addressed by the ethical codes of counselors, psychologists, social workers, and family therapists.

Giving clients access to their files seems to be consistent with the consumer-rights movement, which is having an impact on the fields of mental health, counseling, rehabilitation, and education. One way of reducing the growing trend toward malpractice suits and other legal problems in the medical profession is to allow patients to see their medical records, even while hospitalized. According to Mappes, Robb, and Engels (1985), it has been considered unprofessional and unethical for professionals to provide mental-health clients with access to their files. They add that in view of the current open-records laws governing public and private information, the right of clients to have access to their files is an ethical concern that merits attention.

*consumer right movement & reduce malpractice*

> Feedback provided by such access may be valuable to both the client and the practitioner. It seems logical that counselors who are not willing to explain and to be open and honest with their clients, to the extent of allowing clients to see their own files, cannot expect to create an atmosphere and relationship of trust and safety sufficient to allow the clients to examine their problems openly and

experiment with new ways of handling their lives. Preventing clients access to their own counseling files risks limiting potential for growth and strength and may suggest a lack of therapist confidence in clients' self-help abilities [Mappes et al., 1985, p. 251].

### Rights Pertaining to Diagnostic Labeling.

One of the major obstacles to the open sharing of files with clients is the need to give clients a diagnostic classification as a requirement for receiving third-party reimbursement for psychological services. Most clients are not informed that they will be so labeled, what those labels are, or that the labels and other confidential material will be given to insurance companies. Clients also do not have control over who can receive this information, nor are they informed of their right not to be labeled (Mappes et al., 1985).

We agree with Smith's position (1981) that one of the basic rights of a client is the freedom to choose to be coded and classified by a psychologist or psychiatrist. He urges that the psychologist obtain the consent of clients when they are diagnosed for the purposes of insurance reimbursement. We think that an open discussion with clients about their condition, including a formal diagnosis if this is a part of the therapy procedure, is one way to demystify the client/therapist relationship. We endorse the maximum possible openness with clients about our procedures, so that they can become active and informed agents in their own therapy and not dependent on the magical healing powers of a therapist.

### Tape-Recording or Videotaping of Sessions.

Many agencies require recording of interviews for training or supervision purposes. Clients have a right to be informed about this procedure at the initial session, and it is important that they understand why the recordings are made, how they will be used, and who will have access to them. Often therapists make recordings because they can benefit from listening to them or perhaps having colleagues listen to their interactions with clients and give them feedback. Again, if this is to be done, clients should be informed and their consent obtained. Frequently, clients are very willing to give their consent if they are approached in an honest way. Clients, too, may want to listen to a taped session during the week to help them remember what went on or to evaluate what is happening in their sessions.

### Personal Relationships and Informed Consent.

Before therapists accept supervisees, students, employees, colleagues, close friends, or relatives as clients, it is essential that they discuss with these prospective clients the problems that may be associated with what is known as a "dual relationship." It should be stressed that most of the ethical codes caution against dual relationships and point to the need to avoid exploitation of clients out of the therapist's needs.

Clients have a right to expect that their therapist will be primarily concerned with their welfare. This concern implies that therapists will have some degree of "therapeutic distance," or objectivity. It also implies that therapists will be aware of their own countertransference feelings, so that they do not unnecessarily complicate the therapy process.

**Alternatives to Traditional Therapy.**    Clients need to know about alternative helping systems. Therefore, therapists must become knowledgeable about community resources so that they can present these alternatives to a client. The following are some examples of alternatives to psychotherapy (Hare-Mustin, Marecek, Kaplan, & Liss-Levinson, 1979):

- *individual self-help:* use of self-help books and bibliotherapy, recreational activities, religious activities, and changes in social relationships or lifestyle
- *programs designed for personal-effectiveness training:* parent-effectiveness training, assertiveness training, and marriage encounter
- *peer self-help groups:* Parents Without Partners, Alcoholics Anonymous, Weight Watchers, consciousness-raising groups, and a variety of support groups
- *crisis-intervention systems:* rape-crisis centers, suicide hot lines, shelters for battered wives, and pregnancy and abortion counseling
- *psychological and psychiatric helping systems:* day-treatment and out-patient hospital programs and partial hospitalization
- *other institutional helping systems:* legal assistance, social-welfare agencies, and medical and other health-care facilities

This information about therapy and its alternatives can be presented in writing, through an audiotape or videotape, or during an intake session. Hare-Mustin and her associates caution practitioners to present alternatives to therapy fairly. They also note that an ethical dilemma may arise when a therapist has clear convictions about what course of action is in the best interests of a given client. Although the therapist may ethically state his or her views when a client is tending toward a different course of action, the therapist who insists on a definite approach diminishes the client's right to free choice. An open discussion of therapy and its alternatives may, of course, lead some clients to choose sources of help other than therapy. For practitioners who make a living providing therapy services, this possibility can produce anxiety. On the other hand, the practice of openly discussing therapy and its alternatives is likely to reinforce many clients' decisions to continue therapy.

■ *Case for discussion.*    During the initial interview Simone asks the counselor how long she might need to be in therapy. The counselor tells her the process will take a minimum of two years of weekly sessions. Simone expresses dismay at such a lengthy process. The counselor says that this is the way she works and that if Simone is not willing to commit herself to this process, she should find another therapist.

- Did the counselor take care of the need for informed consent?
- Did she have an ethical and a professional obligation to explain her rationale for the two years of therapy at this initial session?
- Should the therapist have been willing to explore alternatives to her approach to therapy?

## Involuntary Commitment and Human Rights

The practice of involuntary commitment of people to mental institutions raises difficult professional, ethical, and legal issues. Practitioners must know their own state's laws pertaining to involuntary commitment. Our focus here is not specific legal provisions but, rather, the ethical aspects of involuntary commitment.

White and White (1981) have explored the issue of whether the mental-health profession should impose treatment on unwilling patients who have run afoul of state commitment laws or should keep out of that conflict. In their article on the constitutional right of involuntarily committed patients to refuse treatment, they pose three questions: (1) Does the state have the power to commit people? (2) What are a person's rights to receive treatment? (3) What are a person's rights to refuse treatment? Briefly, their answers to these questions are:

1. The U.S. Supreme Court has held that the states do have a legitimate interest in providing care for people who are not able to care for themselves; the states also have the authority to protect the community from those individuals whose psychological condition makes them dangerous.
2. The legal issue of a committed mental patient's right to treatment is not settled. Although some lower courts have expressed support for such a right, no constitutional basis has been established by the Supreme Court to support this right.
3. Some patients may not be legally competent to exercise their right to decide whether to have treatment or what kind of treatment is in their best interests. Legal incompetence to make decisions concerning treatment hinges on state laws, which vary.

What is the role of the mental-health profession in safeguarding the rights of the committed patient? In answering this question White and White emphasize the role of informed consent. Their position is that committed patients must be given all the information necessary for them to make reasonable and intelligent decisions regarding choice of treatment. For example, patients should be given information about their diagnosis and condition. They should also be told about alternative courses of treatment and be able to discuss the benefits and risks of each approach to treatment. White and White's view is that the patient's informed consent to a specific treatment plan should be obtained and that treatment should be terminated at the patient's demand.

Imagine yourself in the following situation. You're employed as a counselor at a state mental hospital. The ward on which you work is overcrowded, and there aren't nearly enough professionals on the staff to provide for much more than custodial services. You observe patients who seem to be psychologically deteriorating, and the unattractive surroundings reinforce the attitude of hopelessness that is so prevalent among the patients. You become aware that the rights of patients are often ignored, and you see many of the hospital's practices as destructive. For instance, when patients are given medication, there is rarely a consistent evaluation of the effects of the drug treatment and of whether it should be continued. Moreover, you recognize that some of the people who have been hospitalized against their will really don't belong there, yet institutional procedures and policies make it very difficult for them to be released or placed in a more appropriate agency. Finally, although some members of the staff are both competent and dedicated, others who hold positions of power are incompetent.

What do you think you might do if you were involved in this situation? What do you see as your responsibility, and what actions might you take? Check as many of the following statements as you think appropriate:

____ Since I couldn't change the people in power, I'd merely do what I could to treat the patients with care and dignity.

____ I'd bring the matter to public attention by writing to newspapers and talking with television reporters.

____ I'd attempt to rectify the situation by talking to the top administrators and telling them what I had observed.

____ I'd form a support group of my peers and see what we could do collectively.

____ I'd keep my views to myself, because the problem is too vast and complex for me to do anything about it.

____ I'd encourage the patients to revolt and demand their rights.

____ I'd directly confront the people I thought were incompetent or who were violating the rights of patients and attempt to change them.

What other courses of action might you take?

# Confidentiality, Privileged Communication, and Privacy

An important obligation of practitioners in the various mental-health specialties is to maintain the confidentiality of their relationships with their clients. This obligation is not absolute, however, and practitioners need to develop a sense of professional ethics for determining when the confidentiality of the relationship should be broken. It also behooves them to become familiar with the legal protection afforded the privileged communication of their clients, as well as the limits of this protection.

## Definition of Terms

Confidentiality, privileged communication, and privacy are related concepts, but there are important distinctions among them.

**Confidentiality.** Confidentiality is the ethical responsibility of mental-health professionals to safeguard clients from unauthorized disclosures of information given in the therapeutic relationship. Siegel (1979) defines it as follows: "*Confidentiality* involves professional ethics rather than any legalism and indicates an explicit promise or contract to reveal nothing about an individual except under conditions agreed to by the source or subject" (p. 251). According to Shah (1969, 1970a), therapists have a moral, ethical, and professional obligation not to divulge information without the client's knowledge and authorization unless it is in the client's interest to do so. As this definition implies, there are limitations to the promise of confidentiality. Court decisions, for example, have underscored the therapist's duty to warn and protect others, even it it means breaking confidentiality.

*therapist duty*

*belongs to the client*

**Privileged Communication.** Shah (1969) defines *privileged communications* as "the legal right which exists by statute and which protects the client from having his confidences revealed publicly from the witness stand during legal proceedings without his permission" (p. 57). Siegel (1979) defines privilege (privileged communication) as "a legal term involving the right not to reveal confidential information in a legal procedure. Privilege is granted by statute, protects the client from having his/her communications revealed in a judicial setting without explicit permission, and is vested in the client by legislative authority" (p. 251). DeKraai and Sales (1982) assert that a special type of law, known as the privileged-communications law, is needed to protect communications of the client when the psychologist is on the witness stand. They state that the courts have held that confidentiality statutes are designed to protect clients from gossip but that these statutes do not create testimonial privilege.

Privileged communication, then, is a *legal* concept and refers to the right of clients not to have their privileged communications used in court without their consent. If a client waives this privilege, the professional has no grounds for withholding the information. Thus, the privilege belongs to clients and is meant for their protection, not for the protection of the therapists. Some other relationships that are protected in various jurisdictions in the United States include those between attorneys and clients, marital partners, physicians and patients, psychiatrists and clients, priests and penitents, accountants and clients, and nurses and patients.

In an article reviewing privileged-communication laws for therapists Knapp and Vandecreek (1985) make the following important points:

• The waiver belongs to the client, and the therapist has no independent right to invoke the privilege against the client's wishes.

• Privileged-communication laws should be changed to cover communications made in marital and family therapy and should not be waived unless both spouses agree. The only exception should be custody cases arising out of reports of suspected child abuse.

• The greatest threat to the integrity of privileged communication comes from the fact that various mental-health professions are excluded from these laws. Many professionals practice counseling and psychotherapy—psychologists, social workers, psychiatrists, marriage and family therapists, certified clinical mental-health counselors, and pastoral counselors. But the privilege exists only for clients of professionals specifically enumerated in the statutes. In most states the definition of the terms *psychologist*, *psychiatrist*, or *social worker* in the statutes determines which mental-health professionals are included.

• Privileged-communication laws often apply to psychiatrists or psychologists qualified for private practice, but they often do not apply to other professionals who are more likely to work in community mental-health centers. The net effect is to provide a privilege for clients who can afford the services of private practitioners and to deny it to rural or poor clients who have access only to community services.

It is important to consider privileged communication in context. There must be a balance between the person's right to privacy and society's need for information. Also, there are differences among the states with respect to privileged-communication legislation. As of the summer of 1985, for example, such laws extended full or partial protection to the relationships between school counselors and their students, licensed counselors and their clients, or both, in 27 states (Sheeley & Herlihy, 1986). Legislative activity could easily change this picture, of course.

Since the psychotherapist/client privilege is a legal concept, there are certain circumstances under which information *must* be provided by the therapist:

• when the therapist is acting in a court-appointed capacity—for example, to conduct a psychological examination (DeKraai & Sales, 1982)
• when the therapist makes an assessment of a foreseeable risk of suicide (Schutz, 1982)
• when the client initiates a lawsuit against the therapist, such as for malpractice (Denkowski & Denkowski, 1982)
• in any civil action when the client introduces mental condition as a claim or defense (Denkowski & Denkowski, 1982)
• when the client is under the age of 16 and the therapist believes that the child is the victim of a crime—for example, incest, child molestation, rape, or child abuse (Everstine, L., Everstine, D.S., Heymann, True, Frey, Johnson & Seiden, 1980)
• when the therapist determines that the client is in need of hospitalization for a mental or psychological disorder (DeKraai & Sales, 1982; Schutz, 1982)

- when information is made an issue in a court action (Everstine et al., 1980)
- when clients reveal their intention to commit a crime or when they can be accurately assessed as dangerous to society or dangerous to themselves (DeKraai & Sales, 1982; Schutz, 1982)

As an example of an exception to privilege, we consider the client who is assessed as potentially violent and dangerous to others. In group therapy, family therapy, and couples therapy, the therapist must retain confidentiality and can demand it of clients. At this time, however, there is no privilege in court. Thus, disclosures of violent intentions in these treatment approaches may be repeated in court (Schutz, 1982).

From the foregoing discussion it should be clear that privileged communication between therapist and client is *not* an absolute matter. There are exceptions to privilege, and therapists are legally bound to comply with the exceptions stated above. In his discussion of privileged communication Siegel (1979) notes that, because it is a legal concept, there are variances in these exceptions from state to state and from federal to state courts. He writes that the issue involves the balance between the individual's right to privacy and the need of the public to know certain information.

**Privacy.**    Siegel (1979) defines *privacy* as "the freedom of individuals to choose for themselves the time and the circumstances under which and the extent to which their beliefs, behavior, and opinions are to be shared or withheld from others" (p. 251). In discussing some basic issues pertaining to privacy, Everstine and his colleagues (1980) raise the following questions:

- To what extent should beliefs and attitudes be protected from manipulation or scrutiny by others?
- How can it be decided who may intrude on privacy and in what circumstances privacy must be maintained?
- Assuming that privacy has been violated, what can be done to ameliorate the situation?
- Do people have a right to waive their privacy, even when their best interests might be threatened?

Examples of some of the most pressing situations in which privacy is an issue include an employer's access to an applicant's or an employee's psychological tests, parental access to their child's school records and health records, and a third-party payer's access to information about a client's diagnosis and prognosis.

Most of the professional codes of ethics contain guidelines for safeguarding a client's right to privacy. Here are two examples:

  • "The social worker should obtain informed consent of clients before taping, recording, or permitting third party observation of their activities" (NASW, 1979).

  • "Information obtained in clinical or consulting relationships, or evaluative data concerning children, students, employees, and others, are discussed only for professional purposes and only with persons clearly concerned with the case. Written and oral reports present only data germane to the purposes of the evaluation and every effort is made to avoid undue invasion of privacy" (APA, 1981a).

One other area where privacy is an issue involves practitioners who also teach courses, offer workshops, write books and journal articles, and give lectures. If these practitioners use examples from their clinical practices, it is of the utmost importance that they take measures to adequately disguise their clients' identities. We think it is a good practice for them to inform their clients that they are likely to use some of their clinical experience in their writing and in giving lectures. One relevant guideline on this issue of privacy is given by the APA (1981a): "Psychologists who present personal information obtained during the course of professional work in writings, lectures, or other public forums either obtain adequate prior consent to do so or adequately disguise all identifying information."

## Summary of Ethical Codes on Confidentiality

*American Psychiatric Association (1986):*

- "Psychiatric records, including even the identification of a person as a patient, must be protected with extreme care. Confidentiality is essential to psychiatric treatment."
- "A psychiatrist may release confidential information only with the authorization of the patient or under proper legal compulsion."
- "Clinical and other materials used in teaching and writing must be adequately disguised in order to preserve the anonymity of the individuals involved."

*National Association of Social Workers (1979):*

- "The social worker should share with others confidences revealed by clients, without their consent, only for compelling professional reasons."
- "The social worker should inform clients fully about the limits of confidentiality in a given situation, the purposes for which information is obtained, and how it may be used."

*American Association for Marriage and Family Therapy (1985):*

- "Marriage and family therapists cannot disclose client confidences to anyone, except: as mandated by law; to prevent a clear and immediate danger to a person or persons; if there is a waiver previously obtained in writing, and then such information may only be revealed in accordance with the terms of the waiver."

*American Psychological Association (1981a):*

- "Psychologists have a primary obligation to respect the confidentiality of information obtained from persons in the course of their work as psychologists. They reveal such information to others only with the consent of the person or the person's legal representative, except in those circumstances in which not to do so would result in clear danger to the person or to others. Where appropriate, psychologists inform their clients of the legal limits of confidentiality."

## Ethical and Legal Ramifications of Confidentiality

The ethics of confidentiality rests on the premise that clients in counseling are involved in a deeply personal relationship and have a right to expect that what they discuss will be kept private. The compelling justification for confidentiality is that it is necessary to encourage clients to develop the trust needed for full disclosure and for the work involved in therapy. Surely no genuine therapy can occur unless clients trust that what they say is confidential. Professionals therefore have an obligation to discuss with clients the circumstances that might affect the confidential relationship.

When it does become necessary to break confidentiality, it is a good practice to inform the client of the intention to take this action and also to invite the client to participate in the process. This step may preserve the therapeutic relationship and create the opportunity to resolve the issue between the individuals concerned (Mappes et al., 1985). For example, most states have statutes that require professionals who suspect any form of child abuse to report it to the appropriate agencies. Professionals who do report suspected child abuse are immune from prosecution for breaching confidentiality in these cases. When therapists find that they have to report actions such as incest, they can still work toward enlisting the cooperation of the client, and they can be instrumental in securing help for both the child and the parent.

Shah (1970a) raises the question "Whose agent is the psychologist?" He notes that in some governmental agencies and in some institutions the psychologist is _not_ primarily the client's agent. In such cases psychologists might be faced with conflicts between their obligations to the agency or institution and their obligations to their clients. For this reason Shah maintains that any possible conflict should be clarified before a psychologist enters into a diagnostic or therapeutic relationship with a client. In short, clients should be informed about the limits of confidentiality. In agreement with Shah's position are Denkowski and Denkowski (1982), who contend that "it is imperative that counselors inform each client of the potential breaches that are likely to impinge on their relationship. Furthermore it seems ethically required that all reasonable steps be taken to restrict the legally sanctioned dissemination of confidential client information to its bare minimum" (p. 374).

Siegel first took the extreme position that absolute confidentiality is necessary for effective therapeutic relationships, and he argued that psychologists should not break the confidentiality of a client under _any_ circumstances. As he noted, this viewpoint provoked a storm of reactions. He has apparently modified his view of absolute confidentiality to fit within the boundaries of the law: "While the absolute confidentiality notion still seems viable, it cannot be urged that anyone disobey the law. Language that would include the concept that confidential information may not be disclosed without consent, except if required by law, should be supported" (Siegel, 1979, p. 255). Siegel holds that professionals should function within the law while at the same time working toward changes in the laws with which they disagree.

Other writers challenge the position that absolute confidentiality is necessary for effective treatment. Denkowski and Denkowski (1982) make the case for limited and qualified confidentiality. They contend that several recent developments tend to refute the conventional wisdom that there can be no therapy without complete confidentiality. They do, however, give two reasons for the continued safeguarding of client confidentiality: (1) confidentiality is needed to protect the client's interests, especially from the social stigma that is frequently associated with participating in psychotherapy; and (2) confidentiality is grounded in ethical motives of promoting vital client rights, which are essential to the therapist's professed concern for the welfare of the client.

**The Limits of Confidentiality.**   Since confidentiality is not absolute, it becomes necessary to determine under what circumstances it cannot be maintained. These circumstances are not clearly defined by accepted ethical standards, and each therapist must exercise his or her professional judgment. When assuring their clients that what they reveal will ordinarily be kept confidential, therapists should point out that they have obligations to others besides their clients. For instance, they are bound to act in such a way as to protect others from harm. Thus, the AACD's (1981) ethical guidelines state: "When the client's condition indicates that there is clear and imminent danger to the client or others, the member must take reasonable personal action or inform responsible authorities."

All the other major professional organizations have also taken the position that practitioners must reveal certain information when there is clear and imminent danger to an individual or to society. Consistent with these guidelines from the professions is the following specific exception to the right of privileged communication and confidentiality, as created by the California legislature: "There is no privilege if the psychotherapist has reasonable cause to believe that the patient is in such mental or emotional condition as to be dangerous to himself or to the person or property of another and that disclosure of the communication is necessary to prevent the threatened danger."

Any limitations on the confidentiality of the therapeutic relationship should be explained at the outset. These limitations may be greater in some settings and agencies than in others. If clients are informed about the conditions under which confidentiality may be compromised, they are in a better position to decide whether to enter counseling. If they are involved in involuntary counseling, they can decide what they will disclose in their sessions.

Miller and Thelen (1986) conducted a survey to assess the public's knowledge and beliefs about the confidentiality of therapeutic communications. The majority of the respondents (69%) believed that everything discussed with a professional therapist would be held strictly confidential. Further, most of the respondents (74%) thought that there should be no exceptions to maintaining confidential disclosures. The vast majority of respondents (96%) wanted information about confidentiality. Most of them (46%) wanted to be told of the exceptions to confidentiality before the first session, whereas some (29%) preferred discussions at various points throughout the therapeutic process. Miller and Thelen concluded that most of the respondents perceived confidentiality as an all-encompassing mandate for therapists. The authors pointed out that there was apparently a huge gap between what clients expected and standard therapeutic practice with regard to maintaining confidentiality.

Practitioners tend to assume that clients' expectations of confidentiality are an important factor in their being able to trust the therapist and reveal personally significant material. Muehleman, Pickens, and Robinson (1985) designed a study to explore the impact on clients of discussing the limits of confidentiality. Strikingly, they found very little evidence that providing detailed information about the limits of confidentiality inhibited client disclosure. Based on their findings, the authors recommend that practitioners provide accurate, impartial, and comprehensive information to their clients.

**Guidelines for Practitioners.**    Sheeley and Herlihy (1986) suggest that confidentiality, privileged communication, and privacy need to be viewed within the broad context of both society's values and the individual's interests. They offer the following guidelines as ways counselors can meet their obligations to confidentiality:

- Difficulties in the client/counselor relationship can be resolved by working within a spirit of confidence.
- Clients need to be informed that, even in cases where privileged communication does exist by statute, there are circumstances in which practitioners ethically or legally are obliged to breach confidence. These circumstances include when clients present a danger to themselves or others, when they lack capacity (minors or the infirm), when they themselves request it, or when a court requests it.
- Practitioners need to know whether their clients' communications are privileged under state statute and, if a statute exists, what exceptions it specifies. Even when these statutes exist, they do not represent absolute guarantees. Counselors should not assume that an existing statute or their license will exempt them from testifying in court.
- Counselors would do well to maintain strict adherence to the ethical codes pertaining to confidentiality of their professional organization.
- Physical settings should be selected that allow for privacy of communications.
- It is important to ask clients to sign waiver forms before counselors disclose information to third parties.
- Counselors should be aware that courts generally do not consider privileged those communications made in the presence of a third party.

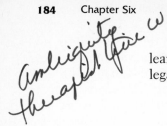

Faced with conflicting standards in certain situations, counselors must learn to live with ambiguity when it comes to knowing what the ethical and legal course of action is. Sheeley and Herlihy put this matter well:

> The combination of multiple and sometimes conflicting considerations—privileged communication law, ethical confidentiality, and societal values—leaves practicing counselors with no easy answers. Yet, it is a mark of professionalism to be able to simultaneously weigh these considerations and to make sound judgments which are in the best interests of both the client and others [1986, p. 147].

**Some Legal Trends in Confidentiality.**    In their discussion of the legal status and implications of client/counselor confidentiality, Denkowski and Denkowski (1982) list several conclusions that evolved from a review of trends and developments in the area:

- There are ethical grounds for the safeguarding of confidentiality, which is a professional requirement.
- How counselors should carry out this professional obligation is increasingly being specified by law.
- Confidentiality cannot be absolutely ensured under a legal framework.
- The therapeutic process seems to proceed adequately without the existence of absolute confidentiality.

Denkowski and Denkowski note that the overall trend seems to be a legislative inclination to bind all mental-health practitioners to confidentiality while at the same time limiting the scope of confidentiality. "Apparently the conviction has sprouted among legislators that confidentiality is necessary for therapy, but it need not be absolute to promote such treatment effectively" (p. 374). They conclude that a "major challenge that will confront counselors over the next decade will be to implement legitimately the increasingly restricted legal definition of confidentiality, while safeguarding client privacy" (p. 374).

Another trend toward legislation that weakens confidentiality involves the stringent regulations imposed on professionals to report a variety of suspected crimes against the person. For example, California has laws regarding the duty to report instances of child abuse, child molestation, and incest. Everstine and his associates (1980) make the point that many professionals are appalled that it has been necessary to pass laws with penalties for failing to report. They conclude that therapists are being called upon to serve as "gatekeepers of the criminal justice system." This raises some questions that should be carefully considered:

- When does a therapist become an informer?
- Can therapists carry out their therapeutic functions effectively and at the same time function as "gatekeepers"?
- What are the therapist's obligations when there are suspicions of crimes but at the same time circumstances that make these suspicions doubtful?

For instance, what might the therapist do when incest is reported by an angry daughter yet denied by the father? What should the therapist do if he or she has serious doubts about the accuracy of the daughter's assertions? Is it the place of the therapist to become a judge?

• If therapists do report a client for a crime (or a suspected crime), what are their obligations to the client? Should they attempt to continue the therapy process if at all possible?

• If your client informed you that he intended to kill his girlfriend but did not disclose her identity, what should you do? Is it incumbent on you to investigate? Are you responsible for contacting the authorities?

The more one considers some of the legal ramifications of the issues that we've raised in this section, the clearer it becomes that most matters are not neatly defined. At a convention a lawyer presented a detailed discussion of the many fine lines that exist in the legal system as it is applied to psychotherapeutic practice. This attorney's central point was that therapists must become familiar with local and state laws that govern their specializations but that this legal knowledge alone would not be enough for them to make sound decisions. Each case is unique; there are many subtle points in the law; there are various and sometimes conflicting ways to interpret a law; and professional judgment always plays a significant role in resolving these cases.

At a recent conference on ethical and legal issues in counseling, a great deal of interest and anxiety was expressed about the issue of dealing with potentially violent clients. Most of the counselors expressed fears of lawsuits and were very concerned about what "exercising sound professional judgment" really means. In discussing the tone of this conference, the three of us became concerned that some counselors are primarily worried about protecting themselves and not about their clients' welfare. Although counselors will surely want to protect themselves legally, we hope that they don't allow this problem to paralyze them and render them useless. While minimizing unnecessary risks, professionals do need to realize that counseling is a risky venture. Although they should be familiar with the laws that govern privileged communications and should know what they can and cannot do legally, counselors should not become so involved in legalism that they cease being sensitive to the *ethical* implications of what they do in their practice.

A question often raised is when the therapist should inform clients that discussions of violent impulses might lead to a breach of confidentiality. Depending on the type of population with whom you work, you might want to consider giving some of this information (including your reasons for disclosing material) to clients in writing at the initial session. Contending that many clients are not violent and have no concerns about violence, Schutz (1982) says that it is best to consider bringing up reasons for breaking confidentiality in those situations when the issue arises, but not as a matter of course to all clients.

## Confidentiality Cases to Consider

To assist you in considering the practical issues involved in confidentiality we present a case study involving drug use. We describe the actions of the counselor and ask you to evaluate her handling of the situation. Then we offer some brief open-ended situations dealing with confidentiality.

■ *An adolescent who uses drugs.*    Larry was 14 years old when he was sent to a family-guidance clinic by his parents. He was seen by a counselor who had nine years of counseling experience. At the first session the counselor saw Larry and his parents together. She told the parents in Larry's presence that what she and Larry discussed would be confidential and that she would not feel free to disclose information acquired through the sessions without Larry's permission. The parents seemed to understand that confidentiality was necessary in order for trust to develop between their son and his counselor.

Larry was reluctant at first to come in for counseling, but eventually he began to open up. As the sessions went on, he told the counselor that he was "heavily into drugs." Larry's parents knew that he had been using drugs at one time, but he had told them that he was no longer using them. The counselor listened to anecdote after anecdote about Larry's use of dangerous drugs, about how he "got loaded" at school every day, and about a few brushes with death when he was under the influence of drugs. Finally, she told the client that she did not want the responsibility of knowing he was experimenting with dangerous drugs and that she would not agree to continue the counseling relationship unless he stopped using them. At this stage she agreed not to inform his parents, on condition that he quit using drugs, but she did tell him that she would be talking with one of her colleagues about the situation.

Larry apparently stopped using drugs for several weeks. However, one night while he was under the influence of PCP, he had a serious automobile accident. As a result of the accident he became paralyzed for life. Larry's parents angrily asserted that they had had a legal right to be informed that he was unstable to the point of committing such an act, and they filed suit against both the counselor and the agency.

1. What is your general impression of the way Larry's counselor handled the case?
2. Do you think the counselor acted in a responsible way toward (a) herself? (b) the client? (c) the parents? (d) the agency?
3. Suppose you had been Larry's counselor and had been convinced that he was likely to hurt himself or others because of his drug use and his emotionally unstable condition. Would you have informed his parents, even though doing so would probably have ended your counseling relationship with him? Why or why not?
4. Which of the following courses of action might you have taken if you had been Larry's counselor? Check as many as you think are appropriate.

___ stating during the initial session the legal limits on you as a therapist

___ consulting with the director of the agency

___ referring Larry for psychological testing to determine the degree of his emotional disturbance

___ referring him to a psychiatrist for treatment

___ continuing to see him without any stipulations

___ insisting on a session with his parents as a condition of continuing counseling

___ informing the police or other authorities

___ requesting supervision and consultation from the agency

___ documenting your decisional process with a survey of pertinent research

5. Discuss in class other specific courses of action you might have pursued.

The following brief cases deal with ethical and legal aspects of confidentiality. What do you think you would do in each of these situations?

*You're a student counselor. For your internship you're working with college students on campus. Your intern group meets with a supervisor each week to discuss your cases. One day, while you're having lunch in the campus cafeteria with three other interns, they begin to discuss their cases in detail, even mentioning names of clients. They joke about some of the clients they're seeing, while nearby are other students who may be able to overhear this conversation. What would you do in this situation?*

___ I would tell the other interns to stop talking about their clients where other students could overhear them, and I would say that I thought they were behaving unprofessionally.

___ I would bring the matter up in our next practicum meeting with the supervisor.

___ I wouldn't do anything, since the students who could overhear the conversation would most likely not be that interested in what was being said.

___ I wouldn't do anything, because it's natural to discuss cases and make jokes to relieve one's own tensions.

___ I would encourage them to stop talking and to continue their discussion in a private place.

*You're leading a counseling group on a high school campus. The members have voluntarily joined the group. In one of the sessions several of the students discuss the drug traffic on their campus, and two of them reveal that they sell marijuana and various pills to their friends. You discuss this matter with them, and they claim that there is nothing wrong with using these drugs. They argue that most of the students on campus use drugs, that no one has been harmed, and that there isn't any difference between using drugs (which they know is illegal) and relying on alcohol (which many of them see their parents doing). What would you do in this situation?*

_____ Since their actions are illegal, I'd report them to the police.

_____ I'd do nothing, because their drug use doesn't seem to be a problem for them and I wouldn't want to jeopardize their trust in me.

_____ I would report the *condition* to the school authorities, while keeping the identities of the students confidential.

_____ I would let the students know that I planned to inform the school authorities of their actions and their names.

_____ I wouldn't take the matter seriously, because the laws relating to drugs are unfair.

_____ I would explore with the students their reasons for making this disclosure.

*You're counseling children in an elementary school. Barbara was referred to you by her teacher because she was becoming increasingly withdrawn. After several sessions Barbara tells you that she is afraid that her father might kill her and that he frequently beats her as a punishment. Until now she has lied about obvious bruises on her body, claiming that she fell off her bicycle and hurt herself. She shows you welts on her arms and back but tells you not to say anything to anyone because her father threatened a worse beating if she told anyone. What would you do in this situation?*

_____ I would respect Barbara's wishes and not tell anyone what I knew.

_____ I would report the situation to the principal and the school nurse.

_____ I would immediately go home with Barbara and talk to her parents.

_____ I would take Barbara home with me for a time.

_____ I would report the matter to the police.

_____ I would ask Barbara why she was telling me about the beatings if she didn't want me to reveal them to anyone else.

_____ I would tell Barbara that I had a legal obligation to make this situation known to the authorities but that I would work with her and not leave her alone in her fears.

# Duty to Warn and Protect

Mental-health professionals, spurred by the courts, have come increasingly in recent years to the realization of a double duty: to protect other people from potentially dangerous clients and to protect clients from themselves. In this section we look first at therapists' responsibility to warn and protect potential victims and then at the problems posed by suicidal clients.

## The Duty to Protect Potential Victims

As created by the courts, the responsibility to protect the public from dangerous acts of violent clients entails liability for civil damages when practitioners neglect this duty by (1) failing to diagnose or predict dangerousness, (2) failing to warn potential victims of violent behavior, (3) failing to commit dangerous individuals, and (4) prematurely discharging dangerous clients from the hospital (APA, 1985). The first two of these legally prescribed duties are illustrated in the case of *Tarasoff* v. *Board of Regents of the University of California*, which has been the subject of extensive analysis in the psychological literature.

**The Tarasoff Case.**    In August 1969 Prosenjit Poddar, who was a voluntary outpatient at the student health service on the Berkeley campus of the university, was in counseling with a psychologist named Moore. Poddar had confided to Moore his intention to kill an unnamed woman (who was readily identifiable as Tatiana Tarasoff) when she returned from an extended trip in Brazil. In consultation with other university counselors, Moore made the assessment that Poddar was dangerous and should be committed to a mental hospital for observation. Moore later called the campus police and told them of the death threat and of his conclusion that Poddar was dangerous. The campus officers did take Poddar into custody for questioning, but they later released him when he gave evidence of being "rational" and promised to stay away from Tarasoff. He was never confined to a treatment facility. Moore followed up his call with a formal letter requesting the assistance of the chief of the campus police. Later, Moore's supervisor asked that the letter be returned, ordered that the letter and Moore's case notes be destroyed, and asked that no further action be taken in the case. It should be noted that Tarasoff and her family were never made aware of this potential threat.

Shortly after Tarasoff's return from Brazil, Poddar killed her. Her parents filed suit against the Board of Regents and employees of the university for having failed to notify the intended victim of the threat. A lower court dismissed the suit, the parents appealed, and the California Supreme Court ruled in favor of the parents in 1976, holding that a failure to warn an intended victim was professionally irresponsible. The court's ruling requires that therapists breach confidentiality in cases where the general welfare and safety of others are involved. Since this was a California case, courts in other states are not bound to decide a similar case in the same way.

Under the *Tarasoff* decision the therapist must first accurately diagnose the client's condition for behaving in dangerous ways toward others. This first duty is judged by the standards of professional negligence. In this case the therapist did not fail in this duty. He even took an additional step of requesting that the dangerous person be detained by the campus police. But the court held that simply notifying the police was insufficient to protect the identifiable victim (Laughran & Bakken, 1984).

In their discussion of the implications of the *Tarasoff* case Everstine and his associates (1980) note that the crucial point of the Supreme Court decision involved the failure of the psychologist and his supervisor to provide a warning of violence to the intended victim or to her parents. In its conclusion the court affirmed the guiding principle that was basic to its decision: "The public policy favoring protection of the confidential character of patient-psychotherapist communications must yield to the extent to which disclosure is essential to avert danger to others. The protective privilege ends where the public peril begins."

In their assessment of *"Tarasoff:* Five Years Later," Knapp and Vandecreek (1982) make the point that variations in state laws make the procedures involved in the "duty to warn" a difficult matter. In the *Tarasoff* case the identity of the victim was known. However, therapists are often concerned about their legal responsibility when the identity of the intended victim is unknown. What are the therapist's obligations in cases of generalized statements of hostility? What is the responsibility of the therapist to predict future violence? In their recommendations to therapists Knapp and Vandecreek (1982) write: "Psychotherapists need only follow reasonable standards in predicting violence. Psychotherapists are not liable for the failure to warn when the propensity toward violence is unknown or would be unknown by other psychotherapists using ordinary skill" (pp. 514–515).

Their point is that therapists should not become intimidated by every idle fantasy, for every impulsive threat is not evidence of imminent danger. In their opinion recent behavioral acts can best predict future violence. In addition to warning potential victims, Knapp and Vandecreek suggest, practitioners should consider other alternatives that could diffuse the danger and, at the same time, satisfy their legal duty. They recommend seeking consultation with other professionals who have expertise in dealing with potentially violent people, and also documenting the steps taken.

In commenting on the Supreme Court's decision in the *Tarasoff* case Siegel (1979) asserts that "this was a day in court for the law and not for the mental health professions" (p. 253). He argues that, if absolute confidentiality had been the policy, the psychologist might have been able to keep Poddar in treatment, ultimately saving the life of Tarasoff. According to Siegel, the potential protection of Tarasoff was eliminated when the therapist contacted the police, but it might not have been eliminated if the psychologist had kept Poddar in treatment. However, other professionals are willing to accept the duty to warn, and it appears that for the indefinite future this will remain a legal requirement in California. There are certain conditions under which a therapist must exchange the professional role for the role of a citizen; therapists cannot hide behind the shield of privileged communication (Everstine et al., 1980).

In his assessment of the *Tarasoff* case Schutz (1982) points out the risk factors that led the court to determine that a duty to warn was a valid expression of due care in this case. First of all, the therapist did indeed make the prediction of violence based on the client/therapist relationship. Then this prediction came to pass, which reinforced the principle of foreseeability of risk through special knowledge. Finally, in the view of the court the unsuccessful attempt to commit Poddar was poorly handled.

The decision in *Tarasoff* has been criticized by both the legal and the mental-health professions. In spite of this criticism, the doctrine that therapists have a duty to protect potential victims has been endorsed by several other state and federal courts. These include courts in New Jersey, Nebraska, Indiana, Georgia, Michigan, Washington, and Kansas. In a New Jersey case a court held a psychiatrist liable for failing to protect a former girlfriend who was killed by an adolescent patient, even though the patient had never expressed any intent to harm her and had talked only about his jealousy. Some courts, however, have limited the duty to protect to victims who were known and identifiable (Levine, 1987).

**The Bradley Case.**    A second case illustrates the duty not to negligently release a dangerous client. In *Bradley Center* v. *Wessner* the patient, Wessner, had been voluntarily admitted to a facility for psychiatric care. Wessner was upset over his wife's extramarital affair. He had repeatedly threatened to kill her and her lover and had even admitted to a therapist that he was carrying a weapon in his car for that purpose. He was given an unrestricted weekend pass so that he could visit his children, who were living with his wife. He met his wife and her lover in the home and proceeded to shoot and kill both of them. The children filed a wrongful death suit, alleging that the psychiatric center had breached a duty to exercise control over Wessner. The Georgia Supreme Court ruled that a physician has a duty to take reasonable care to prevent a potentially dangerous patient from inflicting harm (Laughran & Bakken, 1984).

**The Jablonski Case.**    A third legal ruling underscores the duty to commit a dangerous individual. The intended victim's knowledge of a threat does not relieve therapists of the duty to protect, according to the decision in *Jablonski* v. *United States*. Meghan Jablonski filed suit for the wrongful death of her mother, Melinda Kimball, who was murdered by Philip Jablonski, the man with whom she had been living. Earlier, Philip Jablonski had agreed to a psychiatric examination at a hospital. The physicians determined that there was no emergency and thus no basis for involuntary commitment. Kimball later again accompanied Jablonski to the hospital and expressed fears for her own safety. She was told by a doctor that "you should consider staying away from him." Again, the doctors concluded that there was no basis for involuntary hospitalization and released him. Shortly thereafter Jablonski killed Kimball.

The Ninth U.S. Circuit Court of Appeals found that failure to obtain Jablonski's prior medical history constituted malpractice. The essence of *Jablonski* is a negligent failure to commit (Laughran & Bakken, 1984).

**The Hedlund Case.**    The decision in *Hedlund* v. *Superior Court* extends the duty to warn not only to the potential victim but also to anyone who might be near the intended victim and who might also be in danger. LaNita Wilson and Stephen Wilson had received psychotherapy from a psychological assistant, Bonnie Hedlund. During treatment Stephen told the therapist that he intended to harm LaNita. He later did assault her, in the presence of her child. The allegation was that the child had sustained "serious emotional injury and psychological trauma."

In keeping with the *Tarasoff* decision, the California Supreme Court held (1) that a therapist has a duty first to exercise a "reasonable degree of skill, knowledge, and care ordinarily possessed and exercised by members [of that professional specialty] under similar circumstances" in making a prediction about the chances of a client's acting dangerously to others and (2) that therapists must "exercise reasonable care to protect the foreseeable victim of that danger." One way to protect the victim is by giving a warning of peril. The court in the *Hedlund* case held that breach of such a duty with respect to third persons constitutes "professional negligence" (Laughran & Bakken, 1984).

In the *Hedlund* case the duty to warn of potentially dangerous conduct was owed to the mother, not to her child, against whom no threats had been made. However, the duty to both could have been fulfilled by warning the mother that she and her child were in danger.

The duty to exercise due care is independent of the duty to warn a potential victim, which can arise only if the intended victim is known. This is consistent with the *Tarasoff* decision—that once a dangerous patient is identified, the therapist "bears a duty to exercise reasonable care to protect the foreseeable victim of the danger."

■ *A case to consider.* You're working with a young man, Kevin, whom you think is potentially violent. During his sessions with you Kevin talks about his impulses to hurt others and himself, and he describes times when he has seriously beaten his girlfriend. He tells you that she is afraid to leave him because she thinks he'll beat her even more savagely. He later tells you that sometimes he gets so angry that he comes very close to killing her. You believe that he is very likely to seriously harm and possibly even kill the young woman. Which of the following would you do?

____ I would notify Kevin's girlfriend that she might be in grave danger.

____ I would notify the police or other authorities.

____ I would keep Kevin's threats to myself, because I couldn't be sure that he would act on them.

____ I would seek a second opinion from a colleague.

____ I would inform my director or supervisor.

____ I would refer Kevin to another therapist.

____ I would arrange to have Kevin hospitalized.

What else might you do?

**Guidelines for Dealing with Dangerous Clients.** Stimulated mainly by the *Tarasoff* ruling, most college counseling centers have developed guidelines regarding the duty to warn and protect when the welfare of others is at stake. These guidelines generally specify how to deal with emotionally disturbed students, violent behavior, threats, suicidal possibilities, and other circumstances in which counselors may be legally and ethically required to breach confidentiality.

The question raised by these documents is "What are the responsibilities of counselors to their clients or to others when, in the professional judgment of the counselor, there is a high degree of probability that a client will seriously harm another person or destroy property?" Many counselors find it difficult to predict when clients pose a serious threat to others. Clients are encouraged to engage in open dialogue in therapeutic relationships; believing that what they say is confidential, they may express feelings or thoughts about doing physical harm to others. Generally, these are expressions of feelings, and relatively few of these threats are actually carried out. Counselors should therefore *not* be expected to routinely reveal all threats, for such a policy of disclosure could seriously disrupt clients' relationships with their therapists or with the persons who are "threatened." Counselors have the obligation not to disclose confidential material unless such disclosures are necessary to prevent harm to clients or to others.

What is expected of counselors is that they exercise reasonable professional judgment and apply practices that are commonly accepted by professionals in their specialty. If they determine that clients pose a serious danger of violence to others, they are obliged to exercise reasonable care to protect the would-be victims. Some guidance can be obtained from the procedures in the accompanying box, developed by the Organization of Counseling Center Directors in Higher Education.

## Counseling Center Procedures for Dealing with Threats

I. Notice to counselors
A counselor has a legal responsibility (*Tarasoff*) to follow these procedures when he/she becomes aware of potentially violent behavior on the part of the counselee, i.e., homicide.

II. Evidence of potentially violent behavior
The following two factual ingredients are sufficient cause for notification to the intended victim and for the invocation of these procedures:
A. a threat to others or to property which could reasonably cause bodily injury, (as defined in I above), made in your presence
B. a threat as defined in A above, and a known history of violent attacks towards others by client
Additional factors to be considered in this assessment include:
A. The intended action is sufficiently identifiable.
B. The client has or potentially could have the ability to carry out the threat.

III. Procedure
A. As part of the process of identifying the intended violent action (threatened violence towards a specified victim), the counselor should immediately notify the Counseling Center Director, Associate Director, or other professional personally designated by the Director.

*(continued)*

*(continued)*
   1. This conversation should be noted in writing and signed by both parties.
   2. One may wish to assess the potential for violence by referring to the checklist attached.
  B. Based upon this consultation, a mutual decision shall be made with respect to the danger and whether to begin the procedures.
   1. It is recommended that an Emergency Procedures Panel, of at least two staff, be appointed by the Director in each Counseling Center to assess danger and determine a course of action.
   2. In cases where there appears to be reasonable concern for danger, a decision may be made to undertake further evaluation. In those instances, steps C through G may be initiated so long as there remains reasonable concern.
  C. In addition, a second optional step may be taken:
  The Emergency Procedures Panel may meet to determine a treatment plan or intervention strategies to consider other options, such as:
   1. further psychological assessment, including the administering of individual psychological tests
   2. referral to a staff counselor or consulting psychiatrist for further differential diagnosis and opinion on possible medical or neurological involvement
   3. other appropriate medical diagnostic or laboratory procedures to document the need for ongoing medical/psychiatric collaboration
  D. Continual contact with the Director, Associate Director, or other professional designated by the Director to document and review steps taken in carrying out the above.
  E. Notify the client at the time of disclosure, as set out in Section II above, that you have a duty to warn the intended victim and the campus police and/or city police.
  F. Notify the campus police, Health Center, or other appropriate agencies. This should include the community police of the intended victim. Be specific about the threat and the nature of the assistance required.
  G. Notify the intended victim. Be specific regarding the nature of the threat and other steps then in process or intended, i.e., telephone, certified mail.
  H. In the case of an intern seeing the client, the direct supervisor becomes responsible for the implementation of the above procedures and guidelines. Depending upon the level of experience and skills of the intern, a decision must be made about the appropriateness of the intern continuing as the primary counselor.
IV. Criteria for judgment of violent behavior
 The clinician may evaluate the following four elements of potential violent behavior. Generally, a positive answer to two or more would warrant notification of an intended victim, and/or other precautionary measures. This checklist is not intended as an exhaustive list. The counselor should exercise reasonable professional judgment in adding to or subtracting from this list in light of the particular circumstances of the case.
   1. Has the client expressed some specific intention to commit violence, as against transitory thoughts or expression of feelings?

                            Yes ___ No ___
    a. Has the client identified the kind of action he/she intends?

                            Yes ___ No ___
    b. Does the client have the ability to carry out the action (i.e., weapon, proximity to victim, etc.)?

                            Yes ___ No ___
   2. Has the client identified an intended victim and/or plan of action?

                            Yes ___ No ___

*(continued)*

*(continued)*

3. Is the client able to understand what he/she is doing *and* capable of exercising self control? (History of prior violence would be negative indication.)

Yes ___ No ___

4. Is the client capable of collaborating with the therapist in maintaining control of his/her behavior?

Yes ___ No ___

From "The Psychotherapist's Responsibility toward Third Parties under Current California Law," by W. Laughran and G. M. Bakken, 1984, *Western State University Law Review, 12,* pp. 32–34.

## The Duty to Protect Suicidal Clients

Many therapists inform their clients that they have an ethical and legal obligation to break confidentiality when they have good reason to suspect suicidal behavior. Even if clients argue that they can do what they want with their life, including taking it, therapists do have a duty to protect suicidal clients. In the preceding discussion we emphasized the therapist's obligation to warn and to protect *others,* but these principles apply also to the client. The crux of the issue is knowing when to take a client's hints seriously enough to report the condition. Certainly not every mention of the possibility of taking one's own life justifies extraordinary measures.

The evaluation and management of suicidal risk is a source of great stress for most therapists. It brings to the surface many of the troublesome issues that clinical practitioners must face, such as their degree of influence, competence, level of involvement with a client, responsibility, legal obligations, and ability to make life-or-death decisions. Szasz (1986) has noted that failure to prevent suicide is now one of the leading reasons for successful malpractice suits against mental-health professionals and institutions.

**Guidelines for Assessing Suicidal Behavior.**    Although it is not possible to prevent every suicide, it is possible to recognize the existence of common crises that may precipitate a suicide attempt and reach out to people who are experiencing these crises. Counselors must take the "cry for help" seriously and have the necessary knowledge and skills to intervene once they make an assessment that a client is suicidal (Fujimura, Weis, & Cochran, 1985). The following guidelines are important factors to consider in making the evaluation of suicidal risk. Although this is a partial list, it does give some idea about what to be alert for in making an assessment (Fujimura et al., 1985; Pope, 1985c).

- Direct verbal warnings must be taken seriously, as they are one of the most useful single predictors of a suicide.
- The therapist should pay attention to previous suicide attempts, as these are the best single predictor of lethality. Up to 80% of suicides were preceded by a prior attempt.

- One common characteristic that all suicide victims share is a feeling of depression. Sleep disruption, which can intensify depression, is a key sign. For people with clinical depression the suicide rate is about 20 times greater than that of the general population.
- A sense of hopelessness seems to be closely associated with suicidal intentions. Individuals may feel helpless, desperate, and worthless.
- Definitiveness of a plan is an indicator. The more definite the plan, the more serious is the situation. Suicidal individuals should be asked to talk about their plans. They should be asked to explore their suicidal fantasies.
- Clients who have a history of severe alcohol or drug abuse are at greater risk than the general population. Between one-fourth and one-third of all suicides are associated with alcohol as a contributing factor.
- Giving prized possessions away, finalizing business affairs, or revising wills may be critical signs.
- The suicide rate for men is about three times greater than that of women. More men than women succeed in committing suicide. The suicide rate rises rapidly for men until the age of 35.
- Living alone tends to increase the risk of suicide. Single individuals are twice as likely as married people to commit suicide.
- Unemployment increases the risk for suicide.
- A history of previous psychiatric treatment or hospitalization is a pertinent factor. Clients who have been hospitalized for emotional disorders are more likely to be inclined to suicide.
- Clients who do not have resource and support systems available are more at risk. A person's refusal to use these systems signifies a cutting off of communication and makes the intent more serious.

**The Case for Suicide Prevention.**   Fujimura and her associates (1985) contend that most suicides could be prevented if those who work with suicidal clients could learn to recognize, evaluate, and intervene effectively in crisis situations. Suicidal individuals are often hoping that somebody will listen to their cry. Many of these clients are struggling with short-term crises, and if they can be given help in learning to cope with the immediate problem, their potential for suicide can be greatly reduced.

Therapists have the responsibility to prevent suicide if they can reasonably anticipate it. Once a counselor determines that a significant risk does exist, appropriate action must be taken. Failure to take action can result in the therapist's being held liable (Schutz, 1982). Liability generally arises when counselors fail to act in such a way as to prevent the suicide or do something that might contribute to it.

Once the therapist makes the assessment of foreseeable risk, what are some possible courses of action? What are some ethical and legal options to consider? How can counselors take appropriate steps to demonstrate that a reasonable attempt is being made to control the suicidal client? The following guidelines in managing suicidal behavior of clients are adapted from the writings of Schutz (1982), Pope (1985c), and Fujimura and her colleagues (1985).

• Obtain training for suicide prevention and for crisis-intervention methods. Keep up to date with current research, theory, and practice.

• Recognize the importance of knowing how, when, and where to appropriately refer clients whose concerns are beyond the boundary of your competence. Know your personal and professional limits.

• Be aware of the hospitals where you can make referrals. Know the procedures for both voluntary and involuntary hospitalization of suicidal clients. If the client is assessed as being suicidal and unable to control self-destructive impulses, psychiatric hospitalization becomes the most logical course of action. A commitment procedure may be called for as a way of protecting the client.

• When considering hospitalization, weigh the benefits, the drawbacks, and the possible effects. If the client does enter a hospital, pay particular attention to the increased risk of suicide immediately after discharge.

• Become familiar with the legal standards as they affect this area of practice.

• If suicidal issues arise, consult an attorney with expertise in this area.

• Be clear and firm with the client, and do not allow yourself to be manipulated by threats. Also, give clear messages to the client. The literature reveals the dangers of using techniques such as paradoxical intention with suicidal clients.

• Especially in crisis counseling, make an assessment of your clients for suicidal risk during the early phase of therapy, and keep alert to this issue during the course of therapy.

• For services that take place within a clinic or agency setting, ensure that clear and appropriate lines of responsibility are explicit and are fully understood by everyone.

• Work with clients so that suicidal instruments are not within easy access. If the client possesses any weapons, make sure that they are in the hands of a third party.

• Consider increasing the frequency of the counseling sessions.

• Work with the client's strengths and desires to remain alive.

• Attempt to communicate realistic hopes.

• Develop a therapeutic contract with suicidal clients. If a client says that when life gets too unbearable he or she will commit suicide, the therapist can firmly point out that the client is probably sabotaging their work together. Many therapists call a client in crisis at appointed times or encourage the client to call them in the event of serious loss of hope.

• Be willing to communicate your caring. Suicidal people sometimes interpret the unwillingness of others to listen as a sign that they do not care. People may be driven to suicide by an avoidance of the topic on the part of the listener. Remember that caring entails some specific actions and setting of limits on your part.

• Do not make yourself the only person responsible for the decisions and actions of your clients. Take your share of professional responsibility, but do not accept all of the responsibility. Your clients must share in the responsibility of their ultimate decisions. Also, in working with clients in crisis attempt to develop a supportive network of family and friends to help them face their struggles. Of course, let your clients know that you are trying to create a social-support system, and enlist their help in building this resource of caring people.

• Let the client know that you will be seeking consultation and discussing possible courses of action. It is a good idea to document in writing the steps you take in crisis cases, for documentation may be necessary to demonstrate that you did use sound professional judgment and acted within acceptable legal and ethical parameters.

• Remember that clients are ultimately responsible for their actions and that there is only so much that you can reasonably do to prevent self-destructive actions. Even if you take specific steps to lessen the chances of your clients' committing suicide, they can still take this ultimate step at some time.

**The Case against Suicide Prevention.**     Now that we have looked at the case for suicide prevention, we explore another point of view. Szasz (1986) challenges the perspective that mental-health professionals have an absolute professional duty to try to prevent suicide. He presents the thesis that suicide is an act of a moral agent who is ultimately responsible, and opposes coercive methods of preventing suicide, such as forced hospitalization. Szasz argues that by attempting to prevent suicide, mental-health practitioners often ally themselves with the police power of the state and resort to coercion, therefore identifying themselves as foes of individual liberty and responsibility. In taking this course of action professionals assume the burden of responsibility of keeping clients alive, depriving their clients of their rightful share of accountability for their own actions. It is the client's responsibility to choose to live or to die. According to Szasz, if clients seek professional help for their suicidal tendencies, the helper has an ethical obligation—and in some cases a legal obligation—to provide the help being sought. On the other hand, Szasz argues, if clients do not seek such help and actively reject it, then the professional's duty is either to persuade them to accept help or to leave them alone. He puts the core of his argument as follows:

> Because I value individual liberty highly and am convinced that liberty and responsibility are indivisible, I want to enlarge the scope of liberty and responsibility. In the present instance, this means opposing policies of suicide prevention that minimize the responsibility of individuals for killing themselves and supporting policies that maximize their responsibility for doing so. In other words, we should make it more difficult for suicidal persons to reject responsibility for deliberately taking their own lives and for mental health professionals to assume responsibility for keeping such persons alive [1986, p. 810].

It should be noted that Szasz is not claiming that suicide is always good or a morally legitimate option; rather, his key point is that the power of the state should not be used to either prohibit or prevent people from taking their own life. The right to suicide implies that we must abstain from empowering agents of the state to coercively prevent it.

**Your Stance on Suicide Prevention.**   You will recall that in Chapter 3 we explored the issue of the right to die. Your own value system will have a lot to do with the actions you would be likely to take. Considering the arguments for and against suicide prevention, what is your stance on this complex issue? Where do you stand with respect to your ethical obligations to recognize, evaluate, and intervene with potentially suicidal clients? To what degree do you agree with the guidelines listed earlier? Which are the ones that make the most sense to you? Do you take a contrary position on at least some cases of suicide? How do you justify your position? To what extent do you agree or disagree with the contention of Szasz that current policies of suicide prevention displace responsibility from the client to the therapist and that this needlessly undermines the ethic of self-responsibility?

After clarifying your own values underlying the professional's role in assessing and preventing suicide, reflect on the following case of a client who is threatening suicide. If he were your client, what course of action would you take?

■ *A client who threatens suicide.*   Emmanuel was a middle-aged man who complained of emptiness in life, loneliness, depression, and a lack of will to live any longer. He was in individual therapy for seven months with a clinical psychologist in private practice. Using psychodiagnostic procedures, both objective tests and projective techniques, she determined that he had serious depressive tendencies and was potentially self-destructive. Emmanuel had come to her for therapy as a final attempt to find some meaning that would show him that his life had significance. In their sessions he explored in depth the history of his failures, the isolation he felt, the meaninglessness of his life, and his bouts with feelings of worthlessness and depression. With her encouragement he experimented with new ways of behaving in the hope that he would find reasons to go on living. Finally, after seven months of searching, he decided that he wanted to take his own life. He told his therapist that he was convinced he had been deluding himself in thinking that anything in his life would change for the better and that he felt good about finally summoning the courage to end his life. He informed her that he would not be seeing her again.

The therapist expressed her concern that Emmanuel was very capable of taking his life at this time because so far he had not been able to see any light at the end of the tunnel. She acknowledged that the decision to commit suicide was not a sudden one, for they had discussed this wish for several sessions, but she let him know that she wanted him to give therapy more of a chance. He replied that he was truly grateful to her for helping him to find his answer within himself and that at least he could end his life with dignity in his own eyes. He stated firmly that he didn't want her to attempt to obstruct his plans in any way. She asked that he postpone his decision for at least a week and return to discuss the matter more fully. He told her he wasn't certain whether he would keep this appointment, but he agreed to consider it.

The therapist did nothing further. During the following week she heard from a friend that Emmanuel had committed suicide by taking an overdose of sleeping pills.

1. What do you think of the way the therapist dealt with her client?
2. What is your view of suicide?
3. What might you have done differently if you had been Emmanuel's therapist?
4. How do you think that your viewpoint regarding suicide influenced your answer to the preceding question?
5. Which of the following courses of action might you have pursued if you had been Emmanuel's counselor?
   ____ committing him to a state hospital for observation, even against his will, for a period of 48 hours
   ____ consulting with another professional as soon as he began to discuss suicide as an option
   ____ respecting his choice of suicide, even if you didn't agree with it
   ____ informing the police and reporting the seriousness of his threat
   ____ informing members of his family of his intentions, even though he didn't want you to
   ____ bargaining with him in every way possible in an effort to persuade him to keep on trying to find some meaning in life
6. Discuss in class any other steps you might have taken in this case.

## Chapter Summary

All the ethical codes of mental-health organizations specify the centrality of informed consent. One of the best guarantees of protecting the rights of clients is for therapists to develop procedures that will aid their clients in making informed choices. We have seen that, legally, informed consent entails the client's ability to act freely in making rational decisions. The process of informed consent includes providing information about the nature of therapy as well as the rights and responsibilities of both the therapist and the client. A basic challenge therapists face is to provide accurate and sufficient information to clients yet at the same time not overwhelm them with too much information too soon. Thus, informed consent can best be viewed as an ongoing process during the early course of therapy that is aimed at increasing the range of choices and responsibility of the client as an active therapeutic partner.

Confidentiality in therapy has both ethical and legal aspects that demand careful consideration. The purpose of confidentiality is to protect clients from unauthorized disclosures by professionals. Generally, therapists have a moral, ethical, legal, and professional obligation not to breach confidentiality without the client's knowledge and authorization unless it is in the client's interest to do so or unless the law requires disclosure of certain information. It is essential that clients learn about the limitations of confidentiality. Related to confidentiality is privileged communication, which is a legal concept. It refers to the rights of clients not to have their disclosures used in court without their consent. If clients waive their privilege, however, the professional does not have grounds for withholding the information. The privilege belongs not to the therapist but to clients for their protection. In most states the statutes determine which mental-health professionals are included under the privileged-communication concept. Therapists can be held legally responsible for violating a client's right to confidentiality. Many therapists are under the mistaken assumption that, if their clients do not have privileged communication by statute, the responsibilities for confidentiality are less or do not exist. Therapists have an obligation to maintain the privacy of their clients' communications except in compelling circumstances.

Court decisions have provided an expanded perspective on the therapist's duty to protect the public. As a result of the *Tarasoff* case, for instance, therapists are now becoming aware of their responsibility to the potential victims of a client's violent behavior. This duty spans interventions from warnings to threatened individuals to involuntary commitment of clients. Therapists are vulnerable to malpractice action when they demonstrate negligent failure to diagnose dangerousness, negligent failure to warn a known victim once such a diagnosis has been made, negligent failure to commit a dangerous person, or negligent failure to keep a dangerous client committed.

Therapists also have a duty to protect clients who are likely to injure or kill themselves. This responsibility implies that practitioners develop skills in making accurate assessments of potentially suicidal persons. Once they diagnose a client as a danger to himself or herself, they are responsible for preventing suicide by acting in professionally acceptable ways. A dissenting opinion on this issue is that of Szasz (1986), who challenges the assumption that therapists should be held accountable for a client's decision to die. He believes that suicide is an ultimate right and responsibility of the client and that it is unethical for therapists to employ coercive measures aimed at preventing it.

In dealing with either potentially violent clients or suicidal clients, professionals must know their state laws and their profession's ethical code. Although this knowledge is essential, it alone is not sufficient. Professional judgment always comes into the picture. To assist you in refining your judgment, we have presented guidelines for dealing with dangerous clients and guidelines for intervention with suicidal clients. It is important to re-

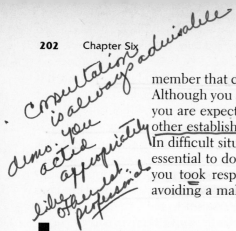

Consultation is always advisable. Demo: you acted appropriately like other professional.

member that consultation with colleagues is always advisable in these cases. Although you are not expected to be perfect in your professional judgments, you are expected to demonstrate that you are able to act in ways that most other established professionals would judge as appropriate and responsible. In difficult situations such as those we have highlighted in this chapter it is essential to document your actions in writing. If you are able to show that you took responsible actions in problematic situations, your chances of avoiding a malpractice suit are greatly increased.

## Suggested Activities

1. As a class project form small groups, and create an informed-consent document. What does your group think clients must be told either before therapy begins or during the first few sessions? How might you implement your informed-consent procedures?

2. Working in small groups in class, explore the topic of the rights clients have in counseling. One person in each group can serve as a recorder. When the groups reconvene for a general class meeting, the recorders for the various groups share their lists of clients' rights on a three-point scale: "extremely important," "important," and somewhat important." What rights can your class agree on as the most important?

3. Select some of the open-ended cases presented in this chapter to role-play with a fellow student. One of you chooses a client you feel you can identify with, and the other becomes the counselor. Conduct a counseling interview. Afterward, talk about how each of you felt during the interview, and discuss alternative courses of action that could have been taken.

4. Providing clients with access to their files and records seems to be in line with the consumer-rights movement, which is having an impact on the human-services professions. What are your own thoughts on providing your clients with this information? What information would you want to share with your clients? In what ways might you go about providing them with this information? What might you do if there were a conflict between your views and the policies of the agency that employed you?

5. As a class project several students can investigate the laws of your state pertaining to confidentiality and privileged communication and then present their findings to the class. What kinds of mental-health providers in your state can offer their clients privileged communication? What are the exceptions to this privilege? Under what circumstances are you legally required to breach confidentiality? Regarding confidentiality in counseling minors, what are the laws of your state that you should know?

6. In small groups discuss specific circumstances in which you would break confidentiality, and see whether you can agree on some general

guidelines. When your class reconvenes for a general meeting, the results of the small groups can be discussed.

7. Discuss some ways in which you can prepare clients for issues pertaining to confidentiality. How can you teach them about the purposes of confidentiality and the legal restrictions on it? Examine how you would do this in various situations, such as school, group work, marital and family counseling, and counseling with minors.

8. In a class debate one side can take the position that absolute confidentiality is necessary to promote full client disclosure. The other side can argue for a limited confidentiality that still promotes effective therapy.

9. In small groups discuss the cases and guidelines presented in this chapter on the duty to protect potential victims from violent clients. If you found yourself faced with a potentially dangerous client, what specific steps might you take to carry out this duty? Each group elects a recorder, and when the class reconvenes, each group shares the trend that emerged.

10. A class debate can be structured around the *case for* versus the *case against* suicide prevention. Failure to prevent suicide is currently one of the main reasons for successful malpractice suits against mental-health professionals and institutions (Szasz, 1986). Divide the class into teams for a lively exchange on this controversial issue.

■
## Suggested Readings

We again suggest that you review the ethical codes presented in the Appendix with reference to those principles that apply to the topics we raise in this chapter.

For both sides of the question "Is involuntary commitment to mental institutions immoral?" see Levine (1987). On informed consent see Goodyear and Sinnett (1984), Bray, Shepherd, and Hays (1985), Lindsey (1984), Deardorff, Cross, and Hupprich (1984), Miller and Thelen (1986), Muehleman, Pickens, and Robinson (1985), Mappes, Robb, and Engels (1985), Smith (1981), Woody (1984), and Handelsman, Kemper, Kesson-Craig, McLain, and Johnsrud (1986). In "The Ethics of Confidentiality and Privileged Communication" Sheeley and Herlihy (1986) discuss the variations between states with respect to privileged communication in counseling; they also provide guidelines for practitioners on the disclosure of information. On privileged-communication laws for therapists see Knapp and Vandecreek (1985), and Woody (1984). On ethical and legal ramifications of confidentiality see Mappes et al., (1985). On the public's knowledge and beliefs about confidentiality see Miller and Thelen (1986) and McGuire, Toal, and Blau (1985). On the limits of confidentiality see Muehleman, Pickens, and Robinson (1985) and Denkowski and Denkowski (1982). For discussions of landmark court cases, the duty to warn and duty to protect, and guidelines for dealing with dangerous clients see Laughran and Bakken (1984) and APA (1985). Woody (1984) also provides a helpful discussion of duty to warn. For a discussion of both sides of the question "Is it a therapist's duty to protect potential victims of violence?" see Levine (1987).

For guidelines on the assessment of suicidal behavior see Fujimura, Weis, and Cochran (1985), Pope (1985c), Ray and Johnson (1983), T. E. Ellis (1986), and Schutz (1982). For the case against suicide prevention see Szasz (1986). For both sides of the question "Can suicide be rational?" see Levine (1987).

# SEVEN

# The Client/Therapist Relationship, Unethical Behavior, and Malpractice Issues

- Pre-Chapter Self-Inventory
- Introduction
- Client Dependence as an Ethical Issue
- Manipulation as Unethical Behavior
- Dual Relationships and Sexual Contact
- Dealing with Unethical Behavior
- Malpractice Issues in the Helping Professions
- Chapter Summary
- Suggested Activities
- Suggested Readings

# Pre-Chapter Self-Inventory

*Directions:* For each statement, indicate the response that most closely identifies your beliefs and attitudes. Use the following code:

3 = I *agree*, in most respects, with this statement.
2 = I am *undecided* in my opinion about this statement.
1 = I *disagree*, in most respects, with this statement.

_____ 1. A therapist should be aware of any client dependency, since it is counterproductive in therapy.

_____ 2. Mystification of the client/therapist relationship tends to increase client dependence and decrease clients' ability to assert their rights in therapy.

_____ 3. A good therapist gets involved in the client's case without getting involved with the client emotionally.

_____ 4. A therapeutic relationship should be maintained only as long as it is clear that the client is benefiting.

_____ 5. Much of therapy is really the "purchase of friendship."

_____ 6. Touching, whether erotic or not, is best avoided in counseling, because it can easily be misunderstood by the client.

_____ 7. Therapists who touch clients of the opposite sex, but not those of the same sex, are guilty of sexist practice.

_____ 8. Although it may be unwise to form social relationships with clients while they are in counseling, there should be no ethical or professional prohibition on social relationships *after* the termination of counseling.

_____ 9. If I were sexually attracted to a client, I am quite sure I would feel guilty.

_____ 10. If I were counseling a client who was sexually attracted to me, I think I might refer this client to another counselor.

_____ 11. I might be inclined to barter my therapy services for goods if I were working with needy clients.

_____ 12. Sexual involvement with a client is never ethical, even after therapy has ended.

_____ 13. Unethical behavior is best defined as anything that is in violation of a professional code of ethics.

_____ 14. Unethical behavior is anything that results in harm to the client.

_____ 15. If another professional were doing something I considered to be unethical, I would report him or her to the state licensing agency.

_____ 16. I should devote some time to thinking about ways to lessen the chances of unethical behavior on my part.

_____ 17. Following the ethical codes of my profession implies that I will avoid unethical behavior.

_____ 18. It is inappropriate for a professional organization to have the power to sanction its members for unethical conduct.

___ 19. Personally, the potential of a malpractice suit concerns me greatly and makes me want to practice conservatively.

___ 20. I should think about specific ways to protect myself from malpractice suits.

# Introduction

In this chapter we discuss unethical practice relating to the client/therapist relationship. Although some of the issues and cases we present may seem clear-cut to you, in the sense that you might judge certain behavior to be clearly unethical, others may not be so cut-and-dried. In these cases it becomes a personal challenge to make an honest appraisal of your behavior and its impact on clients. To us, unethical behavior is behavior that reflects a lack of awareness or concern about the impact of the behavior on clients. For some counselors, it may take the form of placing their personal needs above the needs of their clients, at the expense of their clients' welfare. Since this abuse of clients is often done in a subtle way, you might think about specific ways of recognizing when and how you might be meeting your needs at the expense of your clients. We hope you will develop your own guidelines for determining when you're exploiting your clients.

Consider the following list of behaviors, and ask yourself whether you think these practices are ethical. Use the following code:

A = This is unethical.
B = I can't decide.
C = This is ethical.

___ 1. consistently putting the focus on yourself in a session by talking about your present or past problems

___ 2. encouraging your client to have more frequent sessions, mainly because you need money

___ 3. not referring a client, even when you doubt whether you can be useful to the person, because you don't want to admit that you can't work with everyone

___ 4. deceiving a client, under the guise of being helpful

___ 5. accepting close friends or relatives as clients

___ 6. imposing your values on clients by subtly steering them toward goals you think are worthwhile

___ 7. consulting with a colleague about a specific client without that client's permission

___ 8. agreeing to enter into a counseling relationship with a minor without first securing parental permission

___ 9. deliberately fostering client dependency, with the rationale that it is essential for clients to relive early-childhood wishes and dependencies in the therapy situation before they can become autonomous

___ 10. keeping clients unaware of the process of therapy and increasing the mystery of therapy, on the ground that it gives the therapist the power and influence necessary to effect significant change

___ 11. ignoring unethical practices by a colleague out of fear that any action would create an unpleasant strain in your working situation

Now decide which of these behaviors you consider to be the most serious breaches of professional ethics. What are your reasons for considering them unethical? Are there any conditions under which you think they might be ethical?

We give the topic of *dual relationships* central attention in this chapter because of the ethical problems raised by mixing one's professional relationship with a client with another kind of relationship. In addition, since malpractice suits are on the rise, as well as anxiety over being sued, we provide a discussion of the main causes of such suits and suggest some guidelines for protecting yourself. We also review a few trends in legal liability in the helping professions.

## Client Dependence as an Ethical Issue

Clients frequently experience a period of dependence on therapy or on their therapist. This temporary dependence isn't necessarily a bad thing. Some clients are people who have exaggerated the importance of being independent. They see the need to consult a professional as a sign of weakness. When these people do allow themselves to need others, their dependence doesn't necessarily present an ethical issue.

An ethical issue does arise, however, when counselors *encourage* dependence on the part of their clients. They may do so for any number of reasons. Counselor interns need clients, and sometimes they may keep clients coming to counseling longer than is necessary because they will look bad if they "lose" a client. Some therapists in private practice might fail to challenge clients who show up and pay regularly, even though they appear to be getting nowhere. Some therapists foster dependence in their clients in subtle ways out of a need to feel important. When clients play a helpless role and ask for answers, these counselors may readily tell them what to do. Dependent clients can begin to view their therapists as all-knowing and all-wise; therapists who have a need to be perceived in this way may act in ways that will keep their clients immature and dependent, thus feeding off the dependency needs of clients in order to gain a sense of significance.

A related issue involves attempts by professionals to keep the therapeutic process mysterious. This effort can have the result of encouraging clients to remain powerless. Mystification of the client/therapist relationship tends to intensify clients' dependence and also reduces their ability to assert their rights in the therapy process (Hare-Mustin, Marecek, Kaplan, & Liss-Levinson, 1979). Gross (1979) also comments on ways in which therapists promote client dependency by keeping therapy a mysterious venture: "Professionals must keep clients mystified and dependent to maintain their power" (p. 36).

Stensrud and Stensrud (1981) observe that counseling can be hazardous to health, for it can teach people to be powerless instead of teaching them to trust themselves. They describe powerlessness as a "learned state of generalized helplessness in which clients (a) believe they are unable to have an impact on their environment, and (b) need some external force to intercede on their behalf" (p. 300). These authors note that clients can develop a self-fulfilling prophecy, whereby their expectation of powerlessness feeds into their experience of being powerless. They urge that clients participate actively in the entire therapy process. They also caution that, since people often produce the behavior that is expected of them, if therapists relate to clients in ways that tell the clients that they are not responsible for themselves, these clients are taught to feel dependent and helpless. Yet there are counselors who feel a sense of personal power and who do not need to keep clients dependent to maintain this power. Counselors who themselves feel a sense of powerlessness will have difficulty in preventing their clients from feeling powerless.

*Ethically warns about dependency*

The ethical guidelines of the AACD (1981) warn about creating dependency: "The consulting relationship must be one in which client adaptability and growth toward self-direction are encouraged and cultivated. The member must maintain this role consistently and not become a decision maker for the client or create a future dependency on the consultant."

Like many of the other ethical issues discussed in this chapter, the issue of encouraging dependence in clients is often not a clear-cut one in practice. Since our main purpose here is to stimulate you to think of possible ways that you might foster dependence or independence in your clients, we'll present a couple of illustrative cases and ask you to respond to them.

*Marcia is single and almost ready to graduate from college. She tells you that she has ambivalent feelings about graduating, because she feels that now she's expected to get a job and live on her own. This prospect frightens her, and she doesn't want to leave the security she has found as a college student. As she puts it, she doubts that she can "make it in the real world." Marcia doesn't trust her own decisions, because when she does make choices, the result, in her eyes, is disastrous. Her style is to plead with you to advise her whether she should date, apply for a job, leave home, go on to graduate school, and so forth. Typically, Marcia gets angry with you because you aren't being directive enough. She feels that you have more knowledge than she does and should therefore give her more guidance. She says: "Why am I coming here if you won't tell me what to do? If I could make decent decisions on my own, I wouldn't need to come here in the first place!"*

- How do you imagine you'd feel if Marcia were your client?
- How might you respond to her continual prodding for answers?
- How do you imagine you'd feel about her statement that you weren't doing your job and that you weren't being directive enough?
- What steps would you take to challenge her?
- In what ways do you think it would be possible for you to tie into her

dependency needs and foster her dependence on you for direction, instead of freeing her from you?

*Ron, a young counselor, encourages his clients to call him at home at any time and as often as they feel like it. He frequently lets sessions run overtime, lends money to clients when they're "down and out," devotes many more hours to his job than he is expected to, and overtaxes himself by taking on an unrealistically large case load. Ron says that he lives for his work and that it gives him a sense of being a valuable person. The more he can do for people, the better he feels.*

- In what ways could Ron's style keep his clients dependent on him?
- What could he be getting from being so "helpful"? What do you imagine his life would be like if there were no clients who needed him?
- If you were Ron's colleague and he came to you to talk about how "burnt out" he felt because he was "giving so much," what would you say to him?
- Can you identify with him in any ways? Do you see yourself as potentially needing your clients more than they need you?

On the issue of termination of a therapeutic relationship, a matter that is related to client dependency, the code of ethics of the NASW (1979) states: "The social worker should terminate service to clients, and professional relationships with them, when such service and relationships are no longer required or no longer serve the clients' needs or interests."

*[handwritten margin note: ethics speaks to termination]*

In spite of the fact that most professional codes have guidelines that call for termination whenever further therapy will not bring significant gains, some therapists do have difficulty in letting go of their clients. They run the risk of unethical practice because of either financial or emotional needs. On the financial issue, we contend that ethical practitioners will continually examine whether they are resistant to termination because it would mean a decline in income. Obviously, termination cannot be mandated by ethical codes alone but rests on the honesty and goodwill of the therapist. We agree with Wolman's position that "every therapist has the moral obligation to terminate his or her work as soon as further work will not bring additional and significant therapeutic gains" (1982, p. 195). Wolman contends that the therapist's need to feel useful can unconsciously cause him or her to postpone the end of therapy. He sees the mark of good therapists as the ability to help their clients reach the stage of autonomy, where they no longer need a therapist.

The APA (1981a) states: "Psychologists terminate a clinical or consulting relationship when it is reasonably clear that the consumer is not benefiting from it. They offer to help the consumer locate alternative sources of assistance." A similar guideline is provided by the AACD (1981):

> If the member determines an inability to be of professional assistance to the client, the member must either avoid initiating the counseling relationship or immediately terminate that relationship. In either event, the member must suggest appropriate alternatives. In the event the client declines the suggested referral, the member is not obligated to continue the relationship.

*What criteria do you initiate termination*

These ethical principles of the APA and AACD raise several questions we'd like you to consider:

- What criteria can you use to determine whether your client is benefiting from the therapeutic relationship?
- What do you do if your client feels he or she is benefiting from therapy but you don't see any signs of progress?
- What do you do if you're convinced that your client is coming to you seeking friendship and not really for the purpose of changing?

Put yourself, as a therapist, in each of the following two situations. Ask yourself what you would do, and why, if you were confronted with the problem described.

*After five sessions your client, George, asks: "Do you think I'm making any headway toward solving my problems? Do I seem any different to you now than I did five weeks ago?" Before you give him your impressions, you ask him to answer his own questions. He replies: "Well, I'm not sure whether coming here is doing that much good or not. I suppose I expected resolutions to my problems before now, but I still feel anxious and depressed much of the time. It feels good to come here, and I usually continue thinking after our sessions about what we discussed, but I'm not coming any closer to decisions. Sometimes I feel certain this is helping me, and at other times I wonder whether I'm just fooling myself."*

- What criteria can you employ to help you and your client assess the value of counseling for him?
- Does the fact that George continues to think about his session during the rest of the week show that he is probably getting something from counseling? Why or why not?
- Does it sound as if George has unrealistic expectations about finding neat solutions and making important decisions too quickly? Is he merely impatient with the process?

*Joanne has been coming regularly to counseling for some time. When you ask her what she thinks she is getting from the counseling, she answers: "This is really helping. I like to talk and have somebody listen to me. I often feel like you're the only friend I have and the only one who really cares about me. I suppose I really don't do that much outside, and I know I'm not changing that much, but I feel good when I'm here."*

- If it became clear to you that Joanne wasn't willing to do much to change her life and wanted to continue counseling only because she liked having you listen to her, do you think you'd be willing to continue working with her? Why or why not? Would you say that she is benefiting from the relationship with you? If so, how?
- Is it ethical to continue the counseling if Joanne's main goal is the "purchase of friendship"? Why or why not?
- If you thought that Joanne was using her relationship with you to remain

secure and dependent but that she believed that she was benefiting from the relationship, what might you do? How do you imagine you'd feel if you continued to see Joanne even though you were convinced that she wasn't changing?

# Manipulation as Unethical Behavior

If psychotherapy is basically a process that teaches people how to be honest with themselves, it is of the utmost importance for therapists to be honest with their clients. Unfortunately, there are many ways for therapists to deceive or manipulate clients, often under the guise of being helpful and concerned. Therapists who have plans for what they want their clients to do or to be and who keep these plans hidden are manipulative. Other therapists may attempt to control their relationships with their clients by keeping therapy a mysterious process and maintaining a rigid "professional stance" that excludes the client as a partner in the relationship. Therapy thus becomes a matter of the therapist's *doing* therapy on an unquestioning client.

To offset the danger of manipulating clients toward ends they have not chosen, some therapeutic approaches emphasize strategies designed to ensure that clients will have an active role in deciding what happens to them in the therapeutic relationship. As we saw in Chapter 4, many therapists use a contract as a basic prerequisite for continuing therapy. The contract contains a specific statement of goals and criteria for evaluating when these goals have been effectively met. The nature of the therapeutic relationship is thus defined by the contract, which is agreed on by both the client and the therapist. Its proponents claim that this procedure emphasizes the partnership of client and therapist, demystifies the therapeutic process, and minimizes the chance that clients will be manipulated toward ends that well-intentioned therapists have for them.

Sidney Jourard contrasts manipulation with dialogue. He sees psychotherapy as "an invitation to authenticity" in which the therapist's role is to be an exemplar. Therapists can foster their clients' honesty and invite them to drop their pretenses only by dropping their own and meeting their clients in an honest manner. Jourard (1968) says "I believe that the psychotherapist is the teacher in the therapeutic dance, and the patient follows the leader" (pp. 64–65). One of the best ways for therapists to demonstrate their goodwill is by avoiding manipulation and being open, trusting, and thus vulnerable to their clients. If counselors manipulate their clients, they can expect manipulation in return; if they are open, however, their clients may be open as well. Jourard (1968) expresses this concept descriptively as follows:

> If I want him to be maximally open, but I keep myself fully closed off, peeking at him through chinks in my own armor, trying to manipulate him from a distance, then in due time he will discover that I am not in that same mode; and he will then put his armor back on and peer at me through chinks in it, and he will try to manipulate me [p. 64].

Manipulation can work in subtle ways. Consider the degree to which you think the behaviors of the therapists in the following two examples are manipulative and unethical.

■ *The patients of Jobe.*   Among Dr. Jobe's patients is Josephine, a middle-aged widow. She has been seeing him for three years on a regular basis because of her loneliness and depression. Much of the dialogue of the sessions is now social in nature. Josephine continually tells Dr. Jobe how she enjoys the sessions and how meaningful they are to her. She has connections with a professional sports franchise and has been able to obtain choice tickets for him. At times he lets it be known when he needs tickets for specific events.

• Is it unethical for Dr. Jobe to continue to see Josephine when the nature of the sessions is primarily social?
• Is it ethical to continue to accept the tickets?
• Could this relationship be construed as manipulation of transference feelings?
• Would mere enjoyment of the sessions warrant continuation?

■ *The case of Barbara.*   Barbara is 20 years old and has been in therapy with Dr. Smart for over a year. She has developed a high degree of respect and fondness for her therapist, whom she sees as a father figure. She tells Dr. Smart that she is thinking of discontinuing therapy because she has lost her job and simply has no way of paying for the sessions. Barbara is obviously upset over the prospect of ending the relationship with her therapist, but she sees no alternative. Dr. Smart informs her that he is willing to continue her therapy even if she is unable to pay. He suggests that as an exchange of services Barbara can become the baby-sitter for his three children. She gratefully accepts this offer, only to find after a few months that the situation is becoming difficult for her. Eventually, Barbara writes a note to Dr. Smart telling him that she cannot handle her reactions to his wife and their children. It makes her think of all the things she missed in her own family. She writes that she has found this subject difficult to bring up in her sessions, so she is planning to quit both her services and her therapy.

• What mistakes, if any, do you think that Dr. Smart made?
• How would you have dealt with this situation? What might you have done differently?
• Do you think that it was unethical for the therapist to suggest that Barbara do baby-sitting for him? In doing so, to what degree did he take into consideration the nature of the transference relationship?

# Dual Relationships and Sexual Contact

Dual relationships, which can take many forms, have been called a violation of ethical, legal, and clinical standards (Pope, 1985a). In situations where a professional relationship is potentially impaired because of a combining of incompatible roles, a dual relationship exists. A few examples of dual relationships, as described by Keith-Spiegel and Koocher (1985), are combining the roles of teacher and therapist (which we discussed in Chapter 2); trading therapy for goods or services; bartering with needy clients; providing therapy to a friend's relative; socializing outside therapy sessions; becoming emotionally or sexually involved with a client or former client; and combining the roles of supervisor and therapist (discussed in Chapter 5).

The reasons that dual relationships are prohibited are as varied as the forms they can take. Pope (1985a) contends that such relationships tend to impair professional judgment; that there is a danger of exploiting the client, since the professional occupies the more powerful position; and that clients are put in a vulnerable position by the power of the transference relationship. For example, the therapeutic relationship could suffer if a client bartered services for therapy. If a client were expected to provide several hours of work on the therapist's car in exchange for a therapy session, he might become resentful over the imbalance of the exchange. Furthermore, the therapist might resent the client if her car were not repaired properly.

We do not wish to assert dogmatically that all dual relationships are always unethical. What we are doing is challenging you to think about certain relationships that could place you in professional jeopardy. Rather than unequivocally condemn bartering of goods or services for therapy, for example, we ask you to honestly reflect on how such an arrangement could complicate the therapeutic relationship. In this section we discuss the various forms that dual relationships assume between client and therapist. Our discussion proceeds from social relationships to sexual attractions, non-erotic contact, and sexual contact. We invite you to think through the possible benefits and risks of being involved in such relationships, both to your client and to yourself.

## Social Relationships with Clients

Do social relationships with clients necessarily interfere with therapeutic relationships? Some would say no—that counselors and clients are able to handle a social relationship in conjunction with a therapeutic one, as long as it is clear where the priorities lie. They see this as being particularly true with clients who aren't deeply disturbed and who are seeking personal growth. Some peer counselors, for example, claim that friendships before or during counseling are actually positive factors in establishing trust and good, productive therapeutic relationships.

Other counselors take the position that counseling and friendship should not be mixed. They argue that attempting to manage a social and professional relationship simultaneously can negatively affect the therapy process, the friendship, or both. Some of the reasons they offer for discouraging the practice of accepting friends as clients or becoming socially involved with clients are (1) counselors might not be as confrontive with clients they know socially; (2) counselors' own need to be liked and accepted may lead them to be less challenging, lest the friendship or social relation-ship be jeopardized; (3) counselors' own needs may interlock with those of their clients to the point that objectivity is lost; and (4) by the very nature of the counseling relationship, counselors are in a more powerful position than clients, and the danger of exploiting clients becomes more likely when the relationship becomes other than a professional one.

Obviously, this is not a closed issue that can be resolved with a dogmatic answer. We question the assumption that, if counselors become socially involved with a client other than in the office, they are therefore less willing to risk challenging the client and are less objective. Although the danger exists that therapists may be less confrontive because of their fear of losing the relationship, we do not think that social involvements per se necessarily preclude honest and effective confrontation. We would ask therapists to consider if there is a discrepancy between the way they treat their clients and the way they treat their friends. Counselors need to be aware of their own motivations, as well as the motivations of their prospective clients, and they must honestly assess the impact a social relationship might have on the client/therapist relationship. This issue can take several forms. To illustrate, we'll ask you to respond to a specific case.

*You are an intern in a college counseling center, and one of your clients says to you: "I really like working with you, but I hate coming over here to this cold and impersonal office. I always feel weird waiting in the lobby as if I were a 'case' or something. Why can't we meet outside on the lawn? Better yet, we could get away from campus and meet in the park nearby. I'd feel more natural and uninhibited in a more informal setting."*

- Would you agree to meet your client outside the office? Why or why not?
- Would your decision depend on how much you liked or were attracted to your client? Would your client's age and sex have much to do with your decision?

*Later, your client invites you to a party that he or she is having and lets you know that it would mean a lot if you were to come. Your client says: "I'd really like to get to know you on a personal basis, because I'm being so deeply personal in here. I really like you, and I'd like more time with you than the hour we have each week."*

- What are your immediate reactions? Assuming that you like your client and would like to go to the party, do you think it would be wise to attend? What would your decision be, and what would you say to your client?
- What effect do you think meeting your client on a social basis would have on the therapeutic process?

**Another Point of View.**   One of the reviewers of this book took the position that social relationships with clients are never appropriate. The reviewer argued that counselors make themselves quite vulnerable legally if they enter into such relationships. Ethically, there is the problem that therapists are not so superhuman that they can manage dual relationships that demand different responses.

Although we do not agree that social relationships with clients are never appropriate, we do see problems with such arrangements. They do demand a great deal of honesty and self-awareness on the part of the therapist. They also take a high degree of maturity on the client's part. It is important to consider the client's ability (or inability) to keep the two relationships separate. Clients may well become inhibited during the therapy hour out of fear of alienating their therapist. They may fear losing the respect of a therapist with whom they have a friendship. They may censor their disclosures so that they do not threaten this social relationship. At this point, what are your thoughts on this issue from the *client's* perspective?

## Sexual Attractions in the Client/Therapist Relationship

In a pioneering study, "Sexual Attraction to Clients: The Human Therapist and the (Sometimes) Inhuman Training System," Pope, Keith-Spiegel, and Tabachnick (1986) develop the theme that there has been a lack of systematic research into the sexual attraction of therapists to their clients. This silence gives the impression that therapists are incapable of experiencing sexual attraction to those they serve or that the phenomenon is a regrettable aberration limited to the few who sexually act out with clients. Many therapists feel that, if they do experience sexual attractions toward clients, they are guilty of therapeutic errors. The authors of this study provide clear evidence that attraction to clients is a prevalent experience among both male and female therapists. Because there are taboos on such topics, however, there have been no systematic studies of it. Graduate training programs and clinical internships leave trainees completely unprepared for successfully dealing with their sexual attractions to clients. The authors investigated questions such as the following: "What is the frequency of sexual attraction to clients by therapists? Do therapists feel guilty or uncomfortable when they have such attractions? Do they tend to tell their clients about their attractions? Do they consult with colleagues? Do therapists believe that their graduate training provided adequate education on attraction to clients?"

The investigators conducted a study that involved 585 respondents. Only 77 reported never having been attracted to any client. (We wonder whether these 77 people were telling the truth or if they were denying such feelings!) The vast majority reported that they had never seriously considered actual sexual involvement with a client (82%). Further, the majority of respondents reported never having had sexual relations with their clients (93.5%). Therapists gave a number of reasons for refraining from acting out their attractions to clients, most of which expressed professional values, a concern about the welfare of the client, or personal values compatible with professional standards. Although fears of negative consequences were mentioned, they were less frequent than values pertaining to client welfare.

Most respondents (69%) believed that sexual attractions to clients were useful or beneficial, at least in some instances, to the therapy. With respect to the client's being aware of the therapist's attraction, 71% believed that the client was probably not aware. Most therapists (81%) believed that the attraction had been mutual. Over half (55%) indicated that they had received no education on the subject of sexual attraction to clients in their graduate training and internships. Twenty-four percent had received "very little," 12% had received "some," and 9% thought that they had received adequate preparation in dealing with sexual attraction to clients. Those who had had some graduate training in this area were more likely to have sought consultation (66%) than were those with no such training.

What are the implications for training programs? According to Pope, Keith-Spiegel, and Tabachnick, a training approach must acknowledge the value of a serious consideration of sexual attraction in the client/therapist relationship. The taboo must be lifted so that therapy trainees can recognize and accept their sexual attractions as human responses. The investigators maintain that a discussion of sexual attraction should be a part of all clinical and professional course-work and training. Educational programs must provide a safe environment in which trainees can acknowledge and discuss feelings of sexual attraction. If students sense a judgmental attitude from their professors, they are not likely to explore this issue openly. Further, students need to feel that such a discussion will not be taken as seductive or as inviting a sexual relationship with their educators.

> Educators must display the same frankness, honesty, and integrity regarding sexual attraction that they expect their students to emulate. Psychologists need to acknowledge that they may feel sexual attraction to their students as well as to their clients. They need to establish with clarity and maintain with consistency unambiguous ethical and professional standards regarding appropriate and inappropriate handling of these feelings [Pope et al., 1986, p. 157].

**Dealing with Sexual Feelings toward a Client.** Assume that for several months you've been working with a client whom you find attractive and exciting. You're aware that your client has loving feelings toward you and would be willing to become sexually involved with you. Your own feelings are growing in intensity, and you often have difficulty paying attention during sessions because of your own fantasies.

1. Would you interpret this situation in any of the following ways?
   - This is a sure sign of the beginning of countertransference.
   - My feelings are acceptable and can easily be hidden from the client.
   - This is something to be discussed immediately with the client, with a strong recommendation for referral.
   - My own needs have become more important than my client's needs.
   - I need to consult with a colleague.
2. What do you think about the appropriateness of each of the following courses of action?

- I could ignore my feelings for the client and my client's feelings toward me and focus on other aspects of the relationship.
- I could tell my client of my feelings of attraction, discontinue the professional relationship, and then begin a personal relationship.
- I could openly express my feelings toward my client by saying: "I'm glad you find me an attractive person, and I'm strongly attracted to you as well. But I don't want to act on my sexual feelings, because that's not what this relationship is all about, and I'm sure that's not why you came here."
- If there were no change in the intensity of my feelings toward my client, I could arrange for a referral to another therapist.
- I could consult with a colleague or seek professional supervision.

*honesty?*

Which of the above courses of action would you not take, and why? Can you think of another direction in which you might proceed besides the alternatives given above? Why would you choose this direction?

## Nonerotic Physical Contact with Clients

*acting on these feelings is unethical!*

Although we contend that acting on sexual feelings and engaging in erotic contact with clients is unethical, we do think that nonerotic contact is often appropriate and can have significant therapeutic value. It is important to stress this point, because there is a taboo against touching clients. Sometimes therapists hold back when they feel like touching their clients affectionately or compassionately. They may feel that touching can be misinterpreted as exploitative; they may be afraid of their impulses or feelings toward clients; they may be afraid of intimacy; or they may believe that to physically express closeness is unprofessional.

In a study by Holroyd and Brodsky (1977), 27% of the therapists who responded said they had occasionally engaged in nonerotic hugging, kissing, or affectionate touching with opposite-sex clients; 7% said they had done so frequently or always. The percentages varied with different kinds of therapists; 25% of humanistic therapists engaged in nonerotic contact frequently or always, but fewer than 10% of eclectic therapists and fewer than 5% of psychodynamic, behavior-modification, or rational-cognitive therapists did so. Approximately half of the therapists took the position that nonerotic physical contact would be beneficial for clients at least occasionally. Most of the suggestions fell into four categories of appropriate nonerotic contact: (1) with socially or emotionally immature clients, such as those with histories of maternal deprivation; (2) with people who were experiencing acute distress, such as grief, depression, or trauma; (3) for providing general emotional support; and (4) for greeting or at termination.

*of Beneful! 'hug' ✱ 4 categories of appropriateness*

In a later study Holroyd and Brodsky (1980) explored the question "Does touching patients lead to sexual intercourse?" Their results indicated that respondents who admitted having had sexual intercourse with their clients more often advocated and participated in nonerotic contact with opposite-sex clients but not with clients of the same sex. Also, male therapists who had had intercourse were likely to have used and to advocate affectionate touching with female but not male clients, even though the male clients might have initiated contact. Based on the data from questionnaires received from 347 male therapists and 310 female therapists, Holroyd and Brodsky came to the following conclusions:

• Touching that does not lead to intercourse is associated with older and more experienced therapists.
• It is the practice of restricting touching to opposite-sex clients, not touching itself, that is related to intercourse.

Holroyd and Brodsky observe that it is difficult to determine where "nonerotic hugging, kissing, and affectionate touching" leave off and "erotic contact" begins. They also suggest that any therapeutic technique that is reserved for one gender can be suspected of being sexist. They conclude: "The use of nonerotic touching as a mode of psychotherapeutic treatment requires further research. Moreover, the sexist implications of differential touching of male and female patients appear to be an important professional and ethical issue" (1980, p. 810).

There are two sides to the issue of touching, for some studies support it and other studies do not. After reviewing both this research and clinical data, Willison and Masson (1986) found some indication that touching could be therapeutic when used appropriately. They also found little evidence of negative effects of appropriate touching. By appropriate touching they mean nonsexual contact that fosters therapeutic progress and serves the client's needs. Some clinicians, however, have a bias against any form of physical contact between counselors and clients, on the grounds that it can promote dependency, that it will interfere with the transference relationship, that it can be misread by clients, and that it can become sexualized.

Willison and Masson concluded that there was value in an optimal level of touching as a medium of communication. Some of their findings were that touch seems to be effective with infants and younger children; that women are more comfortable than are men in being touched; that both women and men are more comfortable in accepting touch from women; and that touching can increase the client's positive evaluation of the experience and tends to increase the client's self-disclosure. Willison and Masson came to the following conclusions about the implications of touching in therapy:

> Because the evidence indicates that touch does not lead to negative consequences in any counseling context, counselors may wish to reconsider reservations regarding therapeutic touch with clients. Counselor training focused exclusively on verbal skills and traditional nonverbal behaviors may not be adequate for preparing counselors to engage a client effectively. The introduction of touch concepts into graduate programs could expand the communication capabilities of practitioners [1986, p. 499].

Our own position is that touching should be a spontaneous and honest expression of the therapist's feelings. We think it is unwise for therapists to touch a client if it is not congruent with what they feel for the client. A nongenuine touch will be detected by a client and could erode the trust in the relationship. Counselors need to be sensitive to how touching might be received by the client as well as when it could be counterproductive. There are times when touching clients has the impact of distracting them from what they are feeling at the moment. There are also times when a touch that is given at the right moment can convey far more empathy than words can. In this area therapists need to be aware of their own motives and to be honest with themselves about the meaning of the physical contact. They also need to be sensitive to factors such as the client's readiness for physical closeness, the client's cultural messages concerning touching, the client's reaction, the impact such contact is likely to have on the client, and the level of trust that they have built with the client.

Think about your position on the ethical implications of the practice of touching as a part of the client/therapist relationship by answering these questions:

- In light of the conclusions of Willison and Masson, to what degree might you reconsider any reservations about the role of touching in therapy? To what degree do you think your professional training has prepared you to determine when touching is appropriate and therapeutic?
- What criteria could you use to determine whether touching your clients was therapeutic or countertherapeutic?
- How could you honestly answer the question "Are my own needs being met at the expense of my client's needs?"
- What factors do you need to consider in determining the appropriateness of touching clients? (Examples are age, gender, type of client, nature of client's problem, and setting in which therapy occurs.)
- Do you agree or disagree with the conclusions of Holroyd and Brodsky concerning the sexist implications of differential touching of male and female clients?
- If you are favorably inclined toward the practice of touching clients, are you likely to restrict this practice to opposite-sex clients? same-sex clients? attractive opposite-sex clients? Explain.

## Sexual Contact with Clients

The issue of sexual relations with clients is a very controversial one that is frequently the subject of symposia or panels at professional conventions. Holroyd and Brodsky (1977) reported the results of a nationwide survey of 500 male and 500 female licensed psychologists, all Ph.D.s, which was conducted to assess their attitudes and practices with respect to erotic and nonerotic contact with clients. Holroyd and Brodsky reported a 70% return rate. Their findings included the following:

1. Erotic contact and intercourse are almost always between male therapists and female clients.
2. Therapists who crossed the sexual boundary once were likely to repeat

this practice. Of those therapists who reported intercourse with patients, 80% repeated it.

*500 male*

3. Of the male therapists, 5.5% reported having had sexual intercourse with clients; for female therapists the figure was .6%.

4. Only 4% of the respondents thought that erotic contact might be beneficial. Seventy percent of male therapists and 88% of female therapists took the position that erotic contact is *never* beneficial to clients. *never beneficial*

Most of the psychologists responding strongly disapproved of erotic contact in therapy and stated that it should never occur in a professional relationship. They took the position that such contact is totally inappropriate and is an exploitation of the relationship by the therapist. Erotic contact with clients was thus viewed as unprofessional, unethical, and antitherapeutic. One therapist made the comment that "I feel without qualification that erotic patient-therapist contact is unethical at best and devastating at worst—it reflects pathological needs on the part of the therapist" (Holroyd & Brodsky, 1977, p. 848).

**A Continuum of Sexual Contact with Clients.**    Coleman and Schaefer (1986) write that sexual abuse of clients by counselors can best be considered along a continuum consisting of psychological, covert, and overt abuse. They conceptualize this problem on the following three levels: (1) In *psychological abuse* the client is put in the position of becoming the emotional caretaker of the counselor's needs. Therapists may meet their own needs for intimacy through the client, reverse roles with the client, or self-disclose without aiding the client. (2) In *covert abuse* the counselor's boundary confusion with the client becomes more pronounced as he or she displays behaviors with intended sexual connotations to the client, with the result of intruding further into the client's intimacy boundaries. Common forms of this level of abuse include sexual hugs, professional voyeurism, sexual gazes, overattention to the client's dress and appearance, and seductiveness through dress and gestures. (3) At the far end of the continuum are overt forms of sexual misconduct. This category includes the most clearly recognized forms of counselor abuse: sexual remarks, passionate kissing, fondling, sexual intercourse, oral or anal sex, and sexual penetration with objects.

**Ethical Standards on Sexual Intimacy.**    Virtually all of the professional organizations now have a specific statement condemning sexual intimacies in the client/therapist relationship, as can be seen in the summary of relevant codes in the accompanying box.

*condemning*

It is clear from the statements of the major mental-health professional organizations that these principles go beyond merely condemning sexual relationships with clients. There are also implications for counseling with close friends or relatives, for forming social and personal relationships with clients, and for developing or maintaining any kind of relationship that is

## Sexual Relations in Therapy: Summary of Codes of Ethics

*American Association for Counseling and Development (1981):*

- "Dual relationships with clients that might impair the member's objectivity and professional judgment (e.g., as with close friends or relatives, sexual intimacies with any client) must be avoided and/or the counseling relationship terminated through referral to another competent professional."

*American Psychological Association (1981a):*

- "Psychologists make every effort to avoid dual relationships that could impair their professional judgment or increase the risk of exploitation. Examples of such relationships include, but are not limited to, research with and treatment of employees, students, supervisees, close friends, or relatives. Sexual intimacies with clients are unethical."

*American Psychiatric Association (1986):*

- "The necessary intensity of the therapeutic relationship may tend to activate sexual and other needs and fantasies on the part of both patient and therapist, while weakening the objectivity necessary for control. Sexual activity with a patient is unethical."

*American Association for Marriage and Family Therapy (1985):*

- "Marriage and family therapists . . . make every effort to avoid dual relationships with clients that could impair their professional judgment or increase the risk of exploitation. Examples of such dual relationships include, but are not limited to, business or close personal relationships with clients. Sexual intimacy with clients is prohibited."

*National Association of Social Workers (1979):*

- "The social worker should under no circumstances engage in sexual activities with clients."

*American Psychoanalytic Association (1983):*

- "Sexual relationships between analyst and patient are antithetical to treatment and unacceptable under any circumstances. Any sexual activity with a patient constitutes a violation of this principle of ethics."

likely to impair one's ability to function in a professional manner. Further, it is clear that, if a client/therapist relationship does develop into a relationship that could potentially be countertherapeutic (or if there is a risk of exploiting the client), then ethical practice calls for a termination of the counseling relationship and a referral to another professional.

Those therapists who are convinced that sexual intimacy between a therapist and client is both unethical and professionally inappropriate state a number of grounds for their position. The general argument typically involves the abuse of the power that therapists have by virtue of their function and role. Clients reveal deeply personal material about their hopes, sexual desires and struggles, and intimate relationships, and in many ways they become vulnerable to their therapists. It's easy to take advantage of this trust and exploit it for personal motives. Although it may be true that some clients provoke and tease their therapists, those who consider sexual intimacies to be unethical professional behavior contend that therapists should refuse to collaborate in such sexual game playing and instead confront their clients with what is occurring.

 Another reason given by those who oppose erotic contact in therapeutic relationships is that it fosters dependence. Clients can easily come to think of their therapists as ideal persons when they see them only in the limited context of the office. Instead of forming meaningful relationships with others, clients may begin to live for the affection and attention they receive from their therapists once a week. Further, many would argue that, when sexual activity becomes a part of therapy, the objectivity of the therapist is lost. Therapists are likely to become more concerned about the feelings their clients have toward them than about challenging their clients to take an honest look at their own lives.

Another argument against sexual involvement with clients is that they often feel taken advantage of and may discount the value of any part of their therapy. They may become embittered and angry, and they may terminate therapy with psychological scars. The problem is compounded if they are deterred from initiating therapy with anyone else because of the traumatic experience and thus feel stuck with their unresolved feelings.

**Why Therapists Become Sexually Involved.**  According to Pope and Bouhoutsos (1986), therapists typically offer the "I didn't know any better" explanation for sexual involvement with clients. Yet many of these therapists are well-established mental-health professionals in their 40s and 50s with a long history of training and experience. Writing that the evidence indicates that most therapists do indeed "know better," Pope and Bouhoutsos describe four common misconceptions that could influence the therapist's decision to engage in sexual intimacies with a client.

1. *Sexual involvement with clients is acceptable if it takes place outside the therapy session.*   There are no situations in which this defense has been successfully used in ethics proceedings, licensing actions, or civil court actions.

2. *Only sexual involvement that occurs before the termination of therapy is illegal or unethical.*   Some therapists have attempted to defend themselves with the argument of terminating a therapeutic relationship so that they could begin a sexual relationship. However, there are no instances in which the therapist was cleared on this basis.

3. *Sexual involvement is acceptable if the client initiates it.*   Although this contention is made by some attorneys, it has no merit. Even in cases in which the client behaves seductively, the responsibility for the relationship always rests with the therapist.

4. *If one's professor or supervisor was involved with a client, then one can also be involved without sanctions.*   The authors mention that this unstated misperception is rarely used in a hearing, yet it does often determine the attitude about sexual involvements with clients taken by professionals establishing a practice.

*Ends here!* (handwritten)

**Harmful Effects of Sexual Intimacy on Clients.**    Bouhoutsos, Holroyd, Lerman, Forer, and Greenberg (1983) suggest that when sexual intercourse begins, therapy as a helping process ends. In their study, once sexual activity began, therapy ended immediately for one-third of the clients. When sex is involved in a therapeutic relationship, the therapist loses control of the course of therapy. The researchers concluded that sexual contact was especially disruptive if it began early in the relationship and if it had been initiated by the therapist. Ninety percent of 559 clients who became sexually involved with their therapists were adversely affected. This harm ranged from mistrust of opposite-sex relationships to hospitalization and, in some cases, suicide. Other effects of sexual intimacies on clients' emotional, social, and sexual adjustment included negative feelings about the experience, a negative impact on their personality, and a deterioration of their sexual relationship with their primary partner. The authors contend that the harmfulness of sexual contact in therapy validates the ethical codes barring such conduct and provides a rationale for enacting legislation prohibiting it.

depression ✱ (handwritten)
alcohol
emotional
disturbance
social malady (handwritten)

Commenting on the study by Bouhoutsos and her colleagues, Coleman and Schaefer (1986) describe other negative outcomes such as depression and other emotional disturbances, impaired social adjustment, and substance abuse. Many clients found that their primary relationships deteriorated. Even though these clients felt that their emotional problems had increased, they also found it more difficult to seek out further therapy because of their previous negative experience.

The consequences of sexual intimacy are described as follows by Pope and Bouhoutsos (1986) in their pioneering book, *Sexual Intimacy between Therapists and Patients*:

> Clinically, patients may complain of tension, apprehension, dissociation, fatigue, lassitude, lack of motivation, depression, and/or anxiety. There may be frequent tears or numbness and an inability to cry. Despair and pessimism may be so powerful that functioning is severely limited. The deterioration of familial relationships, inability to work, self-blame, and self-hate may continue and worsen with time unless there is intervention; if there is no intervention, these are the patients at risk for suicide [p. 66].

✱ (handwritten) According to Coleman and Schaefer (1986), the psychological and covert forms of abuse may be more damaging than overt abuse. In cases involving overt actions there is no question about the ethical violation, and clients often feel justified in considering themselves abused. With either psychological or covert abuse, however, clients are likely to feel more confusion, guilt, and shame.

Research conducted by Holroyd and Bouhoutsos (1985) suggests that the estimate that 90% of involved clients were harmed may even be low. This study found that therapists who reported that clients had not been harmed admitted a greater prevalence of sexual intimacy with their clients than did therapists in the population at large. Thus, biased reporting may be a significant factor in the estimate that 10% of clients were unharmed.

*Malpractice sued*

## Legal Sanctions against Sexual Violators.    Therapists who engaged in sex with their clients have been sued for malpractice. Psychologists found guilty, for example, have been given sanctions, have been expelled from membership in the APA, have had their licenses revoked or suspended by the state, and have been ordered to undergo therapy to resolve their problems.

Some states have legal sanctions in cases of sexual misconduct in the therapeutic relationship. A California statute, for example, gives specific authority to all licensing and regulatory boards in the healing arts "to suspend or revoke the license of a person who has committed an act of sexual abuse, misconduct or sexual relations with a patient or client in the course of his/her professional duties" (Psychology Examining Committee *Newsletter*, 1980). Included under this law are psychologists, clinical social workers, marriage and family therapists, physicians, psychiatrists, dentists, nurses, and others. It is clear that professionals cannot argue that the client seduced them. The law states that the ultimate ethical and legal burden of responsibility to avoid such situations rests squarely on the licensed professional. Consistent with this law is the position of Coleman and Schaefer (1986) that the counselor must take responsibility for setting appropriate sexual and intimacy boundaries for the client, communicate these boundaries, and keep the relationship a professional rather than a personal one.

Other states (15, as of 1983) have passed legislation making it considerably easier to remove licenses in situations involving sexual misconduct. In those states it is no longer necessary to prove that damage has resulted from sexual intimacy with a therapist; rather, the only question is whether the sexual intimacy occurred (Holroyd & Bouhoutsos, 1985).

In 1984 the Minnesota legislature created a task force on sexual exploitation by psychotherapists after numerous complaints by victims who were clients. In Minnesota it is a felony if a counselor has sexual contact with a client during the therapy session. In certain cases the counselor may be found guilty of sexual misconduct even if the contact occurs outside the session. Client consent cannot be used as a defense (Coleman & Schaefer, 1986).

Many cases of sexual misconduct probably go unreported because of the clients' shame and guilt, as well as their reluctance to pursue the matter in the courts. It appears, however, that female clients have recently become more willing to sue male therapists. The news media have reported cases in which therapists exploited their clients; some of these therapists have taken the extreme position that the sexual involvement did not interfere with the therapy and often enhanced it. As Fitzgerald and Nutt (1986) have concluded, however, erotic contact with clients is based on the counselor's need for power, reassurance, or sexual gratification and is not engaged in for the benefit of the client.

What are the ethics of beginning an intimate or sexual relationship once therapy has ended? In the absence of clear guidelines, according to Coleman and Schaefer (1986), counselors must make their own ethical deci-

*unreported*

*ended therapy ..... guideline for relationship ??*

*ethical violator now bldg.*

sions. The authors add that sentiment seems to be building that such contact is an ethical violation. Much of the testimony from clients at a task-force hearing in Minnesota involved complaints against psychotherapists who had become sexually involved with clients once the professional relationship had ended.

In another study, Sell, Gottlieb, and Schoenfeld (1986) take the position that it is ethically questionable to assume that the therapeutic relationship ends at a finite point and that a social or sexual relationship with a former client would then be permissible. This presumption has not been found to be an adequate defense against charges of sexual impropriety. State licensing boards and ethics committees have tended to rule against psychologists who use that defense. Sell and his colleagues believe that the only realistic way to deal with the problem of therapists who are sexually involved with former clients is to prohibit posttreatment sexual relations altogether. They recommend that the ethical principles of the APA (1981) should be amended to read (added portion in italics): "Sexual intimacy with clients *or with former clients* is unethical." Sell and his colleagues take a position that they recognize as being controversial and one that leaves no room for compromise. "We contend that sexual relationships with former clients are exploitive and unethical if they follow any therapeutic relationship, regardless of the elapsed time" (p. 507).

*APA unethical*

At this point you might reflect upon your own stand on this issue:

- Do you think that counselors should be free to formulate their own practices about developing a sexual relationship with former clients?
- Do you think that sexual relationships with former clients are unethical, regardless of the elapsed time? Do you see any exceptions that might justify developing intimate relationships with former clients?

**Ethical Sanctions.**    There are definite procedures for filing and processing ethical complaints against psychologists, and such complaints are dealt with by the state professional associations and by the APA's Committee on Scientific and Professional Ethics and Conduct. Sanders and Keith-Spiegel (1980) present a summary of an investigation of a psychologist who was accused of becoming sexually involved with his female client after two years of therapy. The psychologist promptly terminated the therapeutic relationship, according to the client, yet no attempt was made to resolve the therapeutic issues remaining. The sexual relationship continued for about a year, on a weekly basis, until it was finally cut off by the client because of her guilt and disgust over the situation. The psychologist made two attempts to resume the affair, but the client refused to become involved.

*APA Licensure Board Fla.*

Although the psychologist at first flatly denied the client's charges, he eventually admitted that they were true. He also said that he loved his client, that he was struggling with a mid-life crisis, and that he was having severe marital problems. He added that he was willing to seek personal therapy to work on his problems.

In this case the state psychological association voted to monitor the psychologist's personal therapy and have his practice reviewed for one year. In his hearing before the APA's ethics committee he gave a progress report on his personal therapy and attempted to convince the committee members that the insights he had gained would preclude the recurrence of this sort of ethical violation in the future. The committee offered a stipulated resignation from the APA for a period of five years, after which he might reapply if no further ethical violations had been brought to the APA. The committee concluded that this psychologist did appear remorseful, that he would be rehabilitated, and that he seemed to have the self-determination to do so.

In thinking about this case, attempt to answer these questions:

- Do you think that this psychologist should have been allowed to continue his professional practice? Why or why not?
- If you had been a member of the ethics committee that reviewed this case, what action would you have recommended?
- If the psychologist was aware that he had fallen in love with his client and wanted to become sexually involved with her (yet had not done so), what ethical course of action could he have taken? Is termination of the professional relationship enough?

**Conclusions.**   It is unwise, unethical, and in some states illegal to become sexually involved with clients. This is not to say that counselors aren't human beings or will never have strong feelings of attraction toward certain clients. Counselors impose an unnecessary burden on themselves when they believe that they shouldn't have such feelings for clients or when they try to convince themselves that they should not have more feeling toward one client than toward another. What is important is how counselors decide to deal with these feelings as they affect the therapeutic relationship. Referral to another therapist isn't necessarily the best solution, unless it becomes clear that one can no longer be effective with a certain client. Instead, counselors may recognize a need for consultation or, at the very least, for an honest dialogue with themselves. It may also be appropriate to have a frank discussion with the client, explaining that the decision not to act on one's sexual feelings is based on a commitment to the primacy of the therapeutic relationship.

When we've discussed with students the issue of sexual involvement with clients, we've found that they almost universally see it as an unethical practice. However, we want to point out that the issue of erotic contact in therapy is not simply a matter of whether to have sexual intercourse with a client. Even if you decide intellectually that you wouldn't engage in sexual intimacies with a client, it's important to realize that the relationship between therapist and client can involve varying degrees of sexuality. Therapists may have sexual fantasies; they may behave seductively with their clients; they may influence clients to focus on romantic or sexual feelings toward them; or they may engage in physical contact that is primarily intended to arouse or satisfy their sexual desires. Although these therapists may not reach the point of having sexual intercourse with clients, their behavior is clearly sexual in nature and can have much the same effect as direct sexual involvement would have. Romantic overtones can easily distort the therapeutic relationship as the seductive play of the client and therapist becomes the real focus of the sessions. This is clearly an area in which counselors need to be able to recognize what they're doing. It's also crucial that they learn how to accept their sexual feelings and that they consciously decide how to deal with them in therapy.

## ■ Dealing with Unethical Behavior

A particularly touchy issue relates to your obligation when you know of colleagues, peers, or supervisors who are engaging in unethical practices. In our classes and workshops many students have raised the question "What course of action should I take when I know of other therapists who consistently engage in unethical behavior?" To sharpen your thinking on this question, reflect for a few moments on the possibility of your being involved in the following situations:

• You know of a colleague who clearly lacks the competencies to effectively carry out therapeutic functions in an agency. The person is employing techniques in his therapy with psychotic patients that he has not been trained to use. He is also not receiving adequate supervision. What would you do?

• You are aware of a therapist who charges sessions to a client's insurance that were not actually held. The therapist says that "double billing" is a common practice, and he sees nothing wrong with it. What would you do?

• You are aware that a clinical supervisor has made it a practice to have sexual relationships with several of her supervisees. Some of these students are friends of yours, and they tell you that they felt pressure to comply, since they were in a vulnerable position. What would you do?

• You know of a colleague who does not believe in informed consent. She tells you that it is counterproductive to give clients too much information about the therapy process. She admits that she strives to keep the therapeutic relationship a mysterious one, and she claims that it works for her. What would you do?

• A colleague has what you consider to be a rigid set of values, and he sees it as his function to impose them on his clients. He tells you that it is his job to "straighten out" his clients, that they typically do not know what is best for them, and that he finds many ways to indirectly move them in the direction of his thinking. What would you do?

• You know a student intern who makes it a practice to initiate social relationships with his clients. He says that this is acceptable, because his clients are consenting adults, and he argues that by dating some of his clients he actually gets to know them better, which helps him in his role as a therapist. What would you do?

No doubt you can come up with some other actions that you would consider unethical. You may find yourself uncertain of the appropriate course of action. You may wonder whether it is your place to judge the practices of colleagues or other practitioners whom you know. Even if you are convinced the situation involves clear ethical violations, you may be in doubt about the best way to deal with it. Should you first discuss the matter with the person? Assuming that you do and that the person becomes defensive, should you take any other action, or simply drop the matter? When would a violation be serious enough that you would feel obligated to bring it to the attention of an appropriate local, state, or national committee on professional ethics?

Most professional organizations have specific ethical standards that clearly place the responsibility for confronting recognized violations squarely on members of their profession. Further, to ignore an ethical violation is considered a violation in itself. See the accompanying box on codes dealing with unethical behavior of colleagues.

## Unethical Behavior by Colleagues: Ethical Codes

*American Psychological Association (1981a):*

- "When psychologists know of an ethical violation by another psychologist, and it seems appropriate, they informally attempt to resolve the issue by bringing the behavior to the attention of the psychologist. If the misconduct is of a minor nature and/or appears to be due to lack of sensitivity, knowledge, or experience, such an informal solution is usually appropriate. Such informal corrective efforts are made with sensitivity to any rights to confidentiality involved. If the violation does not seem amenable to an informal solution, or is of a more serious nature, psychologists bring it to the attention of the appropriate local, state, and/or national committee on professional ethics and conduct."

*American Association for Counseling and Development (1981):*

- "Ethical behavior among professional associates, both members and nonmembers, must be expected at all times. When information is possessed that raises doubt as to the ethical behavior of colleagues, whether Association members or not, the member must take action to attempt to rectify such a condition. Such action shall use the institution's channels first and then use procedures established by the state Branch, Division, or Association."

We hope that you are willing to develop the attitude of honest self-examination in looking at your own behavior. It is sometimes easier to see the faults in others and to judge their behavior. You can make a commitment to continually reflect on what you are doing personally and professionally to determine the quality of this behavior. It seems to us that being your own judge is more realistic and valuable than being someone else's judge. The intention of this book is to provide a catalyst for this self-inquiry.

In a survey of graduate students in APA-approved clinical training programs, the students were asked what they *should* do in a hypothetical situation in which a friend and colleague had violated APA ethical principles, and then what they *would* do (Bernard & Jara, 1986). Approximately half of these students said they would not live up to their own interpretation of what the ethical codes required of them as professionals. In general, although they knew what they should do as an ethical psychologist in a certain situation, they said they would choose not to follow this course of action. Bernard and Jara contend that the problem in training professionals is not how to communicate ethical codes more clearly to students but, rather, how to motivate them to apply their knowledge of ethical standards. "Psychologists need to carefully examine this question and to arrive at ways to reorder priorities so that their responsibility to monitor their own practices is taken more seriously" (1986, p. 315).

# Malpractice Issues in the Helping Professions

Can mental-health professionals be sued for failing to practice in a professional manner? How vulnerable are they to malpractice actions? What are some practical safeguards against being involved in a lawsuit?

## What Is Malpractice?

Practitioners are expected to abide by legal standards and adhere to the ethical codes of their profession in providing care to their clients. Unless they take due care and act in good faith, they are liable to a civil suit for failing to do their duties as provided by law. Civil liability means that an individual can be sued for not doing right or for doing wrong to another. Malpractice can be seen as the opposite of acting in good faith. It is defined as the failure to render proper service, through ignorance or negligence, resulting in injury or loss to the client. Professional negligence consists of departing from usual practice or not exercising due care. The primary problem in a negligence suit is determining which standards of care apply to determine whether a counselor has breached a duty to a client. The question relates to whether a reasonably prudent counselor in the same situation would have acted in a similar way. Counselors are judged according to the standards that are commonly accepted by the profession in their region (Hopkins & Anderson, 1985). In discussing professional standards of conduct Woody (1984) points out that human-service professionals need not be superior but must possess and exercise the knowledge and skill of a member of the profession in good standing.

Three conditions must be present in malpractice litigation: (1) the therapist must have had a duty to the client, (2) the therapist must have acted in a negligent or improper manner, and (3) there must be a causal relationship between that negligence and the damage claimed by the client (Van Hoose & Kottler, 1985).

## Causes of Malpractice Suits

Violations of confidentiality and sexual misconduct have received the greatest attention in the literature as grounds for malpractice suits. In order to be liable, psychotherapists must violate client confidentiality under those circumstances mandated by ethical guidelines or by state laws. It is suggested that practitioners inform clients before therapy of the limitations on confidentiality. Generally, therapists should attempt to obtain the written consent of the client whenever disclosure becomes necessary (Deardorff, Cross, & Hupprich, 1984). Sometimes, however, the therapeutic relationship is negatively affected when therapists develop too many forms of self-protection. How can practitioners expect their clients to trust them when they do not trust their clients?

According to the American Psychological Association Insurance Trust, which is the major insurance carrier for practicing psychologists, sexual relationships between client and therapist represent the greatest cost to the APA insurance program. Although the actual number of claims is relatively small, they account for 45% of the payments made under the professional liability plan for the last ten years and 20% of the total reported claims. As a way of reducing the impact of this type of unethical practice on the insurance premium charged to all psychologists, the APA insurance carrier has placed a $25,000 cap on payments for damages when sexual misconduct is alleged in a lawsuit.

A review of the literature reveals the following as other frequent causes of malpractice actions against human-service professionals: a countersuit for fee collection; the improper death of a client or other person; abandonment; the failure to supervise properly; misrepresenting one's professional training and skills; the failure to respect the client's integrity and privacy; the failure to exercise reasonable care in cases of suicide; the failure to warn and to protect others from a violent client; the failure to refer a client when it becomes clear that the person needs intervention that is beyond the worker's level of competence; the failure to consult; improper diagnosis and utilization of assessment techniques; improper methods of collecting fees; making inappropriate public statements (libel and slander); illegal search; unethical research practices; striking or physically assaulting a client as a part of the treatment; providing birth control and abortion information to minors (as opposed to making appropriate referrals for such help); prescribing and administering drugs inappropriately; breaching of a contract with a client; the failure to keep adequate records; the failure to treat clients properly; and the failure to provide for informed consent (Hopkins & Anderson, 1985; Reaves, 1986; Van Hoose & Kottler, 1985; Woody & Associates, 1984).

In recent cases counselors have been held liable for damages when poor advice was given. If clients rely on the advice given by a professional and suffer damages as a result, they can initiate civil action. Professional health-care providers would do well to avoid the temptation to try to work with all clients, regardless of their level of competence to render appropriate service.

## Ways to Protect Yourself from Malpractice Suits

*Be competent honestly*

One of the best ways to protect yourself from becoming embroiled in malpractice actions is by taking the preventive measure of acting within the scope of your competence. Another precaution against malpractice is personal and professional honesty and openness with clients. Although you may not always be able to make the "right choice" for every situation, what is crucial is that you know your limitations and remain open to seeking consultation in difficult cases. Below are some additional safeguards against malpractice:

- Clearly define issues pertaining to fees at the outset of therapy. If it is your practice to increase your fees periodically, tell clients that fees are subject to change with notice. Some practitioners avoid raising fees for current clients.
- Do not barter services. Exchanging of services is likely to lead to resentment on both your part and your client's.
- Keep adequate business records. In a case of a suit, if you admit that you don't keep records, you will probably be perceived as unprofessional. It should be stressed that it is a matter of preference as to how detailed you make your clinical notes.
- Keep client records for five to seven years. Write records in such a way that you would be willing to let your client read them.
- Avoid involvement in searches of students (Hopkins & Anderson, 1985). When school counselors take on monitoring and policing duties or become guardians of school lockers, they open themselves to the risk of invading the student's privacy.
- Since you can be sued for abandonment, make sure that you provide coverage for emergencies when you are going away. Consider an answering service so that you can be reached in times of crisis.
- Always consult with colleagues when you are in doubt. Since the legal standard is based on the practices of fellow professionals, the more consensus you have, the better chance you have of prevailing.
- Make use of informed-consent procedures and use contracts to clarify your professional relationships with clients. Realize that there is a wide variation in age of consent, depending on what is being consented to. Present information to your clients in clear language. Before discussing your clients or releasing their records, obtain their written permission.
- Be aware of the limits of confidentiality, and clearly communicate these to your clients. Attempt to obtain written consent whenever disclosure becomes necessary.
- Do not accept gifts from your clients. Although you can be friendly and personal with clients, your relationships should be primarily professional.
- In counseling minors be aware of sources to whom you can send clients who want specific information about birth-control methods and abortion.
- Learn about landmark court decisions and be aware of those rulings when you are required to warn and protect others.

- Learn how to assess and intervene in cases in which clients pose a danger to themselves and others. Knowing the danger signs of suicidal clients is the first step toward prevention.
- Become aware of local and state laws that limit your practice, as well as the policies of agencies you may work for.
- Be open in communications with clients and take an interest in their welfare (Van Hoose & Kottler, 1985).
- Engender positive feelings between yourself and clients, since good relationships substantially reduce the likelihood of a malpractice action (Knapp, 1980).
- Have a theoretical orientation to guide your practice, including a rationale for employing techniques.
- Familiarize yourself with statutes on privileged communication and general rules of confidentiality.
- Carefully document a client's treatment plan. Records might include notes of symptomatology, a diagnosis, treatment, documents verifying informed consent, relevant consultations and their outcomes, and a copy of the therapeutic contract (Knapp, 1980).
- Create reasonable expectations about what psychotherapy can and cannot do. It is especially important to test innovative therapeutic approaches before they are used with the general public (Schutz, 1982).

## Trends in Legal Liability

The public's use of the legal system for resolving grievances against mental-health professionals is increasing. This trend, which may reach crisis proportions (Reaves, 1986), suggests that private practitioners are becoming more vulnerable and are likely to find themselves involved in more litigation than in the past. However, this change can have a positive side, for it can stimulate professionals to offer higher-quality service and can protect clients from injustice (Deardorff, Cross, & Hupprich, 1984). It is a good idea to have access to an attorney for consultation in matters that are problematic. Furthermore, it is wise to have professional liability insurance.

Schutz (1982) predicted that legal liability for therapists would change in the 1980s, partly because of changes in the practice of psychotherapy. It seems clear that his forecast is coming true. Some of Schutz's predictions are:

- There will be an increase in the use of the informed-consent doctrine in cases of negligence.
- Malpractice suits will be more effective against those therapeutic approaches that are highly directive and active, because of the ease of establishing proximate cause.
- As a result of the increase of therapy with elderly people, there will be an increase of undue-influence suits.
- There will be an increase in suits over therapeutic approaches that have

not been as prompt and as effective as short-term therapies in achieving therapeutic results.

- If insurance claims are rejected because the treatment plan is found to have been inadequate, clients may be allowed to recover the fees they paid for services.
- Family therapy will prompt suits by family members who are dissatisfied with the outcomes. Therapeutic approaches that focus solely on the family as a system will be particularly affected. With such a perspective it is possible to lose sight of the individual rights.

This brief discussion of malpractice is not aimed at increasing your anxiety level. Rather, we hope that this entire chapter has helped to familiarize you with legal and ethical standards as a guide to your practice. Although no professional is expected to be perfect, it is beneficial for practitioners to evaluate what they are doing and why they are practicing as they are. At this point you might be interested in further reading in the area of legal liability in counseling and psychotherapy, as well as malpractice issues. Suggestions are given at the end of this chapter.

# Chapter Summary

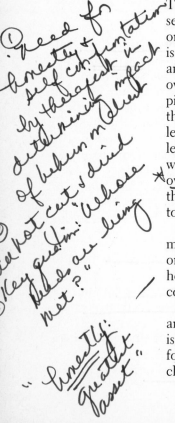

The underlying theme of this chapter has been the need for honesty and self-confrontation by therapists in determining the impact of their behavior on clients. Although certain behaviors are clearly unethical, most of the issues we raised are not cut-and-dried. Resolving them requires personal and professional maturity and a willingness to continue to question one's own motivations. A key question is "Whose needs are being met, the therapist's or the client's?" Perhaps a sign of good faith on the part of therapists is their willingness to openly share their questions and struggles with colleagues. Such consultation may help to clear up many foggy issues or at least suggest a different perspective. We have discussed sexual involvement with clients, which is an obvious affront to their welfare. We should not overlook some of the more subtle and perhaps insidious behaviors of the therapist that may in the long run cause as much, or perhaps more, damage to clients.

Becoming a therapist doesn't make you perfect or superhuman. You'll make some mistakes. What we want to stress is the importance of reflecting on what you're doing and on whose needs are primary. A willingness to be honest with yourself in your self-examination is your greatest asset in becoming an ethical practitioner.

We suggest that you review your responses to the open-ended questions and cases presented in the last three chapters and make a list of the ethical issues that are most significant to you at this time. Bringing these issues up for discussion with fellow students can be an excellent way of beginning to clarify them for yourself.

# Suggested Activities

1. Develop a panel in your class to explore the question of what unethical behavior in counseling is and what forms it can take. Try to select the issues that have the most significance to you and that you think will lead to a thought-provoking class discussion.
2. Review the cases and situations presented in this chapter, and role-play some of them in dyads. By actually experiencing these situations, you may be able to clarify some of your thoughts. If you do the role play in your small group, the others can give you valuable feedback concerning how they experienced you as a client or as a counselor.
3. Interview practicing counselors about some of the most pressing ethical concerns they encounter in their profession and how they have dealt with these concerns.
4. What are your views about forming social relationships with clients during the time they're in counseling with you? After they complete counseling?
5. What guidelines would you employ to determine whether nonerotic touching was therapeutic or countertherapeutic? Would the population you work with make a difference in terms of your touching practices? Would the work setting make a difference? How comfortable are you in both receiving and giving touching? What are your ethical concerns about touching?
6. Consider inviting an attorney who is familiar with the legal aspects of the client/therapist relationship to address your class. Possible questions for consideration are "What are the legal rights of clients in therapy? In addition to the ethical aspects, what are the legal implications of dual relationships in the client/therapist relationship?"
7. What kinds of unethical behavior by your colleagues do you think you would report, if any? How might you proceed if you knew of the unethical practice of a colleague?
8. In small groups explore your concerns about becoming involved in a malpractice suit as a therapist. Come up with as many ways as you can think of to protect yourself from a malpractice action.

# Suggested Readings

For a discussion of dual relationships see Pope (1985a), Stadler (1986), and Keith-Spiegel and Koocher (1985). On the issue of sexual attraction to clients see Pope, Keith-Spiegel, and Tabachnick (1986), Claiborn (1985), Hollingsworth (1985), and Ponzo (1985). On the role of touching in therapy see Willison and Masson (1986) and Holroyd and Brodsky (1977, 1980).

Two excellent books deal with the subject of sexual intimacy in the therapeutic relationship. One is the pioneering work of Pope and Bouhoutsos (1986), *Sexual Intimacy between Therapists and Patients*. This book explores issues such as risks for therapists, vulnerabilities of clients, consequences of therapist/client sexual involvement, specific techniques and principles of the subsequent therapy undertaken by the client with another therapist, filing of complaints, legal proceedings, and prevention of sexual involvement. The other book, *Sexual Dilemmas for the Helping Professional* (Edelwich with Brodsky, 1982), deals with issues such as seduction, power, opportunity and vulnerability, self-interest, morality, relationships among staff colleagues, legal considerations, and malpractice actions.

For journal articles on issues of sexual intimacy in the client/therapist relationship see Bouhoutsos (in press), Bouhoutsos, Holroyd, Lerman, Forer, and Greenberg (1983), Coleman and Schaefer (1986), Glaser and Thorpe (1986), Holroyd (1983), Holroyd and Bouhoutsos (1985), Holroyd and Brodsky (1977, 1980), Pope, Schover, and Levenson (1980), Fitzgerald and Nutt (1986), and Robinson and Reid (1985). For a discussion of the ethics of social and romantic relationships with present or former clients see Sell, Gottlieb, and Schoenfeld (1986). Brodsky (1986) contains an excellent chapter on sexual intimacy with an exploitation of clients.

On malpractice see Van Hoose and Kottler (1985), Hopkins and Anderson (1985), Deardorff, Cross, and Hupprich (1984), Schutz (1982), DePauw (1986), Knapp (1980), Wright (1981), and Reaves (1986). On legal issues in counseling and therapy see Hopkins and Anderson (1985), Knapp, Vandecreek, and Zirkel (1985), Schutz (1982), and Woody and Associates (1984).

# EIGHT

# Ethical Concerns in Multicultural Counseling

- Pre-Chapter Self-Inventory
- Introduction
- Ethical Codes in Multicultural Counseling
- Cultural Values and Assumptions in Therapy
- Matching Client and Counselor
- Multicultural Training of Counselors
- Chapter Summary
- Suggested Activities
- Suggested Readings

# Pre-Chapter Self-Inventory

*Directions:* For each statement, indicate the response that most closely identifies your beliefs and attitudes. Use the following code:

3 = I *agree*, in most respects, with this statement.
2 = I am *undecided* in my opinion about this statement.
1 = I *disagree*, in most respects, with this statement.

____ 1. Therapists who are well-trained, sensitive, and self-aware and who do not impose their values can be considered effective cross-cultural counselors.

____ 2. To counsel effectively I must be of the same ethnic background as my client.

____ 3. As a condition for state licensure, counselors should be able to demonstrate knowledge and competency in multicultural counseling.

____ 4. I must challenge cultural stereotypes when they become obvious in counseling situations.

____ 5. Contemporary counseling theories have applicability for all cultural populations.

____ 6. A sensitive cross-cultural counselor is a spokesperson for the particular culture from which the client comes.

____ 7. I see myself as willing to examine my behavior and attitudes to determine the degree to which cultural bias might influence the interventions I make with clients.

____ 8. I agree with those writers who emphasize the need for special guidelines for counseling members of minority groups.

____ 9. Ethnic and cultural differences must be taken into account whenever counselors work with clients from a different background.

____ 10. The primary function of majority-group counselors is to alert their clients to the choices available to them in the mainstream culture.

____ 11. An effective counselor facilitates the assimilation of the minority client into society.

____ 12. Ethical practice demands that counselors become familiar with the various value systems of diverse cultural groups.

____ 13. I would have no trouble working with someone from a culture very different from mine, because we would be more alike than different.

____ 14. If I just listen to my clients, I will know all I need to know about their cultural background.

____ 15. Client resistance is typically encountered in multicultural counseling and must be eradicated before major changes can take place.

____ 16. The ability to observe and work with nonverbal communication is an aspect of effective cross-cultural counseling.

___ 17. Establishing a trusting relationship is more difficult in a multicultural counseling situation.

___ 18. Unless practitioners have been educated about cultural differences, they cannot determine whether they are competent to work with diverse populations.

___ 19. As a condition for licensure all counselors should have specialized training and supervised experience in multicultural counseling situations.

___ 20. At this point in my educational career I feel well prepared to counsel culturally diverse client populations.

# Introduction

This chapter focuses on the *ethical* implications of a multicultural perspective in the helping professions. Even then we do not cover all the issues. This is not a comprehensive treatment of all the ramifications of multicultural counseling, for the field is complex and is developing rapidly. Also, we do not treat separate ethnic groups in this chapter, except by way of providing examples of some groups. We encourage you to go further by consulting some of the suggested readings at the end of the chapter.

## The Problem of Cultural Tunnel Vision

A faculty member overheard one of our students inquiring about possibilities for a fieldwork placement in a community agency. The student made a remark to the effect that "I don't want a placement where I'll have to work with poor people or minority groups." The faculty member, who teaches our multicultural course, was aghast. This brief sentence revealed much about the student's attitudes and beliefs about both people and the helping professions. In our experience this case represents an all-too-prevalent attitude of many middle-class students.

We have found that many students come into training with cultural tunnel vision. They have limited cultural experiences, and in many cases they see it as their mission to teach their clients about their view of the world. As Triandis (1985) writes, "The gap between the middle-class therapist who comes from a highly predictable environment and the lower-class client who comes from an unpredictable one can be large" (p. 26). Triandis believes that middle-class helpers of all cultural groups come from an environment that is too predictable and that their life experiences are limited. Because of this they may have difficulty in empathizing with others whose experiences significantly vary from their own. We think that specialized training to offset this cultural narrowness is an essential component of any program in the helping professions.

*familiar culture*

Helpers often say, explicitly or implicitly, that minorities are unresponsive to professional psychological intervention because of their lack of motivation to change or their "resistance" to seeking professional help. Lorion and Parron (1985) contend that mental-health professionals must appreciate and be prepared to respond to the needs of minority groups whose social, psychological, and behavioral disorders are accentuated by realities such as economic hardship, racism, discrimination, and environmental stress. In discussing therapy outcomes they point out that the treatment of low-income and minority clients may be influenced either positively or negatively by the client's perception of the initial attitudes and expectations of the therapist. Thus, helpers from all cultural groups need to honestly examine their own expectations and attitudes about the helping process as it applies to working with various cultural and ethnic groups. Lorion and Parron note the importance of such self-examination:

> Our argument simply stated is that the therapist's attitude toward low-income and minority groups has, to date, been a major obstacle to the delivery of effective mental health services. Our concern is that, if unchanged, these attitudes will defeat any attempts to respond to the increasing and multiple needs of low-income and minority people. Hopefully, our comments will help reverse a trend whereby generations of therapists have been trained and, in turn, trained others to assume that the poor, the uneducated, and the minority populations are unresponsive to contemporary treatment modalities [p. 80].

We are aware that in this chapter we may seem at times to be stereotyping certain cultures. Some generalizations are unavoidable, and we have tried to reduce them to a minimum.

## The Trend toward Cultural Awareness

Counselors need to know of specific cultural differences and to realize how certain cultural values find their way into the counseling situation. These are issues to be considered not merely by middle- or upper-middle-class Anglo counselors but also by counselors from any race or culture. To achieve these ends we will explore several issues:

- the scope and limitations of ethical codes for multicultural counseling
- proposed revisions in ethical standards for cross-cultural counseling
- contrasts between Western and Eastern therapeutic approaches and their implications for counselors
- the need to challenge stereotypical assumptions
- imperatives for ethnic and cultural relevance in counselor training programs
- characteristics of the culturally skilled counselor
- the culture and ethnicity of the counselor

*growing*

There is a growing awareness of and sensitivity to ethnic and cultural issues in the helping professions. A variety of multicultural concerns have been receiving increased attention for the last decade. These recent developments can be partially summarized as follows: (1) There is a trend toward acquiring knowledge of culturally different clients and gaining experience in working with minority clients. (2) There is a concern for adapting techniques and interventions in ways that are relevant for the culturally different client. (3) There is a recognition that counselor self-awareness is as important as cultural awareness in multicultural counseling situations. (4) There are implications for practice in the value orientations and differing basic assumptions underlying Eastern and Western therapeutic systems.

## The Need for a Multicultural Emphasis

The mental-health fields have yet to fully address the problems and issues involved in the counseling of culturally diverse populations. Pedersen (1985b) has noted that, although the field of multicultural counseling is a rapidly developing one and is receiving ever-increasing attention, there are few degree-oriented programs at the university level to train counselors in the special skills required.

Although almost any counseling situation involves some cultural differences, certain clients require much more attention and sensitivity. Clients bring with them specific values, beliefs, and actions conditioned by their experiences related to race, ethnicity, sex, religion, age, historical experience with the dominant culture, socioeconomic status, political views, lifestyle, and geographic region.

Multicultural counseling takes into consideration all of these aspects of our culturally pluralistic society. It is the consensus of writers in the field that the theories and practices of counseling need to be adapted to this multicultural perspective (Katz, 1985; Pedersen, 1985a; Smith, 1985b). Such a perspective respects the special needs and strengths of diverse client populations, and it recognizes the environmental experiences of these clients. Thus, it is essential for counselors to carefully examine the appropriateness of counseling practices in multicultural situations and to learn the knowledge, skills, and competencies that will enable them to function effectively and ethically in a multicultural society.

## Key Terms

It is helpful to define some of the terms that we will be using in this chapter: *ethnicity*, *culture*, *minority group*, *multicultural*, *pluralistic counseling*, and *ethnic-sensitive practice*.

*Ethnicity* is a sense of identity that stems from common ancestry, nationality, religion, and race. An ethnic group shares a unique social and cultural heritage passed on from generation to generation. Ethnicity provides a sense of identity, cohesion, and strength. It is a powerful unifying force that offers a sense of belonging and sharing based on commonality (Axelson, 1985; Lum, 1986, pp. 42–43).

*Culture* is a broader term than ethnicity. Pedersen (1986) describes it as including *demographic* variables such as age, gender, and place of residence; *status* variables such as social, educational, and economic background; and formal or informal *affiliations* to one group or special population. In this broad view culture includes institutions, language, values, religious ideals, and patterns of social relationships.

*Minority group* has come to refer to a category of people who have typically been discriminated against or subjected to unequal treatment. These groups have been characterized as subordinate, dominated, and powerless. Although the term *minority* has traditionally referred to national, racial, linguistic, and religious groups, the term now also applies to women, people with a gay or lesbian life-style, the aged, the physically handicapped, and the behaviorally deviant (Lum, 1986).

*Multicultural* is a generic term that we tend to use rather than *cross-cultural*, *transcultural*, or *intercultural*. It is a term that more accurately reflects the complexity of culture and avoids any implied comparison. In describing *multicultural counseling* Axelson (1985) notes that, although people share a common denominator in general society, many also belong to groups that are identified by their beliefs, values, thought patterns, feelings, and behaviors, which are conditioned by factors such as ethnicity, gender, age, socioeconomic status, and life-style. According to Axelson, multicultural counseling considers the aspects of many different cultural environments in a pluralistic society, along with the relevant theories and techniques in counseling practice. Padilla and De Snyder (1985, p. 160) define a related term, *"pluralistic counseling,"* as "a therapeutic intervention that recognizes and understands a client's culturally based beliefs, values, and behaviors." This approach takes into account clients' personal life experiences, family history, and socio-cultural factors that affect them. Pluralistic counseling aims at helping clients clarify their personal and cultural standards so that they can orient their behavior to these standards.

*Ethnic-sensitive practice* focuses on the present-day influences of the daily life of ethnic-minority groups. Going beyond the concerns of the individual, this type of practice addresses the consequences of racism, poverty, and discrimination on the group; it aims to change those institutions that perpetuate these conditions (Devore, 1985).

# Ethical Codes in Multicultural Counseling

Most of the codes of professional organizations mention the practitioner's responsibility for recognizing the special needs of diverse client populations. For example, the *Ethical Standards* of the AACD (1981) specify that counselors must guard the individual rights and personal dignity of the client through an awareness of the negative impact of both racial and sexual stereotyping and discrimination. The code of ethics for the American

School Counselor Association (1984) outlines the following guiding principles and basic tenets in the counseling process:

- Each person has the right to respect and dignity as a human being and to counseling services without prejudice as to person, character, belief or practice.
- Each person has the right to self-direction and self-development.
- Each person has the right of choice and responsibility for decisions reached.

The ethical code of the National Association of Social Workers (1979) makes specific references to the ethical responsibility to recognize and respect the special needs of diverse clients and to work actively against any form of discrimination. There is a commitment to the primacy of the client's welfare and best interests, and specific sections of the code spell out the ethical responsibility to the diverse range of clients.

- The social worker should not practice, condone, facilitate, or collaborate with any form of discrimination on the basis of race, color, sex, sexual orientation, age, religion, national origin, marital status, political belief, mental or physical handicap, or any other preference or personal characteristic, condition, or status.
- The social worker should not engage in any action that violates or diminishes the civil or legal rights of clients.

Social workers are also mandated to promote conditions that encourage respect for the diversity of cultures that constitute American society. (See the NASW code in the Appendix.)

## The Limitations of Existing Codes

Pedersen and Marsella (1982) address the question "Are the APA ethical guidelines adequate for cross-cultural counseling and therapy?" Some of their main points are as follows:

- The ethical crisis of cross-cultural counseling results from the use of mental-health assumptions and interventions that were developed in one cultural context but implemented in a totally different one.

 APA unethical

- Counseling of people of culturally diverse backgrounds by therapists who are not trained or competent to work with such groups should be regarded as unethical.
- The multiplicity of cultural values in our society has been neglected. Too often psychologists are culturally biased, and the services they render are more suited to the dominant culture than to the unique needs of various ethnic groups.
- Ethical guidelines are frequently insensitive to the client's cultural values. The dominant culture's values are often used to describe people in other cultures without its having been proved that the findings can be validly generalized from the dominant to the minority cultures.

According to Pedersen and Marsella, there have been numerous attempts to define ethical guidelines for cross-cultural situations, but not many of them have been successful. They see existing guidelines as inadequate in a cross-cultural context. They conclude:

> A serious moral vacuum exists in the delivery of cross-cultural counseling and therapy services because the values of a dominant culture have been imposed on the culturally different consumer. Cultural differences complicate the definition of guidelines even for the conscientious and well-intentioned counselor and therapist [p. 498].

In essence, their point seems to be that, even though practitioners are conscientiously following the established guidelines of the professional organization, they can still be practicing unethically.

The APA Committee on International Relations in Psychology organized a symposium at the 1986 annual meeting of the association to discuss what, if any, changes should be recommended in the existing APA ethical principles to increase their appropriateness for a multicultural population. The purpose of this symposium was to explore Pedersen's (1986) question "Are the APA ethical principles culturally encapsulated?" *Cultural encapsulation* (Wrenn, 1985) implies stereotypical thinking and ignoring of cultural differences. In most cases counselors who are encapsulated are not aware of it.

Cultural variables are specifically mentioned three times in the existing APA *Ethical Principles of Psychologists* (1981a): Principle 1.a., on responsibility; Principle 2.d., on competence; and Principle 3.b., on moral and legal standards. Pedersen contends that the APA standards are indeed culturally encapsulated and makes these key points:

- To the extent that these codes are based on stereotyped values from the dominant culture's perspective, they may need to be revised so that the interests of minority groups are taken into account as well as those of the majority group.
- To the extent that these codes are grounded on a single standard of normal and ethical behavior, they may require revision to incorporate a variety of culturally defined alternatives.
- To the extent that the codes are "technique oriented," they may need to be made congruent with a wide range of multicultural situations.

Ibrahim (1986), giving a resounding *yes* to Pedersen's question whether the APA ethical principles are culturally encapsulated, proposes the following revisions of them:

- In the Preamble the fact that much of human behavior is learned in a social context needs to be emphasized. People understand themselves and others through the perspective of their own beliefs, values, assumptions, and worldviews.
- Principle 1 (Responsibility) needs to incorporate the psychologist's responsibility to understand the role of cultural factors in shaping human behavior, resulting in different philosophies and worldviews.

- Principle 2 (Competence) should have a stronger statement regarding the need for appropriate education and training to work with diverse populations. Unless practitioners have been educated about cultural differences, they cannot determine whether they are competent to work with certain populations.
- Principle 4 (Public Statements) should be revised to require practitioners to specify their level of training to work with diverse populations.
- Principle 5 (Confidentiality) should state that people from different cultural backgrounds have different conceptions of the limits of confidentiality, and this matter needs to be appropriately communicated to clients from diverse cultures.

According to Casas (1986), the AACD ethical standards (1981) are no better than the APA ethical principles with respect to providing for specific guidelines for serving ethnic minority groups. Casas contends that sensitivity and understanding are lacking among most counseling psychologists because most traditional counseling programs have ignored the existence of ethnic minorities and have ethnocentrically assumed that the education and training provided could be equally applicable to all groups. He agrees that most counseling students and teachers are not aware of their culturally biased values and attitudes. He concludes that the accreditation guidelines for programs approved both by the APA and the AACD need to be revised so they more directly address ethnic variables. Guidelines should contain specific criteria in the area of course work and experiences for the assessment of a program's effort to effectively address culture and race.

Recognizing that the existing ethical codes are limited, Ibrahim and Arredondo (1986) recommend that the AACD's present ethical standards be extended to address cross-cultural perspectives. They propose standards in the areas of (1) preparing culturally effective counselors, (2) providing ethical and effective counseling for diverse cultural and ethnic groups, (3) selecting and using culturally appropriate assessment devices, and (4) conducting culturally appropriate research. With regard to the *preparation of counselors* the authors propose the addition of these two standards:

1. Counselor-preparation programs, in their policies, procedures, and curricula, should recognize and respond to the cultural diversity among students, faculty, and clients.
2. Counselor educators should be prepared to teach and to supervise competently about cross-cultural factors in counseling practice.

With regard to *counseling practice*, Ibrahim and Arredondo recommend the addition of these two standards:

1. Counselors need to incorporate into their practice a knowledge of the client's general cultural system and specific worldview.
2. Counselors need to recognize, assess, and accept their own worldviews, cultural contexts, and biases.

*unethical*

*✳*

## Toward Ethical Multicultural Practice

Counselors may misunderstand clients who are of a different sex, race, age, social class, or sexual orientation. Counselors who do not integrate these cross-cultural factors into their practice infringe on the client's cultural autonomy and basic human rights, and they lessen the chances of establishing an effective therapeutic relationship. Therefore, the failure to address these factors constitutes unethical practice (Cayleff, 1986).

In his article "Ethics and Multicultural Therapy: An Unrealized Dream," Ivey (1986) concludes that our present codes of ethics are not fully ethical, because they are bound by the discourse of Western culture. He adds that much of our research and practice is culturally encapsulated without our awareness. He proposes the following steps as ways of moving toward an ethical multicultural practice:

- Put the issue of multicultural awareness at the center of professional codes of ethics by making it the starting point for practice.
- Place the issue of multicultural practice at the core of our publications and research journals.
- Initiate a long-term program of public and professional awareness of ourselves as cultural beings.
- Open our ethical codes and practice for more involvement with the public.

We think that Albert Ellis takes a challenging and thought-provoking position that could provide a basis for a practitioner's ability to practice ethically in a multicultural context:

> If psychologists follow the psychotherapeutic code of fully accepting all their clients even when they personally disagree with some of these clients' strong preferences and tastes, the place of prejudice in psychology, as well as the unethical conduct of psychologists that frequently accompanies prejudice, will not be completely abolished. But I strongly hypothesize that it will be significantly diminished [1986].

Before you continue, reflect on this situation: Consider a well-trained counselor who is culturally sensitive to the client, is aware of his or her own values and biases, and does not impose them on clients. Do these attributes alone make for an effective cross-cultural counselor? Do these qualities eliminate the chances of ethical transgression? What do you think needs to be added for effective multicultural counseling?

At this point we suggest that you review the professional codes of ethics, found in the Appendix, to determine for yourself the degree to which they take cultural and racial dimensions into account. From a multicultural perspective, what are their shortcomings? To what degree do you think that most of them are culturally encapsulated? What revisions and additions can you think of as a basis for mental-health practitioners to function ethically in today's multicultural world?

# Cultural Values and Assumptions in Therapy

In this section we explore the difference between Western and Eastern assumptions about therapy, examine the importance of the counselor's values in multicultural therapy, and discuss the need for therapists to challenge stereotypical beliefs.

## Western versus Eastern Values

Recently two of us (Marianne Corey and Jerry Corey) observed mental-health practices in China. We discussed contrasts between Western and Eastern therapeutic approaches with David Ho of the University of Hong Kong. Ho (1985) has described the value assumptions of various approaches and has called for a creative synthesis of Western and Eastern values. The categories *Eastern* and *Western* are not geographic terms but represent social, political, and cultural value orientations. When we speak of the Eastern and Western worlds, we are not implying a discrete distinction between these two. It is not a matter of all Easterners thinking alike and all Westerners thinking alike.

Contemporary theories of therapy and therapeutic practices are grounded in Western assumptions. Yet most of the world is not like mainstream U.S. culture. Saeki and Borow (1985) discuss some contrasts between the Eastern and Western systems. Western culture places prime value on choice, the uniqueness of the individual, self-assertion, and the strengthening of the ego. Therapeutic outcomes that it emphasizes include improving assertive coping by changing the environment, changing one's coping behavior, and learning to manage stress. This position advocates ways of changing objective reality to improve one's way of life. By contrast, Eastern views stress interdependence, underplay individuality, and emphasize the losing of oneself in the totality of the cosmos. The Asian counseling perspective, for example, typically mirrors the life values associated with inner enlightenment and acceptance of one's environment.

Being oriented toward change is part of the Westernized approach. In many Eastern countries people have little chance—or inclination—to move out of their cultural context. Therapeutic approaches in China and in Japan rely much more on resources within the community. There is more of a social framework than a focus on the development of the individual. Applying the Western world model of therapy to the Chinese culture does not work. Likewise, this model has major limitations when it is applied to minority groups such as Asian Americans, Hispanics, Native Americans, and Blacks. Seeking psychological professional help is not typical for many minority groups. In fact, in most non-Western cultures informal groups of friends and relatives provide a supportive network. Informal counseling consists of the spontaneous outreach of caring people to others in need (Brammer, 1985b).

According to Ho, Asian Americans underuse professional therapy. Although they may seek formal therapy, they do so when other informal sources of help have not worked. Ho proposes a creative synthesis of collectivism and individualism, whereby it is possible to draw from both worlds. Agreeing with Ho are Saeki and Borow (1985), who believe that the aims of treatment in both worlds are linked to striving for the good life as defined in the respective dominant cultures. "Eastern and Western systems both address the nature and control of intrapersonal conflict but do so in different ways" (p. 225). In the accompanying table we describe general characteristics that, according to Ho, differentiate these two perspectives.

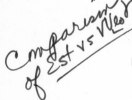

### A Comparison of the Western and Eastern Systems

| West | East |
| --- | --- |
| **Values** | |
| Primacy of individual | Primacy of relationship |
| Democratic orientation | Authoritarian orientation |
| Nuclear family structure | Extended family structure |
| Emphasis on youth | Emphasis on maturity |
| Independence | Interdependence |
| Assertiveness | Compliance |
| Nonconformity | Conformity |
| Competition | Cooperation |
| Conflict | Harmony |
| Freedom | Security |
| **Guiding Principles for Action** | |
| Fulfillment of individual needs | Achievement of collective goals |
| Individual responsibility | Collective responsibility |
| **Behavior Orientation** | |
| Expression of feelings | Control of feelings |
| Uniqueness of individual | Uniformity |
| Self-actualization | Collective actualization |
| **Time Orientation** | |
| Future orientation | Traditionalism |
| Innovation | Conservatism |
| **Ethical Orientation** | |
| Morality anchored in person | Morality linked to relationships |

■ *The case of two immigrants.*  An Asian immigrant couple come to a marriage counselor in a small midwestern American city with concerns for the future of their marriage. The husband is quiet and controlled; the wife cries often and also says little.

Dan, their counselor, has just completed a workshop in cross-cultural counseling and is immediately conscious of their silence and the importance of respecting this behavior. He is aware that in Oriental culture the wife typically defers to the husband and that he should respect that. In other words, he needs to be careful in prompting the wife to speak lest he be guilty of a cultural faux pas. The result is that Dan becomes silent and feels stifled and useless to them as a counselor.

- How would you proceed to work with this couple?
- Even though the problem of marital discord seems straightforward, what are some of the potential cultural issues the therapist may need to consider?
- What would you do or not do with this couple?

**Cultural Contradictions.**   According to Ho (1985), there is a basic contradiction between the traditional moralistic and authoritarian orientation of Eastern perspectives and the psychological and therapeutic orientation of Western approaches. He contends that to follow the Western orientation in the East would lead eventually to a head-on collision with entrenched traditional values. These cultural contradictions often apply in multicultural counseling situations in the United States, especially when Anglo counselors function within the framework of the model we have just described. Likewise, a minority counselor working with an Anglo client from mainstream society would surely falter if he or she did not give sufficient consideration to cultural variables.

Ho contends that research is needed on clients' belief systems, on perceptions of psychological services, and on the effectiveness of treatment in cross-cultural counseling. He also maintains that Western approaches need to examine their underlying value assumptions. Indeed, we want to stress that all approaches need to examine basic assumptions that influence practice.

**A Creative Synthesis of Individualism and Collectivism.**   Can Western approaches be transplanted? Are Asian and Western systems of psychotherapy mutually exclusive because of contrasting philosophical bases?

> It seems reasonable to anticipate that transactions between East and West, as they explore one another's counseling forms, will continue and that a selective sorting and adopting of principles and techniques appropriate to the respective cultures will occur. Should that happen, the psychotherapies of both East and West will have attained a new maturity [Saeki & Borow, 1985, p. 229].

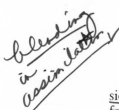

Individualism affirms the uniqueness, autonomy, freedom, and intrinsic worth of the individual, and it insists that each one assume responsibility for his or her conduct, well-being, and salvation. Many of the contemporary counseling theories do have a bias with a focus on the individual. Behavior is explained largely as a function of inner dynamics, and sociocultural factors are generally not given this same emphasis. By contrast, collectivism affirms the value of preserving and enhancing the well-being of the group as the main principle guiding social action. The challenge, according to Ho (1985), is to find a way to integrate elements of collectivism and individualism after exploring these issues with the client and letting the client decide.

This synthesis entails the collective actualization of individuals-in-society and, at the same time, the actualization of the individual.

Patterson (1985b) criticizes the conclusion of many writers that the methods of Western therapeutic approaches are not appropriate in other cultures. And he denies that traditional goals and methods must be adapted to conform to the characteristics of other cultures. He also contends that the Eastern and Western cultures must move toward each other. "Eastern cultures must change in the direction of greater concern for individual personal development. Western culture must move in the direction of greater concern for the influence of the individual upon others and upon their development, and of cooperation in fostering personal development in others" (p. 188).

■ **The case of Claude.**     Claude, an Anglo counselor, takes over as director of a clinic that has a large percentage of Oriental immigrants. At a staff meeting he sums up his philosophy of counseling in this fashion: "People come to counseling to begin change or because they are already in the process of change. Our purpose is to challenge them to change. This holds true whether the client is White, Oriental, or some other minority. If the clients are slow to speak, our job is to challenge them to speak, because the majority of this American culture deals with problems through talking. Silence may be a mark of the Oriental culture, but it does not work in this culture, and the sooner they learn this the better for them."

• To what degree, if any, do you think Claude has "tunnel vision"?
• Do you detect any signs of cultural bias?
• To what degree do you agree or disagree with Claude, and why?

## The Counselor's Values

It is crucial that counselors be aware of their values and be willing to examine the potential impact of these values on clients with different cultural experiences. In addition, counselors must resist making value judgments of clients who are culturally different. They need to understand and accept clients who have a different set of assumptions about life, and they need to be alert for the likelihood of imposing their worldview.

Before you read the next section, we suggest that you reflect on the case example and on the questions that follow as a way of examining some of your own assumptions about the helping process as applied to culturally different clients.

■ **The case of MacInany.**     MacInany, a White middle-class psychologist, is very vocal in his denunciation of "all this cross-cultural stuff." He sees it as more trendy than useful. "I do not impose my values. I do not tell clients what to do. I listen, and if I need to know something, I ask. How am I to know whether a Japanese-American client is more American than Japanese or vice versa unless I ask him? My motto is that the client will tell you all you need to know."

- What stereotypical beliefs and assumptions do you hold?
- Do you focus mainly on the weakness of values different from your own?
- Do you assume that all your clients will be ready to engage in self-disclosure? What interventions might you make, assuming that the client's hesitancy to disclose is cultural rather than a sign of resistance?
- To what extent do you value assertiveness? Is this a value that you expect most of your clients to acquire? How might you react to clients who are culturally conditioned not to be assertive?
- What assumptions about culture and the helping relationship do you have that may either help or hinder you in establishing effective therapeutic relationships with culturally diverse clients?
- What do you think of the view of Patterson (1985b), who argues that it is not necessary, or desirable, to design new approaches for counseling clients from other cultures, because universal human values provide the common goal and methods of counselors in all cultures?

## Challenging Stereotypical Beliefs

Counselors may think they are not biased, yet they may hold some stereotypical beliefs that could well affect practice. Examples are "Failure to change is due to a lack of motivation." "People have choices, and it is up to them to change their life." Counselors who make such assumptions are ignoring that some people do not have a wide range of choices because of environmental factors beyond their control. Another assumption is that "talk therapy" works best, ignoring the fact that many cultures rely more on nonverbal expression.

**Three Oversimplifications.** Lorion and Parron (1985) have identified three stereotypical assumptions that they believe interfere with establishing an effective therapeutic relationship with low-income or minority clients. We list each inaccurate assumption and then add their reply.

1. *Low-income or minority clients are a homogeneous group.* The fact is that diversity characterizes people of any group. Also, poor groups and minority groups are not identical, for minority populations are represented at all economic levels.

2. *Low-income or minority individuals experience lives that are continuously bleak, without any positive moments.* Although they do have a stressful and demanding life, they also experience warmth, humor, joy, and enjoyment. They have many strengths that mental-health practitioners often fail to notice and to use in therapy.

3. *Low-income or minority segments of society are unreliable, impulsive, and irresponsible.* Again, the heterogeneity of the population must be recognized. Although clients from these groups may arrive late for appoint-

ments in a community mental-health agency, therapists need to understand the hardships and efforts that are frequently associated with simply getting to the session. There is also the myth that poor or minority people cannot become self-actualized, primarily because of their struggle for survival.

Low-income or minority clients tend to terminate professional treatment earlier than do wealthier or mainstream clients. Rather than putting the total responsibility on them, however, it is useful for counselors to examine their own attitudes and assumptions. Lorion and Parron (1985) contend that professional helpers often communicate negative expectations to such clients. Whether intentionally or unintentionally, through their words and behavior, helpers reveal their views about a client's appropriateness for therapy. To a large extent these communications and the assumptions on which they are based influence the length of time clients will remain in therapy to gain benefit. Lorion and Parron offer the advice "Know thyself *and* thy client!"

**Assumptions about Self-Disclosure.**    Another assumption is that clients will be ready to talk about their intimate personal issues. This assumption ignores that in some cultures such self-disclosure is taboo and that some European ethnic groups stress keeping problems "in the family." Asian Americans who seek therapy are frequently described as the "most repressed of all clients" (Sue & Sue, 1985). Such Asian-American clients who are considered repressed or resistive may in fact be holding true to their cultural background. Disagreeing with this view are those who say that the inability to self-disclose is something to be overcome, not accepted. Patterson (1985b) contends that, if this obstacle cannot be overcome, the client is unable to participate in the therapeutic relationship. Unless clients are willing to verbalize and communicate their thoughts, feelings, attitudes, and perceptions, he argues, there is no basis for empathic understanding by the therapist.

■ *The case of Lily.*    Lily, a licensed counselor, has come to work in a family-life center that deals with many immigrant families. She often becomes impatient over the slow pace of her clients' disclosures. It is sometimes like squeezing blood from the proverbial turnip. Lily decides to teach her clients by modeling for them. With one of her reticent couples she says: "My husband and I have many fights and disagreements. We express our feelings openly and clear the air. In fact, several years ago my husband had an affair, which put our relationship into a turmoil. I believe it was my ability to vent my anger and express my hurt that allowed me to work through this terrible event."

- What do you think of Lily's self-disclosure? Would such a disclosure be helpful to you if you were her client?
- Might you be inclined to make a similar type of disclosure to your clients? Why or why not?

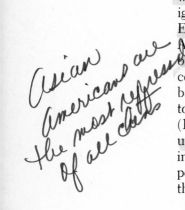

- What possible positive or negative outcomes might occur after such a disclosure?
- Is it a culturally sensitive thing to do with those who have not known such candor in their own experience?

**Assumptions about Assertiveness.**  Most counselors assume that clients are better off if they can behave in assertive ways, such as telling people directly what they think and what they want. In fact, much of therapy consists in teaching clients the skills to take an active stance toward life. Sue and Sue (1985) report a widespread view that Asian Americans are nonassertive and passive. They contend, however, that this assumption has not been supported by research. These authors do stress that traditional counseling practices may act as barriers to effective cross-cultural helping, and they call for culturally appropriate intervention strategies, or culture-specific methods, that are congruent with the value orientation of Asian-American clients.

**Assumptions about Self-Actualization and Trusting Relationships.**  Another assumption made by mental-health professionals is that it is important for the individual to become a fully functioning person. A counselor may often focus on what is good for the individual and neglect the impact of the individual's change on the significant people in that person's life or the impact of those significant people on the client. It is not a question of individual versus group but, rather, a creative synthesis between these two dimensions.

Patterson (1985b) again has another point of view. For him, the purpose and goal of counseling is to help people who are hampered in their personal development to become more self-actualizing. He maintains that, for personality change to occur in the direction of self-actualization, three core conditions of the therapeutic relationship are necessary. These conditions—empathic understanding, respect, and therapeutic genuineness— are viewed as essential in cross-cultural counseling, since the striving for self-actualization is assumed to be common to all cultures.

Another assumption pertains to the development of a trusting relationship. Anglo Americans tend to form quick relationships and to talk easily about their personal lives. This characteristic is reflected in our counseling approaches. We expect clients to come to therapy open and willing to explore personal issues with a counselor who is a total stranger. Among many cultures it takes a long time to develop such a relationship. Many Asian Americans, Hispanics, and American Indians have been brought up not to speak until spoken to, especially when they are with the elderly and authority figures (Sue, 1981a). Counselors may interpret the client's hesitancy to speak as resistance when it is only a sign of respect.

**Assumptions about Nonverbal Behavior.**  Many cultural expressions are subject to misinterpretation, including personal space, eye contact, hand-shaking, dress, formality of greeting, perspective on time, and so forth. Mainstream Americans frequently feel uncomfortable with periods of silence, and so they tend to fill the air with words. In some cultures silence may be a sign of respect and politeness rather than a lack of a desire to continue to speak. Certain cultures, such as the Japanese, place value on indirectness and nonverbal communication. As Henkin (1985) has observed, the Western counselor, whose confrontational style involves direct eye contact, broad physical gestures, and probing personal questions, may be seen as offensively intrusive by Japanese-American clients and by clients from many other cultures. Wolfgang (1985) writes about the need for counselor sensitivity to the different meanings of nonverbal behaviors such as eye contact, distance, and gestures. Increased eye contact, smiling, and head nods are often seen as signs of positive nonverbal reinforcement. But, there is evidence that some ethnic minorities consider prolonged eye contact as confrontive.

Western counselors are often systematically trained in attending skills, which include keeping an open posture, maintaining good eye contact, and leaning toward the client (Egan, 1986). Although these behaviors are aimed at creating a positive therapeutic relationship, individuals from certain ethnic groups may have difficulty in responding positively or understanding the intent of such posturing. In American culture eye contact is considered a sign of attentiveness and presence, and a lack thereof is viewed as being evasive. Devore (1985) cautions that Asians and American Indians may view direct eye contact as a lack of respect. Thus, it is a mistake to prematurely label clients as "resistive" or "pathological" if they avoid eye contact and do not respond to the invitation of the attending behavior. In some cultures lack of eye contact may even be a sign of respect and good manners. Sue (1981a, p. 42) gives a good example of how counselors often feel that their Black clients are hostile and angry and may misread certain other behaviors. Nonverbal behaviors that are misinterpreted include the intense "stare," the diminished personal space, and the greater body activity when speaking. In writing about American Indians, Attneave (1985) indicates that direct eye-to-eye gaze generally indicates aggressiveness; in cross-gender encounters it usually means sexual aggressiveness.

It should be clear that there are no universal meanings of nonverbal behaviors. Thus, it is essential for counselors to acquire sensitivity to cultural differences in order to reduce the probability of miscommunication, misdiagnosis, and misinterpretation of behavior (Wolfgang, 1985, p. 100).

**Assumptions about Directness.**    Western therapeutic approaches prize directness. Yet some cultures see it as a sign of rudeness and as something to be avoided. The counselor could assume that a lack of directness is evidence of pathology or at least as a sign of lack of assertiveness, rather than a sign of respect. Although getting to the point immediately is a prized value in White, Anglo-American culture, certain other cultures could see this type of behavior as inappropriate. Counselees from other cultures might be seen as wanting to avoid dealing with their problems.

■ ***The case of Miguel.***    Miguel, a Mexican American born in the United States, has completed his Ph.D. and is currently working at a community clinic in family therapy. In his training he has learned of the concept of triangulation, or the tendency of two persons who are in conflict to involve a third person in their emotional system in order to reduce the stress (Brown & Christensen, 1986). Miguel is on the watch for evidence of this tendency. While he is counseling an Mexican-American family, the father says to his son, "Your mother wants you to show her more respect than you do and to obey her more." Miguel says to the mother: "Do you always allow your husband to speak for you? Can you say this directly to your son yourself, rather than speaking through your husband?" The room falls silent, and there is great discomfort.

Was Miguel culturally sensitive with his statement? How would you have handled this situation differently, especially if you saw "triangulation" as leading to family pathology?

**A Personal Illustration.**    A few years ago Marianne Corey and Jerry Corey conducted a training workshop with native counselors from a Latin-American country. Marianne was criticized by a male participant for being too direct and assertive. He said that he had difficulties with Marianne's active leadership style and indicated that it was her place to defer to Jerry by always letting him take the lead. Recognizing and respecting our cultural differences, we were able to arrive at a mutual understanding of different values.

Jerry had difficulty with the tardiness of the participants and had to accept the fact that we could not follow a rigid time schedule. Typically we have thought that, if people were late or missed a session, group cohesion would be difficult to maintain. Because the issue was openly discussed in this situation, however, the problem did not arise. We quickly learned that *we* had to adapt ourselves to their view of time. To insist on interpreting such behavior as resistance would have been to ignore the cultural context.

■

## Matching Client and Counselor

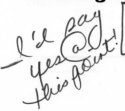

*Does the counselor have to share the racial and cultural backgrounds of the client to be effective?* This is a difficult question to answer, and the research in this area is inconclusive. Some argue that successful interracial counseling is highly improbable because of the cultural and racial barriers involved. Others argue that well-trained and sensitive counselors may be able to establish effective counseling relationships with their culturally different clients.

Lorion and Parron (1985) write that there is little scientific evidence supporting the position that minority clients should always be treated by minority therapists. They add that low-income or minority clients tend to respond most positively to therapists who are warm, open, and sensitive to the demands they struggle with, regardless of the therapist's race. The critical variable seems to be a willingness to learn about the realities of minority life.

We are in agreement with the position that you can work with clients who differ from yourself in gender, race, culture, socioeconomic background, age, or life-style orientation. But, our position is tempered by certain reservations and conditions. First of all, counselors must be trained specifically in multicultural perspectives, both on an academic and an experiential level. Second, as in any counseling situation there must be an agreement between a particular client and a particular counselor with respect to their ability to develop a working therapeutic relationship. Third, counselors must be flexible in applying theories to specific client situations. The counselor who has an open stance has a greater likelihood of success than someone who rigidly adheres to a single theoretical system. Sue (1981a, p. 52) writes "It is my contention that cross-cultural helping cannot be approached through any one theory of counseling."

Fourth, the counselor must be open to being challenged and tested in order to earn trust and credibility. In multicultural counseling situations there is a greater likelihood that clients will exhibit suspicion and distrust. Consider the situation of a Black client and a White counselor. Blacks may tend to perceive Whites as potential enemies unless proved otherwise. Minority members may use many defenses as survival strategies to prevent Whites from knowing their true feelings. A Black client who has had the experience of discrimination and pain at the hands of a White society will not easily—and understandably so—trust a representative of that White culture, no matter how sensitive and skillful the counselor may be. White counselors are often perceived as symbols of the Establishment, and the minority client is likely to project past experiences onto the present situation. Even though the White counselor has admirable motives, the client may distrust the counselor simply because he or she is White. Counselors who see themselves as culturally skilled and sensitive may have a difficult time withstanding this kind of testing. Counselors who become excessively defensive in such situations will most likely lose the client. Minorities may not have faith in the counseling process because the White counselor often proposes White solutions to the client's concern. Yet these solutions may not fit for the non-White client. Clients may feel that they would have to reject their own culture to accept the counselor's values or solutions.

Fifth, it becomes even more important in multicultural counseling situations that counselors be aware of their value system, of potential stereotyping, and of any traces of prejudice. Counselors who view themselves as devoid of all prejudices can in some ways be more dangerous than those who are more open with their prejudices. The counselor who says "When I look at you, I see a person, not a Black person" may encounter mistrust from clients who have had no previous experience with such "openness."

Further, it may be difficult for these clients to discuss their anger toward their negative experiences of prejudice with such an understanding counselor. Smith (1985a) indicates that the life concerns of Black women are both similar to and different from those of White women, and she therefore cautions counselors not to overgeneralize. On this issue Jones (1985) makes the excellent point that a therapist's self-knowledge and continual self-awareness are at least as important as cultural understanding in effectively treating the Black client. Jones concedes that culture and race do play a key role but adds that they should not be overplayed to the extent that they blur the unique individuality of the client.

Finally, counselors need to be aware of their reactions to unusual behavior. The definition of abnormal behavior has a cultural bias. When counselors observe such unusual behavior, it is essential to examine this behavior within the minority client's cultural context. Thus, minority clients may be suspicious and may declare that people are out to get them. They may not be suffering from clinical paranoia but, indeed, be reacting to the realities of an environment in which they have suffered oppression and prejudice. In speaking of the Japanese-American client Henkin (1985) contends that feelings of victimization, suspicion, distrust, and hostility may actually result from genuine persecution.

Ridley (1984) asserts that individual verbal therapies often place the Black client in a paradoxical situation. Although self-disclosure is typically considered essential for maximizing therapy outcomes, there are complex intrapersonal, interpersonal, and social factors that affect the Black client's willingness to be open. Clients are expected to be highly verbal and articulate for successful therapy to occur, and this is the basis of "talking therapies." In this light the goals of most traditional therapies appear to be incongruous with the disclosing tendencies of many Black clients. Through the process of self-disclosure Blacks open themselves up to hurt from racism and oppression. Yet to make therapeutic movement, disclosure is necessary. According to Ridley, this is the therapeutic paradox.

We suggest that you pause here to think about these questions:

- What is your position on whether the counselor needs to share the racial and cultural backgrounds of the client to be effective?
- If you were to encounter considerable "testing" from a minority client, how do you think you would react? What are some ways that you could work therapeutically, rather than being defensive?
- What experiences have you had with discrimination? How do you think your own experiences could either help or hinder you in working with clients who have been discriminated against?

In the case that follows consider this well-intentioned counselor's lack of sensitivity to the needs of minority clients. As you read the case, think about ways in which you could increase your own sensitivity to working with individuals from ethnic and cultural groups different from your own.

■ *The case of John O'Brien.*  John O'Brien, who comes from a lower-middle-class neighborhood in an Eastern city, has struggled to get a college degree and has finally attained a master's degree in counseling. He has moved to the West Coast, proud of his accomplishments, yet he considers himself sensitive to his own background and to those who struggle with similar problems. He has been hired to work in a clinic in a neighborhood with a large minority population.

At the clinic John starts a group for troubled adolescents. His goals for this group are as follows: (1) to instill pride in his group members so that they will see that their present environment is an obstacle to be overcome, not to suffer with; (2) to increase self-esteem in his group members and to challenge them to fight the negativism they may encounter in their home environments; (3) to teach them to minimize their differences in terms of the larger community (for example, he points out how some of their idioms and ways of speaking separate them from the majority and reinforce differences and stereotype); and (4) to teach them how one can overcome obstacles and achieve a graduate degree with minimal help from one's environment. He tells them, not in an arrogant way, "If I can do it, you can do it too."

John does not work very closely with the other staff members. He views them as being more interested in politics and red tape and as actually giving very little energy to working in the community. He has little to do with the families of the adolescents, because he sees them as being too willing to accept handouts and welfare and not very interested in being self-sufficient and independent. He tells his group members: "What you have at home with your families has obviously not worked for you. What you have in this group is the opportunity to change and to have that change appreciated."

- Do you see John O'Brien as possessing the competencies necessary to qualify as a cross-cultural counselor? Why or why not?
- Does he demonstrate an understanding of the unique needs of this minority group? If so, how?
- What, if any, cultural prejudices does John exhibit in the way he deals with his group members? What prejudices, if any, do his goals for his adolescent group imply?
- What effect might it have had on John's goals if he had become familiar with the environment of his group?
- In what position do you think that John put himself in order to learn something about the culture with which he is working?
- What potential risks has John exposed his group members to after the group is finished?
- What difficulties do you anticipate John might encounter because of his attitude toward his colleagues in the clinic? Do you think he might be open to criticism from the parents? Explain.
- What stereotyping might John be doing in terms of his attitudes toward the parents of his adolescents?
- What reactions do you have to the manner in which John set up group goals?

- If you were a colleague of John's, what trouble might you have with him? If you were a member of John's group, what difficulties might you encounter?
- If you had no major differences with John's goals for his adolescent group, would you go about implementing the project any differently? What might you do differently, and why?

*Commentary.*    John O'Brien is an illustration of a well-intentioned counselor who demonstrates in so many ways an almost complete lack of sensitivity to the particular needs of this minority community. We disagree with his axiom that, simply because he could obtain a graduate degree (against difficult odds), anybody could meet with the same degree of success. John made no attempt to become aware of the unique struggles or values of his clients. An obvious oversight is that he failed to include the adolescents in the development of goals that would guide their group. He stereotyped in a very indirect, but powerful, fashion the parents of his group members. John imposed majority values in terms of language and upward mobility. He set up potential conflict between his members and their families by the way he downplayed and labeled their families' value systems.

The point we wish to make is that, even though this may be an extreme example of a well-intentioned, but nevertheless insensitive, counselor, John's attitude typifies the mentality of many of those who come from the majority community to work with the minority community. The counselor's own struggles to achieve his goals do not necessarily make him competent to deal with another's life situation. The counselor entering the minority community has at least as much to learn as to teach, and if any real work is to be done, it must be accomplished on a cooperative basis.

## Multicultural Training of Counselors

Some writers charge that trainees in the psychotherapeutic professions have been taught to use counseling techniques as if cultural differences in clients were unimportant. They contend that too few training programs have prepared therapists for effective practice with culturally diverse clients (Arredondo, 1985; Axelson, 1985; Lefley & Pedersen, 1986; Pedersen, 1985b; Ridley, 1985; Sue, 1983; Sue, Akutsu, & Higashi, 1985; Wrenn, 1985). "Evidence suggests that training programs are not sufficiently preparing trainees to work with ethnic-minority groups. Consequently, mental-health services are not adequately addressing the multitude of problems encountered by minority groups" (Sue et al., 1985, p. 280).

Sue (1983) contends that for too long trainees have simply been admonished to be sensitive, open, flexible, and knowledgeable when working with culturally dissimilar clients. He adds that for these characteristics to fully mature, actual contact with clients must occur.

Casas, Ponterotto, and Gutierrez (1986) summarize findings indicating that faculty members in training programs are generally not committed to providing training of relevance to minority groups. They raise these questions: How can counselors avoid working unethically? Without specialized training how can they understand and appreciate the important role of sociocultural variables in the mental health of persons from racial and ethnic minority groups? How will they be able to provide services in the best interests of these clients?

## The Need for Multicultural Training Programs

Ridley (1985) asserts that a focus on ethnic and cross-cultural training is not only desirable but also mandatory. The discussion below is largely based on a summary of Ridley's proposal, which includes five "imperatives" for ethnic and cultural relevance in training programs.

( 1.) *Professional-participation imperative.*    Although there is pluralistic growth in many cities, there is a monocultural focus in the profession rather than a multicultural emphasis. If professional psychology is to retain its integrity, it must represent more than the interests of the dominant culture, which will rapidly become the minority culture.

( 2. ) *Ethical imperative.*    It is now generally agreed that the treatment of culturally different clients by professionals who lack specialized knowledge, skills, and competencies is unethical. In 1973 the APA sponsored a conference in Vail, Colorado (Korman, 1974). This conference clarified that it is the ethical obligation of all service agencies to employ competent persons or to provide continuing education for the present staff to meet the needs of the culturally diverse population that it serves. This group also suggested that professional psychologists should be required to obtain training and continuing education in the special issues of different religious, ethnic, sexual, and economic groups.

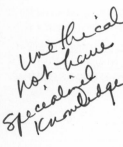
*unethical not have specialized knowledge*

( 3. ) *Cultural-context imperative.*    Mental-health practice occurs in a cultural context. Future professionals need to be prepared to work with clients from contemporary cultures as well as those who come from more traditional backgrounds. This guideline is consistent with the recommendations of the Association for Counselor Education and Supervision (ACES), which is a division of the AACD. According to the ACES, curricula should contain studies of change, ethnic groups, subcultures, changing roles of women, sexism, urban and rural societies, cultural mores, and differing life patterns. ACES standards call for supervised counseling practicum experiences that include people from the environments in which the trainee is preparing to work.

( 4. ) *Scholarly imperative.*    There is a need to correct the inadequate and incorrect presentation of ethnic minorities in the psychological literature. Accurate ethnic and cultural content must be integrated into the mainstream of training programs. Some of the criticisms of the scholarly and professional literature include the following: there is a perpetuation of stereotypes; there is a lack of systematic research and an overemphasis on quantitative research; there is too much emphasis on psychopathology and little recognition of the strengths of ethnic and cultural groups; there is a failure to address the impact of social inequities and pressures on minority-group behavior; there is inappropriate use of culturally biased instruments; ethnic minorities are evaluated by using White middle-class norms; and research is not contributing to improvement of the groups being studied (see also Casas et al., 1986; Ibrahim & Arredondo, 1986). Wehrly and Watson-Gegeo (1985) suggest an ethnographic perspective on research, requiring an active stance by the counselor/researcher as a participant/observer in the world of the culturally different client. The procedures of ethnography provide a holistic understanding of the cultural meanings of behavior exhibited by clients from other cultures. To gain this understanding, Wehrly and Watson-Gegeo point out, it is necessary for counselors to leave their offices and get out into the "real world" of their clients. As ethnographers, they must be willing to modify their research questions as they do their work in the field.

5. *Legal imperative.*   Practitioners who work with culturally diverse groups without having the appropriate knowledge and skills are, in effect, violating the civil rights of their clients. Knowledge of and respect for those rights are essential for effective multicultural counseling (Axelson, 1985).

## Characteristics of the Culturally Skilled Counselor

Sue (1981a, 1981b) has done considerable work in identifying characteristics of the culturally skilled counselor and in developing essential components of cross-cultural counseling. Some of the major points concerning culturally skilled counselors are listed below.

1. Culturally effective counselors understand their own values and assumptions of human behavior and recognize that those held by others may differ.
2. They understand that external sociopolitical forces may have influenced culturally different groups.
3. They are able to share the worldview of their clients, rather than being culturally encapsulated. Worldviews tend to be associated with an individual's cultural heritage and experiences. When there is a sharing of worldviews, the credibility and attractiveness of the counselor tend to be high.
4. Culturally effective counselors are truly eclectic. They use skills, methods, and goals that are appropriate to the experiences and life-styles of the culturally different.

Writing from a social-work perspective, Devore (1985) advocates a model for ethnic-sensitive practice that does not seek to replace valid approaches to practice; rather, it encourages practitioners to be aware of ethnicity and to begin to incorporate this awareness into practice. According to

Devore, workers need (1) knowledge about personality and behavior in the social environment, life-span human development, and the functioning of social institutions; (2) self-awareness, including an understanding of how one's own ethnicity and culture influence practice; and (3) knowledge about ethnicity, culture, and social class as they influence the client.

Sue and his associates (1982) developed minimal cross-cultural counseling competencies to be incorporated into training programs. The characteristics in the accompanying box are based on an adaptation of their position paper and on other sources (Levine & Padilla, 1980; Pedersen, 1985a; Pedersen, Draguns, Lonner, & Trimble, 1981; Sue, 1981b).

## Essential Components of Cross-Cultural Counseling

1. *Beliefs and attitudes of culturally skilled counselors*
   - They are aware of their own values, attitudes, and biases and of how they are likely to affect minority clients. They monitor their functioning through consultation, supervision, and continuing education.
   - They can appreciate diverse cultures, and they feel comfortable with differences between themselves and their clients in terms of race and beliefs.
   - They believe that there can be a unique integration of different value systems that can contribute to both therapist and client growth.
   - If necessary, they are willing to refer a client because of their limitations in cross-cultural counseling.
2. *Knowledge of culturally skilled counselors*
   - They understand the impact of oppression and racist concepts on the mental-health professions and on their personal and professional lives.
   - They are aware of institutional barriers that prevent minorities from making full use of psychological services in the community.
   - They understand how the value assumptions of the major theories of counseling may interact with the values of different cultural groups.
   - They are aware of culture-specific (or indigenous) methods of helping.
   - They possess specific knowledge about the historical background, traditions, and values of the group they are working with.
3. *Skills of culturally skilled counselors*
   - They are able to utilize counseling styles that are congruent with the value systems of different minority groups.
   - They are able to modify and adapt conventional approaches to counseling and psychotherapy in order to accommodate cultural differences.
   - They are able to send and receive both verbal and nonverbal messages accurately and appropriately.
   - They are able to employ institutional intervention skills on behalf of their clients when necessary or appropriate.
   - They are able to make out-of-office interventions when necessary by assuming the role of consultant and agent for change.

## Approaches to Multicultural Training

How can we train counselors to deal with counselees from different cultures? How can we effectively counsel clients who present special difficulties stemming from class or cultural circumstances? Otherwise well-prepared counselors often face fearful, resistant, and noncommunicative individuals who come from other ethnic and economic groups. The barriers are very different life-styles and values, which appear to get in the way of creating the communication needed for a working client/therapist relationship.

**The Triad Model.** Pedersen (1981) believes that the traditional way of selecting and training counselors both reflects and reinforces cultural bias. As an alternative, he has developed a training approach known as the triad model, which helps the student understand a culturally different client's internal dialogue. This model involves role-playing cross-cultural counseling with three persons. One person (the student) assumes the role of counselor. The other two persons have been trained in their roles. The second person plays a client from a different culture. The third person, called the "anticounselor," acts as an antagonistic agent by capitalizing on cultural differences and stereotypes and exacerbating the potential for creating a cultural gap. This third person highlights issues relevant to the cross-cultural relationships by pointing out unique cultural values and their impact on the interaction.

Pedersen (personal communication, September 11, 1986) explains the triad as follows. Every conversation has three dialogues: (1) what we say to each other; (2) what I think but don't say; and (3) what you think but don't say. I know what we say together, and I know what I'm thinking, but I don't know what you're thinking. The more culturally different we are, the less I will know about what you are thinking. I do know, however, that some of the things you are thinking are "positive" (pro), and other things are "negative" (anti). The approach involves selecting two persons who are culturally similar to the coached client to be an anticounselor and a procounselor and instructing them to say aloud what they are thinking, whether the messages are negative or positive. This process demonstrates to observers the inner dialogue that is probably going on in the client's mind. By hearing that dialogue as it is taking place within the context of a role-played interview, participants and observers can learn the skill of (1) perceiving a problem from the client's perspective, (2) recognizing resistance in specific terms, (3) reducing their own defensiveness, and (4) recovering after having said or done the wrong thing. This approach provides a safe context for counselors to learn about a culture in an experiential way.

Pedersen (1981) writes that there are many applications of triad counseling, including training counselors to work with welfare clients, alcoholics, the handicapped, foreign students, prisoners, and other special groups that are likely to have values different from the counselor's.

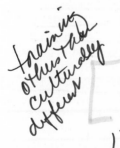

**A Multifaceted Approach to Training.** Parker, Valley, and Geary (1986) describe a multiple approach to the acquisition of cross-cultural knowledge that is a culmination of experiences and activities they have used in a course called Counseling Ethnic Minorities. Their approach is based on the assumption that knowledge and cultural awareness can be achieved through a combination of cognitive, affective, and behavioral procedures. The first part of the course consists of an assessment of the students' level of knowledge and experience with ethnic minorities. The second part of the course includes reading and subsequent discussions of ethnic literature. Students felt that this reading helped them develop empathy toward minority groups and increased their appreciation of the values held by these groups. The third phase of the course involves a series of behavioral procedures designed to help students gain cultural knowledge and increase sensitivity toward ethnic minorities. Students choose from a variety of multicultural experiences, including touring an ethnic community, making contact with minority groups, and spending time in the home of an ethnic family. In the final segment the students cooperate to make small-group presentations that are aimed at contributing to the advancement of cross-cultural knowledge, skills, or understanding.

From the perspective of the students taking this course, the multifaceted approach is a valuable experience for acquiring cross-cultural knowledge and sensitivity. Most of the students viewed the course as the beginning of a lifelong process of learning.

**Our Views on Multicultural Training.** We believe that as a way of introducing trainees to the multicultural dimension of a counseling program, some type of self-exploratory class should be required to help them identify their cultural and ethnic blind spots. This course would ideally be required for all trainees in the mental-health professions and would be taught by someone with experience in multicultural issues. It is an ethical obligation of counselor educators to identify, and perhaps even screen out of such a program, those students who exhibit and maintain rigid notions of the way people ought to live, regardless of their cultural backgrounds. In addition to this introductory course, we would like to see at least one course dealing exclusively with cross-cultural issues and ethnic-minority groups in a multicultural society. Since there are an increasing number of articles and books on ethnic-minority groups, students should have this literature available to them.

It is also extremely important that this multicultural perspective be integrated throughout the rest of the curriculum. The teaching of theories and techniques of counseling, for example, can emphasize how such concepts and strategies can be adapted to the special needs of diverse client populations and how some theories may be quite inappropriate for culturally different clients. Wherever possible, representatives of these diverse cultures can be invited to give direct experience to the students. These persons also can address social, economic, and culture-specific factors that may affect mental-health treatment.

Beyond formal course work there should be at least one required internship in which trainees have multicultural experiences. Ideally, the supervisor at this agency will be well-versed in the cultural variables of that particular setting and also skilled in cross-cultural understanding. Further, trainees will ideally have access to both individual and group supervision on campus from a faculty member. Here the emphasis will be more on the counselor's dynamics than on dealing with client cases. This would provide the trainee with ongoing self-exploration in dealing with members from another culture. Sue and his colleagues (1985) contend that understanding the culture of clients is necessary, but not sufficient, in effectively counseling ethnic-minority clients. Although they value didactic methods of acquiring knowledge, they emphasize the value of actual experience in working in ethnic communities and working with a large number of clients.

Finally, we would highly recommend that through reading and travel trainees expose themselves in a variety of ways to people in other cultures. Students can also make use of films and videotapes and can attend seminars and workshops that focus on multicultural issues in the helping professions.

*During a counseling staff meeting that you are attending, a White male colleague says to the group: "Based on my years of counseling experience, I've found that I'm 'color-blind.' It doesn't make any difference in my counseling if the client is yellow, red, Black, or White. I still do the same things with the same results. This whole business of minority counseling is a camouflage for the real issues. Some counselors just don't have it!"*

- To what degree do you agree or disagree with his statements?
- What might you be thinking and feeling in this situation?
- How might you respond to this man?

# Chapter Summary

A number of writers over the last decade have urged that counselors learn about their own culture and become aware of how their experiences affect the way they work with others who are culturally different. By being ignorant of the values and attitudes of clients who are of a different race, age, sex, social class, or culture, therapists open themselves up to criticism. Imposing one's own vision of the world on clients not only leads to negative therapeutic outcomes but also constitutes unethical practice.

We are all limited by our cultural and ethnic experiences. Yet we can increase our awareness by direct contact with a variety of ethnic and cultural groups, by reading, and by special course work. It is essential that our practices be appropriate for the clients with whom we work. This entails being willing to modify our theories and techniques to their unique needs and not being rigidly stuck on applying interventions in the same manner to all clients.

Perhaps the starting point is to realize that sensitivity to cultural differences is essential for sound practice. We encourage you to carefully examine your assumptions, attitudes, and values so that you can determine how they could influence your practice.

## Suggested Activities

1. Select two or three cultures or races different from your own. What attitudes and beliefs about these cultures did you hold while growing up? How have these attitudes changed, if any, and what contributed to the changes?

2. What values do you owe primarily to your culture? With the passing of time have any of your values changed, and, if so, how? How might these values influence the way you work with clients who are culturally different from you?

3. What cross-cultural life experiences have you had? Did you learn anything about your potential prejudices? What prejudices, if any, did you feel directed at you? You might bring your experiences to class. Also, we suggest that you interview other students or faculty members who identify themselves as ethnically or culturally different from you. What might they teach you about differences that you as a counselor would need to take into consideration in order to work more effectively with them?

4. Invite speakers to class to talk about cross-cultural factors as they relate to values. Speakers representing special concerns of various ethnic groups can address the topic of certain values unique to their group and can discuss the implications of these values for counseling.

5. To what degree have your courses and field experience contributed to your ability to work effectively with people from other cultures? What training experiences would you like to have to better prepare you for multicultural counseling?

6. Divide into groups of three in your class. One person becomes a minority client. A second person assumes the counselor role. And the third person acts as an alter ego for the client, as the anticounselor. You might have the minority client be somewhat reluctant to speak. The counselor can deal with this silence by treating it as a form of resistance, using typical therapeutic strategies. During this time the anticounselor expresses the cultural meaning of the silence. Now, devise a way to deal with silence from this frame of reference, without using traditional therapeutic techniques.

7. Assume that you were asked this question: "Minorities are often put under strong pressure to give up their beliefs and ways in favor of adopting the ideals and customs of the dominant culture. What do you think your approach would be in working with clients who feel such pressure? How might you work with clients who see their own ethnicity or cultural heritage as a handicap that is to be overcome?"

## Suggested Readings

For an excellent reference book that reviews the history, present status, assumptions, theories, future directions, and specializations within the field of cross-cultural counseling and therapy see Pedersen (1985a). This hand-book contains 40 chapters written by experts in the field.

For useful textbooks in the field of multicultural counseling see Axelson (1985), Lum (1986), and Sue (1981a). For ethical issues in counseling groups that are distinct with respect to gender, race, or culture see Cayleff (1986) and Sundal-Hansen (1985). On the limitations of existing codes for cross-cultural counseling situations see Pedersen and Marsella (1982); Casas, Ponterotto, and Gutierrez (1986), and Ibrahim and Arredondo (1986). For a discussion of the issue of the cultural encapsulation of ethical codes, see Casas (1986), Ellis (1986), Ibrahim (1986), Ivey (1986), and Pedersen (1986). For an analysis of the life stresses that ethnic minorities face see Smith (1985b). For a discussion of the sociopolitical nature of counseling see Katz (1985). On value assumptions underlying therapeutic systems see Ho (1985), Saeki and Borow (1985), and Patterson (1985b). On stereotypical assumptions about minority groups see Lorion and Parron (1985) and Sue and Sue (1985). On the importance of nonverbal language in cross-cultural counseling see Wolfgang (1985). For specific guidelines in counseling special client populations see Attneave (1985), Sue and Sue (1985), Padilla and De Snyder (1985), Espin (1985), Jones (1985), and Smith (1985a). For a provocative critique of current perspectives and practices of cross-cultural counseling, see Chapter 10 of Patterson (1985b). On training programs in a multicultural perspective see Lefley and Pedersen (1986), Sue, Akutsu, and Higashi (1985), Arredondo (1985), Sue (1983), Ridley (1985), Pedersen (1985b), Wrenn (1985), Casas (1985a, 1985b), and Casas et al. (1986). For recommendations in planning and implementing a training program in multicultural counseling see Arredondo (1985) and Arredondo and Gawelek (1982). For an interesting description of a multifaceted approach to teaching a course in Counseling Ethnic Minorities see Parker, Valley, and Geary (1986). For an annotated bibliography of human rights issues in counselor training and supervision see Okoawo and Arredondo (1983). On the characteristics of the culturally skilled counselor see Sue (1981a, 1981b). On ethnic-sensitive practice in social work see Lum (1986) and Devore (1985). On issues pertaining to research and practice in cross-cultural counseling see Lonner and Sundberg (1985), Atkinson (1985), Saeki and Borow (1985), and Suinn (1985).

# NINE

# The Counselor in the Community and in a System

# Pre-Chapter Self-Inventory

*Directions:* For each statement, indicate the response that most closely identifies your beliefs and attitudes. Use the following code:

3 = I *agree*, in most respects, with this statement.
2 = I am *undecided* in my opinion about this statement.
1 = I *disagree*, in most respects, with this statement.

___ 1. In general, it's important to include members of the client's environment in his or her treatment.

___ 2. Counselors ought to take an active role in dealing with the social and political conditions that are related in human suffering.

___ 3. Mental-health experts should devote more of their energies to prevention of emotional and behavioral disorders, rather than treatment.

___ 4. With increasing attention being paid to the community mental-health approach, the role of the professional must be expanded to include a variety of indirect services to clients as well as direct clinical services.

___ 5. The use of paraprofessionals is a valuable and effective way of dealing with the shortage of professional help.

___ 6. Paraprofessionals who receive adequate training and close supervision are capable of providing most of the direct services that professionals now provide.

___ 7. In working with minority groups in the community, counselors must be skilled in out-of-office strategies such as outreach, consulting, and working as an agent for change. They must view some counseling problems as residing outside of the minority clients themselves.

___ 8. I generally don't like to challenge the people I work for.

___ 9. It's possible to work within the framework of a system and still do the things I'm convinced are most important to do.

___ 10. When I think of working in some agency or institution, I feel a sense of powerlessness about initiating any real change in that organization.

___ 11. I frequently have good ideas and proposals, and I see myself as willing to do the work necessary to translate these plans into actual programs.

___ 12. If I'm honest with myself, I can see that I might have a tendency to blame external sources for a failure on my part to do more professionally.

___ 13. I see myself as a fighter in a system, in the sense that I'll work to change things I don't approve of.

___ 14. Although I might be unable to bring about drastic changes in an institution or system, I do feel confident that I can make changes within the boundaries of my own position.

___ 15. I can see that I might fall into complacency and rarely question what I'm doing or how I could do my work more effectively.

___ 16. Counselors who no longer raise questions or struggle with ethical concerns have stopped growing professionally.

___ 17. It would be unethical to accept a position with an agency whose central aims I disagreed with philosophically.

___ 18. Ethical concerns are not simply answered once and for all; to become an ethical practitioner, I must be willing to continually raise questions about what I'm doing.

___ 19. As a counselor I'm part of a system, and I have a responsibility to work toward changing those aspects of the system that I think need changing.

___ 20. I feel a personal need for meaningful contact with colleagues so that I don't become excessively narrow in my thinking.

# Introduction

Working with people who come to them for counseling is only one way in which professionals can use their skills to promote mental and emotional health. It can be easy to neglect the fact that the aspirations and difficulties of clients intertwine with those of many other people and, ultimately, with those of the community at large. Many people would argue that professional helpers can foster real and lasting changes only if they have an impact on this social setting of people's lives.

Part of this chapter is concerned with the community mental-health movement, which originated in the mid-1960s in the United States. According to Iscoe (1982), this movement resulted in part from a recognition that mental hospitals had departed radically from their original functions of asylum and treatment. This approach to mental health also grew out of a conviction that individual and group psychotherapy were not appropriate in developing and applying a model based on health and prevention. Iscoe observes that the community mental-health thrust arose as a strong protest against orthodox clinical methods, which aimed at curing disorders but lacked proper attention to their prevention. Thus, the goal of the community perspective to mental health was to apply the knowledge of behavioral science to improving the functioning of people in their environments and to preventing serious emotional dysfunction.

In this chapter we explore the counselor's responsibility to the community. We begin by looking at the community mental-health movement, an approach that emphasizes the social setting of the counselor's work. Then we focus on an issue of particular importance to the community mental-health worker—namely, how the system affects the counselor.

In addition to their degrees, training, and professional competencies counselors working in the community must also have the ability to deal with the rules and regulations of agencies. Such counselors typically have little say in the formulation of agency policies. As opposed to private practice, where practitioners deliver their services directly to their clientele, practitioners working in agency settings must mediate not only with clients but also with the system. The following are some examples of the organizations we are talking about:

- a city or county mental-health agency
- a free clinic
- a church counseling agency
- a school system, including a college counseling center
- a state mental hospital
- a community halfway house

As counselors, we need to decide what our styles for working within a system will be and how we can be most effective. Some counselors who are dissatisfied with the system decide to subvert it in as many ways as they can. Others conform to institutional policies for fear of losing their positions. Some counselors find ways of making compromises between institutional demands and their personal requirements; others find it impossible to retain their personal and professional dignity and still work within an institutional framework. It will be up to you to find your own answers to questions such as these:

- What stance will I take in dealing with a system?
- How can I meet the requirements of an institution and at the same time do what I most believe in?
- In what ways can I work to change a particular system?
- At what point does the price of attempting to work within an organized structure become too high? Can I work within an institutional framework and still retain my dignity?
- What special ethical obligations are required of helpers working in a system?

## The Community Mental-Health Orientation

Many therapists see a need for new approaches to augment the process of individual therapy. Since only a relatively small number of people can be effectively reached by traditional therapeutic approaches, these practitioners support the idea of innovative measures that will make maximum use of the professional resources available. The need for diverse and readily accessible treatment programs has been a key factor in the development of the community mental-health orientation.

Another major factor in this trend is the notion that people can be helped more effectively in their communities than in mental institutions. Returning psychiatric patients to the community, it is hoped, will lead to their reintegration into society. On this issue Bloom (1983) writes that "the community-mental-health movement grew out of the conviction that mental hospitals were as much a cause of chronic mental disorder as a cure and that hospitalization was probably as often harmful as it was helpful" (p. 42).

Taking a community approach to mental health involves abandoning the view that the role of practitioners is to sit back and wait for people to come to them for help. A broader conception of the practitioner's role might include the following:

- using informal groups in cross-cultural counseling
- developing social-support networks
- being aware of cross-cultural issues in counseling and being willing to modify traditional therapeutic practices to meet the needs of diverse ethnic and cultural groups
- developing abilities that will lead to one's being better able to reach minority groups in the community
- actively reaching out to potential clients
- initiating programs aimed at preventing problems rather than merely treating them
- drawing on and improving the skills of paraprofessionals and laypeople to meet the many different needs of clients
- educating consumers about existing resources
- developing strategies to effectively deal with problems such as drug and alcohol abuse, child abuse, violence, and sexual abuse
- attempting to redistribute power and control in society so that the "disenfranchised" can develop and use their strengths (Goldenberg, 1983)
- consulting with a variety of social agencies about programs in gerontology, welfare, child care, and rehabilitation and helping community workers apply psychological knowledge in their work
- evaluating human-services programs by designing research to assess agencies' intervention efforts
- functioning as a liaison with community agencies so that services can be best delivered to those who need help

It is our view that an increasing number of people are unable to cope with the demands of their environment and are receptive to the idea of professional assistance. As more people overcome the stigma attached to seeking psychological help, the demand for community services increases. In our opinion psychotherapy can no longer afford to be tailor-made for the upper-middle-class group. People who are unable to afford the services of professionals in private practice are entitled to adequate treatment programs. Consequently, community clinics are needed to serve people of all ages and backgrounds and with all types and degrees of problems.

The need for community mental-health programs is compounded by such problems of our contemporary society as poverty, absent parents, broken homes, child abuse, unemployment, tension and stress, alienation, addictions to drugs and alcohol, delinquency, and neglect of the elderly.

These are merely a few of the formidable challenges the community approach faces in preventing and treating human problems.

## Characteristics of a Community Mental-Health Center

The community mental-health orientation is based on concepts from fields such as psychology, sociology, social welfare, education, mental hygiene, and public health. The characteristics of the comprehensive mental-health center, as described by Bloom (1983), Dugger (1980), and Goldenberg (1983), include the following:

- The center focuses on a person's interactions with others in the environment and on the impact of social forces on behavior. Treatment emphasizes linking individuals with their communities through the use of new kinds of facilities, such as day-treatment and other outpatient centers.
- Treatment is available to a wide range of people with all types of problems.
- The term *comprehensive* implies a wide range of services, including consultation, direct care, education, and prevention.
- The center's programs reach people who have not previously been helped, particularly the poor.
- A major emphasis is on the provision of services for children.
- A variety of treatment approaches are offered, including crisis intervention, groups, therapeutic communities, and family therapy.
- The center is controlled by the community.
- Fees are based on the ability to pay.
- The center develops a program of in-service education for the staff.
- Roles and leadership are determined more by competence than by professional identification.
- Training and supervision of paraprofessionals is an important function of the center. Paraprofessionals can frequently assume roles previously limited to professionals.
- Periodic program evaluation is necessary to determine the degree to which the center is meeting the needs of the community.
- The center aims at reaching large numbers of people through the use of brief therapies and crisis intervention.
- Behavior disorders are studied from the vantage point of environmental factors that contribute to these problems, rather than the inner conflicts of individuals.

## The Outreach Approach

Outreach strategies are particularly important in reaching ethnic minorities. The complex issues involved in working with minority groups within the framework of the majority community have been well-documented in the literature (Atkinson, Morten, & Sue, 1979; Levine & Padilla, 1980; Pedersen,

Draguns, Lonner, & Trimble, 1981; Sue, 1981a). If practitioners hope to reach and effectively deal with a cultural group different from their own, they must acquire a broad understanding of the group and begin to study the subtle factors that affect the interpersonal interactions within it. In other words, they need to understand how various behaviors and attitudes are viewed within specific populations (Blustein, 1982). Blustein makes a case for using indigenous support systems and informal groups to reach minority groups. Examples include peer groups in schools, self-help groups, church groups, street-corner groups, and work groups. People in minority groups often turn to members of their own and extended families, to friends, and to community members when they need help, rather than turning to professional practitioners within the dominant culture. As Blustein notes, these indigenous networks of support are particularly important to groups living in a culture that is inconsistent with their own. Thus, he encourages counselors to create interventions that are a natural extension of the informal helping networks of their client population.

Mental-health practitioners might imagine themselves doing more outreach work in the territory of their clients. They might function on the steps of a tenement, at a hospital bedside, at a place of work, or in other places where clients live. The outreach approach could include developmental and educational efforts such as psychological education, education of the community about mental health, and consultation in a variety of systems. This shift in the counselor's role truly involves a challenge!

## Other Ways of Becoming Involved in the Community

It is relatively easy for counselors to believe that they can effectively meet the needs of their clients through one-to-one sessions in the office. But many problems demand a broader approach if real change is to occur. We suggest that you consider the responsibility you may have to teach clients to use the resources available to them in their communities.

What follows is a list of things you might do to link your clients to the community in which they live. Rate each of these activities, using the following code: A = I would do this routinely; B = I would do this occasionally; C = I would do this rarely.

_____ 1. familiarize myself with available community resources so that I could refer my clients to appropriate sources of further help

_____ 2. with my clients' permission, contact people who have a direct influence in their lives

_____ 3. try to arrange sessions that would involve both a client and the significant people in his or her life so that we could explore ways of changing certain relationships

_____ 4. as a part of the counseling process, teach my clients how to take advantage of the auxiliary support systems in the community

_____ 5. suggest homework assignments or use other techniques to get my clients thinking about ways that they could apply what they learn in the individual sessions to their everyday lives

____ 6. use natural leaders as a part of outreach work in setting up a liaison with professional practitioners and agencies

____ 7. train natural leaders of various cultural groups in peer-counseling skills so that they could work with groups that might resist seeking professional services from an agency

____ 8. connect with informal groups and social networks by becoming a participant/observer in a variety of these groups

____ 9. after observing a variety of informal groups to learn about the values and beliefs of a given culture, design outreach programs that are a natural extension of these informal helping networks

____ 10. consider joining some type of informal group of another culture so that I could better understand a different world (examples: a church group, a community group, a social group)

Now think of other options for encouraging your clients to find ways of meeting their needs besides the traditional approaches of individual and group counseling.

# The Professional's Role in Educating the Community

Too often counselors wait for clients to come to them in their offices. As a consequence many prospective clients never appear. There are many reasons why people do not make use of available resources: they may not be aware of their existence; they may have misconceptions about the nature and purpose of counseling; they may be reluctant to recognize their problems; or they may harbor the attitude that they should be able to take charge of their lives on their own.

Because of these reasons, we think, educating the public and thus changing the attitudes of the community toward mental health is a primary responsibility of professionals. Perhaps the most important task in this area is to demystify the notion of mental illness. Unfortunately, many people still cling to archaic notions of mental illness. They may make a clear demarcation between people they perceive as "crazy" and those they perceive as "normal." Some of the misconceptions that are still widespread are that, once people suffer from mental illness, they can never be cured; that people with emotional or behavioral disorders are merely deficient in "will power"; and that the mentally ill are always dangerous and should be separated from the community lest they "contaminate" or harm others. Professionals face a real challenge in combating these faulty notions.

Psychotherapy is another area that needs to be demystified. Some of the misconceptions of psychotherapy include that it is some form of magic; that it is only for people with extreme problems; that therapists provide clients with answers; that therapy is only for weak people; and that people should be able to solve their problems without professional help. These misconceptions often reinforce the resistance people already have toward seeking professional help. Unless professionals actively work on presenting psychotherapy in a way that is intelligible to the community at large, many people who could benefit from professional help may not seek it out.

To illustrate how widespread ignorance concerning available resources can be, one of us regularly asks upper-division classes of students in human services and counseling whether they know where the college counseling center is located. Generally, only about a quarter of the class members know where the center is; even fewer are aware of the kinds of services offered. If this lack of knowledge is common among people who will eventually be involved in community mental health, how much more common must it be among the general public? And if future professionals are not aware of available resources, how can they educate others to use them? Moreover, we've found that these students, who might be expected to be somewhat sophisticated regarding psychological counseling, often have misconceptions about therapy and resist seeking help when they need it for themselves.

Of course, the problem does not originate entirely with students. We've found that many college counselors are unwilling to do much public-relations work. They tend to resist going outside their offices and making themselves known to students through direct contacts. Some of these counselors assume that it's up to the students to take the initiative to find help if they want it. This same attitude is shared by many counselors who work in community agencies. They stay within the agency and do very little to develop a public-relations program that will make the community more aware of existing services and how to utilize them. It is hardly surprising that many people who need psychological help never get it if no one has set up an effective program to educate the public and deal with people's resistance in getting the help they need.

## Ethical Issues in Consultation

Consulting in the human-services professions can be defined as helping another responsible person (usually a practitioner), with a work-related problem. The consultation process is aimed at helping people to work more effectively, and with greater self-satisfaction, on the individual, group, organizational, or community level. Consultation is emerging into a specialized professional process, and it is being carried out by many different groups in diverse work settings (Kurpius, 1986).

We are including the topic of consulting in this chapter because a major role of helping professionals in communities and systems is to provide indirect services to a variety of populations. Through the consulting process, it is hoped, consultees can better provide their clients with tools and skills for coping with their concerns.

## The Need for a Code of Ethics

It is essential that consultants have a set of ethical standards to ensure that their services are competent and that the consumer receives professional service. One of the ethical issues in consulting is that it creates a potentially imbalanced power relationship. The consultant has certain skills or abilities that the consultee desires. This situation places the consultant in a powerful position, and there is a high potential for abuse (Tokunaga, 1984). Practitioners who function as consultants come from many disciplines, and thus there are few ethical guidelines from specific professional organizations that encompass this diversity. Because the field of consulting is relatively new and complex and because ethical codes are lacking, many otherwise qualified persons do not know how to deal with ethical dilemmas they face. Such dilemmas are particularly serious because of the potentially large number of people who are indirectly affected by a consultant's ethical principles and decisions. With these problems in mind, Gallessich (1982) asserts that a code of ethics for consultants is urgently needed to protect the public. Other writers agree with the need for guidelines for consultants, yet they argue that the responsibility for ethical behavior ultimately rests with the consultant (Robinson & Gross, 1985; Tokunaga, 1984).

Ethical principles assume a well-defined body of knowledge and generally accepted rules for professional behavior. According to Lowman (1985), these factors do not exist in organizational consulting. Therefore, he argues, it is unrealistic to expect ethical principles in a field that has not decided what constitutes good professional practice.

What follows is an adaptation and description of a consultant's code of ethics that Gallessich (1982) has proposed for adoption. She developed it from her own experiences, from previous articles, and from existing guidelines of professional associations such as the APA and the American Society for Training and Development. We are summarizing their guidelines and also including guidelines provided by Robinson and Gross (1985) and by the AACD's (1981) *Ethical Standards*.

## Summary of Ethical Principles for Consultants

1. The consultees' interests and needs are supreme, and consultants do not put their needs and motives before the welfare of their clients.

2. Consultants inform consultees about the process of consultation, the potential benefits, and any potential risks. They also protect the confidentiality of both their consultees and client agencies.

3. Consultants present their professional qualifications and knowledge so as to avoid misrepresenting themselves. They do not accept a contract for activities beyond their education and training. They assume the responsibility for keeping current with the theoretical and technical developments in their field.

4. The consulting relationship is based on an agreement between the

consultant and the consultee on what the problem is, the goals for change, and the predicted outcomes of the interventions selected.

5. When consultants perceive a consultee behaving in an unethical manner, they express their observations to the person involved.

6. Consultants avoid dual relationships that by their very nature may create conflicts of interest and thus interfere with their effectiveness. They avoid entanglements in roles that are incompatible with their stated purposes and contract.

7. Consultants assist clients in moving toward self-direction and growth; they avoid manipulating consultees and creating dependence. They exercise care not to "push" their values or point of view.

8. Regardless of established codes, published guidelines, or sanctions, the responsibility for ethical behavior lies with the consultant.

9. Consultants establish a clear contract with well-defined limits, respect their contract, and communicate its terms to all who are participating in consulting activities. Any changes in the contract are made only through explicit agreement with staff members and the administration. Before initiating a contract, consultants investigate the goals of the agency to determine whether they can support such goals. When consultants become aware of value clashes, they do not negotiate a contract.

10. Consultants must choose assessment devices that are consistent with the needs and purposes of the consultees.

11. Consultants attempt to evaluate the outcomes of their services. At the outset of the consulting process it is helpful to clarify procedures for gathering information and using it. Who will have access to the consultant's findings as well as the limits of confidentiality should be established before gathering the data.

12. Consultants establish policies related to confidentiality to safeguard the staff members who participate. They remind staff members and administrators of the limits of confidentiality as established during contract negotiations. Certain information that is given confidentially may be useful when it is presented anonymously to an administrator.

13. Consultants protect the freedom of consultees to decline to be involved in activities that require discussion of personal values, beliefs, feelings, and personal issues. They do not attempt to coerce people to do what they really do not want to do.

14. Consultants are aware of their biases, which may distort the interpretation of their observations and their recommendations. They terminate certain consultative activities when their biases interfere with their responsibilities to clients.

15. Consultants ask for feedback from consultees on a regular basis and use this information to assess their strengths and weaknesses. They work with colleagues and in teams to maximize their learning.

16. Consultants donate time to agencies that are unable to pay.

17. Consultants increase their knowledge through research and experimentation.

18. Consultants are aware of personal conditions that interfere with their effective functioning, and they do not practice when such conditions would impair their services. They meet their personal needs outside the consulting relationship so as to avoid using clients for that purpose.

19. Consultants must be reasonably certain that the organization employing them has the resources to give the kind of help that its clients need and that appropriate referral resources are available to the consultant.

20. Consultants make a clear differentiation among the terms *consultation*, *supervision*, and *psychotherapy*. They respect the nature of the contracted consultation relationship and make referrals for supervision and psychotherapy for consultees when appropriate.

# The Use of Paraprofessionals

The question of how best to deliver psychological services to the people who are most in need of them is a controversial one. It is clear that there are not enough professionally trained people to meet the demand for psychological assistance. Faced with this reality, many people in the mental-health field have concluded that nonprofessionals should be given the training and supervision they need to provide some psychological services. There has therefore been a trend toward the use of paraprofessionals in counseling and related fields.

One important reason for the increasing use of paraprofessionals is economic. Service agencies have discovered that paraprofessionals can indeed provide some services as effectively as full professionals, for much lower salaries. However, as Goldenberg (1983) observes, this is not the only advantage to the use of paraprofessionals: "Many paraprofessionals are being trained for new service functions and roles that some psychologists believe they are better able than professionals to fulfill because of their special relationships, as residents, to the communities they serve" (p. 366).

Not all mental-health professionals are enthusiastic about the potential of the paraprofessional movement. Some point to the danger that inadequately trained people might do more harm than good; others claim that the poor who need treatment will receive inferior service; still others fear that more and more paraprofessionals will be allowed to practice without the close supervision and intensive training they need. In addition, as Goldenberg points out, paraprofessionals represent a threat to the economic interests of some professionals. Despite the opposition of some professionals, however, there seems to be little chance that the trend toward the use of paraprofessionals will be reversed. We agree with Goldenberg when he says: "Professionals have a social responsibility to train paraprofessionals. If they fail to carry out this responsibility, the public will turn to individuals with little or no training and the results may in the long run prove to be most unfortunate for all" (1983, p. 370).

## Types of Paraprofessional Mental-Health Workers

There are three general types of nontraditional mental-health workers.

(1.) Many community colleges offer two-year programs in the human services. Students in these programs receive specialized training that is aimed at preparing them to work in community mental-health centers, hospitals, and other human-services agencies. In addition, many colleges and universities have established four-year undergraduate programs in human services that stress practical experience, training, and supervision in mental-health work.

(2.) Lay volunteers from the community are also receiving training and supervision in therapeutic intervention with a wide range of clients. These volunteers work on hot lines, co-lead groups, and engage in other types of supportive activities. Many professionals contend that, although the use of community volunteers is not a cure-all for the shortage of available personnel, trained volunteers can augment the work of professional therapists.

(3.) The use of former patients is another promising way of meeting the increasing demand for mental-health services. Former addicts play a role through substance-abuse programs in rehabilitating others who are addicted to drugs. Alcoholics Anonymous is well known for its contributions in keeping alcoholics sober through the efforts of people who have learned that they can no longer handle alcohol. In many places former mental patients are helping others make the transition from state hospitals to their communities. Besides helping to alleviate the shortage of personnel, these nonprofessionals may actually be more effective in reaching certain people, because they have experienced similar problems and learned to deal with them successfully.

Looking at the community mental-health approach in retrospect, Iscoe (1982) contends that one of its failures is that it has not developed sufficient understanding of the daily lives and values of lower-middle-class groups or developed interventions to meet their psychological needs. He adds that many paraprofessionals (drug and alcohol counselors, crisis workers, mental-health workers, and community specialists) have not been traditionally trained and typically work without supervision from professionals. It appears that a large part of the success of community mental-health programs will depend on these nontraditional workers' receiving the training and supervision they need to develop the skills for effective intervention. Mental-health professionals can be expected to spend less time in providing direct services to clients so that they will have time for teaching and consulting with community workers.

The trend toward the increased use of paraprofessionals means that professionals will have to assume new and expanding roles. Rather than devoting the bulk of their time to direct services, such as one-to-one counseling, they may need to spend considerable time offering in-service workshops for paraprofessionals and volunteer workers. Other activities that could assume priority include educating the public about the nature of mental health, consulting, working as change agents in the community, designing new programs, conducting research, and evaluating existing programs.

## Training Standards and Programs for Paraprofessionals

It is a mistake to assume that paraprofessionals are merely volunteers with little or no formal academic training. In fact, in the last decade there has been an increase in the number of human-service training programs throughout the country. The Council for Standards in Human Service Education (1983) has clarified the difference between baccalaureate and associate-degree programs and has developed detailed standards to evaluate programs for training paraprofessionals.

In the area of curriculum the CSHSE specifies standards and curriculum components that define the three levels of human-service training and education: technical (nondegree), associate degree, and bachelor's degree. These standards specify that human-service workers at all three levels should have an understanding of the dynamics of individuals, groups, and communities; cultural differences; normal and deviant behavior; and methods and strategies for intervening at the individual, group, and community levels. The guidelines include providing skill training in working with a diversity of client populations. It is expected that the curriculum will provide opportunities for students to master skills that are appropriate to their level of training.

Human-service training programs are expected to provide interpersonal skills, administrative skills, and opportunities for students to explore their values and attitudes related to the helping process. The CSHSE stresses the importance of self-development in these programs. Since paraprofessionals must rely on their life experiences in helping clients, it is essential that they be aware of their own values, cultural biases, philosophy, and interpersonal style.

Supervised field experience is a major component of any training program. The CSHSE has established minimal requirements for all education and training programs that seek to obtain approval of their program. These standards emphasize that fieldwork must be an integral part of any program. This field experience is a process of experiential learning that integrates the knowledge, skill, and attitudes being taught in the classroom. Although students in these programs are expected to be exposed to human-service agencies and clients, the council stresses that maximal learning will occur only when both the field site placement and the college provide quality supervision. Thus, practicum and internship courses offer structured opportunities for learning. At the beginning level, observation and learning of specific skills are stressed, and as students progress, there is an increase of responsibility. At all levels, however, clients are protected while the interns learn by doing. There is on-the-job supervision in agency settings as well as weekly seminars at the college that provide group supervision and opportunities for students to discuss their fieldwork experiences.

At the undergraduate level, human-services programs typically stress applications of knowledge and skills to a variety of work settings. An example of one such program is the human-services major at California State University, Fullerton. The curriculum is structured around four interrelated components: (1) theoretical foundations and intervention strategies, (2) client populations and cultural diversity, (3) research and evaluation, and (4) skills development and field experiences. Many of those who graduate secure a job as a paraprofessional worker in a community agency; others elect to pursue a master's degree in social work, psychology, or counseling (see Coley, Corey, Garcia, Moline, Ramirez, Russell, & Wright, 1986).

Paraprofessional workers can play a vital role in providing quality service to a wide clientele in the community. As can be seen, however, it is essential that these human-service workers be given adequate education, training, and supervision so that the welfare of these clients is safeguarded. Paraprofessionals without knowledge and skills who are allowed to practice without careful supervision can do more harm than good. Ethical practice dictates that clients be exposed only to helpers who have the level of training appropriate to their duties.

## Graduate Training Programs in Community-Agency Counseling

Many paraprofessionals secure employment in the mental-health field after a two-year or four-year undergraduate program. Later, some decide to enter one of the helping fields as a professional. In order to make this career shift, they must obtain a graduate degree and further specialized training. For example, some students with a bachelor's in social work enter graduate school with the goal of obtaining a master's or even a doctorate in social work.

Richardson and Bradley (1985) conducted a comprehensive national survey of trends and characteristics in graduate programs in community-agency counseling. This report contains a wealth of information for those who want more information on this topic. The study showed a definite trend in counselor-education programs toward designing and offering a graduate specialization in community-agency counseling. In fact, the authors found that programs in this area account for the majority of graduate student enrollment at the master's level and that this is the fastest growing specialization area in counselor-preparation programs. This change can be attributed partially to new legislation and partially to a growing awareness by employers of the need for expanding the roles and skills of helping professionals in meeting the demands of new client populations in community-agency settings.

Richardson and Bradley describe the following employment trends for people in graduate programs of community-agency counseling: Community mental-health centers represent the most frequent employer of master's level graduates in community-agency counseling. However, these graduates are also employed in a variety of agencies emphasizing the delivery of community mental-health services. These agencies include juvenile and adult probation departments, social services for family and children, and alcohol and drug abuse programs. Graduates are employed by agencies serving a range of client populations, both from a preventive and from a remedial perspective.

## Working within a System

*"strains"*

One of the reasons that systems put an added strain on the counselor is that the providers of their funding may require monumental amounts of paperwork to justify their continued existence. Another source of strain is counselors' relations with the power structure of the institution. The people who administer the agency or institution may have long forgotten the practicalities involved in providing direct services to a range of clients. On the other hand, practitioners who deal with clients directly may have little appreciation for the struggles of administrators who must fight for the continued funding of their programs. Thus, if there is inadequate communication, as there often is, tension is inevitable.

*"system"*

Many professionals struggle with the issue of how to work within a system while retaining their dignity, vitality, and convictions. Although working in any organization can be frustrating, we've observed a tendency on the part of some counselors to put the blame too readily on institutions when their efforts to help others don't succeed. Although bureaucratic obstacles can certainly make it difficult to implement sound ideas, we assume that it's possible to learn ways of working within an institution with dignity and self-respect. Consequently, we emphasize the need for honest self-examination in determining the degree to which the "system" is actually hindering you as you try to put your ideas into practice.

### The Tendency to Avoid Responsibility

We've alluded to the tendency to blame institutions for failing to implement effective programs. So often we hear the "If only it weren't for—" argument, which absolves the speaker of responsibility and diminishes his or her personal power at the same time. Take a moment now to reflect on some typical statements of this kind and apply them to yourself. How likely are you to resort to these statements as a way of deflecting responsibility to external sources? Rate each one, using the following code:

A = I feel this way often, and I can hear myself making this statement frequently.

B = I feel this way at times, and I might be inclined to say this occasionally.
C = I rarely feel this way.
D = I can't see myself using this statement as a way of absolving myself of personal responsibility.

_____ 1. You have to play politics if you want to get your programs through.
_____ 2. I can't do what I really want to do, because my director or supervisor wouldn't allow it.
_____ 3. If the community were more receptive to mental-health programs, my proposals and projects would be far more successful than they are.
_____ 4. I'm not succeeding because my clients aren't motivated.
_____ 5. I can't really say what I think, because I'd lose my job.
_____ 6. The bureaucratic system makes it almost impossible to develop innovative and meaningful programs.
_____ 7. If I were given more time off, I could develop exciting projects; as it is now, all my time is consumed by busywork.
_____ 8. I'm not free to pursue my own interests in my job, because the institution dictates what my interests will be.
_____ 9. The system makes it difficult to engage in the kind of counseling that would produce real change.
_____ 10. My own individuality and professional identity must be subordinate to the policies of the institution if I expect to survive in the system.

What other statements might you make about your difficulties as a professional working in a system?

**The Reality of Working in a System.**   Are you oriented toward what *can* be done or what *cannot* be done? As you reflect on this question, consider some of the following sources of frustration that are part of working in any system:

- The system is not responsive to client needs. It seems that clients are neglected in favor of administrative requirements and the politics of power.
- The system is typically not responsive to the people working in it. Workers are often not given responsibility or consulted about decisions, and they are overlooked in many ways.
- Workers are often not appreciated by their clients. This lack of appreciation occurs most frequently when the clients do not want the help of the worker to begin with. It leads workers to wonder what their purpose is and why they continue in a situation in which they do not seem to be making any significant differences in the lives of their clients.
- There is too much paper work, which distracts workers from what they most want to do.
- Many workers complain that they are not adequately trained for the difficult jobs they are expected to do.

If you accept this description of the "givens of the system," the question is "How can I constructively deal with these real barriers that make my job difficult?"

**The Results of Evading Personal Responsibility.**   Counselors who put the blame on the "system" when they fail to act in accordance with their beliefs are bound to experience a growing sense of powerlessness. This feeling is sometimes expressed in words such as "I really can't change anything at all! I may as well just do what's expected and play the game." The temptation to submit to this stance of professional impotence constitutes a real ethical concern. It is the kind of attitude that feeds on itself.

Another way of evading personal responsibility is to settle into a comfortable rut. We've seen many counselors who have found a niche in the system and who have learned to survive with a minimum of effort. In order to remain comfortable they continue to do the same thing over and over for weeks, months, and years. They rarely question the effectiveness of their efforts or give much thought to ways of reaching a greater number of people more effectively. They neither question the system in which they're involved nor develop new projects that would give them a change of pace. Although we appreciate their difficulties, we think that this kind of complacency is just as deadly a form of powerlessness as the defeated feeling of those who decide they can't really change things.

Defeatism and complacency are both attitudes that cheat the *clients* whom counselors are trying to serve. For this reason, we ask you to consider how ethical it is for counselors to give in to these feelings. We believe that counselors have a responsibility to look at their own tendency to become comfortable to the degree that they make the system work for them instead of those it is intended to serve.

## Assuming Power within a System

If counselors recognize that there are obstacles to overcome in any system, they may be able to acquire a sense of personal power to make significant changes. Our central aim in the rest of this chapter is to encourage you to define a style of working within a system that suits your personality. Although we cannot prescribe a universal method of getting along in an institution, we can present some strategies that we have found helpful and ask you to determine how appropriate these strategies are for you. In addition, we hope that you can think of other ways of preserving your individuality while working as part of a system.

Your first opportunity to assert your individuality is in the job interview. Often people being interviewed for a position confine themselves to answering the questions that are asked of them. However, job interviews can be mutual exchanges in which you explore the requirements and expectations of a position and assess its suitability for yourself. It's important to recognize that accepting a position with an agency entails agreeing to work within a certain philosophical framework. By asking relevant questions you begin to assume a stance of power, for you are exploring how much you want a particular job and what price you're willing to pay for it.

Our experience has been that most established organizations resist change but that small and subtle changes can be significant. If you devote most of your energy to trying to change the people who defend the status quo, your positive programs may become a lesser priority. You'll need to decide for yourself how much energy you're willing to expend on dealing with the resistive forces you encounter. If you attempt radical, system-wide changes, you might feel overwhelmed or paralyzed. If you focus instead on making changes within the scope of your position, you'll stand a better chance of extending your influence. For instance, a social worker whose goal is to correct fundamental inequities in the social-welfare system may soon feel discouraged and helpless. By directing his attention to ways of dealing more humanely with the people he comes into contact with, he may experience a sense of power and accomplishment as he makes less grandiose but still significant changes. To take another example, a school counselor may give up in exasperation if she directs most of her efforts to changing her colleagues' view of their role. If she concentrates instead on defining her own role so that she can do the kind of counseling she believes in, she may succeed in making a smaller but still meaningful change.

Another way to assume power to make changes is to learn the reasons for the policies of the organization you work for. Perhaps there are good reasons why certain policies have been established, even if they seem to restrict your freedom in your job. On the other hand, if a policy is not in the best interest of your clients, you can begin to challenge the assumptions on which the policy is based. You can suggest alternative policies, and you can find out whether others on the staff share your view. A sound understanding of the aims of the agency can strengthen your assessment of existing policies and make your suggestions more acceptable to those in charge. Consulting with colleagues can put you in a better position to suggest changes than operating in isolation.

Often people remain powerless because they don't make the effort to order their priorities and work on them systematically. We've found it helpful to determine what we *most* wanted to accomplish in a given position. We recognize that we don't have total autonomy while we're associated with a system, and so at times we're willing to negotiate and compromise. By ordering our priorities we can decide which compromises we can make without sacrificing our integrity and which positions cannot be compromised in good faith. Knowing what we consider to be most important puts us in a much better position to ask for what we want. In conjunction with this, good communication with directors and supervisors is essential. We try to keep the people to whom we report informed about how we're using our time and why. Many times a proposal fails to be accepted not because it's unsound but because the person responsible for approving it has not been adequately informed of its rationale or design. Since supervisors or directors are the ones who will be on the receiving end of any complaints, they may thwart a plan or block certain activities because they haven't been convinced of their merit.

One essential element in learning how to work effectively within a system is to realize that you're a vital part of that system, that "the institution" is not something that can be divorced from you. This implies that your relationships with other staff members are a central part of the system. Ignoring this reality and attempting to function in isolation will probably diminish your effectiveness. More positively, colleagues can be nourishing and supportive, and your interactions with them can give you a fresh perspective on some of your activities. Furthermore, genuine relationships with your coworkers can be a way of gaining power to make changes with the help of others who share your cause.

Unfortunately, although interactions with others in the institution can be energizing, they can also be debilitating. Instead of developing support groups within an agency, some people develop cliques, harbor unspoken hostility, and generally refuse to confront the conflicts or frictions that keep the staff divided. Often there are hidden agendas at staff meetings, and only superficial matters are discussed while real issues are kept secret. We want to underscore the importance of finding ways to establish working relationships that enrich your professional life instead of draining your energy. It's strange that counselors, who are supposed to be experts in helping others to establish nourishing relationships, often complain that they miss meaningful contacts with their colleagues. If you feel isolated, you can decide to take the initiative and arrange for fruitful interactions with others on the staff. For example, you could suggest a regular meeting time during which several colleagues could share their concerns and experiences. Working with others on special projects is a good way to renew yourself and a source of inspiration that can suggest new directions.

In thinking about the questions we pose below, clarify your position on ways that you could increase your chances of assuming power within the system.

- What are some questions that you would want to raise in a job interview?
- What experiences have you had in encountering resistance to ideas that you wanted to put into practice?
- What would you do if the organization you worked for instituted some policies to which you were strongly opposed?
- What would you do if you strongly believed that some fundamental changes needed to be made in your institution but your colleagues disagreed?
- What would you do if your supervisor continually blocked most of your activities, despite your efforts to keep him or her informed of the reasons for them?

- How would you attempt to make contact with other colleagues if members of your staff seemed to work largely in isolation from one another?
- If your staff seemed to be divided by jealousies, hostilities, or unspoken conflicts, what do you think you would do about the situation?
- What do you consider to be the ethics involved in staying with a job after you've done everything you can to bring about change, but to no avail? (Consider that you are being asked to do things that are against your basic philosophy.)

## Two Case Examples

The following two cases are designed to illustrate some of the issues we've discussed in this chapter. Try to imagine yourself in each of these situations, and ask yourself how you would deal with them.

■ *The case of Sarah.*    Sarah works in a community mental-health clinic, and most of her time is devoted to dealing with immediate crisis situations. The more she works with people in crises, the more she is convinced that the focus of her work should be on preventive programs designed to educate the public. Sarah comes to believe strongly that there would be far fewer clients in a state of crisis if people were effectively contacted and motivated to participate in growth-oriented educational programs. She develops detailed, logical, and convincing proposals for programs she would like to implement in the community, but they are consistently rejected by the director of her center on the ground that the primary purpose of the clinic is to intervene in crisis situations. Because the clinic is partially funded by the government for the expressed purpose of crisis intervention, the director feels uneasy about approving any program that doesn't relate directly to this objective.

If you were in Sarah's place, what do you think you would do? Which of the following courses of action would you be likely to take?

____ I'd probably do what the director expected and complain that the bureaucratic structure inhibited the implementation of imaginative programs.
____ Rather than take the director's no as a final answer, I'd try to work toward a compromise. I'd do what was expected of me while finding some way to make room for my special project. I'd work with the director until I convinced her to permit me to launch my program in some form.
____ If I couldn't do what I deemed important, I'd look for another job.
____ I'd get several other staff members together in order to pool our resources and look for ways to implement our program as a group.

■ *The case of George.*    George is a social worker in a school district. He is expected to devote most of his time to checking on children who are habitually truant and to do social-welfare work with dependent families.

Although he knew his job description before he accepted the position, he now feels that his talents could be put to better use if he were allowed to do intensive counseling with families as units. Referral sources in the area are meager, and the families he works for cannot afford private treatment. Although George has the training to do the type of family counseling that he thinks is sorely needed, his school administrator makes it clear that any kind of therapy is outside the province of the school's responsibility. George is told to confine himself to tracking down truant children, doing legal work, and processing forms.

If you were in George's position, what do you think you would do?

____ I'd present a written plan to the local school board, showing that family counseling was needed and that public facilities were inadequate to meet this need.

____ I'd go ahead and do the family counseling without telling my administrator.

____ I wouldn't make waves, because I wouldn't want to lose my job.

## Chapter Summary

The primary thrust of this chapter has been to suggest ways of going beyond the limitations of one-to-one counseling. Counselors not only need to get involved in the community but also need to find ways of helping their clients make the transition from individual counseling to their everyday lives. The community mental-health orientation is an example of *one* way to meet the increasing demand for psychological services. Too often mental-health professionals have not been creative in devising programs that are addressed to the diverse needs of the community. For this reason some alternatives to conventional therapy have arisen, creating new roles for professional counselors and therapists.

Many of you who are reading this book may be looking forward to a full-time career in a system. We think it is essential to consider how to make the system work *for* you, rather than *against* you. We have challenged you to think of ways to accept the responsibility of surviving and working effectively in an organization and thus increase your power as a person. Finally, we've asked you to reflect on the major causes of the disillusionment that often accompanies working in a system and to find creative ways to remain vital as a person and as a professional.

*How to make the system work for you...*

*major cause disillusionment*

## Suggested Activities

1. In small groups explore specific ways of becoming involved in the community or using community resources to assist you in working with your clients. After you've explored these issues, the class can reconvene to pool ideas.

2. Several students who are interested in the use of paraprofessionals in the human-services field can investigate the issue and present their results in the form of a panel discussion. The discussion can focus on the advantages and disadvantages of the use of paraprofessionals, current trends, and other issues the panel deems important.

3. An issue you may well face in your practice is how to get through the resistance that people have toward asking for psychological assistance. Ask yourself how you should respond to clients who have questions such as "What will people think if they find out that I'm coming for professional help?" Shouldn't I really be able to solve my problems on my own? Isn't it a sign of weakness that I need others to help me?" "Aren't most people who come to a community clinic really sick?" "Will I really be able to resolve my problems by consulting a mental-health professional?" After you've thought through your own responses, you can share them in dyads or in small groups.

4. For this exercise, begin by working in dyads. One student assumes the role of a person in some type of crisis. The student who will role-play the client should be able to identify in some way with the crisis situation. The other student becomes the crisis counselor and conducts an intake interview that does not exceed 30 minutes. Alternatively, a crisis situation can be presented to the entire class, and several students can show what immediate interventions they would make. Students who participate as counselors should be given feedback, and alternative intervention techniques should be discussed.

5. How aware are you of the resources that exist in your community? Would you know where to refer clients for special help? How aware are you of the support systems that exist in your community? Individually or with other students, investigate a comprehensive community mental-health center in your area. In doing so, find the answers to questions such as these:
   • Where would you send a family who needed help?
   • What facilities are available to treat drug and alcohol abuse?
   • What kinds of crisis intervention are available? What are some common crises?
   • Are health and medical services available at the center?
   • What kinds of groups are offered?
   • Is individual counseling available? For whom? At what fee? Long-term? Short-term?
   • Where would you refer a couple seeking marital counseling?
   • Are hot-line services available?
   • What provisions are there for emergency situations?
   • What do people have to do to qualify for help at the center?

6. As a small-group discussion activity, explore the topic of how you see yourself in relation to the educational system of which you are a part. Discuss the implications your style as a learner may have for the style you'll develop when you work for some institution or agency. Some

questions for exploration are "How active am I in the process of my own education? What specific things do I do to make my education more meaningful? Am I willing to talk with instructors if I feel that they aren't offering me a valuable course? Am I willing to suggest constructive alternatives if I'm dissatisfied with a class or with my program? Do I often feel powerless as a student and thus assume the stance that there's nothing I can do to really change the things I think most need changing?"

After you've had enough time to discuss this issue in small groups, the class can reconvene and compare results. Are there any common characteristics in the learning styles of the class members? How might these characteristics affect the way you work in a system as a professional?

7. With another student, role-play a job interview. One person is the director of a counseling center, and the other is the applicant. After 10 to 15 minutes switch roles. Discuss how you felt in each position, and get feedback from your partner after both of you have had a chance to play each role. Some questions the interviewer might ask include:
   - Why are you applying for this job?
   - What are your expectations if you get the position?
   - Since there are many applicants and only a few positions, tell me why we should select you for the job. What do you have to offer that is unique?
   - Could you briefly describe your philosophy of counseling?
   - What do you most hope to accomplish as a counselor, and how would you evaluate whether you were accomplishing your goals?
   - What kinds of clients could you *least* effectively counsel? What kinds of clients would you be *most* effective with?

8. Several students can interview a variety of professionals in the mental-health field about the major problems they encounter in their institution. What barriers do they meet when they attempt to implement programs? How do they deal with obstacles or red tape? How does the system affect them? You can divide this task up so that a wide range of professionals and paraprofessionals are interviewed, including some who have been in the same job for a number of years and others who are just beginning. It would be interesting to compare the responses of experienced and inexperienced personnel. The students who do the interviewing can share their impressions and reactions without revealing the identities of the persons interviewed.

■
# Suggested Readings

For a comprehensive survey and national assessment of trends in graduate programs in community-agency counseling see Richardson and Bradley (1985). On training standards for paraprofessionals see the Council for Standards in Human Service Education (1983). For a description of an undergraduate curriculum in human services designed to prepare paraprofessionals to do work in community agencies with diverse client populations see Coley, Corey, Garcia, Moline, Ramirez, Russell, and Wright (1986). For using paraprofessionals see Easton, Platt, and Van Hoose (1985) and Goldenberg (1983). For outreach strategies in reaching ethnic groups in the community, see Atkinson, Morten, and Sue (1979), Levine and Padilla (1980), Pedersen, Draguns, Lonner, and Trimble (1981), and Sue (1981a). For a discussion of psychotherapy as a professional relationship see Reisman (1986). On the community mental-health orientation see Bloom (1983). For a description of the basic elements required of helpers to function effectively as consultants see Kurpius (1986). On ethical issues in consultation see Tokunaga (1984), Robinson and Gross (1985), Gallessich (1982), Brown (1985), and Crego (1985).

# TEN

# Ethical and Professional Issues in Marital and Family Therapy

- Pre-Chapter Self-Inventory
- Introduction
- Ethical Standards in Marital and Family Therapy
- Contemporary Professional Issues
- Values in Marital and Family Therapy
- Responsibilities of Marital and Family Therapists
- Confidentiality in Marital and Family Therapy
- Informed Consent in Marital and Family Therapy
- Ethical and Legal Issues in Counseling Children and Adolescents
- Counseling Women: A Special Case?
- Ethical and Professional Issues in Sex Therapy
- Chapter Summary
- Suggested Activities
- Suggested Readings

# Pre-Chapter Self-Inventory

*Directions:*  For each statement, indicate the response that most closely identifies your beliefs and attitudes. Use the following code:

3 = I *agree*, in most respects, with this statement.
2 = I am *undecided* in my opinion about this statement.
1 = I *disagree*, in most respects, with this statement.

___  1. A person who comes from a troubled family is generally a poor candidate to become a good family therapist.

___  2. I would never divulge in a family session any secrets given to me privately by one of the members.

___  3. In practicing marriage counseling, I would see my clients only in conjoint therapy.

___  4. Counselors have an ethical responsibility to encourage spouses to leave partners who are physically and psychologically abusive.

___  5. I would not be willing to work with a couple in marital therapy if I knew that one of them had had an affair unbeknownst to the other.

___  6. Therapists with very traditional values are unlikely to be effective in counseling women.

___  7. It is ethical for family therapists to use pressure and even coercion to get a reluctant client to participate in family therapy.

___  8. It is appropriate for therapists who work with children and adolescents to serve as their advocates in certain legal situations.

___  9. When a child is in psychotherapy, the therapist has an ethical and legal obligation to provide the parents with information they request.

___  10. Minors should be allowed to seek psychological assistance regarding pregnancy and abortion counseling *without* parental consent or knowledge.

___  11. I would consider it unethical to work with a child unless I had obtained the informed consent of both the child and his or her parent or guardian.

___  12. Therapists who feel justified in imposing their own values on a couple or a family can potentially do considerable harm.

___  13. In couples or family therapy I would explain my policies about confidentiality at the first session.

___  14. Most family therapists, consciously or unconsciously, proselytize for maintaining a family way of life.

___  15. There are ethical problems in treating only one member of a couple in sex therapy.

___  16. I would be willing to work with a single member of a family and eventually attempt to bring the entire family into therapy.

___  17. Before accepting a family for treatment, I would obtain supervised training in working with families.

___ 18. Before working with families, I need to explore issues in my own family of origin.
___ 19. Skills in family-therapy techniques are far more important to success in this area than knowing my own personal dynamics.
___ 20. I favor requiring continuing education in the field of marital and family therapy as a condition for renewal of a license in this area.

# Introduction

For a decade there has been a rapid increase in the development of theories and techniques of marital and family therapy. Separate graduate programs in the field have grown, and many master's programs in counseling now offer a specialization in relationship counseling or marital and family therapy. In addition, there has been an increased focus on ethical, legal, and professional issues that are unique to a systems perspective. Systems theory is a therapeutic approach that emphasizes individuals' marital system, family system, community system, and the other larger systems of which they are a part. From this orientation marital dysfunction is treated by working with the couple as well as with other significant family members (Baruth & Huber, 1984); Huber & Baruth, 1987). Many of the ethical issues that we have already discussed take on special significance when therapists work with more than one client, especially when these clients live together as some form of family. Most graduate programs in marital and family therapy require a separate course in ethics and the law pertaining to this specialization.

You may not choose to obtain a degree or license in this specialization, but you are likely to eventually work with couples and families in various settings. This chapter introduces you to some of the ethical and professional issues that you are bound to face in this work. We begin the chapter with a discussion of the ethical codes of conduct that have been developed by the American Association for Marriage and Family Therapy (AAMFT), the major professional organization in the field. We also briefly treat contemporary professional issues in marital and family therapy, including educational and training standards.

The role of the family therapist's values cannot be overstressed. Values pertaining to marriage, the preservation of the family, divorce, traditional and nontraditional life-styles, child rearing, and extramarital affairs can all influence the therapist's interventions. Counselors who feel justified in imposing their own values on a couple or a family can potentially do considerable harm. Ethical issues pertaining to therapists' pushing of their own values and misusing power deserve considerable attention. This chapter also focuses on certain other responsibilities of marital and family therapists, such as the responsibility to consult, to give courtroom testimony in custody cases, and to provide for informed consent.

We have included ethical and legal issues involved in counseling children and adolescents in this chapter, because family therapy typically includes working with youngsters and because parents are often involved in their children's treatment program. The topic of confidentiality, explored in Chapter 6, takes on special meaning in the counseling of couples and families. Also included are issues pertaining to therapy for women, with a focus on sex roles and stereotypical views, and how these views affect a practitioner's interventions in working with couples and families. Women's issues deserve a place in this chapter because therapists tend to be men and clients tend to be women. Even though the roles of women and men have changed drastically in recent decades, many therapists still operate on outdated assumptions.

Finally, we also explore issues pertaining to sex therapy, since this is another area where ethics assume a significant role. Sex therapy is often an integral part of relationship counseling.

# Ethical Standards in Marital and Family Therapy

The *Code of Ethical Principles for Marriage and Family Therapists* (AAMFT, 1985) provides a framework for many of the ethical issues that we will consider in this chapter. The code covers seven areas. A statement of each of these main principles follows, along with a brief commentary and questions. (Consult the Appendix for the complete AAMFT code.)

( 1.)*Responsibility to clients.* "Marriage and family therapists are dedicated to advancing the welfare of families and individuals, including respecting the rights of those persons seeking their assistance, and making reasonable efforts to ensure that their services are used appropriately."

More specifically, marriage and family therapists do not refuse their professional services to individuals because of their race, sex, religion, or nationality; enter into dual relationships with clients; exploit clients; develop sexual relationships with a client or a client's partner; continue counseling once clients are no longer benefiting; or abandon or neglect clients without making reasonable arrangements for the continuation of their treatment.

We raise the questions "To whom does the marriage and family therapist have a primary responsibility; that is, who is the client in family therapy? Is the client the family as a whole? Is it either one or both of the spouses? Is it a child?" Morrison, Layton, and Newman (1982) pose further questions: Whose interest is the therapist ethically bound to serve? Should the therapist work with one client and then eventually attempt to bring the entire family into therapy? What is the proper course in cases involving reluctant children and adolescents? Later we consider these and other issues pertaining to the responsibilities of marital and family therapists.

2. *Confidentiality.* "Marriage and family therapists have unique confidentiality problems because the 'client' in a therapeutic relationship may be more than one person. The overriding principle is that marriage and family therapists respect the confidences of their client(s)."

This principle implies that marriage and family therapists do not disclose what they learn through the professional relationship, except (1) in cases as mandated by law, such as physical or psychological child abuse, incest, neglect, and abuse of the elderly; (2) when it is necessary to protect the client from harming himself or herself or to prevent a clear and immediate danger to others; and (3) in cases when the therapist is involved in court proceedings. If therapists use any material from their practice in teaching, lecturing, and writing, they take care to preserve the anonymity of their clients.

As we discuss later, confidentiality assumes unique significance in the practice of marital and family therapy. Confidentiality issues within the family itself arise, such as how secrets should be dealt with. Incest, extramarital affairs, or physical or psychological abuse of a wife or children may be involved. Should the therapist attempt to have families reveal all their secrets, even if some members are likely to suffer from extreme anxiety or loss of respect from the other members (Morrison et al., 1982)?

3. *Professional competence and integrity.* "Marriage and family therapists are dedicated to maintaining high standards of professional competence and integrity."

This principle implies that therapists seek professional help when their own personal problems are likely to negatively affect their professional work or impair their clinical judgment. It also implies that they keep abreast of developments in the field through continuing education and clinical experiences. It is considered unethical for practitioners to diagnose or treat clients when doing so would exceed their level of training. On a related point, Morrison and his colleagues stress care in using diagnostic labeling, since such diagnoses may ultimately be used by others in child-custody disputes.

4. *Responsibility to students, employees, and supervisees.* "Marriage and family therapists do not exploit the trust and dependency of students and supervisees."

The code cautions practitioners to avoid dual relationships, which are likely to impair clinical judgment. Sexual harassment and sexual intimacies with students, employees, and supervisees are specifically prohibited.

5. *Responsibility to the profession.* "Marriage and family therapists respect the rights and responsibilities of professional colleagues; carry out research in an ethical manner; and participate in activities which advance the goals of the profession."

Ethical practice implies measures of accountability to professional standards. In conducting research family therapists function within the framework of the laws and regulations governing the use of human subjects. Research practices are done in an ethical manner and reported accurately. It is expected that marriage and family therapists will contribute time to the betterment of society, including donating services.

6. *Fees.* "Marriage and family therapists make financial arrangements with clients that conform to accepted professional practices and that are reasonably understandable."

This principle makes explicit that marriage and family therapists do not accept payment for making referrals, exploit clients financially for services, or change fee structures without giving reasonable notice. Ethical practice dictates a disclosure of fee policies at the onset of therapy.

7. *Advertising.* "Marriage and family therapists engage in appropriate informational activities, including those that enable laypersons to choose marriage and family services on an informed basis."

Ethical practice dictates that practitioners accurately represent their competence, education, training, and experience in marital and family therapy. Professional standards are used in announcing services. Therapists do not advertise themselves as specialists (for example, in sex therapy) without being able to support this claim by virtue of their education, training, and supervised experience.

## Ethical Problems for Family Therapists

In a study by Green and Hansen (1986) family therapists who responded listed the eight ethical dilemmas they most often faced, in the following order:

1. treating a family if one member does not want to participate
2. keeping abreast of family-therapy developments
3. feeling confident of one's training or qualifications
4. seeing one family member without the others present
5. informing clients of values implicit in the mode of therapy
6. dealing with parental requests for information differently from children's requests for information
7. sharing of one's values and biases with families
8. development of laws and regulations pertaining to family therapy

In a review of the literature on ethical problems facing family therapists, Green and Hansen found a number of issues that are not included in the *Ethical Principles for Family Therapists* (AAMFT, 1984). They found that family therapists encountered dilemmas that were *not* included in the *Principles* more often than they did with regard to those that *were* included. The authors concluded that, although the ethical principles were helpful, further guidelines must be developed.

# Contemporary Professional Issues

In this section we identify a few of the current professional issues in the practice of marital and family therapy. These include the personal, academic, and experiential qualifications necessary to practice in the field.

## Personal Characteristics of the Therapist

A debate surrounds the issue of the preparation of marital and family therapists. In Chapter 2 we discussed personal characteristics of effective counselors. According to Humphrey (1983), of all the professional issues in marital therapy the least studied and most controversial one is what personal qualities are associated with an effective family therapist. Humphrey points out that research data are scant in this area, and he raises these questions: Who should do the training of marital and family therapists? Who will make the decisions about which people are permitted to train people for this profession? How will decisions be made? What criteria will be used? As difficult and complex as these questions are, the profession must strive to answer them.

## Educational Requirements

The AAMFT has developed minimum academic standards for marital and family therapists. Candidates are expected to demonstrate that they have successfully completed a graduate program from an accredited institution, with a minimum of a master's degree. Specific requirements include course work in human development, marital and family studies, research methods, and professional studies (including ethics and family law). The requirements also include a minimum of a year of supervised clinical experience in relationship counseling. These standards require that therapists understand humans from an individual and a social perspective and that they have the knowledge and skills necessary to intervene in treating dysfunctional couples and family relationships.

**Training, Supervision, and Clinical Experience.**    We agree with a number of writers who give primary emphasis to the quality of supervised practice and clinical experience in the training of marital and family therapists. Above all, therapists need to be skilled and sensitive clinicians. Mere knowledge of theories of marriage and family systems and theories of therapeutic intervention are of limited practical value if therapists are not able to use themselves as persons constructively in sessions with couples and families (Humphrey, 1983). It is in supervised practicum and internship that academic knowledge comes alive and that trainees learn how to use and sharpen their intervention skills.

In terms of methods of training, both didactic and experiential methods, in combination with supervised practice, are typically employed in most graduate programs. Didactic methods include classroom lectures, readings, demonstrations, viewing of films and videotapes of family therapy sessions, role playing, and discussion. Experiential methods include both personal therapy and working with one's own family of origin. A rationale for personal therapeutic experiences is that they enable trainees to increase their awareness of transference and countertransference. The AAMFT recommends such therapy. A rationale for exploration of the family of origin is that it enables trainees to relate more effectively to the families they will meet in their clinical practice. (For a discussion of our perspectives on the value of this type of therapeutic experience for any type of therapist, review our discussion in Chapter 2.)

Concerning the objectives of professional training, Goldenberg and Goldenberg (1985) contend that there is neither a single theoretical perspective of family process nor a single set of intervention techniques for helping dysfunctional couples and families. They write that learning family therapy requires a theoretical understanding of personality, family structure, group dynamics, systems theory, and cross-cultural studies. Yet they assert that direct contact with families is the most important component of training. It is through these encounters, under close supervision, that trainees develop their own style of interacting with families.

**Continuing Education.**   Obtaining a graduate degree in marital and family therapy does not end the need for education (see our discussion in Chapter 5). Marriage is not a static institution, in that there are changes in values and life-styles. There are new developments in theories and techniques of family intervention, along with emerging professional issues. Furthermore, legislative and judicial decisions have a major impact. Therapists who are not aware of these changes will not be able to provide the highest quality of professional service. "Such a situation would appear to be both unethical and professionally self-destructive for therapists and possibly harmful to clients" (Humphrey, 1983, p. 213).

# Values in Marital and Family Therapy

In Chapter 3 we explored the impact of the therapist's values on the goals and direction of the therapy process. Values take on special significance in counseling couples and families. Goldenberg and Goldenberg (1985) write that family therapy implies a set of moral values that is primarily middle class. This value orientation includes a respect for the institution of marriage and stability in family life, the importance of using child-rearing methods that fit the needs of each child, the desire to transmit the family's cultural values to the next generation, and the belief that a family is necessary for maintaining psychological health. The Goldenbergs assert that "most family therapists—deliberately or unwittingly, consciously or unconsciously—proselytize for maintaining a family way of life" (p. 249).

The value system of therapists has a crucial influence on their formulation and definition of the problems they see in a family, the goals and plans for therapy, and even the direction the therapy takes. We want to emphasize again that we do not see it as the function of any therapist to make decisions for the client. Family therapists should not decide for the members of a family how they should change. From our perspective, the role of the family therapist is to help family members see with more clarity what they are doing, to help them make an honest evaluation of how well their present patterns are working for them individually and for the family as a whole, and to assist and encourage them to make the changes they decide on.

In this section we invite you to think about your own values and to reflect on the impact that they are likely to have on the interventions you make with couples and families. To assist you in formulating your personal position on these issues, we provide cases to consider and raise value-laden questions.

Suppose you have a 25-year-old client, Sharon, who says: "I'm never going to get married, because I think marriage is a drag! I don't want kids, and I don't want to stay with one person forever." What is your reaction to this statement? Perhaps your values clash with Sharon's desire to be free of responsibility. If so, you might tell her that a refusal to accept any responsibility in life is a sign of immaturity and that she will have a more complete life if she has a family of her own. Or perhaps you envy her independence and wish that you didn't have to be responsible for anyone except yourself. In what ways do you think that you might work with Sharon differently, depending on what your own attitude toward family life is? If you don't feel comfortable with a commitment to marriage and a family, do you think you could be objective enough to help her explore some of the possibilities she might be overlooking? Or might your doubts be useful in your work with Sharon?

■ ***The case of a couple seeking marriage counseling.***    During the past few years Frank and Judy have experienced many conflicts in their marriage. Although they have made attempts to resolve their problems by themselves, they have finally decided to seek the help of a professional marriage counselor. Even though they have been thinking about divorce with increasing frequency, they still have some hope that they can achieve a satisfactory marriage.

We will present the approaches of three marriage counselors, each holding a different set of values pertaining to marriage and the family. As you read these responses, think about the degree to which they represent what you might say and do if you were counseling this couple.

***Counselor A.***    At the first session this counselor states his belief in the preservation of marriage and the family. He feels that many couples take the easy way out by divorcing too quickly in the face of difficulty. He says that he sees most couples as having unrealistically high expectations of what constitutes a "happy marriage." The counselor lets it be known that his experience continues to teach him that divorce rarely solves any problems but instead creates new problems that are often worse. The counselor urges Frank and Judy to consider the welfare of their three dependent children. He tells the couple of his bias toward the saving of the marriage so that they can make an informed choice about initiating counseling with him.

• What are your personal reactions toward the orientation of this counselor?
• Is it ethical for him to state his bias so obviously?

- What if he were to keep his bias and values hidden from the couple and accept them into therapy. Do you see any possibility that he could work objectively with this couple? Explain.

*Counselor B.*    This counselor has been married three times herself. Although she believes in the institution of marriage, she is quick to point out that far too many couples stay in their marriages and suffer unnecessarily. She explores with Judy and Frank the conflicts that they bring to the sessions. The counselor's interventions are leading them in the direction of divorce as the desired course of action, especially after they express this as an option. She suggests a trial separation and states her willingness to counsel them individually, with some joint sessions. When Frank brings up his guilt and reluctance to divorce because of the welfare of the children, the counselor confronts him with the harm that is being done to them by a destructive marriage. She tells Frank that it is too much of a burden to put on the children to keep the family together at any price.

- Do you see any ethical issues in this case? Is this counselor exposing or imposing her values?
- Do you think that she should be a marriage counselor, given her bias and her background of three divorces?
- What interventions made by the counselor do you agree with? What are your areas of disagreement?

*Counselor C.*    This counselor believes that it is not her place to bring her values pertaining to the family into the sessions. She is fully aware of her biases regarding marriage and divorce, but she does not see it as her place to impose her values or to expose them in all cases. Her primary interest is to help Frank and Judy discover what is best for them as individuals and as a couple. She sees it as unethical to push her clients toward a definite course of action, and she lets them know that her job is to help them be honest with themselves.

- What are your reactions to this counselor's approach?
- Do you see it as possible for a counselor to keep his or her values out of the therapy process in a case such as this?

*Commentary.*    The preceding case illustrates that the value system of the counselor determines the direction that counseling will take. The counselor who is dedicated to the mission of preserving marriage and family life is bound to function differently from the counselor who puts prime value on the welfare of an individual family member. What might be best for a given person might not necessarily be in the best interests of the entire family. It is essential, therefore, for counselors who work with couples and families to be aware of how their values influence the goals and procedures of therapy. We take the position that ethical practice challenges clients to clarify their own values and to choose a course of action that is best for them.

# Responsibilities of Marital and Family Therapists

Margolin (1982) argues persuasively that difficult ethical questions confronted in individual therapy become even more complicated when a number of family members are seen together in therapy. She observes that the dilemma with multiple clients is that in some instances an intervention that serves one person's best interests could burden another family member or even be countertherapeutic. For example, under the family-systems model, therapists do not focus on their responsibility to the individual but on the family as a system. Such therapists avoid becoming agents of any one family member since they believe that all family members contribute to the problems of the whole family. It should be clear that therapists are ethically expected to declare the nature of their commitments to each member of the family.

Therapist responsibilities are also a crucial issue in couple counseling or marriage counseling. This is especially true when the partners do not have a common purpose for seeking counseling. An interesting question is raised when one person wants divorce counseling and the other is coming to the sessions under the expectation of saving the marriage or improving the relationship. In such a situation, who is the primary client? How do therapists carry out their ethical responsibilities when the two persons in the relationship have differing expectations?

In addition to clinical and ethical considerations, Margolin mentions legal provisions that can decide when the welfare of an individual takes precedence over that of a relationship. A clear example of a therapist's legal obligations is a case of child neglect or child abuse. The law requires family therapists to inform authorities if they suspect such abuse or become aware of physical or emotional abuse during the course of therapy. Even though reporting this situation may have possible negative consequences for the therapeutic relationships with some members of the family, the therapist's ethical and legal responsibility is to help the threatened or injured person. It becomes clear that there are some situations in which interventions to help an individual become more important than the goals of the family as a system, and clients should be informed of these situations during the initial session.

Margolin (1982) summarizes the complex responsibilities of a therapist who works with more than one client in a family as follows:

> Attempting to balance one's therapeutic responsibilities toward individual family members and toward the family as a whole involves intricate judgments. Since neither of these responsibilities cancels out the importance of the other, the family therapist cannot afford blind pursuit of either extreme, that is, always doing what is in each individual's best interest or always maintaining the stance as family advocate [p. 790].

Morrison, Layton, and Newman (1982) agree with Margolin's position that family therapists may face more ethical conflicts than most other therapists. They write that family therapists sometimes face accusations that they are the agents of the parents against the children, the children against the parents, or of one parent against the other. Again, family therapists often wrestle with the question of whose agent they are.

## The Responsibility to Consult

At times marriage and family therapists must struggle over the issue of when they must consult with another professional. This is especially true of situations in which a person (or couple or family) is already involved in a professional relationship with a therapist and seeks the counsel of another therapist. What course of action would you take if a husband sought you out for private counseling while he and his wife were also seeing another therapist for marriage counseling? Would it be ethical to enter into a professional relationship with this man without the knowledge and consent of the other professional? What might you do or say if the husband told you that the reason for initiating contact with you was to get another opinion and perspective on his marital situation and that he did not see any point in contacting the other professional?

■  *An open-ended case.*  In this situation a couple is seeing the same therapist for marriage counseling. The husband decides to quit the joint sessions and begins private sessions with another therapist. The wife remains in individual therapy with the original therapist. In the course of individual therapy the husband comes to realize that he does not want to terminate the marriage after all. He persuades his wife to come with him for a joint session with *his* therapist to pursue the possibility of keeping the marriage intact.

- What are the ethical obligations of the husband's therapist? Does he have the responsibility of consulting with the wife's therapist?
- Do the two therapists need to get permission of their clients to consult with each other?
- Would it be ethical for the husband's therapist to do marital therapy with the couple, ignoring the work being done by the wife's therapist?

## The Family Therapist as an (Agent of Change)

Minuchin (1974) and his colleagues work with the structural aspects of the family system toward the goal of changing the system so that it will no longer support the symptom. The structural approach focuses on how the family organizes itself, on how its members communicate, and on how dysfunctional patterns develop. Since structural family therapy is an action-oriented approach that requires the therapist to take a highly active role in the therapeutic process, certain ethical issues are raised. Does this approach impose the therapist's value system on the family? Should the primary responsibility for change within the family rest with the therapist rather than with the individual family members? According to Minuchin, the tool of structural family therapy is to modify the present, not to explore and interpret the past. To accomplish this, family therapists join that system and then use themselves to transform it. Minuchin writes that the family system is organized around certain functions of its members (such as support, nurturing, control, and socializing). The therapist's responsibility is clear: "Hence, the therapist joins the family not to educate or socialize it, but rather to repair or modify the family's own functioning so that it can better perform these tasks" (1974, p. 14).

Structural family therapy does emphasize the role and power of the therapist, and this power is seen as a major variable in bringing about therapeutic change. In Minuchin's words: "Change is seen as occurring through the process of the therapist's affiliation with the family and his restructuring of the family in a carefully planned way, so as to transform dysfunctional transactional patterns" (p. 91).

## The Use and Misuse of Power and Influence in Family Therapy

The therapist's use of power is a critical issue in family therapy. Although power is a vital component in any therapeutic relationship and of itself is not a negative force, there are dangers in using power to keep clients dependent. If power is misused, clients may attribute to the therapist magical qualities to effect lasting change and bring about a "cure" to their troubles. They may thus be discouraged from looking within and tapping their own resources to being about constructive change. O'Shea and Jessee (1982) note that a position of power and influence is seen by most marital and family therapists as particularly important in working with couples and families. They write: "The therapist's process of establishing rapport and joining with family members requires deciphering the communications and cracking the role of the family's meaning pattern. This enables the therapist to recognize, intervene, and assign new meaning to, and ultimately change, destructive interactional patterns in the family" (p. 5). They conclude that for a family therapist to be effective, he or she needs to be influential. Systems therapists gain this influence by being active and directive during the early phases of therapy.

Fieldsteel (1982) notes that the ethical issues raised by the structural approach involve recognizing the possible differences between the value systems of the therapist and the family. She pinpoints the danger of the therapist's assuming an inordinate share of the responsibility for change in family systems: "There is the danger that the role of the therapist as a more active agent for change may shift the responsibility for the direction of change from the patient to the therapist" (p. 262).[1] Fieldsteel raises the ethical issue of the therapist's encouraging clients to accept the therapist's perceptions as truth while at the same time the clients suspend their own perceptions by placing more trust in the therapist than in themselves. She also points out that some therapists assume that, by virtue of their professional expertise, they have the right to impose a new set of beliefs and values on the family. We agree with her position that family therapists should be aware of their clients' tendencies to attribute inordinate powers to them. These tendencies are often based on transference projections and the longing for a powerful and all-knowing parent to protect and direct them.

As we've already noted, power and influence are factors in any therapeutic relationship, yet they assume even more importance in family therapy. Thus, family therapists have the obligation of continually examining the ways in which they can use or misuse personal power, for the misuse of power keeps families dependent.

## Responsibilities in the Courtroom

It is critical that marital and family therapists have a basic understanding of the law as it relates to families. The legal areas in which they need to be knowledgeable include malpractice and legal liability, courtroom testimony, divorce and child custody, and the lawyer/therapist relationships (Brown & Christensen, 1986). Earlier we mentioned that confidentiality is limited when family therapists are called on to give expert testimony, which is the situation in child-custody cases. If a family therapist is asked to make an evaluation in a custody case, an ethical issue arises as to the criteria for such an evaluation. Is the child evaluated independently of the family system or as a part of the family system? Some family therapists assert that an evaluation independent of the family system is inaccurate and misleading. They argue that this evaluation must take into account power struggles, triangles, coalitions, alliances, and family boundaries (Brown & Christensen, 1986, p. 284). It might be added that a consultation with an expert in family assessment is appropriate. This is especially important if the therapist is unfamiliar with the field of assessment for legal purposes.

# Confidentiality in Marital and Family Therapy

There are some special confidentiality issues in marital and family therapy. Therapists hold differing views on this topic. One view is that therapists should not divulge in a family session any information given to them by

[1] From "Ethical Issues in Family Therapy," by N. Fieldsteel. In M. Rosenbaum (Ed.), *Ethics and Values in Psychotherapy: A Guidebook.* Copyright 1982 by The Free Press, a division of Macmillan Publishing Company. This and all other quotations from the same source are reprinted by permission.

individuals in earlier private sessions. In the case of marriage counseling, some practitioners are willing to see each spouse for individual sessions. Information given to them by one spouse is honored as confidential, which means that it is not brought into individual sessions with the other spouse without the explicit consent of the disclosing client. Some therapists, however, reserve the right to bring up certain issues in a joint session, even if one person brought up the issue in a private session.

Some therapists who work with entire families, in contrast, have the policy of refusing to keep information secret that was shared individually. The view here is that secrets are counterproductive for open family therapy. Therefore secrets and "hidden agendas" are seen as material that should be brought out into the open during a family session. Still another view is that therapists should inform their clients that any information given to them during private sessions will be divulged as they see fit in accordance with the greatest benefit for the couple or the family. These therapists reserve the right to use their professional judgment about whether to maintain individual confidences. In our opinion this latter approach is the most flexible, in that it avoids putting the counselor in the awkward position of having to either divulge secrets or keep secrets at the expense of the welfare of the family. According to Margolin (1982), therapists who have not promised confidentiality have more options open and thus must carefully consider the therapeutic ramifications of their actions.

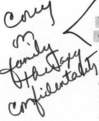

What we think is absolutely essential to ethical practice is that each marital and family therapist make his or her stand on confidentiality clear to each family member from the outset of therapy. In this way each family member can decide whether to participate in therapy and can then decide how much to disclose to the therapist. For example, a husband might disclose less in a private session if he knew that the therapist was assuming the right to bring these disclosures out in joint sessions. We think that Baruth and Huber (1984) put this matter in perspective: "The bottom line in how the issue of confidentiality should be handled is that a therapist must determine a policy that is compatible with his or her approach to conducting therapy, and this policy must be explained to the couple" (p. 284).

■ *A case of therapist quandary.*  A husband is involved in one-to-one therapy to resolve a number of personal conflicts, of which the state of his marriage is only one. Later, his wife comes in for some joint sessions. In their joint sessions much time is spent on how betrayed the wife feels over having discovered that her husband had an affair in the past. She is angry and hurt but has agreed to remain in the marriage and to come to these therapy sessions as long as the husband agrees not to resume the past affair or to initiate new ones. Reluctantly, the husband agrees to her demands. The therapist does not explicitly state her views of confidentiality, yet the husband assumes that she will keep to herself what she hears in both the wife's private sessions and his private sessions. During one of the joint sessions the therapist does state her bias that, if they are interested in working on their relationship, then maintaining or initiating an affair is counter-productive. She states that it is her strong preference that, if they both want to work on improving their marriage, they agree not to have extramarital affairs.

In a later individual session the husband tells the therapist that he has begun a new affair. He brings this up privately with his therapist because he feels some guilt over not having lived up to the agreement. But he maintains that the affair is not negatively influencing his relationship with his wife and has helped him to tolerate many of the difficulties that he has been experiencing in his marriage. He also asks that the therapist not mention this in a joint session, for he fears that his wife will leave him if she finds out that he is involved with another woman.

Think about these questions in taking your position on the ethical course of action:

- Since the therapist has not explicitly stated her view of confidentiality, is it ethical for her to bring up this matter in a joint session?
- How does the therapist handle her bias and conviction regarding affairs in light of the fact that the husband tells her that it is actually enhancing, not interfering with, the marriage?
- Does she attempt to persuade the husband to give up the affair? Does she persuade the client to bring up this matter himself in a joint session? Is the therapist colluding with the husband against the wife by not bringing up this matter?
- Do you think that she could have avoided getting herself into this dilemma? If so, how?
- Does the therapist discontinue therapy with this couple because of her strong bias? If she does suggest termination and referral to another professional, might not this be tantamount to admitting to the wife that the husband is having an affair? What might the therapist say if the wife is upset over the suggestion of a referral and wants to know the reasons?

## Informed Consent in Marital and Family Therapy

In Chapter 6 we examined the issue of informed consent and clients' rights within the framework of individual therapy. As Margolin (1982) notes, informed consent and the right to refuse treatment are also a critical ethical issue in the practice of marital and family therapy. When therapists work with an entire family, there are both ethical and practical reasons for taking the time to obtain informed consent from everyone. When this is done, the message is conveyed that no one member is the "crazy person" who is the source of all the family's problems. Margolin suggests that the therapist explore with the family the following topics at the outset: the purposes and procedures of therapy; the role and function of the person doing the therapy; the risks involved; the benefits that can be expected, along with the price that must be paid for these benefits; the option that each family member can withdraw his or her consent and discontinue participation in therapy at any time; and the possibility that family therapy will lead to outcomes deemed undesirable by some participants but advantageous by others in the same family.

Most family therapists consider it essential that all members of the family participate. This raises ethical questions about exerting pressure on an individual to participate, even if that person is strongly against being involved. Although coercion of a reluctant person is generally viewed as unethical, many therapists strongly suggest to such a person that he or she give a session or two a try to determine what potential value there might be to family therapy. Some resistance can arise from the feeling that a family member will be "ganged up on" and will be the focus of the sessions. In several sessions this resistance can be lessened and perhaps even eliminated if the therapist does not allow the family to use one member as the scapegoat. Although getting the informed consent of each member of the family is ideal from an ethical point of view, actually carrying out this practice may involve difficulties. On this point, Margolin (1982) writes:

> Thus, even though clients deserve an accurate portrayal of therapy in informed consent procedures, complete objectivity and openness may not be possible. At the same time that families need factual information to make an informed decision about therapy, they also need the therapist's support, encouragement, and optimism for taking this risky step [p. 795].

As does Margolin, Haas and Alexander (1981) contend that there are ethical problems in insisting that all the family members must attend sessions. They indicate that the therapist who requires all members to be a part of therapy may be colluding with the most resistant family member in keeping the more willing members from beginning or continuing therapy as a family. This position is often taken when the family therapist identifies the client as "the family" or "the system."

Protecting children's rights is typically made easier by treating the whole family, according to Haas and Alexander. They note that parents are generally considered to retain the legal authority to consent to (or prohibit) their children's treatment and to know what is occurring in this therapy. Family therapy eliminates certain problems, including the parents' "right to know," since they are a part of the therapy process. The issue of informed consent is open for discussion as a family topic, avoiding a conflict that might involve the therapist's siding with either the child or the parent. Haas and Alexander recommend that family therapists establish ground rules for dealing with matters such as family secrets or the confidences of an individual member. If these rules are made a part of the informed-consent procedure at the initial session(s), then issues of confidentiality are less likely to become a problem as therapy progresses.

Haas and Alexander contend that family therapists are responsible for clarifying their basic ethical positions and must communicate their views to their clients. They write:

> The general guideline is that one's position should be articulated; if the therapist does not know where he or she stands on a given issue such as rights of women, proper role of secrets in the family, aspects of children's independence, etc. then it is incumbent upon that therapist to start the process of finding out [1981, p. 9].

We are in basic agreement with their position. We think that, if therapists are able to clarify their positions to all the family members from the outset of treatment, the chances are greatly increased that these members will be willing to cooperate in the therapy. At the least, any member of the family can then argue with the therapist's views.

Hare-Mustin (1980) has observed that family therapy may be dangerous to one's health. Since it requires the involvement of the entire family, it may not be in the best interests of individual family members. The priority placed on the good of the family as a unit may lead to individual risks. Further, by being required to participate in therapy, members may have to subordinate their own goals and give up limited confidentiality. Hare-Mustin suggests that ethical practice demands a method of minimizing these risks for individual members. This can be done by encouraging them to question the goals of family therapy, so that they can understand how their own needs relate to the family goals. Also, it is the therapist's responsibility to open for discussion the subject of how one member's goals are incompatible with family goals or perhaps even unacceptable to other members. She emphasizes the importance of discussing the limits of confidentiality and privacy at the beginning of family sessions. Members have the right to know the rules about disclosure and how this sharing of information will be used (both in the sessions and out of the sessions).

The implications of informed consent for family therapists and systems-oriented therapists are discussed by Bray, Shepherd, and Hays (1985). These writers encourage systems-oriented therapists to tell prospective clients that they look beyond treating a specific and diagnosed problem to a broader view of the client's health. Clients have a right to know that the family system will be the focus of the therapeutic process, as well as to know about the practical implications of this theoretical perspective. The authors suggest that professionals have the responsibility to make reasonable disclosures to their clients of all significant facts, the nature of the procedures that will be used, the more probable consequences of these procedures, alternative treatment procedures, and risks of therapy. However, they do not see it as realistic to discuss every possible risk. They offer the guideline that a risk be disclosed when the client might find it important in deciding whether to consent to therapy. Further, family members should be encouraged to ask questions about therapy, and it is well to inform them that they are always free to withdraw their consent and terminate treatment at any point.

# Ethical and Legal Issues in Counseling Children and Adolescents

Consistent with the increasing concern over children's rights in general, more attention is being paid to such issues as the minor's right of informed consent. There are legal and ethical trends toward granting greater rights to children and adolescents in these areas (Glenn, 1980). According to Koocher (1976), ethical standards in counseling with minors deserve attention, because often "the standards of professional associations do not specifically address children as a unique subset of the population" (p. 3). Some of the legal and ethical questions faced by therapists who work with children and adolescents are: Can minors consent to treatment without parental consent? Can minors consent to treatment without parental knowledge? To what degree should minors be allowed to participate in setting the goals of therapy and in providing consent to undergo it? What are the limits of confidentiality in counseling with minors? What does informed consent consist of in working with minors? In this section we consider some of these questions and focus on the rights of children when they are clients.

## The Right to Treatment

In most states parental consent is legally required for minors to enter into a relationship with health-care professionals. There are exceptions to this general rule; some state statutes grant adolescents the right to seek counseling about birth control, abortion, substance abuse, and other crisis concerns. An example is a Virginia law of 1979 that is the broadest statute in the country on the rights of children and adolescents to consent to therapy. This law implies that "mature minors" should be able to consent to psychotherapy independently on grounds of personal privacy and liberty (Melton, 1981b). More specifically, a minor is deemed an adult for the purposes of consenting to:

1. health services needed to determine the presence of or to treat venereal disease or any infections or contagious disease that the State Board of Health requires to be reported
2. health services required in case of birth control, pregnancy, or family planning
3. health services needed in the case of outpatient care, treatment, or rehabilitation for substance abuse
4. health services needed in the case of outpatient care, treatment, or rehabilitation for mental or emotional illness

In keeping with this law, counselors in Virginia have the duty to keep information in the above areas confidential, even from parents. This duty challenges the commonly accepted premise that, before a counselor accepts a minor as a client, he or she is required to inform the parents and obtain their consent (Swanson, 1983).

Like Virginia, California provides for certain exceptions. Minors who have reached the age of 12 may consent to mental-health treatment if certain conditions are met: the minors must be mature enough to participate intelligently in mental-health treatment on an outpatient basis (in the opinion of the therapist), *and* they must present a danger or serious physical or mental harm to themselves or others *or* have been the alleged victims of incest or child abuse. Minors who meet the above stipulations may consent to receive outpatient mental-health services from sources such as licensed marriage and family counselors, licensed clinical social workers, licensed psychologists, or any governmental agency or community crisis center with qualified practitioners (Board of Medical Quality Assurance, 1980).

The justification for allowing children and adolescents to seek treatment without parental consent is that they might not obtain this needed treatment in some circumstances without such a right. There is some evidence that adolescents who seek help when given independent access might not have done so without the guarantee of privacy (Melton, 1981a). This is especially true in cases where the presenting problems involve family conflict, psychological or physical abuse, drug or alcohol abuse, and pregnancy or abortion counseling.

Counselors who are faced with the issue of when to accept minors as clients without parental consent must consider various factors. What is the competence level of the minor? What are the potential risks and consequences if treatment is denied? What are the chances that the minor will not seek help or will not be able to secure parental permission for needed help? How serious is the problem? What are the laws pertaining to providing therapy for minors without parental consent? Melton recommends to practitioners who must make decisions about accepting minors without parental consent that they seek legal advice about the relevant statutes in their state. He also advises them to consult with other professionals in weighing the ethical issues involved in each case.

## Informed Consent of Minors

Therapists who work with children and adolescents must often function as an advocate for these people. They have ethical responsibilities to provide information that will help minors become active participants in their treatment. On this matter the guideline provided by the APA (1981a) is as follows: "When working with minors or other persons who are unable to give voluntary, informed consent, psychologists take special care to protect these persons' best interests."

Allowing children and adolescents to consent to therapy may have the benefits of increasing their participation in decision making about treatment when they enter *with* parental consent (Melton, 1981b). It is a good policy to provide children with treatment alternatives and enlist their participation in defining goals for their therapy. There are both ethical and therapeutic reasons for involving minors in their treatment. By giving them the maximum degree of autonomy within the therapeutic relationship, the therapist demonstrates respect for them. Also, it is likely that therapeutic change is promoted by informing children about the process and enlisting their involvement in it. On this issue Melton (1981a) concludes: "Available research suggests that involvement of children in treatment planning increases the efficacy of treatment and that the presumption of incompetence to consent to treatment may be invalid for many adolescents" (p. 246).

In cases where children do not have the capacity to give full unpressured consent, some writers have recommended that there be a child advocate to examine and protect the child's interests, especially when the child is reluctant to participate in therapy (Koocher, 1976). This advocate should be a person other than the parent or the therapist. If children lack the background to weigh risks and benefits and if they cannot give complete informed consent, therapists should still attempt to provide some understanding of the therapy process. If formal consent cannot be obtained, then even partial understanding is better than proceeding with therapy without any attempt to explain the goals and procedures of the process (Margolin, 1982).

At this point we suggest that you think about some of the legal and ethical considerations in providing therapy for minors.

- Some argue that it is the right of parents to know about matters that pertain to their adolescent daughters and sons. They assert, for example, that parents have a right to be involved in decisions about abortion. What is your position?
- There are those who argue for the right of minors to seek therapy without parental knowledge or consent, on the ground that needed treatment might not be given to them otherwise. When, if at all, do you think that you would counsel a minor without parental knowledge and consent?
- What are your thoughts on the kinds of information that should be provided to children and adolescents before they enter a therapeutic relationship?
- Do you think that therapists who do not provide minors with the information necessary to make informed choices are acting unethically? Why or why not?
- Glenn (1980) suggests that the child therapist should be able to function as the advocate of the child in certain legal situations and that he or she should be able to function as a social, political, and legal agent for change. What are your reactions to this viewpoint?

**Counseling Reluctant Children and Adolescents.**   Taylor, Adelman, and Kaser-Boyd (1985) contend that most children and adolescents seen in psychotherapy are referred by others and that many (79%) manifest significant reluctance and dissatisfaction toward therapy. The most significant negative impact of this reluctance is seen in the large number of minors who either refuse to consent to therapy or who drop out. The authors' findings suggest that reluctance among minors with regard to entering and staying in therapy is often a problem and that, given the opportunity to do so, a significant number will decline to participate. This study revealed that the initial reluctance of a few did give way to positive attitudes once they had engaged in counseling, but the majority remained negative toward the experience. The study also showed that a large number of youngsters had insufficient information about the positive features of therapy and felt that the choice of entering therapy had been made for them. Rather than "resistance," this reluctance to become involved in the treatment process can be interpreted as a rational and reactive effort to cope and avoid or as the result of failure to establish a clear and mutually agreeable contract.

One interpretation of the finding that many minors have negative perceptions of therapy is that these reactions are often based on previous experiences. Some young people simply resent not having a choice about entering a therapeutic relationship. Adolescents often resist therapy because they become the "identified patient" and the focus is on changing them. These adolescents are frequently aware that they are only a *part* of the problem that rests in the family unit. Although many minors indicate a desire to participate in treatment decisions, few are given the opportunity to become involved in a systematic way. The message here is that resistance to therapy can at least be minimized if therapists are willing to openly and nondefensively explore the reasons behind this resistance.

■ *The case of a reluctant adolescent.* Consider Frank's situation in light of the discussion above. Frank was expelled from high school for getting explosively angry at a teacher, who, according to Frank, had humiliated him in front of his class. Frank was told that he would not be readmitted to school unless he sought professional help. His mother called a therapist and explained the situation to her, and the therapist agreed to see him. Although Frank was uncomfortable and embarrassed over having to see a therapist, he was nevertheless willing to talk. He told the therapist that he knew he had done wrong by lashing out angrily at the teacher but that she had provoked him. He said that, although he was usually good about keeping his feelings inside, this time he "just lost it."

After a few sessions the therapist made a determination that there were many problems in Frank's family, that he lived with an extreme amount of stress, and that to work effectively with him it would be essential to see the entire family. Indeed, he did have a problem, but he was not *the* problem. He was covering up many family secrets, including a verbally abusive stepfather and an alcoholic mother. Hesitantly, he agreed that it would be a good idea to have the entire family come in for therapy. When the therapist contacted the family, the other members totally rejected the idea of family therapy. The mother asserted that the problem was with Frank and that the therapist should concentrate her efforts on him. A few days before his next scheduled appointment his mother called to cancel, saying that they had put him on independent study and that he therefore no longer required counseling.

    ***Commentary.***   One of the ethical problems in this case is the treatment of the individual as opposed to the treatment of the family system. There was an alcoholism problem within the family. Frank's expulsion from school was more a symptom of the family dysfunction than of his own disturbance. Indeed he did need to learn anger management, as both the school and the mother contended, yet there was more going on within this family that needed pressing attention. In this case it might have been best for the therapist to stick to her initial convictions of family therapy as the treatment of choice. If the parents would not agree to this, she could have made a referral to another therapist who would be willing to see Frank in individual counseling.

    Reflect on these questions:

- What are the ethical responsibilities of the therapist?
- Should Frank be seen as a condition of returning to school?
- What other strategies could the therapist have used?
- What would you have done differently, and why?
- Should the therapist have seen Frank and the teacher?
- Did the family interfere with Frank's right to treatment by being uncooperative?
- Should the therapist have encouraged Frank to continue his therapy even if his family refused to undergo treatment?

## Specialized Training for Counseling Children and Adolescents

An important ethical and professional issue is the necessity of obtaining adequate training to counsel children and adolescents effectively. As we noted in Chapter 5 in a discussion of therapist competence, the ethical codes of the major professional organizations specify that it is unethical to practice in areas for which one has not been trained. Many human-service professionals have been trained and supervised in "verbal therapies." Yet there are distinct limitations of applying these therapeutic interventions, which may work well with adults, to children. Practitioners who want to counsel children may have to acquire supervised clinical experience in methods such as play therapy, art and music therapy, and recreational therapy. These practitioners also must have a knowledge of developmental issues pertaining to the population with which they intend to work. They need to become familiar with laws relating to minors, to be aware of the limits of their competence, and to know when and how to make appropriate referrals. It is essential to know about community referral resources, such as the Child Protective Service.

Counselors working with children and adolescents also must have training in dealing with special issues, such as confidentiality. For example, therapists cannot guarantee minors blanket confidentiality. If the parents or guardians of minors request some information about the progress of the counseling, the therapist is expected to provide some feedback. It is essential that areas that either will or will not be disclosed to parents or guardians be discussed at the outset of therapy with both the child or adolescent and the parent or guardian. If this matter of confidentiality is not clearly explored with all parties involved, it is almost certain that problems will emerge later in the course of therapy.

# Counseling Women: A Special Case?

Effective communication with women in counseling relationships is often undermined by stereotypical views. Male counselors need to recognize the issues that women struggle with and the ways in which their own biases and views of sex roles might restrict the autonomous decision-making capacity of their female clients. Cayleff (1986) writes that true autonomy for women may require distinguishing women's own beliefs from society's traditional view of their tendency to please and accommodate others. This perspective implies a therapeutic relationship that avoids paternalism, emphasizes the welfare of the client, and validates women's desire for autonomy. Cayleff makes the point that counseling women by encouraging them to comply with personal and professional sex-role expectations does indeed violate their autonomy and harm their welfare.

## Sex Roles and Stereotypes

According to Hare-Mustin (1980), therapists who work with couples and families need to clarify their own values pertaining to traditional and nontraditional family arrangements and should also be open in divulging these values. She further contends that therapists should be prepared to explain to the family their views on issues such as stereotyped sex-role requirements, role functions, and the distribution of power between spouses and between parents and children. Such explanations are a good way to begin the process of counseling couples and families, for the clients can know from the outset what views and values are likely to influence the nature of the therapy.

Before counselors can be open in a discussion with clients about sex roles, it is essential that they be aware of their own conditioning. It is critical to become aware of the socialization process and the way in which sex-role stereotyping develops. Nutt (1979) has summarized some stereotyped attitudes toward women held, in Nutt's view, by many counselors:

• Women are "kept in their place" through lessons they are taught about their role and their abilities while they are children.

- For adults, sex-role socialization has these effects: Men are providers; they are seen as strong, economically powerful, lacking in emotion, independent, and competitive. Women are viewed as the nurturers; they are typically wives and mothers, and they are often characterized as dependent, submissive, helpless, weak, and highly emotional.
- A particularly negative outcome of sex-role stereotyping is related to the aging process. With increasing age men are often considered distinguished and respected. In contrast, older women are viewed as sexually undesirable, usually powerless, unattractive, and aggressive, and they are often the victims of economic discrimination.

In writing about feminist therapy, Gilbert (1980) summarizes the viewpoints of writers who question the usefulness of traditional therapeutic approaches. Such approaches focus exclusively on how people learn and maintain cultural and social values, and their aim is adjustment to societal norms. Gilbert points out that our society's ideology has encouraged women to accommodate without strain to a set of discriminatory role behaviors and sex-typed personality characteristics. She challenges many of the traditional approaches as encouraging women to adjust to the expectations of society. In its place, she recommends several research priorities in the area of feminist therapy.

Those who counsel couples and families need to appreciate the fact that sex-role stereotypes are functional, and thus die hard. As Scarato and Sigall (1979) have observed, a woman faces a dual problem: dealing with a partner who is unwilling or unprepared to share domestic tasks and letting go of roles that were a basic part of her identity and gave her value.

Along with an increasing number of other writers, Scarato and Sigall assert that counselors who work with couples and families must be aware of the history and impact of sex stereotyping as it is reflected in the socialization process in families. They emphasize that effective practitioners must continually evaluate their own beliefs about appropriate family roles and responsibilities, child-rearing practices, multiple roles for women, and nontraditional vocations for women. Counselors also must have the knowledge to help women explore educational and vocational goals that they previously deemed unreachable.

Hare-Mustin (1979), in her article "Family Therapy and Sex Role Stereotypes," asserts that traditional family therapists who aim to restore family functioning by reinforcing conventional roles may be perpetuating the causes of conflict within families. She gives several specific recommendations of interventions that could lead to a change in the oppressive consequences of stereotyped sex roles (see box on p. 318).

Margolin (1982) has given a number of recommendations on how to be a nonsexist family therapist and how to use the therapy process to challenge the oppressive consequences of stereotyped roles and expectations in the family. One recommendation is that family therapists examine their own behavior for unwitting comments and questions that imply that the wife and

## Principles for Avoiding Role Stereotypes

1. *Knowledge.* Counselors doing family therapy are aware of:
   - the impact of generational problems and age expectations on family members
   - the effects of power and distribution of family resources on family members
   - the impact of stereotypical role assignments on family members
2. *Skills.* Counselors doing family therapy:
   - possess skills in contracting, assigning tasks for shifting functions of family members, establishing rules for balancing communication, and training people to be assertive
   - are able to develop alliances across generations
3. *Attitudes.* Counselors doing family therapy are aware of their attitudes toward family roles.

Adapted from "Family Therapy and Sex Role Stereotypes" by R. Hare-Mustin, 1979, *The Counseling Psychologist*, 8(1), 31–32. Reprinted by permission.

husband should perform different roles and hold a different status. For example, a therapist can show bias in subtle and nonverbal ways, such as looking at the wife when talking about rearing children or addressing the husband when talking about decisions that need to be made. Further, Margolin contends that family therapists are particularly vulnerable to the following biases: (1) assuming that remaining married would be the best choice for a woman; (2) demonstrating less interest in a woman's career than in a man's career; (3) encouraging couples to accept the belief that child rearing is solely the responsibility of the mother; (4) showing a different reaction to a wife's affair than to a husband's; and (5) giving more importance to satisfying the husband's needs than to satisfying the wife's needs. She raises two very important questions dealing with the ethics of doing therapy with couples and families:

1. How does the therapist respond when members of the family seem to agree that they want to work toward goals that (from the therapist's vantage point) are sexist in nature?
2. To what extent does the therapist accept the family's definition of sex-role identities rather than trying to challenge and eventually change these attitudes?

In light of the foregoing discussion, we present several open-ended cases for you to consider. What are your values with regard to each of these cases? How do you think your values might affect your manner of counseling in each case?

■ *The case of the traditional couple.* Marge and Fred come to marriage counseling to work on the stress that they are experiencing in rearing their two adolescent sons. The couple directs the focus toward what their sons are doing and not doing. In the course of therapy it develops that both have full-time jobs outside of the home. In addition, Marge has assumed another full-time job—mother and homemaker—but her husband flatly refuses to share any domestic responsibilities. Marge never questions her dual career and very much feels that this is her station in life. Neither Marge nor Fred shows much interest in exploring the possibility that they have uncritically adopted cultural stereotypes pertaining to what women and men "should" be. Instead, they tend to draw the attention during their sessions to getting advice on how to handle the problems with their sons.

- Is it ethical for the therapist to focus simply on the expressed concerns of Marge and Fred, or is there a responsibility to at least challenge them to look at how they have defined themselves and their relationship through assumptions about sex roles?
- If you were counseling this couple, what might you do? What are your values, and how do you think they would influence the interventions you might make in this case?
- What would you do with their presenting problem, their trouble with their sons? What else might the behavior of the sons imply?

Wyman and McLaughlin (1979) point out the shortcomings of the accepted models used in studying wife and mother roles, and they describe some nontraditional perspectives on the stereotypical female roles. They make the case that women who are unhappy with the traditional feminine roles are labeled neurotic. They add that research shows that women who totally accept their traditional roles also experience reduced chances of happiness. They offer some specific principles for working with traditional wives and mothers, which are presented in the accompanying box.

### Principles for Counseling Traditional Wives and Mothers

1. *Knowledge*. Therapists are aware of factors that decrease a woman's power in marriage, of the results of unequal power distributions, and of satisfiers and dissatisfiers in the marriage relationship.
2. *Skills*. Counselors working with traditional wives and mothers:
   - are able to assess a particular relationship in terms of the potential for personal growth for both parties
   - are able to help women develop a support system outside the nuclear family if desired
3. *Attitudes*. Therapists are aware of their own attitudes and values toward marriage, family, women's careers, and sex roles.

Adapted from "Traditional Wives and Mothers" by E. Wyman and M. McLaughlin, 1979, *The Counseling Psychologist*, 8(1), 24–25. Reprinted by permission.

At this point ask yourself the degree to which you agree or disagree with the main points and recommended principles made by Wyman and McLaughlin. As you think about the following case, ask yourself how your values that relate to traditional wives and mothers might affect your relationship with a client like Melody.

■ ***The case of Melody.***    Melody, 38, is married and has returned to college to obtain a teaching credential. During the intake session she tells you that she is going through a lot of turmoil and is contemplating some major changes in her life. She has met a man who shares her interest and enthusiasm for school as well as many other aspects of her life. She is considering leaving her family to pursue her own interests for a change.

The following statements represent some possible responses that counselors might have to Melody, whether or not they actually voiced them to her. Which of these statements can you see yourself making to Melody? Which of them represent reactions you might have but would keep from her?

- "This is just a phase you're going through. It happens to a lot of women who return to college. Maybe you should slow down and think about it."
- "You'll never forgive yourself for leaving your children."
- "You may have regrets later on if you leave your children in such an impulsive fashion."
- "I really think that what you're doing is terrific. You have a lot of courage. Many women in your position would be afraid to do what you're thinking about doing. Don't let anybody stop you."
- "I hate to see you divorce without having some marriage counseling first to determine whether that's what you both want."
- "Maybe you ought to look at the prospects of living alone for a while. The idea of moving out of a relationship with your husband and right into a new relationship with another man concerns me."

If Melody were your client, which of your own values might influence your counseling with her? For example, what do you think of divorce? Would you want her to use divorce only as a last resort? How much do you value keeping her family intact?

■ ***The case of a woman who wants to pursue a law career.***    The White family (consisting of wife, husband, four children, and the wife's parents) has been involved in family therapy for several months. During one of the sessions, Noel (the wife) expresses the desire to return to college to pursue a degree in law. This wish causes a tremendous resistance on the part of every other member of her family. The husband says that he wants her to continue to be involved in his professional life and that, although he admires her ambitions, he simply feels that it would put too much strain on the entire family. Noel's parents are shocked by their daughter's desire, viewing it as selfish, and they urge her to put the family's welfare first. The children express their desires for a full-time mother. Noel feels great pressure from all sides, yet she seems committed to following through with her professional plans. She is aware of the sacrifices that would be associated with her studies, but she is asking for everyone in the family to be willing to make adjustments so that she can accomplish some goals that are important to her. She is convinced that her plans would not be detrimental to the family's welfare.

The family therapist shows an obvious bias by giving no support to Noel's aspirations and by not asking the family to consider making any basic adjustments. Although the therapist does not openly say that Noel should give up her plans, his interventions have the result of reinforcing the family's resistance.

- Do you think that this therapist is guilty of furthering sex-role stereotypes? With his interventions, is he showing his interest in the well-being of the entire family?
- Are there any ethical issues involved in this case? If so, what are they?
- Being aware of your own bias regarding sex roles, how would you work with this family?
- Assume that the therapist had an obvious bias in favor of Noel's plans and even pushed the family to learn to accept her right to an independent life. Do you see any ethical issue in this approach? Is it unavoidable for a therapist to take sides?

## Special Guidelines for Counseling Women

To deal with the problem of sex-biased therapy, the APA has devoted special attention to the study of the oppression of women, including sex-role stereotyping in therapeutic practice. In 1978 the APA's Division of Counseling Psychology approved "Principles Concerning the Counseling and Therapy of Women" as an official policy statement for the division. More recently the division reviewed and revised a list of principles for competent practice with women. The final version was approved by the division at a 1984 meeting. These principles are presented in the box on p. 322. (See Fitzgerald and Nutt, 1986, for a discussion of the background and rationale for each principle as well as suggestions for implementation).

## Specialized Training in Women's Issues

Lewis (1985) makes the assumption that to achieve the goal of ethical and responsible counseling, practitioners need specialized training in the psychology of women. Such training is the first step in ensuring ethical, responsible, and sensitive counseling for female clients. Adequate training would involve systematic and comprehensive information on historical perspectives, personality development theory, and counseling theory applicable to women. Nonsexist research methods and personal exploration of sex bias would be an integral part of such training. There are several approaches to the inclusion of psychology of women in APA-approved doctoral programs, including requiring formal courses or treating these issues in other courses in the program in an integrated manner.

Lewis (1985) designed a study to explore the question "Have APA-approved training programs in counseling psychology begun to pay systematic attention to the psychology of women?" Lewis's study revealed that the topics most likely to be included in courses or programs included feminist

## Principles Concerning the Counseling and Psychotherapy of Women

Counselors and therapists:

1. Are knowledgeable about women, particularly with regard to biological, psychological, and social issues that have impact on women in general or on particular groups of women in our society.
2. Are aware that the assumptions and precepts of theories relevant to their practice may apply differently to men and women. They are aware of those theories and models that proscribe or limit the potential of women clients, as well as those that may have particular usefulness for women clients.
3. Continue to explore issues related to women, including the special problems of female subgroups, throughout their professional careers.
4. Recognize and are aware of all forms of oppression and how these interact with sexism.
5. Are knowledgeable and aware of verbal and nonverbal process variables (particularly with regard to power in the relationship) as these affect women in therapy so that counselor/client interactions are not adversely affected. The need for shared responsibility between clients and counselors is acknowledged and implemented.
6. Have the capability of utilizing skills that are particularly facilitative to women in general and to particular subgroups of women.
7. Put no preconceived limitations on the direction or nature of potential changes or goals in counseling for women.
8. Are sensitive to circumstances in which it is more desirable for a woman client to be seen by a female or male therapist.
9. Use nonsexist language in counseling, supervision, teaching, and journal publications.
10. Do not engage in sexual activity with their women clients under any circumstances.
11. Are aware of and continually review their own values and biases and the effects of these on their women clients. Therapists understand the effects of sex-role socialization on their own development and functioning and the consequent values and attitudes they hold for themselves and others. They recognize that behaviors and roles need not be sex based.
12. Are aware of how their personal functioning may influence their effectiveness in counseling with women clients. They monitor their functioning through consultation, supervision, or therapy so that it does not adversely affect their work with women clients.
13. Support the elimination of sex bias toward institutions and individuals.

Adapted from "Principles Concerning the Counseling/Psychotherapy of Women" by the American Psychological Association, Division of Counseling Psychology, 1986, *The Counseling Psychologist, 14*(1), 180–216. (See Fitzgerald and Nutt, 1986). Copyright 1986 by the American Psychological Association. Reprinted by permission of Sage Publications, Inc.

theory, professional identity, eating disorders, sense of self, sexual identity and sexuality, violence against women, depression, stereotyping, and therapist/client gender dyads.

Lewis found that the implementation of the APA's "Principles Concerning the Counseling and Therapy of Women" had been incomplete and inconsistent. She concluded that there was little to suggest that training programs were producing more sensitive and better informed graduates than they did before the principles were published.

## Separate Guidelines: A New Form of Sexism?

Many of the writers we have cited contend that specialized knowledge, skills, and attitudes are needed for effectively working with women clients. We should point out that other writers are opposed to such separate principles on the ground that they are a new form of sexism. One of these writers is Spiegel (1979), who was among a group of women's advocates who attempted to institute changes in response to the growing evidence that women clients were at a marked disadvantage in counseling and therapy when compared with men. She rejects the premise that counseling women is sufficiently different from counseling men to warrant a separate set of standards of practice. According to Spiegel, separate standards merely change the form of sexism in therapy rather than alleviate it. Her position is that there is a need to reduce sexism in counseling but that this can best be accomplished within a single set of standards that applies to all practitioners:

> With regard to values, sexism follows when a double standard exists. Thus I am opposed to developing a separate set of values, no matter how optimal and generally applicable they may appear to be, if they are enforced only for those who choose to work with women clients. Since nonsexist values are the basis for all good therapy, a single set of standards should be adopted for all counselors/therapists [p. 50].

We think that Spiegel's case is well worth considering. Our position is that women are one of the groups that have not been treated justly by the mental-health profession. We agree that women have many times been expected to adjust to the traditional values of society and to accept their roles with a minimum of disruption of the status quo. Thus, we agree with the spirit of the principles and recommendations for counseling various subgroups of women. However, we do not agree with the view that holds that women can receive effective counseling only from other women. In general, it is a mistake to assume that the specialization strategy is the only effective way to proceed. We question the assumption that gay and lesbian clients can be genuinely understood and helped only by gay and lesbian counselors, that the concerns of certain ethnic or cultural groups can be addressed meaningfully only by counselors of that particular group, or that religious clients necessarily ought to seek out a counselor with the same beliefs.

What is essential is that counselors understand the feelings, values, life experiences, and concerns of whatever population they accept as clients. Therefore, to effectively counsel a woman contemplating an abortion, the counselor need not have faced the same issue, but he or she must have the capacity to understand the values, struggles, and feelings of the client. We think that ethical practice requires that counselors determine *with whom* and *in what circumstances* they are unable to be effective and that they then make an appropriate referral. Further, we agree with Spiegel's contention that work with subgroups may require specialized knowledge, skills, and attitudes but that what have been identified as "women's issues" should be within the province of all effective counselors. Spiegel presents the case of a hypothetical Black, Protestant, married, professional woman who is a mother of three children. Which set of qualifications would her counselor need to have? Some would argue that only a Black female counselor is appropriate to help her deal with racial and sexual issues. Some would say that her religious upbringing during childhood is critical and that the counselor must have shared the same Christian views and experiences. Some would urge her to seek a counselor with expertise in women's issues, since some of her conflicts may deal with the multiple roles of wife, mother, and professional woman. Our position is that well-trained counselors (who are aware of their values and do not impose them) should be able to work with all of her concerns.

# Ethical and Professional Issues in Sex Therapy

A relatively new issue in professional practice concerns the ethical and professional dimensions of sex therapy. There is some confusion regarding this issue, since clear standards have not been developed, and practitioners are frequently left to exercise their own judgment.

Reporting that the field of sex therapy is in enormous flux because innovative techniques are being used and because the field enters the realm of strongly held values, Lief (1982) asserts that ethical considerations are therefore of particular importance. He writes:

> In the absence of standards of treatment and with uncertain methods of accreditation, safeguarding the welfare of the patient through providing informed consent so that he knows and agrees in advance to the form of treatment, protecting his confidentiality and rights of privacy, ensuring the patient's freedom from exploitation and assuring the competence of the therapist are much more difficult than is the case in types of psychotherapy which have been practiced for generations [p. 269].

Legislation in California mandates training in human sexuality as a condition of licensure, both for those being licensed for the first time and for those seeking renewal of their licenses. This legislation applies to the following licensed practitioners: marriage, family, and child counselors; social workers; and psychologists. The content and length of the required training is very unclear, but the law does illustrate the growing importance attached to sex therapy as a part of counseling and psychotherapy. In this section we briefly explore some of the central questions regarding ethical conduct in this specialized area of counseling.

## Qualifications of Sex Therapists

One of the most basic issues in this area is the question of who is qualified to do sex therapy. Ask yourself these questions:

*Who Can Do: answer —*

- What personal and professional qualifications do I have that might eventually prepare me to do sex therapy?
- Is a single course in human sexuality enough academic preparation to do this type of counseling?
- What preparation am I receiving in my training program to do this kind of therapy?
- What kind of practicum, specialized training, and supervision is essential if I am to become involved in sex therapy?

In many programs students are exposed to no more than a single general course in human sexuality; yet, when they begin practicing, many of their clients will bring in sexual difficulties that demand attention. At the very least, counselors who lack the knowledge and skills needed to work in depth with sexual problems can be aware of their limitations and refuse to attempt counseling they're not competent to perform, even if their licenses allow them to counsel people with sexual dysfunctions. They can recognize the importance of referring clients who are in need of this specialized treatment. To do so, they must be able to recognize when sex therapy is indicated, and they must be aware of good referral sources.

## The Scope of Sex Therapy

Some people criticize the sex-therapy movement on the grounds that too much attention is paid to "fixing plumbing" and not enough to the emotional aspects of sexuality. They argue that sex therapists focus too much on symptoms and physical functioning, whereas effective treatment must include a consideration of the individual's psychodynamics, the factors that led to the problem to begin with, and the nature of the relationship between the client and his or her sexual partner.

Therapy for sexual difficulties doesn't have to be mechanistic, however, or focused only on removal of symptoms. Some sex therapists are aware of the need for a more comprehensive approach. For example, they may stress the acquisition of more effective social skills at the same time as they work on sexual dysfunctions. Also, even though they may *begin* by working with obvious symptoms, they are fully aware that in-depth and meaningful treatment must go beyond symptoms and concern itself with the total life of the client.

Typically, the sex-therapy model prescribes working with both partners in a sexual relationship. The assumption is that one partner's sexual dysfunction is related in some way to the relationship with the other person. According to Kaplan (1974), the primary objective of sex therapy is to modify the couple's relationship and sexual life so that both persons are satisfied. Conjoint treatment, as opposed to separate treatment for each partner or for one partner alone, is also viewed as valuable because the shared sexual experiences of the couple become the central aspects of the treatment.

Of course, conjoint therapy depends on the willingness of both partners. What are the issues involved when one partner desires sex therapy and the other refuses to cooperate in any type of counseling? Suppose a woman wanted sex therapy and her husband refused treatment. Would it really help to work with her alone? Would any change occur? If she did become free of her sexual dysfunction, what kinds of problems might this pose for her if her husband had not been involved in the therapy? Would you refuse treatment for her until her husband agreed to participate in the program? Would you encourage her to change, even if her husband was rigid and would fight any of her changes? Would you consider employing a sex surrogate in this case? These are just some of the difficult questions that arise when conjoint therapy is not possible.

## Dealing with Transference

In Chapter 2 we discussed transference and countertransference as problems that most counselors and therapists eventually need to confront. In sex therapy these issues become even more vital. Because of the focus on the intimate details of the client's sexual behavior, feelings, and fantasies, there is a greater danger that the client will develop an erotic transference toward the therapist (Kaplan, 1974). This raises the ethical issue of therapists' encouragement of this erotic transference, which may be done seductively out of a need to be perceived as sexually attractive and desirable persons. Kaplan warns that, if therapists' clients fall in love with them with regularity, it can be inferred that the therapists' countertransference feelings are producing the situation.

Clearly, therapists' unawareness of their needs and their distorted vision because of their unresolved conflicts in regard to sex can greatly interfere with the therapy process. In order to achieve competence in the practice of sex therapy, Kaplan believes, therapists should be relatively free from their own sexual conflicts, guilt, and competitiveness, or at least be aware of how this personal material can influence the way they work with their clients in sex therapy. Therapists must be aware and responsive persons, not simply technicians.

## Informed Consent  *a must in sex Therapy*

In all forms of psychotherapy the therapeutic relationship is determined to a large extent by informed-consent procedures. Some therapists structure the therapeutic relationship on the basis of a contract that spells out the rights and duties of both the client and the therapist. In the field of sex therapy informed consent becomes particularly crucial, especially when the therapist assigns certain behavioral tasks to carry out at home. We are in agreement with Lief's position (1982) that it is essential for those practicing sex therapy to explain to the client or to the couple the nature of the therapy, the approximate number of sessions, the approximate length of time the therapy will take, the fees involved, and the specialized techniques that will be used. Part of informed consent involves a full discussion with clients about their feelings about expanding their sexual repertoire, with attention given to their values.

# Chapter Summary

The field of marital and family therapy is rapidly expanding and developing. With an expansion in educational programs being offered comes the need for specialized training and experience. A thorough discussion of the ethical issues unique to this field must be part of such programs. A few of these issues are determining who is the primary client, dealing with confidentiality, providing informed consent, using and misusing power and control, counseling with minors, and exploring the role of values in family therapy.

The job of the therapist is to help the family or couple sort through their own values, not to have them conform to the therapist's value system. In the counseling of women, for example, it is essential for family therapists to be aware of any sex-role bias and to challenge their own stereotypical views. A number of writers have proposed specialized training in women's issues, given the fact that many therapists are male and many clients are female.

The particular considerations in counseling children and adolescents demand specialized training. One of the challenges of working with minors is creating a trusting climate and at the same time being aware of the limitations of confidentiality. Another is to keep abreast of the referral resources in the community.

Those who hope to practice as sex therapists must also have specialized training. Therapists who offer relationship counseling will be expected to develop some level of knowledge and skill in exploring sexual concerns in relationships. It is essential that counselors who provide these interventions recognize and respect the boundaries of their competence and know when and where to make appropriate referrals.

# Suggested Activities

1. In the practice of marital and family therapy informed consent is especially important. As a class-discussion topic explore some of these issues: What are the ethical implications of insisting that all members of a family participate in family therapy? What kind of information should a family therapist present from the outset to all those involved? Are there any ethical conflicts in focusing on the welfare of the entire family rather than on what might be in the best interests for an individual?
2. What guidelines do you think are important for those who claim to be qualified to offer sex therapy? What are some of the major professional and ethical issues involved in sex therapy?

3. In small groups in your class, examine some of the questions we raised in this chapter concerning sex therapy. For example, you might discuss the following: (a) When does a person know that he or she is adequately trained to do sex therapy? (b) What are some of the special problems that therapists must be alert to in regard to the therapist/client relationship in sex therapy? What are the potential problems that can surface if transference and countertransference feelings are dealt with poorly? (c) How can the danger of treating only the symptoms of sexual problems be averted?

4. Several students can investigate ethical and legal issues pertaining to psychotherapy with children and adolescents and bring the findings to class. Some topics to consider: What are the rights of children in treatment? What legal considerations are involved in therapy with minors? What obligations does the therapist have toward the parents of these children? Should parental consent always be required?

5. As a project you can investigate the status of regulating professional practice in marital and family therapy in your state. What are the academic and training requirements, if any, for certification or licensure in this field?

6. In small groups you might focus on what you consider to be the major ethical problem facing marital and family therapists. Consider issues such as confidentiality, enforced therapy involving all family members, qualifications of effective family therapists, imposing the values of the therapist on a family, and practicing beyond one's competence.

7. Consider designing a project in which you study your own family of origin. Interview as many relatives as you can. Look for patterns in your own relationships, including problems you currently struggle with, that stem from your family of origin. What advantages do you see in studying your own family as one way to prepare yourself for working with families?

8. Suppose that you were participating on a board to establish standards—personal, academic, training, and experiential—for family therapists. What would you see as being minimum requirements to prepare a trainee to work with families? What would your ideal training program for marital and family therapists look like?

## Suggested Readings

For ethical considerations in marital and family therapy see Margolin (1982). On the use and misuse of power in family therapy see O'Shea and Jessee (1982) and Fieldsteel (1982). On informed consent in marital and family therapy see Hare-Mustin (1980), Haas and Alexander (1981), and Bray, Shepherd, and Hays (1985). On informed consent in counseling children and adolescents see Taylor, Adelman, and Kaser-Boyd (1985) and Kaser-Boyd, Adelman, and Taylor (1985). For issues in counseling women see Cayleff (1986), Wyman and McLaughlin (1979), APA (1978), Fitzgerald and Nutt (1986), Lewis (1985), Spiegel (1979), and Downing and Roush (1985).

For training issues in marital and family therapy see Goldenberg and Goldenberg (1985) and Humphrey (1983). On engaging all family members in therapy see Wilcoxon (1986). For contemporary issues in family counseling see Wilcoxon and Comas (1986). If you'd like to read a more in-depth treatment of ethical issues in sex therapy, we think you'll find Lief (1982) especially meaningful. A book that we recommend for a more comprehensive coverage of all these issues is *Ethical, Legal, and Professional Issues in the Practice of Marriage and Family Therapy* (Huber & Baruth, 1987).

# ELEVEN

# Ethical and Professional Issues in Group Work

# Pre-Chapter Self-Inventory

*Directions:* For each statement, indicate the response that most closely identifies your beliefs and attitudes. Use the following code:

3 = I *agree*, in most respects, with this statement.
2 = I am *undecided* in my opinion about this statement.
1 = I *disagree*, in most respects, with this statement.

_____ 1. A group leader's actual behavior in a group is more important than his or her theoretical approach.

_____ 2. Ethical practice requires that prospective group members be carefully screened and selected.

_____ 3. It's important to prepare group members so that they can derive the maximum benefit from the group.

_____ 4. Requiring people to participate in a therapy group raises ethical issues.

_____ 5. It is unethical to allow a group to exert pressure on one of its members,

_____ 6. Confidentiality is less important in groups than it is in individual therapy.

_____ 7. Socializing among group members is almost always undesirable, since it inevitably interferes with the functioning of the group.

_____ 8. Ethical practice requires making some provision for evaluating the outcomes of a group.

_____ 9. A group leader has a responsibility to devise ways of minimizing any psychological risks associated with participation in the group.

_____ 10. People are not competent to be group leaders until they have completed a structured program of education and training approved by one of the major mental-health professions.

_____ 11. It is unethical for counselor educators to lead groups with their students in training.

_____ 12. Verbal abuse and subsequent emotional casualties are more likely to occur in groups than in individual counseling.

_____ 13. Adequate training in and of itself is sufficient for effective co-leading of groups.

_____ 14. It is the group leader's responsibility to make prospective members aware of their rights and their responsibilities and to demystify the process of a group.

_____ 15. Group members should know that they have the right to leave the group at any time.

_____ 16. Before people enter a group, it is the leader's responsibility to discuss with them the personal risks involved, especially potential life changes, and help them explore their readiness to face these risks.

_____ 17. It is a sound practice to provide written ethical guidelines to group members in advance and discuss them in the first meeting.

___ 18. Group therapists who do not keep the content of group sessions confidential are legally and ethically liable, and they can be sued for breach of confidence.

___ 19. Under certain circumstances it may be ethical for a group leader to tape a group session without the prior knowledge and consent of the members, *if* the leader tells the members at the end of the session that they were taped.

___ 20. It is unethical for group leaders to employ a technique unless they are thoroughly trained in its use or under the supervision of an expert familiar with it.

___ 21. Ethical practice demands that leaders inform members about any research activities that might be a part of the group.

___ 22. Confrontation in groups is almost always destructive and generally inhibits the formation of trust and cohesion.

___ 23. A group leader has a responsibility to teach members how to translate what they've learned in the group setting to their lives outside the group.

___ 24. A group leader has a responsibility to ask potential members who are already being counseled to consult with their therapists before joining the group.

___ 25. One way of minimizing psychological risks to group participants is to negotiate contracts with the members.

# Introduction

We are giving group therapy special attention, as we did with marital and family therapy, because it raises unique ethical concerns. Practitioners who work with groups encounter a variety of situations that differ from those encountered by therapists who work with individuals. Groups continue to increase in popularity, and in many agencies and institutions they are the primary therapeutic avenue. They are also considered the most cost effective.

Our illustrations of important ethical considerations are drawn from a broad spectrum of groups, including therapy groups, personal-growth groups, marathon groups, human-relations training groups, and different types of counseling groups. Obviously, these groups differ with respect to their member population, purpose, focus, and procedures, as well as in the level of training required for their leaders. Although these distinctions are important, the issues we discuss are common to most groups.

This chapter is to a large degree structured around the *Ethical Guidelines for Group Leaders*, as developed and approved by the Association for Specialists in Group Work (ASGW), which is a branch of the American Association for Counseling and Development (AACD). The ASGW guidelines (1980) are intended to complement the broader standards of the AACD

(1981) by clarifying the ethical responsibility of the counselor in a group setting.

# Training and Supervision of Group Leaders

Training of group leaders is a professional issue because the various disciplines have differing views and standards. Group workers in psychology, for example, receive different training from psychiatric workers. Social workers are taught group work from a perspective that is sometimes different from that of counselors. The activities and minimum number of hours suggested for clinical training and supervision in group work differ from one professional organization to another.

## Professional Standards for Training and Supervision

In its *Professional Standards for Training of Group Counselors*, the ASGW (1983) sets out knowledge competencies, skill competencies, and suggested supervised clinical group experience for leaders.[1] In the first area the ASGW takes the position that the qualified group leader has demonstrated specialized *knowledge* in the following aspects of group work:

- the major theories of group counseling, including their differences and common concepts
- the basic principles of group dynamics and the key ingredients of group process
- one's own strengths and weaknesses, values, and other personal characteristics that have an impact on one's ability to function as a group leader
- ethical and professional issues special to group work
- updated information on research in group work
- the facilitative and debilitative roles and behaviors that group members may assume
- the advantages and disadvantages of group work and the situations in which it is appropriate or inappropriate as a form of therapeutic intervention
- the characteristics of group interaction and counselor roles involved in the stages of a group's development

In the second area the ASGW contends that qualified group leaders should be able to demonstrate a mastery of the following *skills:*

- being able to screen and assess the readiness of clients to participate in a group

---

[1] Adapted from *Professional Standards for Training of Group Counselors* (ASGW, 1983) and reproduced by permission of the ASGW, a division of the American Association for Counseling and Development, 5999 Stevenson Avenue, Alexandria, VA 22304.

- having a clear definition of group counseling and being able to explain its purpose and procedures to group members
- diagnosing self-defeating behaviors in group members and being able to intervene in constructive ways with members who display such behaviors
- modeling appropriate behavior for group members
- interpreting nonverbal behavior in an accurate and appropriate manner
- using skills in a timely and effective fashion
- intervening at critical times in the group process
- being able to make use of major techniques, strategies, and procedures of group counseling
- promoting therapeutic factors that lead to change both in a group and within an individual
- being able to use adjunct group procedures, such as homework
- being able to work effectively with a co-leader
- knowing how to effectively bring a group session to a close and how to terminate a group
- using follow-up procedures to maintain and support group members
- using assessment procedures to evaluate the outcomes of a group

In the third area the ASGW specifies the following types of supervised *experience* in group work:

- critiquing of group tapes
- observing group counseling sessions
- participating as a member in a group
- co-leading groups with supervision
- practicum experience—leading a group alone with critical self-analysis of performance as well as a supervisor's feedback
- internship—practice as a group leader with on-the-job supervision

How realistic are the ASGW training standards described above? In a critique of these standards Zimpfer, Waltman, Williamson, and Huhn (1985) conclude that they have some definite limitations. Some of their findings are:

- The standards are offered for consideration but lack a vehicle for enforcement.
- Most training programs in group counseling appear to fall short of the standards.
- Didactic classroom learning is given more emphasis than actual supervised clinical practice. Fewer than two-thirds of the programs require their students to lead a group other than their own in-class group.
- Before the current standards can be used in accreditation, certification, or licensure, a clearer and more specific delineation of the competencies needs to be developed.
- The standards should include the need for continuing education after graduation from a training program.

## Programs of Professional Preparation

What are graduate counselor-education programs doing to prepare students for group work? Huhn, Zimpfer, Waltman, and Williamson (1985) conducted a survey to answer this question. A summary of their findings is given below.

With respect to *areas of training*, nearly all of the programs sought to develop leader skills and competencies, an understanding of small-group dynamics, and an understanding of group leadership and intervention.

In terms of the *training content*, all of the programs dealt with group-process issues, and almost all dealt with the practical considerations in setting up groups, dealing with problems encountered in groups, leadership styles, ethical and professional issues, group dynamics, and intervention techniques. Many programs covered theories and models of group counseling, dealing with problem group members, and special types of groups.

With respect to *teaching methods*, programs reported using lectures, discussion, personal-growth experience, supervised practicum, demonstration, laboratory experience, co-leading of groups, role playing, videotaping, films, simulations, and self-directed group experience.

For *methods of assessment*, the survey showed that all programs assessed knowledge of the subject, 97% assessed skill proficiency, and 89% assessed personal growth. Self-report methods were the favored methods of evaluating personal growth.

## Our Views on Training

We do not think that professional codes, legislative mandates, and institutional policies alone will ensure professional group leadership. We think that students in group-leadership training must be presented with the typical dilemmas they will face in practice and must learn ways to clarify their views on these issues. This can best be done by including ethics in the formal content of the trainees' academic program as well as discussing ethical issues that grow out of the students' experiences in practicum, internship, and fieldwork. We have found that one effective way to teach the process of ethical decision making is presenting trainees with case vignettes of typical problems that occur in group situations and then encouraging open discussion of the ethical issues and the pertinent guidelines for these situations (Corey, Corey, & Callanan, 1982). In our own approach to training and supervising group leaders we emphasize that they will not have the answers to many of the ethical dilemmas that they encounter in practice, because ethical decision making is an ongoing process that takes on a new form and increased meaning as the practitioner gains experience. What is critical is that group leaders develop a receptivity to self-examination and to questioning the professionalism of their group practice.

We highly recommend at least three experiences as adjuncts to a training program for group workers: (1) personal (private) psychotherapy; (2)

experience in group therapy, group counseling, or a personal-growth group; and (3) participation in a supervision and training group.

**Personal Psychotherapy.**   We agree with Yalom's (1985) recommendation that extensive self-exploration is necessary if trainees are to perceive countertransference feelings, recognize blind spots and biases, and use their personal attributes effectively in groups. Although video-taping, working with a co-leader, and supervision all are excellent sources of feedback, Yalom maintains that personal therapy is usually necessary for fuller understanding and correction. We think that group leaders should demonstrate the courage and willingness to do for themselves what they expect members in their groups to do—expand their awareness of self and the effect of that self on others.

**Self-Exploration Groups.**   As an adjunct to a group leader's formal course work and internship training, participation in some kind of therapeutic group can be extremely valuable. In addition to helping interns resolve personal conflicts and develop increased self-understanding, a personal-growth group can be a powerful teaching tool. One of the best ways to learn how to assist group members in their struggles is to work yourself as a member of a group. The ASGW and the American Group Psychotherapy Association (AGPA) recommend personal-group experiences as a part of a comprehensive training program for group counselors. The two groups have suggested 15 hours and 60 hours, respectively, as a minimum requirement for participating in a group experience. Yalom (1985) also strongly recommends a group experience for trainees. Some of the benefits, he suggests, are experiencing the power of a group, learning what self-disclosure is about, coming to appreciate the difficulties involved in self-sharing, learning on an emotional level what one knows intellectually, and becoming aware of one's dependency on the leader's power and knowledge. Yalom cites surveys indicating that 60% to 70% of group-therapy training programs offer some type of personal group experience. About half of the programs offer an optional group, and the other half, a mandatory group.

**Participation in a Training and Supervision Group.**   We have found workshops most useful in helping group trainees develop the skills necessary for effective intervention. Also, the interns can learn a great deal about their response to criticism, their competitiveness, their need for approval, their concerns over being competent, and their power struggles. In working with both university students learning about group approaches and with professionals who want to upgrade their group skills, we have found an intensive weekend workshop to be effective and dynamic. In these workshops the participants have ample opportunity to lead their small group for a designated period of time. After a segment in which the participants lead their group, we intervene by giving feedback and by promoting a discussion by the entire group. By the end of the weekend each participant has led the group at least twice (for an hour each time) under direct supervision. Corey and Corey (1986) describe a framework for such a weekend or a week-long residential training and supervision workshop using experiential and didactic methods to help participants refine their skills as group leaders.

As you consider issues related to group leaders' competence, answer these questions for yourself:

- Who is qualified to lead groups? What are the criteria for determining the competence of group leaders?
- What do you think of the training in clinical practice suggested in the ASGW's *Guidelines for Training Group Leaders*?
- Does ethical practice demand that group leaders receive some form of personal therapy? Should this be group therapy or experience in a personal-growth group? How important are continuing education and training once one has completed a professional program?
- What are your reactions to the suggestions we offered for the training of group workers?

# Co-Leadership

If you should decide to get involved in groups, it is possible that you'll work with a co-leader at some time. We think there are many advantages to the co-leader model. The group can benefit from the insights and feedback of two leaders. The leaders can complement and balance each other. They can grow by discussing what goes on in the group and by observing each other's style, and together they can evaluate what has gone on in the group and plan for future sessions. Also, with co-leaders the total burden does not rest with one person. While one leader is working with a particular member, the other can be paying attention to others in the group.

The choice of a co-leader is crucial. A group can suffer if its leaders are not working together toward a common goal. If much of the leaders' energy is directed at competing with each other or at some other power struggle or hidden agenda, there is little chance that the group will be effective.

We think that the selection of a co-leader should involve more than attraction and liking. Each of the leaders should be secure enough that the group won't have to suffer as one or both of them try to "prove" themselves. We surely don't think it's essential that co-leaders always agree or share the same perceptions or interpretations; in fact, a group can be given vitality if co-leaders feel trusting enough to express their differences of opinion. Mutual respect and the ability to establish a relationship based on trust, cooperation, and support are most important. Also, each person should be autonomous and have his or her own style yet be able to work with the other leader as a team.

In our view it's essential for co-leaders to spend some time together immediately following a group to assess what happened. Similarly, we believe that they should meet at least briefly before each group session to talk about anything that might affect their functioning in the group.

The three of us have worked as a team leading groups for 15 years. Philosophically we share values that have an impact on our view of group work. We're fortunate in this regard; if we had divergent philosophical and theoretical orientations, it would be difficult, if not impossible, to work together as an effective team. Our styles are very different, and the ways in which we work and participate in our groups reflect our particular personalities. However, we have a high degree of respect and liking for one another, and our differences in style and personality actually seem to enhance our functioning in our groups. Before a group session we do spend time together to prepare ourselves psychologically for the group. We meet again after each session to share our perceptions, discuss what is occurring in the group, talk about what we're feeling, challenge one another, and plan for future sessions. Working together in this way has been most rewarding for us and has enhanced the quality of our leadership abilities.

At this point we ask you to draw up your own guidelines for selecting a co-leader.

- What are the qualities you'd look for in a co-leader?
- What kind of person would you *not* want to lead with?
- If you found that you and your co-leader clashed on many issues and approached groups very differently, what do you think you'd do?
- What ethical implications are involved when a great deal of time during the sessions is taken up with power struggles and conflicts between the co-leaders?
- In what ways could you be most helpful to your co-leader?

# Ethical Issues in Group Membership

## Recruitment and Informed Consent

Professional issues are involved in publicizing a group and recruiting members. How can group leaders make potential members aware of the services available? What information do clients have a right to expect before they decide to attend a group?

The ASGW ethical standards (1980) clarify the group leader's responsibility for providing information about services to prospective clients. Two of the guidelines that are relevant here are (1) "Group leaders shall fully inform group members, in advance and preferably in writing, of the goals in the group, qualifications of the leader, and procedures to be employed." (2) "Group leaders shall explain, as realistically as possible, exactly what services can and cannot be provided within the particular group structure offered."

People have a right to know what they are getting into before they make a commitment to become a part of any group. It is the group leader's responsibility to make prospective members aware of their rights and their responsibilities and to demystify the process of a group. Some of the things that it is important for people to know before they decide to join a group are the fees and any other related expenses; the division of responsibility of the leader and the participants; any experimental techniques or any research that might be a part of the group; the potential risks involved in group participation; notice of any observations of the group through one-way mirrors or any recording of group sessions; the duration of the group and the number of participants; whether follow-up service is included in the fee; the education, training, and special group qualifications of the leader; and the limitations of confidentiality, including the use of information acquired during sessions outside the group structure.

## Screening and Selection of Group Members

Group leaders are faced with the difficult task of determining who should be included in a group and who should not. Are groups appropriate for all people? To put the question in another way, is it appropriate for *this* person to become a participant in *this* type of group, with *this* leader, at *this* time?

Many group leaders do not screen prospective participants. This is particularly true of weekend workshops that are essentially experiential groups and of marathon groups where strangers meet for one intensive weekend. Assuming that not everyone will benefit from a group experience—and that some people will be psychologically harmed by certain group experiences—is it unethical to fail to screen prospective group candidates? Some writers argue that truly effective screening is impossible. Others take the position that ethical practice demands the careful screening and preparation of all candidates.

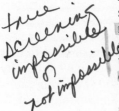
true screening impossible or not impossible

Yalom (1985) argues that, unless careful selection criteria are employed, group-therapy clients may end up discouraged and unhelped. Yalom maintains that it is easier to identify the people who should be excluded from group therapy than those who should be included. Citing clinical studies, he lists the following as poor candidates for a heterogeneous outpatient intensive-therapy group: brain-damaged people, paranoid individuals, hypochondriacs, those who are addicted to drugs or alcohol, acute psychotics, and sociopaths. In terms of criteria for inclusion, he contends that the client's level of motivation to work is the most important variable. From his perspective, groups are useful for people who have problems in the interpersonal domain, such as loneliness, inability to make or maintain intimate contacts, feelings of unlovability, fears of being assertive, and dependency issues. Clients who lack meaning in life, who suffer from diffuse anxiety, who are searching for an identity, who fear success, and who are compulsive workers might also profit from a group experience.

In the *Ethical Guidelines for Group Leaders* (ASGW, 1980) the following principle is given:

> The group leader shall conduct a pre-group interview with each prospective member for purposes of screening, orientation, and, in so far as possible, shall select group members whose needs and goals are compatible with the established goals of the group; who will not impede the group process; and whose well-being will not be jeopardized by the group experience.[2]

Are practitioners who meet their groups without screening or orienting the members behaving unethically? We think that one alternative is to use the initial session for screening and informed consent. Screening is most effective when the leader interviews the members and the members also have an opportunity to interview the leader. While prospective group members are being screened, they should be deciding whether they want to work with a particular leader and whether the group in question is suitable for them. Group candidates should not passively allow the matter to be decided for them by an expert. Leaders should welcome the opportunity to respond to any question or concerns prospective members have, and they should actively encourage prospective participants to raise questions about matters that will affect their participation.

In our own approach to screening we've often found it difficult to predict who will benefit from a group experience. We realize that pregroup screening interviews are like any interviews in that people may tend to say what they think the interviewer expects. Often people who are interviewed for a group feel that they must sell themselves or that they are being evaluated and judged. Perhaps these feelings can be lessened somewhat if leaders take the initiative to emphasize that these interviews are really designed as a two-way process in which leaders and prospective members can decide together whether a particular group, with a particular leader, at a particular time, is in the best interests of all concerned. Although we do have difficulty in predicting who will benefit from a group, we have found screening interviews most helpful in excluding some people who we believed would probably have left the group with negative feelings or who would have drained and sapped the group of the energy necessary for productive work.

It often happens that both the prospective member and the group leader are unsure whether a particular group is indicated for that person. For this reason, in a group that will be meeting several times the first few sessions can be considered exploratory in nature. Members can be encouraged to come to the first session or two and then consider whether the group is what they're looking for. In this way leaders encourage a process of self-selection that gives members the responsibility of deciding what is right for them. Actually experiencing the group for a time enables members to make an

*Screen both ways — leaders + participant*

*hard to tell who'll last!*

*exploratory*

---

[2] From *Ethical Guidelines for Group Leaders*, by the Association for Specialists in Group Work. Copyright 1980 by the American Association for Counseling and Development. This and all other quotations from the same source are reprinted by permission.

informed decision about participation. If, after a few sessions, either the leader or a particular member has any reservations, a private meeting to explore these concerns can be arranged.

## The Preparation of Group Participants

To what extent are group leaders responsible for preparing participants to get the maximum benefit from their group experience? Many group practitioners do very little to systematically prepare members for a group. In fact, some therapists and group leaders are opposed to systematic preparation on the ground that it will bias the members' experience. Many encounter-group leaders assume that part of the task of group members is to flounder and struggle and eventually define their own goals and give their group direction without much intervention by the leader. These leaders think that preparation and structuring on the part of the leader inhibits a group's spontaneity and autonomy.

Others take the position that members must be given some preparation in order to derive the maximum gains from a group experience. As we saw in the previous section, the ASGW's ethical guidelines (1980) emphasize the importance of both screening and orientation in helping members gain the maximum benefit from a group experience.

Yalom (1985) is an advocate of systematic preparation for people in group therapy. His preparation includes exploring misconceptions and expectations, predicting early problems, and providing a conceptual framework that includes guidelines for effective group behavior. His preparatory interviews contain some of the following elements:

- A brief explanation of the interpersonal theory of psychiatry is given.
- Members are given guidelines for how they can best help themselves. This step includes talking about trust, self-disclosure, members' rights to privacy, risk taking, and experimentation with new behavior.
- Stumbling blocks are predicted.
- Members are told that the goal of the therapy group is to change behavior and attitudes, that treatment will take at least a year, and that significant changes should not be expected for months.
- Members are told about the history of group therapy.
- Confidentiality and extragroup socializing are discussed.

Yalom views this preparatory process as more than the dissemination of information. He claims that it reinforces the therapist's respect for the client, demonstrates that therapy is a collaborative venture, and shows that the therapist is willing to share his or her knowledge with the client. He writes that the cognitive approach to preparation has the goals of providing a rational explanation of the group process, clarifying expectations in terms of behavior, and raising expectations about what the group can accomplish.

It is our practice to systematically prepare participants, whether they are in weekly therapy groups, ongoing growth groups, or residential weekend or

*Resistance w/o knowledge goal clarity*

*How Corey plans for group success!*

week-long personal-growth workshops. In our training workshops we have seen much resistance that can be attributed to a lack of knowledge of group process and a lack of clarity of goals. What we say here applies to all types of groups, with some modifications. At both the screening session and the initial group meeting, we explore the members' expectations, clarify goals and objectives, discuss procedural details, explore possible risks and values of group participation, and discuss guidelines for getting the most from a group experience (see Corey & Corey, 1987, pp. 105–112; Corey, Corey, Callanan, & Russell, 1982b, pp. 46–51). As part of member preparation we include a discussion of the values and limitations of groups, the psychological risks involved in group participation, and ways of minimizing these risks. We also allow time for dealing with misconceptions that people have of groups and for exploring any fears or resistances the members may have. In most of our groups members do have certain fears about what they will experience, and, until we acknowledge these fears and talk about them, very little other productive work can occur. Further, we ask members to spend time before they come to the group defining for themselves what they most want to get from the group experience. To make their goals more concrete, we usually ask them to develop a contract that entails areas of concern that they're willing to work on in the group. We also ask them to do some reading and to write about their goals and about the significant turning points in their lives.

At this point, we ask you to write down a few things you might want to do to prepare people for a group. What is your position on the ethical aspects of failing to prepare group members for their experience in the group? What do you think would occur if you did little in the way of preparing group members?

## Voluntary and Involuntary Participation

Should group membership always be voluntary? Are there situations in which it is ethical to require or coerce people to participate in a group? What are the problems involved in mandatory group participation? How is informed consent especially critical in groups where attendance is mandatory?

The ASGW's (1980) guideline is "Group leaders shall inform members that participation is voluntary and that they may exit from the group at any time." We have some reservations about this guideline. First, some practitioners lead groups that are composed of involuntary clients. Second, once members make a commitment to the group, they also have responsibilities to the group, and it is not responsible simply to drop out without any discussion.

**Involuntary Clients.** When group participation is mandatory, much effort needs to be directed toward fully informing members of the nature and goals of the group, procedures to be used, the rights of members to decline certain activities, the limits of confidentiality, and what effect their level of participation in the group will have on critical decisions about them outside of the group. An example will help make our point. The three of us provide in-service training workshops for staff members who lead involuntary groups at a state mental hospital. Groups are the basic type of treatment for "those incompetent to stand trial," "sociopathic criminals," and "mentally disordered sex offenders." One of the factors involved in the determination of patients' release from the hospital and return to the community is their cooperation in the treatment program, which includes participation in regular group-therapy sessions. If patients do not show up for a group, they are likely to have their "hall cards" taken from them, which means that they are restricted to their wards. In such cases where attendance at group sessions is mandatory, informed consent implies that leaders explore with members, during an orientation session, what the group will be about, so that members will understand clearly what their rights and responsibilities are.

**The Freedom to Leave a Group.**   We contend that the leader's attitudes and policies about the freedom of exit should be spelled out and discussed at the onset of a group or, better, at a preliminary meeting. Corey, Corey, Callanan, and Russell (1982b) take the position that clients have a responsibility to the leader and other members to explain why they want to leave. There are several reasons for this policy. It can be deleterious to members to leave without being able to discuss what they considered threatening or negative in the experience. Further, it is unfortunate for members to leave a group because of a misunderstanding about some feedback they have received. It can surely be harmful in terms of developing group cohesion, for the members who remain may think that they "caused" a particular member's departure. We tell our members that they have an obligation to attend all sessions and to inform us and the group should they decide to withdraw. If members even consider withdrawing, we encourage them to bring this up for exploration in a session. We do not think that it is ethical to use undue pressure to keep these members, and we are alert to other members' pressuring a person to stay.

*In a prison group an inexperienced leader senses how counterproductive the therapy is in an involuntary group. In an attempt to lessen the members' resistances she tells them that she does not want anybody to be part of the group who is not willing to participate freely in the sessions. She neglects to inform them that their refusal to attend group sessions will be documented and will be considered in the decision about their release. Thus, the members are operating under the false assumption that they have freedom of choice, yet they do not have all the information they need to make a real choice.*

- What do you think of the ethical decision of this leader?
- Does this leader's desire for an effective group justify her practice? Explain.
- Do you think that members can benefit from a group experience even if they are required to attend? Why or why not?

• What strategy might she have used that would have enabled her to have more effective group participation while still giving the patients true freedom of choice?

## Psychological Risks

The fact that groups can be powerful catalysts of personal change means that they are also risky. We don't think groups should be free of risk, because learning how to grow entails taking risks. In our view, however, ethical practice demands that group leaders at least inform prospective participants of the potential risks involved in the group experience. We also believe that group leaders have an ethical responsibility to take precautionary measures to reduce unnecessary psychological risks. Our view is that merely informing participants of the possible risks does not absolve leaders of all responsibility. Certain safeguards can be taken during the course of a group to avoid disastrous outcomes. In this section we discuss some of the risks that we believe participants should know about.

1. One risk of group participation is that members may experience major disruptions in their lives as a result of their work in the group. Of course, this risk is present in any type of therapy, not simply in groups. Members should be aware, however, that others in their lives may not appreciate their changes. This situation could lead to decisions that will change their lifestyles. On this point of discussion of risks, the ASGW's (1980) guideline is as follows: "Group leaders shall stress the personal risks involved in any group, especially regarding potential life-changes, and help group members explore their readiness to face these risks."

2. Often group participants are encouraged to "let it all hang out." In this quest for complete self-revelation, privacy is sometimes invaded. Participants must learn the difference between appropriate and facilitative self-disclosure and disclosure that leaves nothing private. Group leaders need to be alert to attempts to force people to disclose more than they are ready to share. Otherwise participants may withdraw, feeling a sense of shame for having said more than they were ready and willing to say.

3. The risk of invasion of privacy brings up the related risk of group pressure. In most groups there are pressures to be open, to be honest, to take risks, to talk about personal matters, and to try new behavior. These behaviors are then positively reinforced. At times group pressure to get people to join in certain activities or to change their ideas and behavior can be very strong. More often it appears as a subtle pressure to conform unquestioningly to group norms and expectations. We think it's important to recognize that group pressure is inevitable and that it can even be useful in encouraging participants to take an honest look at themselves. However, it can be misused. In our view the participants' right not to explore certain issues or to stop at a certain point should be respected. Also, members should not be coerced into participating in an exercise. One of the ASGW's

guidelines is relevant here: "Group leaders shall protect member rights against physical threats, intimidation, coercion, and undue peer pressure insofar as it is reasonably possible."

4. Scapegoating is another potential hazard in groups. We question the ethical sensitivity of leaders who fail to intervene actively when they see participants "ganging up" on a certain group member. Unchallenged projection and dumping can have dire effects on the person who is under attack.

5. Confrontation can be used or misused in groups. At times participants may view confrontation in a negative way, seeing it as destructive tearing down of defenses that leaves a person highly vulnerable. To be sure, confrontation can be done in a way that results in a devastating attack. Leaders and participants alike need to learn how to recognize this destructive type of behavior and prevent it from going on in a group. On the other hand, confrontation can be an act of caring, and it can be done in such a way that a member is *challenged*. Confrontation can be an invitation for people to examine their behavior and its consequences more carefully. When confrontation is positive, the confronters share their reactions to the person being confronted. Harmful attacks on others should not be permitted under the guise of "sharing."

6. Another risk involved in groups is that what members disclose may not always be kept confidential. Even though a leader may continue to stress the necessity of not discussing what goes on in the group with outsiders, there is no guarantee that all members will respect the confidential nature of what occurs in their group.

7. On occasion people have been physically injured in groups as a result of such activities as wrestling, pushing, holding down, fighting with bataccas (soft, felt-covered clubs), and other forms of releasing aggression. We have seen irresponsible leaders goad participants to "let out your anger" and then watch helplessly, clearly unprepared for the ensuing violent outbursts of rage. In short, we think that it's unethical for leaders to work toward eliciting aggressive feelings unless they are competent to deal with the likely results. One safeguard is to tell members not to strike one another but to beat a pillow to release aggressive feelings in a symbolic way.

There are several guidelines for preventing injury when using certain physical techniques (see Corey, Corey, Callanan, & Russell, 1982b):

- Leaders should protect group members from harm; they should be prepared to deal with unforeseen directions that the physical exercise might take.
- Such techniques should not be used with clients whom the group leader does not know well. The nature of the client/therapist relationship and the client's personality are critical variables in deciding whether to use physical techniques and exercises.
- Beginning group leaders should use physical techniques only when direct

supervision is available or when they are co-leading with an experienced group leader.

- It is both unethical and unwise to push members into physical exercises. It is essential that members be invited to participate and given the clear option of refraining. If the leader explains the general purpose of such exercises and asks whether members want to participate, the chance of a negative outcome is minimized.

One way of minimizing psychological risks in groups is to use a contract approach, whereby leaders specify what their responsibilities are and members specify what their commitment to the group is by declaring what they're willing to explore and what they're willing to do. If such an approach is used, many of the risks we've mentioned can be reduced. If members and leaders operate under a contract that clarifies expectations, we believe, there is less chance for members to be exploited or to leave a group feeling that they've had a bad experience.

Of course, a contract approach is not the only way to reduce potential risks, nor is it sufficient, by itself, to do so. Probably one of the most important safeguards is the leader's training in group processes. Group leaders have the major responsibility for preventing needless harm to members, and to fulfill this role they need to have a clear grasp of the boundaries of their competence. This implies that leaders conduct only those types of groups for which they have been sufficiently prepared. A counselor may be trained to lead a group of peers in a personal-growth or consciousness-raising group yet be ill prepared to embark on a marathon or therapy group. Sometimes people who have attended a few marathon groups become excited about doing this type of group as leaders, even though they have little or no training and no opportunity for supervision. They soon find that they are in over their heads and are unable to cope with what emerges in the group. Working with an experienced co-leader is one good way to learn and also a way of reducing some potential risks.

## Confidentiality in Groups

The ethical, legal, and professional aspects of confidentiality (discussed in Chapter 6) have a somewhat different meaning in group situations. Are members of a group under the same ethical and legal obligation as the group leader not to disclose the identities of other members or the content of what was shared in the group? In law, a privilege is waived if a third party is present. Therefore, there is no privileged communication in groups. Plotkin (1978) observed that there were no judicial decisions, and little legal commentary, concerning breaches of confidentiality or invasion of privacy as a result of group experience. From an ethical perspective, however, members have an obligation to respect the communications of others in the group.

Plotkin contends that confidentiality is the "ethical cornerstone" of the client/therapist relationship and that leaders should raise the issue in their groups. For a more detailed review of the ethical dimensions of confidentiality in groups see Corey and Corey (1987).

## How to Encourage Confidentiality

Although most writers on ethical issues in group work make the point that confidentiality cannot be guaranteed, most of them also talk about the importance of teaching the members ways to avoid breaking confidences. Davis and Meara (1982) make the point that group confidentiality is difficult to enforce. Since group members cannot assume that anything they say or hear in the group will remain confidential, they should be able to make an informed choice about how much to reveal to the group. According to Davis and Meara, members should know about the difficulties in enforcing confidentiality, and leaders must spend time on this issue beyond merely discussing the topic at the initial sessions. They draw the following conclusion: "There are many reasons members break confidentiality and the leader cannot prevent all violations. If confidentiality becomes a norm for a cohesive group, there is a greater likelihood that members' secrets will remain in the group; however, there are no guarantees" (p. 153).

It is our position that leaders need to periodically reaffirm to group members the importance of not discussing with others what occurs in the group. In our own groups we talk with each prospective member about the necessity of confidentiality in establishing the trust and cohesion required if participants are to risk revealing themselves in significant ways. We discuss this point during the screening interviews, again during the pregroup or initial group meetings, at times during the course of a group when it seems appropriate, and again at the termination of the group. Since the three of us have done many intensive residential groups in which as many as 16 participants live together for an entire week, we have been concerned about maintaining the confidential character of the group. It has been our experience that most people in our groups do not maliciously attempt to hurt others by talking with people outside the group about specific members. However, it's tempting for members to share the nature of their experience with other people, and in so doing they sometimes make inappropriate disclosures. This is particularly true of participants in intensive, time-extended (marathon) groups, who are likely to be asked many questions when they return home about what it was like. Because of this tendency to want to share with outsiders, we repeatedly caution participants in any type of group about how easily and unintentionally the confidentiality of the group can be compromised.

If you were to lead any type of group, which of the following measures might you take to ensure confidentiality? Check any of the following statements that apply:

___ I'd repeatedly mention the importance of confidentiality.

___ I'd require group members to sign a statement saying that they would maintain the confidential character of the group.

___ I'd let members know that they would be asked to leave the group if they violated confidentiality.

___ I'd have a written document on hand describing the dimensions of confidentiality that all the members could refer to.

___ With the permission and knowledge of the members, I'd tape-record all the sessions.

___ I'd say very little about confidentiality and leave it up to the group members to decide how they would deal with the issue.

## Exceptions to Confidentiality

The AACD (1981) cautions counselors that they must set a norm of confidentiality regarding all group participants' disclosures. But the group's ethical standards do make exceptions. "When the client's condition indicates that there is clear and imminent danger to the client or others, the counselor must take reasonable personal action or inform responsible authorities. Consultation with other professionals must be used where possible."

In basic agreement with the AACD position is the APA's ethical standard of the obligation of psychologists to respect the confidentiality of clients. The APA (1981a) qualifies this position with:

> They reveal information to others only with the consent of the person or the person's legal representative, except in those unusual circumstances in which not to do so would result in clear danger to the person or to others. Where appropriate, psychologists inform their clients of the legal limits of confidentiality.

> *About halfway into the life span of a group, around the seventh week, a male member expresses his rage toward his ex-wife. He gives indications that he has plans for inflicting grave harm on her and her boyfriend as a means of righting the wrong done to him. The group leader treats this as a symptom of repressed anger and has the member act out his fantasies in a group, on the assumption that this will defuse his anger. The leader fails to notice that the member is still agitated when the session is over. He assumes that this release of anger has made the man safe. The group leader did not tell members during the first group session of a therapist's obligation to inform potential victims, and at no time during this group session does the leader tell this angry member of the legal "duty to warn" in such cases.*

- The member in fact does not harm his ex-wife and the boyfriend. Does this make the leader's behavior ethical and legal?
- If you were the leader in this case, what guidelines would you use to determine whether the member would be likely to act out his violent fantasies?
- If you had a similar situation occur in a group you were leading, how might you proceed?

# Uses and Abuses of Group Techniques

Group techniques can be used to facilitate the movement of a group and as catalysts to deepen and intensify certain feelings. We think it's important for leaders to have a clear rationale for using each technique. This is an area in which theory can be a useful guide for practice.

Techniques can also be abused or used in unethical ways. Some of the ways in which leaders can use techniques unprofessionally are:

- using techniques with which they are unfamiliar
- using techniques merely as gimmicks
- using techniques to serve their own hidden agendas or to enhance their power
- using techniques whose sole purpose is to create an explosive atmosphere
- using techniques to pressure members or in other ways rob them of dignity or the respect of others

We value techniques when they are appropriate ways of intensifying the experience of group participants. When we began leading groups together, we experimented with a variety of planned exercises that were designed to stimulate interactions and to elicit certain intense feelings. In fact, we were tempted to judge the effectiveness of these groups by the intensity of the feelings that were stirred up and expressed. We discovered, however, that significant learning and change occurred among people who did not have cathartic experiences. We also discovered that cathartic experiences *in and of themselves* did not seem sufficient to produce long-term changes. We therefore began to resist initiating many planned exercises designed to bring out certain feelings or to make things happen in the group. Still, we remain willing to invent techniques or to draw on techniques we've borrowed from others when these procedures seem appropriate to what a participant is experiencing and when we think they will help a person work through some conflict. This kind of appropriateness has become our guideline for using techniques effectively. Of course, group leaders will need to develop their own guidelines for determining whether and when to use techniques.

Following are guidelines we use in our practice to avoid abusing techniques in a group:

- There should be a therapeutic purpose and grounding in some theoretical framework.
- The client's self-exploration and self-understanding should be fostered.
- At their best, techniques are invented in each unique client situation, and they assist the client in experimenting with some form of new behavior.
- Techniques are not used to cover up the group leader's incompetence; rather, they are used to enhance the group process.
- Techniques are introduced in a timely and sensitive manner, and they are abandoned if they are not working.

- The tone of a leader is consistently invitational, in that members are given the freedom to participate or not participate in a given experiment.
- It is important that leaders use techniques they have some knowledge about and that they be aware of the potential impact of these techniques.

Although it is unrealistic for us to expect that leaders will always know exactly what will result from an intervention, they should be able to cope with unexpected outcomes. For example, guided fantasies into times of loneliness as a child or physical exercises designed to release anger can lead to intense emotional experiences. If leaders use such techniques, they must be ready to deal with any emotional release.

## Therapist Competence

The ASGW's (1980) basic principle is that "group leaders shall not attempt any technique unless thoroughly trained in its use or under supervision by an expert familiar with the intervention." How can leaders determine whether they have the competence to use a certain technique? Although some leaders who have received training in the use of a technique may hesitate to use it (out of fear of making a mistake), other overly confident leaders without training may not have any reservations about trying out new techniques. It is a good policy for leaders to have a clear rationale for any technique they use. Further, it is useful if leaders have experienced these techniques as members of a group.

■ *The case of an inexperienced leader.*   An inexperienced group leader has recently graduated from a master's-degree program in counseling. As a part of his job as a community mental-health counselor, he organizes a weekly two-hour group. He realizes that his training in group approaches is limited, so he decides to attend a weekend workshop on body therapy. He does some intensive personal work himself at the workshop, and he comes away impressed with the power of what he has witnessed. He is eager to meet his group on Tuesday evening so that he can try out some of these body-oriented techniques designed to "open the feelings." (He has not been trained in these techniques in graduate school, nor is he receiving any direct supervision in the group that he is leading.)

At the next session of the group a member says "I feel choked up with pain and anger, and I don't know how to deal with my feelings." The leader intervenes by having the member lie down, while he pushes on the client's abdomen and encourages her to scream, kick, shout, and release all the feelings that she's been keeping locked up inside of her. The client becomes pale and her breathing becomes shallow and fast. She describes tingling sensations in her arms, a numbness, and a tight mouth, and she says that she is scared and cannot breathe. The leader encourages her to stay with it and get out all those pent-up feelings that are choking her up. At the same time others in the group seem frightened, and some are angry with the leader for pushing the client.

- Do you think that most leaders would be competent to use body-oriented techniques after one weekend workshop?
- Was this leader's behavior inappropriate, unethical, or both? If the leader had had a qualified supervisor at the session, would your answer be different?
- How can a conscientious group leader determine when he or she is "thoroughly trained" in the use of a technique?
- Do you agree with the ASGW guideline that group leaders should not use *any* technique without being "thoroughly trained"? Why or why not?

## Unfinished Business

Another major issue pertaining to the use of group techniques relates to providing immediate help for any group member who shows extreme distress at the end of a group session, especially if techniques were used to elicit intense emotions. Although some "unfinished business" promotes growth, there is an ethical issue in the use of a technique that incites strong emotional reactions if the client is abandoned at the end of a session because time has run out. Leaders must take care to allow enough time to deal adequately with the reactions that were stimulated in a session. Techniques should not be introduced in a session when there is not enough time to work through the feelings that might result or in a setting where there is no privacy or where the physical setup is such that it would be physically harmful to employ certain techniques.

Our position on the ethical use of techniques is that group leaders must learn about their potential effects. One way for group leaders to learn is by taking part in group therapy themselves. By being a group member and first experiencing a range of techniques, they can develop a healthy respect for using techniques appropriately for the client's needs, not for the enhancement of the therapist's ego. In our training workshops for group leaders we encourage spontaneity and inventiveness in the use of techniques, but we also stress the importance of striking a balance between creativity and irresponsible lack of caution.

In our opinion the reputation of group work has suffered because of irresponsible practitioners, mostly those who use techniques as gimmicks without the backing of a clear rationale. We believe that, if the group leader has a sound academic background, has had extensive supervised group experience, has experienced his or her own therapy or some type of personal-growth experience, and has a basic respect for clients, he or she is not likely to abuse techniques (Corey, Corey, Callanan, & Russell, 1982a).

# Issues Concerning Termination

The final phase of a group and the departure to the outside world are among the most important stages of the group experience. This is true for therapy groups as well as for encounter groups, and it is true for groups that meet on an ongoing basis as well as for concentrated group experiences such as marathon or residential groups. The final stage of a group provides an opportunity for members to clarify the meaning of their experience, to consolidate the gains they've made, and to make decisions about the new behaviors they want to carry away from the group and apply to their everyday lives. We see the following professional issues involved in the termination of a group:

- What responsibilities do group leaders have for assisting participants to develop a conceptual framework that will make sense of, integrate, and consolidate what they've learned in their group?
- To what degree is it the leader's responsibility to ensure that members aren't stuck with unnecessary psychological turmoil at the end of the group?
- How can group leaders help participants translate what they've learned as a result of the group into their daily lives? Should leaders assume that this translation will occur automatically, or must they prepare members for maximizing their learning?
- What are some ways of minimizing postgroup depression?

A common criticism of groups is that people are often stuck with feelings of depression, resentment, and anger after a group ends, without any means of dealing with and resolving these feelings. However, our contention that group members should not be left with unnecessary psychological turmoil does *not* mean that we think they should be comfortable and free of conflict when they leave. On the contrary, we're convinced that a certain amount of anxiety due to unfinished business can be a stimulus for continued growth. It is the leader's task to recognize when anxiety is counterproductive.

Group leaders have other tasks to perform when a group ends. They can minimize postgroup depression by pointing out that members often experience a sense of loss and depression after a group ends. Further, they need to prepare members for dealing with those they are intimate with. The group should be reminded that others in their lives may not have changed as they have and may not be ready for their changes. We routinely caution people in our groups to give people on the outside a chance to get used to their changes. Before the group ends, we do much role playing to give members an opportunity to practice responding to others in different ways. They have the advantage of receiving feedback from the rest of the group on how they come across. We also announce to our groups our availability for some individual sessions at no extra fee after the conclusion of a group, should members feel the need for such consultation. Finally, we spend time talking about where they can continue their personal work. Many group participants become aware of areas in their lives that they want to explore in more depth in individual sessions. Others may want to pursue specific types of groups or workshops. For this reason we mention specific referral resources where participants can continue working on making the changes they've begun.

As a stage in the life of the group, termination has its own meaning and significance. Yalom (1985) observes that therapy groups tend to avoid the difficult work of terminating by ignoring or denying their concerns about it; therefore, it is the leader's task to keep the members focused on the ending of their group. His view is that termination is more than the end of therapy. Rather, it is an integral part of the therapeutic process, which, if properly understood and managed, can be a major force in promoting and maintaining change. In addition, therapists need to look at their feelings about the termination process, for they sometimes unnecessarily delay a member's termination because of their own perfectionistic expectations or their lack of faith in their client's being able to function effectively without the group. Yalom describes the termination of a group as a real experience of "loss" and suggests that therapists can help members deal with this reality by disclosing their own feelings about separating.

> Therapists, as well as patients, will miss the group. For us, too, it has been a place of anguish, conflict, fear, and also of great beauty: some of life's truest and most poignant moments occur in the small and yet limitless microcosm of the therapy group [p. 374].

## Follow-Up

What kind of follow-up should be provided after the termination of any group? What professional obligation does the group leader have to systematically evaluate the outcomes of a group? How can leaders assist members to evaluate the effectiveness of their group experience?

Follow-up services are suggested by the ASGW (1980) in the following guideline: "Group leaders shall provide between-session consultation to group members and follow-up after termination of the group, as needed or requested." We support this guideline, for we think it is a good practice for leaders to provide between-session intervention in cases where this is justified. Further, we agree that follow-up procedures are especially important for marathon groups or residential groups that meet for a few days to a week and then disband. Follow-up can be done in a number of ways. Both short-term (after one month) and long-term (after three months to a year) group sessions can be invaluable accountability measures. Since the members know that they will come together to evaluate their progress toward their stated goals, they are frequently more willing to work actively at making changes. Participants can develop contracts at the final sessions that involve action between the termination and the follow-up session (or sessions). These sessions are valuable not only because they offer the leader an opportunity to evaluate the effectiveness of the group but also because they provide members with the opportunity to gain a more realistic assessment of the impact the group had on them. If a meeting of the entire group is impractical, one-to-one sessions can be scheduled with each member of the group or as many members as can be contacted. In this postgroup interview the participants can discuss what the group meant to them in retrospect. In addition, this private session provides an ideal opportunity to discuss referral resources, should they be indicated. As another alternative (or in conjunction with the group follow-up and the private interview), questionnaires can be sent to members at some point after the termination of a group as a method of evaluating a group experience (see Corey & Corey, 1987, pp. 217–218; Corey, Corey, Callanan, & Russell, 1982b, pp. 154–157).

In the week-long groups the three of us lead together, we have made it a practice to schedule a follow-up session around three months after the group ends. These sessions have been most valuable both for the group members and for ourselves. Through these sessions we get a more realistic picture than we would otherwise have of the impact of the group on the members' everyday lives; the postsessions enable us to see whether members have actually applied what they learned in the group. For their part, members can share what their reentry was like for them and discuss any problems they're having in implementing what they learned in the group in their transactions with others. They have a chance to express and work through any afterthoughts or feelings left over from the group experience, and they can report on the degree to which they have fulfilled their contracts since they left the group. They also have a chance to receive additional feedback and reinforcement from the other members. Even for groups that meet on a weekly basis, we think it's wise to set a time for a group follow-up session to discuss the experience and put it in perspective.

## Evaluation

On the question of evaluating the results of a group, we admit that we find it difficult to objectively assess outcomes. Generally, we've relied on subjective measures; for example, after our groups terminate, we ask the members to write reaction papers in which they evaluate what the experience meant for them. We do think it's important to teach members how to recognize the ongoing changes they're making that are partially the result of what they learned in the group. Members have a tendency to discount what they actually did in a group, and they may not be aware of the subtle changes they continue to make after the group ends. We think it's our responsibility to teach them how to evaluate the nature and degree of their changes.

# Other Ethical Guidelines for Group Work

In this section we list some other ethical guidelines as developed by the ASGW (1980) and briefly comment on these issues.

## Experimentation and Research

"Group leaders shall provide prospective clients with specific information about any specialized or experimental activities in which they may be expected to participate" (ASGW, 1980). Group members should be informed of any research involving the group, and their consent should be obtained in writing (Gazda & Mack, 1982). If leaders intend to write journal articles or books, it is essential that they take measures to adequately safeguard the confidentiality of the material explored in the group. The same care should be taken to disguise identities if the leaders talk with colleagues about the progress of their groups. Those who conduct group work in institutions, such as community mental-health clinics and schools, will probably face the issue of preparing written reports for the institution. The members have a right to know what kinds of information will appear in an institutional report.

## Handling Difficult Members

"Group leaders shall ensure to the extent that it is reasonably possible that each member has the opportunity to utilize group resources and interact within the group by minimizing barriers such as rambling and monopolizing time" (ASGW, 1980). It is the leader's responsibility to help members use the resources within the group to an optimal degree. At times certain members may display problematic behaviors such as monopolizing time, engaging in storytelling, asking many questions and making interpretations for others, chronically jumping in and giving advice or reassurance when it is not appropriate, and so forth. The group leader does not have to take full responsibility for these interventions with difficult members, for the group, too, has a share of the responsibility. However, it is the leader's task to make certain interventions so that some members do not sap the energy of the group and make it difficult for others to do productive work or to meet their needs.

## Individual Treatment

"Group leaders shall make every reasonable effort to treat each member individually and equally" (ASGW, 1980). Leaders sometimes burden themselves with the unrealistic expectation that they should be absolutely impartial at all times to all members. They may think that they should like each member to the same degree, give each member equal time, and be equally interested in each. If they do not feel this universal caring, some leaders develop guilt feelings.

What seems most important in reference to this guideline is that leaders do not cling to initial impressions of a member and that they keep themselves open to changing their reactions. Although it is true that some members may present themselves in ways that make it difficult for them to be liked or interesting, a leader who hopes to have a therapeutic effect on these members will be willing to look at each of them as a unique person and will give each an equal chance of getting attention and fair treatment in the group setting.

## Personal Relationships

"Group leaders shall abstain from inappropriate personal relationships with members throughout the duration of the group and any subsequent professional involvement" (ASGW, 1980). What criteria can a group leader use to determine the degree of appropriateness of personal and social relationships with group members? A key question that leaders need to ask of themselves is whether the social relationship is interfering with the therapeutic relationship. The crux of the matter is to avoid abusing one's power and misusing one's professional role to make personal or social contacts. Although what constitutes "inappropriate personal relationships" is not always clear, trying to determine it does demand honesty in examining one's own motivations and needs.

In the process of being honest about one's motivations, a group leader needs to keep in mind that there is a tendency on the part of some members to glorify the group leader and, in doing so, to lessen their own power. Ethical group leaders do not take advantage of this tendency, nor do they exploit group members in the service of their ego needs.

## Promoting Autonomy of Members

"Group leaders shall help promote independence of members from the group in the most efficient period of time" (ASGW, 1980). Ultimately, the goal of group participation is assisting members to make their own decisions and to function as autonomous people. However, some group leaders actually promote the dependence of their members. Some of the reasons for this practice are the need to be needed; the need to depend on their work as a confirmation of their worth; and the need to make money. Whatever the reason or reasons for keeping members dependent, group leaders need to continually look at their practices to determine whether they are fostering the growth of their clients or are encouraging their members to rely on them for direction.

## Alcohol and Drugs

"Group leaders shall not condone the use of alcohol or drugs directly prior to or during group sessions" (ASGW, 1980). Although many group leaders agree that using alcohol or drugs before or during group sessions is not productive and do not condone such practices, they may have some difficulty in dealing with members who come to a session under the influence. It is possible that leaders may not take a stand out of the fear of being seen as authoritarian. Or they may simply decide to tolerate members who come to sessions under the influence of drugs or alcohol because they feel powerless to change the situation. It is important that group leaders be prepared to give a rationale for any "no-drugs-or-alcohol" rule, rather than simply laying it down as an edict. Members might be testing the limits of the leader by coming to a session somewhat inebriated or stoned. If leaders give in to the pressure and do not challenge this testing, they are likely to lose the respect of the members. The setting of realistic limits by leaders, including the prohibition of coming to sessions under the influence of drugs or alcohol, can be one way to gain the respect that is necessary to conduct an effective group.

# Questions for Review and Reflection

The following questions can help clarify how you see your role as a professional and your responsibilities as a group practitioner.

- How do you effectively screen potential group members? Can you confidently differentiate between those who are suitable for a group and those who are not?
- How do you adequately prepare people for group membership? How do you inform prospective participants of their rights and obligations, of the goals of the group, of the procedures and techniques you intend to use, of the expectations you have, of the possible psychological risks, and of any other factors that might affect them in deciding whether to become involved?
- How and when do you stress the importance of confidentiality? How do you increase the probability that members will maintain confidences?
- Are you alert to symptoms of psychological debilitation in group members, indicating that they should not continue in the group? Are you available for individual consultations? Do you have referral resources?
- Do you have a rationale for the group exercises, techniques, and procedures you employ?
- How do you help participants apply what they learn in the group to their everyday lives?
- Do you arrange follow-up group sessions to determine the impact the group experience had on the members? Do you hold individual interviews after the group ends to discuss and evaluate what the experience meant privately to each member?
- What procedures do you use for improving your groups? How do you get feedback, and what do you do with it? What research and evaluation methods do you use to assess the processes and outcomes of the groups you lead?
- What do you do to enhance your skills as a leader? Do you attend ongoing training programs? Do you get adequate supervison and consultation from other professionals when you need them? If you work with a co-leader, do you take the time to exchange ideas?
- How often do you think about the ethical and professional issues of group leadership that have been raised or implied here? What are you doing to clarify your position on specific moral issues that emerge in your groups?

# Chapter Summary

Along with the growing popularity of group approaches to counseling and therapy comes a need for ethical and professional guidelines for those who lead groups. In this chapter we have focused on some of the most important issues in group work, and we have encouraged you to take your own position on these issues.

There are many types of groups, and there are many possible uses of groups in various settings. Our attempt has been to select the issues that are related to most types of groups. Some of these questions are: How does a leader's theoretical view of groups influence the way that a group is structured? What are some key elements in recruiting, screening, selecting, and preparing group members? What ethical, professional, legal, and practical issues concerning confidentiality are involved in any type of group? To what degree should participants be prepared for a group before the group begins? What are some ethical issues in the selection and training of group leaders? In what ways can group techniques be used or abused? What responsibility do group leaders have in terms of follow-up and evaluation? With respect to these and other issues, we have stressed the importance of formulating your own guidelines for ethical practice in leading groups.

# Suggested Activities

1. In your own class you can experience the initial session of a group. Two students can volunteer to be co-leaders, and approximately ten other students can become group members. Assume that the group is a personal-growth group that will meet for a predetermined number of weeks. The co-leaders' job is to orient and prepare the members by describing the group's purpose, by giving an overview of group-process concepts, and by talking about ground rules for effective group participation. If time allows, members can express any fears and expectations they have about being involved in the group, and they can also raise questions they would like to explore. This exercise is designed to give you practice in dealing with concerns that both group leaders and members often have at the beginning of a group.

2. This exercise is designed to give you practice in conducting screening interviews for potential group members. One person volunteers to conduct interviews, and another student can role-play a potential group member. Allow about ten minutes for the interview. Afterward, the prospective client can talk about what it was like to be interviewed, and the group leader can share his or her experience. This exercise can be done with the entire class watching, in small groups, or in dyads.

3. Suppose you're expected as part of your job to lead a group composed of people who are *required* to be part of the group and who really don't want

to be there. How will the nature of the group affect your approach? What might you do differently with this group, compared with a group of people who want the experience? This is a good situation to role-play in class, with several students playing the reluctant members while others practice dealing with them.

4. You're leading a counseling group with high school students on their campus. One day a member comes to the group obviously under the influence of drugs. He is incoherent and disruptive. How do you deal with him? What might you say or do? Discuss how you would deal with this situation in class, or demonstrate how you might respond by having a fellow student role-play the part of the adolescent.

5. Again, assume that you're leading a high school counseling group. An angry father who gave written permission for his son's participation comes to your office and demands to know what's going on in your group. He is convinced that his son's participation in the group is an invasion of family privacy. As a group leader, how would you deal with this angry father? To make the situation more real and interesting, someone can role-play the father.

6. The issue of selecting a co-leader for a group is an important one, for not all matches of co-leaders are productive. For this exercise form dyads and negotiate with your partner to determine whether the two of you would be effective if you were to lead a group together. You might discuss matters such as potential power struggles, competitiveness, compatibility of views and philosophy, your differing styles and how they might complement or interfere with each other, and other issues that you think would have a bearing on your ability to work together well as a team.

7. Form a panel in class to explore the topic of the uses and abuses of group techniques. The panel can look at specific ways in which group techniques can be used to enhance learning, as well as ways in which they can be misused.

8. Review the excerpts from *Ethical Guidelines for Group Leaders* (ASGW, 1980) that are listed in this chapter. Which of these guidelines do you consider to be most important? Are there any guidelines with which you do not agree? We suggest that you form small groups in your class to discuss specific guidelines that stimulate the greatest controversy.

■
## Suggested Readings

For a more detailed description of the various groups and the differences among them see Corey and Corey (1987) and Duncan and Gumaer (1980). For a comprehensive discussion of the major contemporary theories of group counseling see Corey (1985), Gazda (1982), and Yalom (1985). For training standards for group leaders see ASGW (1983) and Zimpfer, Waltman, Williamson, and Huhn (1985). For a survey of programs of professional preparation for group counseling see Huhn, Zimpfer, Waltman, and

Williamson (1985). For ethical standards for group leaders see ASGW (1980). On ethical and professional issues in screening and preparation of group members see Yalom (1985), Corey, Corey, Callanan, and Russell (1982a, 1982b), Corey (1984), and Corey and Corey (1987). For a casebook dealing with ethical issues for group leaders see Corey, Corey, and Callanan (1982). On training group leaders in ethical decision making see Gumaer and Scott (1985). For group leaders' perceptions of ethical and unethical behavior of group leaders see Gumaer and Scott (1986). For perspectives on group research programs see Morran and Stockton (1985). For a description of an experiental/didactic training and supervision workshop for group leaders see Corey and Corey (1986).

## ■ Some Concluding Ideas

In these chapters we've raised some of the ethical and professional issues that you will be most likely to encounter in your counseling practice. Instead of providing answers, we've tried to stimulate you to think about your own guidelines for professional practice and to initiate a process of reflection that you can apply to the many other issues you will face as a counselor.

If there is one fundamental question that can serve to tie together all the issues we've discussed, it is this: *Who has the right to counsel another person?* This question can be the focal point of your reflection on ethical and professional issues. It can also be the basis of your self-examination each day you meet with clients. You can continue to ask yourself: "What makes me think I have a right to counsel others? What do I have to offer the people I'm counseling? Am I doing in my own life what I'm encouraging my clients to do?" At times, if you answer these questions honestly, you may be troubled. There may be times when you feel that you have no ethical right to counsel others, perhaps because your own life isn't always the model you would like it to be for your clients. Yet this occasional self-doubt is far less damaging, in our view, than a failure to examine these questions. Complacency will stifle your growth as a counselor; honest self-examination, though more difficult, will make you a more effective helper.

We want to close our discussion by returning to the theme that has guided us throughout this book—namely, that developing a sense of professional and ethical responsibility is a task that is never really finished. There are no final or universal answers to many of the questions we have posed. For ourselves, we hope we never fall into the deadening trap of thinking that we "have it made" and no longer need to reexamine our assumptions and practices. We've found that the kinds of issues raised in this book have demanded periodic reflection and an openness to change. Thus, although we hope you've given careful thought to your own ethical and professional guidelines, we also hope you'll be willing to rethink your positions as you gain more experience.

Refer to the multiple-choice survey at the end of Chapter 1 on attitudes and beliefs regarding ethical and professional issues. We suggest that you cover your initial answers and retake the inventory now that you've come to the end of the course. Then you can compare your responses to see whether your thinking has changed. In addition, we suggest that you circle the ten questions that are most significant to you or that you're most interested in pursuing further. Bring these to class, and discuss them in small groups. Afterward, a survey can be conducted to get some idea of the issues that were most important to the students in your class.

As a way to review this book and the course you are completing, write down a few of the most important things you have learned. You might also write down some of the questions that this book and your course have left unanswered for you. After you've made your two lists, form small groups and exchange ideas with other students. This can be an excellent way to get some sense of the most crucial areas and topics that were explored by your fellow students and a fine way to wrap up the course.

Once the course is over, where can you go from here? How can you maintain the process of reflection that you've begun in this course? One excellent way to keep yourself alive intellectually is to develop a reading program. We suggest that you begin by selecting some of the books that we've listed in the References and Reading List. We'd also like to suggest that you dip into this book again from time to time. It can be valuable to reread various chapters as you take different courses that deal with the issues we've considered. In addition, periodically reexamining your responses can stimulate your thinking and provide a measure of your professional and intellectual growth. We hope you'll find other ways to make this book meaningful for yourself as you continue your search for your own direction.

# References
# and Reading List

Adair, J. G., Dushenko, T. W., & Lindsay, R. C. L. (1985). Ethical regulations and their impact on research practice. *American Psychologist, 40*(1), 59–72.

Adelman, H. S., Lusk, R., Alvarez, V., & Acosta, N. K. (1985). Competence of minors to understand, evaluate, and communicate about their psychoeducational problems. *Professional Psychology: Research and Practice, 16*(3), 426–434.

Allen, G. J., Szollos, S. J., & Williams, B. E. (1986). Doctoral students' comparative evaluations of best and worst psychotherapy supervision. *Professional Psychology: Research and Practice, 17*(2), 91–99.

Allen, V. B. (1986). A historical perspective of the AACD ethics committee. *Journal of Counseling and Development, 64*(5), 293.

American Association for Counseling and Development. (1981). *Ethical standards* (rev. ed.). Alexandria, VA: Author.

American Association for Marriage and Family Therapy. (1984). *Ethical principles for family therapists* (pamphlet). Washington, DC: Author.

American Association for Marriage and Family Therapy. (1985). *Code of ethical principles for marriage and family therapists.* Washington, DC: Author.

American Association of Sex Educators, Counselors, and Therapists. (1981). *Ethical standards.* Washington, DC: Author.

American College Personnel Association. (1980). *Statement of ethical and professional standards.* Alexandria, VA: American Association for Counseling and Development.

American Group Psychotherapy Association. (1978). *Guidelines for the training of group psychotherapists.* New York: Author.

American Mental Health Counselors Association. (1980). *Code of ethics for certified clinical mental health counselors.* Falls Church, VA: Author.

American Personnel and Guidance Association. (1981). *Ethical standards* (rev. ed.). Falls Church, VA: Author.

American Personnel and Guidance Association. (1982). *Guidepost, 25*(9).

American Psychiatric Association. (1980). *Diagnostic and statistical manual of mental disorders* (3rd ed.). Washington, DC: Author.

American Psychiatric Association. (1986). *Principles of medical ethics, with annotations especially applicable to psychiatry.* Washington, DC: Author.

American Psychoanalytic Association. (1983). *Principles of ethics for psychoanalysts and provisions for implementation of the principles of ethics for psychoanalysts.* New York: Author.

American Psychological Association. (1967). *Casebook on ethical standards of psychologists.* Washington, DC: Author.

American Psychological Association. (1973a). *Ethical principles in the conduct of research with human participants*. Washington, DC: Author.

American Psychological Association. (1973b). Guidelines for psychologists conducting growth groups. *American Psychologist, 28*(10), 933.

American Psychological Association. (1977a). *Standards for educational and psychological tests*. Washington, DC: Author.

American Psychological Association. (1977b). Standards for providers of psychological services. *American Psychologist, 32*, 495–505.

American Psychological Association. (1978). Guidelines for therapy with women. *American Psychologist, 30*, 1122–1123.

American Psychological Association. (1981a). *Ethical principles of psychologists* (rev. ed.). Washington, DC: Author.

American Psychological Association. (1981b). Specialty guidelines for the delivery of services. *American Psychologist, 36*(6), 639–681.

American Psychological Association. (1981c). *Specialty guidelines for the delivery of services by clinical psychologists*. Washington, DC: Author.

American Psychological Association. (1981d). *Specialty guidelines for the delivery of services by counseling psychologists*. Washington, DC: Author.

American Psychological Association. (1981e). *Specialty guidelines for the delivery of services by industrial/organizational psychologists*. Washington, DC: Author.

American Psychological Association. (1981f). *Specialty guidelines for the delivery of services by school psychologists*. Washington, DC: Author.

American Psychological Association. (1985). *White paper on duty to protect*. Washington, DC: Author.

American Psychological Association, Committee on Professional Standards. (1982). Casebook for providers of psychological services. *American Psychologist, 37*(6), 698–701.

American Psychological Association, Division of Counseling Psychology. (1979). Principles concerning the counseling and therapy of women. *The Counseling Psychologist, 8*(1), 21.

American School Counselor Association. (1984). *Ethical standards for school counselors*. Alexandria, VA: Author.

Anderson, W. (1986). Stages of therapist comfort with sexual concerns of clients. *Professional Psychology: Research and Practice, 17*(4), 352–356.

Anderten, P., Staulcup, V., & Grisso, T. (1980). On being ethical in legal places. *Professional Psychology, 11*(5), 764–773.

Appelbaum, P. (1981). Tarasoff: An update on the duty to warn. *Hospital and Community Psychiatry, 32*, 14–15.

Arredondo, P. (1985). Cross-cultural counselor education and training. In P. Pedersen (Ed.), *Handbook of cross-cultural counseling and therapy* (pp. 281–289). Westport, CT: Greenwood Press.

Arredondo, P. M. (1986). Immigration as a historical moment leading to an identity crisis. *Journal of Counseling and Human Service Professions, 1*(1), 79–87.

Arredondo, P., & Gawelek, M. A. (1982). *Human rights training manual*. Alexandria, VA: Association for Counselor Education and Supervision.

Arredondo-Dowd, P. M., & Gossalves, J. (1980). Preparing culturally effective counselors. *Personnel and Guidance Journal, 58*(10), 657–661.

Ascher, L. M. (1986). Several suggestions for the future of paradox in therapy. *The Counseling Psychologist, 14*(2), 291–296.

Association for Specialists in Group Work. (1980). *Ethical guidelines for group leaders*. Alexandria, VA: Author.

Association for Specialists in Group Work. (1983). *Professional standards for training of group counselors*. Alexandria, VA: Author.

Atkinson, D. R. (1985). Research on cross-cultural counseling and psychotherapy: A review and update of reviews. In P. Pedersen (Ed.), *Handbook of cross-*

*cultural counseling and therapy* (pp. 191–197). Westport, CT: Greenwood Press.

Atkinson, D. R., Morten, G., & Sue, D. W. (1979). *Counseling American minorities*. Dubuque, IA: William C. Brown.

Attneave, C. L. (1985). Practical counseling with American Indian and Alaska native clients. In P. Pedersen (Ed.), *Handbook of cross-cultural counseling and therapy* (pp. 135–140)., Westport, CT: Greenwood Press.

Axelson, J. A. (1985). *Counseling and development in a multicultural society*. Monterey, CA: Brooks/Cole.

Baldick, T. (1980). Ethical discrimination ability of intern psychologists: A function of training in ethics. *Professional Psychology, 11*, 276–282.

Baruth, L. G., & Huber, C. H. (1984). *An introduction to marital theory and therapy*. Monterey, CA: Brooks/Cole.

Baumrind, D. (1985). Research using intentional deception. *American Psychologist, 40*(2), 165–174.

Bayles, M. D. (1981). *Professional ethics*. Belmont, CA: Wadsworth.

Bazelon, D. L. (1982). Veils, values, and social responsibility. *American Psychologist, 37*(2), 115–121.

Bennett, C. C. (1984). "Know thyself." *Professional Psychology: Research and Practice, 15*(2), 271–283.

Bennett, G. (1986). Faculty interventions: How far should you go? In C. D. Scott & J. Hawk (Eds.), *Heal thyself: The health of health care professionals*. New York: Brunner/Mazel.

Berger, Milton. (1982). Ethical problems in the use of videotape. In M. Rosenbaum (Ed.), *Ethics and values in psychotherapy: A guidebook*. New York: Free Press.

Berger, Morton. (1982). Ethics and the therapeutic relationship: Patient rights and therapist responsibilities. In M. Rosenbaum (Ed.), *Ethics and values in psychotherapy: A guidebook*. New York: Free Press.

Bernard, J. L., & Jara, C. S. (1986). The failure of clinical psychology graduate students to apply understood ethical principles. *Professional Psychology: Research and Practice, 17*(4), 313–315.

Bernot, D. J. (1983). Ethical and professional considerations in psychological assessment. *Professional Psychology: Research and Practice, 14*(5), 580–587.

Bernstein, B. L., & Lecomte, C. (1981). Licensure in psychology: Alternative direction. *Professional Psychology, 12*(2), 200–208.

Beutler, L. E. (1983). *Eclectic psychotherapy: A systematic approach*. Elmsford, NY: Pergamon Press.

Biskin, B. H. (1985). Peer reviewer evaluations and evaluations of peer reviewers: Effects of theoretical orientation. *Professional Psychology: Research and Practice, 16*(5), 671–680.

Bloom, B. (1983). *Community mental health: A general introduction* (2nd ed.). Monterey, CA: Brooks/Cole.

Blustein, D. L. (1982). Using informal groups in cross-cultural counseling. *The Journal for Specialists in Group Work, 7*(4), 260–265.

Board of Medical Quality Assurance, Psychology Examining Committee, State of California Department of Consumer Affairs. (1980). *Newsletter*. Sacramento, CA: Author.

Boice, R., & Myers, P. E. (1986). Stresses and satisfactions of chairing in psychology. *Professional Psychology: Research and Practice, 17*(3), 200–204.

Bouhoutsos, J. (in press). Sexual intimacy between psychotherapists and clients: Policy implications for the future. In L. Walker (Ed.), *Women and mental health policy*. Beverly Hills, CA: Russell Sage Foundation.

Bouhoutsos, J., Holroyd, J., Lerman, H., Forer, B. R., & Greenberg, M. (1983). Sexual intimacy between psychotherapists and patients. *Professional Psychology: Research and Practice, 14*(2), 185–196.

Brabeck, M. M., & Wolfel, E. R. (1985a). Counseling theory: Understanding the trend toward eclecticism from a developmental perspective. *Journal of Counseling and Development*, 63(6), 343–348.

Brabeck, M. M., & Wolfel, E. R. (1985b). Truth in counseling theory: A rejoinder to Patterson and Rychlak. *Journal of Counseling and Development*, 63(6), 354–355.

Brammer, L. M. (1985a). Counseling services in the People's Republic of China. *International Journal for the Advancement of Counseling*, 8, 125–136.

Brammer, L. M. (1985b). Nonformal support in cross-cultural counseling and therapy. In P. Pedersen (Ed.), *Handbook of cross-cultural counseling and therapy* (pp. 87–92). Westport, CT: Greenwood Press.

Brammer, L., & Shostrom, E. (1982). *Therapeutic psychology: Fundamentals of counseling and psychotherapy* (4th ed.). Englewood Cliffs, NJ: Prentice-Hall.

Bray, J. H., Shepherd, J. N., & Hays, J. R. (1985). Legal and ethical issues in informed consent to psychotherapy. *The American Journal of Family Therapy*, 13(2), 50–60.

Brickman, P., Rabinowitz, V., Karuza, J., Coates, D., Cohn, E., & Kidder, L. (1982). Models of helping and coping. *American Psychologist*, 37(4), 368–384.

Brodsky, A. M. (1986). The distressed psychologist: Sexual intimacies and exploitation. In R. R. Kilburg, P. E. Nathan, & R. W. Thoreson (Eds.), *Professionals in distress: Issues, syndromes, and solutions in psychology*. Washington, DC: American Psychological Association.

Brown, D. (1985). The preservice training and supervision of consultants. *The Counseling Psychologist*, 13(3), 410–425.

Brown, F. (1982). The ethics of psychodiagnostic assessment. In M. Rosenbaum (Ed.), *Ethics and values in psychotherapy: A guidebook*. New York: Free Press.

Brown, J. E., & Slee, P. T. (1986). Paradoxical strategies: The ethics of intervention. *Professional Psychology: Research and Practice*, 17(6), 487–496.

Brown, J. H., & Christensen, D. N. (1986). *Family therapy: Theory and practice*. Monterey, CA: Brooks/Cole.

Burton, A. (1972). *Interpersonal psychotherapy*. Englewood Cliffs, NJ: Prentice-Hall.

Calhoun, J. F., & Green, C. (1984). Perspectives of psychology training clinics from training and clinic directors. *Professional Psychology: Research and Practice*, 15(3), 371–378.

California Association of Marriage and Family Counselors. (1978, January). *Newsletter*. Los Angeles: Author.

Callis, R., Pope, S. K., & DePauw, M. E. (1982). *Ethical standards casebook* (3rd ed.). Alexandria, VA: American Association for Counseling and Development.

Carroll, M. A., Schneider, H. G., & Wesley, G. R. (1985). *Ethics in the practice of psychology*. Englewood Cliffs, NJ: Prentice-Hall.

Casas, J. M. (1985a). A reflection on the status of racial/ethnic minority research. *The Counseling Psychologist*, 13(4), 581–598.

Casas, J. M. (1985b). The status of racial- and ethnic-minority counseling: A training perspective. In P. Pedersen (Ed.), *Handbook of cross-cultural counseling and therapy* (pp. 267–273). Westport, CT: Greenwood Press.

Casas, J. M. (1986). *Falling short of meeting the counseling needs of racial/ethnic minorities: The status of ethical and accreditation guidelines*. Unpublished manuscript, University of California at Santa Barbara.

Casas, J. M., Ponterotto, J. G., & Gutierrez, J. M. (1986). An ethical indictment of counseling research training: The cross cultural perspective. *Journal of Counseling and Development*, 64(5), 347–349.

Cavell, T. A., Frentz, C. E., & Kelley, M. L. (1986). Acceptability of paradoxical interventions: Some nonparadoxical findings. *Professional Psychology: Research and Practice*, 17(6), 519–523.

Cayleff, S. E. (1986). Ethical issues in counseling gender, race, and culturally distinct groups. *Journal of Counseling and Development, 64*(5), 345–347.

Cerney, M. S. (1985). Countertransference revisited. *Journal of Counseling and Development, 63*(6), 362–364.

Child abuse: The legal aspects. *Child abuse prevention handbook.* Sacramento, CA: Crime Prevention Center.

Claiborn, C. D. (1985). The counselor and physical attractiveness: A response. *Journal of Counseling and Development, 63*(8), 486–487.

Claiborn, W. L., Stricker, G., & Bent, R. J. (Eds.). (1982). Peer review and quality assurance [Special issue]. *Professional Psychology, 13*(1).

Clark, M. M. (1986). Personal therapy: A review of empirical research. *Professional Psychology: Research and Practice, 17*(6), 541–543.

Coleman, E., & Schaefer, S. (1986). Boundaries of sex and intimacy between client and counselor. *Journal of Counseling and Development, 64*(5), 341–344.

Coley, S. M., Corey, G., Garcia, M., Moline, M., Ramirez, J., Russell, J. M., & Wright, J. (1986). The human services program at California State University, Fullerton. *Journal of Counseling and Human Service Professions, 1*(1), 156–165.

Combs, A. W. (1986). What makes a good helper? A person-centered approach. *Person-Centered Review, 1*(1), 51–61.

Commission on Rehabilitation Counselor Certification. *Code of Ethics.* Arlington Heights, IL: Author.

Coombs, R. H., & Fawzy, F. I. (1986). The impaired-physician syndrome: A developmental perspective. In C. D. Scott & J. Hawk (Eds.), *Heal thyself: The health of health care professionals.* New York: Brunner/Mazel.

Corey, G. (1981). Description of a practicum course in group leadership. *The Journal for Specialists in Group Work, 6*(2), 100–108.

Corey, G. (1982). Practical strategies for planning therapy groups. In P. Keller (Ed.), *Innovations in clinical practice: A sourcebook.* Sarasota, FL: Professional Resource Exchange.

Corey, G. (1983). An introduction to group counseling. In B. Pate & J. Brown (Eds.), *Being a counselor: Directions and challenges for the '80s.* Monterey, CA: Brooks/Cole.

Corey, G. (1984). Ethical issues in group therapy. In P. Keller (Ed.), *Innovations in clinical practice: A sourcebook.* Sarasota, FL: Professional Resource Exchange.

Corey, G. (1985). *Theory and practice of group counseling* (2nd ed.) and *Manual.* Monterey, CA: Brooks/Cole.

Corey, G. (1986a). *Case approach to counseling and psychotherapy* (2nd ed.). Monterey, CA: Brooks/Cole.

Corey, G. (1986b). *Theory and practice of counseling and psychotherapy* (3rd ed.) and *Manual.* Monterey, CA: Brooks/Cole.

Corey, G., with Corey, M. S. (1986). *I never knew I had a choice* (3rd ed.). Monterey, CA: Brooks/Cole.

Corey, G., & Corey, M. (1987). *Groups: Process and practice* (3rd ed.). Monterey, CA: Brooks/Cole.

Corey, G., Corey, M., & Callanan, P. (1981). In-service training for group leaders in a prison hospital: Problems and prospects. *The Journal for Specialists in Group Work, 6*(3), 130–135.

Corey, G., Corey, M., & Callanan, P. (1982). A *casebook of ethical guidelines for group leaders.* Monterey, CA: Brooks/Cole.

Corey, G., Corey, M., Callanan, P., & Russell, J. M. (1980). A residential workshop for personal growth. *The Journal for Specialists in Group Work, 5*(4), 205–215.

Corey, G., Corey, M. S., Callanan, P., & Russell, J. M. (1982a). Ethical considerations in using group techniques. *The Journal for Specialists in Group Work, 7*(3), 140–148.

Corey, G., Corey, M., Callanan, P., & Russell, J. M. (1982b). *Group techniques.* Monterey, CA: Brooks/Cole.

Corey, M. S., & Corey, G. (1986). Experiential/didactic training and supervision workshop for group leaders. *Journal of Counseling and Human Service Professions, 1*(1), 18–26.

Cormier, L. S., & Bernard, J. M. (1982). Ethical and legal responsibilities of clinical supervisors. *Personnel and Guidance Journal, 60*(8), 486–490.

Cormier, L. S., Cormier, W. H., & Weisser, R. J. (1984). *Interviewer and helping skills for health professionals.* Monterey, CA: Wadsworth.

Corsini, R. (Ed.). (1981). *Handbook of innovative psychotherapies.* New York: Wiley.

Corsini, R. (Ed.). (1984). *Current psychotherapies* (3rd ed.). Itasca, IL: F. E. Peacock.

Cottingham, H. F. (1980). Some broader perspectives on credentialing counseling psychologists. *The Counseling Psychologist, 9*(1), 19–22.

Cottone, R. R. (1985). The need for counseling licensure: A rehabilitation counseling perspective. *Journal of Counseling and Development, 63*(10), 625–629.

Council for the National Register of Health Service Providers in Psychology. (1980). *National register of health service providers in psychology.* Washington, DC: Author.

Council for Standards in Human Service Education. (1983). *National standards for human service worker education and training programs.* Montpelier, VT: Author.

Courtois, C. A. (1979). Victims of rape and incest. *The Counseling Psychologist, 8*(1), 38–40.

Cramer, D. (1986). Gay parents and their children. A review of research and practical implications. *Journal of Counseling and Development, 64*(8), 504–507.

Crego, C. A. (1985). Ethics: The need for improved consultation training. *The Counseling Psychologist, 13*(3), 473–476.

Davis, J. W. (1981). Counselor licensure: Overkill? *Personnel and Guidance Journal, 60*(2), 83–85.

Davis, K. L., & Meara, N. M. (1982). So you think it is a secret. *The Journal for Specialists in Group Work, 7*(3), 149–153.

Deardorff, W. W., Cross, H. J., & Hupprich, W. R. (1984). Malpractice liability in psychotherapy: Client and practitioner perspectives. *Professional Psychology: Research and Practice, 15*(4), 590–600.

DeKraai, M. B., & Sales, B. D. (1982). Privileged communications of psychologists. *Professional Psychology, 13*(3), 372–388.

Delisle, J. R. (1986). Death with honors: Suicide among gifted adolescents. *Journal of Counseling and Development, 64*(9), 558–560.

DeNelsky, G. Y., & Boat, B. W. (1986). A coping skills model of psychological diagnosis and treatment. *Professional Psychology: Research and Practice, 17*(4), 322–330.

Denkowski, K. M., & Denkowski, G. C. (1982). Client-counselor confidentiality: An update of rationale, legal status, and implications. *Personnel and Guidance Journal, 60*(6), 371–375.

DePauw, M. E. (1986). Avoiding ethical violations: A timeline perspective for individual counseling. *Journal of Counseling and Development, 64*(5), 303–305.

Deutsch, C. J. (1984). Self-reported sources of stress among psychotherapists. *Professional Psychology: Research and Practice, 15*(6), 833–845.

Deutsch, C. J. (1985). A survey of therapists' personal problems and treatment. *Professional Psychology: Research and Practice, 16*(2), 305–315.

Devore, W. (1985). Developing ethnic sensitivity for the counseling process: A social-work perspective. In P. Pedersen (Ed.), *Handbook of cross-cultural counseling and therapy* (pp. 93–98). Westport, CT: Greenwood Press.

Dowd, E. T., & Milne, C. R. (1986). Paradoxical interventions in counseling psychology. *The Counseling Psychologist, 14*(2), 237–282.

Downing, N. E., & Roush, K. L. (1985). From passive acceptance to active commitment: A model of feminist identity development for women. *The Counseling Psychologist, 13*(4), 695–709.

Dugger, J. (1980). *The new professional: Introduction for the human services mental health worker* (2nd ed.). Monterey, CA: Brooks/Cole.

Duncan, J., & Gumaer, J. (1980). *Developmental groups for children.* Springfield, IL: Charles C Thomas.

Earley, T. M., & Hulse, D. (1986). Humanizing a technological society: Ethical implications for the counselor. *Journal of Counseling and Development, 64*(5), 334–336.

Easton, M. J., Platt, C. P., & Van Hoose, C. L. (1985). A cost-effective training program for paraprofessionals at a university counseling center. *Journal of Counseling and Development, 64*(2), 151–153.

Ebert, B. W. (1986). The mental health response team: An expanding role for psychologists. *Professional Psychology: Research and Practice, 17*(6), 580–585.

Edelwich, J., with Brodsky, A. (1980). *Burn-out: Stages of dissillusionment in the helping professions.* New York: Human Sciences Press.

Edelwich, J., with Brodsky, A. (1982). *Sexual dilemmas for the helping professional.* New York: Brunner/Mazel.

Egan, G. (1986). *The skilled helper: A systematic approach to effective helping* (3rd ed.). Monterey, CA: Brooks/Cole.

Elliott, S. N., Witt, J. C., Galvin, G. A., & Moe, G. L. (1986). Children's involvement in intervention selection: Acceptability of interventions for misbehaving peers. *Professional Psychology: Research and Practice, 17*(3), 235–241.

Ellis, A. (1973). *Humanistic psychotherapy: The rational-emotive approach.* New York: McGraw-Hill.

Ellis, A. (1986). *Meeting the culture-related requirements of APA's ethical principles.* Unpublished manuscript, Institute for Rational-Emotive Therapy, New York.

Ellis, T. E. (1986). Toward a cognitive therapy for suicidal individuals. *Professional Psychology: Research and Practice, 17*(2), 125–130.

Espin, O. M. (1985). Psychotherapy with Hispanic women: Some considerations. In P. Pedersen (Ed.), *Handbook of cross-cultural counseling and therapy* (pp. 165–171). Westport, CT: Greenwood Press.

Everstine, L., Everstine, D. S., Heymann, G. M., True, R. H., Frey, D. H., Johnson, H. G., & Seiden, R. H. (1980). Privacy and confidentiality in psychotherapy. *American Psychologist, 35*(9), 828–840.

Farber, B. A. (1983a). Psychotherapists' perceptions of stressful patient behavior. *Professional Psychology: Research and Practice, 14*(5), 697–705.

Farber, B. A. (1983b). *Stress and burnout in the human service professions.* New York: Pergamon Press.

Farber, B. A., & Heifetz, L. J. (1982). The process and dimensions of burnout in psychotherapists. *Professional Psychology, 13*(2), 293–301.

Fieldsteel, N. (1982). Ethical issues in family therapy. In M. Rosenbaum (Ed.), *Ethics and values in psychotherapy: A guidebook.* New York: Free Press.

Fitting, M. D. (1984). Professional and ethical responsibilities for psychologists working with the elderly. *The Counseling Psychologist, 12*(3), 69–78.

Fitting, M. D. (1986). Ethical dilemmas in counseling elderly adults. *Journal of Counseling and Development, 64*(5), 325–327.

Fitzgerald, L. F., & Nutt, R. (1986). The Division 17 principles concerning the counseling/psychotherapy of women: Rationale and implementation. *The Counseling Psychologist, 14*(1), 180–216.

Fretz, B. R., & Mills, D. H. (1980). *Licensing and certification of psychologists and counselors.* San Francisco: Jossey-Bass.

Freudenberger, H. J. (1986). The health professional in treatment: Symptoms, dynamics, and treatment issues. In C. D. Scott & J. Hawk (Eds.), *Heal thyself: The health of health care professionals.* New York: Brunner/Mazel.

Frisz, R. H. (1986). Peer counseling: Establishing a network in training and supervision. *Journal of Counseling and Development, 64*(7), 457–459.

Fujimura, L. E., Weis, D. M., & Cochran, J. R. (1985). Suicide: Dynamics and implications for counseling. *Journal of Counseling and Development, 63*(10), 612–615.

Gallessich, J. (1982). *The profession and practice of consultation.* San Francisco: Jossey-Bass.

Gallessich, J. (1985). Toward a meta-theory of consultation. *The Counseling Psychologist, 13*(3), 336–354.

Garfield, S. L. (1980). *Psychotherapy: An eclectic approach.* New York: Wiley.

Garfield, S. L. (1987). Ethical issues in research on psychotherapy. *Counseling and Values, 3*(2), 115–125.

Gazda, G. (1982). *Basic approaches to group psychotherapy and group counseling* (3rd ed.). Springfield, IL: Charles C Thomas.

Gazda, G., & Mack, S. (1982). Ethical practice guidelines for group work practitioners. In G. M. Gazda (Ed.), *Basic approaches to group psychotherapy and group counseling* (3rd ed.). Springfield, IL: Charles C Thomas.

Gehring, D. D. (1982). The counselor's "duty to warn." *Personnel and Guidance Journal, 61*(4), 208–210.

Gelso, C. J., & Carter, J. A. (1985). The relationship in counseling and psychotherapy: Components, consequences, and theoretical antecedents. *The Counseling Psychologist, 13*(2), 155–243.

Gendlin, E. T. (1986). What comes after traditional psychotherapy research? *American Psychologist, 41*(2), 131–136.

Gibbs, J. T. (1985). Can we continue to be color-blind and class-bound? *The Counseling Psychologist, 13*(3), 426–435.

Gilbert, L. A. (1980). Feminist therapy. In A. M. Brodsky & R. T. Hare-Mustin (Eds.), *Women and psychotherapy: An assessment of research and practice.* New York: Guilford Press.

Gill, S. J. (1982). Professional disclosure and consumer protection in counseling. *Personnel and Guidance Journal, 60*(7), 443–446.

Glaser, R. D., & Thorpe, J. S. (1986). Unethical intimacy: A survey of sexual contact and advances between psychology educators and female graduate students. *American Psychologist, 41*(1), 42–51.

Glenn, C. M. (1980). Ethical issues in the practice of child psychotherapy. *Professional Psychology, 11*(4), 613–619.

Goldberg, C. (1977). *Therapeutic partnership: Ethical concerns in psychotherapy.* New York: Springer.

Goldenberg, H. (1977). *Abnormal psychology: A social/community approach.* Monterey, CA: Brooks/Cole.

Goldenberg, H. (1983). *Contemporary clinical psychology* (2nd ed.). Monterey, CA: Brooks/Cole.

Goldenberg, I., & Goldenberg, H. (1985). *Family therapy: An overview* (2nd ed.). Monterey, CA: Brooks/Cole.

Goodyear, R. K., & Sinnett, E. R. (1984). Current and emerging ethical issues for counseling psychologists. *The Counseling Psychologist, 12*(3), 87–98.

Graham, D. L. R., Rawlings, E. I., Halpern, H. S., & Hermes, J. (1984). Therapists' need for training in counseling lesbians and gay men. *Professional Psychology: Research and Practice, 15*(4), 482–496.

Grater, H. A. (1985). Stages in psychotherapy supervision: From therapy skills to skilled therapist. *Professional Psychology: Research and Practice, 16*(5), 605–610.

Grayson, H. (1982). Ethical issues in the training of psychotherapists. In M. Rosenbaum (Ed.), *Ethics and values in psychotherapy: A guidebook*. New York: Free Press.

Green, S. L., & Hansen, J. C. (1986). Ethical dilemmas in family therapy. *Journal of Marital and Family Therapy, 12*(3), 225–230.

Greenburg, S. L., Lewis, G. J., & Johnson, J. (1985). Peer consultation groups for private practitioners. *Professional Psychology: Research and Practice, 16*(3), 437–447.

Gross, S. (1977). Professional disclosure: An alternative to licensure. *Personal and Guidance Journal, 55*, 586–588.

Gross, S. J. (1978). The myth of professional licensing. *American Psychologist, 33*, 1009–1016.

Gross, S. J. (1979, September/October). Comment on licensing. *APA Monitor*, p. 15.

Gumaer, J., & Scott, L. (1985). Training group leaders in ethical decision making. *The Journal for Specialists in Group Work, 10*(4), 198–204.

Gumaer, J., & Scott, L. (1986). Group workers' perceptions of ethical and unethical behavior of group leaders. *The Journal for Specialists in Group Work, 11*(3), 139–150.

Guy, J. D., & Liaboe, G. P. (1986). The impact of conducting psychotherapy upon the interpersonal relationships of the psychotherapist. *Professional Psychology: Research and Practice, 17*(2), 111–114.

Guy, J. D., & Liaboe, G. P. (undated a). *Personal therapy for the experienced psychotherapist: A discussion of its usefulness and utilization*. Unpublished paper.

Guy, J. D., & Liaboe, G. P. (undated b). *Suicide among psychotherapists: Review and discussion*. Unpublished paper.

Guy, J. D., & Souder, J. K. (1986). Impact of therapists' illness or accident on psychotherapeutic practice: Review and discussion. *Professional Psychology: Research and Practice, 17*(6), 509–513.

Haas, L. J., & Alexander, J. F. (1981). *Ethical and legal issues in family therapy*. Paper presented at the meeting of the American Psychological Association, Los Angeles.

Haas, L. J., Malouf, J. L., & Mayerson, N. H. (1986). Ethical dilemmas in psychological practice: Results of a national survey. *Professional Psychology: Research and Practice, 17*(4), 316–321.

Haley, J. (1976). *Problem-solving therapy*. New York: Harper & Row.

Handelsman, M. M. (1986a). Ethics training at the master's level: A national survey. *Professional Psychology: Research and Practice, 17*(1), 24–26.

Handelsman, M. M. (1986b). Problems with ethics training by "osmosis." *Professional Psychology: Research and Practice, 17*(4), 371–372.

Handelsman, M. M., Kemper, M. B., Kesson-Craig, P., McLain, J., & Johnsrud, C. (1986). Use, content, and readability of written informed consent forms for treatment. *Professional Psychology: Research and Practice, 17*(6), 514–518.

Hansen, J. C. (Ed.). (1982). *Values, ethics, legalities and the family therapist* (Family Therapy Collection No. 1, L. L'Abate, issue editor). Rockville, MD: Aspen.

Hansen, J., Stevic, R., & Warner, R. (1977). *Counseling: Theory and process* (2nd ed.). Boston: Allyn & Bacon.

Hansen, J., Warner, R., & Smith, E. (1980). *Group counseling: Theory and process* (2nd ed.). Chicago: Rand McNally.

Hare-Mustin, R. T. (1979). Family therapy and sex role stereotypes. *The Counseling Psychologist, 8*(1), 31–32.

Hare-Mustin, R. T. (1980). Family therapy may be dangerous to your health. *Professional Psychology, 11*(6), 935–938.

Hare-Mustin, R. T., & Hall, J. E. (1981). Procedures for responding to ethics complaints against psychologists. *American Psychologist, 36*(12), 1494–1505.

Hare-Mustin, R. T., Marecek, J., Kaplan, A. G., & Liss-Levinson, N. (1979). Rights of clients, responsibilities of therapists. *American Psychologist, 34*(1), 3–16.

Hargrove, D. S. (1986). Ethical issues in rural mental health practice. *Professional Psychology: Research and Practice, 17*(1), 20–23.

Hart, G. M. (1978). *Values clarification for counselors.* Springfield, IL: Charles C Thomas.

Hart, G. M. (1982). *The process of clinical supervision.* Baltimore: University Park Press.

Hayman, P. M., & Covert, J. A. (1986). Ethical dilemmas in college counseling centers. *Journal of Counseling and Development, 64*(5), 318–320.

Hedgeman, B. S. (1985). Rehabilitation counselor certification. *Journal of Counseling and Development, 63*(10), 609–610.

Henkin, W. A. (1985). Toward counseling the Japanese in America: A cross-cultural primer. *Journal of Counseling and Development, 63*(8), 500–503.

Herink, R. (Ed.). (1980). *The psychotherapy handbook.* New York: New American Library.

Herron, W. G., & Sitkowski, S. (1986). Effect of fees on psychotherapy: What is the evidence? *Professional Psychology: Research and Practice, 17*(4), 347–351.

Hess, A. K., & Hess, K. A. (1983). Psychotherapy supervision: A survey of internship training practices. *Professional Psychology: Research and Practice, 14*(4), 504–513.

Hillerbrand, E., & Stone, G. L. (1986). Ethics and clients: A challenging mixture for counselors. *Journal of Counseling and Development, 64*(7), 419–420.

Hines, P. M., & Hare-Mustin, R. T. (1978). Ethical concerns in family therapy. *Professional Psychology, 9,* 165–171.

Hinkeldey, N. S., & Spokane, A. R. (1985). Effects of pressure and legal guideline clarity on counselor decision making in legal and ethical conflict situations. *Journal of Counseling and Development, 64*(4), 240–245.

Ho, D. Y. F. (1985). Cultural values and professional issues in clinical psychology: Implication from the Hong Kong experience. *American Psychologist, 40*(11), 1212–1218.

Hogan, D. B. (1979). *The regulation of psychotherapists: A handbook of state licensure laws* (4 vols.). Cambridge, MA: Ballinger.

Hollingsworth, D. K. (1985). The counselor and physical attractiveness: A response. *Journal of Counseling and Development, 63*(8), 488–489.

Hollis, J. W., & Wantz, R. A. (1983). *Counselor preparation 1983–85.* Muncie, IN: Accelerated Development.

Holroyd, J. (1983). Erotic contact as an instance of sex-biased therapy. In J. Murray & P. Abramson (Eds.), *Bias in psychotherapy* (pp. 285–308). New York: Praeger.

Holroyd, J., & Bouhoutsos, J. C. (1985). Biased reporting of therapist: Patient sexual intimacy. *Professional Psychology: Research and Practice, 16*(5), 701–709.

Holroyd, J., & Brodsky, A. (1977). Psychologists' attitudes and practices regarding erotic and nonerotic physical contact with patients. *American Psychologist, 32*(10), 843–849.

Holroyd, J. C., & Brodsky, A. (1980). Does touching patients lead to sexual intercourse? *Professional Psychology, 11*(5), 807–811.

Hopkins, B. R., & Anderson, B. S. (1985). *The counselor and the law* (2nd ed.). Alexandria, VA: AACD Press.

Huber, C. H., & Baruth, L. G. (1987). *Ethical, legal, and professional issues in the practice of marriage and family therapy.* Columbus, OH: Merrill.

Huddleston, J. E., & Engels, D. W. (1986). Issues related to the use of paradoxical techniques in counseling. *Journal of Counseling and Human Service Professions, 1*(1), 127–133.

Huey, W. C. (1986). Ethical concerns in school counseling. *Journal of Counseling and Development, 64*(5), 318–320.

Huhn, R. P., Zimpfer, D. G., Waltman, D. E., & Williamson, S. K. (1985). A survey of programs of professional preparation for group counseling. *The Journal for Specialists in Group Work, 10*(3), 124–133.

Humphrey, F. G. (1983). *Marital therapy.* Englewood Cliffs, NJ: Prentice-Hall.

Ibrahim, F. A. (1985a). Effective cross-cultural counseling and psychotherapy: A framework. *The Counseling Psychologist, 13*(4), 625–638.

Ibrahim, F. A. (1985b). Human rights and ethical issues in the use of advanced technology. *Journal of Counseling and Development, 64*(2), 134–145.

Ibrahim, F. A. (1986). *Cultural encapsulation of the APA ethical principles.* Unpublished manuscript, University of Connecticut, Storrs.

Ibrahim, F. A., & Arredondo, P. M. (1986). Ethical standards for cross-cultural counseling: Counselor preparation, practice, assessment, and research. *Journal of Counseling and Development, 64*(5), 349–352.

Imber, S. D., Glanz, L. M., Elkin, I., Sotsky, S. M., Boyer, J. L., & Leber, W. R. (1986). Ethical issues in psychotherapy research: Problems in a collaborative clinical trials study. *American Psychologist, 41*(2), 137–146.

Iscoe, I. (1982). Toward a viable community health psychology: Caveats from the experiences of the community mental health movement. *American Psychologist, 37*(8), 961–965.

Ivey, A. E. (1986). *Ethics and multicultural therapy: An unrealized dream.* Unpublished manuscript, University of Massachusetts, Amherst.

Ivey, A. E., Ivey, M. B., & Simek-Downing, L. (1987). *Counseling and psychotherapy: Integrating skills, theory, and practice* (2nd ed.). Englewood Cliffs, NJ: Prentice-Hall.

Jaffe, D. T. (1986). The inner strains of healing work: Therapy and self-renewal for health professionals. In C. D. Scott & J. Hawk (Eds.), *Heal thyself: The health of health care professionals.* New York: Brunner/Mazel.

Jason, L. A. (1985). Using the media to foster self-help groups. *Professional Psychology: Research and Practice, 16*(3), 455–464.

Johnson, M. (1986). Paradoxical interventions: From repugnance to cautious curiosity. *The Counseling Psychologist, 14*(2), 297–302.

Jones, E. E. (1985). Psychotherapy and counseling with black clients. In P. Pedersen (Ed.), *Handbook of cross-cultural counseling and therapy* (pp. 173–179). Westport, CT: Greenwood Press.

Jourard, S. (1968). *Disclosing man to himself.* New York: Van Nostrand Reinhold.

Jourard, S. (1971). *The transparent self* (rev. ed.). New York: Van Nostrand Reinhold.

Kagehiro, D. K., Mejia, J. A., & Garcia, J. E. (1985). Value of cultural pluralism to the generalizability of psychological theories: A reexamination. *Professional Psychology: Research and Practice, 16*(4), 481–494.

Kahn-Edrington, M. (1979). Abortion counseling. *The Counseling Psychologist, 8*(1), 37–38.

Kaplan, H. S. (1974). *The new sex therapy.* New York: Brunner/Mazel.

Kaplan, H., & Sadock, B. (Eds.) (1983). *Comprehensive group psychotherapy* (2nd ed.). Baltimore: Williams & Wilkins.

Kaser-Boyd, N., Adelman, H. S., & Taylor, L. (1985). Minors' ability to identify risks and benefits of therapy. *Professional Psychology: Research and Practice, 16*(3), 411–417.

Kaslow, F., & Steinberg, J. (1982). Ethical divorce therapy and divorce proceedings: A psycholegal perspective. In J. Hansen (Ed.), *Values, ethics, legalities and the family therapist.* Rockville, MD: Aspen.

Kaslow, N. J., & Rice, D. G. (1985). Developmental stresses of psychology internship training: What training staff can do to help. *Professional Psychology: Research and Practice, 16*(2), 253–261.

Katz, J. H. (1985). The sociopolitical nature of counseling. *The Counseling Psychologist, 13*(4), 615–624.

Keilin, W. G., & Bloom, L. J. (1986). Child custody evaluation practices: A survey of experienced professionals. *Professional Psychology: Research and Practice, 17*(4), 338–346.

Keith-Spiegel, P., & Koocher, G. (1985). *Ethics in psychology: Standards and cases.* New York: Random House.

Kempler, W. (1973). Gestalt therapy. In R. Corsini (Ed.), *Current psychotherapies.* Itasca, IL: F. E. Peacock.

Kilburg, R. R., Nathan, P. E., & Thoreson, R. W. (Eds.). (1986). *Professionals in distress: Issues, syndromes, and solutions in psychology.* Washington, DC: American Psychological Association.

Kingdon, M. A. (1979). Lesbians. *The Counseling Psychologist, 8*(1), 44–45.

Kitchener, K. S. (1984a). Guest editor's introduction. *The Counseling Psychologist, 12*(3), 15–18.

Kitchener, K. S. (1984b). Intuition, critical evaluation and ethical principles: The foundation for ethical decisions in counseling psychology. *The Counseling Psychologist, 12*(3), 43–55.

Kitchener, K. S. (1986). Teaching applied ethics in counselor education: An integration of psychological processes and philosophical analysis. *Journal of Counseling and Development, 64*(5), 306–310.

Klagsbrun, S. C. (1982). Ethics in hospice care. *American Psychologist, 37*(11), 1263–1265.

Knapp, S. (1980). A primer on malpractice for psychologists. *Professional Psychology, 11*(4), 606–612.

Knapp, S., & Vandecreek, L. (1982). Tarasoff: Five years later. *Professional Psychology, 13*(4), 511–516.

Knapp, S. J., & Vandecreek, L. (1985). Psychotherapy and privileged communicaiton in child custody cases. *Professional Psychology: Research and Practice, 16*(3), 398–410.

Knapp, S. J., Vandecreek, L., & Zirkel, P.A. (1985). Legal research techniques: What the psychologist needs to know. *Professional Psychology: Research and Practice, 16*(3), 363–372.

Kobocow, B., McGuire, J. M., & Blau, B. I. (1983). The influences of confidentiality conditions on self-disclosure of early adolescents. *Professional Psychology: Research and Practice, 14*(4), 435–443.

Kolko, D. J., & Milan, M. A. (1986). Acceptability of paradoxical interventions: Some paradoxes of psychotherapy research. *Professional Psychology: Research and Practice, 17*(6), 524–527.

Koocher, G. P. (1976). A bill of rights for children in psychotherapy. In G. P. Koocher (Ed.), *Children's rights and the mental health professions.* New York: Wiley.

Korelitz, A., & Schulder, D. (1982). The lawyer-therapist consultation team. *Journal of Marital and Family Therapy, 8*(1), 113–119.

Korman, M. (1974). National conference on levels and patterns of professional training in psychology. *American Psychologist, 29,* 441–449.

Kottler, J. A. (1982). Unethical behaviors we all do and pretend we do not. *The Journal for Specialists in Group Work, 7*(3), 182–186.

Kottler, J. A. (1985). The pursuit of excellence between the ideal and real in group counseling. *The Journal for Specialists in Group Work, 10*(3), 144–146.

Kottler, J. A. (1986). *On being a therapist.* San Francisco: Jossey-Bass.

Kurpius, D. J. (1986). Consultation: An important human and organizational intervention. *Journal of Counseling and Human Service Professions, 1*(1), 58–66.

LaFromboise, T. D. (1985). The role of cultural diversity in counseling psychology. *The Counseling Psychologist, 13*(4), 649–655.

Laing, R. D. (1967). *The politics of experience.* New York: Pantheon.

Lakin, M. (1986). Ethical challenges of group and dyadic psychotherapies: A comparative approach. *Professional Psychology: Research and Practice, 17*(5), 454–461.

Laliotis, D. A., & Grayson, J. H. (1985). Psychologist heal thyself: What is available for the impaired psychologist. *American Psychologist, 40*(1), 84–96.

Landman, J. T., & Dawes, R. M. (1982). Psychotherapy outcome. *American Psychologist, 37*(5), 504–516.

Laughran, W., & Bakken, G. M. (1984). The psychotherapist's responsibility toward third parties under current California law. *Western State University Law Review, 12*(1), 1–33.

Lefley, H. P. (1985). Mental-health training across cultures. In P. Pedersen (Ed.), *Handbook of cross-cultural counseling and therapy* (pp. 259–266). Westport, CT: Greenwood Press.

Lefley, H. P., & Pedersen, P. (Eds.). (1986). *Cross-cultural training for mental health professionals.* Springfield, IL: Charles C Thomas.

Leininger, M. M. (1985). Transcultural caring: A different way to help people. In P. Pedersen (Ed.), *Handbook of cross-cultural counseling and therapy* (pp. 107–115). Westport, CT: Greenwood Press.

Levenson, J. L. (1986). When a colleague practices unethically: Guidelines for intervention. *Journal of Counseling and Development, 64*(5), 315–317.

Levine, C. (1987). *Taking sides: Clashing views on controversial bioethical issues* (2nd ed.). Guilford, CT: Dushkin Publishing Group.

Levine, E. S., & Padilla, A. M. (1980). *Crossing cultures in therapy: Pluralistic counseling for the Hispanic.* Monterey, CA: Brooks/Cole.

Lewis, R. E. (1985). *Educating effective counselors for women clients: A survey of training practices.* Paper presented at the annual meeting of the American Psychological Association, Los Angeles.

Lief, H. (1982). Ethical problems in sex therapy. In M. Rosenbaum (Ed.), *Ethics and values in psychotherapy: A guidebook.* New York: Free Press.

Lifton, W. M. (1985). Reaction to "Professional training standards in group counseling: Idealistic or realistic?" *The Journal for Specialists in Group Work, 10*(3), 147–149.

Lindsey, R. T. (1984). Informed consent and deception in psychotherapy research: An ethical analysis. *The Counseling Psychologist, 12*(3), 79–86.

Lindsey, R. T. (1985). *Moral sensitivity: The relationship between training and experience.* Paper presented at annual convention of the American Psychological Association, Los Angeles.

Lipsitz, N. E. (1985). *The relationship between ethics training and ethical discrimination ability.* Paper presented at annual meeting of the American Psychological Association, Los Angeles.

Liss-Levinson, N. (1979). Women with sexual concerns. *The Counseling Psychologist, 8*(1), 36–37.

Loewenberg, F., & Dolgoff, R. (1985). *Ethical decisions for social work practice* (2nd ed.). Itasca, IL: F. E. Peacock.

Lonner, W. J., & Sundberg, N. D. (1985). Assessment in cross-cultural counseling and therapy. In P. Pedersen (Ed.), *Handbook of cross-cultural counseling and therapy* (pp. 199–205). Westport, CT: Greenwood Press.

Lorion, R. P., & Parron, D. L. (1985). Countering the countertransference: A strategy for treating the untreatable. In P. Pedersen (Ed.), *Handbook of cross-cultural counseling and therapy* (pp. 79–86). Westport, CT: Greenwood Press.

Lowman, R. L. (1985). Ethical practice of psychological consultation: Not an impossible dream. *The Counseling Psychologist, 13*(3), 466–472.

Lum, D. (1986). *Social work practice and people of color: A process-stage approach.* Monterey, CA: Brooks/Cole.

Lurie, B. D. (1985). *A summary of California mental health confidentiality laws.* Unpublished manuscript.

Mabe, A. R., & Rollin, S. A. (1986). The role of a code of ethical standards in counseling. *Journal of Counseling and Development, 64*(5), 294–297.

Mahoney, M. J. (1986). Paradoxical intention, symptom prescription, and principles of therapeutic change. *The Counseling Psychologist, 14*(2), 283–290.

Mappes, D. C., Robb, G. P., & Engels, D. W. (1985). Conflicts between ethics and law in counseling and psychotherapy. *Journal of Counseling and Development, 64*(4), 246–252.

Margolin, G. (1982). Ethical and legal considerations in marital and family therapy. *American Psychologist, 37*(7), 788–801.

Maslach, C. (1982). *Burnout: The cost of caring.* Englewood Cliffs, NJ: Prentice-Hall (Spectrum).

Maslow, A. (1968). *Toward a psychology of being* (2nd ed.). New York: Van Nostrand Reinhold.

Maslow, A. (1970). *Motivation and personality* (2nd ed.). New York: Harper & Row.

May, R. (1967). *Psychology and the human dilemma.* New York: Van Nostrand Reinhold.

McGoldrick, M., Pearce, J. K., & Giordano, J. (Eds.). (1982). *Ethnicity and family therapy.* New York: Guilford Press.

McGuire, J. M., Toal, P., & Blau, B. (1985). The adult client's conception of confidentiality in the therapeutic relationship. *Professional Psychology: Research and Practice, 16*(3), 375–384.

Melton, G. B. (1981a). Children's participation in treatment planning: Psychological and legal issues. *Professional Psychology, 12*(2), 246–252.

Melton, G. B. (1981b). Effects of a state law permitting minors to consent to psychotherapy. *Professional Psychology, 12*(5), 647–654.

Messer, S. B. (1986). Behavioral and psychoanalytic perspectives at therapeutic choice points. *American Psychologist, 41*(1), 1261–1272.

Messina, J. J. (1985). The National Academy of Certified Clinical Mental Health Counselors: Creating a new professional identity. *Journal of Counseling and Development, 63*(10), 607–608.

Meyer, R., & Smith, S. (1977). A crisis in group therapy. *American Psychologist, 32*(8), 638–643.

Miller, D. J., & Thelen, M. H. (1986). Knowledge and beliefs about confidentiality in psychotherapy. *Professional Psychology: Research and Practice, 17*(1), 15–19.

Mills, D. H. (1984). Ethics education and adjudication within psychology. *American Psychologist, 39*(6), 669–675.

Minuchin, S. (1974). *Families and family therapy.* Cambridge, MA: Harvard University Press.

Morran, D. K., & Stockton, R. (1985). Perspectives on group research programs. *The Journal for Specialists in Group Work, 10*(4), 186–191.

Morrison, J., Layton, B., & Newman, J. (1982). Ethical conflict in clinical decision making: A challenge for family therapists. In J. Hansen (Ed.), *Values, ethics, legalities and the family therapist.* Rockville, MD: Aspen.

Moses, A. E., & Hawkins, R. O. (1982). *Counseling lesbian women and gay men: A life issues approach.* St. Louis: C. V. Mosby.

Muehleman, T., & Kimmons, C. (1981). Psychologists' views on child abuse reporting, confidentiality, life, and the law: An exploratory study. *Professional Psychology, 12*(5), 631–638.

Muehleman, T., Pickens, B. K., & Robinson, F. (1985). Informing clients about the limits to confidentiality, risks, and their rights: Is self-disclosure inhibited? *Professional Psychology: Research and Practice, 16*(3), 385–397.

National Association of Social Workers. (1979). *Code of ethics.* Silver Spring, MD: Author.

National Federation of Societies for Clinical Social Work. (1985). *Code of Ethics.* Silver Spring, MD: Author.

Negligence: Walking the liability tightrope. (1985). *California State Psychologist*, *20*(4).

Neimeyer, G. J., Fukuyama, M. A., Bingham, R. P., Hall, L. E., & Mussenden, M. E. (1986). Training cross-cultural counselors: A comparison of the pro-counselor and anti-counselor triad models. *Journal of Counseling and Development*, *64*(7), 437–439.

Newman, A. S. (1981). Ethical issues in the supervision of psychotherapy. *Professional Psychology*, *12*(6), 690–695.

Nielsen, T. (1983). Sexual abuse of boys: Current perspectives. *Personnel and Guidance Journal*, *62*(3), 139–142.

Norcross, J. C., & Prochaska, J. O. (1983). Clinicians' theoretical orientations: Selection, utilization, and efficacy. *Professional Psychology: Research and Practice*, *14*(2), 197–208.

Nutt, R. L. (1979). Review and preview of attitudes and values of counselors of women. *The Counseling Psychologist*, *8*(1), 18–20.

Okoawo, R. A., & Arredondo, P. M. (Eds.). (1983). *Human rights issues in counselor training and supervision: Annotated bibliography*. Alexandria, VA: Association for Counselor Education and Supervision.

Okun, B. F. (1986). Incest in family systems. *Journal of Counseling and Human Service Professions*, *1*(1), 67–78.

O'Shea, M., & Jessee, E. (1982). Ethical, value, and professional conflicts in systems therapy. In J. Hansen (Ed.), *Values, ethics, legalities and the family therapist*. Rockville, MD: Aspen.

Padilla, A. M., & De Snyder, N. S. (1985). Counseling Hispanics: Strategies for effective intervention. In P. Pedersen (Ed.), *Handbook of cross-cultural counseling and therapy* (pp. 157–164). Westport, CT: Greenwood Press.

Palmer, J. O. (1980). *A primer of eclectic psychotherapy*. Monterey, CA: Brooks/Cole.

Paradise, L., & Siegelwaks, B. (1982). Ethical training for group leaders. *The Journal for Specialists in Group Work*, *7*(3), 162–166.

Parker, W. M., Valley, M. M., & Geary, C. A. (1986). Acquiring cultural knowledge for counselors in training: A multifaceted approach. *Counselor Education and Supervision*, *26*(1), 61–71.

Parloff, M. B. (1979). Can psychotherapy research guide the policymaker? *American Psychologist*, *34*(4), 296–306.

Patterson, C. H. (1985a). New light for counseling theory. *Journal of Counseling and Development*, *63*(6), 349–350.

Patterson, C. H. (1985b). *The therapeutic relationship: Foundations for an eclectic psychotherapy*. Monterey, CA: Brooks/Cole.

Patterson, C. H. (1986). *Theories of counseling and psychotherapy* (4th ed.). New York: Harper & Row.

Pedersen, P. (1977). The triad model of cross-cultural counselor training. *Personnel and Guidance Journal*, *56*, 94–100.

Pedersen, P. (1978). Four dimensions of cross-cultural skill counselor training. *Personnel and Guidance Journal*, *56*, 480–484.

Pedersen, P. (1981). Triad counseling. In R. Corsini (Ed.), *Innovative psychotherapies*, (pp. 840–855). New York: Wiley.

Pedersen, P. (1983, August). *Developing interculturally skilled counselors: A training program*. Paper presented at the annual meeting of the American Psychological Association, Anaheim, CA.

Pedersen, P. (Ed.). (1985a). *Handbook of cross-cultural counseling and therapy*. Westport, CT: Greenwood Press.

Pedersen, P. (1985b). Intercultural criteria for mental-health training. In P. Pedersen (Ed.), *Handbook of cross-cultural counseling and therapy* (pp. 315–321). Westport, CT: Greenwood Press.

Pedersen, P. B. (1986). *Are the APA ethical principles culturally encapsulated?* Unpublished manuscript, Syracuse University.

Pedersen, P., Avelondo, P. M., Lefly, H. P., Johnson, S. E., Trimble, J. E., & Murase, K. (1983, August). *Symposium: Cross-cultural training programs for counselor education.* Paper presented at the annual meeting of the American Psychological Association, Anaheim, CA.

Pedersen, P., Holwill, F., & Shapiro, J. (1978). A cross-cultural training procedure for classes in counselor education. *Counselor Education and Supervision, 17,* 233–237.

Pedersen, P. B., Draguns, J., Lonner, W., & Trimble, J. (Eds.). (1981). *Counseling across cultures* (rev. ed.). Honolulu: University Press of Hawaii.

Pedersen, P. B., & Marsella, A. J. (1982). The ethical crisis for cross-cultural counseling and therapy. *Professional Psychology, 13*(4), 492–500.

Pelsma, D. M., & Borgers, S. G. (1986). Experience-based ethics: A developmental model of learning ethical reasoning. *Journal of Counseling and Development, 64*(5), 311–314.

Pfifferling, J. H. (1986). Cultural antecedents promoting professional impairment. In C. D. Scott & J. Hawk (Eds.), *Heal thyself: The health of health care professionals.* New York: Brunner/Mazel.

Pine, G. J., & Boy, A. V. (1980). What counselors might like to read about counseling and values: An annotated bibliography. *Personnel and Guidance Journal, 58*(9), 631–634.

Pines, A., & Aronson, E., with Kafry, D. (1981). *Burnout: From tedium to personal growth.* New York: Free Press.

Pines, A. M. (1986). Who is to blame for helpers' burnout? Environmental impact. In C. D. Scott & J. Hawk (Eds.), *Heal thyself: The health of health care professionals.* New York: Brunner/Mazel.

Pinney, E. L. (1983). Ethical and legal issues in group psychotherapy. In H. Kaplan & B. Sadock (Eds.), *Comprehensive group psychotherapy* (2nd ed.). Baltimore: Williams & Wilkins.

Plotkin, R. (1978, March). Confidentiality in group counseling. *APA Monitor,* p. 14.

Ponzo, Z. (1985). The counselor and physical attractiveness. *Journal of Counseling and Development, 63*(8), 482–485.

Pope, K. S. (1984). New guidelines for reporting dangerousness and abuse. *California State Psychologist, 19*(4), 3–4.

Pope, K. S. (1985a). Dual relationships: A violation of ethical, legal, and clinical standards. *California State Psychologist, 20*(3), 3–5.

Pope, K. S. (1985b). Standards for psychological assistants. *California State Psychologist, 20*(2), 3–5.

Pope, K. S. (1985c). The suicidal client: Guidelines for assessment and treatment. *California State Psychologist, 20*(5), 3–7.

Pope, K. S. (1985d). When a client files an ethical complaint against you: Some initial steps to take. *California State Psychologist, 20*(4), 3–4.

Pope, K. S., & Bouhoutsos, J. C. (1986). *Sexual intimacy between therapists and patients.* New York: Praeger.

Pope, K. S., Keith-Spiegel, P., & Tabachnick, B. G. (1986). Sexual attraction to clients: The human therapist and the (sometimes) inhuman training system. *American Psychologist, 41*(2), 147–158.

Pope, K. S., Levenson, H., & Schover, L. R. (1979). Sexual intimacy in psychology training: Results and implications of a national survey. *American Psychologist, 34*(8), 682–689.

Pope, K. S., Schover, L. R., & Levenson, H. (1980). Sexual behavior between clinical supervisors and trainees: Implications for professional standards. *Professional Psychology, 10,* 157–162.

Portwood, D. (1978, January). A right to suicide? *Psychology Today,* pp. 66–74.

Powell, C. J. (1982, August). *Adolescence and the right to die: Issues of autonomy, competence and paternalism.* Paper presentation at the meeting of the American Psychological Association, Washington, DC.

Powell, C. T. (1984). Ethical principles and issues of competence in counseling adolescents. *The Counseling Psychologist, 12*(3), 57–68.

Price, A., Omizo, M., & Hammett, V. (1986). Counseling clients with AIDS. *Journal of Counseling and Development, 65*(2), 96–97.

Prochaska, J. (1984). *Systems of psychotherapy: A transtheoretical analysis* (2nd ed.). Homewood, IL: Dorsey Press.

Prochaska, J. O., & Norcross, J. C. (1983). Psychotherapists' perspectives on treating themselves and their clients for psychic distress. *Professional Psychology: Research and Practice, 14*(5), 642–655.

Psychology Examining Committee. (1980). *Newsletter.* Sacramento, CA: Author.

Quackenbos, S., Privette, G., & Klentz, B. (1986). Psychotherapy and religion: Rapprochement or antithesis? *Journal of Counseling and Development, 65*(2), 82–85.

Ray, L. Y., & Johnson, N. (1983). Adolescent suicide. *Personnel and Guidance Journal, 62*(3), 131–135.

Reaves, R. P. (1986). Legal liability and psychologists. In R. R. Kilburg, P. E. Nathan, & R. W. Thoreson (Eds.), *Professionals in distress: Issues, syndromes, and solutions in psychology.* Washington, DC: American Psychological Association.

Reisman, J. M. (1986). Psychotherapy as a professional relationship. *Professional Psychology: Research and Practice, 17*(6), 565–569.

Rest, J. R. (1984). Research on moral development: Implications for training counseling psychologists. *The Counseling Psychologist, 12*(3), 19–29.

Richardson, B. K., & Bradley, L. J. (1985). *Community agency counseling: An emergency specialty in counselor preparation programs.* Alexandria, VA: American Association for Counseling and Development.

Ridley, C. R. (1984). Clinical treatment of the nondisclosing black client: A therapeutic paradox. *American Psychologist, 39*(11), 1234–1244.

Ridley, C. R. (1985). Imperatives for ethnic and cultural relevance in psychology training programs. *Professional Psychology: Research and Practice, 16*(5), 611–622.

Ridley, C. R., & Tan, S. Y. (1986). Unintentional paradoxes and potential pitfalls in paradoxical psychotherapy. *The Counseling Psychologist, 14*(2), 303–308.

Ritchie, M. H. (1986). Counseling the involuntary client. *Journal of Counseling and Development, 64*(8), 516–518.

Roberts, A. L. (1982). Ethical guidelines for group leaders. *The Journal for Specialists in Group Work, 7*(3), 174–181.

Roberts, G. T., Murrell, P. H., Thomas, R. E., & Claxton, C. S. (1982). Ethical concerns for counselor educators. *Counselor Education and Supervision, 22*, 8–14.

Robinson, D. N. (1984). Ethics and advocacy. *American Psychologist, 39*(7), 787–793.

Robinson, S. E., & Gross, D. R. (1985). Ethics of consultation: The Canterville ghost. *The Counseling Psychologist, 13*(3), 444–465.

Robinson, S. E., & Gross, D. R. (1986). Counseling research: Ethics and issues. *Journal of Counseling and Development, 64*(5), 331–333.

Robinson, W. L., & Reid, P. T. (1985). Sexual intimacies in psychology revisited. *Professional Psychology: Research and Practice, 16*(4), 512–520.

Roeske, N. C. A. (1986). Risk factors: Predictable hazards of a health care career. In C. D. Scott & J. Hawk (Eds.), *Heal thyself: The health of health care professionals.* New York: Brunner/Mazel.

Rogers, C. (1942). *Counseling and psychotherapy.* Cambridge, MA: Houghton Mifflin.

Rogers, C. (1951). *Client-centered therapy*. Boston: Houghton Mifflin.

Rogers, C. (1961). *On becoming a person*. Boston: Houghton Mifflin.

Rogers, C. (1980). *A way of being*. Palo Alto, CA: Houghton Mifflin.

Rokeach, M., & Regan, J. F. (1980). The role of values in the counseling situation. *Personnel and Guidance Journal*, 58(9), 576–582.

Romero, D. (1985). Cross-cultural counseling: Brief reactions for the practitioner. *The Counseling Psychologist*, 13(4), 665–671.

Rosenbaum, M. (1982a). Ethical problems of group psychotherapy. In M. Rosenbaum (Ed.), *Ethics and values in psychotherapy: A guidebook*. New York: Free Press.

Rosenbaum, M. (Ed.). (1982b). *Ethics and values in psychotherapy: A guidebook*. New York: Free Press.

Roth, L. H., & Meisel, A. (1977). Dangerousness, confidentiality and the duty to warn. *American Journal of Psychiatry*, 13(4), 508–511.

Royer, R. I. (1985). *Ethical orientation of mental health practitioners: A comparative study*. Paper presented at the annual convention of the American Psychological Association, Los Angeles.

Ruback, R. B. (1982). Issues in family law: Implications for therapists. In J. Hansen (Ed.), *Values, ethics, legalities and the family therapist*. Rockville, MD: Aspen.

Ruback, R. B. (1984). Family law. In R. Woody (Ed.), *The law and the practice of human services*. San Francisco: Jossey-Bass.

Rubin, S. S. (1986). Cheating, ethics, and graduate training in professional psychology: Crime and punishment on misjudgment and repair. *Professional Psychology: Research and Practice*, 17(1), 10–14.

Rychlak, J. F. (1985). Eclecticism in psychological theorizing: Good and bad. *Journal of Counseling and Development*, 63(6), 351–353.

Saeki, C., & Borow, H. (1985). Counseling and psychotherapy: East and West. In P. Pedersen (Ed.), *Handbook of cross-cultural counseling and therapy* (pp. 223–229). Westport, CT: Greenwood Press.

Sanders, J. R., & Keith-Spiegel, P. (1980). Formal and informal adjudication of ethics complaints against psychologists. *American Psychologist*, 35(12), 1096–1105.

Savickas, M. L., Marquart, C. D., & Supinski, C. R. (1986). Effective supervision in groups. *Counselor Education and Supervision*, 26(1), 17–25.

Savitsky, J. C., & Karras, D. A. (1984). Rights of institutionalized patients. In R. Woody (Ed.), *The law and practice of human services*. San Francisco: Jossey-Bass.

Scarato, A. M., & Sigall, B. A. (1979). Multiple role women. *The Counseling Psychologist*, 8(1), 26–27.

Schmidt, L. D. (1986). Some questions about paradoxical interventions. *The Counseling Psychologist*, 14(2), 309–312.

Schneider, M. G., & Tremble, B. (1986). Training service providers to work with gay or lesbian adolescents: A workshop. *Journal of Counseling and Development*, 65(2), 98–99.

Schneider, W. J., & Pinkerton, R. S. (1986). Short-term psychotherapy and graduate training in psychology. *Professional Psychology: Research and Practice*, 17(6), 574–579.

Schutz, B. (1982). *Legal liability in psychotherapy*. San Francisco: Jossey-Bass.

Schwitzgebel, R. L., & Schwitzgebel, R. K. (1980). *Law and psychological practice*. New York: Wiley.

Scott, C. D., & Hawk, J. (Eds.). (1986). *Heal thyself: The health of health care professionals*. New York: Brunner/Mazel.

Secrest, L., & Hoffman, P. E. (1982). The philosophical underpinnings of peer review. *Professional Psychology*, 13(1), 14–18.

Sell, J. M., Gottlieb, M. C., & Schoenfeld, L. (1986). Ethical considerations of social/romantic relationships with present and former clients. *Professional Psychology: Research and Practice, 17*(6), 504–508.

Sesan, R., Fraerk, K., & Murphy, S. (1986). The support network: Crisis intervention for extrafamilial child sexual abuse. *Professional Psychology: Research and Practice, 17*(2), 138–146.

Seymour, W. (1982). Counselor/therapist values and therapeutic style. In J. Hansen (Ed.), *Values, ethics, legalities and the family therapist*. Rockville, MD: Aspen.

Shah, S. (1969). Privileged communications, confidentiality, and privacy: Privileged communications. *Professional Psychology, 1*(1), 56–69.

Shah, S. (1970a). Privileged communications, confidentiality, and privacy: Confidentiality. *Professional Psychology, 1*(2), 159–164.

Shah, S. (1970b). Privileged communications, confidentiality, and privacy: Privacy. *Professional Psychology, 1*(3), 243–252.

Sheeley, V. L., & Herlihy, B. (1986). The ethics of confidentiality and privileged communication. *Journal of Counseling and Human Service Professions, 1*(1), 141–148.

Shimberg, B. (1981). Testing for licensure and certification. *American Psychologist, 36*(10), 1138–1146.

Siegel, M. (1979). Privacy, ethics, and confidentiality. *Professional Psychology, 10*(2), 249–258.

Smith, D. (1981). Unfinished business with informed consent procedures. *American Psychologist, 36*(1), 220–226.

Smith, D. (1982). Trends in counseling and psychotherapy. *American Psychologist, 37*(7), 802–809.

Smith, D. K., & Lyon, M. A. (1986). School psychologists' attributions for success and failure in consultations with parents and teachers. *Professional Psychology: Research and Practice, 17*(3), 205–209.

Smith, E. M. J. (1985a). Counseling black women. In P. Pedersen (Ed.), *Handbook of cross-cultural counseling and therapy* (pp. 181–187). Westport, CT: Greenwood Press.

Smith, E. M. J. (1985b). Ethnic minorities: Life stress, social support, and mental health issues. *The Counseling Psychologist, 13*(4), 537–579.

Smith, R. L., & Karpati, F. S. (1985). Credentialing career counselors. *Journal of Counseling and Development, 63*(10), 611.

Snow, J. S., & Paternite, C. E. (1986). Individual and family therapy in the treatment of children. *Professional Psychology: Research and Practice, 17*(3), 242–250.

Sophie, J. (1982). Counseling lesbians. *Personnel and Guidance Journal, 60*(6), 341–345.

Spiegel, S. B. (1979). Separate principles for counselors of women: A new form of sexism. *The Counseling Psychologist, 8*(1), 49–50.

Spitizer, R. L., Skodol, A. E., Gibbon, M., & Williams, J. (1981). *DSM-III Case book*. Washington, DC: American Psychiatric Association.

Sporakowski, M. J. (1982). The regulation of marital and family therapy. In J. Hansen (Ed.), *Values, ethics, legalities and the family therapist*. Rockville, MD: Aspen.

Sporakowski, M. J., & Staniszewski, W. P. (1980). The regulation of marriage and family therapy: An update. *Journal of Marital and Family Therapy, 6*(3), 335–348.

Stadler, H. A. (1986). To counsel or not to counsel: The ethical dilemma of dual relationships. *Journal of Counseling and Human Service Professions, 1*(1), 134–140.

Stadler, H., & Paul, R. D. (1986). Counselor educators' preparations in ethics. *Journal of Counseling and Development, 64*(5), 328–330.

Steinberg, J. L. (1980). Towards an interdisciplinary commitment: A divorce lawyer proposes attorney-therapist marriages or, at the least, an affair. *Journal of Marital and Family Therapy, 6*(3), 259–268.

Steindler, E. M. (1986). The role of professional organizations in developing support. In C. D. Scott & J. Hawk (Eds.), *Heal thyself: The health of health care professionals.* New York: Brunner/Mazel.

Steininger, M., Newell, J. D., & Garcia, L. T. (1984). *Ethical issues in psychology.* Homewood, IL: Dorsey Press.

Stensrud, R., & Stensrud, K. (1981). Counseling may be hazardous to your health: How we teach people to feel powerless. *Personnel and Guidance Journal, 59*(5), 300–304.

Stern, S. (1984). Professional training and professional competence: A critique of current thinking. *Professional Psychology: Research and Practice, 15*(2), 230–243.

Stiles, W. B., Shapiro, D. A., & Elliott, R. (1986). "Are all psychotherapies equivalent?" *American Psychologist, 41*(2), 165–180.

Stolz, S., & Associates. (1978). *Ethical issues in behavior modification.* San Francisco: Jossey-Bass.

Stone, L. A. (1985). National board for certified counselors: History, relationships, and projections. *Journal of Counseling and Development, 63*(10), 605–606.

Stricker, G. (1982). Ethical issues in psychotherapy research. In M. Rosenbaum (Ed.), *Ethics and values in psychotherapy: A guidebook.* New York: Free Press.

Stricker, G., Claiborn, W. L., & Bent, R. J. (1982). Peer review: An overview. *Professional Psychology, 13*(1), 5–8.

Strong, S. R. (1980). Christian counseling: A synthesis of psychological and Christian concepts. *Personnel and Guidance Journal, 58*(9), 589–597.

Strupp, H. H. (1986). Psychotherapy: Research, practice, and public policy (How to avoid dead ends). *American Psychologist, 41*(2), 120–130.

Stude, E. W., & McKelvey, J. (1979). Ethics and the law: Friend or foe? *Personnel and Guidance Journal, 57*(9), 453–456.

Sue, D. W. (1981a). *Counseling the culturally different: Theory and practice.* New York: Wiley.

Sue, D. W. (1981b). *Position paper on cross-cultural counseling competencies.* Education and Training Committee report delivered to Division 17, APA Executive Committee.

Sue, D. W., Bernier, J. E., Durran, A., Feinberg, L., Pedersen, P., Smith, E. J., & Nuttall, E. V. (1982). Position paper: Cross-cultural counseling competencies. *The Counseling Psychologist, 10*(2), 45–52.

Sue, D. W., & Sue, D. (1985). Asian-Americans and Pacific islanders. In P. Pedersen (Ed.), *Handbook of cross-cultural counseling and therapy* (pp. 141–146). Westport, CT: Greenwood Press.

Sue, S. (1983). Ethnic minority issues in psychology. *American Psychologist, 38*(5), 583–592.

Sue, S., Akutsu, P. D., & Higashi, C. (1985). Training issues in conducting therapy with ethnic-minority-group clients. In P. Pedersen (Ed.), *Handbook of cross-cultural counseling and therapy* (pp. 275–280). Westport, CT: Greenwood Press.

Suinn, R. M. (1985). Research and practice in cross-cultural counseling. *The Counseling Psychologist, 13*(4), 673–684.

Sundal-Hansen, L. S. (1985). Sex-role issues in counseling women and men. In P. Pedersen (Ed.), *Handbook of cross-cultural counseling and therapy* (pp. 213–222). Westport, CT: Greenwood Press.

Swanson, C. (1983). The law and the counselor. In B. Pate & J. Brown (Eds.), *Being a counselor: Directions and challenges for the '80s.* Monterey, CA: Brooks/Cole.

Szasz, T. (1974). *The myth of mental illness: Foundations of a theory of personal conduct* (rev. ed.). New York: Harper & Row.

Szasz, T. (1986). The case against suicide prevention. *American Psychologist, 41*(7), 806–812.

Talbutt, L. C. (1981). Ethical standards: Assets and limitations. *Personnel and Guidance Journal, 60*(2), 110–112.

Taylor, L., Adelman, H. S., & Kaser-Boyd, N. (1985). Exploring minors' reluctance and dissatisfaction with psychotherapy. *Professional Psychology: Research and Practice, 16*(3), 418–425.

Tennyson, W. W., & Strom, S. A. (1986). Beyond professional standards: Developing responsibleness. *Journal of Counseling and Development, 64*(5), 298–302.

Thackrey, M. (1985). Breakdown in professional self-monitoring: Private practice announcements. *Professional Psychology: Research and Practice, 16*(2), 163–166.

Theaman, M. (1984). The impact of peer review on professional practice. *American Psychologist, 39*(4), 406–414.

Thomas, C. W. (1985). Counseling in a cultural context. *The Counseling Psychologist, 13*(4), 657–663.

Thoreson, R. W., Budd, F. C., & Krauskopf, C. J. (1986). Perceptions of alcohol misuse and work behavior among professionals: Identification and intervention. *Professional Psychology: Research and Practice, 17*(3), 210–216.

Tokunaga, H. T. (1984). Ethical issues in consultation: An evaluative review. *Professional Psychology: Research and Practice, 15*(6), 811–821.

Tremblay, J. M., Herron, W. G., & Schultz, C. L. (1986). Relation between therapeutic orientation and personality in psychotherapists. *Professional Psychology: Research and Practice, 17*(2), 106–110.

Triandis, H. (1985). Some major dimensions of cultural variation in client populations. In P. Pedersen (Ed.), *Handbook of cross-cultural counseling and therapy* (pp. 21–28). Westport, CT: Greenwood Press.

Triandis, H. C., & Brislin, R. W. (1984). Cross cultural psychology. *American Psychologist, 39*(9), 1006–1016.

Tryon, G. W. (1986). Abuse of therapists by patients: A national survey. *Professional Psychology: Research and Practice, 17*(4), 357–363.

Tymchuk, A. J. (1981). Ethical decision making and psychological treatment. *Journal of Psychiatric Treatment and Evaluation, 3*, 507–513.

Tymchuk, A. J., & Associates. (1979). Survey of training in ethics in APA-approved clinical psychology programs. *American Psychologist, 34*(12), 1168–1170.

Tymchuk, A. J., Drapkin, R., Major-Kinsley, S., Ackerman, A. B., Coffman, E. W., & Baum, M. S. (1982). Ethical decision making and psychologists' attitudes toward training in ethics. *Professional Psychology, 13*(3), 412–421.

Uomoto, J. M. (1986). Examination of psychological distress in ethnic minorities from a learned helplessness framework. *Professional Psychology: Research and Practice, 17*(5), 448–453.

Upchurch, D. W. (1985). Ethical standards and the supervisory process. *Counselor Education and Supervision, 75*(2), 90–98.

Van Hoose, W. (1986). Ethical principles in counseling. *Journal of Counseling and Development, 65*(3), 168–169.

Van Hoose, W. H., & Kottler, J. A. (1985). *Ethical and legal issues in counseling and psychotherapy* (2nd ed.). San Francisco: Jossey-Bass.

Vitulano, L. A., & Copeland, B. A. (1980). Trends in continuing education and competency demonstration. *Professional Psychology, 11*(6), 891–897.

Wahl, W. K., & Guy, J. D. (undated). *The utilization of individual therapy by psychologists practicing psychotherapy.* Unpublished paper.

Ward, D. E. (1983). The trend toward eclecticism and the development of comprehensive models to guide counseling and psychotherapy. *Personnel and Guidance Journal, 62*(3), 154–157.

Warnath, C. F. (1979). Counselor burnout: Existential crisis or a problem for the profession? *Personnel and Guidance Journal, 57*(7), 325–330.

Watkins, C. E. (1983). Transference phenomena in the counseling situation. *Personnel and Guidance Journal, 62*(4), 206–210.

Watkins, C. E. (1985). Countertransference: Its impact on the counseling situation. *Journal of Counseling and Development, 63*(6), 356–359.

Watzlawick, P., Weakland, J., & Fisch, R. (1974). *Change: Principles of problem formulation and problem resolution.* New York: Norton.

Weeks, G. R., & L'Abate, L. (1982). *Paradoxical psychotherapy: Theory and practice with individuals, couples, and families.* New York: Brunner/Mazel.

Wehrly, B., & Watson-Gegeo, K. (1985). Ethnographic methodologies as applied to the study of cross-cultural counseling. In P. Pedersen (Ed.), *Handbook of cross-cultural counseling and therapy* (pp. 65–71). Westport, CT: Greenwood Press.

Welfel, E. R., & Lipsitz, N. E. (1984). The ethical behavior of professional psychologists: A critical analysis of the research. *The Counseling Psychologist, 12*(3), 31–42.

White, M. D., & White, C. A. (1981). Involuntary committed patients' constitutional right to refuse treatment. *American Psychologist, 36*(9), 953–962.

Widiger, T. A., & Rorer, L. G. (1984). The responsible psychotherapist. *American Psychologist, 39*(5), 503–515.

Wilcoxon, S. A. (1986). Engaging non-attending family members in marital and family counseling: Ethical issues. *Journal of Counseling and Development, 64*(5), 323–324.

Wilcoxon, S. A., & Comas, R. E. (1986). Contemporary issues in family counseling: Implications for counselors. *Journal of Counseling and Human Service Professions, 1*(1), 118–126.

Willison, B. G., & Masson, R. L. (1986). The role of touch in therapy: An adjunct to communication. *Journal of Counseling and Development, 64*(8), 497–500.

Winkelpleck, J. M., & Westfeld, J. S. (1982). Counseling considerations with gay couples. *Personnel and Guidance Journal, 60*(5), 294–345.

Witmer, J. M., Wedl, L., & Black, B. (1986). Genetic counseling: Ethical and professional role implications. *Journal of Counseling and Development, 64*(5), 337–340.

Wolfgang, A. (1985). The function and importance of nonverbal behavior in intercultural counseling. In P. Pedersen, (Ed.), *Handbook of cross-cultural counseling and therapy.* Westport, CT: Greenwood Press.

Wolman, B. (1982). Ethical problems in termination of psychotherapy. In M. Rosenbaum (Ed.), *Ethics and values in psychotherapy: A guidebook.* New York: Free Press.

Woodman, N. J., & Lenna, H. R. (1980). *Counseling with gay men and women.* San Francisco: Jossey-Bass.

Woody, R. (1984). Professional responsibilities and liabilities. In R. Woody (Ed.), *The law and the practice of human services.* San Francisco: Jossey-Bass.

Woody, R. H., & Associates. (1984). *The law and the practice of human services.* San Francisco: Jossey-Bass.

Wrenn, C. G. (1985). Afterword: The culturally encapsulated counselor revisited. In P. Pedersen (Ed.), *Handbook of cross-cultural counseling and therapy* (pp. 323–329). Westport, CT: Greenwood Press.

Wright, R. H. (1981). What to do until the malpractice lawyer comes: A survivor's manual. *American Psychologist, 36*(12), 1535–1541.

Wyman, E., & McLaughlin, M. E. (1979). Traditional wives and mothers. *The Counseling Psychologist, 8*(1), 24–25.

Yalom, I. (1985). *The theory and practice of group psychotherapy* (3rd ed.). New York: Basic Books.

Ziegler, J. L., & Kanas, N. (1986). Coping with stress during internship. In C. D.

Scott & J. Hawk (Eds.), *Heal thyself: The health of health care professionals.* New York: Brunner/Mazel.

Zimpfer, D. G. (1976). Professional issues in groups. In D. G. Zimpfer (Ed.), *Group work in the helping professions: A bibliography.* Washington, DC: Association for Specialists in Group Work.

Zimpfer, D. G. (1985). Demystifying and clarifying small-group work. *The Journal for Specialists in Group Work, 10*(3), 175–181.

Zimpfer, D. G., Waltman, D. E., Williamson, S. K., & Huhn, R. P. (1985). Professional training standards in group counseling: Idealistic or realistic? *The Journal for Specialists in Group Work, 10*(3), 134–143.

# Appendix

- A. *Ethical Standards*, American Association for Counseling and Development (1981)
- B. *Code of Ethical Principles for Marriage and Family Therapists*, American Association for Marriage and Family Therapy (1985)
- C. *Code of Ethics*, National Association of Social Workers (1979)
- D. *Code of Ethics*, National Federation of Societies for Clinical Social Work (1985)
- E. *Principles of Medical Ethics, with Annotations Especially Applicable to Psychiatry*, American Psychiatric Association (1986)
- F. *Ethical Principles of Psychologists*, American Psychological Association (1981)
- G. *Ethical Standards for School Counselors*, American School Counselor Association (1984)
- H. *Code of Ethics*, Commission on Rehabilitation Counselor Certification (1974)
- I. Counselor Certification
- J. A Guide to Professional Organizations
    1. American Association for Counseling and Development
    2. American Association for Marriage and Family Therapy
    3. National Association of Social Workers
    4. American Psychological Association
    5. American Psychoanalytic Association

# A. Ethical Standards,
## American Association for Counseling and Development

(Approved by Executive Committee upon referral of the Board of Directors, January 17, 1981.)

## PREAMBLE

*The American Personnel and Guidance Association is an educational, scientific, and professional organization whose members are dedicated to the enhancement of the worth, dignity, potential, and uniqueness of each individual and thus to the service of society.*

*The Association recognizes that the role definitions and work settings of its members include a wide variety of academic disciplines, levels of academic preparation and agency services. This diversity reflects the breadth of the Association's interest and influence. It also poses challenging complexities in efforts to set standards for the performance of members, desired requisite preparation or practice, and supporting social, legal, and ethical controls.*

*The specification of ethical standards enables the Association to clarify to present and future members and to those served by members, the nature of ethical responsibilities held in common by its members.*

*The existence of such standards serves to stimulate greater concern by members for their own professional functioning and for the conduct of fellow professionals such as counselors, guidance and student personnel workers, and others in the helping professions. As the ethical code of the Association, this document establishes principles that define the ethical behavior of Association members.*

## Section A: General

1. The member influences the development of the profession by continuous efforts to improve professional practices, teaching, services, and research. Professional growth is continuous throughout the member's career and is exemplified by the development of a philosophy that explains why and how a member functions in the helping relationship. Members must gather data on their effectiveness and be guided by the findings.

2. The member has a responsibility both to the individual who is served and to the institution within which the service is performed to maintain high standards of professional conduct. The member strives to maintain the highest levels of professional services offered to the individuals to be served. The member also strives to assist the agency, organization, or institution in providing the highest caliber of professional services. The acceptance of employment in an institution implies that the member is in agreement with the general policies and principles of

the institution. Therefore the professional activities of the member are also in accord with the objectives of the institution. If, despite concerted efforts, the member cannot reach agreement with the employer as to acceptable standards of conduct that allow for changes in institutional policy conducive to the positive growth and development of clients, then terminating the affiliation should be seriously considered.

3. Ethical behavior among professional associates, both members and nonmembers, must be expected at all times. When information is possessed that raises doubt as to the ethical behavior of professional colleagues, whether Association members or not, the member must take action to attempt to rectify such a condition. Such action shall use the institution's channels first and then use procedures established by the state Branch, Division, or Association.

4. The member neither claims nor implies professional qualifications exceeding those possessed and is responsible for correcting any misrepresentations of these qualifications by others.

5. In establishing fees for professional counseling services, members must consider the financial status of clients and locality. In the event that the established fee structure is inappropriate for a client, assistance must be provided in finding comparable services of acceptable cost.

6. When members provide information to the public or to subordinates, peers or supervisors, they have a responsibility to ensure that the content is general, unidentified client information that is accurate, unbiased, and consists of objective, factual data.

7. With regard to the delivery of professional services, members should accept only those positions for which they are professionally qualified.

8. In the counseling relationship the counselor is aware of the intimacy of the relationship and maintains respect for the client and avoids engaging in activities that seek to meet the counselor's personal needs at the expense of that client. Through awareness of the negative impact of both racial and sexual stereotyping and discrimination, the counselor guards the individual rights and personal dignity of the client in the counseling relationship.

## Section B: Counseling relationship

This section refers to practices and procedures of individual and/or group counseling relationships.

The member must recognize the need for client freedom of choice. Under those circumstances where this is not possible, the member must apprise clients of restrictions that may limit their freedom of choice.

1. The member's *primary* obligation is to respect the integrity and promote the welfare of the client(s), whether the client(s) is (are) assisted individually or in a group relationship. In a group setting, the member is also responsible for taking reasonable precautions to protect individuals from physical and/or psychological trauma resulting from interaction within the group.

2. The counseling relationship and information resulting therefrom [must] be kept confidential, consistent with the obligations of the member as a professional person. In a group counseling setting, the counselor must set a norm of confidentiality regarding all group participants' disclosures.

3. If an individual is already in a counseling relationship with another professional person, the member does not enter into a counseling relationship without first contacting and receiving the approval of that other professional. If the member discovers that the client is in another counseling relationship after the counseling relationship begins, the member must gain the consent of the other professional or terminate the relationship, unless the client elects to terminate the other relationship.

4. When the client's condition indicates that there is clear and imminent danger to the client or others, the member must take reasonable personal action or inform responsible authorities. Consultation with other professionals must be used where possible. The assumption of responsibility for the client's behavior must be taken only after careful deliberation. The client must be involved in the resumption of responsibility as quickly as possible.

5. Records of the counseling relationship, including interview notes, test data, correspondence, tape recordings, and other documents,

are to be considered professional information for use in counseling and they should not be considered a part of the records of the institution or agency in which the counselor is employed unless specified by state statute or regulation. Revelation to others of counseling material must occur only upon the expressed consent of the client.

6. Use of data derived from a counseling relationship for purposes of counselor training or research shall be confined to content that can be disguised to ensure full protection of the identity of the subject client.

7. The member must inform the client of the purposes, goals, techniques, rules of procedure and limitations that may affect the relationship at or before the time that the counseling relationship is entered.

8. The member must screen prospective group participants, especially when the emphasis is on self-understanding and growth through self-disclosure. The member must maintain an awareness of the group participants' compatibility throughout the life of the group.

9. The member may choose to consult with any other professionally competent person about a client. In choosing a consultant, the member must avoid placing the consultant in a conflict of interest situation that would preclude the consultant's being a proper party to the member's efforts to help the client.

10. If the member determines an inability to be of professional assistance to the client, the member must either avoid initiating the counseling relationship or immediately terminate that relationship. In either event, the member must suggest appropriate alternatives. (The member must be knowledgeable about referral resources so that a satisfactory referral can be initiated). In the event the client declines the suggested referral, the member is not obligated to continue the relationship.

11. When the member has other relationships, particularly of an administrative, supervisory and/or evaluative nature with an individual seeking counseling services, the member must not serve as the counselor but should refer the individual to another professional. Only in instances where such an alternative is unavailable and where the individual's situation warrants counseling intervention should the member enter into and/or maintain a counseling relationship. Dual relationships with clients that might impair the member's objectivity and professional judgment (e.g., as with close friends or relatives, sexual intimacies with any client) must be avoided and/or the counseling relationship terminated through referral to another competent professional.

12. All experimental methods of treatment must be clearly indicated to prospective recipients and safety precautions are to be adhered to by the member.

13. When the member is engaged in short-term group treatment/training programs (e.g., marathons and other encounter-type or growth groups), the member ensures that there is professional assistance available during and following the group experience.

14. Should the member be engaged in a work setting that calls for any variation from the above statements, the member is obligated to consult with other professionals whenever possible to consider justifiable alternatives.

## Section C: Measurement and evaluation

The primary purpose of educational and psychological testing is to provide descriptive measures that are objective and interpretable in either comparative or absolute terms. The member must recognize the need to interpret the statements that follow as applying to the whole range of appraisal techniques including test and nontest data. Test results constitute only one of a variety of pertinent sources of information for personnel, guidance, and counseling decisions.

1. The member must provide specific orientation or information to the examinee(s) prior to and following the test administration so that the results of testing may be placed in proper perspective with other relevant factors. In so doing, the member must recognize the effects of socioeconomic, ethnic and cultural factors on test scores. It is the member's professional responsibility to use additional unvalidated information carefully in modifying interpretation of the test results.

2. In selecting tests for use in a given situation or with a particular client, the member must

consider carefully the specific validity, reliability, and appropriateness of the test(s). *General* validity, reliability and the like may be questioned legally as well as ethically when tests are used for vocational and educational selection, placement, or counseling.

3. When making any statements to the public about tests and testing, the member must give accurate information and avoid false claims or misconceptions. Special efforts are often required to avoid unwarranted connotations of such terms as *IQ* and *grade equivalent scores*.

4. Different tests demand different levels of competence for administration, scoring, and interpretation. Members must recognize the limits of their competence and perform only those functions for which they are prepared.

5. Tests must be administered under the same conditions that were established in their standardization. When tests are not administered under standard conditions or when unusual behavior or irregularities occur during the testing session, those conditions must be noted and the results designated as invalid or of questionable validity. Unsupervised or inadequately supervised test-taking, such as the use of tests through the mails, is considered unethical. On the other hand, the use of instruments that are so designed or standardized to be self-administered and self-scored, such as interest inventories, is to be encouraged.

6. The meaningfulness of test results used in personnel, guidance, and counseling functions generally depends on the examinee's unfamiliarity with the specific items on the test. Any prior coaching or dissemination of the test materials can invalidate test results. Therefore, test security is one of the professional obligations of the member. Conditions that produce most favorable test results must be made known to the examinee.

7. The purpose of testing and the explicit use of the results must be made known to the examinee prior to testing. The counselor must ensure that instrument limitations are not exceeded and that periodic review and/or retesting are made to prevent client stereotyping.

8. The examinee's welfare and explicit prior understanding must be the criteria for determining the recipients of the test results. The member must see that specific interpretation accompanies any release of individual or group test data. The interpretation of test data must be related to the examinee's particular concerns.

9. The member must be cautious when interpreting the results of research instruments possessing insufficient technical data. The specific purposes for the use of such instruments must be stated explicitly to examinees.

10. The member must proceed with caution when attempting to evaluate and interpret the performance of minority group members or other persons who are not represented in the norm group on which the instrument was standardized.

11. The member must guard against the appropriation, reproduction, or modifications of published tests or parts thereof without acknowledgement and permission from the previous publisher.

12. Regarding the preparation, publication and distribution of tests, reference should be made to:

a. *Standards for Educational and Psychological Tests and Manuals*, revised edition, 1974, published by the American Psychological Association on behalf of itself, the American Educational Research Association and the National Council on Measurement in Education.

b. The responsible use of tests: A position paper of AMEG, APGA, and NCME. *Measurement and Evaluation in Guidance*, 1972, 5, 385–388.

c. "Responsibilities of Users of Standardized Tests," APGA, *Guidepost*, October 5, 1978, pp. 5–8.

## Section D: Research and publication

1. Guidelines on research with human subjects shall be adhered to, such as:

a. *Ethical Principles in the Conduct of Research with Human Participants*, Washington, D.C.: American Psychological Association, Inc., 1973.

b. Code of Federal Regulations, Title 45, Subtitle A, Part 46, as currently issued.

2. In planning any research activity dealing with human subjects, the member must be aware of and responsive to all pertinent ethical principles and ensure that the research problem, design, and execution are in full compliance with them.

3. Responsibility for ethical research practice lies with the principal researcher, while others involved in the research activities share ethical obligation and full responsibility for their own actions.

4. In research with human subjects, researchers are responsible for the subjects' welfare throughout the experiment and they must take all reasonable precautions to avoid causing injurious psychological, physical, or social effects on their subjects.

5. All research subjects must be informed of the purpose of the study except when withholding information or providing misinformation to them is essential to the investigation. In such research the member must be responsible for corrective action as soon as possible following completion of the research.

6. Participation in research must be voluntary. Involuntary participation is appropriate only when it can be demonstrated that participation will have no harmful effects on subjects and is essential to the investigation.

7. When reporting research results, explicit mention must be made of all variables and conditions known to the investigator that might affect the outcome of the investigation or the interpretation of the data.

8. The member must be responsible for conducting and reporting investigations in a manner that minimizes the possibility that results will be misleading.

9. The member has an obligation to make available sufficient original research data to qualified others who may wish to replicate the study.

10. When supplying data, aiding in the research of another person, reporting research results, or in making original data available, due care must be taken to disguise the identity of the subjects in the absence of specific authorization from such subjects to do otherwise.

11. When conducting and reporting research, the member must be familiar with, and give recognition to, previous work on the topic, as well as to observe all copyright laws and follow the principles of giving full credit to all to whom credit is due.

12. The member must give due credit through joint authorship, acknowledgement, footnote statements, or other appropriate means to those who have contributed significantly to the research and/or publication, in accordance with such contributions.

13. The member must communicate to other members the results of any research judged to be of professional or scientific value. Results reflecting unfavorably on institutions, programs, services, or vested interests must not be withheld for such reasons.

14. If members agree to cooperate with another individual in research and/or publication, they incur an obligation to cooperate as promised in terms of punctuality of performance and with full regard to the completeness and accuracy of the information required.

15. Ethical practice requires that authors not submit the same manuscript or one essentially similar in content, for simultaneous publication consideration by two or more journals. In addition, manuscripts published in whole or in substantial part in another journal or published work should not be submitted for publication without acknowledgment and permission from the previous publication.

## Section E: Consulting

*Consultation* refers to a voluntary relationship between a professional helper and help-needing individual, group or social unit in which the consultant is providing help to the client(s) in defining and solving a work-related problem or potential problem with a client or client system. (This definition is adapted from Kurpius, DeWayne. Consultation theory and process: An integrated model. *Personnel and Guidance Journal*, 1978, 56.)

1. The member acting as consultant must have a high degree of self-awareness of his-her own values, knowledge, skills, limitations, and needs in entering a helping relationship that involves human and-or organizational change and that the focus of the relationship be on the issues to be resolved and not on the person(s) presenting the problem.

2. There must be understanding and agreement between member and client for the problem definition, change goals, and predicated consequences of interventions selected.

3. The member must be reasonably certain that she/he or the organization represented has the necessary competencies and resources for giving the kind of help that is needed now or may develop later and that appropriate referral resources are available to the consultant.

4. The consulting relationship must be one in which client adaptability and growth toward self-direction are encouraged and cultivated. The member must maintain this role consistently and not become a decision maker for the client or create a future dependency on the consultant.

5. When announcing consultant availability for services, the member conscientiously adheres to the Association's *Ethical Standards*.

6. The member must refuse a private fee or other remuneration for consultation with persons who are entitled to these services through the member's employing institution or agency. The policies of a particular agency may make explicit provisions for private practice with agency clients by members of its staff. In such instances, the clients must be apprised of other options open to them should they seek private counseling services.

## Section F:  Private practice

1. The member should assist the profession by facilitating the availability of counseling services in private as well as public settings.

2. In advertising services as a private practitioner, the member must advertise the services in such a manner so as to accurately inform the public as to services, expertise, profession, and techniques of counseling in a professional manner. A member who assumes an executive leadership role in the organization shall not permit his/her name to be used in professional notices during periods when not actively engaged in the private practice of counseling.

 The member may list the following: highest relevant degree, type and level of certification or license, type and/or description of services, and other relevant information. Such information must not contain false, inaccurate, misleading, partial, out-of-context, or deceptive material or statements.

3. Members may join in partnership/corporation with other members and-or other professionals provided that each member of the partnership or corporation makes clear the separate specialties by name in compliance with the regulations of the locality.

4. A member has an obligation to withdraw from a counseling relationship if it is believed that employment will result in violation of the *Ethical Standards*. If the mental or physical condition of the member renders it difficult to carry out an effective professional relationship or if the member is discharged by the client because the counseling relationship is no longer productive for the client, then the member is obligated to terminate the counseling relationship.

5. A member must adhere to the regulations for private practice of the locality where the services are offered.

6. It is unethical to use one's institutional affiliation to recruit clients for one's private practice.

## Section G:  Personnel administration

It is recognized that most members are employed in public or quasi-public institutions. The functioning of a member within an institution must contribute to the goals of the institution and vice versa if either is to accomplish their respective goals or objectives. It is therefore essential that the member and the institution function in ways to (a) make the institution's goals explicit and public; (b) make the member's contribution to institutional goals specific; and (c) foster mutual accountability for goal achievement.

 To accomplish these objectives, it is recognized that the member and the employer must share responsibilities in the formulation and implementation of personnel policies.

1. Members must define and describe the parameters and levels of their professional competency.

2. Members must establish interpersonal relations and working agreements with supervisors and subordinates regarding counseling or clinical relationships, confidentiality, distinction between public and private material, maintenance, and dissemination of recorded information, work load and accountability. Working

agreements in each instance must be specified and made known to those concerned.

3. Members must alert their employers to conditions that may be potentially disruptive or damaging.

4. Members must inform employers of conditions that may limit their effectiveness.

5. Members must submit regularly to professional review and evaluation.

6. Members must be responsible for inservice development of self and-or staff.

7. Members must inform their staff of goals and programs.

8. Members must provide personnel practices that guarantee and enhance the rights and welfare of each recipient of their service.

9. Members must select competent persons and assign responsibilities compatible with their skills and experiences.

## Section H: Preparation standards

Members who are responsible for training others must be guided by the preparation standards of the Association and relevant Division(s). The member who functions in the capacity of trainer assumes unique ethical responsibilities that frequently go beyond that of the member who does not function in a training capacity. These ethical responsibilities are outlined as follows:

1. Members must orient students to program expectations, basic skills development, and employment prospects prior to admission to the program.

2. Members in charge of learning experiences must establish programs that integrate academic study and supervised practice.

3. Members must establish a program directed toward developing students' skills, knowledge, and self-understanding, stated whenever possible in competency or performance terms.

4. Members must identify the levels of competencies of their students in compliance with relevant Division standards. These competencies must accommodate the para-professional as well as the professional.

5. Members, through continual student evaluation and appraisal, must be aware of the personal limitations of the learner that might impede future performance. The instructor must not only assist the learner in securing

remedial assistance but also screen from the program those individuals who are unable to provide competent services.

6. Members must provide a program that includes training in research commensurate with levels of role functioning. Para-professional and technician-level personnel must be trained as consumers of research. In addition, these personnel must learn how to evaluate their own and their program's effectiveness. Graduate training, especially at the doctoral level, would include preparation for original research by the member.

7. Members must make students aware of the ethical responsibilities and standards of the profession.

8. Preparatory programs must encourage students to value the ideals of service to individuals and to society. In this regard, direct financial remuneration or lack thereof must not influence the quality of service rendered. Monetary considerations must not be allowed to overshadow professional and humanitarian needs.

9. Members responsible for educational programs must be skilled as teachers and practitioners.

10. Members must present thoroughly varied theoretical positions so that students may make comparisons and have the opportunity to select a position.

11. Members must develop clear policies within their educational institutions regarding field placement and the roles of the student and the instructor in such placements.

12. Members must ensure that forms of learning focusing on self-understanding or growth are voluntary, or if required as part of the education program, are made known to prospective students prior to entering the program. When the education program offers a growth experience with an emphasis on self-disclosure or other relatively intimate or personal involvement, the member must have no administrative, supervisory, or evaluating authority regarding the participant.

13. Members must conduct an educational program in keeping with the current relevant guidelines of the American Association for Counseling and Development.

# B. Code of Ethical Principles for Marriage and Family Therapists, American Association for Marriage and Family Therapy

The Board of Directors of AAMFT hereby promulgate, pursuant to Article II, Section (1)(C) of the Association's Bylaws, a Revised Code of Ethical Principles for Marriage and Family Therapists.

## 1. Responsibility to clients

*Marriage and family therapists are dedicated to advancing the welfare of families and individuals, including respecting the rights of those persons seeking their assistance, and making reasonable efforts to ensure that their services are used appropriately.*

1.1 Marriage and family therapists do not discriminate against or refuse professional service to anyone on the basis of race, sex, religion, or national origin.

1.2 Marriage and family therapists are cognizant of their potentially influential position with respect to clients, and they avoid exploiting the trust and dependency of such persons. Marriage and family therapists therefore make every effort to avoid dual relationships with clients that could impair their professional judgement or increase the risk of exploitation. Examples of such dual relationships include, but are not limited to, business or close personal relationships with clients. Sexual intimacy with clients is prohibited.

1.3 Marriage and family therapists do not use their professional relationship with clients to further their own interests.

1.4 Marriage and family therapists respect the right of clients to make decisions and help them to understand the consequences of these decisions. Marriage and family therapists clearly advise a client that a decision on marital status is the responsibility of the client.

1.5 Marriage and family therapists continue therapeutic relationships only so long as it is reasonably clear that clients are benefiting from the relationship.

1.6 Marriage and family therapists assist persons in obtaining other therapeutic services if a marriage and family therapist is unable or unwilling, for appropriate reasons, to see a person who has requested professional help.

1.7 Marriage and family therapists do not abandon or neglect clients in treatment without making reasonable arrangements for the continuation of such treatment.

## 2. Confidentiality

*Marriage and family therapists have unique confidentiality problems because the "client" in a thera-*

*peutic relationship may be more than one person. The overriding principle is that marriage and family therapists respect the confidences of their client(s).*

2.1 Marriage and family therapists cannot disclose client confidences to anyone, except: (1) as mandated by law; (2) to prevent a clear and immediate danger to a person or persons; (3) where the marriage and family therapist is a defendant in a civil, criminal or disciplinary action arising from the therapy (in which case client confidences may only be disclosed in the course of that action); or (4) if there is a waiver previously obtained in writing, and then such information may only be revealed in accordance with the terms of the waiver. In circumstances where more than one person in a family is receiving therapy, each such family member who is legally competent to execute a waiver must agree to the waiver required by sub-paragraph (4). Absent such a waiver from each family member legally competent to execute a waiver, a marriage and family therapist cannot disclose information received from any family member.

2.2 Marriage and family therapists use clinical materials in teaching, writing, and public presentations only if a written waiver has been received in accordance with sub-principle 2.1(4), or when appropriate steps have been taken to protect client identity.

2.3 Marriage and family therapists store or dispose of client records in ways that maintain confidentiality.

## 3. Professional competence and integrity

*Marriage and family therapists are dedicated to maintaining high standards of professional competence and integrity.*

3.1 Marriage and family therapists who (a) are convicted of felonies, (b) are convicted of misdemeanors (related to their qualifications or functions), (c) engage in conduct which could lead to conviction of felonies, or misdemeanors related to their qualifications or functions, (d) are expelled from other professional organizations, or (e) have their licenses or certificates suspended or revoked, are subject to ter-

mination of membership or other appropriate action.

3.2 Marriage and family therapists seek appropriate professional assistance for their own personal problems or conflicts that are likely to impair their work performance and their clinical judgement.

3.3 Marriage and family therapists, as teachers, are dedicated to maintaining high standards of scholarship and presenting information that is accurate.

3.4 Marriage and family therapists seek to remain abreast of new developments in family therapy knowledge and practice through both educational activities and clinical experiences.

3.5 Marriage and family therapists do not engage in sexual or other harassment of clients, students, trainees, or colleagues.

3.6 Marriage and family therapists do not attempt to diagnose, treat, or advise on problems outside the recognized boundaries of their competence.

3.7 Marriage and family therapists attempt to prevent the distortion or misuse of their clinical and research findings.

3.8 Marriage and family therapists are aware that, because of their ability to influence and alter the lives of others, they must exercise special care when making public their professional recommendations and opinions through testimony or other public statements.

## 4. Responsibility to students, employees, and supervisees

*Marriage and family therapists do not exploit the trust and dependency of students and supervisees.*

4.1 Marriage and family therapists are cognizant of their potentially influential position with respect to students, employees and supervisees, and they avoid exploiting the trust and dependency of such persons. Marriage and family therapists therefore make every effort to avoid dual relationships that could impair their professional judgement or increase the risk of exploitation. Sexual harassment or exploitation of students, employees, or supervisees is prohibited.

4.2 Marriage and family therapists do not permit students, employees or supervisees to perform or to hold themselves out as competent to perform professional services beyond their training, level of experience, and competence.

## 5. Responsibility to the profession

*Marriage and family therapists respect the rights and responsibilities of professional colleagues; carry out research in an ethical manner; and participate in activities which advance the goals of the profession.*

5.1 Marriage and family therapists remain accountable to the standards of the profession when acting as members or employees of organizations.

5.2 Marriage and family therapists assign publication credit to those who have contributed to a publication in proportion to their contributions and in accordance with customary professional publication practices.

5.3 Marriage and family therapists who are the authors of books or other materials that are published or distributed should cite appropriately persons to whom credit for original ideas is due.

5.4 Marriage and family therapists who are the authors of books or other materials published or distributed by an organization take reasonable precautions to ensure that the organization promotes and advertises the materials accurately and factually.

5.5 Marriage and family therapists, as researchers, must be adequately informed of and abide by relevant laws and regulations regarding the conduct of research with human participants.

5.6 Marriage and family therapists recognize a responsibility to participate in activities that contribute to a better community and society, including devoting a portion of their professional activity to services for which there is little or no financial return.

5.7 Marriage and family therapists are concerned with developing laws and regulations pertaining to marriage and family therapy that serve the public interest, and with altering such laws and regulations that are not in the public interest.

5.8 Marriage and family therapists encourage public participation in the designing and delivery of services and in the regulation of practitioners.

## 6. Fees

*Marriage and family therapists make financial arrangements with clients that conform to accepted professional practices and that are reasonably understandable.*

6.1 Marriage and family therapists do not offer or accept payment for referrals.

6.2 Marriage and family therapists do not charge excessive fees for services.

6.3 Marriage and family therapists disclose their fee structure to clients at the onset of treatment.

## 7. Advertising

*Marriage and family therapists engage in appropriate informational activities, including those that enable laypersons to choose marriage and family services on an informed basis.*

7.1 Marriage and family therapists accurately represent their competence, education, training, and experience relevant to their practice of marriage and family therapy.

7.2 Marriage and family therapists claim as evidence of educational qualifications only those degrees (a) from regionally-accredited institutions or (b) from institutions accredited by states which license or certify marriage and family therapists, but only if such regulation is recognized by AAMFT.

7.3 Marriage and family therapists assure that advertisements and publications, whether in directories, announcement cards, newspapers, or on radio or television, are formulated to convey information that is necessary for the public to make an appropriate selection. Information could include:
1. office information, such as name, address, telephone number, credit card acceptability, fee structure, languages spoken, and office hours;
2. appropriate degrees, state licensure and/or certification, and AAMFT Clinical Member status; and
3. description of practice.

7.4 Marriage and family therapists do not use a

name which could mislead the public concerning the identity, responsibility, source, and status of those practicing under that name and do not hold themselves out as being partners or associates of a firm if they are not.

7.5 Marriage and family therapists do not use any professional identification (such as a professional card, office sign, letterhead, or telephone or association directory listing), if it includes a statement or claim that is false, fraudulent, misleading, or deceptive. A statement is false, fraudulent, misleading, or deceptive if it (a) contains a material misrepresentation of fact; (b) fails to state any material fact necessary to make the statement, in light of all circumstances, not misleading; or (c) is intended to or is likely to create an unjustified expectation.

7.6 Marriage and family therapists correct, wherever possible, false, misleading, or inaccurate information and representations made by others concerning the marriage and family therapist's qualifications, services, or products.

7.7 Marriage and family therapists make certain that the qualifications of persons in their employ are represented in a manner that is not false, misleading, or deceptive.

7.8 Marriage and family therapists may represent themselves as specializing within a limited area of marriage and family therapy, but may not hold themselves out as specialists without being able to provide evidence of training, education, and supervised experience in settings which meet recognized professional standards.

7.9 Marriage and family therapist Clinical Members—not associates, students or organizations—may identify their membership in AAMFT in public information or advertising materials.

7.10 Marriage and family therapists may not use the initials AAMFT following their name in the manner of an academic degree.

7.11 Marriage and family therapists may not use the AAMFT logo. The Association (which is the sole owner of its name, logo, and the abbreviated initials AAMFT) and its committees and regional divisions, operating as such, may use the logo. A regional division of AAMFT may use the AAMFT insignia to list its individual members as a group (*e.g.*, in the Yellow Pages); when all Clinical Members practicing within a directory district have been invited to list themselves in the directory, any one or more members may do so.

7.12 Marriage and family therapists use their membership in AAFMT only in connection with their clinical and professional activities.

Violations of this Code should be brought to the attention of the AAMFT Committee on Ethics and Professional Practices, in writing, at the central office of AAMFT, 1717 K Street, N.W., Suite 407, Washington, D.C. 20006.

# C. Code of Ethics,
*National Association of Social Workers*

## PREAMBLE

*This code is intended to serve as a guide to the everyday conduct of members of the social work profession and as a basis for the adjudication of issues in ethics when the conduct of social workers is alleged to deviate from the standards expressed or implied in this code. It represents standards of ethical behavior for social workers in professional relationships with those served, with colleagues, with employers, with other individuals and professions, and with the community and society as a whole. It also embodies standards of ethical behavior governing individual conduct to the extent that such conduct is associated with an individual's status and identity as a social worker.*

*This code is based on the fundamental values of the social work profession that include the worth, dignity, and uniqueness of all persons as well as their rights and opportunities. It is also based on the nature of social work, which fosters conditions that promote these values.*

*In subscribing to and abiding by this code, the social worker is expected to view ethical responsibility in as inclusive a context as each situation demands and within which ethical judgement is required. The social worker is expected to take into consideration all the principles in this code that have a bearing upon any situation in which ethical judgement is to be exercised and professional intervention or conduct is planned. The course of action that the social worker chooses is expected to be con-* *sistent with the spirit as well as the letter of this code.*

*In itself, this code does not represent a set of rules that will prescribe all the behaviors of social workers in all the complexities of professional life. Rather, it offers general principles to guide conduct, and the judicious appraisal of conduct, in situations that have ethical implications. It provides the basis for making judgements about ethical actions before and after they occur. Frequently, the particular situation determines the ethical principles that apply and the manner of their application. In such cases, not only the particular ethical principles are taken into immediate consideration, but also the entire code and its spirit. Specific applications of ethical principles must be judged within the context in which they are being considered. Ethical behavior in a given situation must satisfy not only the judgement of the individual social worker, but also the judgement of an unbiased jury of professional peers.*

*This code should not be used as an instrument to deprive any social worker of the opportunity or freedom to practice with complete professional integrity; nor should any disciplinary action be taken on the basis of this code without maximum provision for safeguarding the rights of the social worker affected.*

*The ethical behavior of social workers results not from edict, but from a personal commitment of the individual. This code is offered to affirm the will and zeal of all social workers to be ethical and to act ethically in all that they do as social workers.*

This Code of Ethics as adopted by the 1979 NASW Delegate Assembly, effective July 1, 1980, and reapproved by the 1984 NASW Delegate Assembly is reprinted with the permission of the National Association of Social Workers.

*The following codified ethical principles should guide social workers in the various roles and relationships and at the various levels of responsibility in which they function professionally. These principles also serve as a basis for the adjudication by the National Association of Social Workers of issues in ethics.*

*In subscribing to this code, social workers are required to cooperate in its implementation and abide by any disciplinary rulings based on it. They should also take adequate measures to discourage, prevent, expose, and correct the unethical conduct of colleagues. Finally, social workers should be equally ready to defend and assist colleagues unjustly charged with unethical conduct.*

## I. The social worker's conduct and comportment as a social worker

A. *Propriety.* The social worker should maintain high standards of personal conduct in the capacity or identity as social worker.
  1. The private conduct of the social worker is a personal matter to the same degree as is any other person's, except when such conduct compromises the fulfillment of professional responsibilities.
  2. The social worker should not participate in, condone, or be associated with dishonesty, fraud, deceit, or misrepresentation.
  3. The social worker should distinguish clearly between statements and actions made as a private individual and as a representative of the social work profession or an organization or group.
B. *Competence and professional development.* The social worker should strive to become and remain proficient in professional practice and the performance of professional functions.
  1. The social worker should accept responsibility or employment only on the basis of existing competence or the intention to acquire the necessary competence.
  2. The social worker should not misrepresent professional qualifications, education, experience, or affiliations.
C. *Service.* The social worker should regard as primary the service obligation of the social work profession.

1. The social worker should retain ultimate responsibility for the quality and extent of the service that individual assumes, assigns, or performs.
2. The social worker should act to prevent practices that are inhumane or discriminatory against any person or group of persons.
D. *Integrity.* The social worker should act in accordance with the highest standards of professional integrity and impartiality.
  1. The social worker should be alert to and resist the influences and pressures that interfere with the exercise of professional discretion and impartial judgment required for the performance of professional functions.
  2. The social worker should not exploit professional relationships for personal gain.
E. *Scholarship and research.* The social worker engaged in study and research should be guided by the conventions of scholarly inquiry.
  1. The social worker engaged in research should consider carefully its possible consequences for human beings.
  2. The social worker engaged in research should ascertain that the consent of participants in the research is voluntary and informed, without any implied deprivation or penalty for refusal to participate, and with due regard for participants' privacy and dignity.
  3. The social worker engaged in research should protect participants from unwarranted physical or mental discomfort, distress, harm, danger, or deprivation.
  4. The social worker who engages in the evaluation of services or cases should discuss them only for the professional purposes and only with persons directly and professionally concerned with them.
  5. Information obtained about participants in research should be treated as confidential.
  6. The social worker should take credit only for work actually done in connection with scholarly and research endeavors and credit contributions made by others.

## II. The social worker's ethical responsibility to clients

F. *Primacy of clients' interests.* The social worker's primary responsibility is to clients.

1. The social worker should serve clients with devotion, loyalty, determination, and the maximum application of professional skill and competence.

2. The social worker should not exploit relationships with clients for personal advantage, or solicit the clients of one's agency for private practice.

3. The social worker should not practice, condone, facilitate, or collaborate with any form of discrimination on the basis of race, color, sex, sexual orientation, age, religion, national origin, marital status, political belief, mental or physical handicap, or any other preference or personal characteristic, condition, or status.

4. The social worker should avoid relationships or commitments that conflict with the interests of clients.

5. The social worker should under no circumstances engage in sexual activities with clients.

6. The social worker should provide clients with accurate and complete information regarding the extent and nature of the services available to them.

7. The social worker should apprise clients of their risks, rights, opportunities, and obligations associated with social service to them.

8. The social worker should seek advice and counsel of colleagues and supervisors whenever such consultation is in the best interest of clients.

9. The social worker should terminate service to clients, and professional relationships with them, when such service and relationships are no longer required or no longer serve the clients' needs or interests.

10. The social worker should withdraw services precipitously only under unusual circumstances, giving careful consideration to all factors in the situation and taking care to minimize possible adverse effects.

11. The social worker who anticipates the termination or interruption of service to clients should notify clients promptly and seek the transfer, referral, or continuation of services in relation to the clients' needs and preferences.

G. *Rights and prerogatives of clients.* The social worker should make every effort to foster maximum self-determination on the part of clients.

1. When the social worker must act on behalf of a client who has been adjudged legally incompetent, the social worker should safeguard the interests and rights of that client.

2. When another individual has been legally authorized to act in behalf of a client, the social worker should deal with that person always with the client's best interest in mind.

3. The social worker should not engage in any action that violates or diminishes the civil or legal rights of clients.

H. *Confidentiality and privacy.* The social worker should respect the privacy of clients and hold in confidence all information obtained in the course of professional service.

1. The social worker should share with others confidences revealed by clients, without their consent, only for compelling professional reasons.

2. The social worker should inform clients fully about the limits of confidentiality in a given situation, the purposes for which information is obtained, and how it may be used.

3. The social worker should afford clients reasonable access to any official social work records concerning them.

4. When providing clients with access to records, the social worker should take due care to protect the confidences of others contained in those records.

5. The social worker should obtain informed consent of clients before taping, recording, or permitting third party observation of their activities.

I. *Fees.* When setting fees, the social worker should ensure that they are fair, reasonable, considerate, and commensurate with the service performed and with due regard for the clients' ability to pay.

1. The social worker should not divide a fee or accept or give anything of value for receiving or making a referral.

## III. The social worker's ethical responsibility to colleagues

J. *Respect, fairness, and courtesy.* The social worker should treat colleagues with respect, courtesy, fairness, and good faith.

1. The social worker should cooperate with colleagues to promote professional interests and concerns.
2. The social worker should respect confidences shared by colleagues in the course of their professional relationships and transactions.
3. The social worker should create and maintain conditions of practice that facilitate ethical and competent professional performance by colleagues.
4. The social worker should treat with respect, and represent accurately and fairly, the qualifications, views, and findings of colleagues and use appropriate channels to express judgments on these matters.
5. The social worker who replaces or is replaced by a colleague in professional practice should act with consideration for the interest, character, and reputation of that colleague.
6. The social worker should not exploit a dispute between a colleague and employers to obtain a position or otherwise advance the social worker's interest.
7. The social worker should seek arbitration or mediation resolution for compelling professional reasons.
8. The social worker should extend to colleagues of other professions the same respect and cooperation that is extended to social work colleagues.
9. The social worker who serves as an employer, supervisor, or mentor to colleagues should make orderly and explicit arrangements regarding the conditions of their continuing professional relationship.
10. The social worker who has the responsibility for employing and evaluating the performance of other staff members should fulfill such responsibility in a fair, considerate, and equitable manner, on the basis of clearly enunciated criteria.
11. The social worker who has the responsibility for evaluating the performance of employees, supervisees, or students should share evaluations with them.

K. *Dealing with colleagues' clients.* The social worker has the responsibility to relate to the clients of colleagues with full professional consideration.

1. The social worker should not solicit the clients of colleagues.
2. The social worker should not assume professional responsibility for the clients of another agency or a colleague without appropriate communication with that agency or colleague.
3. The social worker who serves the clients of colleagues, during a temporary absence or emergency, should serve those clients with the same consideration as that afforded any client.

## IV. The social worker's ethical responsibility to employers and employing organizations

L. *Commitments to employing organization.* The social worker should adhere to commitments made to the employing organization.

1. The social worker should work to improve the employing agency's policies and procedures, and the efficiency and effectiveness of its services.
2. The social worker should not accept employment or arrange student field placements in an organization which is currently under public sanction by NASW for violating personnel standards, or imposing limitations on or penalties for professional actions on behalf of clients.
3. The social worker should act to prevent and eliminate discrimination in the employing organization's work assignments

and in its employment policies and practices.

4. The social worker should use with scrupulous regard, and only for the purpose for which they are intended, the resources of the employing organization.

## V. The social worker's ethical responsibility to the social work profession

M. *Maintaining the integrity of the profession.* The social worker should uphold and advance the values, ethics, knowledge, and mission of the profession.

1. The social worker should protect and enhance the dignity and integrity of the profession and should be responsible and vigorous in discussion and criticism of the profession.

2. The social worker should take action through appropriate channels against unethical conduct by any other member of the profession.

3. The social worker should act to prevent the unauthorized and unqualified practice of social work.

4. The social worker should make no misrepresentation in advertising as to qualifications, competence, service, or results to be achieved.

N. *Community service.* The social worker should assist the profession in making social services available to the general public.

1. The social worker should contribute time and professional expertise to activities that promote respect for the utility, the integrity, and the competence of the social work profession.

2. The social worker should support the formulation, development, enactment, and implementation of social policies of concern to the profession.

O. *Development of knowledge.* The social worker should take responsibility for identifying, developing, and fully utilizing knowledge for professional practice.

1. The social worker should base practice upon recognized knowledge relevant to social work.

2. The social worker should critically examine and keep current with emerging knowledge relevant to social work.

3. The social worker should contribute to the knowledge base of social work and share research knowledge and practice wisdom with colleagues.

## VI. The social worker's ethical responsibility to society

P. *Promoting the general welfare.* The social worker should promote the general welfare of society.

1. The social worker should act to prevent and eliminate discrimination against any person or group on the basis of race, color, sex, sexual orientation, age, religion, national origin, marital status, political belief, mental or physical handicap, or any other preference or personal characteristic, condition, or status.

2. The social worker should act to ensure that all persons have access to the resources, services, and opportunities which they require.

3. The social worker should act to expand choice and opportunity for all persons, with special regard for disadvantaged or oppressed groups and persons.

4. The social worker should promote conditions that encourage respect for the diversity of cultures which constitute American society.

5. The social worker should provide appropriate professional services in public emergencies.

6. The social worker should advocate changes in policy and legislation to improve social conditions and to promote social justice.

7. The social worker should encourage informed participation by the public in shaping social policies and institutions.

# D.  Code of Ethics,
## National Federation of Societies for Clinical Social Work

## PREAMBLE

*Ethical principles affecting the practice of clinical social work are rooted in the basic values of society and the social work profession. The principal objective of the profession of clinical social work is to enhance the dignity and well-being of each individual who seeks its services. It does so through use of clinical social work theory and treatment methods, including psychotherapy.*

*The following represents codified ethical principles which serve as a standard for clinical social workers as psychotherapists and in their various other professional roles, relationships, and responsibilities. The clinical social worker is expected to take into consideration all the principles in this code that have a bearing upon any situation in which ethical judgment is to be exercised, and to select a course of action consistent with the spirit as well as the letter of the code.*

*Members of State Societies for Clinical Social Work adhere to these principles. When clinical social workers' conduct is alleged to deviate from these standards, they agree to abide by the recommendations arrived at by State Society disciplinary panels.*

*It is recognized that the practice of clinical social work is complex and varied and does not lend itself to limitation by a set of rules which will particularize all of its functions. The primary goal of this code is not to restrict the practice of clinical*

*social workers, but to offer general principles to guide their conduct and to inspire their will to act according to ethical principles in all of their professional functions.*

## I.  General responsibilities of clinical social workers

*Clinical social workers maintain high standards of the profession in all of their professional roles. Clinical social workers value professional competence, objectivity and integrity. They consistently examine, use, and attempt to expand the knowledge upon which practice is based, working to ensure that their services are used appropriately and accepting responsibility for the consequences of their work.*

a.  As psychotherapy practitioners, clinical social workers bear a heavy responsibility because their recommendations and professional actions may alter the lives of others. The social worker's primary responsibility is to the client. However, when the interest of the individual patient or client conflicts with the welfare of his family or of the community at large, the clinical social worker weighs the consequences of any action and arrives at a judgment based on all considerations.

b.  As employees of institutions or agencies, clinical social workers are responsible for remaining alert to and attempting to moderate institutional pressures and/or policies that conflict with the standards of their profession. If such conflict arises, clinical social workers' primary responsibility is to uphold the ethical standards of their profession.

c. As teachers, clinical social workers are responsible for careful preparation so that their instruction maintains high standards of scholarship and objectivity.

d. Clinical social workers practice only within their sphere of competence. They accurately represent their abilities, education, training, and experience. They avail themselves of opportunities for continuing professional education to maintain and enhance their competence. When indicated, they seek consultation from colleagues or other appropriate professionals.

e. Clinical social workers do not exploit their professional relationships sexually, financially, or for any other personal advantage. They maintain this standard of conduct toward all who may be professionally associated with them, such as clients, colleagues, supervisees, employees, students, and research participants.

f. Clinical social workers refrain from undertaking any professional activity in which their personal problems or conflicts might lead to the inadequate provision of service. If involved in such a situation, they seek appropriate professional assistance to help them determine whether they should suspend, terminate, or limit the scope of their professional involvement.

## II. Responsibility to clients

*The clinical social worker's primary responsibility is to the client. Clinical social workers respect the integrity, protect the welfare, and maximize the self-determination of the clients with whom they work.*

a. Clinical social workers inform clients of the extent and nature of services available to them as well as the limits, rights, opportunities, and obligations associated with service which might affect the client's decision to enter into or continue the relationship.

b. Clinical social workers enter and/or continue professional relationships based on their ability to meet the needs of the client appropriately. The clinical social worker terminates service to clients, and professional relationships with them, when such service and relationships are no longer required or no longer serve the clients' best interests. The clinical social worker who anticipates the interruption or termination of service to clients gives reasonable notification and provides for transfer, referral or continuation of service in relation to the clients' needs and preferences. Clinical social workers do not withdraw services precipitously except under extraordinary circumstances, giving careful consideration to all factors in the situation and taking care to minimize possible adverse effects.

c. Clinical social workers use care to prevent the intrusion of their own personal needs into relationships with clients. They recognize that the private and personal nature of the therapeutic relationship may unrealistically intensify clients' feelings toward them, thus increasing their obligation to maintain professional objectivity. Therefore, specifically:

1. Clinical social workers avoid entering treatment relationships in which their professional judgment will be compromised by prior association with or knowledge of a client. Examples might include treatment of one's family members, close friends, associates, employees, or others whose welfare could be jeopardized by such a dual relationship.

2. Clinical social workers do not engage in or condone sexual activities with clients.

3. Clinical social workers do not initiate, and should avoid when possible, personal relationships or dual roles with current clients, or with any former clients whose feelings toward them may still be derived from or influenced by the former professional relationship.

d. The clinical social worker takes care to ensure an appropriate setting for practice to protect both the client and the social worker from actual or imputed mental and/or physical harm. If the clinical social worker judges that there is a threat to safety, reasonable steps are taken to prevent the client from causing harm to self or others.

e. When the clinical social worker must act on behalf of a client, the action should always safeguard the interests and concerns of that client. When another person has been authorized to act on behalf of a client, the clinical social worker should deal with that person with the client's best interests in mind.

## III. Relationships with colleagues

*Clinical social workers act with integrity in their relationships with colleagues and members of other professions. They know and take into account the traditions, practices, and areas of competence of other professionals and cooperate with them fully for the welfare of clients.*

a. The clinical social worker treats with respect and represents accurately the views, qualifications, and findings of colleagues, and, when expressing judgment on these matters, does so fairly and through appropriate channels.

b. Clinical social workers know that a client's health and safety may depend on their receiving appropriate service from members of other professional disciplines. They are responsible for maintaining knowledge of, and appropriately utilizing, the expertise of such professionals on the client's behalf.

c. In referring clients to allied professionals, clinical social workers ensure that those to whom they refer clients are recognized members of their own disciplines and are competent to carry out the professional services required.

d. If a clinical social worker's services are sought by an individual who is already receiving similar services from another professional, consideration for the client's welfare shall be paramount. It requires the clinical social worker to proceed with great caution, carefully considering both the existing professional relationship and the therapeutic issues involved.

e. As supervisors or employers, clinical social workers accept their responsibility to provide competent professional guidance to colleagues, employees, and students. They foster working conditions that ensure fairness, privacy, and protection from physical or mental harm. They evaluate fairly and with consider-

ation the performance of those under their supervision, and share evaluations with supervisees. They do not abuse the power inherent in their position.

f. Clinical social workers take appropriate measures to discourage, prevent, expose, and correct unethical or incompetent behavior by colleagues, but take equally appropriate steps to assist and defend colleagues unjustly charged with such conduct. They do not encourage the unsupervised practice of social work by those who fail to meet accepted standards of training and experience (i.e., a master's degree in social work from a school of social work accredited by the Council on Social Work Education, or a doctoral degree in social work, that included a sequence of clinically oriented course work and supervised clinical field placement, plus at least 2 years or its part-time equivalent of post-master's or doctoral fulltime supervision in direct-service clinical experience in a clinical setting. Standards for Health Care Providers in Clinical Social Work, National Federation of Societies for Clinical Social Work, 1974.)

## IV. Remuneration

*Fees set by clinical social workers are in accord with professional standards that protect the client and the profession.*

a. In establishing rates for professional services, clinical social workers take into account both the ability of the client to pay and the charges made by other professionals engaged in comparable work. Financial arrangements are explicitly established and agreed upon by both the clinical social worker and the client.

b. Clinical social workers do not give or receive any fee or other consideration to or from a third party for the referral of a client.

c. Clinical social workers employed by an agency or clinic and also engaged in private practice conform to agency regulations regarding their dual role.

## V. Confidentiality

*The safeguarding of the client's right to privacy is a basic responsibility of the clinical social worker.*

*Clinical social workers have a primary obligation to maintain the confidentiality of material that has been transmitted to them in any of their professional roles, including the identity of the client.*

a. Clinical social workers reveal confidential information to others only with the informed consent of the client, except in those circumstances in which not to do so would violate the law or would result in clear and imminent danger to the client or to others. Unless specifically contraindicated by such situations, clients should be informed in advance of any limitations of confidentiality, and informed and written consent should be obtained from the client before confidential information is revealed. Such consent includes telling the client about the purposes for which information is obtained and how it may be used.

b. When confidential information is used for the purposes of professional education, research, consultation, etc., every effort will be made to conceal the true identity of the client. Such presentations will be limited to material necessary for the professional purpose, and this material will be shared only with other responsible individuals.

c. Special care needs to be taken regarding confidentiality when the client is a vulnerable adult or minor child. In disclosing information to parents, guardians, the court, or others, the clinical social worker acts to protect the best interest of the primary client. Clinical social workers uphold their obligation to observe applicable law, including state mandates to report actual or potential abuse.

d. In keeping client records, clinical social workers remain aware of the limits of confidentiality and of the conditions under which they may be required to reveal recorded information. Accordingly, they maintain records adequate to ensure proper diagnosis and treatment, but take precautions to minimize the exposure of the client to any harm that might result from improper disclosure. Clients are permitted to examine their records if they request access. Clinical social workers make provisions for maintaining confidentiality in the storage and disposal of these records, whether written or on audio or visual tape.

## VI.  Societal and legal standards

*Clinical social workers show sensible regard for the social codes and ethical expectations in their communities, recognizing that violations of accepted societal, ethical, and legal standards on their part may compromise the fulfillment of their professional responsibilities or reduce public trust in the profession.*

a. Clinical social workers do not, in any of their capacities, practice, condone, facilitate, or collaborate with any form of discrimination on the basis of race, sex, sexual orientation, age, religion, socioeconomic status, or national origin.

b. Clinical social workers practice their profession in compliance with legal standards. They do not participate in arrangements undermining the law. However, when they believe laws affecting clients or their practice are in conflict with the principles and standards of the profession, clinical social workers make known the conflict and work toward change that will benefit the public interest.

c. Clinical social workers recognize a responsibility to participate in activities contributing toward improved social conditions within their community.

## VII.  Pursuit of research and scholarly activities

*In planning, conducting, and reporting a study, the investigator has the responsibility to make a careful evaluation of its ethical acceptability, taking into account the following additional principles for research with human subjects. To the extent that this appraisal, weighing scientific and humane values, suggests a compromise of any principle, the investigator incurs an increasingly serious obligation to seek advice and to observe stringent safeguards to protect the rights of the research participants.*

a. In conducting research in institutions or organizations, clinical social workers obtain appropriate authority to carry out such research. Host organizations are given proper credit for their contributions.

b. Ethically acceptable research begins with the establishment of a clear and fair agreement between the investigator and the research participant that clarifies the responsibilities of each. The investigator has the obligation to honor all promises and commitments included in that agreement.

c. Responsibility for the establishment and maintenance of acceptable ethical practice in research always remains with the investigator. The investigator is also responsible for the ethical treatment of research participants by collaborators, assistants, students, and employees, all of whom, however, incur parallel obligations.

d. Ethical practice requires the investigator to inform the participant of all features of the research that might reasonably be expected to influence willingness to participate, and to explain all other aspects of the research about which the participant inquires. Failure to make full disclosure imposes additional force to the investigator's abiding responsibility to protect the welfare and dignity of the research participant. After the data are collected, the investigator provides the participant with information about the nature of the study in order to remove any misconceptions that may have arisen.

e. The ethical investigator protects participants from physical and mental discomfort, harm, and danger. If a risk of such consequences exists, the investigator is required to inform the participant of that fact, secure consent before proceeding, and take all possible measures to minimize distress. A research procedure must not be used if it is likely to cause serious or lasting harm to a participant.

f. The methodological requirements of the study may necessitate concealment, deception, or minimal risk. In such cases the investigator is required to justify the use of these techniques and to ensure, as soon as possible, the participant's understanding of the reasons and sufficient justification for the procedure in question.

g. Ethical practice requires the investigator to respect the individual's freedom to decline to participate in or withdraw from research, and to so inform prospective participants. The obligation to protect this freedom requires special vigilance when the investigator is in a position of power over the participant, as, for example,

when the participant is a student, client, employee, or otherwise is in a dual relationship with the investigator. It is unethical to penalize a participant in any way for withdrawing from or refusing to participate in a research project.

h. Information obtained about the individual research participants during the course of an investigation is confidential unless otherwise agreed in advance. When the possibility that others may obtain access to such information exists, to protect confidentiality, the participants will be informed that it is part of the procedure to obtain informed consent.

i. Investigations of human participants using drugs are conducted only in conjunction with licensed physicians.

j. Research findings must be presented accurately and completely, with full discussion of both their usefulness and their limitations. Clinical social workers are responsible for attempting to prevent any distortion or misuse of their findings.

k. Clinical social workers take credit only for work actually done in scholarly and research endeavors and give appropriate credit to the contributions of others.

## VIII. Public statements

*Public statements, announcements of services, and promotional activities of clinical social workers serve the purpose of providing sufficient information to aid consumers in making informed judgments and choices. Clinical social workers state accurately, objectively, and without misrepresentation their professional qualifications, affiliations, and functions as well as those of the institutions or organizations with which they or their statements may be associated. They should correct the misrepresentations of others with respect to these matters.*

a. In announcing availability for professional services, a clinical social worker may use his or her name; highest relevant academic degree from an accredited institution; specialized postgraduate training; date, type, and level of certification or licensure; address and telephone number; office hours; type of services provided; appropriate fee information; foreign languages spoken; and policy with regard to third-party payments.

b. Brochures or catalogs bearing a clinical social worker's name announcing any services offered shall describe the services accurately, but shall not claim or imply superior personal or professional competence.

c. Advertising communicated to the public by audio-visual means must be pre-recorded and approved for broadcasting by the clinical social worker.

d. Clinical social workers provide diagnostic and therapeutic services only in the context of a professional relationship. Such services are not given by means of public lectures or demonstrations, newspaper or magazine articles, radio or television programs, or anything of a similar nature. Professional use of the media or other public forum is appropriate when the purpose is to educate the public about professional matters regarding which the clinical social worker has special knowledge or expertise.

e. Clinical social workers do not offer to perform any services beyond the scope permitted by law or beyond the scope of their competence. They do not engage in any form of advertising which is false, fraudulent, deceptive, or misleading. They do not solicit or use recommendations or testimonials from clients, nor do they use their relationships with clients to promote commercial enterprises of any kind.

f. Clinical social workers respect the rights and reputation of any professional organization with which they are affiliated. They shall not falsely imply sponsorship or certification by such an organization. When making public statements, the clinical social worker will make clear which are personal opinions and which are authorized statements on behalf of the organization.

# E. Principles of Medical Ethics, with Annotations Especially Applicable to Psychiatry, *American Psychiatric Association*

Following are the AMA Principles of Medical Ethics printed separately, along with annotations especially applicable to psychiatry. (Statements in italics are taken directly from the American Medical Association's Principles of Medical Ethics.)

## PREAMBLE

*The medical profession has long subscribed to a body of ethical statements developed primarily for the benefit of the patient. As a member of this profession, a physician must recognize responsibility not only to patients, but also to society, to other health professionals, and to self. The following Principles, adopted by the American Medical Association, are not laws, but standards of conduct which define the essentials of honorable behavior for the physician.*

## Section 1

*A physician shall be dedicated to providing competent medical service with compassion and respect for human dignity.*

1. The patient may place his/her trust in his/her psychiatrist knowing that the psychiatrist's ethics and professional responsibilities preclude him/her gratifying his/her own needs by exploiting the patient. This becomes particularly important because of the essentially private, highly personal, and sometimes intensely emotional nature of the relationship established with the psychiatrist.

2. A psychiatrist should not be a party to any type of policy that excludes, segregates, or demeans the dignity of any patient because of ethnic origin, race, sex, creed, age, socioeconomic status, or sexual orientation.

3. In accord with the requirements of law and accepted medical practice, it is ethical for a physician to submit his/her work to peer review and to the ultimate authority of the medical staff executive body and the hospital administration and its governing body. In case of dispute, the ethical psychiatrist has the following steps available:

   a. Seek appeal from the medical staff decision to a joint conference committee, including members of the medical staff executive committee and the executive committee of the governing board. At this appeal, the ethical psychiatrist could request that outside opinions be considered.

   b. Appeal to the governing body itself.

   c. Appeal to state agencies regulating licensure

of hospitals if, in the particular state, they concern themselves with matters of professional competency and quality of care.

d. Attempt to educate colleagues through development of research projects and data and presentations at professional meetings and in professional journals.

e. Seek redress in local courts, perhaps through an enjoining injunction against the governing body.

f. Public education as carried out by an ethical psychiatrist would not utilize appeals based solely upon emotion, but would be presented in a professional way and without any potential exploitation of patients through testimonials.

4. A psychiatrist should not be a participant in a legally authorized execution.

## Section 2

*A physician shall deal honestly with patients and colleagues, and strive to expose those physicians deficient in character or competence, or who engage in fraud or deception.*

1. The requirement that the physician conduct himself with propriety in his/her profession and in all the actions of his/her life is especially important in the case of the psychiatrist because the patient tends to model his/her behavior after that of his/her therapist by identification. Further, the necessary intensity of the therapeutic relationship may tend to activate sexual and other needs and fantasies on the part of both patient and therapist, while weakening the objectivity necessary for control. Sexual activity with a patient is unethical.

2. The psychiatrist should diligently guard against exploiting information furnished by the patient and should not use the unique position of power afforded him/her by the psychotherapeutic situation to influence the patient in any way not directly relevant to the treatment goals.

3. A psychiatrist who regularly practices outside his/her area of professional competence should be considered unethical. Determination of professional competence should be made by peer review boards or other appropriate bodies.

4. Special consideration should be given to those psychiatrists who, because of mental illness, jeopardize the welfare of their patients and their own reputations and practices. It is ethical, even encouraged, for another psychiatrist to intercede in such situations.

5. Psychiatric services, like all medical services, are dispensed in the context of a contractual arrangement between the patient and the treating physician. The provisions of the contractual arrangement, which are binding on the physician as well as on the patient, should be explicitly established.

6. It is ethical for the psychiatrist to make a charge for a missed appointment when this falls within the terms of the specific contractual agreement with the patient. Charging for a missed appointment or for one not cancelled 24 hours in advance need not, in itself, be considered unethical if a patient is fully advised that the physician will make such a charge. The practice, however, should be resorted to infrequently and always with the utmost consideration of the patient and his/her circumstances.

7. An arrangement in which a psychiatrist provides supervision or administration to other physicians or nonmedical persons for a percentage of their fees or gross income is not acceptable; this would constitute fee-splitting. In a team of practitioners, or a multidisciplinary team, it is ethical for the psychiatrist to receive income for administration, research, education, or consultation. This should be based upon a mutually agreed upon and set fee or salary, open to renegotiation when a change in the time demand occurs. (See also Section 5, Annotations 2, 3, and 4.)

8. When a member has been found to have behaved unethically by the American Psychiatric Association or one of its constituent district branches, there should not be automatic reporting to the local authorities responsible for medical licensure, but the decision to report should be decided upon the merits of the case.

## Section 3

*A physician shall respect the law and also recognize a responsibility to seek changes in those requirements which are contrary to the best interests of the patient.*

1. It would seem self-evident that a psychiatrist who is a lawbreaker might be ethically unsuited to practice his/her profession. When such illegal activities bear directly upon his/her practice, this would obviously be the case. However, in other instances, illegal activities such as those concerning the right to protest social injustices might not bear on either the image of the psychiatrist or the ability of the specific psychiatrist to treat his/her patient ethically and well. While no committee or board could offer prior assurance that any illegal activity would not be considered unethical, it is conceivable that an individual could violate a law without being guilty of professionally unethical behavior. Physicians lose no right of citizenship on entry into the profession of medicine.

2. Where not specifically prohibited by local laws governing medical practice, the practice of acupuncture by a psychiatrist is not unethical per se. The psychiatrist should have professional competence in the use of acupuncture. Or, if he/she is supervising the use of acupuncture by nonmedical individuals, he/she should provide proper medical supervision. (See also Section 5, Annotations 3 and 4.)

## Section 4

*A physician shall respect the rights of patients, of colleagues, and of other health professionals, and shall safeguard patient confidences within the constraints of the law.*

1. Psychiatric records, including even the identification of a person as a patient, must be protected with extreme care. Confidentiality is essential to psychiatric treatment. This is based in part on the special nature of psychiatric therapy as well as on the traditional ethical relationship between physician and patient. Growing concern regarding the civil rights of patients and the possible adverse effects of computerization, duplication equipment, and data banks makes the dissemination of confidential information an increasing hazard. Because of the sensitive and private nature of the information with which the psychiatrist deals, he/she must be circumspect in the information that he/she chooses to disclose to others about a patient. The welfare of the patient must be a continuing consideration.

2. A psychiatrist may release confidential information only with the authorization of the patient or under proper legal compulsion. The continuing duty of the psychiatrist to protect the patient includes fully apprising him/her of the connotations of waiving the privilege of privacy. This may become an issue when the patient is being investigated by a government agency, is applying for a position, or is involved in legal action. The same principles apply to the release of information concerning treatment to medical departments of government agencies, business organizations, labor unions, and insurance companies. Information gained in confidence about patients seen in student health services should not be released without the student's explicit permission.

3. Clinical and other materials used in teaching and writing must be adequately disguised in order to preserve the anonymity of the individuals involved.

4. The ethical responsibility of maintaining confidentiality holds equally for the consultations in which the patient may not have been present and in which the consultee was not a physician. In such instances, the physician consultant should alert the consultee to his/her duty of confidentiality.

5. Ethically the psychiatrist may disclose only that information which is relevant to a given situation. He/she should avoid offering speculation as fact. Sensitive information such as an individual's sexual orientation or fantasy material is usually unnecessary.

6. Psychiatrists are often asked to examine individuals for security purposes, to determine suitability for various jobs, and to determine legal competence. The psychiatrist must fully describe the nature and purpose and lack of confidentiality of the examination to the examinee at the beginning of the examination.

7. Careful judgment must be exercised by the psychiatrist in order to include, when appropriate, the parents or guardian in the treatment of a minor. At the same time the psychiatrist must assure the minor proper confidentiality.

8. Psychiatrists at times may find it necessary, in order to protect the patient or the community from imminent danger, to reveal confidential information disclosed by the patient.

9. When the psychiatrist is ordered by the court to reveal the confidences entrusted to him/her by patients, he/she may comply or he/she may ethically hold the right to dissent within the framework of the law. When the psychiatrist is in doubt, the right of the patient to confidentiality and, by extension, to unimpaired treatment should be given priority. The psychiatrist should reserve the right to raise the question of adequate need for disclosure. In the event that the necessity for legal disclosure is demonstrated by the court, the psychiatrist may request the right to disclosure of only that information which is relevant to the legal question at hand.

10. With regard for the person's dignity and privacy and with truly informed consent, it is ethical to present a patient to a scientific gathering, if the confidentiality of the presentation is understood and accepted by the audience.

11. It is ethical to present a patient or former patient to a public gathering or to the news media only if that patient is fully informed of enduring loss of confidentiality, is competent, and consents in writing without coercion.

12. When involved in funded research, the ethical psychiatrist will advise human subjects of the funding source, retain his/her freedom to reveal data and results, and follow all appropriate and current guidelines relative to human subject protection.

13. Ethical considerations in medical practice preclude the psychiatric evaluation of any adult charged with criminal acts prior to access to, or availability of, legal counsel. The only exception is the rendering of care to the person for the sole purpose of medical treatment.

## Section 5

*A physician shall continue to study, apply, and advance scientific knowledge, make relevant information available to patients, colleagues, and the public, obtain consultation, and use the talents of other health professionals when indicated.*

1. Psychiatrists are responsible for their own continuing education and should be mindful of the fact that theirs must be a lifetime of learning.

2. In the practice of his/her specialty, the psychiatrist consults, associates, collaborates, or integrates his/her work with that of many professionals, including psychologists, psychometricians, social workers, alcoholism counselors, marriage counselors, public health nurses, etc. Furthermore, the nature of modern psychiatric practice extends his/her contacts to such people as teachers, juvenile and adult probation officers, attorneys, welfare workers, agency volunteers, and neighborhood aids. In referring patients for treatment, counseling, or rehabilitation to any of these practitioners, the psychiatrist should ensure that the allied professional or paraprofessional with whom he/she is dealing is a recognized member of his/her own discipline and is competent to carry out the therapeutic task required. The psychiatrist should have the same attitude toward members of the medical profession to whom he/she refers patients. Whenever he/she has reason to doubt the training, skill, or ethical qualifications of the allied professional, the psychiatrist should not refer cases to him/her.

3. When the psychiatrist assumes a collaborative or supervisory role with another mental health worker, he/she must expend sufficient time to assure that proper care is given. It is contrary to the interests of the patient and to patient care if he/she allows himself/herself to be used a a figurehead.

4. In relationships between psychiatrists and practicing licensed psychologists, the physician should not delegate to the psychologist or, in fact, to any nonmedical person any matter requiring the exercise of professional medical judgment.

5. The psychiatrist should agree to the request of a patient for consultation or to such a request from the family of an incompetent or minor patient. The psychiatrist may suggest possible consultants, but the patient or family should be given free choice of the consultant. If the psychiatrist disapproves of the professional qualifications of the consultant or if there is a difference of opinion that the primary therapist cannot resolve, he/she may, after suitable no-

tice, withdraw from the case. If this disagreement occurs within an institution or agency framework, the difference should be resolved by the mediation or arbitration of higher professional authority within the institution or agency.

## Section 6

*A physician shall, in the provision of appropriate patient care, except in emergencies, be free to choose whom to serve, with whom to associate, and the environment in which to provide medical services.*

1. Physicians generally agree that the doctor-patient relationship is such a vital factor in effective treatment of the patient that preservation of optimal conditions for development of a sound working relationship between a doctor and his/her patient should take precedence over all other considerations. Professional courtesy may lead to poor psychiatric care for physicians and their families because of embarrassment over the lack of a complete give-and-take contract.
2. An ethical psychiatrist may refuse to provide psychiatric treatment to a person who, in the psychiatrist's opinion, cannot be diagnosed as having a mental illness amenable to psychiatric treatment.

## Section 7

*A physician shall recognize a responsibility to participate in activities contributing to an improved community.*

1. Psychiatrists should foster the cooperation of those legitimately concerned with the medical, psychological, social, and legal aspects of mental health and illness. Psychiatrists are encouraged to serve society by advising and consulting with the executive, legislative, and judiciary branches of the government. A psychiatrist should clarify whether he/she speaks as an individual or as a representative of an organization. Furthermore, psychiatrists should avoid cloaking their public statements with the authority of the profession (e.g., "Psychiatrists know that . . .").
2. Psychiatrists may interpret and share with the public their expertise in the various psychosocial issues that may affect mental health and illness. Psychiatrists should always be mindful of their separate roles as dedicated citizens and as experts in psychological medicine.
3. On occasion psychiatrists are asked for an opinion about an individual who is in the light of public attention, or who has disclosed information about himself/herself through public media. It is unethical for a psychiatrist to offer a professional opinion unless he/she has conducted an examination and has been granted proper authorization for such a statement.
4. The psychiatrist may permit his/her certification to be used for the involuntary treatment of any person only following his/her personal examination of that person. To do so, he/she must find that the person, because of mental illness, cannot form a judgment as to what is in his/her own best interests and that, without such treatment, substantial impairment is likely to occur to the person or others.

# F. Ethical Principles of Psychologists, *American Psychological Association*

## PREAMBLE

*Psychologists respect the dignity and worth of the individual and strive for the preservation and protection of fundamental human rights. They are committed to increasing knowledge of human behavior and of people's understanding of themselves and others and to the utilization of such knowledge for the promotion of human welfare. While pursuing these objectives, they make every effort to protect the welfare of those who seek their services and of the research participants that may be the objects of study. They use their skills only for purposes consistent with these values and do not knowingly permit their misuse by others. While demanding for themselves freedom of inquiry and communication, psychologists accept the responsibility this freedom requires: competence, objectivity in the application of skills, and concern for the best inter-*
*ests of clients, colleagues, students, research participants, and society. In the pursuit of these ideals, psychologists subscribe to principles in the following areas: 1. Responsibility, 2. Competence, 3. Moral and Legal Standards, 4. Public Statements, 5. Confidentiality, 6. Welfare of the Consumer, 7. Professional Relationships, 8. Assessment Techniques, 9. Research with Human Participants, and 10. Care and Use of Animals.*

*Acceptance of membership in the American Psychological Association commits the member to adherence to these principles.*

*Psychologists cooperate with duly constituted committees of the American Psychological Association, in particular, the Committee on Scientific and Professional Ethics and Conduct, by responding to inquiries promptly and completely. Members also respond promptly and completely to inquiries from duly constituted state association*

*Ethical Principles of Psychologists* (revised edition), by the American Psychological Association. Copyright 1981 by the American Psychological Association. Reprinted by permission of the publisher.

This version of the *Ethical Principles of Psychologists* (formerly entitled *Ethical Standards of Psychologists*) was adopted by the American Psychological Association's Council of Representatives on January 24, 1981. The revised *Ethical Principles* contain both substantive and grammatical changes in each of the nine ethical principles constituting the *Ethical Standards of Psychologists* previously adopted by the Council of Representatives in 1979, plus a new tenth principle entitled "Care and Use of Animals." Inquiries concerning the *Ethical Principles of Psychologists* should be addressed to the Administrative Officer for Ethics, American Psychological Association, 1200 Seventeenth Street, N.W., Washington, D.C., 20036.

These revised *Ethical Principles* apply to psychologists, to students of psychology, and to others who do work of a psychological nature under the supervision of a psychologist. They are also intended for the guidance of nonmembers of the Association who are engaged in psychological research or practice.

Any complaints of unethical conduct filed after January 24, 1981, shall be governed by this 1981 revision. However, conduct (a) complained about after January 24, 1981, but which occurred prior to that date, and (b) not considered unethical under prior versions of the principles but considered unethical under the 1981 revision, shall not be deemed a violation of ethical principles. Any complaints pending as of January 24, 1981, shall be governed either by the 1979 or by the 1981 version of the *Ethical Principles*, at the sound discretion of the Committee on Scientific and Professional Ethics and Conduct.

*ethics committees and professional standards review committees.*

## Principle 1: Responsibility

*In providing services, psychologists maintain the highest standards of their profession. They accept responsibility for the consequences of their acts and make every effort to ensure that their services are used appropriately.*

a. As scientists, psychologists accept responsibility for the selection of their research topics and the methods used in investigation, analysis, and reporting. They plan their research in ways to minimize the possibility that their findings will be misleading. They provide thorough discussion of the limitations of their data, especially where their work touches on social policy or might be construed to the detriment of persons in specific age, sex, ethnic, socioeconomic, or other social groups. In publishing reports of their work, they never suppress disconfirming data, and they acknowledge the existence of alternative hypotheses and explanations of their findings. Psychologists take credit only for work they have actually done.

b. Psychologists clarify in advance with all appropriate persons and agencies the expectations for sharing and utilizing research data. They avoid relationships that may limit their objectivity or create a conflict of interest. Interference with the milieu in which data are collected is kept to a minimum.

c. Psychologists have the responsibility to attempt to prevent distortion, misuse, or suppression of psychological findings by the institution or agency of which they are employees.

d. As members of governmental or other organizational bodies, psychologists remain accountable as individuals to the highest standards of their profession.

e. As teachers, psychologists recognize their primary obligation to help others acquire knowledge and skill. They maintain high standards of scholarship by presenting psychological information objectively, fully, and accurately.

f. As practitioners, psychologists know that they bear a heavy social responsibility because their recommendations and professional actions may alter the lives of others. They are alert to personal, social, organizational, financial, or political situations and pressures that might lead to misuse of their influence.

## Principle 2: Competence

*The maintenance of high standards of competence is a responsibility shared by all psychologists in the interest of the public and the profession as a whole. Psychologists recognize the boundaries of their competence and the limitations of their techniques. They only provide services and only use techniques for which they are qualified by training and experience. In those areas in which recognized standards do not yet exist, psychologists take whatever precautions are necessary to protect the welfare of their clients. They maintain knowledge of current scientific and professional information related to the services they render.*

a. Psychologists accurately represent their competence, education, training, and experience. They claim as evidence of educational qualifications only those degrees obtained from institutions acceptable under the Bylaws and Rules of Council of the American Psychological Association.

b. As teachers, psychologists perform their duties on the basis of careful preparation so that their instruction is accurate, current, and scholarly.

c. Psychologists recognize the need for continuing education and are open to new procedures and changes in expectations and values over time.

d. Psychologists recognize differences among people, such as those that may be associated with age, sex, socioeconomic, and ethnic backgrounds. When necessary, they obtain training, experience, or counsel to assure competent service or research relating to such persons.

e. Psychologists responsible for decisions involving individuals or policies based on test results have an understanding of psychological or educational measurement, validation problems, and test research.

f. Psychologists recognize that personal problems and conflicts may interfere with professional effectiveness. Accordingly, they refrain from undertaking any activity in which their personal problems are likely to lead to inadequate performance or harm to a client, colleague, student, or research participant. If engaged in such activity when they become aware of their personal problems, they seek competent professional assistance to determine whether they should suspend, terminate, or limit the scope of their professional and/or scientific activities.

## Principle 3:  Moral and legal standards

*Psychologists' moral and ethical standards of behavior are a personal matter to the same degree as they are for any other citizen, except as these may compromise the fulfillment of their professional responsibilities or reduce the public trust in psychology and psychologists. Regarding their own behavior, psychologists are sensitive to prevailing community standards and to the possible impact that conformity to or deviation from these standards may have upon the quality of their performance as psychologists. Psychologists are also aware of the possible impact of their public behavior upon the ability of colleagues to perform their professional duties.*

a. As teachers, psychologists are aware of the fact that their personal values may affect the selection and presentation of instructional materials. When dealing with topics that may give offense, they recognize and respect the diverse attitudes that students may have toward such materials.
b. As employees or employers, psychologists do not engage in or condone practices that are inhumane or that result in illegal or unjustifiable actions. Such practices include, but are not limited to, those based on considerations of race, handicap, age, gender, sexual preference, religion, or national origin in hiring, promotion, or training.
c. In their professional roles, psychologists avoid any action that will violate or diminish the legal and civil rights of clients or of others who may be affected by their actions.
d. As practitioners and researchers, psychologists act in accord with Association standards and guidelines related to practice and to the conduct of research with human beings and ani-

mals. In the ordinary course of events, psychologists adhere to relevant governmental laws and institutional regulations. When federal, state, provincial, organizational, or institutional laws, regulations, or practices are in conflict with Association standards and guidelines, psychologists make known their commitment to Association standards and guidelines and, wherever possible, work toward a resolution of the conflict. Both practitioners and researchers are concerned with the development of such legal and quasi-legal regulations as best serve the public interest, and they work toward changing existing regulations that are not beneficial to the public interest.

## Principle 4:  Public statements

*Public statements, announcements of services, advertising, and promotional activities of psychologists serve the purpose of helping the public make informed judgments and choices. Psychologists represent accurately and objectively their professional qualifications, affiliations, and functions, as well as those of the institutions or organizations with which they or the statements may be associated. In public statements providing psychological information or professional opinions or providing information about the availability of psychological products, publications, and services, psychologists base their statements on scientifically acceptable psychological findings and techniques with full recognition of the limits and uncertainties of such evidence.*

a. When announcing or advertising professional services, psychologists may list the following information to describe the provider and services provided: name, highest relevant academic degree earned from a regionally accredited institution, date, type, and level of certification or licensure, diplomate status, APA membership status, address, telephone number, office hours, a brief listing of the type of psychological services offered, an appropriate presentation of fee information, foreign languages spoken, and policy with regard to third-party payments. Additional relevant or important consumer information may be included if not prohibited by other sections of these Ethical Principles.

b. In announcing or advertising the availability of psychological products, publications, or services, psychologists do not present their affiliation with any organization in a manner that falsely implies sponsorship or certification by that organization. In particular and for example, psychologists do not state APA membership or fellow status in a way to suggest that such status implies specialized professional competence or qualifications. Public statements include, but are not limited to, communication by means of periodical, book, list, directory, television, radio, or motion picture. They do not contain (i) a false, fraudulent, misleading, deceptive, or unfair statement; (ii) a misinterpretation of fact or a statement likely to mislead or deceive because in context it makes only a partial disclosure of relevant facts; (iii) a testimonial from a patient regarding the quality of a psychologist's services or products; (iv) a statement intended or likely to create false or unjustified expectations of favorable results; (v) a statement implying unusual, unique, or one-of-a-kind abilities; (vi) a statement intended or likely to appeal to a client's fears, anxieties, or emotions concerning the possible results of failure to obtain the offered services; (vii) a statement concerning the comparative desirability of offered services; (viii) a statement of direct solicitation of individual clients.

c. Psychologists do not compensate or give anything of value to a representative of the press, radio, television, or other communication medium in anticipation of or in return for professional publicity in a news item. A paid advertisement must be identified as such, unless it is apparent from the context that it is a paid advertisement. If communicated to the public by use of radio or television, an advertisement is prerecorded and approved for broadcast by the psychologist, and a recording of the actual transmission is retained by the psychologist.

d. Announcements or advertisements of "personal growth groups," clinics, and agencies give a clear statement of purpose and a clear description of the experiences to be provided.

The education, training, and experience of the staff members are appropriately specified.

e. Psychologists associated with the development or promotion of psychological devices, books, or other products offered for commercial sale make reasonable efforts to ensure that announcements and advertisements are presented in a professional, scientifically acceptable, and factually informative manner.

f. Psychologists do not participate for personal gain in commercial announcements or advertisements recommending to the public the purchase or use of proprietary or single-source products or services when that participation is based solely upon their identification as psychologists.

g. Psychologists present the science of psychology and offer their services, products, and publications fairly and accurately, avoiding misrepresentation through sensationalism, exaggeration, or superficiality. Psychologists are guided by the primary obligation to aid the public in developing informed judgments, opinions, and choices.

h. As teachers, psychologists ensure that statements in catalogs and course outlines are accurate and not misleading, particularly in terms of subject matter to be covered, bases for evaluating progress, and the nature of course experiences. Announcements, brochures, or advertisements describing workshops, seminars, or other educational programs accurately describe the audience for which the program is intended as well as eligibility requirements, educational objectives, and nature of the materials to be covered. These announcements also accurately represent the education, training, and experience of the psychologists presenting the programs and any fees involved.

i. Public announcements or advertisements soliciting research participants in which clinical services or other professional services are offered as an inducement make clear the nature of the services as well as the costs and other obligations to be accepted by participants in the research.

j. A psychologist accepts the obligation to correct others who represent the psychologist's professional qualifications, or associations with products or services, in a manner incompatible with these guidelines.

k. Individual diagnostic and therapeutic services are provided only in the context of a professional psychological relationship. When personal advice is given by means of public lectures or demonstrations, newspaper or magazine articles, radio or television programs, mail, or similar media, the psychologist utilizes the most current relevant data and exercises the highest level of professional judgment.

l. Products that are described or presented by means of public lectures or demonstrations, newspaper or magazine articles, radio or television programs, or similar media meet the same recognized standards as exist for products used in the context of a professional relationship.

## Principle 5: Confidentiality

*Psychologists have a primary obligation to respect the confidentiality of information obtained from persons in the course of their work as psychologists. They reveal such information to others only with the consent of the person or the person's legal representative, except in those unusual circumstances in which not to do so would result in clear danger to the person or to others. Where appropriate, psychologists inform their clients of the legal limits of confidentiality.*

a. Information obtained in clinical or consulting relationships, or evaluative data concerning children, students, employees, and others, is discussed only for professional purposes and only with persons clearly concerned with the case. Written and oral reports present only data germane to the purposes of the evaluation, and every effort is made to avoid undue invasion of privacy.

b. Psychologists who present personal information obtained during the course of professional work in writings, lectures, or other public forums either obtain adequate prior consent to do so or adequately disguise all identifying information.

c. Psychologists make provisions for maintaining confidentiality in the storage and disposal of records.

d. When working with minors or other persons who are unable to give voluntary, informed consent, psychologists take special care to protect these persons' best interests.

## Principle 6: Welfare of the consumer

*Psychologists respect the integrity and protect the welfare of the people and groups with whom they work. When conflicts of interest arise between clients and psychologists' employing institutions, psychologists clarify the nature and direction of their loyalties and responsibilities and keep all parties informed of their commitments. Psychologists fully inform consumers as to the purpose and nature of an evaluative, treatment, educational, or training procedure, and they freely acknowledge that clients, students, or participants in research have freedom of choice with regard to participation.*

a. Psychologists are continually cognizant of their own needs and of their potentially influential position vis-à-vis persons such as clients, students, and subordinates. They avoid exploiting the trust and dependency of such persons. Psychologists make every effort to avoid dual relationships that could impair their professional judgment or increase the risk of exploitation. Examples of such dual relationships include, but are not limited to, research with and treatment of employees, students, supervisees, close friends, or relatives. Sexual intimacies with clients are unethical.

b. When a psychologist agrees to provide services to a client at the request of a third party, the psychologist assumes the responsibility of clarifying the nature of the relationships to all parties concerned.

c. Where the demands of an organization require psychologists to violate these Ethical Principles, psychologists clarify the nature of the conflict between the demands and these principles. They inform all parties of psychologists' ethical responsibilities and take appropriate action.

d. Psychologists make advance financial arrangements that safeguard the best interests of and are clearly understood by their clients. They neither give nor receive any remuneration for referring clients for professional services. They contribute a portion of their services to work for which they receive little or no financial return.

e. Psychologists terminate a clinical or consulting relationship when it is reasonably clear that the consumer is not benefiting from it. They offer to help the consumer locate alternative sources of assistance.

## Principle 7: Professional relationships

*Psychologists act with due regard for the needs, special competencies, and obligations of their colleagues in psychology and other professions. They respect the prerogatives and obligations of the institutions or organizations with which these other colleagues are associated.*

a. Psychologists understand the areas of competence of related professions. They make full use of all the professional, technical, and administrative resources that serve the best interests of consumers. The absence of formal relationships with other professional workers does not relieve psychologists of the responsibility of securing for their clients the best possible professional service, nor does it relieve them of the obligation to exercise foresight, diligence, and tact in obtaining the complementary or alternative assistance needed by clients.

b. Psychologists know and take into account the traditions and practices of other professional groups with whom they work and cooperate fully with such groups. If a person is receiving similar services from another professional, psychologists do not offer their own services directly to such a person. If a psychologist is contacted by a person who is already receiving similar services from another professional, the psychologist carefully considers that professional relationship and proceeds with caution and sensitivity to the therapeutic issues as well as the client's welfare. The psychologist discusses these issues with the client so as to minimize the risk of confusion and conflict.

c. Psychologists who employ or supervise other professionals or professionals in training accept the obligation to facilitate the further professional development of these individuals. They provide appropriate working conditions, timely evaluations, constructive consultation, and experience opportunities.

d. Psychologists do not exploit their professional relationships with clients, supervisees, students, employees, or research participants sexually or otherwise. Psychologists do not condone or engage in sexual harassment. Sexual harassment is defined as deliberate or repeated comments, gestures, or physical contacts of a sexual nature that are unwanted by the recipient.

e. In conducting research in institutions or organizations, psychologists secure appropriate authorization to conduct such research. They are aware of their obligations to future research workers and ensure that host institutions receive adequate information about the research and proper acknowledgment of their contributions.

f. Publication credit is assigned to those who have contributed to a publication in proportion to their professional contributions. Major contributions of a professional character made by several persons to a common project are recognized by joint authorship, with the individual who made the principal contribution listed first. Minor contributions of a professional character and extensive clerical or similar nonprofessional assistance may be acknowledged in footnotes or in an introductory statement. Acknowledgment through specific citations is made for unpublished as well as published material that has directly influenced the research or writing. Psychologists who compile and edit material of others for publication publish the material in the name of the originating group, if appropriate, with their own name appearing as chairperson or editor. All contributors are to be acknowledged and named.

g. When psychologists know of an ethical violation by another psychologist, and it seems appropriate, they informally attempt to resolve the issue by bringing the behavior to the attention of the psychologist. If the misconduct is of a minor nature and/or appears to be due to lack of sensitivity, knowledge, or experience, such an informal solution is usually appropriate. Such informal corrective efforts are made with sensitivity to any rights to confidentiality involved. If the violation does not seem amenable to an informal solution, or is of a more serious nature, psychologists bring it to the attention of the appropriate local, state, and/or national committee on professional ethics and conduct.

## Principle 8: Assessment techniques

*In the development, publication, and utilization of psychological assessment techniques, psychologists make every effort to promote the welfare and best interests of the client. They guard against the misuse of assessment results. They respect the client's right to know the results, the interpretations made, and the bases for their conclusions and recommendations. Psychologists make every effort to maintain the security of tests and other assessment techniques within limits of legal mandates. They strive to ensure the appropriate use of assessment techniques by others.*

a. In using assessment techniques, psychologists respect the right of clients to have full explanations of the nature and purpose of the techniques in language the client can understand, unless an explicit exception to this right has been agreed upon in advance. When the explanations are to be provided by others, psychologists establish procedures for ensuring the adequacy of these explanations.

b. Psychologists responsible for the development and standardization of psychological tests and other assessment techniques utilize established scientific procedures and observe the relevant APA standards.

c. In reporting assessment results, psychologists indicate any reservations that exist regarding validity or reliability because of the circumstances of the assessment or the inappropriateness of the norms for the person tested. Psychologists strive to ensure that the results of assessments and their interpretations are not misused by others.

d. Psychologists recognize that assessment results may become obsolete. They make every effort to avoid and prevent the misuse of obsolete measures.

e. Psychologists offering scoring and interpretation services are able to produce appropriate evidence for the validity of the programs and procedures used in arriving at interpretations. The public offering of an automated interpretation service is considered a professional-to-

professional consultation. Psychologists make every effort to avoid misuse of assessment reports.

f. Psychologists do not encourage or promote the use of psychological assessment techniques by inappropriately trained or otherwise unqualified persons through teaching, sponsorship, or supervision.

## Principle 9: Research with human participants

*The decision to undertake research rests upon a considered judgment by the individual psychologist about how best to contribute to psychological science and human welfare. Having made the decision to conduct research, the psychologist considers alternative directions in which research energies and resources might be invested. On the basis of this consideration, the psychologist carries out the investigation with respect and concern for the dignity and welfare of the people who participate and with cognizance of federal and state regulations and professional standards governing the conduct of research with human participants.*

a. In planning a study, the investigator has the responsibility to make a careful evaluation of its ethical acceptability. To the extent that the weighing of scientific and human values suggests a compromise of any principle, the investigator incurs a correspondingly serious obligation to seek ethical advice and to observe stringent safeguards to protect the rights of human participants.

b. Considering whether a participant in a planned study will be a "subject at risk" or a "subject at minimal risk," according to recognized standards, is of primary ethical concern to the investigator.

c. The investigator always retains the responsibility for ensuring ethical practice in research. The investigator is also responsible for the ethical treatment of research participants by collaborators, assistants, students, and employees, all of whom, however, incur similar obligations.

d. Except in minimal-risk research, the investigator establishes a clear and fair agreement with research participants, prior to their participation, that clarifies the obligations and responsibilities of each. The investigator has the obligation to honor all promises and commitments included in that agreement. The investigator informs the participants of all aspects of the research that might reasonably be expected to influence willingness to participate and explains all other aspects of the research about which the participants inquire. Failure to make full disclosure prior to obtaining informed consent requires additional safeguards to protect the welfare and dignity of the research participants. Research with children or with participants who have impairments that would limit understanding and/or communication requires special safeguarding procedures.

e. Methodological requirements of a study may make the use of concealment or deception necessary. Before conducting such a study, the investigator has a special responsibility to (i) determine whether the use of such techniques is justified by the study's prospective scientific, educational, or applied value; (ii) determine whether alternative procedures are available that do not use concealment or deception; and (iii) ensure that the participants are provided with sufficient explanation as soon as possible.

f. The investigator respects the individual's freedom to decline to participate in or to withdraw from the research at any time. The obligation to protect this freedom requires careful thought and consideration when the investigator is in a position of authority or influence over the participant. Such positions of authority include, but are not limited to, situations in which research participation is required as part of employment or in which the participant is a student, client, or employee of the investigator.

g. The investigator protects the participant from physical and mental discomfort, harm, and danger that may arise from research procedures. If risks of such consequences exist, the investigator informs the participant of that fact. Research procedures likely to cause serious or lasting harm to a participant are not used unless the failure to use these procedures might expose the participant to risk of greater harm, or unless the research has great potential benefit and fully informed and voluntary consent is obtained from each participant. The

participant should be informed of procedures for contacting the investigator within a reasonable time period following participation should stress, potential harm, or related questions or concerns arise.

h. After the data are collected, the investigator provides the participant with information about the nature of the study and attempts to remove any misconceptions that may have arisen. Where scientific or humane values justify delaying or withholding this information, the investigator incurs a special responsibility to monitor the research and to ensure that there are no damaging consequences for the participant.

i. Where research procedures result in undesirable consequences for the individual participant, the investigator has the responsibility to detect and remove or correct these consequences, including long-term effects.

j. Information obtained about a research participant during the course of an investigation is confidential unless otherwise agreed upon in advance. When the possibility exists that others may obtain access to such information, this possibility, together with the plans for protecting confidentiality, is explained to the participant as part of the procedure for obtaining informed consent.

## Principle 10: Care and use of animals

*An investigator of animal behavior strives to advance understanding of basic behavioral principles and/or to contribute to the improvement of human health and welfare. In seeking these ends, the investigator ensures the welfare of animals and treats them humanely. Laws and regulations notwithstanding, an animal's immediate protection depends upon the scientist's own conscience.*

a. The acquisition, care, use, and disposal of all animals are in compliance with current federal, state or provincial, and local laws and regulations.

b. A psychologist trained in research methods and experienced in the care of laboratory animals closely supervises all procedures involving animals and is responsible for ensuring appropriate consideration of their comfort, health, and humane treatment.

c. Psychologists ensure that all individuals using animals under their supervision have received explicit instruction in experimental methods and in the care, maintenance, and handling of the species being used. Responsibilities and activities of individuals participating in a research project are consistent with their respective competencies.

d. Psychologists make every effort to minimize discomfort, illness, and pain of animals. A pro-cedure subjecting animals to pain, stress, or privation is used only when an alternative procedure is unavailable and the goal is justified by its prospective scientific, educational, or applied value. Surgical procedures are performed under appropriate anesthesia; techniques to avoid infection and minimize pain are followed during and after surgery.

e. When it is appropriate that the animal's life be terminated, it is done rapidly and painlessly.

# G. Ethical Standards for School Counselors, *American School Counselor Association*

## PREAMBLE

The American School Counselor Association is a professional organization whose members have a unique and distinctive preparation, grounded in the behavioral sciences, with training in clinical skills adapted to the school setting. School counselors subscribe to the following basic tenets of the counseling process from which professional responsibilities are derived:

1. Each person has the right to respect and dignity as a human being and to counseling services without prejudice as to person, character, belief or practice.
2. Each person has the right to self-direction and self-development.
3. Each person has the right of choice and the responsibility for decisions reached.
4. The counselor assists in the growth and development of each individual and uses his/her highly specialized skills to insure that the rights of the counselee are properly protected within the structure of the school program.
5. The counselor-client relationship is private and thereby requires compliance with all laws, policies and ethical standards pertaining to confidentiality.

In this document, the American School Counselor Association has identified the standards of conduct necessary to maintain and regulate the high standards of integrity and leadership among its members. The Association recognizes the basic commitment of its members to the Ethical Standards of its parent organization, the American Association for Counseling and Development, and nothing in this document shall be construed to supplant that code. The Ethical Standards for School Counselors was developed to complement the AACD standards by clarifying the nature of ethical responsibilities of counselors in the school setting. The purposes of this document are to:

1. Serve as a guide for the ethical practices of all school counselors regardless of level, area, or population served.
2. Provide benchmarks for both self-appraisal and peer evaluations regarding counselor responsibilities to pupils, parents, professional colleagues, school and community, self, and the counseling profession.
3. Inform those served by the school counselor of acceptable counselor practices and expected professional deportment.

## A. Responsibilities to pupils

The school counselor:

1. Has a primary obligation and loyalty to the pupil, who is to be treated with respect as a unique individual.
2. Is concerned with the total needs of the pupil (educational, vocational, personal and social)

---

*Ethical Standards for School Counselors* is an adaptation of the ASCA *Code of Ethics* (1972) and the California School Counselor Association *Code of Ethics* (revised, 1984). Adopted by the ASCA Delegate Assembly March 19, 1984.

and encourages the maximum growth and development of each counselee.

3. Informs the counselee of the purposes, goals, techniques, and rules of procedure under which she/he may receive counseling assistance at or before the time when the counseling relationship is entered. Prior notice includes the possible necessity for consulting with other professionals, privileged communication, and legal or authoritative restraints.

4. Refrains from consciously encouraging the counselee's acceptance of values, lifestyles, plans, decisions, and beliefs that represent only the counselor's personal orientation.

5. Is responsible for keeping abreast of laws relating to pupils and ensures that the rights of pupils are adequately provided for and protected.

6. Makes appropriate referrals when professional assistance can no longer be adequately provided to the counselee. Appropriate referral necessitates knowledge about available resources.

7. Protects the confidentiality of pupil records and releases personal data only according to prescribed laws and school policies. The counselor shall provide an accurate, objective, and appropriately detailed interpretation of pupil information.

8. Protects the confidentiality of information received in the counseling process as specified by law and ethical standards.

9. Informs the appropriate authorities when the counselee's condition indicates a clear and imminent danger to the counselee or others. This is to be done after careful deliberation and, where possible, after consultation with other professionals.

10. Provides explanations of the nature, purposes, and results of tests in language that is understandable to the client(s).

11. Adheres to relevant standards regarding selection, administration, and interpretation of assessment techniques.

## B. Responsibilities to parents

The school counselor:

1. Respects the inherent rights and responsibilities of parents for their children and endeavors to establish a cooperative relationship with parents to facilitate the maximum development of the counselee.

2. Informs parents of the counselor's role with emphasis on the confidential nature of the counseling relationship between the counselor and counselee.

3. Provides parents with accurate, comprehensive and relevant information in an objective and caring manner.

4. Treats information received from parents in a confidential and appropriate manner.

5. Shares information about a counselee only with those persons properly authorized to receive such information.

6. Follows local guidelines when assisting parents experiencing family difficulties which interfere with the counselee's effectiveness and welfare.

## C. Reponsibilities to colleagues and professional associates

The school counselor:

1. Establishes and maintains a cooperative relationship with faculty, staff, and administration to facilitate the provision of optimum guidance and counseling services.

2. Promotes awareness and adherence to appropriate guidelines regarding confidentiality, the distinction between public and private information, and staff consultation.

3. Treats colleagues with respect, courtesy, fairness, and good faith. The qualifications, views, and findings of colleagues are represented accurately and fairly to enhance the image of competent professionals.

4. Provides professional personnel with accurate, objective, concise and meaningful data necessary to adequately evaluate, counsel, and assist the counselee.

5. Is aware of and fully utilizes related professions and organizations to whom the counselee may be referred.

## D. Responsibilities to the school and community

The school counselor:

1. Supports and protects the educational program against any infringement not in the best interest of pupils.

2. Informs appropriate officials of conditions that may be potentially disruptive or damaging to the school's mission, personnel, and property.
3. Delineates and promotes the counselor's role and function in meeting the needs of those served. The counselor will notify appropriate school officials of conditions which may limit or curtail their effectiveness in providing services.
4. Assists in the development of (1) curricular and environmental conditions appropriate for the school and community, (2) educational procedures and programs to meet pupil needs, and (3) a systematic evaluation process for guidance and counseling programs, services, and personnel.
5. Works cooperatively with agencies, organizations, and individuals in the school and community in the best interest of counselees and without regard to personal reward or remuneration.

## E. Responsibilities to self

The school counselor:

1. Functions within the boundaries of individual professional competence and accepts responsibility for the consequences of his/her actions.
2. Is aware of the potential effects of personal characteristics on services to clients.
3. Monitors personal functioning and effectiveness and refrains from any activity likely to lead to inadequate professional services or harm to a client.
4. Strives through personal initiative to maintain professional competence and keep abreast of innovations and trends in the profession.

## F. Responsibilities to the profession

The school counselor:

1. Conducts herself/himself in such a manner as to bring credit to self and the profession.
2. Conducts appropriate research and reports findings in a manner consistent with acceptable educational and psychological research practices.

3. Actively participates in local, state, and national associations which foster the development and improvement of school counseling.
4. Adheres to ethical standards of the profession, other official policy statements pertaining to counseling, and relevant statutes established by federal, state, and local governments.
5. Clearly distinguishes between statements and actions made as a private individual and as a representative of the school counseling profession.

## G. Maintenance of standards

Ethical behavior among professional school counselors is expected at all times. When there exists serious doubt as to the ethical behavior of colleagues, or if counselors are forced to work in situations or abide by policies which do not reflect the standards as outlined in these *Ethical Standards for School Counselors* or the AACD *Ethical Standards*, the counselor is obligated to take appropriate action to rectify the condition. The following procedure may serve as a guide:

1. The counselor shall utilize the channels established within the school and/or system. This may include both informal and formal procedures.
2. If the matter remains unresolved, referral for review and appropriate action should be made to the Ethics Committees in the following sequence:
   • local counselor association
   • state counselor association
   • national counselor association

## H. References

School counselors are responsible for being aware of and acting in accord with the standards and positions of the counseling profession as represented in such official documents as those listed below. A more extensive bibliography is available from the ASCA Ethics Committee upon request.

*Ethical Standards* (1981). American Association for Counseling and Development. Alexandria, VA.

*Ethical Guidelines for Group Leaders* (1980). Association for Specialists in Group Work. Alexandria, VA.

*Principles of Confidentiality* (1974). ASCA Position Statement. American School Counselor Association. Alexandria, VA.

*Standards for Educational and Psychological Tests and Manuals* (1974). American Psychological Association. Washington, DC.

*Ethical Principles in the Conduct of Research with Human Participants* (1973). American Psychological Association. Washington, DC.

# H. Code of Ethics,
## Commission on Rehabilitation Counselor Certification

The Rehabilitation Counselor has a commitment to the effective functioning of all human beings; his/her emphasis is on facilitating the functionings or refunctioning of those persons who are at some disadvantage in the struggle to achieve viable goals. While fulfilling this commitment, he/she interacts with many people, programs, institutions, demands and concepts, and in many different types of relationships. In these endeavors, he/she seeks to enhance the welfare of their clients and of all others whose welfare his/her professional roles and activities will affect. He/she recognizes that both action and inaction can be facilitating or debilitating and he/she accepts the responsibility for their action and inaction.

- The primary obligation of the rehabilitation counselor is the client. In all relationships, the rehabilitation counselor will protect the client's welfare and will diligently seek to assist the client towards his/her goals.
- The rehabilitation counselor recognizes that the client's family is typically a very important factor in the client's rehabilitation. He/she will strive to enlist the understanding and involvement of the family as a positive resource in promoting the client's rehabilitation plan and in enhancing the client's continued effective functioning.
- The rehabilitation counselor is obligated to protect the client-employer relationship by adequately apprising the latter of the client's capabilities and limitations. He/she will not participate in placing a client in a position that will result in damaging the interests and welfare of either or both the employer and the client.
- The rehabilitation counselor will relate to his/her colleagues in the profession so as to facilitate their ongoing technical effectiveness as professional persons.
- Typically, the implementation of a rehabilitation plan for a client is a multi-disciplinary effort. The rehabilitation counselor will conduct himself/herself in his/her interdisciplinary relationship in such a way as to facilitate the contribution of all the specialists involved for maximum benefit of the client and to bring credit to the profession of rehabilitation counseling.
- The rehabilitation counselor will be loyal to the agency that employs him/her and to the administrators and supervisors who supervise him/her. They will refrain from speaking, writing, or acting in such a way as to bring discredit on his/her agency.
- The rehabilitation counselor will regard his/her professional status as imposing on him/her the obligation to relate to the community (the public) at levels of responsibility and morality that are higher than are required for persons not classified as "professionals." He/she will use specialized knowledge, special abilities and leadership

*Code of Ethics*, by the Commission on Rehabilitation Counselor Certification, 1974. Reprinted by permission.

A revised version of this *Code of Ethics* has been approved on March 26, 1987.

position to promote understanding and the general welfare of handicapped persons in the community, and to promote acceptance of the viable concepts of rehabilitation and of rehabilitation counseling.

- In relationships with other programs, agencies, and institutions that participate in the rehabilitation plan of the client, the rehabilitation counselor will follow procedures and insist on arrangements that will foster maximum mutual facilitation and effectiveness of services for the benefit of the client.

- The rehabilitation counselor is obligated to keep his/her technical competency at such a level that his/her clients receive the benefit of the highest quality of services the profession is capable of offering.
- The rehabilitation counselor is obligated to assist in the efforts to expand the knowledge needed to serve handicapped persons with increasing effectiveness.
- CRCC does not discriminate on the basis of race, color, religion, national origin, sex, age, handicapped or marital status.

# I. Counselor Certification

## Rehabilitation Counselor Certification

In 1973 the Commission on Rehabilitation Counselor Certification was established. The current registry of certified counselors numbers over 11,000. Since 1980 there has been an increasing tendency for private practitioners to apply. Many graduates of programs accredited by the Council on Rehabilitation Education apply. The certification maintenance rate has been over 50%, with higher percentages in recent years. The commission's *Code of Ethics* and further information are available from:

> Commission on Rehabilitation Counselor Certification
> Division of the Board for Rehabilitation Certification
> 1156 Shure Drive, Suite 350
> Arlington Heights, Illinois 60004
> (312) 394-2104

*Source:* Adapted from Hedgeman (1985).

## National Academy of Certified Clinical Mental Health Counselors

The National Academy of Certified Clinical Mental Health Counselors was developed by the American Mental Health Counselors Association with the goal of establishing the role and identity of counselors. A certified clinical mental-health counselor, as defined by the academy, uses methods and procedures of counseling and psychotherapy with the goal of assisting individuals or groups to achieve optimal mental health by means of personal and social development and adjustment in order to prevent the debilitating effects of certain somatic, emotional, and intrapersonal or interpersonal disorders. Requirements for certified status include a master's degree or two years of graduate work with a minimum of 45 semester hours in clinical mental health or an allied field; or a minimum of two years of post–master's degree experience in a mental health setting with at least 1500 hours of supervised clinical experience, including 50 hours of face-to-face supervision.

The *Code of Ethics for Certified Clinical Mental Health Counselors* has the following specific sections: responsibility, competence, moral and legal standards, public statements, confidentiality, welfare of the consumer, professional relationships, utilization of assessment techniques, and pursuit of research activities.

Further information about this organization, certification requirements and procedures, and the *Code of Ethics* can be obtained from:

> National Academy of Certified Clinical Mental Health Counselors
> 5999 Stevenson Avenue
> Alexandria, VA 22304
> (703) 823-9800

*Source:* Adapted from Messina (1985).

## National Board for Certified Counselors

The National Board for Certified Counselors (NBCC) was incorporated as a nonprofit corporation in July 1982, and as of June 1985 it had certified over 14,000 counselors. Its primary purposes are to establish and monitor a national certification system; to promote professional counselor accountability; to identify to the public and professional peers those counselors who have voluntarily sought and obtained certification; to advance cooperation among groups involved in professional credentialing; to maintain a register of credentialed counselors; and to encourage the continuing professional growth and development of national certified counselors.

Counselors certified by the board are authorized to use the designation National Certified Counselor. Certification is the process by which the board grants formal recognition to an individual who has met specified professional standards. Eligibility requirements include a master's or doctor's degree in counseling or a related field; at least two years of professional counseling experience, including supervised experience; and a counselor certification examination. The examination assesses knowledge in eight areas deemed important for professional counselors, regardless of professional specialization: the helping relationship; group dynamics, group process, and counseling; human growth and development; life-style and career development; professional orientation; appraisal of individuals; social and cultural foundations; and research and evaluation. Further information can be obtained from:

National Board for Certified Counselors
5999 Stevenson Avenue
Alexandria, VA 22304
(703) 823-9800 Ext. 262 or 253

*Source:* Adapted from Stone (1985).

## Credentialing Career Counselors

The National Council for Credentialing Career Counselors (NCCCC) administered its first examination in 1984, and it is estimated that about 1000 professionals had received certification by the end of 1985. In July 1985 the council affiliated with National Board for Certified Counselors. As a result of the merger, the generic certification is a prerequisite for obtaining and renewing the career specialty designation. Specific eligibility requirements for certified career counselors include a graduate degree in counseling, with evidence of course work in career development and assessment; a practicum that involves supervised experience focused on career counseling in a work setting; three years of post–master's degree professional career counseling experience; and passing of the NBCC career counseling specialty examination. Further information can be obtained from:

National Vocational Guidance Association,
A Division of the American Association for
    Counseling and Development
5999 Stevenson Avenue
Alexandria, VA 22304
(703) 823-9800

*Source:* Adapted from Smith and Karpati (1985).

# J. A Guide to Professional Organizations

It is a good idea while you are a student to begin your identification with state, regional, and national professional associations. To assist you in learning about student memberships, we are listing five major national professional organizations, along with a summary of student membership benefits, if applicable. We suggest that you contact your local, state, and regional organizations and get involved in their activities, especially conventions and conferences.

## American Association for Counseling and Development

The AACD has 56 state branches and four regional branch assemblies. Students qualify for a special annual membership rate of $32 and for half-rate membership in any of the 14 divisions. AACD membership provides many benefits, including a subscription to the *Journal of Counseling and Development*, eligibility for professional liability insurance programs, legal defense services, and professional development through workshops and conventions. For further information, write to:

> American Association for Counseling and
>   Development
> 5999 Stevenson Avenue
> Alexandria, VA 22304
> (703) 823-9800

## American Association for Marriage and Family Therapy

The AAMFT has a student membership category. You must obtain an official application, including the names of at least two Clinical Members from whom the AAMFT can request official endorsements. You also need a statement signed by the coordinator or director of a graduate program in marital and family therapy in a regionally accredited educational institution, verifying your current enrollment. Student membership may be held until receipt of a qualifying graduate degree, or for a maximum of five years. Members receive the *Journal of Marital and Family Therapy*, which is published four times a year, and a subscription to six issues yearly of *Family Therapy News*. For applications and further information, write to:

> American Association for Marital and Family
>   Therapy
> 1717 K Street NW #407
> Washington, DC 20006
> (202) 429-1825

## National Association of Social Workers

NASW membership is restricted to those who have graduated from an accredited social-work program. For information on membership categories and benefits, write to:

> National Association of Social Workers
> 7981 Eastern Avenue
> Silver Spring, MD 20910
> (301) 565-0333

## American Psychological Association

The APA has a Student Affiliates category rather than student membership. Journals and subscriptions are extra. Each year in mid-August or late August the APA holds a national convention. For further information write to:

American Psychological Association
1200 17th Street, NW
Washington, DC 20036
(202) 955-7600

In addition to the national organization there are seven regional divisions, each of which has an annual convention. For addresses or information about student membership in any of them contact the main office of the APA or see a copy of the association's monthly journal, *American Psychologist.*

- New England Psychological Association
- Southeastern Psychological Association
- Eastern Psychological Association
- Southwestern Psychological Association
- Western Psychological Association
- Midwestern Psychological Association
- Rocky Mountain Psychological Association

The APA has a number of publications that may be of interest to you. The following can be ordered from:

American Psychological Association
Order Department
P.O. Box 2710
Hyattsville, MD 20784
(703) 247-7705

*Specialty Guidelines for Delivery of Services by Psychologists:*
- "Delivery of Services by Clinical Psychologists"
- "Delivery of Services by Counseling Psychologists"
- "Delivery of Services by School Psychologists"

- "Delivery of Services by Industrial/Organizational Psychologists"

*Careers in Psychology* (pamphlet)

*Graduate Study in Psychology and Associated Fields.* Information on graduate programs in the United States and Canada, including staff/student statistics, financial aid deadlines, tuition, teaching opportunities, housing, degree requirements, and program goals.

*Preparing for Graduate Study: Not for Seniors Only!*

*Ethical Principles in the Conduct of Research with Human Participants*

*Standards for Educational and Psychological Testing.* Revised standards for evaluating the quality of tests, testing practices, and the effects of test use. There are also chapters on licensure and certification and program evaluation. New in this edition are chapters on testing linguistic minorities and the rights of test takers.

## American Psychoanalytic Association

The American Psychoanalytic Association approved a code of ethics in 1975 and revised it in 1983. Some of its sections deal with relationships with patients and colleagues, protection of confidentiality, fees, dispensing of drugs, consultation, sexual misconduct, remedial measures for the psychoanalyst, and safeguarding the public and the profession. These principles of ethics can be secured by writing to:

American Psychoanalytic Association
309 East 49th Street
New York, NY 10017

# Name Index

# Subject Index

To the owner of this book:

Writing *Issues and Ethics in the Helping Professions* (3rd Edition) was both meaningful and challenging to us, and we hope that, as you read it, you found yourself challenged to clarify your positions on the issues we've raised. Only through your comments and the comments of others can we assess the impact of this book and be in a position to improve it in the future.

School: _____ Instructor's name: _____

City _____ State _____ Zip _____

1. In what class did you use this book? _____

2. What did you like *most* about this book? _____

   _____

   _____

3. What did you like *least* about this book? _____

   _____

   _____

4. How useful were the pre-chapter inventories and the other inventories within the chapters?

   _____

   _____

5. How useful were the cases and examples in helping you formulate and clarify your thoughts on the issues? _____

   _____

   _____

6. How valuable were the end-of-chapter activities and exercises? _____

   _____

   _____

7. What issues that we explored were most relevant and most important to you? _____

   _____

   _____

8. What topics do you think should be expanded or added to this book in future editions?

   _____

   _____

9. In the space below or in a separate letter, please write any other comments about the book you'd like to make. We welcome your suggestions! Thank you for taking the time to write to us.

Optional:

Your name: _____ Date: _____

May Brooks/Cole quote you, either in promotion for *Issues and Ethics in the Helping Professions* or in future publishing ventures?

Yes _____ No _____

Sincerely,

*Gerald Corey*
*Marianne Schneider Corey*
*Patrick Callanan*

- - - - - - - - - - - - - - - - - - - - FOLD HERE - - - - - - - - - - - - - - - - - - - -

‖‖‖

NO POSTAGE
NECESSARY
IF MAILED
IN THE
UNITED STATES

┌─────────────────────────────────────┐
│ BUSINESS REPLY MAIL                  │
│ FIRST CLASS     PERMIT NO. 358     PACIFIC GROVE, CA │
└─────────────────────────────────────┘

POSTAGE WILL BE PAID BY ADDRESSEE

ATT: *Corey/Corey/Callanan*

**Brooks/Cole Publishing Company**
**511 Forest Lodge Road**
**Pacific Grove, California  93950-9968**